New Mexico's Quest for Statehood

1846-1912

New Mexico's Quest for Statehood

1846-1912

ROBERT W. LARSON

THE UNIVERSITY OF NEW MEXICO PRESS

For Carole

Preface

A STUDY OF THE MOVEMENT in New Mexico to achieve statehood is a particularly challenging one, because, of all the contiguous territories of the Union, New Mexico remained a territory the longest. To locate information dealing with this prolonged effort, which spanned parts of two centuries, libraries and archives were searched in Santa Fe, Albuquerque, Washington, Denver, and elsewhere. The material, including personal correspondence, newspapers, and public and private documents, was relatively plentiful, especially for the years just prior to President Taft's proclamation of 1912 making New Mexico a state.

The number of people and institutions I am indebted to is very large. To the late Dr. Frank D. Reeve of the University of New Mexico, I owe the initial inspiration to take the entire movement as my project. Dr. Myra Ellen Jenkins, the senior archivist at the State Records Center and Archives in Santa Fe, gave invaluable help, and showed unfaltering interest in my study and complete attentiveness to my many questions and requests. At the National Archives, Mr. Buford Rowland, in charge of the congressional bills and reports, was most considerate, as were the archivists in charge of documents in the Department of State, Department of Interior, and Department of Defense. Dr. John Porter Bloom, editor of the Territorial Papers, kindly helped me locate a rare and important document. To the librarians at the Division of Manuscripts of the Library of Congress I also owe a great debt.

Other people who assisted me in my research were the librarians in charge of the Special Collections Division of the University of New Mexico library, and Dr. J. William Hess, associate curator of the West Virginia Collection in the University of West Virginia library, who was most kind in locating for me pertinent correspondence in the Stephen B. Elkins Papers. Many librarians at the Colorado State College library at Greeley were helpful to me, especially Miss Carol L. Koehmstedt, Mrs. Virginia S. Costello, Mrs. Marjorie M. Johnson, Mr. Gabor Kovacs, Mr. James B. Greer, and Mr. Daniel A. Seager, the head librarian.

Advice and constructive suggestions were offered to me by Dr. Ben Sacks from Baltimore. Mrs. Jacquelyn Kay Otero helped me to translate difficult Spanish documents, and Dean Forrest W. Frease and Professor Marcia I. Willcoxon of Colorado State College were willing consultants on matters of punctuation and style. Mrs. Mary Krape, my typist, was always co-operative and very careful to avoid error. To Mrs. Winifred W. Gregory, my manuscript editor, of the University of New Mexico Press, I am especially indebted for suggestions on how to improve the manuscript. Dr. France V. Scholes, professor emeritus of the University of New Mexico, has my deep gratitude for his guidance on many scholarly matters.

Among the institutions that made this study possible was the American Philosophical Society, through which I received two generous grants enabling me to do research at Santa Fe and at Washington in 1963 and 1964. I am also grateful for the interest shown by many of my colleagues, my family, and old friends and faculty members at the University of New Mexico.

The greatest debt I owe, however, is to my wife, Carole, whose dedicated help in editing the first draft was an integral and essential part of the work. She shared from the beginning the vision of what I proposed to do in chronicling the long history of the New Mexico statehood movement.

                                                          Robert W. Larson

Contents

ONE

Conquest &
Military Rule

I T WAS MID-AUGUST, 1846, when Brigadier General Stephen Watts Kearny led his confident American forces into the ancient capital of Santa Fe, bringing an old era to an end and inaugurating a new one. Since 1610, Santa Fe had been the center of a Spanish civilization established in the Southwestern wilderness and imposed upon Indian cultures ranging from primitive nomadic tribes to more sedentary Pueblos. Kearny's conquest brought a dramatic change, far more drastic than the one that had occurred as a result of Mexican independence. For now the energetic, aggressive Anglo-American civilization would be grafted on the aged and somewhat lethargic Spanish and Indian ones.

The Mexican War unofficially began on April 25, 1846, when a Mexican force of 1,600 men attacked some sixty-three American dragoons in the disputed area between the Rio Grande and Nueces rivers. In the encounter there were American casualties and Americans taken prisoner, so that when the alarming news reached Washington on May 9, the expansion-minded president, James Knox Polk, could deliver a war message with all the indignation of a victim of wanton aggression. In actuality, however, Polk in consultation with his cabinet had already decided to go to war.[1]

Relations between the two countries had been deteriorating for several years. The instability of the Mexican government had resulted in loss of American property in the troubled country amounting to $8,000,000. The annexation of Texas was bitterly resented in Mexico City. Then there was the rejection of the Slidell mission on December 20, 1845. The Mexican government, sensing an overpowering desire on the part of its expanding northern neighbor to acquire by purchase much of Mexico's northern domain, refused to discuss with John Slidell, the special presidential envoy, any question except the annexation of Texas, which was already regarded as a closed matter by the United States. Polk followed up this famous rebuff by dispatching a force under the command of General Zachary Taylor to the Rio Grande. Taylor not only occupied territory claimed by Mexico but blockaded the river so as to prevent supplies from reaching the Mexican town of Matamoros on the other side. Polk apparently had hoped for a quick Mexican response to this move, but when the weeks passed without a skirmish he decided to launch a war which would, in effect, acquire those vast Mexican holdings we wished to purchase. The clash in April only added righteousness to the cause.

The response to Polk's war message was decisive. Soon after its delivery, the Senate voted 40 to 2 for war with Mexico, while the House approved 174 to 14. Congress also voted a $10,000,000 appropriation to support the war and authorized the recruitment of 50,000 volunteers. But even while this action was being taken, hostilities were in process. The Mexican commander, General Mariano Arista, had crossed the Rio Grande and had engaged Taylor's forces in battle from May 8 to 13 at Palo Alto and Resaca de la Palma, but was defeated in both encounters. The victorious Taylor then crossed the river and seized control of Matamoros and began an invasion of northern Mexico which reached its first major climax at the crucial battle of Monterrey in September.

In the meantime, Polk and his cabinet had decided on an invasion of Mexican territory north of the Rio Grande. Kearny, then only a colonel, was instructed to muster his "Army of the West" at Fort Leavenworth, Kansas. A respected officer and rigid disciplinarian, Kearny had been serving on the frontier almost continually since 1819. In 1833, his years of service had been recognized by his elevation to lieutenant colonel of the newly organized First Dragoon Regiment, often regarded as the forerunner of the United States Cavalry. Many subsequent expeditions into the frontier regions west of the Mississippi marked him as a natural leader for such a western invasion. Consequently, he was elevated on June 30 to the rank of brigadier general, and on the same day departed for Santa Fe.[2]

What the result of this American conquest would be no one knew for certain. A few Americans, of course, envisioned some type of union with the United States, and the *Hispano*[3] majority was no doubt apprehensive on that score. But at this point, American policy, at least officially, was one of righteous indignation. Mexico has "shed American blood upon the American soil," repeated Polk's Secretary of State, James Buchanan,[4] in a confidential circular sent as early as May 14 to the United States commercial agent in Santa Fe.

We go to war with Mexico solely for the purpose of conquering an honorable and permanent peace. Whilst we intend to prosecute the war with vigor, both by land and by sea, we shall bear the olive branch in one hand, and the sword in the other; and whenever she will accept the former, we shall sheath the latter.[5]

Kearny's official instructions, however, were less innocent. William L. Marcy, the Secretary of War, directed him to take Santa Fe, then move on to California. If Kearny were successful in New Mexico, he was to establish temporary civil governments. Moreover, he was to retain as many local officials as possible.[6] An ambitious, imperialistic America seemed determined to make the most of the Mexican government's weak control of its northern holdings. That a bloodless conquest also was desired is indicated by an earlier directive which instructed the American leader to take with him to Santa Fe an influential Roman Catholic. President Polk, alarmed that the religious prejudices of the natives had been aroused, made arrangements for a person of high character and good repute in the Roman Catholic church to accompany Kearny on his expedition.[7]

Political precautions were matched by military ones. As the invasion could have sparked a serious conflict, Kearny had assembled a force of 1,568 men including three squadrons of First Dragoons, two companies of infantry, one regiment of Missouri cavalry, and two batteries of artillery. Colonel Sterling Price, who followed later, had under his command 1,200 mounted volunteers from Missouri and members of the colorful Mormon Battalion, a band of 500 men recruited at the Mormon encampment at Council Bluffs, Iowa.[8] The conglomerate army took the mountain branch of the Santa Fe Trail, described by one officer as a difficult, time-consuming journey across 800 miles of uninhabited country.[9]

Before reaching the capital, however, the invading Americans came into contact with native settlements in eastern New Mexico. Here they learned that Mexican Governor Manuel Armijo, once described by the ubiquitous Englishman, George F. Ruxton, as "a mountain of fat," was assembling an army of 3,000 men at Apache Canyon, the gateway to Santa Fe. At this point the experienced Santa Fe trader, James Magoffin, commissioned by President Polk to accompany Kearny, played his crucial role. Accompanied by a staff officer, Captain Philip St. George Cooke, Magoffin rode forward to meet Armijo and dissuaded him from offering resistance to the American invasion. Of greater difficulty was the Mexican governor's chief lieutenant, Colonel Diego Archuleta, who required special persuasion. Magoffin promised him that Kearny would take only that part of New

Mexico east of the Rio Grande, suggesting that Archuleta might lay claim to the western half. Archuleta accepted the suggestion enthusiastically and the will of the Mexican forces to resist collapsed.[10]

A bloodless conquest followed. Don Manuel abandoned his defense of the canyon, returned to Santa Fe, and fled southward, eventually reaching Chihuahua in Old Mexico. On August 18, Kearny's forces entered the old city and replaced the Mexican flag with the Stars and Stripes. "Don Manuel Armijo, the late Governor of this Department, has fled from it—the undersigned has taken possession of it without firing a gun or spilling a single drop of blood . . . ," boasted Kearny in a proclamation to the people issued several days later.

Acting promptly on his instructions to establish a temporary civil government, he then appointed as acting governor Juan Bautista Vigil y Alarid who was Secretary of the Department Assembly when American forces arrived. Kearny's sentiments were reassuring to the inhabitants. He promised to respect the religious institutions of New Mexico and protect the people from their Indian enemies. He announced his intentions to hold the area with its original boundaries as part of the United States under the name "Territory of New Mexico." In this way, Kearny quickly dispelled any notion Archuleta might have of controlling the western half of the territory. "It is the wish and intention of the United States to provide for New Mexico, a free government, with the least possible delay, similar to those in the United States," he vigorously asserted in his proclamation, "and the people of New Mexico will then be called upon to exercise the rights of freemen in electing their own Representatives to the Territorial Legislature." His only harshness was in urging those who had taken up arms against the United States to return to their homes lest they be regarded as enemies and traitors.[11] Could New Mexicans, and particularly the more enthusiastic Anglos, regard these pledges as the first step toward territorial status or possibly even statehood in the not too distant future?

On September 22, 1846, General Kearny issued the Organic Law of the Territory of New Mexico, more popularly known as the Kearny Code. According to one historian this code was a combination of Spanish-Mexican law, the law of the State of Missouri, plus the Livingston Code which had been fashioned for Louisiana upon its acquisition from France.[12]

Kearny assigned major credit for the drafting of the code to one of his chief subordinate officers, Colonel Alexander W. Doniphan of the First Regiment of Missouri volunteers, and to Willard P. Hall, a private in Doniphan's regiment.[13] According to General Kearny, the laws incorporated in the code were "taken, part from the laws of Mexico,—retained as in the original—a part with such modifications as our laws and Constitution made necessary; a part from the laws of Texas and also of Texas and Coahuila, a part from the statutes of Missouri; and remainder from the Livingston Code."[14]

The code divided governmental functions into the three traditional branches. Executive power was to be vested in a governor who would hold office for two years "unless sooner removed by the President of the United States." A secretary for the Territory also would be appointed by the President. The traditional bicameral system was instituted for the legislative authority. The General Assembly was to consist of a House of Representatives, the members of which would be chosen by qualified electors from the counties, and a Legislative Council composed of members elected from districts. The Assembly would convene at Santa Fe on the first Monday in December, 1847, and the first Monday of December every two years thereafter. Judicial power was vested in a Superior Court to consist of three judges appointed by the President, while additional and inferior tribunals were to be established by law. A bill of rights similar to the first ten amendments to the Constitution also was incorporated.[15]

Kearny, claiming presidential authorization, appointed officials to the new civil government on September 22, the same day he proclaimed the new Organic Law. Charles Bent, the famous Taos trader, was made Governor. Donaciano Vigil, a native who had had a distinguished civil and military career under Mexican rule, was appointed Secretary; Richard Dallam, Marshal; Francis P. Blair, Jr., a young Missouri-born lawyer, United States District Attorney; Charles Blummer, Treasurer; and Santa Fe trader Eugene Leitensdorfer, Auditor of Public Accounts. To the Superior Court, Kearny appointed Joab Houghton, former United States consul at Santa Fe, able Antonio Jose Otero, and Charles Beaubien, a French-Canadian who had been a resident of Taos since 1827.[16] Three days later, the general, no doubt feeling he had done his job, took a portion of his army and departed for California leaving Colonel Doniphan in command at Santa Fe.

Kearny's policy as leader of the conquering army had been generous and New Mexicans could feel assured that this conquest would result in some kind of American union. This had been specifically stated in the Kearny Code itself. But it soon became evident that Kearny had gone too far. An indignant Congress, feeling its powers had been usurped, called upon President Polk to clarify the orders and instructions given to American officers regarding civil government for territories which might be or were occupied by American arms. Polk responded by sending a message to the House on December 22, 1846, in which he firmly repudiated those portions of the Kearny Code which purported to establish a permanent government and grant to the citizens of New Mexico political rights which under the Constitution can be "enjoyed permanently only by citizens of the United States."[17]

Secretary of War Marcy wrote Kearny informing him of the President's position. "So far as the code of laws, established in New Mexico by your authority, attempts to confer such . . . [political] rights, it is not approved by the President . . . ." As for the "permanent" government established by Kearny, he was conceded the right to establish a civil government as a means of securing his conquest and protecting the persons and property of New Mexico. But militarily occupied territory acquired from the enemy could not, while the war continued, be regarded as territory permanently annexed to the United States.[18] This position was clarified in a directive to Commodore Robert F. Stockton, one of the leaders in the conquest of California. "The possession of portions of the enemy's territory acquired by justifiable acts of war, gives to us the right of government, during the continuance of our possession, and imposes on us a duty to the inhabitants who are placed under our dominion." The United States would have the right, however, to acquire the territory permanently under the right of *uti possidetis*, or the right of belligerents to territory in their possession at the date of the treaty of peace.[19]

The obvious result of Washington's attitude was to create confusion in New Mexico. Kearny had ignored the Northwest Ordinance of 1787 which gave Congress jurisdiction over the establishment of territories. Moreover, Article IV, section 3, of the Constitution provided that the Congress should have the power "to dispose of and make all needful Rules and Regulations respecting the Territory or other Property belonging to the United States . . . ." But where did this leave the people of New Mexico? What about the government established by General Kearny under the Organic Law which was to bear his name?

In the winter of 1847 occurred the Taos Uprising, a rebellion by both Indians and *Hispanos* who were unhappy with the new American government regardless of its status. The suppression of this insurrection was a clear illustration of the fact that in New Mexico any attempt at self-government would have to be by the grace of the military.

The incident was a product of mounting discontent on the part of many native leaders humiliated by Armijo's quick surrender and apprehensive about the good intentions of the new rulers. The conspirators found leadership in Archuleta, who was understandably bitter over what he believed were broken promises, and Tomas Ortiz, a prominent *Hispano* from Santa Fe. According to one observer, Archuleta was "one of the first adherents to the Government established by General Kearny as an expectant of office . . . and the first to conspire against the Government . . . ."[20] Meeting in the home of Ortiz the conspirators set December 19 as the date for a major uprising. Later the date was postponed to Christmas night in the belief that the celebrating Americans would be less vigilant that evening. Before the target date, however, the American forces in Santa Fe got wind of the plot and the conspiracy soon collapsed. Arrests were made and Archuleta and Ortiz were forced to seek refuge in the south.

Although the plot was centered in Santa Fe, the conspirators had been in touch with native leaders throughout New Mexico, and parts of the territory, such as the area around Taos, were ripe for revolt. An unsuspecting Charles Bent was to be the most prominent victim of the fierce, native backlash. A resident of New Mexico since 1832 and married to a native woman, he believed he had a real understanding of the people of the territory. Traveling to his home in Taos in mid-January, 1847, the Kearny-appointed governor was obviously convinced that all serious danger had passed. But the angry Indians of Taos Pueblo and their *Hispano* allies were eager for action, having been deceived into believing that there would be a general uprising. On the nineteenth, a group of angry rebels quietly entered the snow-covered town in the bitter cold preceding dawn. The citizens of Taos were aroused from their sleep by the discharge of guns, and some fled their homes in terror. An angry rap at Bent's door indicated the insurgents were after the governor himself. A group of Taos Indians under the leadership of Tomasito Romero broke into Bent's house, showered the struggling governor with arrows, and scalped him alive. Bent's family escaped through a quickly dug hole in the back of the adobe house, but five other prominent residents were killed, including Cornelio Vigil, the probate judge and prefect, and Narciso Beaubien, son of Judge Beaubien. Soon the violence spread throughout other parts of northern New New Mexico as *Hispanos* and Indians joined in a series of attacks on Anglo-Americans in Mora, at Arroyo Hondo, and elsewhere.[21]

The avenging of Governor Bent's death at the hands of Taos insurrectionists highlighted the decisive role the American army would play in New Mexico affairs during the coming years. Colonel Sterling Price, who assumed command when Colonel Doniphan was called to Mexico in December, 1846, took the field in wintry weather to arrive at Taos on January 24. With his appearance, the rebels led by Pablo Montoya, self-styled "Santa Anna of the North," took refuge in the town's adobe church, and Price's men had to use scaling ladders to drive them out and break the insurrection. Marcy, in a dispatch commending Price on his effective handling of the Taos Uprising and its aftermath, forcefully asserted that New Mexico's government was in every sense a military one. Earlier he had remarked to the New Mexico commander that the government of New Mexico was strictly military, and not established under the laws and Constitution of the United States.

The subordinate position of civil appointees in Santa Fe was convincingly brought to light on February 16, 1847, when Donaciano Vigil, the acting governor replacing Bent, submitted a letter of resignation to Secretary of State Buchanan. Vigil had hoped that the President would appoint his successor. The Polk administration, however, had different ideas. Marcy assured Price that, as military commander to whom the temporary civil officer was subordinate, it was up to him to make the decision. Should the acting governor wish to retire, he wrote Price, "you or the senior military officer in New Mexico, if convenient or necessary to delegate the power, will select such person as you or he may deem best qualified to exercise the functions of that situation, and duly invest him with them."[22] Consequently, although Vigil remained at the governor's post, the military continued to be the power behind his every action.

A perusal of *The Republican*, a Santa Fe newspaper in publication at this time, reveals that the civilian population was far from happy with the situation. Edited by G. R. Gibson, it expressed Anglo sentiments based upon the constitutional principle that the military should be subordinate to the civil. Calling first for clarification, *The Republican* declared that the

people of New Mexico should have a Government of some kind which they can see and feel and understand, either military or civil—if the military is the only authority they should know it; if they have a Territorial Government all of the acts of which are to be observed and respected let them know it . . . .[23]

The newspaper regretted that the authority of the civil tribunals had been doubted and insisted that the public mind had been kept in a feverish state by conflicting claims of jurisdiction between the civil and military tribunals. It quoted a suggestion made in the *St. Louis Republican* that Congress in the next session should make an inquiry into the present state of government at Santa Fe, to determine its propriety and legality under the Constitution of the United States.

Mere desire for clarification was soon replaced by a determined attitude. *The Republican* praised Kearny and his Organic Law for guaranteeing the civil rights of the people and providing government from the Governor "down to the lowest [offices] of a civil character." Colonel Doniphan was praised, as was Price, for implementing the Kearny Code until the United State Congress could act. However, in spite of these efforts to achieve civil government, there was concern about the growing power of the military. The commanding officer could order the imprisonment of a private citizen and deprive him of a jury trial and prevent his exercise of habeas corpus.

Despite such imposing powers, it was generally believed that Colonel Price would adhere to the Kearny Code and allow the General Assembly to convene on the first Monday of December. But this did not satisfy all. On October 24, a group of distrustful American citizens held a rally at the old Governor's Palace in Santa Fe to voice their resentment of the military's power to decide whether a civil legislature might assemble. They were addressed by Captain William Z. Angeny, a Missourian who had commanded infantry forces used to crush the Taos Uprising; a Major Oxley; and others. The political participation of these two officers seems extraordinary, but the role of the military in the early affairs of conquered New Mexico was an extraordinary one. The group resolved that it was better to have no civil government at all than one in name only. Why convene a legislative body if its acts can be annulled by the will or caprice of the commanding officer? An editorial two weeks later echoed these sentiments feeling it was a matter of "superarrogation" for the legislative assembly to act unless Price was willing to give it more independence.

The General Assembly did meet, however, amid hopes that the deficiencies of the civilian government during the past fifteen and a half months of American occupation would be reviewed and corrected. The first legislative activity under American rule was initiated by Acting Governor Vigil, who addressed a joint session of the General Assembly on December 6. While admitting that there were embarrassments in exercising civil rights at a time when the country was held by military occupation, the governor struck an optimistic note. He urged the legislators to be grateful for the prosperity and agricultural abundance of New Mexico, and advised them to establish a code of laws modeled after the codes of the different states.[24] The Assembly was soon at work. Captain Angeny, one of only four Anglo members, was unanimously elected Speaker of the House of Representatives, while a prominent *Hispano*, Antonio Sandoval, was elected presiding officer of the Legislative Council. Standing committees were established and soon the machinery of self-government was in operation.[25]

In the House, bills were introduced calling for the organization of common schools, the clarification of contracts made under Mexican rule, and the raising of revenue. In the Council, a measure providing for a census in the territory was considered and accepted. Recognizing the bilingual nature of New Mexico, both houses passed a resolution calling for a translation of the United States Constitution. Of particular interest was a proposal to consider the annexation of New Mexico to the United States. Both houses passed a bill calling for a convention to devise ways and means to effect the permanent annexation of New Mexico to the United States, as a territory.

While the legislature was in session, there was much concern over Price's attitude. Although military supremacy was attacked in principle, *The Republican* was always careful to maintain respect for the able colonel, himself a former congressman from Missouri.

. . . We have reason to believe, that the anticipations of the citizens relative to his establishing a Civil Government in this Territory will be realized and that the laws framed by the present legislature will receive his [Price's] sanction.[26]

At a ball given at the United States Hotel in Santa Fe, there was a display of respect and affection for Price. The turnout for the ball was the largest since General Kearny's ball at which the military and residents of Santa Fe became acquainted.

Interestingly enough, despite its continual lambasting of military supremacy, *The Republican* seemed willing to allow Price to intervene in legislative proceedings. This about-face occurred when the overwhelmingly *Hispano* Council rejected laws passed by the House of Representatives. Price was reported as planning an examination of the House measures, and, if they seemed beneficial and necessary to him, he would order them promulgated as laws of the land. Such action, *The Republican* reported, would be heartily approved.

This stand indicated not only a certain ambivalence on the part of New Mexicans concerning the military question, but a division of opinion as well. Of course there was bound to be conflict between *Hispanos* and Anglos, groups with such opposite cultural backgrounds. Basic differences were revealed during the legislative sessions of the General Assembly when bills to establish public cemeteries and the legalization of marriage by magistrates were defeated. The Roman Catholic Church, which had enjoyed great power prior to the American occupation, naturally opposed such measures. The attitude of *The Republican*, which represented a segment of Anglo sentiment in New Mexico, pointed to future tension. It referred to the Catholic priesthood as that

class who, under the pretended sanction of heaven have imposed the most grievous burthens [sic] and exactions for the support of the most shameful and glaring vices. Who, claiming to be teachers of divine origin, have in their lives, both private and public, placed before you examples of the most shocking human depravity.[27]

A letter to the editor signed Conciudadano, or fellow citizen, warned the people to guard against the weakening of "*toleration* of freedom in mind and person—of civil and religious liberty." Asserting that the twenty million citizens of the United States were better off than the eight million of "unhappy Mexico," he claimed this was due not to the soil and climate of the United States, but because the people of the country had "based their first institutions on freedom of the mind."[28]

The sentiments of the *Hispanos* at this time are difficult to gauge accurately. A vanquished people are rarely outspoken. Surely, many of them must have been apprehensive of attempts to secularize certain of their institutions. On the other hand, a number were concerned lest their loyalties to the new government be questioned. A case in point was the petition signed at Taos on December 17, 1847, by Padre Antonio Jose Martinez and other leading *Hispanos*. As Father Martinez has been accused of masterminding the Taos Uprising, which occurred earlier that year, this petition pledging loyalty is significant.

. . . New Mexicans, not through fear, but for the sake of their well-being, avail themselves of the opportunity to seek the good will of the American government of the north . . . [asking] . . . to be numbered among its citizens, with all the privileges and rights awarded to its people.

According to its signers, the petition was drawn up to correct an erroneous impression that they were involved in certain acts of rebellion, including the killing of the late governor.[29]

Notwithstanding this pledge of loyalty by prominent *Hispanos*, the convention called to consider the question of annexation to the United States was to run into trouble. *The Republican* sensed resistance. "We feel deep interest in the pending question of the annexation of the Territory to the United States," but we are "well aware of the strong opposition that will be made at the assembling of the approaching convention . . . ." According to the newspaper's logic if annexation were brought about by a peace treaty, it was certainly desirable for the people of New Mexico to have wanted and requested it. But unfortunately the convention met on February 10, 1848, and adjourned shortly without taking action.[30]

Still no great alarm was caused by this failure, as the determination of the United States government to have the territory, regardless of the wishes of the inhabitants, was recognized. In fact, America's firmness of purpose was demonstrated eight days before New Mexicans even met to discuss annexation. On February 2, after months of delay, the fateful Treaty of Guadalupe Hidalgo was drawn up in Mexico between Nicholas Trist, the American negotiator, and the provisional government of Mexico. Accordingly, New Mexico and California were annexed to the United States, the Rio Grande became the boundary between Mexico and Texas, and the United States paid Mexico $15,000,000 and assumed claims against the government of Mexico "not exceeding" $3,250,000.[31] The "antagonistic character of the Anglo Saxon and Gothic races—the pride, enterprise and determination of the one—the stationary and unjust disposition of the other, in fact the laws of nature had decreed it," crowed the imperialistic *Republican*.

But ratification was necessary. The United States Senate, despite the "exceptional conduct" of Mr. Trist who negotiated the treaty after his dismissal by the impatient President Polk, ratified the treaty on March 10, 1848, by a vote of 38 to 14. The Mexican Congress acted favorably on May 26, but New Mexicans did not hear about it until July 19 when two American soldiers, Lieutenant Heighbanks and Private Tyler, arrived from Las Vegas with the news. A copy of the St. Louis *Union* of June 20, received at about the same time, also carried the exciting news.[32] Thus, the conquest was complete. New Mexico was now part of the United States, but her status in that Union would be a subject of controversy for many years to come.

TWO

First Attempts

T HE TREATY OF GUADALUPE HIDALGO
provided for New Mexico's incorporation into the Union by stating that
it "shall be admitted at the proper time (to be judged of by the Congress
of the United States) according to the principles of the constitution."[1]
With this assurance, several groups in New Mexico began to work for
some type of union with the American states. Territorial status seemed
most likely, but statehood was not outside the realm of possibility.

Numerous and imposing problems were present, however, and would
cause endless difficulty for New Mexicans as the years passed. An immediate challenge was presented by military rule. After the peace treaty
was ratified, the legality of military control and the civil government established by it was questioned. The Anglo-Americans in New Mexico, particularly, began to protest openly against continuing military control.
"There are numerous citizens, native and American[,] who can run affairs
here. The army officers recognize no authority but their own . . . ,"
wrote one prominent citizen of Taos.[2]

Because Congress was deeply involved in the slavery controversy, no
efforts were made to clarify New Mexico's status until Whig Senator John
M. Clayton, from the Committee on Territories, reported a bill on July
19, 1848, proposing territorial governments for Oregon, California, and
New Mexico. Outspoken Thomas Hart Benton, Democratic senator from
Missouri, offered a similar bill on July 31, 1848. President Polk apparently
agreed with these proposals, for as early as December 7, 1847, he had
recommended the "early establishment of territorial governments" in the

areas occupied by American forces. Clayton's bill was passed by the Senate on July 26, 1848,[3] but got no further.

At this point, Senator Benton, whose friendliness to New Mexico stemmed from his state's long interest in the Santa Fe trade, offered advice to the people of the territory. In an open letter on August 28, 1848, to the people of California and New Mexico, he suggested that because Congress had failed to act, they might establish governments themselves. " . . . Meet in convention—provide for a cheap and simple government—and take care of yourselves until congress can provide for you."[4] Polk was very anxious to organize the new territories but distrusted Benton's motives, feeling he was secretly planning to make his son-in-law, Colonel John C. Frémont, governor of California. The President's cabinet agreed that he should send a message to the people of California warning them that such action would be illegal and that they should continue to obey the temporary de facto military government.[5]

Despite presidential resistance and the opposition of New Mexico's new military and civil governor, Lieutenant Colonel John M. Washington,[6] Benton's suggestion struck a responsive chord among the people. Encouraged by Captain Angeny, now a civilian recently returned from Missouri to persuade New Mexicans to pursue Benton's suggestion, a number of people began to talk in favor of such a course. Donaciano Vigil, who had continued to cling to his authority as civil governor, responded to this sentiment by proclaiming a convention to implement Benton's ideas.[7]

Accordingly, some of the most influential citizens of the territory met at Santa Fe on October 10, 1848. Historian Ralph Twitchell claims that these delegates were members of the convention to consider annexation to the United States, originally authorized by the short-lived legislative assembly which Price permitted to convene in December, 1847. Although scheduled to meet in February, the group did not convene until this October gathering.[8] The Santa Fe Republican disagrees with this report and states that a meeting was held on February 10, the delegates to the gathering being popularly elected to membership in January.[9] Whether these same members comprised the October meeting is not clear, but whatever the method of selection it failed to achieve harmony. The start of the convention was so disrupted by discord that many members withdrew. As described by Spruce M. Baird, a critic from Texas, certain members, "principally if not entirely Mexicans," left for a reason that he could not determine.[10] Those who remained chose the intelligent and effective Taos priest, Padre Martinez, as president and J. M. Giddings as clerk. Members of the convention were Francisco Sarracino, a former governor under Mexican rule; Donaciano Vigil; Martinez; Santiago Archuleta; two

Anglo attorneys, Elias P. West and James H. Quinn; Judge Charles Beau-bien; Gregorio Vigil; Manuel A. Otero; Ramon Luna; Jose Pley; Antonio Saenz; and Juan Perea.[11]

On the fourth day of the convention the delegates drafted a memorial asking Congress for "the speedy organization by law of a Territorial Civil Government." The signers petitioned for the right of judicial appeal to the United States Supreme Court, the prompt appointment by the President of officials to public office, and representation in Congress by a delegate The Kearny Code, with some few alterations, was regarded as satisfactory. Of particular importance were the unequivocal provisions concerning the explosive issue of Negro slavery and the Texas claims to eastern New Mexico.

We do not desire to have domestic slavery within our borders and until the time shall arrive for our admission into the Union, as a State, we desire to be protected by Congress against their introduction amongst us.

As for Texas, the members of the convention protested "respectfully but firmly" against the dismemberment of the territory "in favor of Texas, or for any cause."[12]

The memorial was sent to Clayton in hopes that he and Benton would represent the cause of the petitioners in Congress.[13] Judge Joab Houghton, the persuasive Kearny appointee and resident of New Mexico since 1843, in transmitting the memorial strongly endorsed its contents. He em-phasized the impracticability of slavery in competition with "cheap na-tive labor," and denied the validity of Texas land claims along the east bank of the upper Rio Grande. If such territorial claims were recognized, he insisted, New Mexico would lose about half its inhabitants. What would the nation do with the western half of the territory if Texas secured to herself all on the east bank of the Rio Grande?[14]

Clayton and Benton did not disappoint the anxious memorialists. On December 13, 1848, the two legislators introduced the petition for self-government in the Senate. Uncompromising John C. Calhoun of South Carolina immediately branded the petition as insolent. The newly ac-quired territory "belongs to the States of Carolina and Virginia as much as it does to New York and Massachusetts" and the right of a Southerner to go there with his slave property was unquestioned and "supported by the Constitution." He accused the inhabitants of New Mexico of trying to exclude from the territory the very people who had conquered the area during the recent war with Mexico. The provision of the memorial deny-ing Texan claims to eastern New Mexico also was challenged. Senator Thomas J. Rusk of Texas defended "the indisputable title of Texas to all the territory lying on this [the east] side of the Rio Grande."[15]

New Mexico had supporters too. In the North, antislavery societies, friendly newspapers, Northern legislatures with a bias, and citizens' groups filed petitions which enthusiastically supported the New Mexico memorial.[16] *The National Era*, an antislavery newspaper in Washington, compared New Mexico's plea to "a similar prayer [which] was presented by the people of Virginia, when a Colony, to the King of England. Could a petition be more reasonable, more respectful?"[17] The protection against slavery afforded by the Republic of Mexico prior to the acquisition of New Mexico also was cited in defense of the antislavery provision of the memorial.

The slavery question in America had been a burning issue since August 8, 1846, when Representative David Wilmot of Pennsylvania offered his famous proviso which made it a fundamental condition to the acquisition of any territory from the Republic of Mexico that "neither slavery nor involuntary servitude shall ever exist . . . except for crime, whereof the party shall be duly convicted." Wilmot's proviso was never accepted by Congress but it remained a critical issue around which antislavery people rallied. Wilmot was convinced that the Kearny Code proved the existence of slavery in New Mexico because in prescribing the qualifications of electors it used the term "every free male" for those entitled to vote. "Does this not imply that there are males there not free? . . . Slavery is there, sir . . . . It is on the move, sir. It is in New Mexico," shouted Wilmot in a passionate speech made before Congress some months later.[18]

The Santa Fe *Republican* indicated that New Mexicans were acutely aware of the significance of this issue. ". . . The slave question and its final determination is of incalculable importance," *The Republican* admitted. Yet it believed that the resources of New Mexico

. . . together with its most infinite commercial advantages, will cause it at no very distant day, to be thronged with its millions, who actuated by the restless and indomitable enterprise of the race, will cast their [lot] in the new land that will be opened to them. Among these, slave holders, from the fact, that it is nearest and best known to a slave holding population.[19]

Some observers thought the question of slavery had little practical relevance for New Mexico. Lieutenant William H. Emory, whose work in determining the new international boundary between the United States and Mexico was later to bring him fame, wrote in 1846: "The profits of labor are too inadequate for the existence of negro slavery. Slavery, as practiced by the Mexicans, under the form of peonage" has all the advantages. It enables a master to receive the services of an adult while he is in the prime of life "without the obligations of rearing him in infancy, supporting him in old age, or maintaining his family . . . ."[20] The aridity of the area was also noticed. "While the present organization of material creation stands, African slavery can never find a foothold in New Mexico," Senator John Bell of Tennessee argued during the crucial debates preceding the Compromise of 1850.[21] Daniel Webster, in his famous Seventh of March speech, said as much. There was then considerable consensus among knowledgeable men that because of soil, climate, and native labor a perpetual bar to the expansion of slavery existed in New Mexico.[22]

The suitability of slavery to the arid Southwest and the right to bring slaves into it were two different matters, however. To many Southerners, the extension of this "peculiar institution," at least in a legal sense, was of prime importance if the balance of slave states and free states was to be maintained. Texas had a double interest in New Mexico. As a slaveholding state, its people not only wished to expand slavery in the area, but placed great importance upon their claims to eastern New Mexico. Spruce Baird, agent for the Texan claims, no doubt had both of these interests in mind when he described the 1848 memorial as emanating from twelve men authorized to act for no one but themselves. He asserted that the people of New Mexico knew and cared very little about the controversial anti-slavery resolution. It was written in the hope of giving "their application for a territorial government a zest with the abolitionists having no hope in any other quarter."[23]

Texas' claim to part of New Mexico dated back to the Texas Revolution. After winning virtual independence from Mexico at the battle of San Jacinto on April 21, 1836, the congress of the newly established Republic of Texas made sweeping claims. In the Texas Boundary Act of December of that year, the Lone Star Republic insisted that its southwestern border was located in the center of the principal stream of the Rio Grande. In so doing, she not only asserted claims to a part of New Mexico but to lands within Chihuahua, Coahuila, and Tamaulipas as well. Thus, the city of Santa Fe, as well as other settlements east of the upper Rio Grande, were to be under Texas authority. Some of these settlements had been in existence more than a century before the founding of Texas.[24]

The claims of Texas were never successfully implemented prior to the admission of Texas to the Union in 1845. In fact, a Texas expedition sent against Santa Fe in 1841 met with humiliating defeat. Consequently, when Texas was annexed, there was no exact definition of boundaries, the expectation being that these questions could be settled later by negotiations with the government of Mexico. President Polk did, however, indicate in no uncertain terms that he would "not permit an invading enemy to occupy a foot of the soil east of the Rio Grande."[25] But the new state of Texas needed little encouragement. Texans intended to claim all of the unappropriated public domain within the boundaries cited by the

Texas Boundary Act, and, it was argued by many, United States victory in the Mexican War had given these aspirations a solid boost. Her claims would certainly be recognized sooner by the United States government than by a foreign power.

Kearny's easy conquest of New Mexico was particularly heartening, although his proclamation was not. The general, upon taking Santa Fe, announced his intention of holding the area "with its original boundaries (on both sides of the Del Norte)" as part of the United States, and under the name of "Territory of New Mexico."[26] But with Polk's rebuke of the Kearny action, Texans became more aggressive in asserting their claims. On March 15, 1848, after the Treaty of Guadalupe Hidalgo had been signed, the Texas legislature created Santa Fe County which took in much of the disputed area. American response was favorable. The commanding officer at Santa Fe was told by Secretary Marcy not only to refrain from interfering with Texas efforts in this regard, but to "lend aid on proper occasions in sustaining them."[27] Nevertheless, when Baird, appointed by Texas Governor George T. Wood, arrived to serve as judge of the newly created judicial district of Santa Fe, he found Colonel Washington most unco-operative.

Meanwhile, New Mexicans were becoming increasingly determined to have a separate, independent government. Lieutenant Colonel Benjamin Beall, acting in the absence of Colonel Washington, issued a proclamation to elect a full convention of delegates who would consider the problem of a civil government.[28] On September 24, 1849, the nineteen elected delegates assembled in convention at Santa Fe. Father Martinez was again looked to for leadership. He was unanimously elected president, while James Quinn, an Illinois native also from Taos, was chosen as secretary.[29] Delegates were Manuel Armijo y Mestas, Ambrosio Armijo y Ortiz, Bernalillo County; Joseph Naugle, the territorial auditor, Salvador Lucero, Rio Arriba; Gregorio Vigil, Manual Antonio Baca, a former county prefect, San Miguel; Miguel Montoya, Francisco Tomas Baca, Santa Ana; Manuel Alvarez, E. Vaudry Deroin, Angeny, Santa Fe; Father Martinez, Ceran St. Vrain, the colorful early fur trader, Antoine Leroux, Taos; and Juan Jose Sanchez, William Curtis Skinner, Mariano Silva, Judge Antonio Jose Otero, Manuel Antonio Otero, Valencia. At least seven of the delegates had held an office in the government established under the Kearny Code.

On the evening of the first day, Father Martinez appointed a committee of five to prepare a constitution to serve as the basis for a new territorial government. Angeny, Skinner, Naugle, Baca of Santa Ana, and Antonio Jose Otero were selected as members. On September 26, the final day of the gathering, a majority report was presented by Skinner proposing a plan of territorial government, while a minority report, which disagreed in part, was submitted by Naugle. The minority proposal called for statehood if territorial government did not seem feasible, suggesting as a model the constitution of the State of Missouri. If only territorial status was attainable, the minority faction insisted upon an organic act like that of Minnesota Territory or one with "provisions at least as favorable." The convention, after an evening of debate, accepted the majority report with amendments, thus declining the opportunity to request state government.[30]

Members of the convention sidestepped those issues that had made the 1848 memorial so controversial. The issue of slavery was not dealt with directly, rather the delegates unanimously agreed that the right of citizenship be conferred on all "free white male inhabitants residing within the limits of this territory, not already citizens of the United States, but who, on the 2d day of February, 1848, were residents within the territory of New Mexico . . . ." As Americans in the territory already enjoyed citizenship this provision pertained to Hispanos who were to take an oath or make an affirmation before a territorial or federal court renouncing "every foreign prince, potentate, state or sovereignty, whatever."[31] Negroes, by implication, were denied the rights of citizenship by this provision. A stand on the Texas boundary question also was avoided. The boundaries of New Mexico, as proposed by the minority and accepted by the convention, were simply defined as being "north by the Indian Territory; west by California; south by the boundary line between Mexico and the United States; and east by the state of Texas."[32]

Another matter facing the convention was the election of a delegate to represent the territory in Congress. As early as May, 1849, a movement had been started to send a representative to Washington to watch over the affairs of New Mexico, the expenses to be borne by an association of private individuals.[33] Hugh N. Smith was so designated by the group. Smith, a man of very strong views, had formerly served as attorney general of the military-controlled government in the territory. He defeated Major Richard H. Weightman, ex-army paymaster and one of the most ambitious of the new political figures, by an early convention vote of 15 to 3. Joab Houghton received the lone nineteenth vote.

Interestingly enough, none of the candidates to represent New Mexico were convention delegates, although, on the last day, Houghton, along with Donaciano Vigil and Colonel Washington, was invited to take a seat in the convention. The invitation was the result of a motion presented by Armijo y Ortiz of Bernalillo County, who no doubt hoped to soften Washington's attitude by including him in the offer. All three gentlemen, including the reluctant Colonel, accepted, and on the third and final day were escorted into the convention to take their seats near Father Martinez, the presiding officer. A perusal of the record, however, indicates that none of the three participated in any of the voting, as the ballots cast on that day did not exceed nineteen on any one question.[34]

The split vote represented a growing factionalism in New Mexico. Although national political affiliations had not yet developed, continued military supremacy had divided political leaders into two camps. One supported the presence of the military, the other demanded unhampered civil government. The schism had been evident during the 1848 gathering, and continued through the 1849 convention. Generally, the officeholders, men such as Smith and Houghton, supported the military as a source of revenue, and favored territorial government in the belief that continued control of patronage by Washington would insure their retention in public office. During the 1849 convention, for instance, voting delegates such as Quinn, Judge Otero, Manuel Antonio Otero, Naugle, Montoya, Baca, and Lucero had been or were associated with the military-sponsored territorial government which would end with statehood.[35] With the notable exception of Naugle, all of these men leaned toward a continuation of territorial status. The opposition, on the other hand, had had enough.

The convention delegates also dealt with questions concerning the welfare of the native element in New Mexico. As part of his instructions, Smith was to impress upon the Congress of the United States the necessity of a clause in the territorial constitution which would insure New Mexicans of their religious rights as Catholics, and prohibit "all possibility of the interference of either military or civil tribunals with rights and privileges of the Catholic Church." Confirmation of the master and servant contract, the basis of the old *Hispano* system of peonage, also was to be secured. Important to all the inhabitants was a guarantee of protection from Indian attack. Smith was to insist upon the permanent establishment of two regiments of troops within the territory and urge the construction of a fort in the heart of the Navajo country.[36]

The Indian menace was a very real problem to New Mexicans at this time. Indian depredation had been all too common since the conquest. One American officer estimated that, in the summer of 1847 alone, Indian attacks along the Santa Fe Trail had accounted for the loss of 47 American lives, the destruction of 330 wagons, and the plunder and theft of 6,500 head of stock.[37] New Mexico, the western terminus of the Trail, was a particularly violent place because of restless bands of roving Apaches, Navajos, and Utahs. The J. M. White affair, perhaps the most sensational incident of Indian hostility, occurred in 1849, and affected even the political situation in New Mexico by delaying Delegate Smith's mission to Washington.

White, a prominent merchant, was traveling from St. Louis to Santa Fe with his family and a group of emigrants. Upon reaching Point of Rocks, a well-known camping ground in the dry, open stretches of eastern New Mexico, they were set upon by a group of angry braves, probably Jicarilla Apaches. In the ensuing melee, White and several others in the group were killed, and his wife, little daughter, and a female Negro servant were dragged away. Mrs. White was almost rescued a while later by a military force under the command of Major William N. Grier, which approached the Indian camp in the hopes of parleying for the safe return of the unfortunate woman. Almost in the presence of the troops, Mrs. White was slain, her body still warm as Grier moved into the encampment just behind the retreating Indians. A desperate effort to ransom the White girl met with no success. Kit Carson, who served as a guide for the unsuccessful rescue mission, asserted later that one of the chiefs of the raiding party came into Santa Fe sometime later wearing a necklace made from the teeth of the girl's father.

A group of unfortunate Mexican buffalo hunters also came upon the scene at the time of the attack at Point of Rocks. They too were set upon, leaving only a few wounded survivors. One, a lad no more than twelve years old, saved himself by pretending to be dead. Crawling away from the site of the massacre as rapidly as possible, he was seen and rescued by the eastbound party of Delegate Smith. With such evidence of immediate danger, Smith promptly returned to Las Vegas to await further developments.

Referring to the White tragedy, the Santa Fe *New Mexican* angrily demanded that Congress not lose a single day in taking the necessary measures, including the movement of 2,000 mounted troops to the area, the stationing of two companies of dragoons at Arkansas Crossing and at Point of Rocks, and the confinement of the four major tribes of the area within "certain fixed limits . . . compelled to remain [there], under a penalty of utter annihilation."[38]

The Indian problem was only one of many encountered by Smith. Opposition to him within the territory was strong. Colonel Washington, even though he had accepted the invitation to sit in the convention, refused to recognize its proceedings.[39] The territory's first governor, James S. Calhoun, while still serving as Indian agent, expressed the view of many statehood proponents who wanted the delegate to ask for statehood rather than territorial status.

I understand this was a hurried affair, and manageable voters picked up at what ever place found and this arose from extreme anxiety to secure the services of an exceedingly clever man, the Hon. Hugh N. Smith as the delegate of certain influential Citizens of this territory.[40]

Davis claims that Major Weightman and Angeny held several meetings in Santa Fe to oppose Smith's selection. The *New Mexican* added its voice. Feeling Congress would do nothing because of the "vexed slavery question," it cried for action:

> Our brethren all around us are acting for themselves, California . . . has adopted and framed a State Government, and in a short time her Senators and Representatives will present their Constitution and credentials—and demand of Congress a seat in their councils. Who can doubt the result? The Mormon settlement upon the great Salt Lake, north of us, are forming a State government, they are acting upon the known determination of Congress not to do anything for them. With these facts staring them in the face, is it not strange that we, who are so deeply interested, should sit quietly and fold our arms in repose.

Although opposing his effort to achieve territorial status, the newspaper did not call for the political destruction of Smith.

> We do not propose to take anything away from him, our Representative, we only clothe him with additional power and authority, for we feel justified saying, that no one in this territory more justly deserves, or should be so likely to get his present place, if we were to form a State Government, or perhaps be promoted to the station of Senator.[41]

Smith had his strong support too. A circular signed by such influential New Mexicans as Skinner; Padre Martinez; Houghton; St. Vrain; Beaubien; Quinn; Dr. Henry Connelly, close friend of former Mexican Governor Armijo; Judge Otero; Jess Turley; James L. Collins, a Missourian long engaged in the Santa Fe Trade; Donaciano Vigil; Francisco Sarracino; James S. Hubbell; Pedro Jose Perea; and others backed both Smith and his mission.[42] They were responding specifically to attacks by the *New Mexico Gazette*, a new paper published by one of Major Weightman's closest allies, Manuel Alvarez, longtime New Mexico resident and former U.S. commercial agent in Santa Fe during the Mexican rule.[43] Doubt as to the efficacy of a delegate in Washington—"he will not be entitled to a VOTE upon a single question, he can only by courtesy be heard upon questions relative to the Territory"[44]—also was dealt with. "We have elected a Delegate, full of zeal, intelligence, and patriotism to carry our plans and recommendations to Congress," the supporters of Smith insisted. He will attempt to secure help in order to subjugate the Indians and acquire funds for the advancement and education of the people. There was confidence in Smith's prospects, and a belief in the superior merits of territorial status. There would be donations in land and public funds to the Territory of New Mexico, but, with statehood, all that could be expected would be a small donation of land for schools. The alleged proslavery views of Smith's opposition were also belabored.

Despite the best intentions of Smith and the dominant territorial group, the work of the 1849 convention was to come to naught. Smith's strong bid to represent New Mexico was placed in the hands of the important Committee on Elections of the House of Representatives. On April 4, 1850, a majority of the committee submitted a report rejecting Smith's bid.[45] A favorable report supporting Smith's position, however, was submitted eighteen days later, both reports being committed to the House to be made a special order of business on April 29.

In the meantime Smith tactlessly plunged New Mexico deeper into the heated slavery controversy by authoring a pamphlet bitterly critical of slavery and of the slaveholding section of the United States. Appealing to public opinion he accused the "decaying" South and its "selfish, venal, and ambitious" Northern supporters of trying to secure "an equal weight in the Senate of the United States with the rapidly growing progressive population and multiplying free states of the Union." He claimed that slave labor had destroyed the industry of the free race and the prosperity of the South by forcing white Southerners to become "yoke-fellows with the degraded African race." Finally Smith, anticipating the growing sentiment in favor of statehood in New Mexico, urged his fellow New Mexicans to establish a state government interdicting slavery, promising that the time would come when the people of the United States would rally to their support.[46]

Having completely alienated any possible Southern support by this attack and having offended many Northern moderates, Delegate Smith finally received a reception in the House that should have been no great surprise. On July 18, 1850, the House after debating the matter refused to seat Smith by a vote of 92 to 86. The incendiary pamphlet was read on the floor of the House, which did not help Smith's cause or the cause of New Mexico. But there were other compelling reasons for his rejection. The claims of Texas to eastern New Mexico posed a problem. Some feared it might result in a clash between Texas troops and New Mexicans, especially if United States military units became involved. One congressman warned of the "dissolution of the Union" if such a disastrous clash should occur. There were the constitutional questions. If the claims of Texas to the land east of the Rio Grande were valid, then taking this territory away from the former republic would be dividing up the State of Texas without its consent. More basic, perhaps, was the legality of House action on this matter without the concurrence of the Senate or the approbation of the President. Other legal questions included the legitimacy of Smith's bid. It was said that the would-be delegate was not elected by the people of New Mexico but rather by a quasi-territorial government. Recognizing the close association between the military establishment in the territory and the leaders of majority forces at the 1849 Santa Fe convention, one House member accused Smith of attempting to represent a government that was military rather than civil in origin. Finally, there was the news reaching Washington that a new and stronger movement had already resulted in a convention and the establishment of a state government. Does this not constitute a "positive rejection of Mr. Smith as a *Delegate?*"[47]

Smith's fate was sealed on a summer day in 1850. But he was to be one of many spokesmen for the territory to face disappointment in the years ahead. His request in behalf of New Mexico was a modest one, merely the extension of territorial status. Others would ask for statehood and meet a similar fate.

THREE

The 1850 Constitution

E VEN BEFORE HUGH SMITH
had reached Washington to plead the cause of New Mexico, events in the Southwest were reaching a climax. Anglo-Americans in California as well as in New Mexico were demanding some clarification regarding their status in the newly acquired lands. The unwillingness of Congress to take any decisive action during the 1848 session was a disappointment to many who wanted at least a territorial government to guarantee their rights as American citizens. A short session in 1849 also failed to settle the question, and anxiety in the territories increased. The people, meanwhile, were attempting to take action themselves. The 1848 memorial and the 1849 convention which sent Smith to Washington already have been mentioned. In California, the growing influx of gold seekers made clarification there necessary. A number of meetings were held and ringing resolutions passed expressing a growing desire to create a popularly elected government without waiting for congressional action. In February, 1949, a group in the San Francisco area established a government to fill the void. Recognizing the compelling nature of the movement, Brevet Major General Bennet Riley, the military commander and acting governor in California, issued a proclamation on June 3, 1849, calling for a constitutional convention. The convention assembled at Monterey in September, and decided to create a state government rather than a territorial one. Its constitution, which prohibited slavery, was ratified by a 15 to 1 vote on November 13, while state officials and representatives to Congress were chosen the same day.[1] These actions forced Congress into a position that made further delay impossible.

But the legislative body did not meet again until December, 1849, nine months after President Zachary Taylor's term began. The new President, a military man elected over Lewis Cass in 1848, grew increasingly restless in his search for a decisive settlement regarding the land acquired from Mexico. Greatly influenced by that fire-eater, Whig Senator William H. Seward of New York, and by a cabinet predominantly opposed to the expansion of slavery, Taylor was determined to organize the southwestern area without regard to the pros and cons of the slavery controversy. On December 4, 1849, he recommended in his message to the newly convened Congress that California be admitted as a state. The President also warned, but with obvious sympathy and support, that New Mexico "at no very distant period" would be asking for statehood.[2]

Soon a view began to grow in Congress that Taylor himself was responsible for statehood activity in the West, and that the executive branch of government was usurping the powers that rightfully belonged to the legislative branch. On December 31, 1849, the House passed a resolution requesting the President to make available all pertinent information regarding the new agitation. The Senate passed a similar resolution on January 17. Within a few weeks, President Taylor complied with both resolutions and submitted a series of reports prepared by his department heads relating to the rapidly moving events in the territories. In an accompanying message sent from the White House, the stubborn old soldier denied that he was trying to solve the problem without Congress but at the same time outlined views which were definitely favorable to the determined efforts for recognition in California and New Mexico:

I did not hesitate to express to the people of those Territories my desire that each Territory should, if prepared to comply with the requisitions of the constitution of the United States, form a plan of a State constitution and submit same to Congress, with a prayer for admission into the Union as a State; but I did not anticipate, suggest, or authorize the establishment of any such government without the assent of Congress; nor did I authorize any government agent or officer to interfere with or exercise any influence or control over the election of delegates, or over any convention . . . .[3]

To an angry Congress confronted with a dangerous crisis believed to be the making of the President, Taylor's assertion that he did not "anticipate, suggest, or authorize" the establishment of state governments was of paramount importance. Future good relations with Congress depended on the President's ability to prove his good faith. The reports of George Crawford, his Secretary of War, were particularly significant because many outraged Southern congressmen blamed the territorial military commanders for the statehood agitation. Crawford attempted to vindicate General Riley of California and his predecessor, Brevet Brigadier General Richard B.

Mason, on the basis that the two commanders were merely granting to the people a fuller enjoyment of the laws, customs, and usages contemplated in both the Constitution of the United States and the 9th article of the Treaty of Guadalupe Hidalgo. Morever, Crawford argued, some sort of organization was vital because of the dissimilar habits and language of the mushrooming population, and the legislative assemblies springing up throughout California, which he regarded as irregular and "dangerous to the public peace, and the public interests."[4]

The instructions given to T. Butler King, a rather mysterious presidential emissary in California, were also submitted to the House. Written by the new Secretary of State, John Clayton, one month after Taylor took office, they too dramatized the President's rather strange position. King could with propriety suggest to the people of California measures which would promote their peace and happiness.

These measures must, of course, originate solely with themselves. Assure them of the sincere desire of the Executive of the United States to protect them in the formation of any government, republican in its character, hereafter to be submitted to Congress, which shall be the result of their own deliberate choice. But let it be, at the same time, distinctly understood by them that the plan of such a government must originate with themselves, and without interference from the Executive.[5]

The instructions were emphatic, but the fact that King arrived in California at the same time General Riley was issuing his proclamation calling for a constitutional convention was a greater coincidence than many congressional critics could accept.

Suspicion was growing that Taylor's motives were not as innocent as he would have Congress believe. California's constitution contained an antislavery provision, and antislavery men were in the forefront in New Mexico. Both areas were asking for admittance, and admission of both as free states would amount to a stunning defeat for the South. It seemed reasonable to many Southern congressmen and Northern moderates that Taylor was encouraging, if not inciting, statehood activity, with the belief that quick admission of the territories in question would remove the slavery question from public concern.

Evidence of presidential duplicity in New Mexico is especially interesting, and centers around two persons.[6] The first is James Calhoun, the Indian agent and later Indian superintendent in New Mexico. According to William W. H. Davis, who was U.S. District Attorney in the territory during the 1850's, Calhoun was actually a secret emissary of the President. Arriving in Santa Fe on July 22, 1849, the new Indian agent had in his possession secret instructions from Washington to induce the people to form a state government.[7] There is no documentation to support this, but Annie Heloise Abel, who edited Calhoun's official papers in 1915, concluded that Calhoun "was most certainly sent to Santa Fe for a purpose but what the real purpose was does not appear. Somewhere, no doubt, and very probably in the confidential files of Interior, War, or State department, there are papers that hold that secret."[8]

Calhoun did imply, in a letter to the Commissioner of Indian Affairs dated February 2, 1850, that he was very favorable to Taylor's statehood plans. Called to Taos in response to a bitter complaint, Calhoun was told by some sixty-nine members of the Taos pueblo that their *alcaldes* were selected for them by American authority, instead of their old and approved custom of annually electing these officers, and others, in their own pueblo, and by their own people. Moreover, in the election for delegates to the 1849 convention, Calhoun discovered that

in order to secure a result adverse to a State Organization, many of the Indians . . . were brought to the polls and induced to vote, and thereby, the factious purpose of thwarting the supposed policy of the Administration, in regard to New Mexico, was secured; so far as the election of delegates from the county of Taos, could accomplish the reckless design.

In the letter, Calhoun also revealed suspicions that Judge Beaubien and Padre Martinez were behind the pressuring of Indians into voting for delegates favorable to territorial rather than statehood status, but he did accept denials from the influential pair, plus their assurances that they would in the future act with "General Taylor's real friends."

Evidence on the involvement of the second person sent to New Mexico, Brevet Lieutenant Colonel George A. McCall, is more conclusive. McCall was sent to Santa Fe as an agent of the Taylor administration, but it is difficult to ascertain whether he merely encouraged efforts for self-government or was actively sparking political enterprises of the type for which Riley in California was so criticized. The nature of McCall's mission is somewhat revealed in a letter to him from Secretary of War Crawford which requested McCall to pass through Washington for an interview on his way back to New Mexico to join his regiment.[9] The essence of their conference was undoubtedly contained in subsequent instructions from Crawford to McCall dated November 19, 1849. In these Crawford carefully outlined the attitude of the Taylor administration toward a movement for self-government. The failure of Congress to provide suitable governments had necessitated military rule, a duty "falling beyond their [the army's] appropriate spheres of action." Crawford concluded that the people of New Mexico should be supplied with a government of their choice and prompt action on the part of New Mexicans was urged:

. . . It is not believed that the people of New Mexico are required to await the movements of the Federal Government, in relation to the plan of a government proper for the regulation of their own internal concerns.

The Constitution of the United States, and the late Treaty with Mexico guaranty [sic] their admission into the Union of our States, subject only to the judgment of Congress. Should the people of New Mexico wish to take any steps toward this object so important and necessary to themselves, it will be your duty and the duty of others with whom you are associated, not to thwart, but advance their wishes. It is their right to appear before Congress and ask for admission into the Union.

The ambiguous nature of these instructions to McCall, while not totally incriminating, certainly makes evident the reasons for the fury of many congressmen over "old Zach's" part in the statehood activity of California and New Mexico.

When McCall reached Santa Fe on March 21, 1850, he soon discovered that the greatest obstacle to the discharge of his instructions was the attitude of the new leaders in New Mexico. Factionalism was inflicting deep wounds on the body politic of the new territory. This was reflected during the bitterly cold winter months preceding McCall's arrival by harsh feelings and frequent fist fights. It was primarily a continuation of the same factional struggle that had begun soon after the conquest. A few new personalities had been added, but the territorialists remained, by and large, closely tied to the military and beholden to federal patronage.

Calhoun, too, whatever the nature of his mission, had discovered upon his arrival eight months earlier that the territorial group strongly opposed immediate admission. One historian has concluded that it was this stubborn opposition that drove Calhoun to seek the aid of the crafty Weightman in organizing statehood sentiment.[10] This colorful former army officer, a West Pointer, seems to have been successful, for by the time McCall reached Santa Fe the statehood group was quite vocal. Weightman not only managed to corral the support of a majority of the influential *Hispanos* in the territory but had won as an ally, Manuel Alvarez, whose years of residence in New Mexico, along with his earlier consular duties, had won him a strong following. As a matter of fact, opponents frequently used the term "Alvarez faction" to describe the statehood party, although the facts indicate Weightman's leadership.

As for the territorial party, it included men close to the military establishment such as Judge Houghton, Judge Beaubien, and Thomas S. J. Johnson, chief clerk of the army quartermaster. Because of the extraordinary influence of Joab Houghton in this group, it was often referred to as the Houghton faction or the Houghton party. Houghton was an amazing fellow in many ways. Educated as a civil engineer, he combined a financial interest in merchandising with his controversial legal pursuits.

His association with the judicial branch of the military-controlled government in New Mexico accounted for much of the tension between the two parties, as Houghton and his fellow judges were accused of complete subservience to the "wills, whims, and caprices" of the military authority.[11]

McCall's appraisal of the relative strength of these two warring factions is particularly interesting in that it indicates the success of the Houghton faction in maintaining its initial advantage against the persuasive Weightman. Writing about four weeks after his arrival in Santa Fe, McCall found the territorialists in control.

> . . . I found politics the rage, engrossing the attention of all classes of people; the territorial party high in the ascendant—the state party down. The latter had lost the printing press, & the former had got possession of it. Indeed the State party which from all accounts possessed no influence beyond the precincts of the town, evidently exercised so little within those limits that to a mere looker-on, who from sympathy alone felt any solicitude to see N. Mexico present herself for admission into the Union as a state, the prospect would have seemed hopeless indeed.[12]

This evidence of popular enthusiasm brings into question historian Bancroft's evaluation that activity for self-government was manipulated by a few men at Santa Fe and was largely the work of a "few Americans who acted for their own personal interest or that of their party or section in the states, and aroused popular enthusiasm only slightly . . . ."[13]

If Bancroft had misinterpreted the extent of interest in self-government, he had not misread the opportunism that characterized New Mexico politics or the force of certain personalities. Although encouragement, pressure, or both, from the Taylor administration had finally persuaded the territorialists to work with the Weightman faction, the two groups continued to have sharp differences and disagreements. One effort at cooperation was shattered by charges that the Weightman group assumed "too high a tone." When the territorialists decided on a unilateral action and made a persuasive appeal to the native majority, issuing an address in Spanish, the Alvarez, or Weightman, party made a move toward reconciliation, but with the unacceptable stipulation that "their leader (Maj. Weightman) shall be put upon the ticket for U.S. Senator."[14]

Conflicts such as this remained unsettled, but the attempt to create a state government went on. McCall began to pressure Houghton to work with the statehood movement, using as his trump cards the position of the Taylor administration and the Texas boundary claims. He convinced the judge and his followers that they were destined to fail if they opposed statehood, and was strengthened in his resolve when the military gave him backing. After three weeks of negotiation, Colonel McCall won his point as the two sides agreed to combine their efforts. On April 13, 1850, Judge

Houghton and some of his closest associates called for a public meeting to be held on April 20 in Santa Fe at which resolutions would be drafted in favor of statehood.[15] In compliance with this call for a meeting, the citizens of Santa Fe County gathered at the courthouse and by resolution requested Brevet Colonel John Munroe, Colonel Washington's successor as civil and military governor,[16] to call for a constitutional convention. Munroe, at the behest of Colonel McCall, responded to the appeal by proclaiming an election for delegates on May 6, the winners to assemble at the capital on May 15 to draft a state constitution to present to Congress.[17]

The transition from insistence on territorial government to a call for statehood was painful for the Houghton faction, according to Calhoun. The influential Indian agent, and confidant of Weightman and Alvarez, claimed that the Houghton faction "violently opposed a State organization until Governor Munroe *required* them to do otherwise . . ."[18] If Colonel Munroe felt enough pressure from the national administration, as represented by McCall, to force his friends in the territorial administration into a statehood convention, then President Taylor's role was far more forceful than he was willing to admit.

The veracity of this claim of strong pressure from Washington has support. Daniel Webster, Clayton's successor as Secretary of State, admitted in August of 1850 that Munroe had issued the proclamation "in pursuance or in consequence of an order or letter of instructions given . . . to Lt. Col. McCall . . . ." But he claimed McCall and Munroe were not dictating action to be taken by New Mexicans but merely encouraging them to exercise their rights as American citizens in the absence of congressional action. "Their whole duty was confined to what they might be able to perform, subordinate to the wishes of the people." They were to act as the agents of the inhabitants and not as officers of the national government.[19] Munroe himself declared that he had been urged by local citizens through petitions and "personal representations" to issue his proclamation calling for a statehood convention.[20] But the flurry of statehood activity that followed McCall's arrival in New Mexico seems to belie these elaborate explanations.

The small group of New Mexico leaders elected as delegates to the constitutional convention met in the old capital of Santa Fe with the idea of pushing for statehood firmly in mind. Among the familiar names were, of course, Judge Houghton and some of his old associates like Ceran St. Vrain. James Quinn was there and was elected to preside over the proceedings. Others were Padre Jose Manuel Gallegos, the powerful Albuquerque priest who leaned toward the Weightman faction; Jose Maria Martinez; George Gold; Jose Antonio Mansanares, a brilliant *Hispano* from an old Rio Arriba family; Jose Pablo Gallegos; Thomas S. J. Johnson, whose presence further illustrates the role of the military; Francisco Ortiz y Delgado; Levi J. Keithly; Juan Perea, a political power from Bernalillo County; Murray F. Tuley, attorney general of the territory; Charles Overman; Judge Otero; Juan Antonio Baca y Pino; and Ramon Luna. Robert Carey, former prefect of Taos County, and Donaciano Vigil were chosen to serve as secretaries for the convention.[21]

It was obvious from the start that Houghton and his friends would dictate the actions of the assembly. Their majority was a clear one, said by McCall to be 17 to 3.[22] With the old territorial faction holding such an advantage, opposition would seem to be useless. But the Weightman-led faction was determined not to be cut out of all influence and positions of power should a state government actually come into being. Curiously, this group, which had so eagerly desired statehood from the start, now opposed immediate statehood on the grounds that this would mean "forming a state-government without the consent of Texas." The Weightman group, however, was so small that without the tumultous Archuleta affair the convention would have been extremely one-sided and uneventful.

Diego Archuleta had been allowed to participate in the election of delegates despite his part in the conspiracy that led to the Taos Uprising, and he won a seat in the assembly. His election angered many people, especially the friends of slain ex-Governor Bent. Quite a few delegates threatened to withdraw if Archuleta were seated. Upon hearing that his seat would be contested, Archuleta himself declared he would not attend the sessions. But the former Mexican official's friends, many of whom were members of the Weightman faction, realized what havoc could be wrought by a bitter fight over Archuleta's seat.

Archuleta was persuaded by the faction leaders to demand his seat. The response was immediate. The legality of his election was "at once assailed; & after two days of vexatious debate, Archuletta [sic] was finally excluded by a vote of 11 to 7 . . . ." Victory belonged to the Houghton group but the effect of the contest, "as had been anticipated by its originators, was to excite angry feelings among the Mexicans themselves, & at the close of the session, several of them were on the point of withdrawing from the Convention." The following day, May 20, a proposed state constitution was to be presented to the delegates. But the Archuleta affair had had its intended effect. The committee appointed to draft the document now began to differ on points previously agreed upon so that the draft was not ready for presentation, forcing an adjournment until the next day.

The evening of May 20 was diligently used by the old state party to aggravate the "feeling of dissatisfaction and jealousy" felt by native New Mexican delegates. So successful were they that by ten o'clock enough delegates had been won over to deprive the convention of a quorum.

These dissatisfied members, many of them from old and prominent *Hispano* families, were protesting against "the unjustifiable expulsion of Archuletta [sic] by the American members."[23] Houghton and his associates were now forced by the Weightman clique's successful maneuver to reconsider their strategy. To secure a quorum, and the adoption of a constitution without further loss of time, several of Archuleta's more zealous opponents had to sacrifice their individual feelings and allow Archuleta a role in the Santa Fe proceedings for the "good of their State & the Country." On the morning of May 21, Archuleta was seated so that the convention could proceed with its constitution-making.

Four days later the small assembly at Santa Fe completed its labors. A document had been hammered out during the ten days that would be presented to the people for approval on June 20, less than a month away. Houghton was the author, with some assistance from his friend Tuley.[24] The Anglo-Saxon legal and political traditions and staunch antislavery views of the Houghton faction were strongly represented, but the demands vocalized by the state party were recognized by several significant concessions to the Spanish-speaking inhabitants. Published in both Spanish and English,[25] and comparatively brief, the new constitution established the historical and traditional three branches of government with a bicameral legislature, a governor and lieutenant governor to serve four years, and a court system that called for a division of the new state into three judicial circuits.

The burning issue of slavery and its expansion was dealt with firmly in an antislavery provision that refused to equivocate and thereby reduce opposition from Southern states.

All men being born equally free and independent, and having certain natural, inheritant [sic] and inalienable rights, amongst which are the enjoying and defending of life and property, the acquirement, possession and protection of property, and the pursuit of and attainment of happiness; therefore, no male person shall be held by law to serve any person as a servant, slave or apprentice, after he arrives at an age of twenty-one years; nor female in like manner, after she arrives at the age of eighteen years; unless they be bound by their own consent after they arrive at such age, or are bound by law for punishment of crime.[26]

But the delegates wanted to do more than just outlaw the controversial Southern institution. A statement entitled "To the People of N. Mexico," which was included with the constitution, openly expressed not only the hostility of convention delegates toward slavery but also their determination to be forever free of the institution.

Slavery in New Mexico is naturally impracticable, and can never, in reality, exist here;—wherever it has existed it has proved a curse and a blight to the State upon which it has been inflicted,—a moral, social and political evil. The only manner in which this question now affects us is politically; and on grounds of this character, with its general evil tendencies, we have unanimously agreed to reject it—if forever.[27]

This emphatic stand against slavery caused McCall to write his superior about it the very day of its adoption, May 21. Delivery of the letter, however, was delayed four days because of another violent Indian attack. A party of braves struck a group of travelers at Wagon Mound, northeast of Las Vegas, killing eleven persons. Seven of these were members of the unfortunate Brown party, which had earlier lost its mules in a snowstorm and had been forced to take refuge at a place near the Cimarron River.[28] This incident demonstrated again the ever-present Indian threat.

In Santa Fe, the convention wore on, the omnipresent Indian threat notwithstanding, with delegates coping with another serious problem, the Texas boundary dispute. On this issue, the men at Santa Fe also had unequivocal ideas. They not only moved the boundary of the new state eastward from the Rio Grande, but placed it deep inside territory claimed by Texas. They claimed for New Mexico the entire Texas panhandle and a considerable amount of territory to the north and the west of that now claimed by New Mexico. The boundary with Texas was projected all the way "due East to the hundredth parallel . . . ." As for the other boundaries of the State of New Mexico, the eastern boundary line was to be extended northward along the 100th parallel to the Arkansas River, incorporating what is now the Oklahoma panhandle and southeastern Kansas. The northern boundary, starting at a point just southeast of what is today Dodge City, was drawn along the Arkansas to its source in the mountains of modern-day Colorado, and then southwestwardly in "a direct line" to that point where the Colorado River intersects the 111th parallel. The western boundary was extended directly southward through present Utah and east central Arizona to the Gila River. The boundaries of the new state were rounded out by drawing a southern line along the Gila to a point to be determined by an international boundary commission established by the United States and Mexico. The southern boundary would continue along the international boundary to the "Dam in the Rio del Norte, which supplies with water the 'asequia,' [sic] or irrigating canal of the town of El Paso del Norte [Juarez]" and thence eastward back to the starting point on the 100th parallel.[29] The proposed boundary lines were ambitious, but they were not without historical precedent. The eastern and northeastern borders, for instance, followed the international boundary drawn between the United States and Spain in the Transcontinental Treaty of 1819. Texas later claimed these boundaries after she separated from Mexico. Needless to say, had this claim of the 1850 convention stood, the political organization of the Southwest today would be radically different.

The constitution-makers further defied the Texans in their claims to eastern New Mexico by locating the state capital at Santa Fe some twenty miles east of the Rio Grande. This was to be the political center of the new state until or unless another capital was established elsewhere by the legislature of the proposed state.

Other significant provisions were those dealing with the status of the military, the Church, and the native *Hispanos*. In no uncertain terms, the military was subordinated to the civil establishment. Accordingly, no permanent army was to be maintained by the state during time of peace, and the quartering of soldiers in private homes without the consent of owners was disallowed even during wartime, "except in the manner prescribed by law." The protection of the citizen was given particular emphasis. Civilians were not to be subjected to corporal punishment under military law. Soldiers of the United States Army stationed in New Mexico were allowed no vote in the state.

The spiritual monopoly of the Roman Catholic Church was challenged, but an all-out declaration of war was avoided. Freedom of conscience was guaranteed to every individual and, by law, no preference was to be given to "any religious society, [or] mode of worship . . . ." Church control of education was threatened by a provision to establish a system of education to be supported by public taxation. By its terms, the state legislature was to set aside "not less than one-twelfth of the annual revenue of the State, derived from taxation, as a perpetual fund" to be used for the maintenance of the public schools.[30] A religious test could not be required as a qualification for public employment. Realizing that the Church would look upon most of these provisions with distrust, some concessions were made. For instance, divorce could not be granted except by a "special act of the Legislature." Other more positive concessions to the old order were reflected in the section which recognized Hispanic legal tradition. Spanish civil law not "inconsistent" with the 1850 constitution would remain in effect along with compatible practices in common law. As for the right to vote, the members of the convention seemed anxious to bestow this cherished American prerogative upon the native people of New Mexico. All of them except the "uncivilized" Indian were given the vote provided they took an oath "at least six months preceding any election, before some Judge of the Supreme Court in this State, or before a Clerk of any Court of Record in this State . . . renouncing and abjuring all allegiance or fealty to the Government of the Republic of Mexico, and to support the Constitution of the United States and of this State."[31]

Of particular fascination was a provision stating unequivocally that priests and ministers could not be forced to serve in the army, "work on Roads or serve on Juries." The delegates also felt protective toward the humble but honest toilers of the world. "The Legislature shall have the power to lay an income tax, to tax all persons pursuing any trade, occupation or profession; provided, that the term occupation shall not be construed to apply to pursuits either agricultural or mechanical."[32]

Published copies of the constitution were accompanied by a *cédula*, or decree, which called for a referendum to approve the document as well as the election of officials for the proposed state government. Colonel Munroe, responding to that portion of the decree requesting action on his part, issued a proclamation on May 28 calling for a vote on June 20. Two ballots were to be cast. On one, citizens were to vote for or against the new constitution; on the other, votes were to be cast for a governor, lieutenant governor, representative to Congress, and members of the first state legislature. Deferring to the wishes of the convention, the colonel also allowed the legislature to assemble for its first session on July 1 of the same year.

It being provided and understood that the election of all officers in this election can only be valid by the adoption of the Constitution by the people and otherwise null and void; and that all action of the Governor, Lieut. Governor, and of the Legislature, shall remain inoperative until New Mexico be admitted as a State under said Constitution properly before the Congress of the United States.

Munroe followed this precaution with an endorsement of the current territorial government under his jurisdiction. "The present Government shall remain in full force until by the action of Congress another shall be substituted."[33]

Twenty-four hectic days passed between the adoption of the constitution and the day of its popular referendum. As both the Weightman and Houghton factions endorsed the new constitution, the heated and unabated political battle that marked every day of the interim was due to determination on each side to place the most men in official positions in the new government. The Houghton faction, the old territorial party, was most anxious to nominate the popular and longtime resident of New Mexico, Henry Connelly, for governor. Ceran St. Vrain was this group's choice for lieutenant governor, and Hugh Smith, who was still in Washington, was the candidate for the national House of Representatives. Candidates for the state legislature were also selected. McCall, who had many friends among the influential territorialists, expressed the widely held belief that the "Houghton party would carry all before them."[34]

The Weightman faction, however, had a candidate of its own for every office. Thomas Cabeza de Baca and Manuel Alvarez were the respective nominees for governor and lieutenant governor. A New Englander, William S. Messervy, opposed Hugh Smith for the congressional seat. Seats in the state legislature would, hopefully, be filled by such early advocates of statehood as Angeny and Naugle.[35] Control of the state legislature was recognized as essential because of the power it would have in choosing New Mexico's two United States senators.

The Weightman faction took the offensive with a fast-moving campaign appealing for civilian rather than military control in New Mexico. According to McCall, the group called itself "the friends of the people," and adopted as its "rallying cry 'the people against the authorities' and rang the charges [sic] on oppression[,] corruption & maladministration. . . ." Roman Catholics were told that their interests would best be served by the election of the Weightman candidates. Weightman had personally made himself the advocate of the priests and the defender of the Church. Consequently, enthusiasm for the underdog party, the "Angeny, Weightman, Pillons [sic] & Messervy party" as McCall put it,[36] began to mount as election day approached. Only one setback occurred to slow the campaign's drive, and that was the resignation on June 5 of Father Jose Francisco Leyva, the popular priest from San Miguel. The padre, who had been nominated to run for the upper house by the Weightman faction, declined the honor, and announced his intention to retain his Mexican citizenship and leave the territory.[37]

McCall was particularly critical of the Weightman group's badgering of the Pueblo Indians. Having failed to prevent the framing of a constitution, the old state party was determined to control the votes of the Pueblo Indians in order to win the election. "Addresses have been sent to them; advice has been forced upon them in the most formal & authentic shape; & promises & threats have alike been used by Mexicans & Americans to bring them over." The objective was at least 2,000 Pueblo votes, which they believed would be decisive "if there should prove to be, among the Mexicans themselves, any thing like an equality between the parties."

An example of the unfortunate position of the Indians in this struggle for votes is provided by Cochiti Pueblo, situated southeast of Santa Fe. A deputation from the small pueblo came to the capital on June 10 to call upon Munroe and express their bewilderment over the election proceedings. It seems that as early as May, Calhoun, acting in his capacity as Indian agent, told the Cochiti Indians not to vote in the election for delegates to the constitutional convention which met later that month. Sometime thereafter, one of the candidates for governor in the June election, Cabeza de Baca, warned the chief of the Cochitis that the Anglo-American leaders of the Houghton faction were determined to win the votes of the Pueblo Indians, and, if they failed, they would reduce the Pueblos to the "Condition of Nabahoes & Apache's [sic]" and take away their posses-sions. Finally, to completely overwhelm the Cochiti group, Munroe, wish-ing to countcract the confusion, had issued a proclamation on June 6 de-claring the perfect right of the Pueblos to vote for or against the adoption of the State Constitution, "or to abstain from voting altogether, should they prefer to do so."[38]

McCall condemned any intimidation of the Indians as most unwise, for in the future the Pueblo Indians could be valuable auxiliaries in the event of a war with the neighboring wild tribes. On the other hand, if mis-treated, these "10,000 souls," who are "Christianized, intelligent, indus-trious, moral & peaceful" might join the nomadic tribes who were keeping New Mexico in an almost constant state of upheaval. ". . . It would be easy for them to join marauding or war parties of our enemies without fear of detection, should they be goaded on to revenge by their accumulated wrongs." McCall believed that the Pueblos preferred American rule, "as they had always been more or less oppressed by Mexican Officials"; there-fore, alienating them was both stupid and unnecessary.

Suddenly it was voting day, June 20, 1850, a day for assessing the feel-ings of New Mexicans. A desire for statehood was clearly revealed by an overwhelming approval of the new state constitution. Voting for it were 8,371 people, and only 39 cast ballots against it.[39]

The voting for state officials gave the Weightman faction a new role as majority party. Although Dr. Connelly, because of the support he received from both parties in the southern counties,[40] and his prestige and experi-ence, was elected governor in a 4,604 to 2,706 vote victory, the Weight-man candidates won the other top offices. Alvarez became lieutenant gov-ernor, defeating St. Vrain by a vote of 4,586 to 3,465,[41] and Messervy be-came the new national congressman in a 4,934 to 3,424 triumph over the unfortunate Smith.[42] The old state party also gained control of the first state legislature.

Thus, a rather strange new "state" administration was given life. Whether its mandate included electing United States senators, at that time a legislative function, was a moot question. Munroe in his proclama-tion claimed that the newly elected state government would "remain in-operative until New Mexico be admitted as a State"; yet he did permit them to take "the primary steps of organization" so that they could "prop-erly" present the new constitution to Congress. Notwithstanding the con-fusion, the infant government decided to take decisive action. Ten days after their election, members of the new state legislature met, on July 1, and soon "commenced in earnest the maneuvering and log rolling for seats in the U. S. Senate, the great object of the leaders on either side."

Although the Weightman faction held more seats in the legislature, the Houghton group hoped for division among them because three state party men were competing for the two senate seats. Weightman, as the leader, sought one; Calhoun, the other; and Dr. James D. Robinson, a physician described by McCall as being an adventurer grateful for any favors, also hoped to be a senator. The territorialists had as their candidates Judge Houghton and Captain A. W. Reynolds, quartermaster of the military forces stationed in the territory. Division in the Weightman party did not materialize in quite the way Houghton had hoped, and Houghton and Reynolds, lacking votes, were out of the race after a "short struggle." After a few more days Calhoun and Robinson also were removed from consideration, and Major Francis A. Cunningham, an Army paymaster, was selected without solicitation to serve with Weightman as one of the first two senators to represent New Mexico in Congress. Cunningham, at the time, was out of the city with a mail party and the legislators were not certain whether he would accept the designation.[43] It is interesting to note that Weightman too had been an Army paymaster.

The old state party was jubilant over its victory. Calhoun interpreted the election results as a disastrous defeat for the Houghton faction. "The [Houghton] party . . . to whom the Governor [Munroe] had committed the formation of the State Government submitted to an overwhelming defeat, and the party who commenced the agitation of the question during the fall past triumphed."[44] Weightman, whose shrewd opportunism and fluency in Spanish had made him the big winner, offered a similar analysis, but with particular bitterness toward Munroe. "The State party at the late elections triumphed in every county but one, and did so despite the partisan acts of the military commander, despite the almost unanimous opposition of the judges, prefectos, alcaldes . . . who held their offices at the will and pleasure of the military commander, and despite the almost unanimous vote of the employees of the quartermaster's department."[45] As Weightman saw it, Munroe, as the civil and military governor of New Mexico, had two important holds over the populace. Politically, he could exercise control over the civilian territorial officials through Judge Houghton. Economically, he could exercise power over the merchants who supplied the army through his quartermaster, Captain Reynolds. It was no accident, then, that these two men were the candidates of the territorial party for the Senate seats. Houghton was Munroe's "chief judge" and Reynolds his "chief quartermaster," the managers of "two webs of influence, having Santa Fe as their common center, and extending to the frontiers of New Mexico . . . ." While Houghton as "controller of the civil officers," held these officials at the "absolute will and pleasure of Munroe,"

Reynolds exercised a comparable power as "chief of quartermaster's department, 'with its army of employees, with its contracts to let, and with its agencies to purchase the entire surplus of the corn and forage of the country.' "[46]

Weightman was also among the first to shout fraud in connection with a New Mexico election, a charge that was to be echoed time and time again in the future. Writing to Alvarez on October 18, 1850, he complained that the margin of victory for their party would have been much greater if some of the votes had not been suppressed. "You will recollect that our friends the Prefectos in the late election suppressed as many of our majorities as possible in order to give their party the majority."[47]

Obviously the factional struggle which dominated New Mexico's first "state" election had created bitterness that would not disappear easily. There would be very little time for the victorious Weightman party to gloat.

FOUR

Becoming a Territory

New Mexicans had now
framed a constitution, forthrightly denied the legitimacy of slavery in their
domain, and, with equal boldness, defied the claims of Texas. Each of
these actions was certainly open to serious challenge, but the immediate
question was whether the state government created by the convention of
1850 and then ratified by a popular vote of more than 8,000 was legitimate,
or merely an exercise in self-government.

Many people hoped that Colonel Munroe, the military commandant
and civil governor of New Mexico, would follow the precedent set by General Riley of California, who voluntarily surrendered his civil authority
and allowed the new civilian government to begin operating immediately.
Riley, however, had promised to do this in his election proclamation[1] before the convention, while Munroe was limited by his own election proclamation of May 28 which required congressional approval before the state
officials elected in June could legally function. In short, New Mexico's
new state government would remain "inoperative" until Congress granted
statehood. But congressional action would necessarily involve slavery and
the territorial demands of Texas, and the complexity of these issues made
congressmen reluctant to deal with New Mexico.

After the state legislature's election of Weightman and Cunningham in
a spirited contest, the Weightman faction moved to consolidate its power.
The senatorial victory encouraged them to attempt a removal of their opponents from those state offices under jurisdiction of the legislature. According to the Constitution of 1850 this included the judiciary. "The

Judges of the Supreme Court shall be appointed by the Governor, with the consent of both Houses of the Legislature in joint ballot . . . ."[2] In McCall's opinion, the move had reference "principally to the judiciary— the principal object being to oust Houghton, against whom the whole of the leaders of the dominant party were at daggers drawn."[3] The courts had been established by the military under Kearny, and as Munroe had declared that the military-sponsored government would remain in full force until by the action of Congress another shall be substituted, the purge of officials was no small matter.

In the absence of Governor Connelly, who was on business in the states,[4] Alvarez became acting governor. After his inaugural address had been delivered on July 4,[5] he began to apply pressure with "indecent haste,"[6] nominating friends of the faction for judicial posts "without regard to capacity [,] character or principle . . . ." For seats on the high court he suggested Palmer J. Pillans, a former Texas attorney whom Mc-Call contemptuously called a small country-court lawyer;[7] Francisco Tomas Baca, "a sensible well informed Mexican but with no knowledge of law"; Elias P. West, "an illiterate and presumptuous adventurer who has never been able to tarry long in any state [,] place or country"; and the highly controversial Diego Archuleta, whom McCall unequivocally labeled "the mover of the assassination of Gov. Bent in Taos and the excitation of the insurrection of 1847." McCall's bias was unmistakable, and yet one can justifiably assume that he reflected the attitudes and prejudices of many of the Anglo-Americans in New Mexico, particularly those associated with the old territorial party. Alvarez's appointments to executive offices such as secretary of state, comptroller, and state treasurer were regarded with similar distrust.

Acting Governor Alvarez's actions had grave consequences. Most members of the Houghton faction soon withdrew from the legislature in anger. And, according to McCall, there was trouble even within the smaller group left. Some of the "most influential of the (Mexican) members, & probably the most sincere & best men among them declared that, they desired only the removal of two prefects & two or three Alcaldes who had made themselves obnoxious to their constituents . . . ." These insurgents, feeling that Alvarez had gone too far, threatened to leave the legislature and return to their homes. The disaffection was made known to McCall who urged the group of unhappy *Hispano* legislators to take their problem to the military governor, Colonel Munroe, where their objections would receive immediate attention and be promptly acted upon. But to McCall's chagrin, the rebel group backed off and stayed with the ruling Weightman faction. The prejudices of the observant colonel and federal emissary are revealed here. These legislators "like all Mexicans, easily turned [a]round in their opinions & feelings . . . [were] led by the nose, & used as tools" by the leaders of the Weightman faction. McCall also implied that, because of ignorance, the native leaders had even begun "to talk of the day" when American influence would be diminished and *Hispanos* would be masters and sovereign people in their own land.[8]

That Alvarez and his associates intended to implement fully the civilian state administration seemed obvious, in spite of the clarity of Munroe's proclamation denying legal life to the new government until congressional approval was forthcoming. On July 4, Munroe reminded the legislators of his position in his first communication with the legislature by enclosing a copy of the May 28 election proclamation in his message.[9] But the Weightman group "manifested very decidedly their determination (a la California) to put the state Govt. in full operation at once, without waiting for the action of Congress on the subject . . . ." With this in mind, Alvarez; Angeny, the speaker of the lower house; and other leaders, working with a legislature eager to comply, proceeded "to pass certain acts, among which was one requiring an election of Prefects & Alcaldes . . . to be held on the 15th [of] August."[10]

Tensions mounted as Munroe made it apparent that he would not tolerate this defiance by the new legislature, while Alvarez, for his part, publicly and staunchly defended the right of the legislators to organize a civil government without consent of the military. He argued that the military government in New Mexico, currently represented by Munroe, was a temporary, *de facto* government existing by the "presumed consent of the inhabitants" of New Mexico. President Polk himself indicated as early as July 8, 1848, that, with the termination of the war with Mexico, the power of the chief executive "to establish or to continue temporary civil governments over these territories, which existed under the laws of nations whilst they were regarded as conquered provinces, in our military occupations, has ceased." Polk stated in a later speech that with the coming of peace it was the prerogative of Congress, not of the President, to establish a permanent government. If the President did not have the power to impose a government, argued Alvarez, how could Munroe, the commander of the Ninth Military Department and a subordinate, have such a power? Besides, he added, the "*presumed consent*" of the people of New Mexico to be governed by a militarily appointed officialdom had been withdrawn by the people themselves. Consequently, in the absence of pertinent congressional legislation, New Mexicans had as much right to form their own government as the people of New York or Virginia.

Another argument effectively used by Alvarez was one which questioned the colonel's right to permit New Mexico civilians to establish a state government in order to present the constitution to Congress and select two United States senators, and yet not allow this government to go into operation. If it is possible for the legislature to enact one law such as the one drafted to regulate the election of United States senators, is it not also proper for the lawmakers "to make two, or as many as they may deem proper?" As for his own position as lieutenant governor, Alvarez queried, how could he be "an officer with full authority one day, the next without such authority, and on the third vested again with his official dignity and power . . . ?" The concept of two governors for New Mexico also was introduced as part of a bold challenge to Munroe's continuing authority as civil and military governor. If he had been governor for "one hour," proclaimed Alvarez, he was so until his term expired, "and being so, there is no other; for the coexistence of two governors coeval in the same State is impossible, and contrary to all law and experience."[11]

The stand of Alvarez was strong and uncompromising, and he received the unequivocal support of his state legislature. The members of both houses quickly rose to his support, and on July 15 passed a joint resolution which defended point by point the position taken by the acting governor.[12]

Munroe responded to this tough stand by telling Alvarez in a letter that his original position was unchanged, and that the old territorial government which he controlled would remain in operation until appropriate congressional action was taken. Moreover, if the officers nominated by Alvarez attempted in any way to supercede the civil officials under his jurisdiction, Munroe would regard such action as a direct violation of their duties as citizens of the United States.[13] He then emphasized the fact that he had received definite assurances from the leaders of the 1850 constitutional convention that they clearly understood that the state constitution would not go into effect until sanctioned by the Congress.[14] Calhoun realized how dangerous the argument between the newly elected government and Munroe was becoming. And he was convinced that Munroe was determined to sustain, with all the power at his command, the authorized officials under the Kearny Code, who, until recently, were "violently opposed to a State Government."

The charges and countercharges continued. Munroe was accused of using his troops to curb supporters of the new state government, while Munroe's men felt that many citizens had "revolutionary and treasonable designs."[15] Weightman furiously wrote to Alvarez that troops under the command of a Lieutenant Adams were sent to Mora to put down a rebellion, the second of its kind. This was all part of a scheme, wrote Weightman, a plan "to raise reports of revolutions or mal disturbances . . . [and] have the military called out and then argue the unfitness of New Mexico for self govt. and then defeat the State Govt."[16] Calhoun believed that the deployment of troops and the "much talked of insurrectionary designs" had done much to dampen the enthusiasm of the state movement.[17]

An open clash between the two camps occurred on July 23, 1850, when Colonel Munroe, responding to the call of Alvarez and the state legislature for local elections in August, informed the prefects of the counties in New Mexico that they were to ignore "the proclamations, commands, or other acts issued from the hand of Alvarez, vice governor, or any other official under the said state government and hold the same as null and void . . . ." Munroe reiterated his strong stand that the newly established government had no legal existence until New Mexico was admitted into the Union as a state.[18]

As both principals in the controversy were very stubborn men, a more violent collision was possible. Munroe, a tall artillery officer, was a "very determined man in all his acts and doings." An especially aggressive personality in the morning, he preferred to relax in the afternoon and drink in the warm New Mexico sunshine. Once characterized as the best mathematician in the army and the "ugliest looking man" around, Colonel Munroe would "brew his pitcher of toddy at night, & take the first drink of it at noon the next day; after which hour he would not attend to any official business." But when he was on duty, he was a formidable foe.[19]

Despite the low point reached in the deep political division, there is some evidence that both sides wished to avoid reaching a point of no return. Alvarez, in a proclamation dated August 8, conceded that officials elected in the August 12 balloting would not attempt to exercise "any jurisdiction under or by the authority of said State until after the first day of November, A.D. 1850, or until after they are duly commissioned to act as such." He claimed that this decision was initially made in the July 15 joint legislative resolution in support of his position. Munroe seemed to sense an impending compromise. On the following day, he issued instructions to the county prefects that they were not to obstruct or assist in the upcoming elections. "You will not, however," he cautioned, "recognise [sic] those elections as giving the persons chosen any right to assume the duties of the offices to which they may be elected until the competent authority has so decided by giving the act the validity of its sanction."[20]

The proposed local elections apparently were never held, at least not in Santa Fe. Calhoun in referring to political activity in the old capital mentions the scheduled elections but states that none "were held in this city, nor was any attempt made to induce the people to assemble at the polls . . . ."[21] He felt that Munroe's interference with the new state government had "so completely *chilled* the anxieties of those who had been *hon-*

estly desirous of a state organization" that the slight efforts by Alvarez and Munroe to work for a *modus vivendi* could not dispel the general feeling of discouragement.

The boundary between Texas and New Mexico remained undetermined all this time. Since March of 1848, when the Texas legislature had established Santa Fe County, the state had been attempting to formalize its hold on eastern New Mexico. The most recent step had been the enactment of two bills to organize a militia for the new county and establish a judicial district within it. Representation to the lower house of the Texas legislature also was provided.[22] New Mexico's attempt to establish its own unauthorized government in 1850 gave the Texas assembly a welcome opportunity to righteously denounce New Mexicans and request the Texas delegation in Congress to present the state's case to the federal authorities.

The Santa Fe *Republican* indicates that New Mexico leaders were united in adamant resistance to this pressure from Texas. There is "not a citizen, either American or Mexican, that will ever acknowledge themselves as citizens of Texas until it comes from higher authorities." The peppery journal also advised Texas to send with her civil officers for the county a large force, in order that they may have a sufficient bodyguard to escort them back again in safety. "Oh [,] Texas, do show some little sense and drop this question, and not have it publicly announced that Texas['] smartest men were tarred and feathered by attempting to fill the office assigned them!!!"[23]

These were spirited words but in reality there was little that New Mexico's civilians could do about Texas without federal support. Washington had thus far given no official help to either New Mexicans working for statehood or for territorial status. Polk's policy of noninterference with Texas activities was continued under President Zachary Taylor, who took office on March 4, 1849. Secretary of War Crawford issued orders similar to those given under Polk, but without Polk's command to render assistance to Texas when necessary. Consequently, when the Texas legislature on December 31, 1849, reorganized Santa Fe County by reducing its size and creating three additional counties, there was no military opposition.

Santa Fe County was certainly large enough to warrant a division. It extended from what is today southwestern Texas northward along the Rio Grande and through the Rocky Mountains to Wyoming. The new counties created were Presidio to the far south, its boundaries drawn north and south from a point where the Pecos River empties into the Rio Grande; El Paso to the north of Presidio; and Worth to the north of both. Santa Fe County remained immense, taking in territory both north and south of the Oklahoma panhandle, including central Colorado and a portion of southern Wyoming, in addition to New Mexico territory. Important towns along the Rio Grande such as Santa Fe, Taos, and Albuquerque remained in Santa Fe County.[24]

Texas' tough governor, Peter Hansborough Bell, appointed Major Robert S. Neighbors as commissioner to preside over the reorganization of the counties. The selection of Neighbors was an excellent one, the tall, determined Texan having served in many sensitive assignments as an Indian agent. This aggressive move compelled the federal government to make the difficult choice of either interfering with Texas' activities or continuing its policy of complete noninterference. Washington decided upon the latter alternative. Colonel Munroe, in response to Crawford's directions, ordered his subordinates not to interfere with Neighbors' mission.[25]

Neighbors arrived in the southern counties early in 1850 and began to hold elections and circulate messages and addresses from the resolute Texas governor. He met with particular success in El Paso where he had been before, having pioneered a route from El Paso to Austin. He had no opposition from the military, and it was reported in the Texas capital that the people of El Paso were delighted to become a part of Texas.

Convinced of his success, Major Neighbors started north, arriving in Santa Fe on April 8. His optimism soon faded as he was greeted with noisy public denunciations and angry opposition. Judge Baird, the first Texas agent, had utterly failed to pave the way for Neighbors' mission, a fact partially understood in Austin where the state senate had already withheld his pay. Plans to hold a county election were met by a hostile proclamation issued by Judge Houghton, who urged New Mexicans to stay away from the polls and resist any attempt by Neighbors to organize a government in the name of Texas.[26] But problems with Texas were suddenly obscured by Colonel Munroe's proclamation calling for the convention that drafted the constitution of 1850. This totally unexpected action of Munroe not only shocked Neighbors, but revealed President Taylor's deep involvement in New Mexico's statehood efforts. The surprised Neighbors lodged a protest, but to no avail.

There are some controversial accounts that indicate support for the Texas commissioner. Davis, in his book *El Gringo*, claims that the powerful Weightman faction, the state party, "took sides with Mr. Neighbors, while the territorial party, composed of the mass of people, were opposed to the dismemberment of the Territory by Texas."[27] McCall may have been a source for this claim, as he wrote during the 1850 constitutional convention that the state party was "now averse to forming a state-government without the consent of Texas."[28] McCall apparently believed and repeated a rumor circulating in Santa Fe that Weightman agreed to support the claims of Texas in return for Texas' support of his party. As Mc-Call was partial toward the Houghton faction and held Weightman in great contempt,[29] this accusation must be considered carefully, especially in light of the reckless nature of the charges being bandied about by the two feuding factions. Even Hugh Smith, the rabid abolitionist, was accused by Judge Baird of having supported the claims of Texas at the 1848 meeting, which caused heated opposition to his selection as territorial representative at the 1849 convention.[30]

Of all the figures involved, however, Weightman was most frequently mentioned as a conspirator in behalf of Texas. James L. Collins, a resident of New Mexico for many years and a hostile foe of the Weightman faction, accused the controversial leader of being one of the "distinguished lawyers" said by Neighbors to have helped him in organizing Santa Fe County. Weightman had actually worked for a vote favorable to Texas, and led a band of armed Texans to suppress a protest meeting in Santa Fe plaza, according to Collins. A plan to seize the registration books and suggestions for using an armed force from Texas if necessary to maintain authority were other indictments of Weightman. Collins' opinion was that although Major Weightman admitted that the claims of Texas were contrary to "law and justice," his co-operation with Neighbors was in the name of expediency. And, he also was promised a judgeship under the new Texas authority.[31]

The strangest of all Collins' accusations was that Major Weightman had urged Colonel Munroe to word his proclamation calling for a constitutional convention in such a way as to involve only those New Mexicans living in the undisputed region west of the Rio Grande. Thus, by default, eastern New Mexico would fall into the hands of Texas. When Munroe refused to do this, Weightman urged his *Hispano* followers west of the river to organize their own statehood movement. Despite failure of both schemes, this master of deceit denied, according to Collins, any part in the movement to annex part of New Mexico to Texas.[32]

No proof was found to indicate that Weightman was as unscrupulous as Collins says, only bitter accusations, but a friendship between the leaders of the state party and influential Texans like Judge Baird was revealed by a letter in which Weightman praised Baird's later appointment as Indian agent in the warmest terms.[33] More than two years after this letter, Baird successfully defended Weightman against the charge of murdering Francois X. Aubry, the famous trailblazer, in a fatal argument in a Santa Fe store on August 18, 1854. Since many months had passed between Baird's Santa Fe assignment and these subsequent events, the emphasis attached to their later association would be of questionable importance.

Many early adventurers coming to New Mexico stayed in the territory as permanent residents to befriend former enemies.

Certainly, not all members of Major Weightman's group were ready to accept a victory by Texas. Facundo Pino, a member of the state party and as close to the priesthood in New Mexico as Weightman,[34] was the leader of the protest meeting in Santa Fe plaza which, according to Collins, was forcibly dispersed by the unprincipled Weightman. Even if Weightman had been partial to the claims of Texas, and unquestionably he was an opportunist, a large majority of New Mexicans, both Anglo and Spanish-speaking, would never have tolerated the giving to Texas of the towns of Santa Fe, Albuquerque, and Taos, the very heart of the old Spanish domain. If the sentiments of these New Mexicans were ever to be decisive, the frustrating mission of Baird and Neighbors would be doomed from the beginning.

Judge Baird, however, was more determined than even his fellow Texans were willing to admit, and on July 20, 1850, in the midst of the controversial statehood activity inspired by Alvarez and others of the Weightman group, he boldly issued an election proclamation. There would be a vote on local executive and judicial officials for Santa Fe County on August 5, the same day that the State of Texas was having its general election. It was an insistent proclamation in which Baird stated that in case of "failure or refusal of the regular presiding officer to act it will be Lawful for the electors (Voters) present at the precinct to appoint a presiding officer who will as in ordinary cases appoint 2 Judges and 2 Clerks of the election[.] [T]he presiding officers will make their returns to me within Ten days from and after the election In accordance with instructions."[35]

Because of strong opposition, no one showed up at the polls on the scheduled day and this crisis with Texas passed without conflict,[36] but not without Calhoun adding a new charge to the long list of accusations. "You will observe that he [Munroe] speaks in emphatic terms in relation to Governor Alvarez's proclamation, but not a word of allusion to the Texan order."[37] Perhaps Calhoun was unaware of the policy of nonintervention that Munroe was instructed to follow, or perhaps he was simply trying to pin a pro-Texas label on Munroe in the hope that some of the guilt would rub off on the colonel's allies in the Houghton faction. It is clear that neither faction could afford to be identified with the Texas aspirations.

In the meantime, Texas was preparing to claim eastern New Mexico by more forceful methods. A bill was passed by the state senate giving the governor authority to raise an army of 3,000 mounted volunteers to crush the opposition in Santa Fe and Worth counties.[38] Rumors of possible invasion spread all through New Mexico, and the possibility of violence now gave the boundary dispute national significance. Millard Fillmore, who succeeded to the presidency after Taylor's unexpected death on July 9, 1850, acknowledged congressional authority in this sphere, as Taylor had. On August 6, he proposed to Congress that the boundary dispute be settled by a congressionally inspired compact between the United States, of which New Mexico was now a part, and the claimant, Texas. As an alternative to this solution, Fillmore proposed a judicial decision, but he urged congressional action as faster and more likely to avoid bloodshed.[39]

But this was a time of deep division among the American people, clearly reflected in Congress' inability to act decisively. Fillmore realized that Texas might settle the boundary question by armed force long before Congress could arrange a settlement. He, therefore, had his acting Secretary of War, General Winfield Scott, inform Colonel Munroe that about 750 federal recruits were en route to New Mexico. Presumably they would be used as protection against the Indians, although they might later be needed to protect New Mexicans "in the enjoyment of all rights" should Texas send "a large body of troops" into the territory. Munroe was instructed to avoid violence if at all possible by the use of persuasion. But if efforts to dissuade the Texans from invasion failed, he was to "interpose" his troops and be prepared to fight if the invaders arrested "civil functionaries" and seized property.[40]

In the year 1850, any argument over lands in the West quickly became part of the great debate over the extension of slavery, known as the sectional question. If the demands of Texas were satisfied, the result would be a vast area of land open to slavery. On the other hand, if the New Mexico constitution, with its emphatic antislavery provisions, was recognized, the westward spread of slavery would be abruptly halted at the 100th parallel. Wilmot and others leading the antislavery movement would have scored a major victory.

New Mexicans looked with great favor upon attempts to settle the boundary dispute by congressional negotiation. Weightman spoke for many when he praised President Fillmore for urging Congress to deal with the question, for in "the present [situation] . . . Texas can neither conquor [sic] or retire or return into [sic] New Mexico."[41] The focusing of national attention on the problem had an effect in Texas, too. The Texas legislature adjourned on September 6 without authorizing the dispatch of troops to Santa Fe, apparently feeling that this was a move that the people of Texas must approve because of its many serious repercussions. This lessened the immediacy of the crisis, although the issue was far from being resolved.

Before Congress could act on the related issue involving Texas and New Mexico, the two houses of Congress became almost paralyzed by the bitterness surrounding the issue of slavery. Convening for the first time in nine months in December, 1849, it faced an accumulation of sectional problems, the demand for statehood by a free California being the major one. Disunion as a solution began to attract the firebrands. As notable a Southerner as Robert A. Toombs of Georgia uttered the ominous word, secession, while Southerners cheered and shouted.[42]

It was in this setting that the great Henry Clay played his last major role in American history. After seven years of absence, the Kentuckian was returning to the Senate deeply disturbed at the tenseness and division he saw growing throughout the country. On January 29, 1850, he introduced a series of resolutions that were a memorable and sincere effort to save the union of states. The resolutions dealt with all the major issues causing national conflict.

He recommended that California be admitted as a free state, and New Mexico and the rest of the Southwest be organized as territories without any restrictions as to slavery. He presented a solution to the Texas-New Mexico border dispute which favored New Mexico, but compensated Texas for its loss by having the federal government assume the state's public debt. Slave traffic would be abolished in the District of Columbia, but not without the consent of the people of the District and those of adjacent Maryland. As concessions to the South, Congress would abdicate its power over the interstate slave trade, and enact an effective fugitive slave law.

The Clay resolutions, a major effort at compromise, quickly plunged Congress into a debate, which during its long course, produced some of the finest oratory of the Silver Age. Moderates in the Congress, including the eloquent Daniel Webster, generally supported Clay. Grim, old John C. Calhoun and Jefferson Davis attacked the compromise proposals on behalf of the South with great feeling and conviction. From the North, men like Senator William Seward of New York regarded as immoral the proposals that favored slavery. As for President Taylor, during his last months he continued to believe that immediate statehood for both California and New Mexico was the best solution for the sectional conflict, and he, therefore, regarded Clay's resolutions as a challenge. Relations between the Whig President and Clay, the old party leader, had never been particularly warm,[43] and consequently Clay's effort to compromise, opposing as it did the President's plan, was regarded by some people as an attack on the President and an act of party disloyalty. To these charges, Clay responded that he would defend his policy against "a thousand Presidents, be they whom they may."[44]

On April 19, the Senate appointed Henry Clay chairman of a committee of thirteen which was to shape the controversial resolutions into legislative proposals. The May 8 report of this select committee proposed the admission of California as a free state, and the organization of New Mexico into a territory without reference to slavery. Utah, to the north, was to be given territorial status in the same way. In New Mexico and Utah, the slavery issue would not be dealt with at this time. President Taylor's wish that these areas determine their own status was ignored.

The suggested boundary settlement largely denied the aspirations of Texas. ". . . It is proposed to Texas that her boundary be recognised [sic] to the Rio Grande, and up that river to the point commonly called El Paso, and running thence up that river twenty miles, measured thereon by a straight line, and thence eastwardly to a point where the hundredth degree of west longitude crosses the Red river . . . ."[45] This boundary line on the western side of Texas would extend northward from the El Paso area at an angle that would deny Texas the right to most of eastern New Mexico. Texan claims to lands north and east of New Mexico also were denied.[46] These proposals of the Clay committee would have greatly encouraged delegates at the Santa Fe constitutional convention to insist that the 100th meridian was the eastern boundary of New Mexico, but the primitive transportational facilities were such, that unless there had been advance warning, news of the committee's recommendation could not possibly have reached Santa Fe by May 25, the last day of the convention. Presumably, then, the New Mexico action was a bold, unilateral one.

Well aware of the impact of their boundary proposal on the expansionist desires of Texas, the committee of thirteen proposed to compensate Texas with "a large pecuniary equivalent" of the lost lands. The exact amount was not specified, but it was to be enough to extinguish that portion of the Texas debt incurred before annexation, in which the duties on foreign imports into the Lone Star Republic had been pledged for payment. The United States government would pay "in a stock, to be created, bearing five per cent interest annually, payable half yearly, at the treasury of the United States, and the principal reimbursable at the end of fourteen years."[47]

The committee report received substantial support in the Senate, but was denounced by extremists of both North and South, who were quick to make known their views. It soon became evident that the President, too, disagreed with many of the committee's solutions. Speaking through supporters such as John Bell of Tennessee, whose own role as a dedicated compromiser lay in the not too distant future, Taylor expressed his continued determination to see both California and New Mexico admitted as states. Clay responded vigorously, charging the President with an attempt to usurp congressional power. The President had merely recommended the formation of a state constitution for California; only Congress could sanction it, stated Bell in the President's defense.

In a speech aimed at Southern members of the Senate, Bell argued for the views of Taylor that territorial rather than state government for New Mexico was actually not a concession to the South, as advocates of compromise said, because if New Mexico did permit slavery within her borders, the territory would have small chance of being admitted as a slave state. Bell regarded the prospect of slavery in New Mexico as very unlikely, but it was a continual source of agitation on both sides of the Mason-Dixon line. He felt that the South would benefit if New Mexico were admitted immediately into the Union, thereby healing one of the "bleeding wounds" of the nation. Taylor's plan, he concluded, would end the controversy, while the Clay proposals would merely prolong it.[48]

Weeks and then months passed as the debate dragged on. An omnibus bill proposing California statehood, territorial status for New Mexico and Utah, and the Clay boundary settlement, was defeated by a parliamentary maneuver. A tired and disheartened Clay left the Senate to journey to Newport where he hoped to regain his strength. The battle for compromise was carried on by the younger, energetic Stephen A. Douglas of Illinois.

Extremist positions gradually weakened and an atmosphere more conducive to compromise developed. The heated boundary dispute, made more dangerous by the growing hostility of Texas, was the first of the problems pertaining to New Mexico to be solved. Texans were very bitter about the Clay committee's proposals. Texas Senator Thomas J. Rusk was convinced of the legality of his state's claim. "The Constitution is explicit that no State [New Mexico] shall be formed within another State without its consent."

Nor did talk of a judicial settlement of the boundary dispute satisfy Rusk. This solution, embraced by the newly installed President Fillmore as one alternative, had the support of several powerful figures in the capital, including Senator Seward. Seward was a prominent critic of Negro slavery, an institution which, in spite of its legal or constitutional foundation, was in his view "temporary, accidental, partial, and incongruous" in a free society. He had thrown himself into the center of the sectional controversy in his publicized March 11, 1850, speech in which he maintained that there was "a higher law than the Constitution" governing the actions of the United States in the recently acquired Western domain, and that was God's law, which in Seward's view opposed the extension of slavery. The wrath and indignation in the South caused by this moralistic position placed the slight New Yorker in the radical camp, as even Northern moderates were surprised and alarmed by his uncompromising approach. But Seward continued to speak forcefully on the question of slavery extension and on statehood for California and New Mexico.

On July 26, 1850, he spoke in behalf of New Mexico statehood and the right of New Mexicans to have their own representatives on any commission that Congress might authorize to determine the boundary between Texas and New Mexico. Holding a copy of the recently drafted constitution of New Mexico in his hand, sent to him by "one who attended the convention," Seward eloquently pleaded for the admission of New Mexico before Texas could absorb the "most valuable and most densely settled portions" of the territory. Although the new constitution had not been formally presented, Seward insisted that its contents were well known to the members of Congress, and that the document did not create a "kingly" government, as charged by one senator, but was republican in form.

Spurning compromises—"I believe that concession to-day only increases the evils and embarrassments of to-morrow"—the New Yorker insisted that territorial status was insufficient; New Mexico was entitled to immediate admission. The people of the territory might be a vanquished and "subjugated people," but they constituted a community and were entitled to the same rights as the people of any territory, or even of any state within the United States. The Treaty of Guadalupe Hidalgo entitled New Mexico to statehood, and although the consent of Congress was required, Congress could only determine "when," not if, New Mexico should be admitted. With a population of 100,000, "two-thirds as large as Texas, which has two members of Congress," the territory was ready for statehood. More pertinent to the boundary question, New Mexico as a state with representation in Congress could meet the State of Texas on a basis of equality. The issue of the disputed boundary could be presented to the Supreme Court, the logical avenue of settlement provided by the Constitution and the laws of the United States for such controversies. "In the Supreme Court, New Mexico would be an acknowledged party, allowed to speak for and defend herself." In this just atmosphere, a solution would be achieved "without any delay."

But Senator Rusk staunchly opposed any such solution. "Suppose the court should determine, as I have no doubt they would, that it [eastern New Mexico] is within the limits of Texas, the action of Congress will have been directly in the teeth of the Constitution in forming the Government. If you cannot form a State within a State, can you take steps toward it?"[49]

The Texan's firm stand was too late, however, to stop the movement toward a final settlement of the question. On August 5, 1850, nine days before Rusk's angry response, Senator James A. Pearce of Maryland offered Senate bill 307, a compromise measure which drew the Texas-New Mexico boundary along the meridian of 103 degrees west longitude instead of along the 100th meridian. The persuasive Pearce also proposed that Texas be compensated by some ten million dollars for the lands she would surrender. After four days of debate, the Senate passed this measure by a vote of 30 to 20.[50] The House concurred, thus formalizing what is today in all major respects, the boundary line between Texas and New Mexico.

The western boundary of Texas started at the 36° 30' parallel and ran southward along the "meridian of one-hundred and three degrees west from Greenwich" to the 32nd degree of north latitude, and along that parallel to the Rio Grande, following the channel of this great river to its mouth.[51] This charted most of New Mexico's western boundary, and the eastern portion of her southern boundary, which ran eastward from a point some twenty miles northwest of modern El Paso.

Financial compensation for Texas was similar to that suggested by the Clay committee. The United States government was to pay the State of Texas $10,000,000 in stock bearing five per cent interest to be reimbursable at the end of fourteen years, the interest payable on a half-yearly basis at the United States Treasury.[52] The money, representing approximately the amount needed to cancel the public debt owed by Texas, was to be paid as soon as the President of the United States received an "authentic copy of the act of the general assembly of Texas accepting these propositions . . . ."[53] On November 25, the Texas legislature accepted the compromise and on December 13, 1850, President Fillmore declared the new boundary, which had become law by his signature on September 9th, in "full force and operation."[54]

Senate bill 170, calling for the creation of the Territory of New Mexico, accompanied the boundary measure and came up for debate on August 13. Inhabitants of the territory were given the right to decide for themselves whether or not slavery would exist in the territory. An amendment added to the bill by contentious Senator Henry S. Foote of Mississippi specified that eventual statehood would be on terms decided by New Mexicans themselves. ". . . That, when admitted as a State, the said Territory, or any portion of the same, shall be received into the Union, with or without slavery, as their constitution may prescribe at the time of their admission."[55]

Another amendment, offered by Senator Douglas on August 14, defined with uneven exactness the entire territory's boundaries. Beginning at that point where the boundary separating the Republic of Mexico from the United States intersects the Colorado River, the southern boundary of New Mexico was drawn eastward to the Rio Grande, "thence following the main channel of said river to the parallel of the thirty-second of north latitude; thence eastward with said degree to its intersection with the 103d degree of longitude west from Greenwich; thence north with said degree of longitude to the parallel of the 38 degree of north latitude; thence west with said parallel to the summit of the Sierra Madre [Rocky mountains]; thence south with the crest of said mountains to the 37th parallel of north latitude; thence with said boundary line to the place of beginning."[56] The new territory, as defined by the Illinois senator, took in a great deal of the American Southwest. It included not only present-day New Mexico, minus the area acquired later in the Gadsden Purchase, but most of Arizona, plus sizable portions of southern Colorado and Nevada.

The Senate passed the bill on August 15 by a comfortable margin, the vote being 27 to 10. It was then sent with the boundary bill to the House of Representatives. After some discussion of the bill in the House, Congressman Linn Boyd, Democrat of Kentucky, offered an amendment to the Texas boundary bill that would give territorial status to New Mexico. The amendment was so like Senator Douglas' measure, calling for almost exactly the same boundary and governmental organization,[57] that when the Senate considered the House amendment some days later, Douglas suggested that the reading of the amendment be dispensed with. The House amendment, he stated, was "word for word, the New Mexico territorial bill, which passed the Senate some days since, which they have added to the Texas boundary bill, without altering either."

On September 6, the amended bill passed the House of Representatives by a vote of 108 to 97. The victors were jubilant, according to the *Globe* reporter. "The announcement of the result was received with manifestations of applause of various kinds, the most peculiar and attractive of which was a sort of unpremeditated *allegro* whistle, which the Reporter does not remember to have heard before, (certainly never before in the House of Representatives)." The other tokens of gratification, he added, were of a less musical order. The excitement was not confined to partisans in the gallery. "It was evident that a greater portion of the applause, especially at the outset, was on the floor of the Hall itself."[58]

The Senate approved the House alterations on September 9, 1850, and eliminated another problem the same day by giving statehood to California. President Fillmore completed the accomplishment when later, on September 9, he signed into law both the California statehood measure and the bill clarifying the Texas boundary and giving territorial status to New Mexico. Fillmore also gave his life to Utah on that day, the new territory having earlier asked for admittance as the State of Deseret with claims to Arizona overlapping those of New Mexico. Utah was admitted with the right to decide for herself whether slavery would be allowed within her boundaries. Consequently, the principle of "popular sovereignty," first advanced by Lewis Cass, the prominent Democratic politician and unsuccessful presidential candidate, was at last written into a piece of vital legislation pertaining to the sectional problem. As for New Mexico, she failed to achieve statehood because granting her full status would have completely upset the delicate sectional balance, but she did receive an Organic Act because congressional leaders believed that this would compromise the sharp difference in views held by Southern and Northern leaders.

The Compromise of 1850, as these actions came to be called, had resolved without violence the explosive problems posed by the newly acquired lands in the West, and a great feeling of relief passed through the country. This did not mean, though, that the statemakers in New Mexico were pleased with the outcome for the territory. Senator-elect Richard H. Weightman arrived in Washington to claim his congressional seat around September 5, the day before the House of Representatives passed the amended version of the Texas boundary measure.[59] Although disappointed and frustrated, there was little the New Mexico leader could do but hopefully transmit to President Fillmore the state constitution "and accompanying papers."

Weightman later wrote the President a letter, enclosing a memorial from the New Mexico legislature asking for statehood, a memorial in behalf of the 1850 constitution, and Alvarez's inaugural address to the legislators.[60] These were to be forwarded to the Senate. President Fillmore told Weightman personally that had the bill creating New Mexico Territory not been passed, "he would have recommended the admission of N.M. as a State." But in view of the action already taken by Congress, he would, after consulting his cabinet, merely "transmit the Constitution without recommendation of any kind." The following day the President did confer with his cabinet, and with their approval New Mexico's constitution was submitted to the Senate without a statehood recommendation.[61]

Both Weightman and his predecessor in Washington, Hugh Smith, were disappointed but not surprised by Fillmore's apathy in regard to New Mexico. They believed Taylor's death had done irreparable damage to the statehood cause. Although the old soldier in the White House had been ailing, causing great concern within his cabinet,[62] his sudden death in the midst of the great sectional crisis could not have been anticipated. For New Mexico, the unfortunate event meant the passing of her strongest statehood champion. "It is Mr. Hugh Smith's opinion as well as mine," observed Weightman, "that but for the death of General Taylor we would at once have received a State Govt."[63]

Weightman recognized the fait accompli that had made New Mexico a territory. "There will be no legislation in regard to the admission of New Mexico as a State this Session (which terminates the 30th of this month)." But a natural inclination to confidence and optimism kept him from feeling the fight was over. "Had I have arrived here two months earlier there is but one opinion New Mexico would have been a State."

A plan by which statehood might yet be achieved was devised by Weightman. First, a vote would be taken in New Mexico that would illustrate to Congress how persistent the statehood sentiment was in the territory. Second, the new state government in New Mexico would oust Colonel Munroe's military-dominated territorial government. Writing to Alvarez, Weightman said he was convinced statehood could be achieved in the next session of Congress if the people again voted affirmatively for it. "I would very respectfully suggest to you[,] Sir, that this point be submitted to the people and a distinct vote be had to test the preference of the people for a state or Territorial Government—and I wish to be distinctly understood that should the people prefer a State Govt. It [sic] is my opinion *that they can get it.*" If the people decided otherwise, he would consider his mission at an end and return to New Mexico with his family at an early date.

Weightman felt the removal of the military government in New Mexico was necessary so that the superiority of the civil over the military would be "clearly exemplified." What better way of demonstrating the subordination of the military could be devised, Weightman queried, than by forcing Munroe out? "*I think it all important that in any case, the State govt., before the organization of the Territorial Govt., should oust the Military Government if only for a month.*"

Weightman had some reason to hope his scheme might work since the new territorial government might not begin before the approval of Texas was secured. When the Texas legislature adjourned, many felt that the solution to the Texas-New Mexico boundary dispute ought to be submitted to the citizenry of Texas before the provisions of congressional legislation, including New Mexico's territorial government, were implemented. This of course would occupy some time, reasoned Weightman. Perhaps so much time that the territorial government would not go into operation at all, inasmuch as it was his opinion that "N.M. will at the next session be admitted."[64]

Working constantly to secure Munroe's removal from the scene in New Mexico, Weightman saw to it that the heated exchange of opinions between the stubborn colonel and Alvarez was thoroughly publicized in Washington. He presented the state government's side as favorably as possible by publishing letters from Alvarez to Munroe, and forwarded to President Fillmore a telegraph dispatch which effectively stated the Alvarez position. Weightman was optimistic, anticipating prompt action on the part of President Fillmore in regard to the "unjustifiable intereference" by the colonel.[65] Everybody repudiated the military government, he told Alvarez, and the opinion in "high quarters" was that Munroe, "the Anglo-American," had suffered a defeat at the hands of the "*Anglo-Mexican* (yourself)."[66]

Weightman was indeed pleased with his work when he heard that Secretary of War Charles M. Conrad had sent an important dispatch to New Mexico by a special courier named Henry Hardy, who was selected for that purpose.[67] The message was a firm reprimand to Colonel Munroe, commanding him to stop meddling in civilian affairs. It was at all times desirable, warned Conrad,

that the civil and military departments of the government be kept entirely distinct. Although circumstance may occasionally arise which require a temporary departure from this principle, that departure should cease with the necessity which occasioned it. No necessity seems to exist at present for departing from it in regard to New Mexico. The country is represented to be tranquil. . . . Unless, therefore, it should become necessary to suppress rebellion or resist actual hostilities against the United States, (an event hardly to be apprehended) or unless the inhabitants . . . should demand from you . . . protection [,] . . . you are directed to abstain from all further interference in the civil or political affairs of that country.

As for the recently established state government headed by Alvarez, Munroe's charges of dangerous usurpation were not only ignored by the Secretary of War but sternly dismissed. Even though the inhabitants of the territory had undertaken, without the authority of a congressional act, to establish a government, he insisted, there was no reason to believe that they intended to throw off their allegiance to the United States, and as the government they sought to establish was entirely consistent with the lawful authority and dominion of the United States, ". . . the President does not consider himself called upon to suppress it by military force."[68]

Weightman was concerned lest Colonel Munroe neglect to inform the territory's citizens of his new instructions, finally received on October 22.[69] The senator-elect knew the encouragement the dispatch would give civilian elements and especially the Alvarez state government. Despite urging by his friend Weightman, however, Alvarez did not take advantage of Munroe's weakened position by either holding another referendum on statehood, or replacing the military government, even for a short time.

As Weightman's plans were New Mexico's only hope for statehood in 1850, their failure meant statehood was impossible that year. Although the elected state government was no longer regarded as inconsistent "with the lawful authority and dominion of the United States," it was never accredited by the Thirty-first Congress. The national administration, despite professions of sympathy by Fillmore, clearly defined its position in a statement by Secretary of State Daniel Webster on August 5. New Mexico's state government was a "nullity." It had no legal validity until it was recognized and adopted by the "law-making power of the United States."[70]

Weightman and his family remained in Washington in spite of the fact that Congress was now between sessions. Still full of ambitions, ideas, and plans, Weightman often assumed the pretensions of a senator. His letters to Alvarez announced his intention "to keep New Mexico aloof" from the sectional conflict. "The slavery excitement is by no means concluded. The South or rather the Ultras of that section think the Admission of California an outrage on their rights—while the Northern Ultras contemplate resisting the Fugitive Slave Bill—."[71] Weightman also intended to draw national attention to an old and very serious New Mexico problem, the Indian menace. Conditions in the territory were "deplorable," and he would impress upon Congress the necessity of prompt and efficient protection against the Indians.[72]

By the time appointments for the new territorial government were being seriously considered, Weightman had made himself so well heard that he was able to help his political ally, Calhoun, secure appointment as chief executive of the new territorial government. In a letter to Alvarez, he predicted that Calhoun would be selected as governor on the basis that he had given great satisfaction as Indian agent, and to appoint anyone else as governor would amount to "virtually turning him out of office," as the governor of the territory was also the Indian agent.

Weightman also confidently informed his friend Alvarez that he [Alvarez] would be the new Secretary of the Territory. "I am told that Col. Calhoun will be Governor and yourself Sec. of [the] Territory—certain, I think."[73] But to the embarrassment of the would-be senator in Washington, the fight over this appointment dragged on for months until an Anglo named William S. Allen was finally chosen. Allen did not arrive in the territory to assume his secretarial duties until June, 1851, three months after the territorial government had been established. Weightman was, however, able to block Senate confirmation of the appointment of his rival, Hugh Smith, to the coveted position.[74]

The final demise of the opportunist in his role of senator was to come soon, but not before Weightman managed to create one last flurry of controversy in the capital. On September 23, 1850, Whig Senator William C. Dawson of Georgia proposed an amendment to a congressional appropriations bill which would pay $2,000 to Weightman as travel expenses for his journey to Washington. Two votes on the proposal were taken, and both times the mileage allowance was narrowly defeated, 24 to 23 and 20 to 19. But the debate preceding the vote rekindled some of the heated emotions surrounding the Compromise of 1850.

Dawson compared Weightman's mission to the one taken by the California senators to assert their claims. Even if California's bid had been rejected, the Senate "would have consented to pay her Senators." William M. Gwinn, one of California's new senators, denied that the situations were comparable, because New Mexico's state government, unlike California's, had been formed *after* Congress went into session, and it was known by that time that a territorial government was being considered for New Mexico. Other senators jumped into the fray. One dismissed the entire statehood movement in New Mexico as a "flagrant usurpation"; if New Mexico's claims were honored it would be like making states "as cheap as whetstones." Senator Foote of Mississippi sharply criticized the New Mexico statehood policy of the late President Taylor. "Can any man doubt, that if New Mexico had been recognized as a State of this Confederacy, civil war would not have occurred, out of which this blessed Union itself would have been destroyed?"[75]

The two senators from Texas also voiced their opinions on the reimbursement of Weightman. Sam Houston said that, as a former army officer, Weightman, upon discharge, was entitled to travel expenses back to his home, which was the city of Washington. Therefore the $2,000 requested from Congress was additional and constituted a double payment. Protests that a year had lapsed after Weightman's discharge brought Houston's answer that the time passed was irrelevant and Weightman could still collect the payment. The outspoken Houston also observed that Hugh Smith, the other of New Mexico's strange envoys to Washington, had been "fully compensated" for his services. Senator Rusk, the other Texan in the upper house, denied any personal malice toward Weightman—" I am the last man here that would withhold from any individual who came from New Mexico or elsewhere his allowance of mileage or per diem . . ."—but he felt that to recognize Weightman's claims would cause new resentment over the recently settled New Mexico-Texas boundary. "The amendment now pending, I fear, will be seized upon to raise this question anew, and thus to increase and protract the irritation which already exists in Texas."[76]

The months of painstaking negotiation spent in working out the Compromise of 1850, a delicate truce between North and South, resulted in a strong and widespread feeling that adamant, emotional sectional strife must be avoided at any cost. New Mexico had failed to achieve statehood, as had California, in the advantageous climate of change and presidential willingness that existed in 1849 and 1850. Now the territory's ambiguous geographical position, located in both south and west, would cause the issue of her admission to be avoided by all sides as a needless aggravation of the simmering sectional conflict.

FIVE

Internal Strife

T HE 1850'S AND 1860'S
were the saddest and most disruptive years of America's history. Naturally
the myriad problems brought on by slavery, sectional strife, a bloody Civil
War, and the controversial years of Reconstruction left little time for the
nation to attend to the needs of the Territory of New Mexico, despite its
ever-present desire for admission as a state.

No serious effort was made by New Mexicans to achieve statehood in
the 1850's. In the 1860's, perhaps hoping to be recognized for their loyalty
to the Union, New Mexicans again took their case to Congress. But long
before this, the territory had shown its inability to present a picture of stability and unity of purpose to the country. The Southwest, with its Rio
Grande and piñon trees and lore of the *conquistadores*, had become, with
the advent of Anglos in larger numbers, a land of vast cultural, religious,
racial, political, and economic differences among its people. Factions,
feuds, bitterness, and a chronic inability to unite effectively resulted from
these differences.

The Compromise of 1850 left as a legacy for New Mexico popular sovereignty on the matter of slavery. This freedom to choose sides in the
event of becoming a state made the territory a pawn in the struggle between North and South. Both abolitionists and slaveholding Southerners
in the divided nation hopefully sought to insure New Mexico's commitment to their cause, to be paid for by support of the territory's statehood
movement. Political leaders in New Mexico found themselves having to
ally at times with one side or the other, and sometimes, because of their

views on slavery, they were labeled supporters of the North or South even though they often preferred not to be.

Weightman, who became the territory's official delegate to Congress, told, in a long speech which he had published, about the activities of the abolitionists in New Mexico. According to Weightman, the American and Foreign Anti-Slavery Society had sent W. G. Kephart, a Presbyterian minister, to the territory as an agent.[1] This aggressively antislavery missionary arrived even before New Mexico had been made a territory by the Compromise of 1850. An article appearing on February 26, 1852, in Washington's *National Era*, a widely circulated antislavery newspaper, told of Governor Calhoun licensing traders to purchase Indian children as slaves for people in New Mexico.[2] This indictment of New Mexican officials as heartless slave traders was felt by Weightman to have originated with Kephart's exertions on behalf of his cause.

"Padre" Kephart, as Weightman liked to call him, engaged in the most partisan of politics. He regarded the predominant Catholic Church as a prime adversary, accusing it of open political interference. Because Kephart remained in the territory and worked closely with the old military-dominated Houghton faction, the territorial party increasingly became known as the antislavery party. Kephart became the editor of the *Santa Fe Weekly Gazette*, with such co-editors as Houghton and T. S. J. Johnson, Colonel Munroe's "chief clerk of the quartermaster." The newspaper possessed the only printing press in the territory[3] and was owned by Johnson, Collins, and Hugh Smith, all leaders in the Houghton faction.[4] Houghton, himself, had an established reputation as a fierce antislavery partisan.[5] No wonder Weightman believed that all the Houghton people were siding with the North and antislavery.

A pamphlet published by the antislavery society, and brought by Kephart to the territory, urged New Mexicans to spurn slavery and organize a territorial government without the "detestable institution." "BE FIRM AND RESOLUTE IN DECLARING FOR INDEPENDENCE, unless exempted from the curse of slavery, and the whole North will rally in your behalf."[6]

Weightman's position on slavery, important because he was the territory's first recognized representative in Washington, was publicly one of determined neutrality, in line with his plans to keep New Mexico, if possible, aloof from the sectional struggle.

The popular feeling in New Mexico is, I believe, fixedly set against that country being made an arena in which to decide political questions in which people have no practical interest, and all attempts which have heretofore been made, or which hereafter may be made, to induce the people of that country to *take sides* on a question in which they are not at all interested, have been, and will, I trust, forever be, utterly abortive.

Weightman was one of those Americans who, like Stephen A. Douglas, did not regard the slavery question as a moral one. When the question came up, he declared, they would treat it simply as a matter of policy, by which to facilitate admission into the Union. "Once admitted we can do as we choose. We desire the friendship of all; entangling alliances with none." Slavery was also unsuitable for the territory. "*Slave labor will not pay in New Mexico*, and in that is comprised the whole question."[7]

Public professions of neutrality notwithstanding, Weightman was denounced as a slave propagandist in 1850 by members of the constitutional convention who were drafting antislavery provisions. Of the two competing power factions in New Mexico, the Weightman or state party was far less antagonistic to the expansion of slavery. Later, Weightman would prove his ultimate allegiance to the Southern cause by fighting and dying for the Confederacy.[8]

As for Governor Calhoun, he was probably innocent of the charge that he licensed slave traders to kidnap Indian children, but his hostility toward free Negroes cannot be denied. The governor, a Georgian by birth, requested in his first message to the New Mexico legislature that a law be passed preventing the admission of free Negroes into the territory. "Free Negroes are regarded as nuisances in every state and territory in the Union, and where they are tolerated Society is most depraved."[9] This statement, even though it applied only to liberated slaves, was in sharp contrast to the uncompromising stand against slavery taken by Houghton, Kephart, and their associates on the *Gazette*.

During the 1850's, the sentiments of Calhoun became more popular. In 1856, the territorial legislature did enact a law restricting the movement of free Negroes. A free Negro could not remain in the territory longer than thirty days, intermarriage was prohibited, and newly freed Negroes were required to leave New Mexico within a month. The territory's congressional delegate at this time was Miguel A. Otero, an aristocratic *Hispano* leader from New Mexico. His marriage to Mary Josephine Blackwood, a Southern belle from Charleston, South Carolina, had brought him close to the Southern political leadership, and he was anxious to have his associates in New Mexico co-operate with the South.

New Mexico became increasingly pro-Southern under the governorship of Abraham Rencher, a Buchanan appointee and Democrat from North Carolina. A slave code law enacted by the legislature was signed by Rencher on February 3, 1859.[10] The measure, favored by both Governor Rencher and Otero, did not create or legalize the institution in New Mexico, but merely regulated the two or three dozen slaves who had been brought into the territory from the outside. Otero, in his support of the code, had let it be known that if New Mexico expected any favors from Washington, a slave code would be a wise move.[11]

The power struggle in New Mexico had other sources besides the divisive slavery issue. The deep-seated and bitter rivalry between the Houghton and Weightman factions divided the town of Santa Fe into two camps. The atmosphere of hostility was worsened by Calhoun's appointment as the first governor of the new territorial government, and by Weightman's election as territorial delegate to Congress.

President Fillmore's choice of Calhoun for governor was a logical one, for the Georgian had many years of success behind him. A member of the Whig party like the President, Calhoun had had a distinguished business and political career in Georgia before serving with General Taylor in the Mexican War. He had then been Indian agent in New Mexico for twenty months, a period in which his diplomacy and ability to work with people were much needed. Calhoun's appointment passed the scrutiny of a Democratic Senate, giving him some claim to bipartisan support. Foes of Calhoun were in fact most annoyed by his alleged boast "that a man 'nominated by a Whig President, and endorsed by a Democratic Senate' cannot be remiss in his duty."[12]

Calhoun was inaugurated on March 3, 1851, and immediately found himself in the midst of the running battle of personalities. Colonel Munroe, a political enemy of Calhoun from the early days of rivalry between the territorial and state parties, refused to subside into the background despite instructions from Washington to that effect. He continued to cause trouble until replaced by Lieutenant Colonel Edwin V. Sumner in July of 1851. Weightman precisely identified people antagonistic toward Calhoun as "the legitimate successors of that old military party . . . ."[13]

Beginning with an inaugural address at the Palace of Governors in Santa Fe that promised to prepare the territory for "a higher and more glorious position as one of the sovereign and independent states of the Union . . . ,"[14] Calhoun pressed forward without regard to his enemies as he built a working territorial administration. Voters in the eight territorial districts already in existence elected thirteen senators and twenty-six representatives, who met on June 3, 1851, forming the first territorial legislature.[15] Under the new government the first census was taken in April of that year, showing the population of New Mexico to be 56,984.[16] Among the most pressing problems faced by Calhoun and the legislature were education, the problem of Indian attacks, and New Mexico's isolation. About seven-eighths of the population were illiterate.[17] Countless memorials would be sent to Congress as the years passed asking for protection from the Indians, and in the early 1850's the geographical isolation of the territory prompted a group of citizens to petition for semimonthly rather than monthly mail service between Independence, Missouri, and Santa Fe.[18]

Calhoun was prevented from concentrating completely on these problems by the furor accompanying the election of Weightman in September, 1851, as congressional delegate. Captain Reynolds, formerly Munroe's quartermaster, was Weightman's opponent in the balloting held throughout the territory. Calhoun was accused of allowing voting irregularities in behalf of Weightman, for as the returns came in the indignant Reynolds was behind by 592 votes out of 7,638 cast. His loss was further increased by late returns from Abiquiu giving Weightman 150 more votes. Reynolds, denouncing the election as a fraud, sent a memorial to Congress which charged intimidation, violence, and irregular procedures throughout the territory. He was especially critical of Calhoun who had waited until August 8, 1851, to announce the election. The governor did not print the election proclamations until August 13, and delayed their distribution for several days, leaving only two weeks for campaigning in a territory as big as "all of New England!"[19]

Weightman defended his election as an obviously honest one because the entire vote cast for him and his opponent equaled the votes cast for candidates for lesser offices. Moreover "comparison of the votes and statement of the result, was made by Secretary Allen, and not by Governor Calhoun as has been charged."[20] The Weightman camp had their own version of voting irregularities. An American soldier named Burtinett, who along with a group of other Anglos attempting to close down a polling place at Los Ranchos, near Albuquerque, was actually using violence and intimidation in order to delay and prevent voting, thus insuring the election of Reynolds.

Judge Baird, now closely allied with Weightman, told of Burtinett, two army wagonmasters, and nine other men with bottles of liquor in their hands trying to cast illegal votes in Albuquerque first. They voted despite strenuous protest by the election judge, and then the rowdy group moved on to Los Ranchos, where in an effort to close down the polling place, Burtinett was shot and killed.[21]

The death of an American soldier caused alarm and controversy that was only heightened by the Houghton group's attempt to use the incident to drive a wedge between *Hispanos* and friendly Anglos in the territory. William C. Skinner of the old territorial party, who played such a prominent role in the 1849 convention, was sent to Albuquerque to prosecute the case before the Court of Commitment.[22] During his stay in Albuquerque, Skinner angrily entered the store of a native merchant, Juan Cristobal Armijo, after threatening to "cowhide or whip" him. Whether Skinner was responding to opposition to his investigation or had some personal grievance is not clear, but it is known that he had a quarrel with Armijo's brother, the prefect in Bernalillo County, and had told friends prior to entering Armijo's store that "there was no justice in the ranches [Los Ranchos] . . . ." Skinner was waving a pistol as he approached Armijo, and a desperate fight ensued between the two men, and several bystanders, in which Skinner was killed.[23] The news of Skinner's death, brought back to Santa Fe by Merrill Ashurst, a sometime supporter of the Houghton faction, caused near pandemonium in the territory.

It had long been the policy of Weightman, Calhoun, and the old state party to cater to the traditions and attitudes of the Spanish-speaking New Mexicans. According to Chief Justice Grafton Baker of the territorial supreme court, Calhoun did all he could to make *Hispanos* feel like American citizens, including the appointment of many to public office, a source of resentment among many Anglos who felt deprived of political or financial opportunity.[24] A political alliance had thus grown between the Weightman-Alvarez group and the *Hispanos*. The anxiety caused by the Skinner-Armijo incident now gave the Houghton group a chance to discredit Governor Calhoun. In the eyes of frightened citizens, like those who met on September 25 and publicly condemned the "brutal butchery," Calhoun's determination to deal with the matter temperately and lawfully seemed far too tolerant and easygoing. The *Gazette*, mouthpiece of the Houghton party, urged citizens to action with this headline: "Another Horrible Assassination in Bernalillo County." In an effort to force Calhoun into action, a group of angry Santa Feans, led by a committee of two lawyers and three merchants, marched through the town plaza to the Palace of Governors. Calhoun was interrupted, according to Weightman, in the middle of a whist game with friends to listen to the group's demand that he immediately send two hundred armed men to Bernalillo County. One citizen volunteered to raise fifty men at his own expense. The *Gazette* compared the governor's card game to "the *fiddling of Nero over the burning of Rome*."[25]

Instead of sending an armed militia southward, the next day Calhoun himself left for Bernalillo County with his interpreters, a few friends, and two judges, including Chief Justice Baker. Upon arriving in Bernalillo, the governor interviewed the prefect, Ambrosio Armijo, brother of the man accused of murdering Skinner, despite dire warnings that Ambrosio intended to assassinate him. After this peaceful, fact-finding mission, Calhoun allowed the natural processes of the law to go into operation. Juan Cristobal Armijo was required to give the usual bail, and later appeared before the district court of the United States, where the charge presented against him "was ignored by the grand jury."

Armijo's acquittal infuriated Anglo citizens. Collins, a man who felt animosity toward both Calhoun and Weightman, claimed that the indictment failed because the prosecutor, District Attorney Elias P. West, was a law partner of Baird, attorney for the defense, and failed to press the case with vigor. Moreover, the grand jury was composed of "more than one half of the immediate relatives of the Armijos' and that two of its members were known to have been participants in the murder of Burtinett."[26] The *Gazette* tried to make the Skinner-Armijo affair appear to be part of a native insurrection fostered by the ineffective policies of Governor Calhoun. "There is not an American in the Territory who does not feel his head sit more lightly upon his shoulders . . . . We cannot shut our eyes, or close our mind against the conviction that, had our civil authorities taken prompt and efficient action in the murder of the unfortunate Burtinett, instead of manifesting a cold indifference, and in some instances an ill concealed satisfaction, the blood of poor Skinner . . . [would] not this day [have] been upon their guilty souls."[27]

The furious controversy over Weightman's election as delegate and the two deaths was thoroughly made known in Washington through memorials, protests, charges, and countercharges sent to President Fillmore and the Department of State. The territory and its people were placed in the worst possible light by the whole affair with its atmosphere of fraud, confusion, and bitterness. Calhoun, Weightman, and even Justice Baker found their competency and integrity challenged by their political enemies.

Collins wrote the President that Calhoun was so beholden to the native population that "he must protect them or fall."[28] This was why the murders of Burtinett and Skinner had gone unpunished. He also questioned Calhoun's reputation as an Indian agent by accusing him of concluding a treaty with the Navajo nation in 1849 after negotiating with only two chiefs who could not speak for the whole nation.[29] Messervy, who had earlier recommended Calhoun for the governorship, now wrote that the governor was "wholly unfit" for the office. "I deem it my duty to say;—in my humble opinion a sanguinary civil war will ensue in the Territory of New Mexico if James S. Calhoun is longer permitted to occupy the office he now unfortunately fills."[30] The predominantly Spanish territorial legislature, however, rose to Calhoun's defense stating categorically that with very few exceptions the people of New Mexico entirely approved of the acts of the governor.[31]

A letter published in New Mexico and then sent to Washington compared Delegate Weightman to "two great bad men," Benedict Arnold and Aaron Burr, although, the writer added, he lacked the brains of either.[32] Houghton and Collins wrote the President accusing Weightman of robbery and vote fraud, especially in San Miguel and Bernalillo counties.[33]

Daniel Webster, still serving as Secretary of State a few months before his death, prepared a synopsis of the charges for President Fillmore, which included remarks accusing Justice Baker of often being "so drunk he could not open and hold court." The judge, a Mississippi lawyer who brought a Negro servant with him to New Mexico, was especially controversial among the highly vocal abolitionists in the territory. Baker, in his own defense, submitted a statement by twelve jurors denying the charge.

In a letter to Fillmore accompanying the synopsis of charges, Webster very honestly admitted his confusion. "You will see that the testimony is very contradictory. If you should not easily be enabled to form an opinion upon the cases, I will take an early opportunity to examine the papers in order to reach a conclusion upon the point in dispute."[34]

A memorial from Reynolds to the House of Representatives challenged the legality of Weightman's being seated as New Mexico's delegate. Missouri Congressman John S. Phelps introduced the memorial and supported the charges of Captain Reynolds. The strong influences of certain Missourians in the territorial party no doubt prompted the congressman to side against Weightman. In a defense of his seat in Congress, Weightman made a long speech on March 15, 1852, answering the charges and other attacks, one by one.[35] His answer to Phelps, Reynolds, and other denouncers proved to be mainly a vigorous and detailed attack on Colonel Munroe, Houghton, Reynolds, and their territorial party.

Leaders of the old military party were so concerned about Weightman's influence in Washington that, to counteract it and to lobby for federal jobs, they traveled to Washington themselves. "Our friends here muster strong," wrote Weightman to Alvarez on February 9. "There are here Collins, Reynolds, Houghton, Johnson, Tulles, [sic] McGrorty and Quinn. They do a great business walking up and down the Avenue."[36]

Personal enmity increased between the leaders of the two factions, Weightman and Houghton. Weightman called Houghton, among other things, a puppet of Munroe, "the chief judge under the military government," and Colonel Munroe's "Fountain of Justice." He accused the judge of being incompetent and unethical on the bench,[37] which so angered Houghton that he published a reply to the "learned attorney" characterizing Weightman's accusations as "malignant and cowardly slanders."[38]

The judge had once felt himself to be so maligned that he challenged

Weightman to a duel.[39] The contest of honor was held and Weightman
fired at the word of command, while the judge, who was deaf, ducked his
head as the bullet whizzed past. When Houghton shouted "I didn't hear
the command to fire," Weightman put his hands in the air and shouted
back "all right, you have the right to shoot. Fire now." At this point, the
seconds rushed in and persuaded Weightman to apologize. "I'll apologize
so far as being sorry is concerned, but I can't take back what I said, Judge,
for it was so." Fortunately, Houghton accepted this as an apology, but
announced to his opponent that if he were insulted again he would shoot
to kill.[40]

The Spanish-speaking majority in New Mexico was hurt more than any
other group by the political divisions and feuds. Their reputation with a
self-righteous Anglo-Saxon America was precarious at best, and unfortunately, of the two factions in New Mexico, one rather scornfully exploited
the *Hispanos*, and the other patronizingly sought their votes. Neither
seemed able to respectfully accept the customs and traditions of a people
with a strange, foreign heritage. Anglos in the territory customarily assumed that the *Hispanos* would change, certainly not they.

Anglo intolerance of Spanish ways dated back to the first contacts of
Americans with the inhabitants of Mexico's northern holding. Santa Fe's
important position as the terminal point on the Santa Fe Trail brought
traders and Mountain Men to the area long before the conquest of 1846.
Those who kept a written record were often critical, although not
necessarily antagonistic toward the native population.[41] Kearny's victory
brought military Americans who were more critical, and sometimes even
antagonistic or contemptuous.

Accounts left by such military and civilian observers as Lewis Garrard,
Rufus B. Sage, Lieutenant Colonel Philip St. George Cooke, Susan Magoffin, Private Frank S. Edwards, Dr. Adolphus Wislizenus, and others
were frequently scornful of the religion, the social and political habits, and
economic practices of native New Mexicans.[42] These observers, with varying degrees of harshness, called the people superstitious and the priests
corrupt; the native men, indolent and cruel; and the *senoritas* sexually
immoral, despite their admittedly kind and humane attitude. The Roman
Catholic Church was severely blamed for the alleged indifference and
lack of civic responsibility on the part of the people. Social inequalities
and the unjust institution of peonage were reproachfully noted. Americans could not resist comparing Anglo-Saxon virtues with Spanish and
Indian ones, and the native culture was almost always found to be sadly
lacking.

James L. Collins, the outspoken Houghton supporter, had a typical

Anglo attitude toward his fellow New Mexicans even after more than twenty-five years in the territory. He claimed that the widespread illiteracy and ignorance resulted in political apathy. ". . . Consider the great mass of people, and how many of them are able to give an intelligent idea of the form of government under which they live, or who understand 'the true feeling of suffrage.' " Collins wrote a pamphlet in which he condemned the tyranny of the Church in strong terms. He included in the pamphlet a letter from a "friend" which denounced the clergy of Old Mexico, and Collins claimed that the same evils existed in New Mexico. The Church completely dominated education, teaching mostly "dogmas and spiritual terrors" in order to prepare young people for the "final mental slavery to which they are destined." Collins claimed great affection for his *Hispano* neighbors and boasted of his intimate and constant communication with them,[43] but he refused to leave them their integrity and self-respect.

Had the Spanish-speaking people been more aggressively political, the Anglos might well have completely lost influence, for the Anglo population in the 1850's and 1860's was surprisingly small. Weightman claimed in 1852 that the latest census showed only 538 Anglos in the territory, although McCall estimated perhaps 1,200 people "born in the United States and in Europe, who have become citizens" of New Mexico.[44] Obviously, any political group in the territory had to have a certain amount of native support.

The Houghton faction's open hostility toward the Spanish majority did not come until after the faction's leaders had tried and failed to win allegiance from the native people. Captain Reynolds, for instance, had distributed during his delegate campaign an election card printed with a cross and the words "Amigo de los Pobres" (Friend of the Poor).[45] But Reynolds failed to win enough votes from devout *Hispanos*. Padre Jose Manuel Gallegos, an influential priest in Albuquerque, gave his support to Weightman instead of Reynolds, saying, "El senor Reynolds does not seem to be very effective."[46] Gallegos also seemed pleased about the Houghton faction's earlier defeat in the election for state officers on June 20, 1850.[47]

Having failed in a bid for native support, Kephart, a Houghton ally, began to accuse the Catholic priests of actively interfering in politics, a charge that was sure to infuriate Americans in the era of Know-Nothingism. Weightman, who had appealed with great success to Spanish-speaking Catholics, insisted that the only political participation by the priests had been to defend their faith against unfair assaults by Kephart, and other critics of the Houghton faction. They defended themselves by using their influence against their oppressors, in the hope that the Church would be able to arrange its affairs "without intervention of secretaries, judges, prefectos, or alcaldes."

Weightman addressed Congress on this matter, appealing for fairness in judging the Catholic Church in New Mexico. "And now I ask, is it anything extraordinary, that the Catholic clergy of New Mexico have taken part in politics? Imagine, *if you can*," he said addressing the Speaker of the House,

either of the political parties here to have assailed any religious denomination in the United States—the Methodists for instance—as the Catholics in New Mexico were assailed; and let me ask, if you would be surprised to see the clergy of that denomination raise their voices against the party who thus outraged their rights, and the laws of the country.[48]

Weightman's defense of the Catholic Church was praised by some and damned by others. A Baltimore Catholic newspaper was pleased by the delegate's defense of "the right of the Catholic Church and Catholic people to be undisturbed in the exercise of their religion."[49] The Protestant Weightman expressed pride at receiving such praise, although he faced at the same time a barrage of abuse from other quarters. Houghton and other opponents of the clergy in New Mexico sarcastically named Weightman "*El defensor de nuestro religion*" (the defender of our faith), a derisive and harsh judgment prompted no doubt by the frustration felt by the old territorial party at having lost the bulk of the Spanish vote. The spiritual needs of the native Catholics were, in Judge Houghton's opinion, being mishandled by a "base and corrupt priesthood, (in whose baseness and corruption he [Weightman] was a participant in full communion . . . ."[50]

The native *Hispano* population also had its patroitism continually questioned by the same critics who denounced its religion. Colonel Munroe, following the election of 1850 in which most of his supporters were defeated, warned his superiors of the "unstable elements of the Mexican character, the general ignorance of the people, their manifest dislike (although latent) to [sic] Americans, and the strong sympathies a large number entertain for Mexican institutions and its government as opposed to that of the United States . . . ."[51]

The image of the Spanish-speaking majority was also damaged by a memorial sent to the President of the United States by Houghton, Reynolds, Collins, Johnson, Messervy, Quinn, William McGrorty, and John R. Tullis. It requested Calhoun's removal as governor of the territory on the grounds that during the Skinner and Burtinett affairs, the governor had protected the "Mexican" population in the perpetuation of "murder."

We are fully convinced that there is no hope for the improvement of our Territory *unless Americans rule it,* and that the spirit of Mexican rule must be corrupt, ignorant, and disgraceful in a Territory of the United States, and that we know from experience that under such rule, there can be no sufficient guarantees for the secure enjoyment of property, or even life . . . .[52]

Certain as this harsh condemnation was to alienate the native population, Collins made no attempt to soften its impact in a published reply to Weightman who was giving the prejudiced statement wide circulation. "Now, allow me to ask any Mexicans of education," wrote Collins, carefully distinguishing between the ignorant *Hispanos* and the elite, "if . . . all that was said to the President concerning this business [was not] true?"[53]

The Weightman faction made the most of the Houghton group's weak position, claiming that the Anglo minority's intense desire to hold all power motivated their base actions. Thus they insisted that American rule was the only answer, the panacea "to heal the wounds of New Mexico." According to Weightman, the Houghton faction was also eager to re-establish military rule in New Mexico,[54] because this would clearly enhance Anglo influence. Weightman claimed that the faction, in order to make military rule seem necessary, even went so far as to start a rumor that another rebellion was about to break in Taos. United States troops were dispatched north only to find the people of Taos County peacefully cultivating their fields and guarding their flocks. The St. Vrain mills, which ground flour for the government, and had been destroyed according to the rumor, were found untouched. Nevertheless, the rumor had accomplished its purpose of influencing the nation to feel that a military government, or a government of reliable "Americans," was needed in New Mexico.

Certain groups in the territory also desired the presence of the military because of the economic prosperity it brought. Colonel Sumner had arrived with his troops as the new military commander in the summer of 1850, and fifteen days after his arrival in Santa Fe, the body of the troops, which under the command of Colonel Munroe had been stationed in the larger towns, were on the march to the Navajo country. Although in Weightman's view this action satisfied the great majority of New Mexicans, it was a severe economic blow to the "prospects of the post sutlers and traders who dealt with the soldiers and quartermaster's men . . . ," ending their money-making schemes.[55] Consequently, these people too, worked for the return of military dominance in New Mexico.

Summing up New Mexico's internal problems, it becomes clear that by 1852 opponents of New Mexico statehood had already found many reasons for claiming that the territory was unfit for self-government. The charges of corruption, and the deep political division, together with the attacks on the character and reliability of the *Hispanos*, made New Mexico's chances for statehood seem remote indeed, even had there been no slavery question to make all judgments subordinate to sectional interests.

SIX

A Changing Territory

G OVERNOR CALHOUN FOUND
the strain of New Mexico's insoluble conflicts extremely tiring. In poor
health and low spirits, he began a trip to the East in May of 1852, accompanied by his two daughters and their husbands. Although his plans
were to visit Washington and his family home in Georgia, Calhoun's
forebodings were so strong that he took a coffin with him. On the plains
of Kansas, the governor did die, and the small group of travelers carried
his body to Independence, Missouri, for burial. Apparently his grave in
that city is an unmarked one.[1]

President Fillmore appointed William Carr Lane as the second territorial governor. Lane, a man in his early sixties, had a career of public
service to prepare him for a job that would certainly require all his ability
and leadership. While a young man, Lane studied medicine and became
a medical doctor. As a soldier, he fought in the Old Northwest against
Indians led by the powerful Tecumseh, and later his idealism led him
to consider joining Simon Bolívar in the liberation of Latin America, this
plan being cancelled only by his marriage.

The people of St. Louis, Missouri, elected the handsome, athletic Lane
mayor of their city nine times, and it was said that he was so respected
in Missouri politics that he could easily have been elected at any time
to the United States Senate over the influential Thomas Hart Benton. In
1826, he won a Democratic seat in the House of Representatives, but
while in Congress he became disillusioned with his party and particularly
its leader, Andrew Jackson. His subsequent joining of the Whig party

made him a logical man for Whig President Fillmore to appoint as New Mexico's governor.[2]

In compliance with his orders, Lane proceeded west immediately and ended his long journey on September 9, 1852, just north of Santa Fe where he was enthusiastically greeted by a group of citizens[3] led by John Greiner, secretary of the territory and an ardent Whig, who was the creator of William Henry Harrison's campaign song "Tippecanoe and Tyler too."[4] The welcoming committee escorted the new governor to the town's plaza where a "rousing" military salute was given in his honor. The goodwill gesture was not ordered by Colonel Sumner but by his subordinate, Brevet Lieutenant Colonel Horace Brooks, who was reprimanded for the act.

Since Calhoun's departure, Sumner, ignoring Secretary Greiner,[5] had been acting as civil governor of the terirtory, and he felt only resentment toward a new governor who would take his place. Despite widespread civilian support for Lane, including a warm letter of introduction from Delegate Weightman,[6] Sumner used his position to make life very difficult for the new governor. Colonel Sumner arbitrarily removed from the plaza the American flag that had flown in the capital since Kearny's triumphant entry in 1846. When Lane courteously requested a flag, Sumner replied that he had no authority from the government to furnish him with government supplies. Governor Lane was a tall, impatient redhead, a man not inclined to forget such insults, and the exchange led to a personal enmity between the two men. When Colonel Sumner later refused to use five hundred volunteers to fight the marauding Navajos, Lane challenged him to a duel, a challenge declined by Sumner.[7]

In a letter to Colonel Sumner, Lane expressed his frustration with affairs in New Mexico.

Never was an executive officer in a more pitiable plight than I was at this time. I was an utter stranger to my official duties, without having any competent legal adviser, and with scarcely an official document on file to direct or assist my official actions; the secretary of the Territory was likewise lacking in experience[.] . . . [There was] not a cent of money on hand, or known to be subject to the draft of the governor, superintendent of Indian affairs, or the secretary of the Territory; not a cent in the city, county or Territorial treasuries, and no credit for the county. There were no policemen and no constabulary force for either city or county, . . . nor was there a single company of militia organized in the whole Territory, nor a single musket within reach of a volunteer, should there be an offer of service by anyone; and you, Colonel Sumner, must have been, from your official position, duly informed of these things.[8]

On December 7, 1852, Lane delivered his first address to the territorial legislature.[9] It was preceded by a trip through six of the nine counties in

New Mexico, and was a report on conditions as Lane found them. In the governor's Anglo, idealistic view, conditions in the territory were deplorable. Indian protection was totally inadequate. "The county is over-run, with Red and White thieves and robbers." The lack of economic efficiency upset Lane and he seized opportunity to emphasize it. "Agriculture and stock-raising, the two great interests of the Territory, are depressed . . . . Your mines are nearly abandoned . . . . Your high-ways are in a bad condition . . . ." The local government suffered because revenue laws were so defective, that sufficient funds were not provided for the ordinary purposes of government. The "schoolmaster, (an indispensable functionary in popular government,) is rarely seen amongst you." The prevailing use of the Spanish language as the official one was criticized because the "English language is the language of all Departments of the Government of the U.S.," and the same ought to be true of New Mexico. Strangely enough, the governor objected even more to the simultaneous use of both languages than to the use of Spanish as the official tongue. Yet it was precisely this bilingual approach, disliked by Lane, which characterized official business throughout the territorial period.

Lane, with his medical background, recognized the great health potential of New Mexico. "Your country is one of the very healthiest on the globe," he told the legislators. There also were great possibilities of irrigation from well water and from ditches and reservoirs, making the "scarcity of water . . . more apparent, than real." The dignified manners and family life of the native New Mexicans were commended too as the chief executive urged them to continue to use their "beautiful language" in daily intercourse.

Lane was acutely aware of the cultural and political tensions that had existed in New Mexico even in pre-territorial days, and he warned his listeners of "unreasonable jealousies and bickerings . . . between the natives of the country and immigrants." He also criticized the self-rule of the various Pueblo communities, which operated within the civil government of the territory, calling it *"Imperium in Imperio."*[10] As for the charges that the *Hispano* majority was resisting the changes brought to New Mexico by American dominance, the governor cautioned the people of New Mexico to "obey the obvious dictate of common sense" and not resist the Manifest Destiny of the United States. ". . . Embark upon the Anglo-Saxon wave which is now rolling from East to West, across the Continent, and ultimately prosper, instead of attempting to resist it, and perish."

The depressing and dark picture of the territory painted by Lane was characteristic of the general pessimism regarding New Mexico felt by American officials during the early 1850's. Lane unquestionably had the best interests of the territory in mind when he reported on New Mexico's deficiencies, but other officials, who agreed with Lane on the enormity of the problems, allowed their frustration to lead them to suggest that the best solution was simply to abandon New Mexico.

Colonel Sumner, embittered by several Washington reprimands of his surly and unco-operative attitude,[11] suggested, either sincerely or spitefully, that all troops and civil officers be withdrawn, and the government left totally in the hands of native New Mexicans. Let them elect their own civil officials, he urged, and conduct their own governmental affairs under the general supervision of the United States government.

It would probably assume a similar form to the one found here in 1846; viz., a civil government but under the entire control of the governor. This change would be highly gratifying to the people. There would be a pronunciamento every month or two, but these would be of no consequence, as they are very harmless when confined to Mexicans alone.[12]

Sumner believed civil government to be impossible in New Mexico because it could not function without the help of the army, and this fact made any civil government virtually a military one. Lane himself had emphasized the necessity of the military for protection in his legislative address. "The population . . . is widely scattered . . . over an area so immense, that 20 companies of U.S. troops, are insufficient for its protection against the Indians; and your own people are so badly armed that they cannot protect their own property from depredation."[13]

Sumner's rather extreme proposal of abondonment was supported by some Washington officials, to the dismay of many New Mexicans. Secretary of State Webster and Secretary of War Conrad were both quite willing to quit the battle with the problems of New Mexico. Citizens of the territory were enraged by a report given by Conrad on December 4, 1852. Placing the population of New Mexico at approximately 61,000, exclusive of "wild Indians," and estimating the value of the territory's real estate at about $2,700,000, he questioned the efficacy of continued American occupation.

To protect this small population we are compelled to maintain a large military force, at an annual expense nearly equal to half the value of the whole of the real estate of the Territory. Would it not be better to induce the inhabitants to abandon a country which seems hardly fit for inhabitation of the civilized, by remunerating them for their property, in money or in lands situated in more favorable regions?

He justified such a move on the basis of economy. "Even if the Government paid for the property quintuple its value, it would still, merely on the score of economy, be largely the gainer by the transaction; and the troops now stationed in New Mexico would be available for the protection of other parts of our own and of the Mexican Territory." Conrad's major emphasis, however, was on the futility of further involvement by the United States government in New Mexico.[14]

As late as 1874, some American officials were to be found who regarded New Mexico as a valueless nuisance. General William Tecumseh Sherman suggested before a committee of the House of Representatives that we prevail upon the Republic of Mexico to take back the territory.[15]

The feelings of New Mexicans toward talk of withdrawal were undoubtedly influenced by the severity of frequent Indian attacks and the territory's vital need for military protection. Even so, there may have been some *Hispanos* who would have welcomed a return to Mexican citizenship. But the danger from nomadic tribes, combined with the outspoken indignation of the territory's leadership community toward any abandonment proposals, kept dissenting New Mexicans quiet. The small, but highly influential, Anglo community agreed wholeheartedly with the editorial view of Kephart, which denounced Conrad for recommending withdrawal and accused the Secretary of War of ignorance regarding New Mexico and of being a blunderer. Kephart warned his fellow New Mexicans that they must speak out "lest silence be construed into [sic] acquiescence."[16]

Governor Lane was particularly anxious to have the national government's support for New Mexico because of a dispute with Mexico over the international boundary. South of the Gila River and west of the Rio Grande was an area of unknown dimensions and uncertain attributes. Although the extreme eastern portion of the area, bordering the Rio Grande, was a rich, agricultural valley known as *La Mesilla*,[17] the land to the west was arid and inhospitable. In the opinion of many, however, the area was rich in mineral resources and also would be an appropriate place to build a southern transcontinental railroad. Before Governor Lane left Washington for New Mexico, he was urged by Weightman to occupy this southern area by force despite the overlapping claims of the United States and Mexico.

The Treaty of Guadalupe Hidalgo, by which Mexico ceded her vast northern holdings, was unfortunately vague and unclear in its definition of the boundary between the United States and Mexico from the Rio Grande River to the Colorado River. The boundary, as stated in the treaty, ran

westwardly, along the whole southern boundary of New Mexico (which runs north of the town called Paso) to its western termination; thence, northward, along the western line of New Mexico, until it intersects the first branch of the river Gila; (or if it should not intersect any branch of that river, then to the point on the said line nearest to such branch, and thence in a direct line to same;) thence down the middle of said branch and of the said river, until it empties into the Rio Colorado . . . .[18]

The southern and western limits of the Department of New Mexico, as it was known under the Republic of Mexico, were defined in an inaccurate map of Old Mexico published in New York in 1847 by J. Disturnell, and incorporated with the treaty. The joint commission established by the United States and Mexico to determine the exact boundary was consequently forced to ignore the Disturnell map and run a compromise line. As this line was thirty-two miles further north than indicated by the map[19] this compromise was later to be rejected by the United States government.

The inhabitants of the disputed area were concerned and anxious for a settlement, for as a group they illustrated well the ambiguous nature of the region. Many of the first settlers of the Mesilla Valley were, according to John R. Bartlett, who was the American on the commission which drew the compromise line, Mexicans who had lived in Doña Ana east of the Rio Grande and had moved west across the river in alarm at the constant encroachment of Anglo-Americans. These people first arriving in 1849 or 1850, settled and made new homes in the Mesilla Valley, believing they were within the jurisdiction of Mexico. The Mexican government encouraged this belief, despite the unfinished work of the joint commission.

Pressure from Texas speculators and land grabbers was a particularly aggravating cause of migration across the Rio Grande. Given land certificates or "head-rights" by the State of Texas, a number of land-hungry Anglo-Americans flocked to the Rio Grande Valley and settled on land which for more than a century had been in the hands of the old Spanish colonists and their descendants. In desperation, these original inhabitants sought refuge on the west side of the river and soon constituted a sizable part of La Mesilla's population.[20] Anglo settlers, too, came to the Mesilla Valley and they, far from believing themselves residents of Mexico, were hoping to be annexed to the United States, as were "many of the Mexicans" in the opinion of one Texas judge.[21]

Chihuahua, insisting that the boundary settlement of the treaty was final, proclaimed that the disputed region belonged to the Republic of Mexico. This prompted the Anglo settlers, together with a few Mexicans, to petition Governor Calhoun for help,[22] although it was his successor, William Carr Lane, who finally responded to the plea for support.

Hesitating at first, Governor Lane took action when he was notified that the compromise boundary (Bartlett's line) had been rejected by Congress. Lane traveled south toward *La Mesilla,* and when he reached the town of Doña Ana he countered the claims of Chihuahua with a bold proclamation made on March 13, 1853.

I, William Carr Lane, Governor of the Territory of New Mexico, (upon my own official responsibility, and without orders from the cabinet in Washington,) do hereby, in behalf of the U.S., re-take possession of the said disputed Territory, to be held provisionally by the U.S., until the question of Boundary, shall be determined by the U.S. and the Mexican Republic.[23]

A direct confrontation between the Mexican state and the American territory now seemed inevitable. Governor Angel Trias of Chihuahua responded to Lane's proclamation by announcing that he would meet the challenge with force. In April, less than seven weeks after Lane issued his defiant statement, Trias arrived in El Paso with approximately eight hundred men. According to newspaper reports, the central government, headed by that colorful Mexican *caudillo,* President Antonio Lopez de Santa Anna, had ordered two companies of soldiers from the south to Chihuahua.

This left Governor Lane in an extremely difficult position. The American government supported Lane in his claims, but not in his determination to occupy *La Mesilla* with troops. Alfred Conkling, United States minister to Mexico, wrote Lane and strongly urged restraint on his part.[24] More important, Colonel Sumner, no friend of the governor, refused to release his regulars in the event of necessary military action. The governor unhappily realized that he would be forced to rely on Texas and New Mexico volunteers should a fight ensue.

The Govt[.] and the people of the U.S. have disapproved & repudiated the Bartlett[']s line; the Board of Commissioners have been dissolved, . . . the Authorities of the state of Chihuahua have usurped authority, in the acknowledged Territory of New Mexico, & trampled upon the rights of the citisens [sic] of the U.S. . . . and some 350 U.S. Troops who are unemployed, and are within 5 miles of the scene of action; fold their arms, in frigid Tranquility & thereby sustain the enemies of their country![25]

The government's reluctance to occupy the border area with troops, which might have meant war, eventually forced Governor Lane to moderate his adamant position. His successor as chief executive of the territory, David Meriwether, received instructions to take no action which might provoke Mexico. The United States, now under the leadership of recently elected Franklin Pierce, had not changed in its determination to have the Mesilla Valley area, but abandoned force in favor of more diplomatic tactics. Influenced by Southerners and hoping to have a southern transcontinental railroad run through the land, Pierce sent James Gadsden of South Carolina to Mexico to offer to purchase as much land south of the Gila River as the Mexican government would sell. Negotiations in Mexico City continued for several months, finally resulting in a treaty drawn up on December 30, 1853, which became known as the Gadsden Purchase. For the sum of $10,000,000, Mexico gave the expansion-minded Americans approximately 45,000 square miles of land lying between the Colorado and Rio Grande rivers. After some balking at the huge price, Congress accepted the treaty and it became law.[26] New Mexico gained in this expansionist movement of the United States, for the land acquired by the Gadsden Purchase was given to the Southwestern territory.

Although Governor Lane had resigned during the government's efforts to achieve a peaceful solution, his decisive attitude toward the disputed land may have influenced the government in its resolve to acquire La Mesilla rather than accept some compromise settlement.[27] Lane had been criticized and politically hurt by his stand on La Mesilla, but evidently the tall, dignified ex-governor was a fighter, for he remained in New Mexico and was a candidate in the election of a territorial delegate to Congress. The voting on September 5, 1853, gave him a majority of votes, but Congress refused to accept ballots cast by Pueblo Indians, and this left his opponent, Padre Jose Manuel Gallegos, the victor, as he had the votes of those Hispanos under the influence of the Mexican clergy.[28]

Lane was, however, supported by the new, American-sponsored, Catholic clergy whose Vicar Apostolic was the recently appointed Jean B. Lamy. Mostly of French origin, the new priests were under the direction of the Baltimore diocese, and eventually they achieved prominence and authority over the handful of Franciscans who for many years had been directed by the Bishop of Durango in Mexico. Although Gallegos was successful in 1853 with the support of the Mexican clergy, in 1855 he was defeated by Miguel A. Otero who had the support of Bishop Lamy and his friends.[29]

As a delegate, Gallegos had one major drawback. He spoke not a word of English. The efforts of a friendly congressman to obtain an interpreter so that Gallegos could understand the proceedings in Congress painfully revealed the plight of New Mexico's delegate. "Mr. Gallegos does not understand one word of the English language, which is the misfortune of his constituents . . . ." The House refused to suspend its rules so that a resolution allowing an interpreter might be considered,[30] leaving the territory in a ludicrous position.

The issue of slavery continued to influence all congressional decisions regarding New Mexico. When the Territory of Colorado was carved from Kansas in 1861, its southern boundary was drawn along the 37th parallel, giving Colorado a large piece of land which had belonged to New Mexico. This loss, the first of several contractions in size for the territory, was opposed by Delegate Otero,[31] but passed the Senate on February 4, 1861. Two days later, Senator Stephen Douglas, the legislator responsible for New Mexico's original boundaries, proposed a reconsideration of the vote creating Colorado Territory. In an effort to prevent the loss of land for New Mexico, the senator from Illinois pointed out that because the people of the area had originally been Mexican, their laws and customs would be very different from those of the rest of Colorado. New Mexico's slave code, enacted in 1859, led most people to believe that the territory had accepted slavery. Senator Douglas now asked what the status of slavery would be in the portion of New Mexico cut off and given to Colorado. Is the effect of the Colorado bill "to abolish slavery in that part of the territory thus cut off, and make it a free territory?"[32]

Douglas was answered by his colleague, James S. Green from Missouri, who apparently wished to implement an unspoken compromise agreement between the slavery and antislavery forces in Congress, by which slavery would not be referred to in any way in bills which created new territories. Green protested Douglas' assumption that the area taken from New Mexico had been slave territory. He claimed that the Colorado bill "does not cut off five inhabitants, and not a single nigger [sic]." Green's contention was that the new measure did not prohibit or establish slavery anywhere.[33]

The effort to avoid the issue of slavery in the territories was absolutely necessary if the desperately divided nation was to provide governments for the unorganized lands of the West. Realizing this, Congress passed the Colorado bill with relatively slight opposition, and it was signed by President Buchanan on February 28, 1861. New Mexico thus had a new neighbor to the north, a territory which she had unwillingly enlarged.

The peacemaking effects of the Compromise of 1850 had been largely nullified by the Kansas-Nebraska Act of 1854, sponsored by Senator Douglas. This measure created new and tragic problems, such as the fighting in Kansas, by calling for popular sovereignty which would allow the people of the territories to either accept or reject slavery. Former President Fillmore was one of many who felt that the Kansas-Nebraska Act was an important factor in leading the nation to war.

But in an evil hour this Pandora's box of Slavery was again opened by what I conceive to be an unjustifiable attempt to force Slavery into Kansas by a repeal of the Missouri Compromise, and the flood of evil now swelling and threatening to overthrow the constitution and sweep away the foundations of the Government itself and deluge this land with fraternal blood, may all be traced to this unfortunate act.[34]

By the summer of 1861 "fraternal blood" was indeed being shed.

A last attempt to avoid bloodshed was made in the winter of 1861 by supporters of the Crittenden Compromise, which called for the extension of slavery as far as the Pacific Ocean, south of the Missouri Compromise line. During the passionate debate over this proposal, Miguel Otero indicated that New Mexico would accept inclusion in the new slave area, and there was even talk in March of granting immediate statehood to the territory under those terms. Partisans on both sides refused to compromise in this way and both New Mexico's chance for statehood and the Crittenden Compromise were defeated. Otero surprised many when he spoke in favor of a confederation of Pacific states that would side with neither North or South, revealing that perhaps the real desire of New Mexico Territory was simply to avoid involvement in the sectional struggle.[35]

All attempts at compromise having failed, the Civil War began with the firing on Fort Sumter in April, 1861, and New Mexico was soon a part of the struggle, whether she wished to be or not. In July, a Confederate force of Texans under the command of Lieutenant Colonel John R. Baylor marched north and, invading New Mexico, occupied the town of Mesilla and seized the southernmost federal post in the territory, Fort Fillmore. A group of local citizens had paved the way for the Texans by meeting and passing a resolution attaching themselves to the Confederacy. On January 13, 1862, the Confederate Congress at Richmond, Virginia, pleased by the positive results in the Southwest, organized the Confederate Territory of Arizona which took in all of New Mexico south of the 34th parallel (just below the town of Socorro). A government was established which recognized the legality of slavery, and specified that all legislative proceedings would be in English. Baylor had earlier proclaimed himself governor, and Granville H. Oury, an attorney and native of Virginia, was elected delegate to the Confederate Congress. On February 14, 1862, Jefferson Davis officially gave territorial status to Arizona.[36]

But the Confederacy had larger plans than simply occupying southern New Mexico. Ultimate goals included expansion to seize Colorado and California, both areas rich in gold, and annexation of part of northern Mexico as well.[37] With these aspirations in mind, a large Confederate force, commanded by hard-drinking Brigadier General Henry H. Sibley, had launched another invasion of New Mexico in January, 1862. Sibley's brother-in-law, Lieutenant Colonel Edward R. S. Canby, was commander of the opposing Union forces.

Sibley's initial success disturbed the North. Marching up the Rio

Grande with an army of more than three thousand tough, undisciplined Texans, the general seized Albuquerque and Santa Fe and would have captured crucial Fort Union, north of Las Vegas, and the rich goldfields of Colorado, had he not been stopped. Colorado Volunteers dispatched from Fort Union battled the Confederate forces for three days at La Glorieta Pass between Fort Union and Santa Fe. The Union forces were outnumbered and forced to give ground, but on the final day, March 28, the Coloradans destroyed the Confederate supply wagons and forced Sibley to leave the scene of the battle, since regarded as the Gettysburg of the West.[38] The defeated Texans made their way back down the Rio Grande Valley, marching past Mesilla and out of New Mexico. The retreat was none too soon, for Brigadier General James H. Carleton and his Unionist force, the colorful "California Column," arrived from across the desert soon after Sibley's departure.

The *Hispano* majority in New Mexico remained staunchly loyal to the Union throughout the Confederate invasion. Governor Rencher, before he was replaced by Henry Connelly, commented on the pro-Union sympathies of the people of New Mexico.[39] Connelly more emphatically stated that there "was not a disloyal native in the territory."[40] On January 29, 1862, the predominantly Spanish-speaking territorial legislature encouraged New Mexicans to resist. "Drive off the audacious invader. . . . This people will never consent to his rule, his military, his slave despotism. . . . Let every Mexican in the Territory rally to the brave in the field; your fathers, sons and brothers."[41]

The invading Confederates from Texas could testify to the loyalty of native New Mexicans. As early as October 25, 1861, Lieutenant Colonel Baylor pleaded with Sibley for reinforcements because the "Mexican population are decidedly Northern in sentiment, and avail themselves of the first opportunity to rob us or join the enemy."[42] The Confederate commander at El Paso admitted that pro-Northern sympathies of the native people was a factor in Sibley's disastrous retreat. Antagonism toward the Confederacy was only increased when soldiers seized supplies without paying for them because New Mexicans refused to accept Confederate money.[43]

There were some logical reasons for native loyalty to the Union. Not only is an invading army rarely popular, unless it comes to liberate, but this invader was the Texas Confederate force, and Texas had long been a rival of New Mexico. Invasion of the territory by the Texas Republic in 1841, the role of Texas in the Mexican War, and the aggressive actions of Anglos, mostly from Texas, in *La Mesilla*, had all contributed to a general dislike and resentment on the part of *Hispanos*. Thus identification of Texas with the Confederacy doomed any attempts to gain the allegiance of native New Mexicans.[44] The exclusive use of English in all legal proceedings by the Confederate Territory of Arizona only made the territory's Spanish-speaking citizens more positive of the unsuitability of the Southern cause in New Mexico.

Outspoken pro-Union sympathies did not protect the unlucky *Hispano* population from suspicion and dislike by many American military men. Governor Connelly, in a letter to Secretary of State William H. Seward, told of his part in organizing a territorial militia to meet the Texas invasion and the ever-present Indian threat. He pointed out that this was the territory's first militia because, until this time, the government had been fearful of the rebellious nature of the people.[45] Again General Winfield Scott, just three months before his retirement, reported on the unreliability of volunteers from New Mexico.[46] And Canby himself, the commander of the Department of New Mexico, expressed his lack of faith in the volunteer or militia units of the territory, and indicated the need for regular troops to fight the invading Confederates.[47] He later warned of desertions when it was reported that funds for the payment of New Mexico volunteers had been detained at Ft. Leavenworth, claiming that the "Mexican people have no affection for the institutions of the United States . . . ."[48] One can only conclude that the loyalty of *Hispanos* to the Union had little effect upon the majority of Anglos, who continued to regard their customs, ways, and culture as totally alien. This attitude would, of course, be a vital factor in the refusal of Americans to accept New Mexico as an equal partner for so many years.

When the Civil War ended in 1865, Governor Connelly led a movement to seek statehood, hoping to capitalize on the territory's unwavering loyalty to the Union. New Mexicans also had good reason to believe that the longer they remained a territory, the more land they would lose through various congressional actions. On December 6, 1865, Connelly addressed the territorial legislature. "I . . . recommend that the present Legislature, take the necessary steps for calling a convention for the purpose of forming a State constitution, to be submitted to the people for approbation, and asking admittance, as one of the States of the Union."[49]

In a flowery speech packed with analogies, Connelly compared the territorial status of New Mexico with that of a small child, who would never know the results of self-reliance or of independent exertion until he left the paternal roof and was thrown upon his own resources in the "great struggle after competence and fortune for which all have to contend." New Mexico had been dependent upon three parent governments, Spain, Mexico, and the United States, and Connelly felt that this was the cause of her "present retarded position." There was no doubt that New Mexico's neighboring territories were "much in advance of our own."

Yet the governor fully realized that the cost of state government would far exceed that of a territorial one, as the people of New Mexico, "desolated and impoverished as they have been by the savage Indians that surround them," could never bear the expenses of maintaining a state government. But he had an answer: "This would certainly be true if they were not to receive an equivalent in government patronage and protection, which would enable them to bear this additional burden."

Connelly then listed for the attentive legislators, most of whom were of native extraction, the benefits of statehood. The arguments which stressed patronage and representation were familiar ones to any aspiring territory. "Through the voice and influence of two senators, we will have a vote and influence in the United States Senate equal to the state of New York; and in the House, equal to the number of our population." With such representation the means would be secured for the construction of roads, the establishment of schools and colleges, the building of forts and opening to settlement and cultivation the vast regions of vacant and unappropriated public lands within the territory. As for protection, a vital problem in New Mexico, Governor Connelly was convinced that statehood would decisively curb the Indian menace, making the expenses of state government a small price to pay for the "entire subjugation and colonization of the Indian tribes which have so long desolated and retarded the progress of our people . . . ."

Connelly also regarded statehood as the only effective way of stopping the territory's gradual shrinking in size, most of which had occurred during the last four years. Alluding to New Mexico's loss of her northern notch, the governor expressed regret that Colorado had taken the "fairest portion of our northern boundary," containing four thousand inhabitants, and would, without a doubt, be admitted as a state during the present session of Congress. New Mexico's greatest loss, however, occurred when the Territory of Arizona was created in 1863, "perhaps, a region of the greatest mineral wealth that is to be found upon the American continent." Connelly was greatly concerned about the growth of Arizona, claiming that a strong tide of emigration was bringing to Arizona settlers from Mexico, and from California and the rest of the United States. "Impelled by the spirit of self-reliance which has distinguished the pioneers of our mountain Territories, she, too, in a few years, will call for admission as a state, and ask an extension of her boundaries east to the Rio Grande." Secessionist movements to the south also concerned the chief executive, particularly a recent effort to carve a territory called Montezuma out of southern New Mexico and northwestern Texas. "Montezuma has high hopes of a separate territorial existence in a short time, and will include within her limits all of our Territory, east and west, that lies south of Fort Craig or the town of Paraje;[50] so, that when we awake from our lethargy, we will have neither agricultural or pastoral lands for the maintainance [sic] of our citizens, or for the pasture of our stock."

Movements to organize a separate territory in the lower or western part of New Mexico had occurred periodically almost from the time of the Gadsden Purchase. One account claims that as early as December, 1854, six months after the Gadsden Purchase became law, the New Mexico legislature sent a memorial to Congress asking that the territory be divided.[51] A memorial introduced on January 23, 1855, by James A. Lucas, a member of the legislature, called for a new territory in the southern part of New Mexico to be called Pimeria. Only five days before, the territorial legislature had officially annexed the land acquired by the Gadsden Purchase.

In 1856, two memorials were sent to Congress by citizens in southern and western portions of New Mexico, each requesting territorial status. The first was drafted in Mesilla and signed by William Claude Jones, who later became speaker of Arizona's first territorial legislature, and fifty-six others;[52] the second, dated August 29, came from Tucson.[53] Both memorials asked that southern New Mexico be organized as a territory to be called Arizona. Both requested that the northern boundary of the new territory be drawn along the latitude of 34° 20′ N., the former extending from the Colorado River to the Pecos, the latter from the Colorado to the Rio Grande. In both memorials, the reasons cited for separation were lack of governmental protection, inadequate administration, and geographical remoteness from the centers of the territory, particularly the political capital at Santa Fe.

In 1857, the "Kippen Memorial," signed by 519 people with a George Kippen heading the list, was sent to Congress by residents of the western area. The same year approximately a thousand petitioners, mostly *Hispanos* living in or near Mesilla, or along the Rio Grande, signed the "Bradley Memorial."[54]

New Mexico's territorial legislature was inconsistent in its view of these separatist movements. It opposed the 1855 Lucas Memorial,[55] but in 1858 supported the idea of separate status for the section west of the 109th meridian, with the stipulation that all Indians be removed from New Mexico and placed in the new territory north of the 34th parallel.[56] In 1860, the legislature gave full support to the creation of "The Territory of Arizona," admitting its "utter inadequacy" to govern the territory south of the 34th parallel from Texas to the lower Colorado River.[57]

The desire to form a separate territory was also clearly manifested by ten Arizona bills introduced in Congress and five elections for delegate held by 1860. In April, 1860, a convention held in Tucson established a provisional government to administer a new "Territory of Arizona" south of the 33° 40' N. latitude, including by this boundary the southern half of New Mexico.[58] Then, in 1861-1862, there was the shortlived Confederate "Territory of Arizona" followed by a third "Territory of Arizona" proclaimed by the victorious Union officer, General Carleton, on June 8, 1862, after his army had completed its long march from California to Tucson. The government established by the military in Arizona was never given federal approval, so the status of the area remained in doubt until the way was paved for the fourth and final "Territory of Arizona" by Representative James M. Ashley of Ohio, who introduced a bill for territorial status. Supported in the Senate by the powerful Senator Benjamin F. Wade of the same state, the proposal passed both houses of Congress and was signed into law by President Lincoln on February 24, 1863.[59]

The new Arizona, carved out of the western section of New Mexico, rejected the earlier concept of an east-west boundary for a north-south boundary approximately along the 109th meridian.[60] Although the persistent secessionist movements were undoubtedly a factor in achieving an Organic Act for Arizona, probably the most significant reason for success was the belief that there were rich deposits of gold and silver in the territory which would be added to the Union's war chest. Separate territorial administration would insure more effective exploitation of this mineral wealth.[61]

The creation of the Territory of Arizona did not discourage separatist activities in the south of what remained New Mexico Territory. Six months before Connelly recommended statehood in his address to the territorial legislature, a memorial was referred to Congress calling for the creation of the Territory of Montezuma south of the latitude 33° 30' N., east of the new Arizona boundary, and embracing that portion of northwestern Texas adjacent to El Paso. Claiming that four-fifths of the proposed territory was drained by the Rio Grande, the memorialists stressed the wealth and community of interest in Montezuma. The "unlimited" pastoral resources were praised, and the mineral wealth was described as being "as vast as man's comprehension can span." The political and social unity of the people and the commercial ties, made essential because of the great distance from the nearest centers of government in Santa Fe and Austin, also were emphasized.[62]

But this time New Mexico resisted further partition, and the apparent indifference that accompanied the creation of Arizona was not repeated. Governor Connelly took the lead and the territory's newspapers followed in an attack on any further reduction of New Mexico's size. "Montezuma is a useless scare crow," chimed the Santa Fe Weekly Gazette. "It never had any existence outside of a monkey show that was had in Mesilla a little less than three years ago."[63] (This was an obvious reference to the Confederate Territory of Arizona.) The movement for autonomy in Mesilla never gained much impetus, but local efforts persisted as late as 1867 when another appeal to Congress was made.[64] The Santa Fe *New Mexican* regarded these rumblings from Doña Ana County as the work of a "set of malcontents," who would "never make themselves satisfied with the condition of things as they found them."[65]

The *Santa Fe Weekly Gazette* felt that Governor Connelly's 1865 call for statehood had come at the right time. "There appears to be a pretty strong popular current in favor of the movement." The journal predicted early legislative action.[66] A week later, however, the *Gazette* reported that leaders of the territorial legislature were afraid consideration of statehood at this time would be inexpedient and could be injurious to their party prospects in the future. The paper suggested that statehood be made a test question in the next legislative election. As the "present Legislature was not elected with a view to the consideration of the question, and probably would not have thought of it had it not been brought to their attention by the [governor's] message," let the candidates in the next election be divided into state and antistate proponents to determine the will of the people.[67]

The Santa Fe newspaper was proved too pessimistic by a vote taken January 30, 1866, by which the members of the legislature overwhelmingly approved an act authorizing Governor Connelly to call a convention to frame a state constitution. The terms of the measure stated that the governor would immediately issue a proclamation calling for an election of convention delegates on the first Monday of March, 1866. The convention would then meet at Santa Fe on the fifth Monday of April, 1866, and frame a constitution to be submitted to a popular vote on the fourth Monday of June, 1866. If approved by a majority, the new document would be forwarded to Congress. The legislature's reasons for seriously pressing for statehood for the first time since 1850 were clearly stated in a preamble to the authorization act. New Mexicans were fully capable of self-government, and it was, therefore, their duty to organize a state government. Moreover, the Congress of the United States was only waiting to know that a "majority of the people of this Territory wish to organize a State Government with a Constitution republican in form."[68]

Although the full power of the Radicals in Congress had not as yet been felt, the New Mexico legislators had the attitudes of Congress clearly in mind when they amended the authorization act with a voting clause that required only that the voter be a male citizen, over twenty-one years, who had resided in the territory more than one year prior to approval of the act.[69] Knowing fully how vital a favorable attitude from Congress was to its cause, the territorial assembly made a further attempt to please Congress by repealing the restrictive Free Negro law, and also an earlier act which had legalized the system of involuntary peonage in the territory.[70] W. F. M. Arny, secretary of the territory, wrote powerful Senator Wade, a Radical extremist, and carefully pointed out New Mexico's liberal actions. There was no color qualification for voters in the delegate election and the legislature "has *repealled* [sic] the odious so called 'Free Negro law' . . . and amended 'the Peon law' so as to make the servitude *voluntary*." To make sure the senator would get the point, Arny added "If we are admitted as a State, we will be a *Free* State in the full sense of that term."[71]

Governor Connelly approved the legislature's action the day after the authorization act was passed, and on February 2 he announced by proclamation the coming election of convention delegates.[72] Quickly, the legislators followed this up with a memorial to Congress asking for approval of these actions.[73] A friendly Denver newspaper reported at this time that "New Mexico is beginning to see the importance of State organization."[74] Earlier, in December, 1865, the New Mexico legislature requested a ninety day leave of absence for the competent and respected Arny,[75] ostensibly so Arny could travel to Washington and join Delegate J. Francisco Chaves in encouraging capital investment in New Mexico. But the timing of this bid for additional influence in Washington makes it likely that intensive lobbying for statehood was to be done.

In February, before Arny left for the East, all the officials of the territory, including the legislators, held a meeting in Santa Fe and expressed their unanimous enthusiasm for statehood.

By their talk you would have anticipated seeing the State Government entering forthwith, drawn on a triumphal car, by elephants! To be opposed to a State Government there at that time, was neither more nor less than setting yourself down an ass. They patted one another on the back, using endearing expressions the while, and like the Fenians elected themselves to high offices under the new *regime*.[76]

New Mexicans may have been inspired in their statehood activity by the unrelenting pursuit of statehood taking place in the neighboring territories of Colorado and Nebraska. Coloradans had responded to an enabling act that received congressional approval on March 21, 1864, by holding a convention at which candidates for various offices were nominated and a state constitution was prepared. The subsequent rejection of this constitution by the people of Colorado, the failure to successfully implement another constitution which received popular endorsement in 1865, and the opposition of Territorial Governor Alexander Cummings to a determined effort of some Coloradans to organize a state legislature,[77] dampened the spirit of statehood seekers, but only temporarily. The persistence again brought about good prospects for admission by the spring of 1866,[78] and hopes for statehood probably would have been fulfilled had not Andrew Johnson vetoed an enabling act for Colorado passed by Congress. He gave the usual reasons for rejecting the statehood bid—insufficient population, uncertainty about the real wishes of Coloradans concerning statehood, etc.—but the truth was that Colorado was now involved in Reconstruction politics. Johnson felt that no Rocky Mountain territory should be admitted into the Union until the eleven Southern states had been accepted back into the fold.[79] One Colorado historian states that Johnson offered to relent in his opposition if Colorado's two senators-elect, John Evans and Jerome B. Chaffee, would support his reconstruction program. Such support not forthcoming, the President remained adamant.[80]

Colorado's attempt to achieve statehood in the 1860's did fail, but honorably and through no fault of her own. New Mexico's attempt, initiated with such enthusiasm, simply fizzled out within the territory. An election of delegates was held but when the group met in Santa Fe, the lack of a quorum soon caused the convention to quietly disband. The entry in the official territorial journal was very brief. "May 1, 1866—In conformity with the act enacted by the Legislative Assembly and approved January 31st 1866. The members of the state constitutional convention met this day and there not being a quorum, they adjourned *sine-die*."[81] One bitter critic labeled the territory "a mere creeping skeleton" and heaped scorn on the statehood leaders. "Like all their former fumings: the lalk [sic] satisfied the garrulous old fellows, and the thing died out."[82]

During the next few years there was little talk of statehood. Fiery Governor Robert B. Mitchell, who succeeded Connelly, did not even mention statehood in his July 16, 1866, inaugural address. He forecast new immigration comparable to the numbers currently "pouring into Idaho and Montana," boasted of the "sealed treasures of uncoined gold and silver" in New Mexico, and advocated better educational facilities,[83] but avoided any mention of the defunct statehood movement.

It is probable that any eagerness for statehood at this time would have been dampened, in any case, by Mitchell's controversial personality and by the national crisis resulting from President Johnson's stormy administration. The new governor, an ex-Union general with a massive dark beard, clashed almost continuously with the territorial legislature. Although much of the arguing was over petty matters of jurisdiction and authority, Mitchell's allegiance to Johnson, certainly natural as he was a presidential appointee, caused much bitterness. A published letter to the President from Mitchell, Chief Justice John P. Slough, Associate Justices Houghton and Sidney A. Hubbell, and other territorial officials frustrated New Mexicans who were supporters of the Radicals in Congress.

. . . WE HEARTILY ENDORSE YOU in your truly patriotic efforts to stay the threatening tide of RADICALISM, and produce a reunion of the hearts of the people by a firm adherence to the Federal Constitution; and . . . we pledge ourselves, our lives, our liberties, and our sacred honor to you, to aid and sustain you in all your efforts in that direction.[84]

Secretary Arny wrote Seward a letter in which he also gave assurance of support for the President. "Four-fifths of the voters in this Territory are in favor of the President's policy of reconstruction."[85]

Although the President undoubtedly appreciated these sentiments, they did not help the cause of statehood. It is by the authority of Congress and not a president, that a territory receives an enabling act. And the Radicals dominated Congress so strongly that Johnson was only saved from removal from office by one vote. The loyalty of many territorial officials notwithstanding, Radicalism also had vocal support in New Mexico, as evidenced by an 1869 memorial to Congress from the territorial legislature demanding the removal of Justice Houghton. The judge's stormy political career had survived longer than that of most of his colleagues' in the 1850 statehood movement. The memorial charged Houghton with neglect of duty and failure to reside in his own judicial district, and condemned him for having joined Mitchell and the other officials in their support of Andrew Johnson against the Congress of the United States.[86]

Unfortunately, during the difficult decade of the sixties, New Mexico was not able to rid itself of the continuing distrust between Anglo and *Hispano* elements. *The New Mexican* warned of a secret movement made up primarily of newcomers who were bent on undermining "the natives [,] comparing their culture to one below *barbarous Indians*." According to the paper, the plotters had prepared a memorial demanding that the governor and judges of the state supreme court be constituted as a legislative body "to *dictate* our laws and that our legislature which is now composed of members of our own people should be abolished . . . ." Because of legal difficulties, often dating back to the times when Spanish and Mexican land grants were given, New Mexicans were especially concerned about the quality of new emigration to the Southwest.

We need a good solid emigration, when we have any; men who come with their families with the intention of remaining, and not a class of broken down politicians and second rate upstarts who come with the expectation of finding a very ignorant class of people, and swindling them out of a fortune in a year or two.[87]

Although there was little statehood activity in the years following the Civil War, the territory continued to send an elected delegate to Congress. These election contests were often exciting and dramatic, in the best frontier tradition. In one election, in which Gallegos made a comeback against the incumbent, J. Francisco Chaves, emotions became so violent in Mesilla that a riot took place when rival groups of Democrats and Republicans met in front of a local store on August 27, 1871. One Apolonia Barela fired a pistol into the air and, in the melee that followed, nine men were killed and forty or fifty wounded. No indictments were ever returned.[88]

Eastern newspapers were, of course, ready to seize upon such incidents as proof of the barbarous crudity of life in the formerly Mexican land. The influential *New York Times* described Santa Fe as "the heart of our worst civilization . . . [and] seventy miles south is Albuquerque, younger, but with all the signs of ignorance and sloth."[89] The Santa Fe *New Mexican*, however, expressed the hopes of those New Mexicans who were undaunted by Eastern hostility when it pointed out that New Mexico could claim priority of organization to any government in the West.[90]

During the administration of the inept Governor William A. Pile, best known to historians for his responsibility in the loss of much of the Spanish archives, an abortive statehood attempt was made. The effort, beginning in 1869 or the early seventies, was brought to the attention of President Ulysses S. Grant by the charge that Pile, a Republican, made a bargain with New Mexico Democrats whereby he would gain a seat in the United States Senate and Democrats would split state offices if admission were achieved. Pile denied the charge in a letter to the President, claiming he had sacrificed no principles, agreed to no division of office, but had "only contemplated uniting all friends of the movement in its favor . . . ."[91] Possibly of more significance was a concurrent effort in Congress to organize the Territory of New Mexico into the State of Lincoln in honor of the martyred and beloved ex-President.[92] It, too, failed, but New Mexico was on the threshhold of another major statehood drive in 1872, which would ultimately bring the territory to the center of the American political scene.

SEVEN

The Constitution of 1872

O<small>N THE FIRST DAY</small> of September, 1871, a new governor arrived in Santa Fe to succeed William Pile. Marsh Giddings was a prominent and active Republican, whose home state was Michigan. He had been a delegate to the conventions which nominated Abraham Lincoln and Ulysses S. Grant, and he claimed to have been a member of the group that drew up the first Republican platform ever presented to the American people. When Grant became President, he offered Giddings the post of consul general to India, which he declined. But the President's later unsolicited offer of the governorship of New Mexico was accepted.[1]

As he took over the reins of government in New Mexico, with the full support of the national administration, Giddings no doubt was full of confidence and cheerful goodwill toward his new fellow citizens in the territory. His first message to the legislature, delivered on December 7, 1871, was, according to the new governor's own testimony, exceedingly well received. The address was given the highest praise by all the papers in New Mexico without regard to party, and the people were astonished that their new chief executive could in so little time give so perfect and extended a history of New Mexico and its productions, resources, and everything connected with the territory. The legislators requested extra copies of the speech to send to Congress so that its valuable information could receive national exposure.[2]

The nonpartisan, enthusiastic reception given Governor Giddings seemed to augur well for the future of the territory. But before Giddings was even able to settle into the routines of his office, the calm surface erupted, and bitter factionalism once again became the dominant factor in New Mexico. On December 30, 1871, a bill was presented in the territorial legislature that moved Chief Justice Joseph G. Palen from the important first district, in Santa Fe, to the remote and far less vital third district in Mesilla.[3] The Chief Justice of the territory traditionally presided over the court in the capital city, yet this deliberately sought comedown for Palen was quickly passed by both houses without being printed or referred to a committee, and without adequate discussion.

The *Daily Rocky Mountain News* of Denver criticized the legislature's action, stating that the legislators were responding to two decisions handed down by New Mexico's supreme court which were inimical to a large and powerful money interest. "This ring" was taking revenge by banishing Judge Palen to the southern district.[4] There was certainly much intrigue and maneuvering behind the bold attempt to get rid of Palen. Governor Giddings felt that the judge was being attacked because he made no distinction between the rich and poor in his courts, and his judgments could not be bought. There were at this time several prominent citizens of Santa Fe under indictment, including A. P. Sullivan, the postmaster and editor of the Santa Fe *Weekly Post*, "indicted for some criminal act—under the charge of Judge Palen . . . ."[5] Henry Wetter, secretary of the territory, had also been charged with some wrongdoing, and Giddings believed he too was under indictment. Morever, several wealthy parties in Santa Fe had become bound under heavy bonds for the performance of certain duties, and these parties desired a "more facile judge" as their cases were soon to be brought to trial. Justice D. B. Johnson of Mesilla, who would exchange places with Palen in Santa Fe, was a "drinking debauchee . . . [,] too low to be respected" in the governor's opinion. This kind of man would present no problem to the indicted citizens of Santa Fe. The scheming against Palen was made easier by the jealousy felt toward Palen by other judges, such as ex-Chief Justice Kirby Benedict and John S. Watts, one of the original justices on the supreme court.[6]

Governor Giddings was determined to prevent what was, in his eyes, a blatant disregard for justice, and he promptly vetoed the bill moving Palen to Mesilla. This brought on "a terrible war"[7] as Republican legislators, many of whom had voted with the Democrats to remove Palen, now stood by the Republican governor, while the Democrats fought to prevent a vote that would support Giddings' veto. The issue was finally voted upon, the veto being sustained by the House 12 to 4, and this so angered the Democrats that they determined to seize control of both houses of the territorial legislature.

In a power grab that began on January 5, 1872, the Democrats removed three elected Taos Republicans, and secured control of the House by re-placing them with Democrats. Another Democrat was selected to fill the seat of a recently deceased Republican representative from the area.[8] In the Council, Democrats gained a 7 to 6 margin by putting one of their members in a seat made temporarily vacant by a Republican member who had gone home on a leave of absence.[9] Governor Giddings, shocked by these maneuvers, which in the House had only been accomplished by the collusion of several of his party members, including the Republican speaker, decided to restore the four House seats to Republican control.[10]

In a move that caused extreme Democratic resentment, Giddings en-tered the House Chamber and sat by the speaker, Milnor Rudolph, during the stormy sessions of January 9 and 10. While present on the ninth, the governor was informed that the legislators were carrying weapons.[11] By the next day, the confusion was so great that Speaker Rudolph ordered the seargent-at-arms to remove all spectators, but the crowd, "supported and encouraged by all the democratic members," refused to leave. The Demo-cratic sheriff of Santa Fe was asked to help, but he too refused to co-oper-ate. Finally, Rudolph called for an adjournment, but after the Republi-cans had filed out of the chamber, the Democrats immediately began to organize their own legislature, electing John R. Johnson as their new speaker.[12]

The seemingly insoluble division of the legislature generated tense and hostile feelings throughout the old capital, causing Governor Giddings much concern. "For many days a fight seemed inevitable. Riot & blood-shed were imminent & one day I was called on not less than three times by members of the House to go into the House to prevent a hand to hand fight, as it was declared to me every member was armed and at any mo-ment a fight might occur."[13]

Except for the danger of violence, the situation certainly had comical aspects, which were only increased when the newly established Demo-cratic House instructed its seargent-at-arms, H. Clay Carson, to go forth and bring to the House all absent members. The assignment was partially accomplished when ex-Speaker Rudolph was arrested with the help of a posse. Rudolph, however, with the support of the governor, promptly re-quested federal troops to help restore order, and with the protection of the troops, he entered the House on January 11 and declared it Republi-can again by reseating the four Taos Republicans. Far from resolving the problem, this action resulted in two houses, the governor recognizing the Republican one, and the council, or upper house, recognizing the Demo-cratic one.

The comedy continued with the Democrats taking possession of the House chamber on January 13, by forcibly depriving the doorkeeper of his keys. Speaker Rudolph responded to this affront by sneaking into the building two nights later and replacing the old lock with a new one, thus barring entry for the Democrats. During the rest of the month, the two feuding groups of lawmakers met separately, each passing laws and acting as a legal body. The cause of the "Republican House" was strengthened on January 22 when the high court of the territory ruled in behalf of the Republicans and declared the Democratic action "unauthorized, illegal, revolutionary and void."[14] On January 27, Secretary Wetter telegraphed Secretary of State Hamilton Fish and asked him which body should be paid. His answer came at the end of the month from United States Attorney General George H. Williams: neither of the two groups was recognized as the lawful House of Representatives.[15]

Two days before adjournment of the legislative session, leaders of the two factions began to realize the necessity of a compromise. The upper chamber of the legislature, Democratic and favorable to new legislation, agreed to recognize the "Republican House" if a compromise speaker were selected. Giddings, anxious to have the territory progress again, also agreed, and Gregorio N. Otero became the new speaker.[16] Unfortunately, a residue of bitterness was revealed when Secretary Wetter, who had been involved in the thwarted reassignment of Chief Justice Palen, refused to pay House members their per diem allowance. Giddings thought Wetter was determined to disrupt the legislature.

Among the Republican leaders in Santa Fe at this time were several men whose careers would eventually be a fascinating part of New Mexico's story. Thomas B. Catron, an attorney for the territory, came forward and paid House members from his own pocket and, together with friends, provided enough money to keep the legislature functioning.[17] In 1867, the young Catron had left Missouri and moved to New Mexico to practice law. Governor Mitchell had promised the newcomer an appointment as attorney for the third district if he could learn the Spanish language. The strong-willed Catron at once moved to Rio Arriba County and spent much of his time in a little Mexican plaza where there was not another English-speaking person. After six months, he spoke Spanish fluently and received the appointment.[18]

A close ally of Catron was Stephen B. Elkins, another Missourian, who had moved to New Mexico in 1865. Elkins achieved great prominence later in his life as a Senator from West Virginia and Secretary of War in Benjamin Harrison's cabinet, but his political career in New Mexico came first. Having prepared for an active role in the territory by mastering Spanish, the Missourian was elected to the Territorial House of Representatives in 1866. Soon after, he formed a law partnership with Catron, his former classmate at the University of Missouri. Like Catron, Elkins was a staunch supporter of the regular Republican organization, a vital factor during the legislative crisis. He spoke at a Republican convention, held in Santa Fe on January 22, which chose Giddings and Palen as delegates to the national convention to be held later that year in Philadelphia.[19]

The support of such loyal Republicans as Catron and Elkins kept the legislature intact, and in the last few days of the session the lawmakers rallied and passed some important and useful measures. Giddings' pride in this brief period of co-operation led him to state the case strongly. The territorial assembly passed "more really valuable laws within the last two days of the Session than had been secured before by many years of legislation."[20] On the recommendation of Giddings, a tax law was enacted, calling for a levy of one-fourth of one per cent on the entire territorial assessment, this revenue to be used primarily for school support. Another new law to admit aliens and give them the same property-holding rights as native citizens was passed. Also, at the behest of the governor, the "most liberal" railroad laws were enacted to protect the people against the "extortion of railroads."

The climax of the new spirit of enthusiastic progress was the legislature's drafting of a new state constitution. The Daily New Mexican pointed out that although the governor, in making his recommendations to the legislature, had not asked for a statehood movement, the net result of his actions and those of the legislature had been to give to the movement an impetus "greater than twenty years previous legislation . . . ."[21] According to another newspaper account, the move toward statehood was prompted by a strong feeling among the people in the territory that the time for another try for admission had come. So interested were they in this subject that the legislators could not return to their constituents, without having attempted something in the way of a state organization. During the stormy month of January, leaders of both houses decided upon a joint caucus or junta of the two parties to discuss the subject, and for several evenings the matter was thoroughly debated pro and con, and at every meeting the anxiety became greater and the determination more firmly fixed for a state organization. Finally, "with greater unanimity than could have been expected in the midst of intense party excitement on other subjects," it was agreed that a committee of the most competent persons to be found should draft the best constitution they could and submit it to the people for their approval. If approved, the constitution would be submitted to Congress with the request that New Mexico be admitted as a state upon the adoption of the constitution by the people.[22]

A group endeavor, fully supported by "every republican and some of [the] most intelligent and leading democrats," produced a detailed document, which was read aloud by Republican Senator J. Bonifacio Chaves of Valencia, brother of the prominent former delegate, J. Francisco Chaves, at a joint session of both houses called on January 30, 1872.[23] On the same day, Senator Chaves successfully sponsored a bill in the Legislative Council, calling for a popular vote on the state constitution and the election of state officials.[24] The new constitution was accepted by the legislature with a motion for approval made and seconded after the reading of the preamble.[25]

The constitution, to be presented to New Mexicans for approval, was modeled after the constitution of the State of Illinois, and its proponents were sure it was the "best in the United States."[26] Strict provisions for railroad regulation certainly made the document progressive. Restrictions of the railways had been pioneered in Illinois, after successful agitation by shippers, merchants, and Grangers, members of the energetic new farm organizations springing up throughout the Midwest. Now, some seven years before the Atchison, Topeka and Santa Fe laid the first tracks into the territory, the 1872 constitution empowered the state legislature to pass laws to correct abuses and prevent unjust discrimination and extortion in the rates of freight and passenger tariffs, and enforce such laws by adequate penalties.[27] Laws could be enacted from time to time establishing reasonable maximum rates of charges for the transportation of passengers and freight. Railroad corporations were required to maintain a public office in the new state, could not consolidate with any other company owning a parallel or competing line, and were expressly prohibited from initiating any fictitious increase in capital stock. Moreover, a majority of the directors of railroad corporations had to be citizens and residents of the State of New Mexico.[28]

Those who approved the constitution felt that the inclusion of railroad provisions was an intelligent preparation for the advent of rails in the territory, predicted as coming in one or two years. Statehood would bring rail connections, which in turn would create a ready market for products of the territory. Railroad activity would also bring lower prices for consumer goods and reasonable freight rates.[29] Opponents of the constitution viewed the railroad provisions as "obstructive," and The Republican Review of Albuquerque complained that railroad corporations "are the only corporations the projectors of this Constitution condescend to make provisions for . . . ." The section on railroads was "full of provisions" calculated to prevent businessmen living in other states and territories from investing in the construction of railroads in and through New Mexico. The Republican thought railroad legislation should be passed when railroads actually existed in New Mexico, and not before. "When the Atlantic and Pacific Railroad cars are running from this valley eastward, there is not a

Republican in this part of the Territory but will favor a State organization with a *decent* Republican Constitution."[30]

Actually the constitution, so quickly accepted by the New Mexico legislators, was surprisingly liberal for its time and did make an effort to deal with the excesses of corporations in general, not just railroads. A separate section on corporations guaranteed every stockholder the right to vote in person or by proxy in all elections of company directors. Another article prohibited the legislature from granting to any corporation a special or exclusive privilege.[31] The lengthy and special treatment given railroad corporations in the constitution was a natural recognition that this was the age of railroads and that the rail empires were often vast and powerful.

The constitution of 1872 asked for liberal homestead laws and provided for free public schools for all children, at a time when no such system existed in New Mexico. It represented, in many respects, the best of Midwestern agrarian democracy, which was becoming increasingly vocal and defensive as industrialism challenged many of rural America's most cherished beliefs.

The values and traditions of the Midwest, however, were not necessarily those of New Mexico, which was unique in many ways. Under both Spanish and Mexican rule, the Roman Catholic Church had handled all education with little interference from secular forces. The proposed new constitution, with a section which would completely eleminate public support for Church activities, undoubtedly was regarded by Church officials as a threat to the traditional role of Catholicism in the territory.

Neither the General Assembly, nor any county, city, town, township, school district or other public corporation shall ever make any appropriation, or pay from any public fund whatever, anything in aid of any church or sectarian purpose, or help, support or sustain any school, academy, seminary, college, university or other literary or scientific institution, controlled by any church of sectarian denomination whatever, nor shall any grant or donation of land, money or other personal property ever be made by the state or any such public corporation, to any church, or for any sectarian purpose.[32]

Although the legislators who prepared the constitution were overwhelmingly of *Hispano* origin, the document they prepared was surprisingly oblivious of the feelings of Spanish-speaking Roman Catholics. No provision was made for election ballots to be printed in Spanish, the sale of lottery tickets was forbidden, and donations to seminaries and other educational institutions had to be "faithfully applied to the objects for which such gifts and grants were made." Separation of Church and state was clearly spelled out by strong guarantees of freedom of conscience, and tax exemption for church property was enumerated. But although a guarantee that no "preference [was to] be given by law to any religious denomination or mode of worship"[33] would have pleased church officials elsewhere in the United States, in New Mexico this statement was merely a challenge to established church authority.

Because the constitution was a Republican undertaking, apparently having the support of only a scattering of Democrats, opponents of the constitution used these religious provisions as proof of anti-Catholicism among New Mexico Republicans. *The Borderer*, in the spring of 1871, introduced the anti-Catholic issue, reporting that a clause in the New Hampshire state constitution excluded Roman Catholics from public office. Readers were urged to ask Republican leaders in Doña Ana County if they could name "a single Democratic State with such a contemptible provision in its constitution . . . ." The newspaper concluded that the Republican party, where it had the power, had always shown itself hostile to the Catholic religion. Realizing the political damage that could be done if such feelings became prevalent, the *Republican* vigorously denied the anti-Catholic charge and accused *The Borderer* of an editorial fabrication solely to raise religious prejudices against the Republican party, in order to obtain the Roman Catholic vote. "For our part we know not an instance where the Republican party sought to oppress Roman Catholics or any other religious persuasion." Knowing the high regard of many of its readers for the benevolent work of the Sisters of Charity, the *Republican* mentioned a congressional act to remunerate this order of nuns for the destruction of property in Baltimore during the Civil War, which was sponsored by two Protestant Republicans.[34]

Other provisions in the constitution that caused dissension included a specification that only naturalized citizens who obtained "a certificate of naturalization before any court of record" in New Mexico, prior to April 1, 1870, could vote.[35] The *Republican* deplored this discrimination against the foreign born and charged Know-Nothingism. Sections that allowed the grand jury to be abolished by law and made illegal the confiscation of goods after conviction and prevented people convicted of crimes committed in the new state from being sent out of New Mexico, were regarded by the newspaper as being unconstitutional. The term "Copperheadism" was used to describe the provision that would reserve to the State of New Mexico all revenue from "fines, penalties and confiscations" owed to the territory or "*to the people of the United States.*" The backers of statehood were accused of trying to gobble up the property of the United States.[36] A provision for the State of New Mexico to assume all territorial debts brought bitter controversy over the payment of militia claims, debts incurred largely for Indian defense.

In its organization of a state government, the constitution was traditional in establishing three branches of government with a bicameral legislature and a reasonable provision for amending the document, requiring a two-thirds vote in both legislative houses and majority approval by the electorate. The constitution was made unnecessarily long by the inclusion of many details that could have been left for legislative action.

Accompanying the constitution was an act that called for a popular referendum on the new document, to be held the second Monday of June, 1872.[37] Thus, New Mexicans would themselves decide the ultimate fate of the constitution. Newspapers, as molders of public opinion, had more than four months to persuade their readers to either support or reject the new document, and they made the most of it. The powerful Santa Fe New Mexican, which claimed to be the voice of Republicanism in the territory, was a leader in the statehood crusade. The newspaper had only praise for the selfless devotion of Governor Giddings and the legislators to the urgent demands for statehood by constituents. The paper claimed that there was so little partisanship and individual ambition that Giddings had studiously avoided mentioning statehood in his December message to the legislative assembly. The character of the movement did not come from any one person. "Not a government official counseled or encouraged the movement either directly or indirectly, but the representatives acted solely on their own judgment . . . ."[38]

There were other papers, however, such as the The Republican Review of Albuquerque, that questioned the unanimity of Republican support for the constitution. The Republican, a rival voice for Republicanism in New Mexico, also claimed some eight weeks before the referendum was held, that the New Mexican was the only newspaper supporting the document. Three of the seven territorial papers, including the Albuquerque paper, were against it and three had not taken a stand either way.[39] The Las Vegas Mail called the statehood movement an abortion cooked up by a rump legislature. The Borderer of Las Cruces called it an outrage made possible because "the Governor and the ring had the legislature under their thumbs . . . ."[40]

The motives of the statehood seekers were unkindly scrutinized by the press. The Republican was convinced that the state movement was for the "sole benefit of the demagogues who wish to be United State Senators, Governor," or fill other state positions.[41] Although political partisanship certainly entered into these journalistic speculations, the charges of personal ambition undoubtedly had substance. J. Francisco Chaves had been accused in 1871 of conspiring with Elkins and Catron to divide up future federal patronage so as to give the prospective senatorships to himself and Elkins, and a "Supreme Judge's berth" to the ambitious Catron.[42] The active role of Chaves' brother in getting the legislature to submit a state con-

stitution to the people seems quite significant. The passionate outcries
that patronage and public office motivated the "stateites" were summed
up in a poem quoted from the St. Louis *Democrat*:

What Constitutes a State?

A governor at the head
Well paid, well fed!
And fifteen dozen legislators,
All great "inflators,"
A lot of lazy loafers,
To lounge on sofas,
Throughout the winter;
A Public Printer;
An army store-keeper!
A hundred parasites
And blatherskites,
In broad-cloth coats
And red cravats,
With a good sprinkling
Of black cats![43]

The campaign against the constitution was intensified by insinuations
that speculators were backing the statehood movement for personal gain.

If those 'smart lobbist[s] and jobbert [sic]' can make such hauls out of a territorial
government, where the plunder is small, and they are under the chance of being baulked
in their schemes by Congress, how much more will they be apt to steal, when the
plunder is larger and [there is] no Congressional surveillance to dread.[44]

It was charged that lobbyists were scheming to make large profits by forcing the proposed state government to accept financial responsibility for
previously incurred militia warrants. These warrants were claims issued
against the territorial treasury for money the territory had needed for Indian defense and other purposes. The *Republican* estimated that the total
sum of militia warrants amounted to from two to five million dollars, and
that upon adoption of the constitution submitted by the legislature, and
New Mexico's admission as a state, the people would immediately be
burdened with "a *bona fide* debt." Asserting that many of the warrants
were fraudulent and in the hands of speculators, the paper reported that
one person was paid $60,000 in militia warrants for only a few weeks of
service as a clerk. More evidence of shady dealings in the warrants was
given in the case of a man who sold an Albuquerque merchant twenty

thousand dollars in these warrants for only two thousand dollars in merchandise. Speculators in warrants were also accused of attempting to manipulate the funding of the debt in such a way that the initial interest rate would be as high as ten per cent.[45]

Although the opponents of statehood undoubtedly had sincere reasons for their hostility toward the drafters of the constitution, as a group they seemed much like the man who cuts off his nose to spite his own face. For there were, in 1872, some compellingly logical reasons for making an immediate try for statehood. It was generally felt that Congress was in a mood favorable to New Mexico's admission. According to a letter to the New Mexican, it was understood that the territory would probably be admitted if she could present proper qualifications. This is why the territorial legislature voted the necessary taxes for schools, for payment of the debt, interest and current expenses, and a full amount for the "successful running" of a state government.[46]

The actions of New Mexico's neighbor to the north, Colorado, particularly seemed to warrant an immediate try for statehood by the territory. Colorado politicians were accused of planning to annex New Mexico's six northern counties in order to give Colorado a population equal to New Mexico's. In this way, the energetic Anglo territory hoped to insure its admission as a state. Coloradans rationalized that the people of New Mexico were indifferent and took "no interest in becoming a state."[47]

Another ambitious plan was offered in Congress by Colorado delegate Jerome B. Chaffee. To secure faster admission, the Western territories, along with some states, would be consolidated in groups of two, thus presenting Congress with population figures difficult to ignore. Together, Colorado and Wyoming would have a population of 48,982; Dakota and Nebraska, 137,174; Idaho and Montana, 35,994; Washington and Oregon, 114,878; Arizona and the southern part of California, 40,000; Nevada and Utah, 129,277.[48] New Mexico's exclusion from the plan was noted by The Las Vegas Mail which feared New Mexico was being left out in the cold. The antistate Republican, however, was delighted by the omission. We do not wish to be "encumbered with or spliced to any other territory." But there did seem to be some apprehension that the consolidation of Colorado and Wyoming might include part of New Mexico. The Albuquerque journal carefully noted that when New Mexico was ready for statehood, she would be admitted "without division or diminution."[49]

Governor Giddings repeatedly insisted that his own attitude toward the constitution was neutral and free from partisanship. But the fact that the act accompanying the constitution authorized a proclamation by the governor calling for a referendum on the document, placed Giddings at the center of the swirling controversy whether he chose to be there or not. Giddings' actions during the legislative crisis had made him a controversial figure, and now personal attitudes toward the governor would inevitably influence the outcome of the popular vote on statehood. An indignant group from Lincoln County probably spoke for many who opposed statehood when they said "Giddings has lent himself to the schemes of these over-riders of the public wishes . . . ." It was the duty of the people to petition the President to send honest public officers, who would pay more attention to the duties of their offices, and less to "little political tricks in favor of rings."[50] Democratic Delegate Jose M. Gallegos, again serving as New Mexico's spokesman in Congress, wrote a bitter letter to President Grant on March 13. "My people are extremely anxious to have Gov. Giddings removed as Governor; he's an offensive, meddling, disagreeable man to my people."[51] Giddings' son, William, who had served as librarian and adjutant general in the territory, was characterized as a "man of bad habits, bad moral character."[52]

The besieged governor was also accused of gerrymandering following his apportionment of the legislature, which he had undertaken because the legislators had failed to enact an apportionment law themselves.[53] The appointment of his son as adjutant general brought derisive charges of nepotism.[54] The governor fought the charges with a few of his own. He claimed his mail was intercepted, read, and divulged before it reached him. The postmaster was Sullivan, the man who had been indicted in Justice Palen's court and who ran an opposition newspaper which, according to the governor, had been given a $5,000 subsidy by the Democrats.

More trouble came when William Giddings was beaten and left for dead by unknown *Hispano* assailants in the dark streets of Santa Fe. His father denied a charge that William, who was working for Sullivan in the post office, had been robbed of postal funds by the attackers. Giddings revealed bitter Anglo prejudices in his assessment of the entire incident. Could he, his father, be induced to take his only son from his farm stock and business in a quiet farming town in Michigan, twelve miles away from any villages, and bring him into "a Mexican city of 6000 people, and of the lowest class on God[']s earth," just "to disgrace himself & his family, myself & my family . . . ?"[55]

Finally, on April 2, sixty days before the first Monday of June, 1872, in accordance with the law, Giddings issued a proclamation calling for a referendum to be held on June 3 for the sole purpose of determining whether the people of the territory were in favor of the constitution and a state government.[56] The ballot would offer two choices: "For the Constitution and a State" or "Against the Constitution and a State." If the constitution were approved, a second election would be held on the first Monday of

September, 1872, to elect state officials, legislators, and a representative to Congress.[57]

The campaign to win popular approval for the constitution surprisingly enough did not begin until about six weeks after the legislature adjourned. A March 11, 1872, editorial in the *New Mexican* appears to have been the first favorable reference to the document. The influential Republican paper, alone among newspapers in its support of statehood, rather apologetically explained its delay in speaking out. "We should have brought up this subject before but it seemed best to wait until the new Constitution which the last legislature adopted should be placed in the hands of the people for examination. These are now printed and will be circulated as fast as possible . . . ." *The Republican Review* of Albuquerque was sternly denounced for its opposition to statehood.[58] Having taken the cause of the new constitution as its own, the *New Mexican* forcefully used every argument that could be mustered to convince the territory's citizens to vote affirmatively. Somewhat contradictorily, the paper claimed that the statehood movement was a Republican effort, supported by every Republican member of the legislative assembly, and at the same time supported by a majority of citizens, be they Republican or Democrat. The newspaper also absolved Governor Giddings of any selfish motives or any responsibility for the statehood drive.[59]

Anticipating the old and often used argument of cost, the *New Mexican* estimated that admission as a state would cost the taxpayers only about $54,500.[60] Readers were reminded that the last legislature had already made ample provision for the support of a state, and also that the just rights guaranteed the people of New Mexico by the Treaty of Guadalupe Hidalgo would only be obtained if the territory sought admission into the Union at once. The paper attacked the lack of Indian protection, claiming that by the treaty New Mexicans were promised protection from Indian spoliations, which they had enjoyed under the government of Mexico, but not under the government of the United States. But statehood would bring ample protection. State government must be beneficial; why else do "people of all other territories . . . in all cases with a smaller population than ours" seek admission? Economic prosperity would increase after statehood, as "in all instances" territories became more prosperous after they became states. The low prestige accorded a territorial government was noted. "A Territory exists merely by the sufferance of the General Government—it has no voice in its councils, cannot be heard in Congress except by courtesy . . . while a state is sovereign, a part and portion of the government . . . ."

In order to give an air of immediacy to the entire statehood business, the fact was stressed that unless the territory manifested a burning desire for statehood, the national government would certainly not seek to bestow the honor. The initiative must come from New Mexico. Unless the people of the territory took an interest in having the constitution adopted, and expressed a willingness to become a state in the Union, "it will be taken for granted as claimed now by some, that we are indifferent on the subject . . . ."[61]

The opposing press pounded away at the "stateites" using familiar but effective arguments to discredit their movement. The *Republican* challenged the low estimate of statehood cost given by its rival and insisted that a basic sum of nearly $100,000 would be needed to make New Mexico a state. There would also be the interest and principal of an "already existing debt of about $70,000," and militia claims which must be paid, adding up to an excessively high commitment.[62] For this reason the "more intelligent of the middle class which constitute a majority" are strongly opposed to statehood. *The Borderer* cited the plight of Nevada, the last territory admitted before Nebraska achieved full status in 1867. ". . . She stands to-day at the head of the lists of states in excessive taxation . . . with a rate of taxation of $26.34 upon $10000, while eastern states come down to [only] six dollars upon the same amount of property." All this because some of Nevada's more ambitious citizens wanted to go to the Senate, or become governors.[63]

The *Republican* argued that because New Mexico's population fell short by thirty or forty thousand of the 133,000 required by Congress as a ratio of apportionment for House seats, on the basis of the 1870 census,[64] it was foolish to incur the costs of the attempt to become a state.

If a majority of the votes returned . . . be in favor of a State, a State Legislature is to be elected in September, and in November it will organize and elect two United States Senators to go to Washington and demand of Congress, 'in the name of the people of the Territory of New Mexico, its administration as a State under this Constitution.' Congress having determined to admit no state with a population less than 133,000, will of course deny the demand, and who, then, will have to compensate these two 'Senators' for their trouble and expense?

Citizens of the territory, naturally.[65]

As both the *Republican* of Albuquerque and the *New Mexican* of Santa Fe claimed to be the true voice of Republicanism in the territory, tempers grew shorter and the editorial attacks more personal as the heated journalistic duel wore on. The editors of the *Republican* took exception to an assertion that a rejection of statehood would be "a clear and explicit acknowledgement of most degrading imbecility and inferiority." It did not stand to reason, remarked the indignant *Republican*, that because people might differ from the writer that they must necessarily be imbeciles. "We trust the *New Mexican* does not mean that."[66] The Albuquerque paper was also annoyed by an effort to link opposition to the constitution with opposition to support of public schools. "The opponents of the State Constitution, are *not* opposed to the establishment and maintenance of a public school system."[67] A public antistatehood meeting held in Albuquerque on May 5 also emphasized this point in a series of resolutions attacking statehood. The *Republican* pointed out the success of the Territory of Arizona in establishing a public school system and asked why New Mexico could not do the same. "The people are willing enough to be taxed to support schools, but not a State government."[68]

Although the *Republican* often found itself in a defensive position in answering the forceful case for statehood presented by its rival in Santa Fe, it used at least one effectively offensive tactic. Over and over again, the paper published this simple proclamation: "Against the Constitution and a State Election on the First Monday of June, 1872. Let every voter who desires the well-being of New Mexico give his vote on that day, as above!!!"[69]

Charges of election corruption were in the air even before a single vote had been dropped in a ballot box. The *Republican* and *The Borderer* were among the newspapers which exploited this issue to their benefit. The election law, which was published with the constitution, allowed only one week for the probate judges to receive election returns and forward them to Santa Fe. Section 5 of the law stated that if ballots cast on the first Monday of June were in favor of the constitution, the favorable result was to be in full effect the following Monday. "If the majority of the votes cast be in favor of the constitution and a state, the Governor is hereby required to issue his proclamation on the second Monday of June, 1872, announcing the result of said election," and ordering state and congressional elections for September.[70] "Is this provision a piece of political rascality, or stupidity?" asked the *Republican*. There had never been an election held in the territory for delegate requiring less than two weeks to get in the returns, and the election laws, under which this election was to be held, had no provision of ways and means to have all the returns in Santa Fe by the second Monday in June.

The *Republican* quite definitely believed it was "rascality" rather than "stupidity" that accounted for the time specifications in the election law. Even if only a very small portion of the returns were received by the designated day, "*those votes* only are to be counted," and if a bare majority of them were in favor, the governor was to declare the result, no matter what the votes given by the vast majority of voters in the territory.[71] Careful vigilance by statehood opponents was urged. "Efforts will be made to deter or disencorage [sic] voters to come to the polls and after the day of the election, like effort will be made to detain the returns, if unfavorable to the adoption of a State government[,] until such time as, when arrived in Santa Fe, it will be too late to count them." The journal particularly cautioned the counties furthest from the capital to use all laudable means to have the returns in by the second Monday of June.[72]

The Borderer, always aggressive and partisan in approach, went even further than the *Republican* in charging fraud. The paper claimed that the election law itself had been tampered with. "The law [which] stands eurolled [sic] in the office of the secretary of the territory as it was passed . . . requires the Governor to issue his proclamation on the *second Monday of July*" rather than June! This outrage, which Governor Giddings and the ring were more than capable of perpetrating, was not accomplished during the last hectic hours of the legislative session, but was instead the result of an afterthought. Nevertheless, the Las Cruces newspaper made no bones about whom it believed guilty. "Why this silence upon the part of the Governor? Why has the *organ* [the *New Mexican*] been so dumb upon this matter during the weeks we have been calling attention to fraud and violence?" To give credence to its expose of scandal and fraud, *The Borderer* insisted that its information was most positive and could be relied upon. "It comes from a gentleman well known throughout the territory, and who has personally examined the law."[73]

A direct challenge from the *Republican* made it difficult for the embattled *New Mexican* to ignore the issue of fraud. What about the entry in the books of the Secretary of the Territory fixing the time "for the reception of the returns" on the second Monday of July? Was that a fact or not? "Our contemporary [in Santa Fe] has better facilities to learn whether it is or not and ought to inform the people of the fact."[74]

The published laws of the Legislative Assembly of the Territory of New Mexico clearly state that in July the governor would proclaim the results of the election. Giddings was to announce the returns "on the second Monday of July, A.D. 1872," and, if they were favorable to the constitution, order another election for the first Monday of September to elect a governor, lieutenant governor, secretary of state, auditor, treasurer, attorney general, superintendent of public instruction, members of the state legislature, and a representative to the Congress of the United States.[75] This printed document would substantiate the most serious charges leveled at statehood supporters by *The Borderer* and the *Republican*, and bring into serious question the integrity of the leadership in Santa Fe.

The published copy, however, was a translation;[76] the original law in Spanish has not been found.[77] Moreover, the public printer was Giddings' bitter foe, Sullivan, whose quarrels with the governor and the Republican organization were a part of the disruptive feud over control of the legislature. Because of the political chaos of the time in New Mexico, it is dangerous and unwise to draw unequivocal conclusions—Sullivan could have altered the wording of Section 5 to read the second Monday in July.

Even more baffling was the role of the legislators. By law, each of them was to receive three copies of the published pamphlet containing the constitution and the election act.[78] If this was done, the alleged switch in the date from July to June would have been known by the very men who framed the act, and yet, as divided along partisan lines as this group was, there apparently was no outcry against the supposed tampering with the law. Certainly there was no mention of protest in the territorial newspapers until *The Borderer* brought up the charge in early May, and, according to the *New Mexican*, printed copies of the constitution were available and ready for circulation in early March. This would indicate that either no switch was made, a logical assumption, or that there was massive involvement in a serious conspiracy by legislators not particularly known for their harmony. The latter possibility seems remote indeed.

Regardless of whether the charge of fraud was valid or not, the time allowed for returning votes was too short to secure a completely honest vote, and the framers of the election law knew it. As a matter of fact, there is evidence to indicate that the one-week time limit was not common knowledge. One thousand copies of the constitution and the accompanying election act were printed in what opponents contemptuously referred to as the "pamphlet,"[79] but the question of their effective distribution remains unresolved. Leading and informed citizens, in all probability, knew about the one-week time limit, but the average citizen may well have been totally unaware of the deadline for returns, until the *Republican* publicized it in late April. The *New Mexican* avoided the subject until after election day, and even the governor's proclamation announcing the June election, which was published in the newspapers, did not mention the one-week limit.[80] As problems of distance and transportation were so great in New Mexico, this seems an odd omission. It can perhaps be argued that this information was pertinent only to election officials responsible for the quick dispatch of returns to Santa Fe, and these officials were by law to receive the printed pamphlet containing the constitution and the act, which clearly stated the time limit for returns.[81] This does not, however, change the fact that the legislators who drafted the constitution were well aware of the transportation difficulties in a vast territory, where marauding Indians roamed the land, yet they, or at least a sizable faction of them, chose to allow only one week for the return of votes to the capital city.

On the first Monday of June, polling places throughout the territory opened to a disappointingly small number of voters. *The Las Vegas Mail* estimated that only one out of every five qualified voters cast a ballot. *The Borderer* insisted that in Doña Ana County the people looked upon the matter as "a farce and scarcely inquired where the poels [sic] were."[82] Certainly apathy and lack of interest were widespread and disastrously affected the vote on the constitution. Even the *New Mexican* had to admit that in a large number of precincts no election was held at all. The Santa Fe newspaper blamed the indifference of the electorate on Congress. There was a general belief that Congress would not admit New Mexico as a state, and therefore there was no propriety in going through the farce of an election for state officers at great expense, unless Congress should first authorize it and show its willingness to admit New Mexico. The fact that Congress had tabled a statehood bill only a few days before New Mexico's vote on her constitution deepened the frustration felt by statehood supporters.[83]

The election was followed by incessant cries of cheating and corruption as each political group tried to blame the other for the small voter turnout. A Doña Ana citizen wrote "I tried to vote for the state movement, but was intimidated at the polls by a certain Irishman here who had a crowd of his countrymen at his back, all armed with wattles, or vulgarly speaking, clubs." The same letter expressed the opinion that Anglos in the county had voted to remain in ignorance, the writer hoping that a few patriotic and unselfish men in Santa Fe would put a "quietus on the whole thing" if New Mexicans voted against statehood.[84] Antistatehood people, on the other hand, felt that a poll tax enacted by the last legislature had discouraged many voters. Although the tax of one dollar for each male citizen was ostensibly for school purposes,[85] the *Republican* insisted that the requirement kept away from the polls many people who were against the constitution. Thus, in the town of Peralta, forty votes were cast for the constitution, but none against it.[86] In the Mesilla Valley area, too, many voters were deterred from voting by a circulated report that if they did not vote they would save the dollar capitation tax.

Flooding caused by a late spring runoff from the mountains also affected the voting. "In Cruces and Dona Ana nearly all the voters were hard at work at the acequia to prevent an overflow."[87] In Mora County, unsuccessful efforts to prevent flooding occupied most adults prior to and during the election. When the overflow did come, there were several days of destruction during which all the Mora River bridges between Golondrinas and La Junta were swept away.[88]

Opposition newspapers had evidently discouraged many voters by their attacks on the one-week time limit for returns. There seemed to be little purpose in voting when one's vote might not even be counted. In a sarcastic editorial, *The Borderer* commented that there was "no particular need of hurry now; we did intend to take the ride to Santa Fe to carry returns from Dona Ana, but we know our rights and shall not jump at the crack of the whip of any Governor or ring unless the whip [be used] in a lawful manner." Although the Las Cruces paper urged every citizen to vote, telling its readers "Don't let a neighbor remain indifferent,"[89] the prospect of votes being cast in vain hardly generated enthusiasm.

Transported by horseback, wagon, and coach, the marked ballots began arriving in Santa Fe in the days following the election. But even in Santa Fe County, the center of statehood activity, only a small number of returns had been received by Thursday, June 6. The *New Mexican* optimistically predicted a 150-vote majority for statehood in the county, noting that seven precincts had voted for the constitution. Two Pueblo communities, however, had rejected the document,[90] perhaps feeling that the exploitation they had suffered since receiving citizenship in 1867 would only be worse if New Mexico became a state and the Indians were left with less federal protection. The Santa Fe daily also had to report that the precinct of Peñasco in Taos County cast all of its ninety votes against statehood.[91] By Monday, the day of the deadline, however, the *New Mexican* proudly announced victory for statehood in Santa Fe County, 554 votes for the constitution, and 346 against it, a majority of 208 votes.[92] In Grant County, too, a majority of 356 votes was recorded,[93] and several precincts scattered through the territory followed in approving the constitution.

But these few evidences of success could not blur the outline of the harsh truth becoming clearer as the week passed. Bernalillo County, regarded by the *Republican* as the "keystone county of New Mexico," cast a 674-vote majority against the constitution, only 24 people favoring it. "Hurrah! For Bernalillo!!" trumpeted the *Republican*.[94] Valencia and Socorro counties also rejected statehood, a defeat apparently duplicated in San Miguel and Mora counties to the east. A trickle of votes, 45 against the constitution and 32 for it, spelled defeat in Las Vegas, the county seat of San Miguel. In Mora County, the precinct of La Junta voted decisively, casting 19 votes for the constitution and 132 against it.[95]

The steady trend of the returns, small in numbers though they were, clearly indicated defeat for the proposed state government. Governor Giddings and other officials of the territorial administration were well aware of this negative outcome, and, at the end of the week, the small number of votes was used as an excuse to ignore the result of the voting and cancel all further proceedings. New Mexicans were never told whether they had actually voted for or against the constitution. An official explanation was given by Governor Giddings in a message to the legislature some eighteen months later.

The returns of the votes from the several counties were not made in time to be counted as the act of the legislature required, and of course with this failure, all subsequent proceedings were ended. The commission to count and declare the vote had no power to delay, adjourn, or put off the count, nor to send for returns of votes, but was in everything strictly limited to the specific powers designated in the act. . . . The time for returning and counting the vote, and the subsequent action to be taken thereon, was by an evident oversight or mistaken computation of time, made too short, and thus made the whole effort to obtain the views of our people on the subject nugatory.[96]

An accurate assessment of popular sentiment regarding statehood in 1872 cannot be made; it is obvious, though, that pro-statehood sympathy was not strong. There is no record of an actual count of all submitted returns. The commission appointed by the legislative act to make the count consisted of Governor Giddings, the attorney general, and the treasurer of the territory. According to the governor, the commission met on the second Monday in June to examine, count, and declare the vote. But with only partial returns in, there was little it could do, "and with the expiration of the day, expired also the power to act, and of course no legal count was made of the vote, for or against the constitution, and no further action was required either of the commission or the executive in regard to the matter."[97]

The fact that no official count of the vote was ever announced to the public, gave both pro- and anti-statehood forces an opportunity to claim a majority sentiment for their side. The New Mexican, on June 11, admitted that the vote was small, but believed that a fair majority of those who voted favored the constitution. One county, in which there was a very large population with sixteen or seventeen precincts, returned votes only for one precinct, going over four hundred for the state and not a single one against it. Rather eagerly the paper acknowledged the necessity of the commission's having abandoned the job of counting votes. "By an error in fixing the time too short in which to make returns . . . [a] fair expression of the sentiment of the people" could not be obtained. If a majority of the voters in the territory had voted on the question, they thought the ruling would have been different; but if the fact proved to be "that only one-third of the voters turned out then we question, much as we favor a state organization [,] the propriety of calling an election for state officers, even though a majority of the votes cast are in favor of the constitution."

The Republican of Albuquerque naturally felt that the negative results of the election proved they had been right all along. "What a generous organ!" it said of the New Mexican. "They will not force us to swallow the nauseous pill, knowing we dislike it so much . . . ."[98] Again mentioning the issue of the changed deadline for results, the Republican implied that statehood supporters had tried to rig an election, but when the results appeared to be adverse to their cause, they piously supported the governor and the commission in canceling the proceedings. If all available ballots had been counted, a "huge majority" of votes would have been against the constitution and statehood.

Hopes for statehood received a jolting setback in 1872. Those both in the national government and in the territory who opposed New Mexico's becoming a state could easily claim that the territory had "declared by an overwhelming majority that she does not wish to become a State, as yet."[99] The apathetic attitude of so many of the territory's citizens, resulting in only one-third of all eligible voters even casting a ballot, was damning evidence of little desire for statehood. New Mexico's effort to present Congress with a workable, progressive constitution, endorsed by the people, was, unfortunately, a total failure.

EIGHT

The Fateful Handshake

I N 1873, GOVERNOR
Marsh Giddings again quietly attempted to encourage New Mexicans to
pry open the door to statehood. A memorial to Congress in 1874 that
requested an enabling act for New Mexico[1] may well have been the result
of subtle and low-key pressure brought to bear upon the territorial legislature in a speech by the governor. Only the most naive could have been
beguiled by his introductory claim that "I have no opinion to express."[2]
This remark was followed by a list of good reasons for New Mexico becoming a state. Pointing to the statehood recommendation of Governor Connelly eight years before, Giddings noted that other chief executives of the
territory had "adopted like conclusions . . . as the first step in any great
progressive movement for this Territory." New Mexico could claim equal
status in the Senate with the oldest and most populous commonwealths,
and statehood would bring the additional honor of representation in the
lower house of Congress. Fifteen of twenty-four states admitted since the
thirteen original had an average population of less than 63,000, and New
Mexico's population had now reached to 40,000 in excess of that minimum, even excluding approximately 7,000 "industrious, quiet" Pueblo
Indians. With the heavy immigration to the territory of the past three
years, the territory's population might now be as much as 135,000. Was
this not further proof of the territory's worthiness? The governor made a
valiant attempt, however, to conclude his message on a calm note of ob-
jectivity. "Many believe that we shall gain more by aid from the general
government by remaining in a Territorial condition, than in assuming a

state government and paying its expenses . . . I do not deem it best to advise or recommend in the matter . . . ."

If Governor Giddings felt it necessary to be restrained in advocating statehood, New Mexico's delegate to Congress since 1872, Stephen B. Elkins, felt no such restraint back in Washington. With vigor and enthusiasm, Elkins pursued the goal of statehood so actively that the statehood movement gained new life during his two terms in Congress. Ignoring the failure of the 1872 constitution, Elkins introduced a bill on March 9, 1874, "to enable the people of New Mexico to form a constitution and State government, and for the admission of said State into the Union on an equal footing with the original States . . . ."[3]

On May 21, Elkins, a man motivated by a growing interest in acquiring land in the vast territory, as well as political power, made an effective bid for support of his bill in a lengthy speech that was certainly the most complete and persuasive exposition of New Mexico's cause yet heard by the nation's lawmakers.[4] The territory's qualifications for statehood were forcefully advanced. Not only did New Mexico have the requisite population prescribed by law, and the capacity to support a state government, but the population growth rate was ten per cent greater than that of the states of Alabama, Connecticut, Georgia, Arkansas, Delaware, Indiana, Kentucky, Louisiana, Maine, Massachusetts, Mississippi, New Hampshire, New York, North Carolina, South Carolina, Ohio, Pennsylvania, Rhode Island, and Tennessee. Elkins claimed New Mexico's population was 135,000, noting that this growth was achieved despite the loss of Arizona and some territory given to Colorado.[5]

Elkins made full use of the historical argument that New Mexico was entitled to admission "by reason of the promises and assurances made by our Government," previous to the ratification of the Treaty of Guadalupe Hidalgo. The proclamation made by Kearny on August 22, 1846, to the conquered people of New Mexico stated that it was "the wish and intention of the United States to provide for New Mexico a free government with the least possible delay similar to those in the United States . . . ." When the Mexican Congress balked at ratifying the Treaty of Guadalupe Hidalgo for fear that the people of New Mexico would not be admitted to all the rights of American citizens. Secretary of State Buchanan gave full assurance to his counterpart in Mexico by pledging that "Congress will never turn a deaf ear to a people anxious to enjoy the privilege of self-government. Their desire to become one of the States of this Union will be granted the moment it can be done with safety."[6]

Elkins reminded Congress that during the Civil War *Hispanos* had given unfailing loyalty.

. . . When the cause of the Union looked dark and doubtful, and when General Sibley's trained soldiers from the confederate armies were already on the soil, these people as one man rallied under their adopted flag, and fought gallently to preserve the Union into which they now seek admission.

New Mexico also deserved credit for the effective education measure passed by her legislature in 1871, in which she appropriated a larger share of her taxes for the support of public schools than any other state or territory in the Union, and, as yet, had had no help from any source whatever for school purposes. Transportation facilities in New Mexico were improving and lessening the territory's isolation. Five lines of railway were under construction, and pointing to New Mexico: The Texas and Pacific, Atlantic and Pacific, Atchison, Topeka and Santa Fe, Kansas Pacific, and Denver and Rio Grande; three were within ninety miles of her borders, with a fair prospect of being rapidly extended, and three would terminate within the heart of New Mexico, and two it was supposed would become transcontinental. Elkins also appealed to the traditionally penurious nature of Congress. "By applying for admission, New Mexico testifies her willingness to relieve you of the expense of continuing in existence a territorial government, and enables you to reduce your annual appropriations at a time when economy and retrenchment is the popular demand."

A major portion of Elkins' speech was devoted to New Mexico's tremendous resource potential and its salubrious climate. Medical authorities were quoted to show, that the lowest death rate from tubercular disease in America was in New Mexico. The whole territory had always been astonishingly free from epidemic disease, and the climate was unsurpassed by that of any other territory or state in the United States.[7] Elkins himself testified that the territory "is without doubt, the best grazing and stock-producing country in the United States, and will continue to be so." According to the great Baron Von Humboldt, the vinyards produced excellent wines, which were preferred even to the wines of Parras and New Biscay. On top of this, the territory had excellent mineral resources, the coal being as good as the best Pennsylvania, and entirely free from bitumen. Even the famous railroad builder, General William J. Palmer, president of the Denver and Rio Grande Railway Company, had to admit that New Mexico coal was "apparently . . . as good as the Westmoreland coal of Pennsylvania." Elkins also quoted the commissioners of the General Land Office: "Valuable minerals are found in every portion of New Mexico."[8] This storehouse of mineral wealth meant that the territory could become not only a great mining state, but because of her coal resources, a manufacturing center as well.

Although the members of the House were impressed by the strong case Elkins had made for New Mexico, those anxious to block progress for the territory were not silenced. Eastern attitudes toward the predominantly Spanish-speaking territory were well represented by Clarkson Potter, a Democrat from New York State. The eloquent appeal of Delegate Elkins was thoroughly refuted by Potter's attack on New Mexico's statehood qualifications. The New York congressman insisted that General Kearny had promised New Mexicans only a government similar to, but not necessarily identical to, those of the United States. Kearny's proclamation had also assured *Hispanos* that they would have the right to send representatives to a territorial legislature, not a state legislature. The idea that Congress was obligated because of guarantees in the Treaty of Guadalupe Hidalgo to admit New Mexico was dealt with by referring to Article 9 of the treaty which granted to Congress the right to accept or reject a statehood bid at its discretion.

New Mexico's assets and resources, which had been set forth so carefully by her delegate in Congress, were cut down with razor sharpness as Elkins listened helplessly. Potter challenged the population estimate of 135,000, pointing out that the last census had showed only 91,470. The widespread use of interpreters in the territorial legislature and in the courts indicated to Potter that unfortunately a "very considerable portion of the population of the Territory do not [even] speak the English language." Potter emphasized that not only was it dangerous to create a situation in which states with small populations possessed disproportionate influence in the Senate, but there was always the danger of these small commonwealths becoming the private preserves of wealthy men. Congressman George F. Hoar of Massachusetts, although a Republican, supported this Democratic colleague from New York with a vigorous attack on New Mexico's educational system. There had been no public school system in that territory until within three years. A very few years ago the question had been put to a vote of the people there whether they should have a public school system, and the decision was in the negative by a large majority.

Elkins had worked long and diligently to gather support for New Mexico and, when the vote came, New Mexico's supporters withstood, for that day at least, the strong opposition. The fact that H. R. 2418 was very similar to other statehood bills of the recent past also helped. "This is the same bill by which all the new States have been admitted. We have not dotted an 'i' nor crossed a 't'. It is the usual enabling act."[9] But for Elkins and New Mexico it was a victorious day when the statehood bill passed the House of Representatives by a count of 160 to 54 with 76 not voting.

Judging by the lack of popular enthusiasm for the 1872 referendum, there were undoubtedly many New Mexicans who cared little whether a statehood bill passed or did not pass. But this first step toward self-government was hailed with delight by territorial officials and some of the political leaders. William Breeden, chairman of the Republican Central Executive Committee of New Mexico, wrote Elkins "I read your speech yesterday—It does you credit—We all feel proud of you—you have distinguished yourself and the Territory—The vote was very gratifying and quite surprising."[10] Judge S. A. Hubbell of Las Vegas, a statehood proponent for more than fifteen years, was especially pleased by Elkins' speech, feeling it covered the whole ground and would give satisfaction to New Mexicans. ". . . I believe our people are now in a proper frame of mind to support the movement and give an overwhelming majority in favor of it, and to you will be due the credit and honor of establishing a State government for New Mexico . . . ." The judge knew, however, that the bill faced a crucial test in the upper house.[11]

It was almost inevitable that the Senate would offer far more resistance to the making of a new state than had the lower house. The very nature of that august body, in which each state was represented on an equal basis, made the senators reluctant to admit new members. Nine months passed before the Senate dealt with New Mexico's bill. It was ignored during the first session of the 43rd Congress primarily because of complications ensuing from Colorado's effort to achieve statehood.

As early as December 8, 1873, Colorado's territorial delegate, Jerome B. Chaffee, had introduced an enabling act for the territory, followed later the same day by a second such bill sponsored by Republican Representative George Colin McKee of Mississippi. These bills were in response to a message to Congress sent a week earlier by President Grant in which he recommended statehood for Colorado. "It possesses all the elements of a prosperous state, agricultural and mineral, and I believe, has a population now to justify such admission."[12] This strong presidential endorsement of the mountain territory would certainly have hastened the process of admission had it not been for the bitter political feud caused by Grant's reappointment of Edward M. McCook as territorial governor in January, 1874.

McCook had been as Civil War comrade of President Grant, having commanded a division of cavalry in the Army of the West. Then, after serving one controversial four-year term as Governor of Colorado, he was replaced by a prominent resident of the territory, Samuel H. Elbert, who assumed leadership in 1873. Although McCook was deeply embittered by his dismissal and determined to reverse Grant's decision, Delegate Chaffee, a political opponent of McCook, was very pleased with this action by Grant, whom he considered a close friend. However, a gradual cooling off of the friendship between Grant and Chaffee, which, according to one report, was the result of a quarrel during a poker game,[13] was most helpful to McCook in his determined effort to be reinstated as governor. Making the long trip to Washington, McCook used his old army connections to win the confidence and esteem of General Orville E. Babcock, one of the President's closest aides. His approach was effective, for on January 27, 1874, Grant, without the "slightest warning," sent to the Senate for confirmation McCook's name as governor to replace Elbert, and new nominations for the territorial secretary and surveyor general. This gave new credence to the rumor circulating throughout the territory that Grant was unhappy with the results of that poker game with Chaffee.

Rather naturally, Colorado politics were thrown into turmoil by the Grant dismissals and McCook's reappointment. According to Frank Hall, a Chaffee man who had lost his position as secretary of the territory, old wounds were now reopened. "The old State and anti-State factionalism, for some time dormant, reappeared; long buried prejudices were revived."[14] Chaffee attempted to prevent Senate confirmation of McCook's appointment, when, without consulting the President, he strode into the Senate chamber and began organizing his friends there against confirmation. But Chaffee himself was soon to be vitally affected by the fiercely divided Colorado Republican party. Although he had served two terms as delegate, in 1874 Chaffee absolutely refused to accept his party's nomination for re-election and the minority Democrats were able to elect Thomas M. Patterson, an able lawyer, as delegate. The victory was impressive, Patterson carrying nineteen of twenty-five counties against his Republican opponent.[15]

The confused state of Colorado politics slowed action on Chaffee's statehood bill until June 8, 1874, when it was finally passed by the House.[16] Now the two statehood bills, New Mexico's and Colorado's, stood side by side in the race for admission, both waiting for approval from the Senate.

Colorado was fortunate enough to have a champion, Senator William M. Stewart of Nevada, who on June 23, the last day of the session, demanded that Colorado's bill be considered immediately. The brusque and bearded Westerner insisted that the territory had "about the requisite amount of population, is a grand Territory, and it is time it should be admitted." But a motion by one of the hostile New England senators to table consideration passed by a vote of 33 to 20.[17]

Senate action on both statehood measures finally came on February 24, 1875, only one week before adjournment of the second session of the 43rd Congress. Sponsors of the Colorado bill, which was taken up first, were afraid that prolonged discussion and changes in the bill would destroy its chance of passage with so little time left before adjournment. Senator John A. Logan of Illinois expressed concern. "At this late hour in the session, when sending the bill back to the House may probably cause its defeat, it does seem to me that we ought not" make unnecessary changes. Senator Phineas W. Hitchcock, Republican of Nebraska, who presented the bill for the Committee on Territories, echoed these sentiments. "I desire if possible to prevent any amendment being adopted for the reason that I believe it will peril the passage of the bill . . . ."[18] But a small group was determined to amend the enabling act and to the chagrin of many Westerners they were led by a Californian, Senator Aaron A. Sargent.

The changes in the Colorado bill made by Sargent and his supporters were small ones. Section 12 of the enabling act, which gave five per cent of the proceeds from the sale of public lands within the territory to Colorado prior to admission, was changed so that proceeds became Colorado's only after admission. Public lands sold could not be land under the homestead laws of the United States, but should be agricultural lands, all mineral lands to be "excepted from the operation and grants of this act." Efforts to prevent the transfer of certain public lands to the new state were largely unsuccessful.

Two amendments were offered by Republican Senator George F. Edmunds of Vermont, a man with mixed views on the question of new states, in order to delay action on the Colorado bill. The amendments were both accepted, the first one prohibiting the governor from calling for a constitutional convention until ninety days after the first day of September, 1875, and the second stating that the people could not vote to ratify or reject the state constitution until the month of July, 1876. Although Senator Hitchcock objected that the second change was only designed to postpone statehood till some "future and indefinite time," Edmunds claimed that the five or six months between the constitutional convention and the referendum were necessary for "ample time to study the fundamental and most important instrument that can exist in a State and vote upon it intelligently." The second amendment was passed by a vote of 27 to 22.

Colorado statehood supporters dared not fight too hard against the amendments, lest the bill's chances for quick passage be further endangered. But it was necessary to resist increasing attacks on the financial provisions for the proposed state. Sargent even questioned the accepted custom of granting to the state sections 16 and 36 of every township for the support of public education. Ignoring the comparative aridity of Colorado's soil, he noted that Illinois only received section 16 of each township. This attitude seemed to shock Senator Stewart. "That provision has been in . . . [statehood] bills for over twenty years."

A Senate vote of 42 to 12 finally approved the amended Colorado statehood bill, and about half an hour later the New Mexico measure was taken up. "I propose to move *seriatim* the amendments which were made in the case of Colorado," Sargent informed the Senate, "commencing with the first one and going all the way through."[19] A majority agreed with this proposal and the discussion was brisk and concise, as most of the issues had been thoroughly covered during the Colorado debate. Senator Edmunds managed to amend New Mexico's enabling act so that the constitutional convention would be no earlier than the last day of November, 1875, like Colorado's. The final vote approved the bill by 32 to 11.[20] This brought New Mexico to the brink of statehood, with House concurrence on the amendments the only remaining hurdle.

With only a few days left of the second session of Congress, many New Mexicans resented the amendments on which the fate of the bill now hung. The New Mexican, speaking for many statehood supporters, felt that if "the bill is defeated we have Sargent of California, in the main, to thank for the defeat. The amendments of Mr. Sargent were unnecessary and could only come from an oversticklish [sic], carping or cussed nature." Another editorial added that the people of New Mexico had bitter cause for remembering some distinguished solons; to whom could be substantially charged the ultimate defeat of the bill. The changes in the bill made by the Senate were considered worthless by the paper, largely meant to slow its passage.[21]

Newspapers in the East viewed the statehood question from the standpoint of the older, established states and therefore tended to support the Senate's amendments. The Chicago Daily Tribune praised the logic of delaying constitutional conventions and referendums in the proposed states so that the new constitutions could not be presented to Congress until December, 1876, the lame-duck session of the 44th Congress. By this time, the presidential election of 1876 would be over, without the two new states having been able to cast their six electoral votes.[22] Little did the influential Republican paper realize how crucial just one electoral vote would be in 1876.

Although much abuse was heaped on the two aspiring territories following the Senate's approval of the amended bills, more space and attention would undoubtedly have been given to the subject had it not been for the sensational trial of Henry Ward Beecher, accused of seducing the wife of the editor of a religious journal, and a heated congressional debate over another bill to compel the South to carry out Reconstruction measures. The territories themselves, however, could hardly have wished for more attention, as most of what they got was derogatory. The New York Times was especially critical of New Mexico. "That territory is thinly populated, the towns scattered over its vast area are few and ill-regulated, and a large part of the people is ignorant and utterly destitute of enterprise and public spirit." The eminent paper saw no reasonable excuse for making New Mexico a state.[23] The Chicago Tribune was more fair; it saw no excuse for making either of the Western territories a state. As for Colorado, none of its attractions could hide the fact that according to the 1870 census the population was only 39,864, less than half of New Mexico's. The Tribune insisted that a territory should have a minimum population of 130,000, the current unit of representation in Congress. It was wrong in principle to admit any new state to the Union until it had the population requisite to entitle it to at least one representative in Congress. "The present ratio is a very liberal one."[24]

The Chicago paper also objected to the fact that, if admitted, Colorado and New Mexico would join the list of states which were overrepresented in Congress, or in the paper's words, "borough States." The established borough states of Delaware, Florida, New Hampshire, Vermont, and Rhode Island had a combined population of only 1,178,967, not equal to rural Iowa's population of 1,194,020. Yet these rotten boroughs had eleven representatives in Congress and 21 electoral votes, while Iowa had nine representatives and only eleven electoral votes.

The Reconstruction problem of carpetbaggers was also made an issue. The organization of two new states opened an opportunity to that large class of "adventurous politicians" who failing in one place, sought others where promotion to power and place was more possible. A number of those who participated in the troublous organization of Arkansas had already gone into New Mexico and Colorado. Reconstruction was over in all the Southern states. "There are no more bonds to be voted, no more grants and subsidies to be sold, no more debts to be created, no more offices to be held. These States have been squeezed dry. The opening of two new States offers opportunities which that class of politicians are not likely to overlook."

Although it condemned both territories, the Tribune did indicate that if it were forced to choose between the two, Colorado had the most potential. Indeed, it might someday "become comparatively populous."[25] Other Eastern papers also gave the impression of being somewhat less critical of Colorado. The Cincinnati Commercial, although exceptional in the acid severity of its criticisms, did follow a general trend in that it reserved its harshest indictments for New Mexico.[26]

The Commercial, repeating the familiar criticisms, noted that of 91,874 inhabitants recorded in the 1870 census, between seventy and eighty thousand were of "Mexican descent." These people were "almost wholly ignorant" of the English language. In only two of fourteen counties was English understood well enough to be used in jury trials. Most newspapers were published in Spanish. The people of New Mexico "are aliens to us in blood and language." Illiteracy was so widespread that "popular ignorance prevails like a pall throughout the whole Territory, with few and insignificant exceptions." Only 1,899 children attended schools, and of the 44 schools only five were public. The 1870 census had estimated that of the 66,464 inhabitants who were ten years of age or above, 48,836 were unable to read and 52,220 could not write. The *Commercial* concluded that three quarters of the territory's more rational individuals were thus totally illiterate. Ignorance in New Mexico was even greater than in South Carolina and Mississippi, states where illiteracy was among the highest, and "blacks outnumber whites." Even in Utah, to many people a "synonym for darkness and ignorance"—a slap at the Mormons—practically all the people were able to read and write.

The Catholicism of native New Mexicans was used in a particularly insidious way. Although the Know-Nothing movement had died out, and the American Protective Association was not yet established, there was still a strong undercurrent of nativism in the country. The *Commercial* disavowed any intent of arousing bigotry, but pointed out that of the 158 churches in the territory, 152 were Roman Catholic. The handful of Protestant churches had "sittings for only 850 people," while the Catholic churches had room for no less than 80,710 worshipers. It is to the credit of our free institutions that they acknowledge no distinction whatever on the ground of religious belief, the journal commented piously. "We would be among the last to object to admitting to the Union a Catholic State on the grounds of the religious faith of its inhabitants." The paper was on more valid ground in implicating the Catholic Church in the high percentage of illiteracy in the territory. As the Church had enjoyed "uncontrolled sway" over education for generations, this was a highly vulnerable area.

The overwhelming agrarian economy of New Mexico was regarded as a serious liability, leaving the territory far too underdeveloped to merit statehood. "There are few manufacturers, little commerce, . . . [and the] nearest railway does not come within two hundred miles of New Mexican soil."

Although Anglo prejudices against the culture and religion of New Mexico were very real, opposition to statehood for New Mexico and Colorado was also prompted by political consideration. The two territories had long been regarded as Republican, and it is worth noting that the *Cincinnati Commercial* echoed strong Democratic sentiments. The Republicans, having lost twelve senators in the upper branch of Congress, and fearing still further depletions of their number in the next general election, had grasped at a chance of preserving the balance of power in the legislative branch of the government, by securing four more Republican senators, at the expense of making sovereign states "out of a handful of half-breeds, miners and squatters in these remote Territories."[27]

In recent years, the two major parties had indeed become more evenly balanced, culminating in a Democratic triumph in the 1874 congressional election. When the 43rd Congress entered its last week before final adjournment, the Republicans, knowing that they would no longer have control when this lame-duck session was over, were most anxious to pass as much of their legislative program as possible. After March 3, 1875, the Democrats would control the House of Representatives. Although there was some confusion as to whether the statehood bills for Colorado and New Mexico, Republican-sponsored measures, had been totally approved in a Republican caucus, most Republicans were committed to statehood for the territories.[28] Besides statehood, Republican leaders also hoped to use this last remaining chance to enact Reconstruction measures which would help the Southern Negro. The Radicals within the Republican party were aware of the Negro's increasingly abandoned position beneath the firm hand of the resurgent Southern politician. On February 27, a Civil Rights Act requiring Southerners to give equal rights to the Negro in theaters, hotels, public carriers, and all other public facilities, was approved by the Senate and forwarded to President Grant, who signed it on March 1, 1875. Unfortunately, this measure, predating the public accomodations section of the 1964 Civil Rights Act by nearly nine decades, was subsequently declared unconstitutional by the Supreme Court. Another Force Bill, which almost became law, was passed by the House in February. This measure would have given the chief executive the right to suspend the writ of habeas corpus in Alabama, Arkansas, Louisiana, and Mississippi.[29]

The bitterness of the civil rights debate clearly affected the fight of the two territories for statehood, because it increased the antagonism of Southern Democrats toward any Republican effort. Supporters of statehood feared that with only a few crowded days left in the session, united Democratic opposition would prove fatal if the bills were sent through traditional channels. A fateful decision was made. Rather than send the enabling bills to the House Committee on the Territories, where they might lie unreported indefinitely, the friends of New Mexico and Colorado would lay them "upon the speaker's table." According to parliamentary procedure, a two-thirds majority vote of approval would remove a bill from the Speaker's desk for passage or rejection by House members. It was a gamble to try this method of gaining House concurrence on the Senate amendments, but it was felt by one influential participant that "the shoals and quicksands of the committee, and the deadly perils of a filibuster in the very last days of the session, were all avoided."[30]

The flaw in this plan was that the Republicans lacked a two-thirds majority and would only succeed in their scheme if a number of Democrats could be induced to join their side. Colorado was lucky enough to have present in Washington her newly elected and capable Democratic delegate, Patterson, who expressed his willingness to co-operate with both Chaffee and Elkins in behalf of the enabling bills. Patterson campaigned effectively among Democratic House members, arguing statehood for both territories, although his plea for Colorado was obviously more heartfelt. Many Democrats were impressed by the mere fact that he had been elected, for this raised hopes that Colorado might become a Democratic state.[31] It was easier to win support for Colorado than for New Mexico, and talks with influential Senator Allen G. Thurman, Ohio Democrat, and other Democratic legislators, began to win support, especially for Colorado. Patterson deserves admiration, however, for as the week continued, he made it clear that the goal was to have both bills removed from the Speaker's desk, not just one.

On March 3, the last day of the session, while the House was engaged in debating the civil appropriations bill and other less important measures, the Colorado and New Mexico forces went into action. Congressman George G. Hoskins, New York Republican, moved to suspend the rules for the purpose of going to the Speaker's table and concurring in the Senate amendments to House bill No. 435, the Colorado bill, and House bill No. 2418, the New Mexico measure. The opposition immediately objected to considering the two bills in one vote, but a congressman who asked that the bills be called for separately, was overruled. The first vote on the two measures, however, found the statehood supporters somewhat disorganized, and they failed to muster a two-thirds majority, the final tally being 164 to 84. After the balloting, there was great confusion, as some of the Republicans who had voted against the measure were being induced to change their vote. While these "changes were in the making, great interest was manifested, the members crowding in front of the Clerk's desk, and inquiring the result." At this point, the shrewd Democratic leader Samuel J. Randall of Pennsylvania called for a recess until eight o'clock that evening. The New York Times happily regarded the vote as a defeat of the statehood bills, caused by the unresolved Senate amendments, and hoped the matter was ended.[32]

But Elkins, Chaffee, Patterson, and their friends would not accept defeat and lobbied feverishly into the night to round up support for another effort. At eight o'clock, debate began again over a variety of issues and continued past midnight into the following day. Anxiously, statehood supporters waited while a resolution by controversial old Ben Butler of Massachusetts, by which bills could be removed from the Speaker's table by a simple majority, failed to win approval.[33] Shortly after midnight, James G. Blaine, the elegant Speaker of the House, dramatically entered the chamber dressed in full evening clothes and made his way to the chair. Blaine was retiring as Speaker, and had just left a "fashionable dinner function" where he had been the guest of honor. According to Patterson, Blaine's arrival signaled a final test for the statehood cause, for in the opinion of the Colorado delegate, Blaine was a friend of statehood.[34]

The long-awaited opportunity came when Republican Congressman Ellis H. Roberts of New York moved the rules be suspended so that members of the House could go to the Speaker's table and remove the bills there one by one, either by "unanimous consent or a vote of two thirds."[35] This motion was accepted and the House began to act upon measures which, for the most part, had already been passed by the Senate and only required House concurrence. It was early in the morning, probably sometime between one and two, when the Colorado bill was reached, strategists having agreed that consideration of that territory should come before New Mexico.[36] As the suspense mounted, Democratic Congressman Samuel S. Cox of New York called for a reading of the Senate amendments, hoping to delay action. Following this, Speaker Blaine responded to loud demands for a roll call from the Democrats, by ordering that "yeas and nays" be given. For more than thirty-five minutes, the balloting went on. Some tortured legislators declined to vote when their names were called, and cast their votes at the end of the roll call. But the final tally showed Colorado had won the day, or, as Patterson put it, "the night," 164 for statehood, 76 against it, and 48 abstaining.[37] With the tabulation of the required two-thirds majority, the House concurred in the Senate amendments. Enough Democrats had been won for the Colorado cause by high-powered persuasion.

The New Mexico bill was taken up next, as Delegate Elkins prepared to take his own count of the roll call. At first, the balloting seemed to parallel that of Colorado, and hopes for New Mexico were high. But desertions here and there soon made it evident that some Democrats who had supported Colorado were withholding votes from her neighboring territory.[38] When it was over, a truly crestfallen Elkins could count only 154 votes for New Mexico, 87 against, and 47 abstentions, leaving the luckless territory seven short of the necessary two-thirds.[39] The hardworking team of Elkins, Chaffee, and Patterson had accomplished only half their goal, despite powerful Republican support. When the 43rd Congress adjourned later that day, statehood for New Mexico was once again no more than a dream.

Many New Mexicans felt the disappointment keenly, although the editors of the New Mexican philosophically rationalized that New Mexico had achieved no small amount of consideration during the Congress just expired, "notwithstanding the dashing away of that most acceptable cup when so near the lips,—the defeat of that cherish [sic] . . . hope of our people, the enabling act which was to make New Mexico a state of the Union."[40] Delegate Elkins was quite unjustly blamed for the defeat by some journalists. The *Santa Fe Gazette* had already confidently put into type New Mexico's enabling act, and being "terribly disgusted," heaped "bile on poor Elkins" and denounced him for making little effort.[41] *The Borderer*, which had little enthusiasm for statehood anyway, remarked that little good had been done by the delegate.

The *New Mexican* was unstinting in its praise of Elkins and came to his defense by accusing *The Borderer* of partisan zeal. Could the Las Cruces journal name one Democratic delegate who accomplished "more substantial good" in several terms than Mr. Elkins has done in his first term? The *New Mexican* proudly repeated the Denver *Mirror's* claim that no other man in the territory could have done half as much for New Mexico.[42] The passage of an enabling act by both houses of Congress was a high point in the struggle for statehood as all previous efforts to secure consideration of an enabling act had ended with a mere introduction of the bill and reference to the committee. The paper attempted to place the last minute rejection of the territory's bid in proper perspective. With the immense pressure of business in the last days of Congress, it was seldom that any bill received consideration, except those of overwhelming importance, such as finance and annual appropriation bills. Also emphasized was the considerable good done for the territory by Elkins over and above the attempt to secure an enabling act. "With Mr. Elkins in Congress, false impression[s] relative to the territory have been corrected and the croakings and malignings which itinerating bohemians have delighted to pile on the territory have been effectually stopped among all the leading and respectable newspapers of the land."[43] Although this was an optimistic view, it did indicate an awareness of the hostility of the nation's press toward statehood for New Mexico.

The Denver *Tribune* joined in recognizing the vital role played by Elkins in the recent political battle. About a year before, when everyone in Washington representing Colorado in any capacity was engaged in the fight over the governorship, Elkins had framed a bill for the admission of his territory as a state. The Colorado bill, shortly after "tacked on" to the New Mexico measure, soon benefited from the eloquence of New Mexico's delegate. The "able and elegant" speech delivered in the House of Representatives by Elkins was said to have exerted a very powerful influence in securing the large majority, by which the two bills passed that body the previous year. Probably going beyond the facts in its praise, the Denver paper claimed that the idea of statehood for Colorado was suggested by the delegate from New Mexico.[44] *The Chicago Tribune* had earlier evaluated Elkins' contribution in much the same way. "To Delegate El-kins of New Mexico, more than any one man in Washington, is the ad-mission of Colorado due. As the bill to that end was tacked on to the one for the admission of New Mexico, he worked assiduously for both, only to be defeated for his own Territory after a hard-fought battle."[45]

Though pleased by these accolades for New Mexico's delegate, and charitable enough, despite disappointment, to congratulate Colorado on her success, the Santa Fe New Mexican could not help asking "by what rule of logic Colorado is admitted and New Mexico left out . . . ." The paper fell prey to the irresistable temptation of finding scapegoats, and the United States Senate was the first to be cast as villain. "By all rules of fair-ness and of majorities New Mexico ought to have been admitted as a state and would have been, had it not been for a couple of carping busybodies in the Senate, who, in view of the insignificance and immateriality of their amendments to the bill, we cannot conceive of any adequate motive, be-yond that of outright cussedness." Assuming the role of spokesman for residents of the territory, the paper declared that most of the people felt that language was inadequate to give proper expression to their feelings of outraged indignation over this "most unjust interference."

The highly partisan Republican daily also gave the Democrats in Con-gress a proper chastising. The fact that a switch of only seven votes on the final roll call would have given New Mexico the necessary two-thirds was a hard pill to swallow. Were the seven congressmen who had stood be-tween New Mexico and statehood Republicans or Democrats? The New Mexican revealed that only fourteen Republican members, "principally from Massachusetts and New York," voted against the suspension of the rules for both Colorado and New Mexico. Obviously the Republican party, as a party, stood by the enabling act for New Mexico to the end. The Democrats' record was very different. Only nine Democratic House members voted to remove the New Mexico bill from the Speaker's table. Worse yet, on the first crucial vote on Hoskins' resolution to take the two enabling measures together, only three Democrats had voted for suspen-sion of the rules. In this case, the paper claimed that a change of only two votes would have meant passage of the statehood bills together.[46] The "final and immediate defeat" of the enabling act for New Mexico was due to the absence of a few Democratic votes.[47]

The Denver Tribune explained Colorado's greater success in the roll call votes as the result of having an effective Democratic delegate present in Washington. Thomas M. Patterson, "the able and courteous gentleman whom we Republicans allowed the Democrats to . . . elect as Delegate," was in Washington during the last few weeks of the session, and used all the influence he possessed, both personal and official, in behalf of the Colorado measure. It was he who secured the only two Democratic votes cast in the Senate. The eleven Democratic House votes for the mountain territory were also insured either "directly by Mr. Patterson or through use of his name." Patterson also prevailed upon seventeen unfriendly Democrats to cast no vote at all.[48] His strategy was to convince enough Democrats that the admission of Colorado would not be a political liability, and, without question, he succeeded in "alluring" enough of them into the belief that Colorado would come in a Democratic state. House Democrats failed to render similar aid to New Mexico because it was "Republican beyond doubt."[49]

Although partisan politics did affect the vote on New Mexico, it was certainly less than the whole truth to blame the Democrats entirely for defeat. Republican support for statehood in Congress was substantial, but by no means complete. The Senate amendments that necessitated return of the bills to the House for concurrence were the work of two Republican senators, Sargent and Edmunds. There were newspaper reports in various parts of the country indicating that Speaker Blaine was less than enthusiastic about statehood for the territories. One story, which appeared in at least two influential daily papers during the session's final week, claimed that Blaine was exerting himself to kill the bills, because there was a movement to have the delegates from those would-be states to the National Republican Convention instructed to vote for General John A. Logan as candidate for the presidency against Blaine.[50] This is contrary to Patterson's belief that Blaine was a firm supporter of the statehood cause. Blaine himself, in his *Twenty Years of Congress*, more noted for omissions than commissions, says nothing pertinent about the two enabling bills, although he praises both Elkins and Chaffee and comments favorably on Colorado's growth in the years between 1866 and 1875. "The Territory had in the long interval developed great wealth in the precious metals, in rich deposits of iron and coal, and most surprising of all, in its agricultural resources."[51] But there is nothing about the tense days preceding the final roll call votes on both territories.

It seems that although statehood for New Mexico and Colorado was a Republican-supported effort in Congress, the cause was regarded with little enthusiasm east of the Mississippi, even by Republicans. Moreover, an amazingly small amount of news coverage and publicity was given to the issue, even in the final, crucial days of congressional debate. Most newspaper discussion of the territories was limited to devastating criticism of the qualifications they claimed to possess. The occasional article containing favorable information on the subject was usually brief and unenthusiastic. The St. Louis Daily Globe had a good word for the resources, although not the people, of the two territories. Colorado and New Mexico had the "best range on the continent" for stock raising. The Press of Philadelphia noted that southern Colorado and New Mexico produced the cheapest wool in the country, "and the manufacturer who buys his wool at the door of his mill can out-sell any competitor."[52] There was a significant lack of simple human considerations in the national reckoning of whether or not the territories should be states, and often the final judgment of a law-maker or a newspaper was based on the supposed political leanings of the territory.

Any summation of the factors responsible for New Mexico's failure to achieve statehood in 1876 would be incomplete without the inclusion of a strangely fateful political accident. The "Elkins Handshake" story was apparently not made public until Patterson told it to a gathering in Boulder, Colorado, celebrating the twenty-fifth anniversary of statehood for Colorado.[53] Later, in 1906, when another New Mexico statehood bill was under consideration, Patterson, then a senator, repeated the story for his colleagues in the upper house.[54] A more complete account occurred in a special fiftieth anniversary edition of Patterson's Denver newspaper, The Rocky Mountain News.

According to Patterson, the hard work of the territories' delegates had resulted in enough support so that he felt confident, about a week before the final roll call votes, that statehood had the "necessary two-thirds, and the friends of the measure were ready for action." One day, however, while the House was heatedly debating a piece of civil rights legislation, a little-known representative from Michigan named Julius Caesar Burrows rose to speak in behalf of the Force Bill. This bill was the most controversial of the last-minute attempts to legislate Reconstruction measures because it called for the suspension of habeas corpus when necessary to protect the rights of Negroes. In an eloquent and lengthy speech, Burrows, who was rumored to be "a Columbian orator of prodigious carrying power," deliberately "grilled the Southerners from head to foot, and tortured them in the fires of his oratory."[55]

Congressman Burrows passionately defended the actions of Republicans during the Reconstruction period.

Never in the history of the world was there such an exhibition of magnanimity as that manifested by the Federal Government in its dealings with the Southern States. Southern chivalry should be quick to recognize it. . . . Have you forgotten the generous terms of surrender at Appomattox? Have you forgotten that every seceded State has been received back into the Union with full restoration of all its rights? Have you forgotten that not a single man who participated in that conspiracy has ever paid the penalty for his treason?

Southern congressmen listened to the fierce castigation of the South "with gleaming eyes and gritting teeth."[56]

It is true you disbanded your armies, but only to organize the Ku-Klux and White Leagues, oath-bound to secret murder. You have abandoned your warfare against an armed nation only to strike down unseen defenseless citizens. You have accepted the abolition of slavery and the liberty of the black race only to attempt his enslavement by a system of vagrant laws which, if executed, would consign the people to a servitude no less terrible than slavery itself.

Burrows finished midst thunderous Republican applause with a challenge to the vanquished South.

Strip the hideous masks from your outlawed Ku-Klux; disband your White Leagues; visit swift and condign punishment upon your unarrested and untried felons, and enforce State and Federal law with a firm hand. Give to human life some security and to property protection; recognize the equality of all men before the law, . . . Do this, and the whole South will spring from her baptism of blood into the fullness of a new life, and regenerated forever. All hail that auspicious day![57]

Delegate Elkins wandered into the House chamber about five minutes before Burrows had brought his speech to its climactic ending. He entered through a door very close to the desk from which Burrows was speaking. He was immediately attracted by the orator and stood listening to him. He was manifestly carried away by the fervor and swelling voice and earnest manner of Burrows, and when Burrows closed, he rushed up to him, "and was the very first to shake him by the hand and congratulate him upon the mastery of his effort." Scores of other members gathered about Burrows' seat and shook his hand, but Elkins was the first.

Fatal enthusiasm! . . . The Democrats—particularly the Southern ones, those who had been won over to Colorado and New Mexico statehood—witnessed Elkins' rush for Burroughs [sic] and his congratulations with set teeth and ominous mutterings. That evening it was known that a number of them who had been counted friends of statehood would vote against New Mexico, at least, and Colorado might possibly be included in their wrath.

Following the unfortunate handshake, statehood supporters worked frantically to repair the "dislodged fences." They were successful in their effort for Colorado, but the cause for New Mexico was lost.[58]

At the close of the 43rd Congress, New Mexico found itself consigned to territorial status for the indefinite future. Colorado, with a new lease on life, had proceeded to prepare and ratify a state constitution by July, 1876, and was proclaimed a state on August 1 by President Grant. State elections held in October resulted in a slender majority for the Republicans, discrediting Patterson's argument that the territory could become a Democratic state. On November 1, a few days before the presidential election, which later would be known as the "Stolen Election of 1876," Colorado's new legislature convened in Denver and proceeded to select its presidential electors. In discharging this function, required by the new state constitution, the fledgling state was to decide a national election.[59]

On election day, the Republican Rutherford B. Hayes lost in the popular vote to Samuel J. Tilden, the Democratic candidate. But electoral college votes in South Carolina, Florida, and Louisiana were in dispute due to charges and countercharges of vote fraud, and in Oregon an elector was disqualified. For two months, debate raged across the country, and the confusion of the electoral college finally compelled Congress to establish, in January, 1877, a Joint Electoral Commission to decide which electoral returns were legitimate. The Republicans had a majority of one on the commission, which enabled a partisan vote to award the disputed votes to Hayes. This made the final count in the electoral college 185 to 184, in favor of Hayes. If Colorado had not been admitted as a state, however, Tilden would have won by 184 to 182, as Colorado had given her three electoral votes to Hayes. Or, if the three Colorado votes had gone to the Democrats, as Patterson had strongly implied they would, Tilden's margin would have been a more comfortable 187 to 182. Colorado's decisive role caused disappointed Democrats to be suspicious of the other Western territories for many years to come.

NINE

Statehood &
the Santa Fe Ring

Following New Mexico's attempt to achieve statehood in 1875, the Democratic party was understandably reluctant to admit new states to the Union,[1] having been badly burned by the admission of Republican Colorado. And because of the even balance of party strength in Congress, Republicans were unable to support New Mexico statehood effectively, nor were they particularly enthused over the matter. Lack of congressional action, combined with little initiative on the part of the territory's citizens, was to cause a low ebb in the statehood movement that would last for almost thirteen years.

Congress, deadlocked since the controversial Hayes election, seemed unable to act decisively on an issue as explosive as statehood. The presidential elections of 1880 and 1884 did not break the deadlock; they were so close that a shift of less than 5,000 votes in the first and less than 12,000 in the second would have changed their outcomes. In five of the Congresses serving from 1875 to 1889, each party controlled one house. In the 46th Congress, Democrats had majorities in both houses, but Hayes was President. In the 47th, although Republicans dominated the lower house, the number of Republicans and Democrats in the Senate was exactly even. Both parties were apprehensive about admitting a new state that might aid the opposition. New Mexico's fight for statehood was also delayed by the loud cry for statehood from Dakota Territory.

Dakota was one of the Western territories that formed a huge arc around the state of Kansas and encompassed most of the Great Plains and Rocky Mountain region. Of the territories in the arc, only Nebraska and Colorado had achieved statehood, but now Dakota, a vast territory and a growing center of population north of the Jayhawker state, was demanding recognition. To the west of Dakota lay the raw, young territories of Montana, Wyoming, Idaho, and Washington. South of these were Utah, Arizona, and New Mexico, and to the east were Oklahoma, created in 1890, and the Indian Territory, both below Kansas. But Dakota's rapidly increasing population gave her a much stronger case for statehood than her neighbors. Bradford Prince, who later served as territorial governor of New Mexico, realized that the superior claim of Dakota made it "obviously impossible for any less populous Territory to be admitted until her urgent application was heeded."[2]

Thus, the outlook for New Mexico's political future was by all indications, in the late 1870's, indeed static and disheartening. Delegate Elkins had sensed this immediately after the defeat of the 1875 statehood bill, and was glad to leave the turbulent Washington scene and go abroad for several months. He was not, however, to escape that easily from New Mexico's problems. While in Europe, he was again nominated by Republicans in New Mexico for the position of territorial delegate, and, although he gave no formal consent to his candidacy, was elected to the office.[3] Upon returning to Congress, Elkins again illustrated his commitment to statehood by correcting the enabling act which had so nearly been passed by the 43rd Congress, and reintroducing it in the 44th Congress.[4] The bill, however, never emerged from the House Committee on the Territories, a fate common to many New Mexico statehood bills.

The day before Elkins presented his enabling act, a Western senator introduced an enabling act for New Mexico which had some hope of success. Nebraska's newly elected Senator Algernon Paddock, with the support of his colleague, Senator Hitchcock, was aware of the substantial Republican support that had been given New Mexico in the preceding legislative session, and he and his fellow Nebraskan hoped to see another of the Western territories with which they indentified become a state. Two months after the introduction of the Paddock bill on January 11, 1876, it was favorably reported out of the Senate Committee on Territories. On March 10, the Senate debated the bill and approved it by a vote of 35 to 15.[5] The House of Representatives, however, was firmly controlled by the Democrats, and New Mexico's Republican leanings eliminated any chance of approval. The Paddock bill joined the Elkins measure in the House Committee on the Territories, where it too remained untouched.

But the nation's capital, with its legislative intrigues and sophisticated social life, was a great distance from the Territory of New Mexico, both in miles and spirit. Violence and political instability in the sun-drenched territory reached a climax during the governorship of Samuel B. Axtell, appointed to replace Giddings, who had died on June 3, 1875. Upon receiving his new assignment, Axtell moved from Utah, where he had served as territorial governor for four months, to the old capital of Santa Fe and took up residence there on July 30. Within a few months, Axtell was deeply involved in the political rivalries in the territory, and, far from seeking the justice and establishment of order needed to end the feuds, he became an active participant in them. The bloody battle between Murphy supporters and McSween supporters, known as the Lincoln County War, was in full swing, and the governor unfortunately made a mockery of law enforcement by his determined backing of Lawrence G. Murphy, a most unscrupulous man. At the same time, the Colfax County War raged over the disputed rights of settlers to remain on the Maxwell Land Grant, which had been sold to an English-Dutch Company in the early 1870's.

Under Spanish and then Mexican rule, immense pieces of land had been awarded by the government to various individuals and their families. By this time, the question of legitimate title to these lands was made difficult, not only by the large number of descendants of the original owners still living on the land, but also by the new American legal system that had been superimposed on the Mexican one in 1846. And in cases like the Maxwell Grant, the problem was complicated by thousands of poor people of Mexican descent who had long occupied and farmed the vast open spaces of the land grants. Lucien Maxwell, whose father-in-law had been given the land by the Mexican government, had allowed settlers to remain for only a token payment and a share of the produce. But when Maxwell sold the grant to a group of investors, including Jerome Chaffee of Colorado, who in turn sold to the English-Dutch company, the old feudal arrangement was destroyed. The new owners tried to force the "squatters" from the land, as the foreign combine hoped to profit from its new enterprise. Citizens of Colfax County soon divided into two definite groups, one supporting the company's right to evict the settlers, and another group resisting the change and claiming that much land in the Maxwell Land Grant had been added to the original tract over the years by illegal schemes.[6]

Unfortunately, a number of ambitious, unscrupulous Anglo lawyers regarded the confused legal status of the land grants as an ideal opportunity for adding money and land to their personal assets. These men went to such lengths to build their financial empires that those who fought to check their greedy actions labeled them a "ring," referring usually to the notorious Santa Fe Ring, although there were others in the territory of less importance. Residents of Colfax County actually feared the actions of the ring more than those of the English-Dutch Company. Their fears appeared justified when, in September of 1875, a Methodist minister, the Reverend F. J. Tolby, was murdered after attempting to prevent the control of Colfax County by members of the Santa Fe Ring. There were rumors that the new owners of the Maxwell Grant had arranged the killing, but subsequent action by the territorial assembly indicated that a powerful group living on the other side of the Sangre de Cristo Mountains was engaged in an enormous land grab within Colfax County. A measure passed by the territory's legislators authorized the courts to partition land grants or put them upon the sale block, even when only the smallest owners petitioned such action. Another law, enacted in January of 1876, annexed Colfax County to Taos County for judicial purposes for at least two court terms. Taos was in this way given jurisdiction over all land grant cases in Colfax County.

Citizens of Colfax County held a mass protest meeting on November 10, 1875, charging the Santa Fe Ring with full responsibility for the Reverend Tolby's brutal murder.[7] Such leaders in the county as Frank Springer pleaded with Governor Axtell to intervene and investigate the situation. Axtell not only refused to visit the county and hear the arguments presented by residents, but he supported and defended members of the ring, claiming there was no reason to believe any "Ring" or person in Santa Fe had anything to do with Tolby's death. When Axtell was accused of planning the murder of Springer and others opposing him, and when protests were sent to Washington concerning the court's removal from Colfax to Taos, many influential New Mexicans came to the governor's defense. Supporting the governor were Elkins; Don Trinidad Romero, who succeeded Elkins as delegate to Congress; William G. Ritch, territorial secretary; and Breeden, the prominent Republican leader.[8]

The Lincoln County War, 1876 to 1878, began as a personal feud, but snowballed so quickly that it soon involved important people throughout the territory. Murphy, a vital figure in the violence, had come to New Mexico while serving in the army and, like others, had remained after his discharge. He became a merchant of considerable influence and wealth, which he aggressively used to dominate economic life in Lincoln County. As he controlled all business enterprises in the area, owned the only store, and had control of most of the wagon trains, farmers and ranchers in the huge county could do little to challenge his dictatorship. Not until 1875, when a lawyer named Alexander A. McSween settled in Lincoln, did the many enemies of Murphy find a leader. The ambitious McSween, an unusual man on the frontier because he refused to touch alcohol or wear a gun, immediately began to handle cases against Murphy. With the backing of his English friend, John Henry Tunstall, and cattle king John

Chisum, he also challenged Murphy's financial monopoly by building a store and acquiring a ranch and a bank.[9]

The inevitable clash came when the Murphy group, led by James J. Dolan and John G. Riley, successors to Murphy in the mercantile firm, became involved in an effort to recover several thousand dollars which they felt had been unfairly charged by McSween in a legal matter. Although Tunstall's financial partnership with McSween had not yet been formalized, his property was attached by the sheriff of the county, and during this process the sheriff's posse, meeting Tunstall on a road, shot and killed him.[10]

Murphy's influence was so widespread that Tunstall's friends, who included William Bonney, better known as Billy the Kid, were obstructed in every attempt to bring about a just and lawful retribution for his death. Taking matters into their own hands, McSween's men killed Sheriff William Brady and his deputy, both loyal Murphy supporters, on the main street of the town of Lincoln in broad daylight. This and other killings brought on a last bloody showdown, involving about forty men on each side, between July 16 and 19 of 1878. McSween and his allies barricaded themselves in his house and two other homes in the town, but the McSween house was set on fire, and he and three of his supporters were killed in a raging gun battle. Billy the Kid escaped by running toward the nearby Bonita River and losing himself in the darkness. His notorious career continued until his death at the hands of Sheriff Pat Garrett at Fort Sumner on July 14, 1881.

Governor Axtell's role in both the Colfax and Lincoln County wars was that of a weak and unprincipled man. He, with the support of Thomas Catron, United States district attorney general, and Colonel William L. Rynerson, attorney for the Third Judicial District, intervened on numerous occasions in behalf of the powerful Murphy faction.[11] There was little hope of stopping the endless succession of murders and corruption as long as the governor and other officials publicly took sides in the dispute, keeping the emotions of all concerned at the boiling point. Residents of Lincoln County felt so insecure in the midst of continuing violence that many of them left their farms and jobs and moved away. When news of the chaotic situation in New Mexico and Governor Axtell's mishandling of it reached Washington, Axtell was removed from office and replaced by General "Lew" Wallace, famed for his distinguished Civil War service.

When the new governor reached Santa Fe in September, 1878, he was still working on the manuscript of his novel, Ben-Hur. Between literary bouts with the novel, Wallace received presidential assurance of the use of federal troops to maintain law and order, and upon personally investi-

gating the Lincoln County situation in March of 1879, he realized that the
McSween-Tunstall faction was deserving of some sympathy, having now
lost both its leaders in the violence. Earlier, Wallace had greatly eased
tense feelings by announcing on November 13, 1878, a complete amnesty
for those on either side in the feud guilty of "misdemeanors and offenses
committed . . . between the first day of February, 1878," and the day of
his proclamation.[12] But for one more gun-slaying of a lawyer attempting
to settle the McSween estate for his widow, the amnesty ended the Lincoln County War. Hearings, trials, and indictments related to the war,
however, went on for some time.

The natural intolerance of Easterners for New Mexico, and its ways,
was increased by the constant tales of murder and violence in the territory.
And in fact, it would have been quite difficult during the 1870's and
1880's to claim that New Mexico was ready to govern itself as a state.
There were Anglos within the territory, too, who were disenchanted and
annoyed with everything about the place and its people. Governor Wallace's wife Susan was an outspoken critic of "the land of sage brush and
cactus." To her the adobe villages looked "like nothing so much as a collection of brick kilns." Lincoln County was an "asylum for cut throats,"
in which "there was very little worth fighting for." She ridiculed the territory's celebrated healthful climate. "The old Spanish conquerors were
gorgeous liars but there are modern letter writers fit to tread in their
exalted footsteps—these gifted creatures spread their wings when they
talk of climate." On the subject of statehood, she thought that if the territory was made a state, "the Americans would bear the taxes and the
Mexicans hold all the offices—it is not in the interest of the white men to
bring that about."[13]

New Mexico's progress toward statehood was also slowed by a series of
small, but violent and costly, wars with the nomadic Apaches. The Chira-
cahua Apaches were living on the Ojo Caliente reservation in Grant
County when the federal government, at the insistence of local settlers,
decided to relocate them in Arizona on the huge San Carlos reservation.
Trouble began when the great chief, Victorio, who had already twice unsuccessfully attempted to escape, fled the white man's authority in April,
1879, and vowed he would never surrender. He took to the warpath with a
band of followers, and, before his death in 1883, his raids brought death
to 200 New Mexicans, more than 100 soldiers, and 200 citizens of northern
Mexico.[14] His leadership was assumed by younger rebellious Apaches,
among them the determined Geronimo. Geronimo's last gesture of defiance began in 1885. With a tiny, ragged band of 42 men and 96 women
and children, the intrepid warrior raided settlers, kept his people alive in

the hot, mountainous desert, and eluded hundreds of soldiers until he surrendered in a remote canyon in southwestern New Mexico in 1886.[15]

The Apache raids, though confined mostly to southwestern New Mexico, were well publicized in national newspapers, and this tended to strengthen the image of the territory as a wild, primitive land rather than the home of a European civilization that predated the Plymouth Rock landing by several decades. In actuality, the territory was, in spite of its problems, developing in many ways. Census figures show that the population increased by more than 68,000 between 1870 and 1890.[16] In 1879, the Atchison, Topeka and the Santa Fe entered the territory, and, in March of 1881, it met the Southern Pacific at Deming to complete the first rail route across New Mexico. This ended the vital importance of the historic Santa Fe Trail. One historian has noted that Lew Wallace was the last territorial governor to enter New Mexico by horse-drawn stagecoach and the first to leave it in a Pullman car.[17] After the Civil War, gold mining was especially important, although gold had been discovered as early as 1828 in the Ortiz Mountains between Albuquerque and Santa Fe. Gold strikes in 1867 and 1869 brought a boom, and in a short time the precious metal was being mined in most of the territory's counties. Silver resources were also developed, many mines being located in the area around Silver City in southwestern New Mexico. The presence of a railroad in the territory meant the beginning of a substantial coal industry, as Elkins had foreseen. Sheep grazing and farming had long been a vital part of New Mexico's economy, but they expanded after the war along with a new phenomenon, the open-range cattle industry. The fabled cattleman, John Chisum, once owned range land which extended 150 miles up and down the Pecos River from Fort Sumner to the Texas border.[18]

Although statehood was not a major issue during this period of general growth for the territory, there were still many individuals who strongly desired the advantages of self-government. The statehood boosters often included members of the "rings," or as they were at times referred to, "land grabbers." Ring members often gave influential and powerful support to statehood attempts over the years.

When Edmund G. Ross was appointed territorial governor to succeed Lionel A. Sheldon in 1885, he wrote a remarkable description of the rings.[19] "The curse of this Territory is rings," he declared.

Many years ago a few sharp shrewd Americans came here—discovered a number of small Mexican and Spanish Grants—purchased them at nominal prices—learned the Spanish language—ingratiated themselves into favor with the Mexican people, and proceeded to enlarge the Grants they had purchased, and to manufacture at will, titles to still others, and to secure therefor [sic] Congressional recognition. . . .

These "sharp" Americans were lawyers.

As an old soldier of the Mexican war, who settled here on being mustered out, expressed it . . . [they were] 'Americans possessed of some legal lore with a large amount of cheek and an unusual quantity of low cunning and astuteness that always had an inclination to run in a crooked direction.'

According to the old veteran, these attorneys, working together in a "ring," corrupted the legitimate grant owners, "simple Mexicans who never would have thought of claiming more than their papers called for." The native landowners were taught a "few tricks" and learned to "swell" their holdings to "colossal dimensions." Having helped the owners, the "land ring fiends" were repaid with large shares of these grants for their services. The lawyers became "hi-muck-a-mucks" in the territory.

The Mexicans voted them to congress, thus giving them federal as well as territorial power, and anybody who does not know that they played a high old game is ignorant of the history of the Territory.

Governor Ross, a staunch foe of these lawyers, regarded the Land Grant Ring as first and foremost among the scheming groups. Others grew from it as opportunities for "speculation and plunder" developed. "Cattle Rings, Public Land Stealing Rings,[20] Mining Rings, Treasury Rings, and Rings of almost every description" grew until the affairs of the territory came to be run almost exclusively in the interest and for the benefit of these combinations. Santa Fe,

being at the terminus of the great inland highway reaching from St. Louis to the Rio Grande, and capital and commercial centre of the Territory, naturally became the seat of operations of all these combinations, which were organized regardless of political divisions, in one sense, but strictly with reference to politics in another sense, as nearly every law or commercial firm especially the former, contained a Democrat and a Republican, apparently for prudential reasons, so that whichever side, might come uppermost, the dominant party was represented, and there was an average of one lawyer to every ten Americans.

This numerical predominance of lawyers gave the Santa Fe bar a position of great influence. Its members controlled the activities of the Santa Fe Ring, which in turn dictated to all the lesser rings. The governor described the Santa Fe bar as being for all practical purposes, a closed corporation, manipulating the bulk of the territory's legislation. The rings found in other towns in New Mexico were all subservient to the "central head" in Santa Fe.

Ross regarded Elkins and Catron as the principal "originators and manipulators" of the Land Grant Ring,[21] usually considered synonomous with the Santa Fe Ring. The eventful lives of these two men followed the prescribed pattern. Both were early emigrés to the territory who adopted the language and habits of the country in order to achieve their objectives. Both were amazingly successful.

Elkins acquired ownership of a large portion of the extensive Mora Grant in northern New Mexico,[22] after securing congressional confirmation of the grant as delegate.[23] He also was one of the principal owners of the Ortiz Grant north of Albuquerque.[24] Fiercely aggressive in defending his interests, he was once accused of using his influence as Secretary of War in the Benjamin Harrison administration to prevent a resurvey of the Ortiz Grant intended to ascertain whether valuable mineral land had been illegally incorporated into it.[25]

Elkins' closest confidant while in the territory and during the years that followed his departure was Catron, and if any man could be pointed to as the leader of the Santa Fe Ring, that man was Catron. Elkins as well as other members of this group that controlled so much in New Mexico looked to Catron as their representative. His name was continually associated with the Ring's activities, and, when the Ring was blamed for certain maneuvers, Catron was often the scapegoat. A stout man with a gruff manner, he commanded respect in many and fear in others. He had a reputation for being willing to fight anyone,[26] and facts reveal that he won a large per cent of his political battles.

The extent of Catron's landholdings was fantastic. Arriving in New Mexico in 1867, he was reputed to be one of the nation's largest landowners by 1883.[27] With an insatiable hunger for land, he acquired through the years 240,000 acres of the Mora Grant, taking in most of the grant's northern section.[28] But his biggest holding by far was the Tierra Amarilla Grant, comprising 593,000 acres of land located in northern New Mexico and southern Colorado.[29]

Another important member of the Ring, despite the fact that he was often at odds with Catron, was Le Baron Bradford Prince. Prince received his political experience in New York, but during the Republican National Convention of 1876, he had argued with powerful Roscoe Conkling, the New York State boss, and this ended his political career there. When President Hayes later offered him the governorship of the Territory of Idaho, he declined, but in 1879 did accept the offer of Chief Justice of New Mexico.[30] While serving in this position, he was accused of being a Ring member,[31] even though Catron opposed him when he unsuccessfully ran for territorial delegate in 1884.

After this defeat, Prince began a legal career that fulfilled his strong desires in the direction of land and mining speculation.[32] As a highly successful lawyer, he seemed to be well qualified for membership in the Ring, but the great renown he eventually gained rested on his unceasing efforts in behalf of statehood. Although he was a comparative newcomer to the statehood cause, his diligent work prompted some to call him "The Father of New Mexico Statehood." Whether Prince deserved this title may be debatable, but his appearance and bearing, at any rate, did make him an attractive advocate. An Eastern newspaper described him well.

He is a tall man, straight as an Oregon pine, and the extreme dignity of his appearance, enhanced by a flowing beard, is defended from austerity by an expression of the greatest good will . . . .[33]

Catron, Elkins, and Prince were Republicans, but membership in the Ring, as Ross implied, was not limited to those of Republican persuasion. There were several active Democrats in the Ring, among them two law partners of Catron, Charles H. Gildersleeve and William C. Thornton.[34] Gildersleeve was accused of heading a clique of "land grabbers," in which Antonio Joseph, who was elected as New Mexico's Democratic delegate to Congress in 1884, was a member. According to the charge, Gildersleeve was the main Democratic manipulator for the Santa Fe Ring and "the most unscrupulous of all that combination." He supposedly had his henchman, Joseph, elected delegate with the help of the Santa Fe Ring, engineering a split in the Republican party.[35] Gildersleeve collaborated closely and secretively with Catron in land speculation and allegedly had interests in the Ritaca and San Cristobal grants and four other important tracts of land.[36]

Evidently Delegate Joseph was not above resorting to various schemes to acquire land. He was accused of taking advantage of "poor ignorant Mexicans" in procuring his holdings in the Chama and Ojo Caliente grants.[37] Joseph's native background did not make him unique among Ring members, as there were a number of prominent *Hispanos* closely connected with the group. Among them were J. Francisco Chaves and Mariano S. Otero, and also the influential Perea family which controlled much of Bernalillo County.[38]

Max Frost, the editor of the *New Mexican*, must also be mentioned as an important member of the Santa Fe Ring. Frost, who was at one time during his active career indicted in a land fraud prosecution,[39] acted as a journalistic spokesman for the Ring, effectively using the press to discredit foes of the Ring and to place its activities in the best possible light.

The acquisition of statehood was the project most dear to all Ring members, especially Catron, Elkins, and Prince, who continually advocated this step. Their major motive is not difficult to discover. One need only peruse the correspondence of Catron. In a letter to one J. M. Free-man, Catron offered to secure a loan of $200,000 with his vast holdings in the Tierra Amarilla Grant, stating that his property was the "finest large body of land in the arid region of the United States" and that his "selling price for the same is three dollars per acre and with the passage of the statehood bill for New Mexico it will be advanced to not less than $5 per acre."[40] In discussing another tract of land, Catron again em-phasized the importance of statehood to land values in New Mexico. If New Mexico is admitted as a state, "each acre of that land would be worth three pesos otherwise it is not worth more than one now."[41]

As important as this motive was, it does not adequately explain all the desires of individual Ring members. The leaders of this clique were prom-inent and influential citizens and naturally had political ambitions. Statehood would mean two senatorships, and a representative in the lower house, plus a host of state officials to be elected. Not a new or unique reason for statehood support, it nevertheless remained an issue of some importance in the territory.

The *Hillsboro Advocate* of Sierra County sensed the underlying ambi-tion, for in an article quoted in the *Rio Grande Republican* on Septem-ber 28, 1889, it stated that everyone was opposed to statehood in southern New Mexico except for "a few self-seeking politicians."[42]

The desire for a feeling of equality was no doubt another important motive. A majority of the Ring members had come from Eastern states where statehood had been achieved, and they felt that territorial status was a form of second-class citizenship. This view was often expressed in their correspondence and public utterances, always louder and longer than it warranted, when considered in relation to the economic and polit-ical reasons they probably felt to be more important yet were careful to hide from the public.

Whatever the real objectives of Ring members in so eagerly desiring statehood for New Mexico, they never left room for doubt as to their position in this matter. Their policy was forcibly stated by Frost as early as 1870 when he wrote in the *New Mexican*: "As long as we obtain state-hood we do not care how it comes or who brings it about. Statehood is what the people of New Mexico want and statehood they must have in order to prosper and advance."[43]

Governor Ross intensely disliked the idea of New Mexico's future, whether as a territory or a state, being in the hands of the Santa Fe Ring. A man of unflinching courage, it was he who as a senator from Kansas cast the decisive vote against the impeachment of Andrew Johnson in 1868. Savagely attacked for his decision, he had been thrust into political obscurity and eventually moved west to Albuquerque, where he was living when Grover Cleveland recognized his worthiness by appointing him governor.[44] As a fighting journalist, Ross quickly recognized the power of the Ring and identified with its opposition. Hence, although the rest of the territory hailed his appointment, the people of Santa Fe, under the influence of the Ring, fought it. When the new governor first assumed office, members of the Ring made an attempt to win him to their side, but when he refused to co-operate they unsuccessfully agitated to get the President to withdraw his appointment. In this endeavor they naturally received the hearty support of Ring Democrats in the territory. When President Cleveland did not withdraw his support, Ring members conspired to elect a legislature entirely hostile to Ross. According to Ross, this plan succeeded because as a federal official he could not actively fight the Ring and also because of the perfidy of disloyal Democrats.[45] As a result Ross was in constant conflict with the legislature throughout his term.

The governor had his supporters, too, in such Democratic politicians as the incorruptible Harvey B. Fergusson, an able young attorney who had been in New Mexico since 1882, and outspoken Democratic newspapers such as the *Albuquerque Morning Democrat* and the *Socorro Industrial Advertiser*. Nor were native New Mexicans entirely inactive, as indicated by a secret Catholic society called the "Association of the Brotherhood for the Protection of the Rights and Privileges of the People of New Mexico" which vowed "to oppose rings, cliques, monopolies and official corruption of all kinds . . . ."[46]

Although members of the Santa Fe Ring and various others were almost always supporters of statehood, it would be wrong to assume that their opponents were generally against statehood. On the contrary, many of them protested their second-rate status as vigorously as Catron or Prince. They were, however, much concerned about statehood being granted on the "land grabbers'" terms, which they felt would be disastrous for New Mexico. Ross, for instance, was opposed to immediate statehood because the territorial legislature had failed to enact an adequate school bill, and he felt that congressional action must first establish a public school system before admission would be wise. He accused Ring members in general, and Catron specifically, of killing the Kistler bill, which would have established such a school system. He reasoned that the Ring deliberately wanted to keep the people ignorant so it could remain in control.[47] Thus, the forces for statehood were divided against themselves and could not, at least during the mid-eighties, wage an effective battle for an equal place in the Union of States.

TEN

The Constitution of 1889

WITHIN NEW MEXICO, pressure for statehood was negligible during the late seventies and early eighties. Although members of the powerful Santa Fe Ring were for immediate admission, New Mexicans generally were indifferent to the opportunities supporters claimed statehood would bring. As a result of this indifference, New Mexico's political progress toward an enabling act was initiated outside the territory. A number of statehood bills for the Western territories had been presented in Congress only to be denied passage, but an effort by Democratic Congressman William M. Springer of Illinois to secure admission for four territories, including New Mexico, very nearly succeeded.

On March 13, 1888, Springer, the chairman of the House Committee on the Territories, introduced H. R. 8466, an omnibus bill which would "enable the people of Dakota, Montana, Washington and New Mexico to form constitutions and State governments," and be admitted into the Union.¹ New Mexico was also included in S. 400, a separate omnibus bill offered in the Senate on December 12, 1887. A companion measure to this bill was presented in the lower house on January 10, 1888.

It was not merely fondness for New Mexico that dictated the territory's inclusion in these omnibus bills. Congressman Springer was doubtless more interested in New Mexico's Democratic tendency than in her cause, especially as New Mexico was the only one of the four territories in which the Democratic party had a chance for success. This assumption was based mainly upon the election and subsequent re-election of Delegate Joseph

147

to Congress.[2] Partisanship influenced the Senate version of the bill, too, with the added ingredient of a father's ambition for his son. The father was Daniel W. Voorhees of Indiana, Democratic leader of the Senate, who requested a colleague to introduce the bill, and the son was Charles Steward Voorhees, delegate from Washington, who presented the companion measure in the House. The elder Voorhees, a very partisan politician, may have entertained hopes that Washington would become a Democratic state and send his son to sit by his side in the Senate.[3]

Of all the omnibus bills introduced, Springer's bill, H. R. 8466, seemed most likely to win approval. For one thing, unceasing pressure for statehood by the people of Dakota Territory could no longer be ignored. It was assumed that the northwestern territories would all be Republican and that the first act of the next Congress would be to admit them. With this in mind, Democrats, who controlled the House, were willing to remove all opposition to the admission of Dakota, Washington, and Montana, if in return the Republican Senate would allow New Mexico into the Union.[4] After the Republican victory at the polls in November of 1888, Democrats, dislodged from control of the next House, were especially anxious to make this bargain.

As in the past, however, a bid for statehood by New Mexico aroused heated controversy of a kind to which the other territories seemed, at least partially, immune. Eastern and midwestern newspapers, led by the *Chicago Tribune*, criticized bitterly the inclusion of New Mexico,[5] and only accelerated the bitter abuse after the Republican success in 1888. To include New Mexico in the omnibus bill was merely an eager effort to secure a couple of Democratic senators, to offset the senators from Dakota.[6] "Partisan impudence" was the cynical evaluation of the *Indianapolis News*.[7] The *Chicago Tribune* referred to New Mexico's population as "not American, but 'Greaser,' persons ignorant of our laws, manners, customs, language, and institutions." New Mexicans were accused of being lazy, shiftless, and "grossly illiterate and superstitious." Wyoming with its 60,000 fewer people was far more deserving of statehood.[8] Factionalism within the territory was not overlooked either. Under a state government, the greater portion of New Mexicans, being unfamiliar with the English language, would be at the mercy of "unscrupulous rings of politicians."[9]

Despite this vigorous attack by the leading newspaper in Springer's home state, the congressman remained undaunted. He was, after all, a good and loyal Democrat. Moreover, it was his bill that they were attacking, for the Committee on the Territories under his direction had substituted the Springer bill for the Voorhees omnibus bill and the separate bills of statehood for Dakota, Montana, and Washington.

The bill, as finally introduced, was comparatively short and simple,

considering that it was an enabling act for four territories.[10] Those provisions pertaining to New Mexico called for a 75-delegate constitutional
convention empowered to create a full state government. One portion
specified that sections 13 and 36 of every township should be granted to
the states for common schools. Another provided 500,000 acres of land
for the support of public institutions and, recognizing the aridity of the
Southwest, included in the land grant 250,000 acres of land for the establishment of permanent water reservoirs for irrigation.

New Mexicans were disturbed by Section 20 of the bill, which stated
that the constitutional convention was to submit to the people for approval a proposal to change New Mexico's name to Montezuma. Voting
on the name change was to take place on the same day the referendum
for the constitution was held. This section was probably the result of the
"solicitation and influence" of the noted lawyer, David Dudley Field,
who felt so strongly that the territory's name should be changed that he
wrote a number of letters to periodicals and even took the trouble to visit
Washington and interview members of Congress on behalf of this project.
Proponents of the change argued that the name New Mexico was puzzling
and that foreigners, and even Americans from the East, were likely to confuse it with the Republic of Mexico. New Mexicans angrily disagreed with
this reasoning, and a group of citizens met in Santa Fe in the winter of
1888-1889 and appointed a committee to draw up a series of resolutions
demanding that the historic name be kept. These resolutions were presented to the Senate on April 7, 1890.[11]

The Springer bill was accompanied by a majority and a minority report,
each of which reached an entirely different conclusion. The minority report presented by Isaac S. Struble of Iowa, the ranking Republican on the
House Committee on the Territories, recommended that each territory
stand on its own merits rather than be incorporated into an omnibus bill.
It suggested that Washington, Montana, and South Dakota be admitted
into the Union, and that North Dakota be organized as a territory to
receive an enabling act sometime during that session of Congress. New
Mexico would remain a territory.[12]

The paragraphs dealing with New Mexico were biased, unkind, and
deeply cutting. The people were presented as having no desire for statehood and having made no move toward it since 1875. Neither the territorial delegate nor anyone else in recent years had introduced a bill asking
for New Mexico's admission. Delegate Joseph and Governor Ross, who
were in Washington and had been for one month, were said to have made
no effort to urge congressional action. In fact, the only suggestion for New
Mexico's entrance along with the other three territories was made by the
committee chairman, Mr. Springer. The minority members thought it

remarkable that with such an "intelligent and able" delegate and such an experienced governor, himself a former United States senator, it should remain for the chairman of the Committee on the Territories to decide the time and qualifications for New Mexico's admission. They could not understand how the majority could maintain that New Mexico desired statehood when no official expression by the territorial assembly had been offered in fifteen years, when no bill except Springer's had been presented in Congress, and when no convention had been held by the people to give expression on this subject.

The majority report included New Mexico as a candidate for admission and tried to answer the charge of disinterest by citing two documents. The first was the old 1874 memorial of the territorial legislature urging immediate statehood. The memorialists claimed that they spoke for the people and insisted that the territory had the necessary population for statehood. Next, the majority report, after admitting that there had been no authoritative expression by the people of the territory on admission since the failure to get an enabling act during the 43rd and 44th Congresses, cited newspaper discussion on this subject which had ensued since the introduction of Springer's bill, showing that a commanding majority of papers favored statehood. The report emphasized a poll taken by the *Santa Fe New Mexican* in which circular letters had been addressed to prominent citizens and newspapers in the territory to solicit their opinions regarding the advisability of New Mexico's becoming a state. Of the 122 replies from every county in the territory, 91 favored statehood and 31 were against it.[13]

The story behind this poll is an interesting one. The *New Mexican* had received a letter from "a member of congress, a Democrat in politics and a man of great prominence in his party" who desired to know how the people of the territory felt about New Mexico's admission.[14] The inquiring congressman must have been Springer and he could not have selected a more co-operative conspirator than Frost, the chief spokesman for the Ring and a determined advocate of statehood. In view of this, the validity of the poll may be questioned.

Whether the charge that New Mexicans were apathetic toward statehood was correct or not, the introduction of the omnibus bill did bring immediate action. On March 27, 1888, Joseph presented to the Committee on the Territories a memorial from Governor Ross asking for the admission of New Mexico,[15] and separate petitions from the citizens of the territory asking for admission were introduced on March 29, April 2,[16] and April 12.[17]

Another charge made in the Struble report was that New Mexico, although the oldest of the territories, was not yet ready for statehood. This was perhaps not resented as much as the type of evidence introduced to support it. The minority members of the committee presented such old and outdated works as W. W. H. Davis' *El Gringo*, as well as republished critical extracts from the reports of such former governors as Lew Wallace. The effect was to picture New Mexicans as largely illiterate, superstitious, and morally decadent.

So disturbed was Catron over inclusion of the uncomplimentary remarks in *El Gringo* that he wrote influential Senator Orville H. Platt of Connecticut, Republican chairman of the Committee on Territories, stating that the Republican candidate for delegate would have been elected last November had he not been handicapped by the minority report, which incorporated an extract from *El Gringo* "stating the most scandalous, vilifying, abusive and untrue things with reference to the people of this Territory."[18] The burly leader wrote another letter to Elkins telling how Joseph shrewdly included the Republican minority report in a pamphlet, printed in both Spanish and English, which went to "every man and woman in the Territory." Catron felt that "this was the only thing on earth" that elected Joseph.[19]

Bradford Prince also felt it necessary to dispel the bad impression given in the Struble report. In an open letter to the *New York Tribune*, he contended that the population of the territory was 180,000 and not 150,000 as stated by the House committee. His figure gave New Mexico a larger population than that of any other state upon admission. Prince also claimed that illiteracy, although existing among the older elements of the native population, was rapidly being reduced. Furthermore, the Spanish-speaking population was a conservative one and very valuable because of its settled character.[20] Prince was supported in this position by territorial papers such as the *Silver City Enterprise*, which, with far less restraint, denounced the report and took Delegate Joseph to task for remaining silent until after numerous meetings had been held throughout the territory and ringing resolutions passed urging him "to denounce the vile slanders and brand the authors as liars." When Joseph finally did lodge a protest, however, the paper was willing to compliment him.[21]

The strong defense of the territory was helpful, but its effect was unfortunately countermanded by a "Protest of Citizens of New Mexico Against the Admission of that Territory into the Union of States." The petition was addressed to both houses of Congress and signed by a number of prominent commercial people, of whom approximately half were Jewish businessmen[22] from Albuquerque. Two especially prominent signers were Joshua Reynolds, a well-known banker and boyhood friend of William

McKinley, and W. S. Burke, a noted editor. The influential president pro tempore of the Senate, John J. Ingalls of Kansas, presented the petition from New Mexico in January, 1889.[23]

The protest against statehood produced counterpetitions which were sent to the territorial legislature and to Congress. One petition, signed by 178 citizens attending a meeting in Albuquerque, declared that the protest petition did not represent the sentiments of one per cent of the residents of that city.[24]

Nevertheless, the idea that New Mexicans were indifferent to statehood prevailed in Congress. Even before the antistatehood petition had been sent to Washington, Springer had written Governor Ross that the greatest obstacle in New Mexico's path was the distinct impression that the people did not desire the change.[25] When a copy of the protest petition lay on the desk of every member of Congress, this impression was only reinforced. Delegate Joseph was well aware of the danger if this belief persisted, but he also was worried by New Mexico's political support, which he felt was mainly from Democrats, while Republicans opposed statehood for the territory. He urged staunchly Republican Prince to come to his aid, for unless a delegation of prominent Republicans from New Mexico came to Washington to lobby for passage of the statehood bill, it would be defeated when it came to a vote in the House.[26]

Joseph's pessimistic view proved to be wrong. In an action which surprised many, the House in late January, 1889, acted favorably on the Springer bill. At least one territorial newspaper was encouraged and optimistic. "When the bill came up for passage [in the House], it was found that New Mexico had plenty of defenders, and so it will be in the senate."[27] Perhaps this cocky attitude was inspired by more spirited behavior on the part of the territory's citizens. The legislative assembly passed a memorial requesting statehood several days prior to House action, and a statehood convention was held in Santa Fe the same month.[28]

Despite the high hopes of New Mexicans, given added impetus by news that the Colorado legislature was considering a statehood memorial in her behalf,[29] only deep disappointment resulted. The Republican Senate dropped New Mexico from the omnibus bill. The only glimmer of hope for the territory now was in the conference procedure. On February 14, the House was to consider the conference reports of the House and the Senate and reconcile the differences in the two versions. There were three major points of disagreement. First, the House declared for New Mexico, while the Senate opposed inclusion of that territory in the bill. Second, the House wanted to submit the question of Dakota's division to her voters, while the Senate opposed such an action. And, thirdly, the Senate, in order to prevent delay, favored a proclamation by the President to bring in these territories.[30]

The deadlock was finally broken by the vote on an amendment offered by New York Congressman Samuel Cox, an old foe of statehood, who proposed that the House recede from its original position of favoring New Mexico. The amendment also called for the admission of South Dakota by presidential proclamation without a new vote on the question of division. North Dakota, Washington, and Montana were likewise to be admitted by presidential proclamation. Just prior to a decision on this question, another congressman proposed that a separate vote be taken on the provision to exclude New Mexico from the bill. The Speaker having ruled in favor of this motion, a roll call vote was taken on New Mexico. The result was 134 votes in favor of New Mexico's omission, 105 against, with 84 abstentions. A proposal that the vote be laid on the table for reconsideration was carried with 136 yeas, 109 nays, and 77 abstentions.

During the debate that preceded these votes, Congressman Springer, whom one territorial paper called New Mexico's "true friend,"[31] made a last appeal. He cited New Mexico's unsuccessful attempt to gain admittance into the Union in 1850, and the futile effort during the 43rd Congress when Colorado's bid for statehood was accepted and New Mexico's rejected by only a seven vote difference. He made the telling point that New Mexico received strong Republican support in the latter effort and that many prominent Republicans still serving in Congress had voted for her. He concluded by asking, why, if the Republican party felt that New Mexico was entitled to statehood fourteen years ago, would it not feel so now, especially in light of such "wonderful" developments in the territory as the 1,200 miles of railroad track that had been laid, the common school system that had been established, or the growth which gave the territory a greater population than either Montana or Washington.

Despite Springer's bid for Republican support, he had to concede that of all the territories under consideration New Mexico was the only one likely to be Democratic. Congressman Cox recognized this, too, and was quick to reassure his fellow Democrats that his amendment was not destructive to the party's hopes. He pointed out that the last two territorial legislatures were heavily Republican, and that in the current assembly there was a two-thirds Republican majority in each branch. He also claimed that Joseph's victories in 1884 and 1886 were caused by Republican division, and in 1888 his success was simply due to his support of statehood. But this reasoning did not convince Congressman Francis B. Spinola of New York who saw in New Mexico's rejection Republican partisanship. Feeling strongly that New Mexico should be admitted immediately,

Spinola claimed that the Grand Old Party opposed anything that would have "the least shadow of a tendency towards strengthening the Democratic party in this country."

Joseph, too, spoke forcefully on this matter, stating he would rather be a citizen of a Republican state than a Democratic territory. He pointed out that New Mexico was the oldest territory in the Union and that this was the fourth time in which she had come "knocking on the door of Congress" to ask for admission as a state. He brought up the popular argument that the United States Congress was obligated at its discretion under the Treaty of Guadalupe Hidalgo to admit New Mexico at an early date. He also presented the memorial adopted by the territorial assembly and seconded by the Colorado state legislature.

In discussing the economic situation in New Mexico, Joseph probably reflected his own interests as a member of the Santa Fe Ring. He pointed out that the titles of more than 10,000,000 acres of the "best land in the world" were unsettled and doubtful, having been Spanish and Mexican grants. The people of New Mexico had tried for more than forty years to provide a remedy for these defective titles, but had finally come to the conclusion that the only solution lay in statehood.

During Joseph's presentation, criticism came from a most unexpected quarter. Republican Congressman George G. Symes of Colorado, echoing the charges of the Struble report, took Joseph and Governor Ross to task for not pressing New Mexico's cause with the influential Committee on the Territories during the Forty-ninth Congress. He then compared the efforts of the other territories included in the omnibus bill, claiming that the people in each of them held constitutional conventions years ago and adopted constitutions. He said that he would not jeopardize their chances by insisting against the wishes of the Senate that New Mexico remain in the bill.

Throughout the debate the major reason given for dropping New Mexico from the omnibus bill was that if the House did not recede from its position, but continued to insist on the inclusion of New Mexico during its conference with the Senate, it might impair the chances of the other territories for admittance. Several congressmen contended that they were in favor of statehood for New Mexico but not at the expense of denying it to the Dakotas, Montana, or Washington. Nevertheless, two congressmen were not convinced by these protestations of innocence. Representative Spinola claimed that it was poor display of statesmanship to oppose the admission of a territory on account of the religious opinions of a large minority of its inhabitants. Congressman William McAdoo, Democrat of New Jersey, implied that it was the Spanish background of the inhabitants that was keeping the area under territorial status. He attacked the

"narrow minded misrepresentation" of the people of the territory, asserting that the "Spanish Americans of New Mexico are Americans by birth,
sympathy, and education," and had given testimony of this on the field
of battle, furnishing more troops to the Union army during the Civil War
than some of the new states.[32]

Still the most important but least stated reason for New Mexico's omission from the Springer omnibus bill was simply politics. The Democratic
party had held out for New Mexico as its lone hope for partisan advantage.
When it realized that the jig was up, it surrendered, and the four northwestern territories, minus luckless New Mexico, were given their enabling
acts with a stroke of Cleveland's pen on February 22, 1889.[33]

Joseph belatedly introduced a separate bill for statehood the following
day, and presented another bill for separate admission on February 26.
But neither measure had any hope of success, and Congress adjourned on
March 2 without taking action.

Although the Springer bill failed to secure statehood for New Mexico,
it did clarify the various shades of opinion on the subject existing in the
territory. The local press, led by the New Mexican, was predominantly
favorable to the statehood movement. One paper compared territorial
status to the carpetbag rule of the South during Reconstruction days.[34]
There was, however, some opposition, the two strongest objections being
the increased taxation which supposedly would accompany increased expenses brought about by statehood, and fear that native people would
control the new state.[35] Proof that this fear of increased taxation did exist
is found in the Las Vegas Stock-Grower, where it was claimed that cattlemen did not wish to gratify the ambitions of politicians and "grabbers"
by having New Mexico become a state, for to the taxpayer statehood only
meant doubling of the tax assessment.[36]

There were also those who wanted statehood but distrusted the second
section of the Springer bill. Among these was the calculating Catron, who
did not like the provision to allow the present governor, United States
marshal, and federal attorney—all Democrats—to redistrict the territory
for the election of delegates to the constitutional convention. The New
Mexico attorney suggested another plan supported by the heavily Republican territorial assembly whereby there would be three members of the
convention for every one in the lower house, as presently constituted, plus
three from the territory at large.[37]

It was suggested at least twice in Washington during the drive for admission that New Mexico was not interested in statehood because her
people had made no recent effort to draft a constitution to present Congress for inspection. To supporters of the Springer bill in New Mexico,
this fact had not gone unnoticed. Six days after Cleveland authorized

statehood for the Dakotas, Montana, and Washington, Colonel George Pritchard, a leading Republican from San Miguel County, introduced a bill in the territorial council to authorize a constitutional convention to meet in September. The 73 delegates to be elected would be apportioned among the counties in the territory.[38]

No sooner had the bill been introduced than it became the center of a new, more lively controversy. Democratic leaders attacked the bill's apportionment provision, which they felt gave too much representation to Republican counties. The apportionment of delegates was said by one Democratic newspaper, the *Albuquerque Morning Democrat*, to give the Republicans control of the convention, and that would be an iniquitous arrangement considering that the last three elections had shown New Mexico to be Democratic by a majority of from 1,500 to 2,000.[39] Although Ross allowed the bill to reach the statute books without his signature, other Democratic leaders remained adamant and a deadlock soon developed.

The two parties tried to reach some agreement whereby the relative strength of their forces would be more equally balanced. Each appointed members of a committee which met on June 12 to discuss the problem. Prince, Pritchard, and Mariano S. Otero, a former delegate to Congress, represented the Republicans, while the Democrats selected Gildersleeve, F. A. Manzanares, another ex-delegate, and W. B. Childers, an Albuquerque attorney, to represent them. According to Prince, it was conceded at the meeting that Republicans were more than sufficiently represented. The Republicans showed some willingness to accept a majority of seven, while the Democrats offered to concede three. Republican conferees then objected that three was too small a majority and claimed that absences due to sickness would easily destroy this slender advantage. The conference was on the verge of agreeing that five was a fair figure when one of the Democrats arose and exclaimed "our friends in Congress will never be satisfied unless we have half the convention." This torpedoed any chance for agreement.[40]

This account differs from one published in the partisan *Albuquerque Morning Democrat*. According to the newspaper version, the Democrats had offered to allow the Republicans 37 delegates in the convention to their 36, warning that rejection of this proposal would doom prospects for statehood. When the Republicans refused to agree, the Democratic conferees, acting under the instructions of Childers, the chairman of the central committee, declined to take part in any of the convention proceedings.[41]

Each party wanted to blame the other for failure to agree upon fair apportionment. At a meeting of the Democratic Territorial Central Committee held at Santa Fe on June 22, 1889, a vain effort was made to secure the co-operation of the Republican central committee. A perusal of the proposition made by the Democrats would leave little doubt in the mind of the reader as to who was felt to be responsible for the impasse. The report concentrated on the "inequalities of representation" that permeated the system of apportionment for delegates to the convention, claiming that the method was unrealistic to such a degree that several of the most rapidly growing and developing counties were practically disfranchised by a denial of nearly one half the number of delegates to which they were "fairly" entitled, and at the same time other counties were given more than they were entitled to—"the discrimination thus cutting both ways and made doubly odious."

The report admitted that the first requisite in framing a constitution is to make a wise and proper instrument, but that "a very serious part in this connection is that this convention will have the apportioning of the territory for the election of a State Legislature, which legislature will have the selection of two United States senators from the new state." Thus, national political implications were brought to light. Because of the close balance of parties in the Senate, the two senators from New Mexico might "turn the scale of supremacy in that body." Therefore, it must be insured that their selection be "as fair and free as possible from all factitious influence."[42]

Republicans also strove to appear before the public as the injured party, and during the county conventions to nominate candidates to the constitutional convention, the territorial committee expressed regret over the failure to achieve reconciliation between the two parties. Also, as late as June 24, William W. Griffin, chairman of the committee, made a new effort to bring about an agreement. He was supported by the New Mexican which vigorously advocated some sort of adjustment. But no accord was reached.

In compliance with the proposal by the legislative assembly to hold the election for delegates to the convention on the "first Tuesday following the first Monday in August, 1889," Bradford Prince, whom Harrison had recently appointed to succeed Ross as territorial governor,[43] proclaimed on June 24 that the election would be held on August 6.[44] As the controversial election approached, the Rio Grande Republican of Las Cruces tried hard to insert a note of nonpartisanship into the proceedings. It cautioned its readers that this was not "a political contest—not a race for office between democrats and republicans but it is a common cause demanding the united action of all true patriots regardless of their political affiliations."[45] But a growing hostility among Democrats toward this "Republican affair" was evident, particularly in Lincoln County, where the county commissioners refused to perform their duties in compliance with the terms of the act. Governor Prince quickly responded to this defiance and, in a proclamation issued August 3, recommended that the legal voters in each precinct of the county assemble at 9 o'clock on August 6, appoint their election judge, apply to the probate clerk for poll books and ballot boxes, and conduct "said election as nearly as practicable in conformity with the forms of law."[46]

Notwithstanding the forceful role played by the territorial administration, the vote cast for delegates in Lincoln County was noticeably small. The *Las Vegas Daily Optic*, in commenting on the small vote cast in that city, stated that "everything passed off quietly, no one seeming to pay much attention to the matter." The vote was so inconsequential that the *Optic* thought it impossible to prognosticate just how the question of a constitution for the territory would be decided, but common talk seemed to indicate it would not be carried if left to the vote of the people.[47] The *Albuquerque Morning Democrat*, taking a cheerful attitude, stated that the election clearly indicated that the people were opposed to statehood "as promulgated by political bosses such as Perea, Catron, Chaves, Pritchard, etc."[48]

Although voter participation in the election was not impressive, some very prominent and powerful figures in the territory were elected to the convention, which assembled in Santa Fe on September 3. Bernalillo County was represented by Otero, who was once described as the "invincible caudillo of the Republicans,"[49] and by Pedro Perea, a Ring member of considerable influence. A garrulous Irishman by the name of Bernard S. Rodey and Judge L. S. Trimble, the only Democrat to attend the convention, also were included in the large Bernalillo delegation. Santa Fe County had among its representatives such figures as Catron; Major Jose D. Sena, the Civil War hero; and attorney Frank W. Clancy. San Miguel sent Pritchard, Frank Springer, and eight other delegates. J. Francisco Chaves of Valencia was elected to preside over the convention.[50] Chaves' Civil War experiences, his campaigns against the Navajo, and his political leadership made him a popular choice, but his known partisanship did not detract from the Republican stamp so deeply imprinted upon the gathering.

In a last bid for Democratic co-operation, Judge Trimble, the temporary president, made an opening address in which he declared every man at the convention to be "sincerely desirous to make a Constitution free from party bias . . . ." Chaves followed, stating that when Congress had before it the constitution the convention was about to write, New Mexico's future as a state would be secure—all would realize she was capable of self-government. The work of the convention was divided among twelve committees to handle such topics as the legislative and executive departments, the judiciary, a bill of rights, and election procedures.[51] Upon the motion of Catron, a rules committee was formed to set up regulations and the order of business for the convention. Catron, Rodey, Pritchard, Albert J. Fountain, and William G. Ritch served as members. Colonel Fountain's selection was regarded as further evidence of Republican partisanship, for as Speaker of the House during Ross's governorship, Fountain, along with Chaves, the president of the Council, ran roughshod over the governor's vetoes and passed a Republican program.[52]

Once the rules of order were established, the convention had to come to grips with one of the most controversial and deep-rooted problems in the territory: the question of education. The Roman Catholic Church had enjoyed a position of primacy in that field for almost three centuries and looked with suspicion toward any incursions in this sphere. About two months prior to the convention, a secret circular was mailed to Catholics throughout the territory. It bore no signature and was marked "confidential," but was supposed to have come from high authorities in the Church. It warned that it was the "declared intention of the enemies of our religion to send delegates to that convention, who will so form the organic law as to force you to deny your children all kinds of education excepting that of the world." Catholics would be obliged to pay taxes to sustain public schools, the circular warned, and followed up the warning with an admonition that the faithful should not permit their children to be educated in such places.[53] Of a more official nature was the letter of the Most Reverend J. B. Salpointe, Archbishop of Santa Fe. This letter, appearing in the territorial press while the convention was in session, demanded a system of elementary schools which would give citizens of the territory, of every shade of belief, equal facility to educate their children "in a manner they believe will conduce to bring about their happiness."[54]

The message from the archbishop seemed to express the Church's desire for some sort of role in the educational life of the proposed state. Whether it was a plea for a measure of church control in educational affairs or a hint for state support of church schools was not made clear; but, regardless of its intention it was totally ignored. Instead a clause was enacted which would establish a public school system "under the absolute control of the state, and free from sectarian or church control; and no other or different schools shall ever receive any aid or support from public funds."[55] The impact of this strong rejection of the archbishop's point of view could not escape the attention of the territorial press. The Las Vegas Daily Optic stated that the Church leader would by no means consider himself a defeated man, for his "strongest argument is yet in reserve" and he would use it "for all its worth" when the constitution was submitted to the people for ratification. The paper wondered whether Catholic voters would follow the "dictation" of the Church or fall in line with their "old political leaders, Otero, the Pereas, and others of that class, who have agreed to stand by the constitution."[56]

Considering the strong hold the Church had on its believers, it is interesting to consider why such an emphatic position was taken by the convention delegates. Undoubtedly there was strong pressure from the Anglo population, imbued as it was with the tradition of separation of church and state. This was clearly reflected in a letter to Prince in which the writer admitted that the nonsectarian school issue was the most important one, and added the suggestion that an incentive for learning be provided by requiring that qualified voters be able to write their names legibly in the register books and be able to read any four lines in the English version of the state constitution.[57]

Although an efficient secular school system was both needed and wanted, the delegates realized the dangers involved in attempting to establish one. Republicans were particularly aware that the school issue would have political repercussions, and that only Republicans could be hurt politically because they had sole charge of the convention. One observant party member wrote Prince that he could name a hundred people who would stick to the Church and the expression of their families on the school question. He was sure that this affair, in which the Democrats had outgeneraled them, would ruin the Republican party in the territory and prevent New Mexico from becoming a state for at least ten years.[58]

Prince was most receptive to this kind of political argument for he had worked hard to win *Hispano* support for the Republican party. Alarmed because Harrison had not appointed any natives to office in the territory, he wrote the President a letter on July 13, 1889, urging the appointment of Spanish-speaking citizens. They "constitute more than half" the population, and their earlier "lack of acquaintance with the American system of government . . . has long ceased."[59]

If the Republicans sensed the reaction a strong secular school provision might have, and they do seem to have been aware of it, why did they incorporate such an adamant secular school clause into the constitution? An article appearing in the *New York Tribune* a month or so after the convention adjourned seemed to hint strongly that the convention delegates were writing a constitution as much for the eyes of the rest of the nation as for the people of their territory. They were very conscious of the many charges by outsiders that the new state government would be unduly influenced by the priesthood. Thus, the new constitution's school clause was so strongly secular that it even forbade appropriations to private or sectarian institutions.[60] It is interesting to observe that many of the territory's prominent Spanish-speaking Catholics were present at this convention, among them Otero, Chaves, Sena, and Perea. But for Perea, who assented during the convention[61] but later worked against the constitution, these men all enthusiastically supported the education provision. The provision on nonsectarian schools was not alone in creating controversy. A clause stating that the legislature would provide school textbooks at public expense was felt to give the legislature unnecessary control.[62]

The new constitution, a Republican product, was not an advanced document such as the constitution framed in 1872, which included some fairly progressive features. It did reflect a growing national concern about the growth of monopolies, outlawing all combinations which could control prices,[63] but the article pertaining to corporations was not as tough or specific as the antirailroad provisions of the 1872 document. It contained an "irrevocable" article which proclaimed complete religious freedom,[64] no doubt pleasing native *Hispanos*, and decreed that all legal debts of the territory be assumed by the state, no doubt pleasing holders of militia warrants. Several references to religious freedom or religious matters are sprinkled throughout, including a provision reminiscent of the 1850 constitution which prevented the legislature from passing any special or local law affecting the granting of divorce. Obviously, the reaction of the Roman Catholic Church to the controversial educational provisions was being anticipated.

The traditional three branches of government, the bicameral system, and a reasonable amending article, which stipulated that a two-thirds majority of the territorial legislators in each house must propose any constitutional change, were incorporated in the document. A special vote on the constitution on the day of the general election in November, 1890, was provided; although, anticipating an enabling act in recognition of their efforts, the constitution-makers optimistically added that an election could be held as early as ninety days after the passage of a statehood bill.

What angered Democratic newspapers almost as much as the partisan cast of the constitutional convention was a rumor, apparently true, that the constitution would not be submitted to the voters of the territory before it was sent to Congress.[65] The *Albuquerque Morning Democrat* claimed that if this were done, petitions would be sent to Congress which would bury the constitution "too deep for the trump[et] of resurrection ever to revive it."[66] The more reasonable *Optic* maintained that it really made no difference who saw it first as both Congress' and the people's approval were needed.[67] The *Silver City Enterprise*, on the other hand, defended any such action, insisting there were some very good reasons for such a move.[68]

Resistance to the new statehood movement was national as well as local, as Colonel Rynerson, visiting Washington in 1890 with Catron, observed. Alarmed by the extent of the opposition, Rynerson wrote the editor of the *New Mexican* on February 10, strongly urging that a delegation of leading citizens be sent to the national capital as a deterrent to the forces opposing the territory's statehood. This suggestion was gladly accepted by Frost, and then taken up by the Bureau of Immigration, an organization he controlled. The bureau formally requested Governor Prince to appoint a delegation, and eventually a group of twenty-nine New Mexicans reached Washington. The official purpose of the delegation was to lobby for statehood, although most members of the group, and especially Prince, also desired to settle the knotty question of Spanish and Mexican land grants.[69]

The delegation was aided in its mission by the Atchison, Topeka and Santa Fe Railroad which offered half-fare rates on its line to all citizens going to Washington. The *New Mexican* enthusiastically interpreted this gesture as a sincere contribution toward the achievement of statehood. It stated that New Mexico's prosperity and increase in wealth and population, "which are as sure to follow statehood as the day succeeds the night, will increase the business and prosperity of the Santa Fe road, hence the latter extends this help."[70] Although it was probably true that the railroad's business would have increased with statehood, the Santa Fe was not as much concerned with admission as it was with the attempt of the delegation to settle land grant questions. The completely neutral attitude of Judge Henry Waldo, the solicitor of the Santa Fe and a member of the delegation, gives credence to this assertion.[71]

Important as the delegation was in showing strength and unity among New Mexicans, its results would amount to little if Delegate Joseph did not give it his full support. Although no one doubted Joseph's desire for statehood, there was speculation as to whether he would support the Republican constitution. The *New Mexican* claimed he would, and this paper's positive assurances provoked one Democratic organ to state that it was difficult for "a New Mexico republican editor to tell the truth, the whole truth and nothing but the truth." It charged that Joseph's position was being misrepresented as favoring the movement of the "republican bosses" for statehood, when actually the delegate was convinced that statehood could be secured only by the united efforts of all the people in the territory.[72] That this appraisal of Joseph's position was the correct one was soon borne out by the delegate's action in Washington. Even the *New Mexican* was forced to report reluctantly that Joseph was opposed to the constitution, but added happily that the House Committee on the Territories had decided that if New Mexico was to be admitted at all during the present session it would be under the recently written constitution.[73] This report was confirmed several days later in a resolution adopted by the House committee, which postponed consideration of a statehood bill introduced earlier by Joseph and provided that a subcommittee appointed by the chairman should consider reporting an enabling act to admit New Mexico to statehood under the constitution prepared in Santa Fe.[74]

Joseph expressed his views on this proposal the following day in Congress. He claimed that to admit New Mexico under the new constitution would offend all the Democratic voters and three-fourths of the Republicans. The apportionment of delegates to the convention was characterized as a piece of "outrageous partisanship," and this was backed by a letter from former Governor Ross to Congressman Charles H. Mansur of Missouri in which a county-by-county survey of the iniquitous arrangement was cited. Joseph then charged that the framers of the constitution knew well that it would never receive the approbation of the people and therefore, he erroneously asserted, made no provision in it for submission to the people. He pointed out that, of 32,000 voters in New Mexico, only 7,000 participated in the election of convention delegates. Joseph argued strongly that an enabling act should be passed which provided for the framing of a constitution nearer to the reality of the people's wishes.[75]

Joseph's uncompromising position so alarmed the Republicans of the territory that they arranged a meeting at the National Hotel in Washington between Democratic leaders and the delegation headed by Governor Prince. Prior to this gathering, Joseph had told Republicans that he had received a number of letters from leading Democrats who were opposed to admission at present, and he therefore felt guided by their views. Despite the willingness of Republicans to make concessions on apportionment, Joseph, backed by Gildersleeve, remained adamant during the Washington meeting. Both men contended that Democratic leaders in Washington and New Mexico could not possibly favor admission under the present circumstances.

The intransigent stand of Joseph and Gildersleeve can only be explained in terms of political partisanship. Economically, both had a great deal to gain by immediate statehood, as their landholdings and Ring affiliation would testify. A letter from Prince to Gildersleeve written before the constitutional convention reveals much regarding the personal stake of each man. Prince was pleading for Democratic co-operation in the election of convention delegates:

Can't you get back in town to attend to this election—Your people are acting as badly as possible, and unless you come and put some sense into them, we will be criticized all over the country, Statehood may be off for 2 years at best, every chance for a Land Grant bill will be destroyed, and values of real estate will be reduced to nothing. . . . Do take the train and come back. It is worth more to you than whatever you are doing.[76]

On the surface it would seem that Joseph, as a native leader[77] and a Catholic, might conceivably have disliked the constitution because of the secular school provisions, but Joseph's life gives little evidence that this was true. He was seldom seen in church except for Christmas Midnight Mass, and on rare occasions when he paid his respects to certain friends or relatives being married or buried. Moreover, he was a Mason in good standing[78] and had separated from his first wife[79] and later remarried.

Notwithstanding the favor shown the new constitution by the committee, Democratic opposition was having its effect. Democrats found their most effective propaganda weapon to be the argument that the proposed document lacked popular support. The fact that the constitution of Wyoming had been adopted by a popular vote and that the committee report approved this action did not escape the attention of New Mexico's delegation in Washington. Former Governor Axtell, a member of the group, stated later in an address that the delegates had been told in so many words to submit the constitution to the people for their ratification, after which the territory would be admitted if the people gave their approval. Consequently, on June 15, 1890, Chaves, acting in pursuance of the authority invested in him as president of the convention, called for a second meeting to be held in Santa Fe on August 18 for all members of the constitutional convention.[80]

At this meeting, attended by less than half the delegates elected to the first session of the convention, several minor amendments were added to the new instrument and October was chosen as the new date for a referendum. Only one amendment seemed to take cognizance of the politically dangerous school issue. Frank Springer of San Miguel County successfully moved[81] that the fifth section of the education article be amended to make only a vague and general reference about raising the taxes necessary to insure an adequate school system.[82] The original provision had called for school taxation on the lowest local level. Presumably the purpose of this change was to assure the Church that revenue sources for education below the county level would not be entirely absorbed by the public school system.

Another amendment made at the August convention altered the apportionment article so that the new counties of Eddy and Chaves, carved out of Lincoln County, would be represented in the legislature. Also, laws providing for punishment of libel were liberalized. An amendment introduced by Springer authorized the chair to have a public printer make 30,000 copies of the constitution and an equal number of a pamphlet containing addresses of a group called the Committee of Fifteen, established to promote the constitution. Ten thousand copies would be in English and 20,000 in Spanish.

A resolution for the passage of a bill establishing a land court, which was then pending in Congress, received unanimous approval. It was believed that a land court would soon settle the continual conflict over land titles, which was said to have delayed the material progress of the territory.[83] The Republican-dominated convention could count on Democratic support for this resolution, especially from Joseph, who had labored many years for a bill to deal with land grants.[84]

Since it was known that the campaign for popular approval of the constitution would be bitter, a suggestion was made from the floor of the convention that the two party central committees decide together on a unified policy regarding the constitution. Republicans rejected the idea immediately. Chaves said it was useless "to try to teach the democrats any sense." He then ruled the well-intentioned delegate who had made the suggestion out of order.[85] Consequently, Democrat Judge Trimble was to provide the lone example of nonpartisanship, as leading Democrats such as attorney Jacob H. Crist, and Harvey Fergusson and Neill B. Field of Albuquerque, joined Ross, Joseph, Childers, and Gildersleeve in opposing the constitution.

Even while the August amending convention was still in session, the constitution was being vigorously defended before the public by its supporters. Otero and Catron, making public addresses on August 19, urged New Mexicans to vote as freeborn American citizens anxious to obtain admission to the Union. In Catron's words, "Democrats and Republicans Alike . . . [Should] Stand Up For Progress And The Constitution."[86] Friendly newspapers were already busy editorializing on behalf of the constitution. The *Silver City Enterprise* emphasized the fact that New Mexico's laws could be amended, just as the national constitution was amended with the Bill of Rights almost immediately after its adoption.[87] The *Denver Republican* warned the Democrats of New Mexico that they would do the territory a great injury if they stood in the way of this attempt to establish a state government.[88] But Democrats would not be silent, and they unrelentingly attacked alleged iniquities in the constitution. Childers exposed economic unfairness and built-in corruption in his charge that the document's tax provision enabled the land grant holders to escape taxation almost completely.[89] Further charges were made by the *Socorro Industrial Advertiser* which said that through unscrupulous manipulation, assessments on large land grants would be kept down to one-tenth of their value, and furthermore, taxes would be kept small by a constitutional limit of one per cent of taxable property. There was, however, no limit to taxation of "particular articles" and occupations. The paper felt that the constitution shifted the burden of taxation from the landowner to those far less able to bear it, the poor. Catron specifically was accused of abusing his privileges as a landowner. He had favored a clause in the constitution empowering the legislature to levy a tax upon unpatented mines. His reason for this was a shrewd one: in accordance with Spanish mining law, minerals were not reserved on land grants. Therefore, the land was open to outside exploitation. Several mining towns had been established on grants in Santa Fe County held by Catron. As these mines could not be patented, the Santa Fe lawyer realized that if the gross output of the mines was taxed, the miners would be ruined, clearing his land of unwelcome visitors.[90]

Strongly advocating acceptance of the constitution were people who allegedly held hundreds of thousands of dollars worth of militia warrants. Otero and Catron were among the many warrant holders who hoped that the first state legislature would recognize their claims and pay large sums of money for the warrants from state funds.[91] The *Optic*, a paper usually leaning to the Republican side, felt that if the new state legislature paid the warrants, it would merely be the beginning of corrupt control by selfish interests in New Mexico, and it accused the Santa Fe Ring of fraudulently buying the warrants for speculative purposes.[92]

These charges brought into question the economic motives of the convention delegates and did not go unnoticed. Newspapers sympathetic to the Republican cause usually defended them without hesitation. Ridicule was frequently employed by these newspapers with great effectiveness. The *Albuquerque Morning Democrat* reported that in a speech before a large concourse of Democrats at Springer, the remarks of Neill Field and Fergusson were met with a deafening applause.[93] The Springer paper made a point of mentioning soon after that there were only forty present and there was no "deafening applause" except when the chairman and secretary of the meeting were introduced.[94] Ross, back to his old trade of newspaper work, too, was belittled on the basis of an editorial in the *Deming Headlight*, in which he warned cattlemen that a vote for the constitution was a vote for a tax levy on every horse, steer, cow, and calf to make up the deficit of the general tax provided for the support of government, for the great landowners who made the constitution limited the general tax to a sum below the needs of the state government in order to shield their own property from its "fair share of public and necessary taxation." This statement induced the *Colfax County Stockman* to picture Ross as perceiving things through the "optic of a pig" instead of his own mind, and accused him of being willing to tax cattlemen, mining men, and sheepmen if it were for the support of a Democratic state government.[95] Another paper also considered Ross a prime target and said the "old chump verily believes he is a 'bigger man' than George Washington."[96]

The public education issue was used constantly and effectively by the Democrats. The Republicans themselves could not present a completely united front in favor of their public school provision, for there were dissenters in the party on this matter, notably Perea.[97] The question of secular education had class, racial, and linguistic implications as well as religious ones, involving everyone in the territory in one way or another. Church opposition seemed to grow as election day neared. On election eve, it was reported in the New Mexican that ". . . At several points throughout the territory strong sermons were preached advising the people to vote against the constitution and against statehood."[98]

Catron, a most ingenious fighter for statehood, was deeply concerned over this controversy. Knowing that critical Eastern senators were watching New Mexico's actions on the public school issue with great interest, he was determined not to let a weak school clause ruin national support for the territory's admission to statehood. He wrote sympathetic Senator Stewart of Nevada that "many of the priests of the Catholic Church have been delivering sermons against" the constitution.[99] In order to strengthen New Mexico's position, he requested that Stewart introduce a bill that would require jurors in the territories to read or write. However, when it appeared that the presentation of this bill would cause great commotion, Catron became alarmed and asked the senator not to reveal his part in the affair.[100]

There was a great amount of political acrimony in the campaign, and often the school issue overlapped with others. The Democrats, the New Mexican insisted, had been trying, through their "boodle sheets," to turn the Hispanos of the territory against the new instrument, despite the fact that at the constitutional convention thirty or more natives "of Spanish blood and Roman Catholics in religion" voted for the school provision.[101] Employing every political device in order to stop the ratification of the constitution, the Democrats made their biggest effort at Silver City where they formally attacked the new Republican instrument in convention. Their four main objections were set forth as follows: the appellate judges were to be appointed; the governor was to be suspended during impeachment; the state tax was to be limited to only one per cent; and the apportionment was unjust. The attack on the governor's suspension no doubt reflected the influence of former Governor Ross, whose newspaper objected to the practice. Ross's administration had been one of continual conflict with the Republican-controlled legislative branch, and he favored a strong executive with broad appointive powers.[102]

Another issue, important, yet below the surface, was the fear many Anglos had of "Mexican" domination, which they thought might come with statehood. Many Anglos either completely opposed the constitution with this in mind or wanted to insert restrictions to curb native power.[103]

The constitution simply did not have enough support among New Mexico's citizens because of the political, religious, and cultural issues at stake. It was decisively rejected on October 7 by a vote of 16,180 against it and 7,493 approving. It is difficult to determine which factor was most important in the constitution's defeat. Governor Prince denied that the vote indicated any "disinclination on the part of the people to assume the condition of statehood," and blamed the rejection on the apportionment controversy and the subsequent refusal of the Democratic party to participate in the election of convention delegates.[104] But the issue of nonsectarian schools was an equally significant one and closely intertwined with politics as noted by the *Silver City Enterprise*. The paper accused Democrats of such distortion that many citizens believed that "the adoption of one constitution would destroy all the Catholic schools in the territory, and that eventually even their church property would be confiscated, their priests driven from the country and their children converted to the protestant faith."[105] Charges that the 1889 constitution was a "land grabbers'" constitution, which would also enrich unprincipled holders of militia warrants, added to the woes of the statehood advocates.

The effect of this setback on the statehood aspirations of New Mexico was unquestionably important, especially in view of the fact that Congress was under Republican control and could not be expected to overlook the defeat of the local party organization. No doubt the belief among a number of congressmen that New Mexicans were not eager for statehood was reinforced by this action. And the taking of one stand by Joseph and the Democrats while the Republicans took another could only add to the misgivings and confusion.

Despite the smashing defeat the constitution suffered at the polls, a number of prominent Republican leaders continued to defend it for years. A decade after the constitution was rejected, a territorial governor called it "the peer of any similar document in the Union" and "a monument to the wisdom and statesmanship of its framers."[106]

ELEVEN

Free Silver & Populism

T HE DECADE OF THE NINETIES was a difficult one for the western part of the nation, marked by a serious farm depression and by a money crisis. New Mexico, a silver-producing territory, was inevitably drawn into the conflicts of the Populist era, with its emphasis on reform and unceasing demands for "free and unlimited coinage of silver and gold at . . . [a] ratio of 16 to 1." Although New Mexico's silver mining was not as vital to her economy as Colorado's, a state in which the emotional pull of the clarion call for free silver was very strong, nevertheless the production of silver in the territory was of increasing importance and had surpassed the output of gold. A few years earlier the amount of gold mined in New Mexico had far exceeded the amount of silver. From 1846 to 1880, $10,350,000 in gold was mined and only $3,622,000 in silver. But this trend was sharply reversed in the years from 1885 to 1889 when only $3,808,000 in gold was mined, and the production of silver ore increased to $19,113,000.[1] This new importance of silver made the free coinage of silver a major issue in New Mexico politics.

Two men equally dedicated to achieving statehood served as New Mexico's delegates to Congress during most of these troubled years. One was Antonio Joseph, completing his long ten years of service as delegate; the other was Tom Catron. The two were alike in having close connections with the Ring and similar economic motives. But politically Joseph was a strong Democrat, while Catron was the unquestioned leader of the territory's Republicans.

Joseph was first given the Democratic nomination in 1884 when the favorite, Frank Manzanares, an active wholesale merchant from Las Vegas, declined the offer.[2] Joseph was generally regarded as a weak candidate, but a feud within the opposition party split the Republican vote. Fights between Catron and Prince, the regular Republican nominee, were not unusual, and this time Catron left the convention with his followers and at a rump convention nominated Colonel Rynerson, thus dividing Republican support and guaranteeing victory to Joseph.[3] Two years later Joseph was re-elected over a very unpopular Republican choice, and in the 1888 election barely managed a victory over the potent Otero. In this last election, his use of the Struble Report probably gained him more votes than any personal attributes. By 1890, Joseph's advocacy of the statehood movement increased his growing popularity and he was accepted by a majority of New Mexicans for a fourth term.[4]

Joseph was small, quick, and energetic, with a knack for making speeches under any and all circumstances. He entered with facility into almost any group and won many friends with his agreeable manner.[5] Certainly his ingratiating ways had much to do with his success in the politics of New Mexico. As the *Optic* put it, Joseph was elected "not because he was a democrat but because of his personal popularity and his careful attention to the duties entrusted to his charge."[6] For years Joseph operated a sanitarium in Ojo Caliente near the famous hot springs, and was very active in the politics of the area. Accused of being a laggard in the statehood movement during his first two terms,[7] he worked diligently for admission thereafter, introducing two statehood bills in Congress immediately after the elimination of New Mexico from the Springer omnibus bill.[8]

Catron, on the other hand, was an imposing power in the territory. According to one contemporary "he was recognized as the leader of the republican party, framed its policies, wrote its platforms, controlled its conventions, represented the party in national conventions, and was a member of the republican national committee."[9] Among Republicans his unwavering efforts to achieve statehood were only matched by Prince, and it was commonly believed that when statehood came, Catron would be one of New Mexico's first senators.[10] Economically as well as politically powerful, Catron was, when he became the territory's delegate in 1895, the largest taxpayer in the territory.[11] Besides immense landholdings, he had investments in mining and cattle, and an interest in the territory's most prosperous bank, the First National of Santa Fe. Catron was also a successful and able lawyer who represented a number of illustrious clients. He was the local attorney for the Atchison, Topeka and Santa Fe, the Southern Pacific, the Denver and Rio Grande, and the El Paso and

Southwestern railroads. The Wells Fargo Express Company had given him a frank for legal services rendered them.[12]

Joseph, although he had joined his fellow Democrats in the territory in rejecting the constitution of 1889, nevertheless continued his efforts in Washington by introducing in December of 1889 another statehood bill. The measure was accompanied by another bill introduced several weeks later in the upper chamber by Senator Edward O. Wolcott, Republican from Colorado. The Joseph bill provided for a constitutional convention to be held on July 4—a clear rejection of the instrument drafted at Santa Fe earlier in the year. Although it was a Democratic measure, its future was clouded by a bill offered by Democrat Springer, who again tried to achieve admission for the territory with an omnibus package. The new measure called for the admission of Arizona, Idaho, New Mexico, and Wyoming. The inclusion of the two Southwestern territories was intended to balance the Republican territories of Idaho and Wyoming.

The *Denver Republican* was not so sure such a balance would result from the admission of these four states. ". . . The utmost that the Democrats can in reason claim is that they would have an even chance with the Republicans in carrying New Mexico if it were let into the union." The *New Mexican* agreed with this evaluation and said that the people of the territory wanted statehood despite uncertainty as to the dominant party. "Give us statehood and the Republicans of New Mexico will take their chances. Faint heart never won a fair lady."[13] The Santa Fe paper was particularly disturbed by Joseph's insistence in pushing his own enabling act. The only outcome from such action, it reasoned, would be to weaken Springer's bid and undermine the statehood movement. Joseph's action angered territorial Republicans because of the bill's provision for a new constitution, something not required in the Springer measure.[14]

Actually, neither bill had a chance for enactment, although the bills to admit Idaho and Wyoming moved smoothly through both houses. Joseph continued his efforts despite the failure of his bill. While the House was considering the admission of Idaho, he delivered a long and effective address on why New Mexico deserved equal consideration with the two northern territories.[15] Although he protested any intention of disparaging the merits of Wyoming, his speech drew a comparison between the two territories which placed New Mexico in a very favorable light.

Wyoming had 125,000 people; New Mexico had 195,000 to 225,000. Furthermore, the population of New Mexico had shown a "very steady increase" each year since 1880—the increase coming largely from the farm districts of Missouri, Indiana, and Illinois, bringing in "the very best class of settlers."[16] The assessed property of Wyoming in 1889 was $31,500,000, while for New Mexico the latest figures available recorded $48,690,723. Although each territory had about 1,500,000 head of cattle, Wyoming had only 1,250,000 head of sheep to New Mexico's 4,328,735.

Joseph gave the latest statistics on education in New Mexico, stressing the progress that had been made. On October 1, 1889, there were 342 public schools in operation, with an enrollment of 16,803 pupils. "In 143 of these schools nothing but English is taught; in 93 some instruction is included in Spanish, and in 106 the instruction is in the Spanish language, but even in these latter schools the pupils with very few exceptions understand English." More important, Joseph felt that statehood for New Mexico would do more than any one thing to significantly raise the level of education.

Some official figures on New Mexico's agriculture prepared by a statistician from the Department of Agriculture were then presented. More than $1,000,000 were presently going into new irrigation companies as an answer to the oft-repeated claim that the territory was too arid to be an important agricultural region. The companies would soon reclaim 200,000 acres of valuable valley land. Returns from the wheat crop revealed that New Mexico was second only to Utah and Colorado in acres planted, and outranked both areas in growing corn. Ranches "crowded with cattle, sheep, and horses" dotted the countryside, and there were more successful roundups and a smaller percentage of loss in the territory than in any other cattle region of the West. The territory's diversification of mineral wealth also was stressed.

Joseph concluded his argument by saying that he refused to believe the current rumors that the opposition toward New Mexico was largely due to sheer prejudice against the Roman Catholicism of many of its inhabitants. He chose to ignore the prejudice against the Spanish language and culture; he did hasten to point out, though, that there were 100,000 settlers—nearly the whole population of Wyoming—from Eastern states who had "not a drop of Spanish or Mexican blood in their veins."

Joseph's eloquence was persuasive, but nevertheless New Mexico stood by and watched while Wyoming and Idaho were proclaimed states by President Harrison in 1890. A year later, Prince made the comment that "Our people think they have been unjustly debarred from the privileges of statehood. We have a greater population than Wyoming and Idaho combined and in wealth and natural resources surpass either of these states." Prince's only consolation was the creation of the Court of Private Land Claims on March 3, 1891, which in the governor's opinion gave "stability to titles and confidence to investors."[17]

Again, on March 11, 1892, during the 52nd Congress, Joseph made another bid for statehood. The bill he introduced, H. R. 7136, got a good start as it was reported out of the House Committee on the Territories only five days later, accompanied by a 45-page report prepared by Joseph.[18] Calling for a constitutional convention of 75 delegates, the report also extolled the Court of Private Land Claims, regarded by many as the solution to conflicting claims over Spanish and Mexican land grants. An apportionment section reflected Joseph's partisanship as Democratic counties, allegedly underrepresented in the constitution of 1889, were given additional delegates to the proposed constitutional convention, while Republican strength was trimmed. Democratic Doña Ana, for instance, had its delegate strength increased from three to five.[19]

When Joseph's bill reached the floor of the House on June 6, Congressman Joseph E. Washington of Tennessee, a friendly Democrat, moved to suspend the rules, bringing a sharp protest from Representative George D. Perkins, an Iowan who felt he could not stand by while an important bill was rushed through the lower chamber. Perkins, a Republican, was critical of the generous land provisions, contending that the bill would give New Mexico twice the amount of land ever given to a state, regardless of the excuse that this was the proper way to dispose of arid lands. He also objected to the policy of selling these lands at half price because, as the science of irrigation advanced, it would be difficult to determine the value of such land in the future. But the argument upon which Perkins placed most emphasis was the familiar one that the territory did not want statehood. In Joseph's report he found a lack of evidence showing a current and sincere desire for admission. "It is true that about a year ago New Mexico voted for the adoption of a constitution, and rejected it. I do not know but that New Mexico would declare against admission at this time."[20]

The use of Spanish in the courts also brought criticism. Congressman John Lind, Republican of Minnesota, said that as an American citizen he objected to the "perpetuation of a foreign tongue" side by side with the English language. Joseph interceded here with the comment that the business language of New Mexico was English; it was spoken in all courts and taught in every public school. Another defender came forth saying that he had been informed by Joseph that the English language was required by law to be used in the pleadings and official records of court. To this the Minnesotan replied that the records and official proceedings outside the federal courts were kept in both languages, and this he felt ought to be prohibited in the enabling act.

After thirty minutes of debate, the Speaker called for the question on Washington's motion that the rules be suspended and the bill passed. When the motion carried by a vote of 177 to 3,[21] Democrats were jubilant, having also passed an Arizona statehood measure the same day. Chances for increased Democratic strength in the near future suddenly seemed bright.

On June 9, the bill reached the Senate and was sent to the Committee on Territories where Republican Senator Joseph Carey of Wyoming was in charge. The Senator was sympathetic to New Mexico's plight, having lived in Wyoming for many years before it became a state. The bill was amended in Carey's committee and sent forth with changes having been made in the apportionment section and land appropriations section. It was accompanied by a report which highlighted the futility of New Mexico's struggle for statehood with the revelation that fifteen states had been admitted since the territory came under the jurisdiction of the United States, four having been carved from territories formerly under Mexican jurisdiction. New Mexico would have been, the report said, one of "the great and influential states of the Union," had she been admitted under the constitution of 1850.[22]

Prince, always ready to plunge into the statehood fray, wrote to the politically potent chairman of the Senate territorial committee, Orville Platt, and attempted to use his influence on behalf of H. R. 7136. Platt had been instrumental in getting the northwest territories into the Union, and was generally considered a friend of territories seeking admission. Recent events had shown, however, that the senator might not be as favorable to the cause of the other territories. He had clashed with Joseph over a statehood bill's apportionment section in the last Congress[23] and had shown little enthusiasm for New Mexico's efforts. Prince's letter to Platt proudly set forth the progress made in public education, for while the population of the territory had increased 28 per cent from 1880 to 1890, "the number of children enrolled in the schools increased 283 per cent, or ten times as rapidly."[24]

Governor Prince and the New Mexican had been somewhat miffed when the 1889 constitution was defeated and New Mexico remained a territory. The New Mexican, a la Frost, sulked for while and then rejoined the fight for statehood. Prince, however, showed a willingness to forgive and forget almost immediately. He even forgave Joseph's treasonous act of running on an anti-land-grant plank in 1890[25] to secure re-election, and subordinated his disappointment to the cause for which "all good New Mexicans" must unite.[26]

Catron also regained his confidence and used his vast power and prestige to further New Mexico's chances for admission. The Albuquerque Morning Democrat, in a surprisingly charitable mood, defended the New Mexico leader from an attack by the Santa Fe Sun, which had taunted him for his political ambition. The paper admitted he was an "aggressive republican" and would probably be the territory's first United States senator, but lauded his efforts for statehood.[27] This attitude of forbearance changed quickly, however, when Catron made an unsuccessful bid for Joseph's job in 1892, causing the *Democrat* to warn that Catron's election would mean "good-bye to statehood."[28]

Page after page of newsprint was filled with conjectures on the bill's fate in the Senate. President Harrison's attitude was anxiously studied and comments about it constantly made. Two Denver papers confidently predicted presidential approval of the measure,[29] and the *Las Vegas Daily Optic* said that "as the republican platform is pledged to their [New Mexico and Arizona] admission, President Harrison can not but sign the bills."[30] The Republican platform adopted in Minneapolis three weeks before the *Optic*'s prediction did call for the admission of the remaining territories at the earliest practicable date, and was joined in this pledge by the Democratic nominating convention which assembled in Chicago three weeks later.[31] Both political parties had called for statehood in 1888, however, and nothing came of it, although the Republican platform confined its pledge to only "qualified" territories. Nevertheless, pledges were made which were never kept, proving once again that political platforms are a poor basis for confident prediction.

On July 21, Senator Carey, acting under instruction from the Committee on Territories, reported the amended statehood bill to the Senate with recommendation for its passage. Senator Platt, too, addressed the upper chamber on that day, but dissented from the majority, asking permission to submit a minority report. Platt proposed that, before admitting New Mexico, the Committee on Territories or another appropriate committee should be authorized to go to New Mexico and secure needed information, with expenses paid from the contingent fund of the Senate. This resolution was accepted on July 28, but no investigation took place at this time.

Carey tried to save the measure by introducing two amendments during the second session of the 52d Congress, the first providing for the formation of four new states: New Mexico, Utah, Arizona, and Oklahoma; and the second substantially the same but omitting Arizona.[32] He was apparently trying to attract the largest possible vote by including other territories anxious for statehood. With Oklahoma's Republican leanings as a balance to the Democratic proclivities of the other three territories, more Republican support was hoped for.

On February 1, 1893, the bill was passed over by the Senate, and on February 6 the *Optic* had to report that Senator Platt and Senator Matthew Quay of Pennsylvania, two very powerful Republicans, were opposed to the admission of any of the territories on the grounds that they were not prepared for self-government. This prompted Catron to write Platt the following day that New Mexico would be lost to the Democrats if the Republicans "fail or refuse" to admit New Mexico into the Union. He reasoned that the outlook for Democrats and Populists controlling the next Senate was excellent, and that this combination would certainly pass the enabling act. This would be a severe blow to Republican politics in the territory.[33]

The bill was passed over two more times before Congress adjourned, ending all hopes for the passage of Joseph's measure. The *Silver City Enterprise* viewed the setback as only temporary, and began to plan new tactics. New Mexico would "undoubtedly" be admitted by the next Congress.[34] The paper also took the opportunity to needle Joseph for unkept promises. ". . . Hon. Antonio promised us statehood as a Christmas gift some time ago and we are still waiting for it."[35] In another letter, Catron discussed the immense benefit that would result if Republicans originated the measure admitting New Mexico, and he urged Carey to introduce a bill early in the session before Joseph came forth with one.[36]

Carey apparently followed Catron's advice for on August 8, 1893, he laid two bills before the Senate. One would allow New Mexico to be admitted individually on its merits; the other was an omnibus bill incorporating New Mexico, Utah, Arizona, and Oklahoma into one package. Nevertheless, the Joseph bill, introduced about a month later, received the greatest attention. Undoubtedly this was because the Democrats were again at the helm after Grover Cleveland won his second term following a four-year interim. The bill, H. R. 353,[37] was very similar to the one introduced in the last Congress by the New Mexico delegate. The report which accompanied it was possibly more forceful than previous ones. It attacked the contention that statehood should be withheld until every inhabitant had learned to speak and write the English language, because this was contrary to the understanding which had existed among those who signed the Treaty of Guadalupe Hidalgo. The report told of a large and enthusiastic statehood convention in Albuquerque called in September by Governor William T. Thornton, a recent Cleveland appointee. At this meeting Joseph's bill had been given unanimous approbation, expressing the "intense desire of the people of New Mexico for admission into the sisterhood of states."[38]

The silver issue loomed ever larger on the horizon of local as well as national politics. All the territories admitted into the Union since 1864 had some interest in silver mining. Consequently they successfully worked against the protective McKinley tariff until Congress appeased them by passing the Sherman Silver Purchase Act of 1890, which obligated the federal government to buy virtually all the domestic silver produced. Soon after Cleveland took office for his second term, a severe panic gripped the nation, blamed by many Easterners, including the President, upon the drain of gold reserves caused by "cheap" silver. On June 30, 1893, Cleveland with characteristic courage called for a special session of Congress to meet in August to consider repeal of the Sherman Act. Notwithstanding the damage that debate over silver legislation would do to the Democratic party, the President and his supporters in Congress were determined to end the gold drain. They reasoned that the country had been brought to the verge of ruin by putting too much power in the hands of the silver-producing states. Joseph, knowing that New Mexico was included in this criticism of the West, wrote to a friend that he realized there would be some opposition in the Senate to his bill.

The prospects for my enabling act are good. I feel satisfied that we cannot pass an act for immediate admission in the senate, as the anti-silver senators seem to be opposed at this time to increasing the strength of the friends of silver in that body. I believe however they will not oppose an act which provides for admission early in 1895.[39]

The House of Representatives, having voted to repeal the Sherman Act two months before the Senate took the same action on October 30, recovered enough from the violent debate over silver to take surprisingly fast action on the statehood bills just before Christmas. On December 13, 1893, the Utah bill was passed and two days later favorable action was taken on the admission of Arizona. New Mexico, however, did not fare so well. On the day of the Arizona action, following lengthy debate, H. R. 353 was passed over until after the Christmas recess.

New Mexico's troubles were largely the result of an effort to insure admission of Republican Oklahoma along with that of the two Southwestern Democratic territories, Arizona and New Mexico. House Republicans had sought assurance from Representative Joseph Wheeler of Alabama, chairman of the Committee on the Territories, that the majority Democrats would not block the admission of Oklahoma.[40] When Wheeler refused to publicly pledge support of Oklahoma on the grounds that her statehood bill did not adequately provide for the settlement of treaties with the Five Civilized Tribes, Republicans balked at supporting New Mexico. Colorful "Sockless Jerry" Simpson of Kansas, displaying a nativist sentiment attributed by some historians to Populism, was bitter because the Democrats were willing to give statehood to New Mexico, a territory populated by "a race speaking an alien language," while denying statehood to Oklahoma, a region "peopled by the best blood on the American continent."

But to Representative Washington the people of the territory whether of "Spanish or Mexican origin" were just as much citizens of the United States as the people of Kansas, Iowa, or Nebraska, who had come to these states within the last eight or ten years from countries in Europe. Their claim was technically even more legitimate, as most of them had been born in the territory, and those under forty were natural-born American citizens, having been born after the United States acquired New Mexico. The Tennessee Congressman rose to heights of indignation when he discussed the religious question. So much had been said about the religious practices of the Mormons in connection with Utah and the Roman Catholics in connection with New Mexico that he wanted to know "whether a man's religion is to be made a test of his fitness for citizenship in the Union? If so, let it be stated here and now, and let it go forth to the world. If religion is to be also a party test, let it be so declared here and now . . . ."[41]

Despite the loyal support of Democrats, H. R. 353 was handicapped by the untimely absence of Joseph. According to Prince the delegate had suffered a malarial attack and returned to New Mexico, hoping that a few days of its healthy climate would speed his return to the Congress. He inquired of congressional leaders as to the prospects of action on his bill and was assured that there was no chance of the New Mexico bill or any statehood bill reaching the floor before the Christmas recess. But Congress unexpectedly postponed its recess until the day before Christmas. During this time, the Utah bill was announced and passed in the House, despite considerable opposition to Mormonism. After the holiday, it was successfully acted upon by the Senate. Had Joseph been present, it was reasoned, New Mexico would have had the same good fortune.

Prince did not blame Joseph, whom he regarded as an earnest advocate of statehood, but merely chalked up the incident as another in the "series of mishaps" suffered by the territory.[42] Indeed, it might be placed alongside the unhappy Elkins' handshake as an unfortunate quirk of fate. Chairman Wheeler, acknowledging Joseph's absence during debate of H. R. 353, had nothing but praise for Joseph's work and claimed he was in "telegraphic communication" with the ailing delegate. Congressman Springer insisted that no man had ever served his constituents more faithfully than Joseph.

Final action in the House on the New Mexico bill was not taken until the summer of 1894. In the meantime, Joseph continued to push for admittance after his return to Washington, and his efforts were recognized by brief consideration of H. R. 353 in March. This effort failed, too, and Joseph blamed the setback on the Republicans. He termed their opposition "cowardly."[43] The New Mexican, now owned by Governor Thornton, a Democrat, agreed completely, although another territorial paper said the criticism of the Republicans was unjust in view of the majority of 83 that Joseph's Democratic colleagues enjoyed in the lower house.[44]

Disputes among New Mexicans were not confined to which party should receive the blame for the delay in statehood. The bill itself was a subject of controversy even among strong supporters of the territory's claim for admittance. The *Silver City Enterprise* looked with favor at the measure, and after reading the report which accompanied H. R. 353, pronounced it "highly interesting," a document which showed that New Mexico was entitled to statehood.[45] Catron, however, had reservations, and in a letter to Carey he asked the Wyoming senator to use his influence in the House to have the bill amended so that the Republicans would receive a fair deal. He objected to the provision that would delay the selection of delegates to the constitutional convention until the regular election. The "democratic bandits" wanted this delay in order to confuse the election of delegates with the regular general election, hoping to intimidate the unaggressive Spanish-speaking residents into supporting their candidates. His second objection concerned the provision allowing the Democratic secretary, a Cleveland appointee, to count and certify votes rather than the boards of county commissioners in each county.[46] Despite these partisan conflicts, when the time came, Catron and most of his Republican colleagues supported the bill.

H. R. 353 was also a source of controversy in the rest of the country. The Trans-Mississippi Congress, an organization to promote the West in which Prince was very active, sent a resolution to Washington "praying" for the admission of Utah, New Mexico, and Arizona. Although it was undoubtedly beneficial to New Mexico that she was associated with the other two would-be states, liabilities were also evident. Three memorials were introduced in the Senate, where Utah was receiving serious consideration, each of which remonstrated against the admission of Utah, Arizona, and New Mexico because of the alleged strength of the Mormon faith in each territory.

Final action on the bill on June 27 brought attempts to amend the measure and the three-hour rule under which it was to be deliberated. Republican Congressman John F. Lacey of Iowa tried to amend the rule so as to embrace consideration of the Territory of Oklahoma, but was unsuccessful. He thought it a shame to admit that "Aztec civilization" while excluding "300,000 Anglo-Saxons ready for admission into the Union."

Representative Perkins offered another amendment which would change the election of constitutional convention delegates to a date other than the regular election day in November, in order to avoid partisanship. Catron's letter to Carey seems to have had some influence. Delegate Joseph defended the late election date on the grounds that the delay would give

the territorial legislative assembly time to audit and investigate the float-
ing militia debt which the territory had incurred during the Civil War.
Because New Mexico had decided to assume this debt upon achieving
statehood, every citizen and taxpayer in the territory wanted to postpone
admission in order to ascertain why there were more militia warrants in
circulation than there were vouchers for them in the hands of the adjutant
general of the territorial militia. The Perkins' amendment was rejected by
a vote of the House.

The most serious attempt to amend the bill was made by Republican
Representative George W. Smith of Illinois who wanted to incorporate
the phrase: "in all of which public schools the English language shall be
taught." According to Smith, Delegate Joseph had accepted such an
amendment in the 51st Congress when it was pointed out to him that in
many of the public schools of the territory only the Spanish language was
taught. Joseph objected because this suggestion had been made seven or
eight years ago, and since that time the educational system had been expanded so that English was taught in each of the 619 public schools in the
territory.

This amendment was defeated, but another, substantially the same, was
proposed. The substitute, offered by a fellow Republican, Representative
George W. Wilson of Ohio, provided for teaching the English language
as a branch of study in all public schools, but not to the exclusion of other
languages. The amendment differed from the first in that it provided that
the English language be dealt with as an academic subject. Wilson also
maintained that every subject should be taught in English. Joseph was
against this proposal too, and received support from another congressman
who made this observation:

Now, if you say that "all branches" shall be taught, that certainly embraces Spanish.
Consequently according to the language of the amendment, you provide that the Spanish language shall be taught in English. That would seem to be an absurdity.[47]

The Congressman's point was well taken, the amendment was rejected,
and on the following day the bill passed the House.

Two weeks after H. R. 353 had reached the Senate, Joseph gave New
Mexico supporters a reason to cheer. Disclaiming all reports to the contrary, he announced that President Cleveland told him he would sign
the statehood bill. According to a Washington dispatch in the St. Louis
Globe-Democrat, Cleveland felt it was high time that the pledge made
under the Treaty of Guadalupe Hidalgo be redeemed.[48] This report was
contrary to all speculation on the subject. The same St. Louis paper had
editorialized six months before that because of the silver sentiment in

Utah, Arizona, and New Mexico, President Cleveland would have a "strong temptation" to veto the admission of these states.[49] About a month later, the Washington correspondent of the *Globe-Democrat* wrote that the President was "unalterably opposed" to the admission of these three territories, as they would increase the strength of the West at the expense of the East.[50]

The optimistic report on Cleveland's position triggered a wave of enthusiasm among New Mexico Democrats, according to one territorial paper. The provision in the bill regarding apportionment—similar to that found in H. R. 7136—was such that they felt confident of controlling the constitutional convention which, in turn, would fix representation in the state legislature. Already they were gossiping about dividing the spoils. It was conceded that if the "apportionment scheme" worked, Joseph would be one of the United States senators. Other top candidates mentioned included the governor and the chairman of the Democratic Territorial Committee.[51]

Despite the proclaimed Democratic advantages that would accrue from passage of the bill, Catron, probably thinking in terms of his own financial advancement, never wavered in his support of statehood. Although critical of the bill, the Santa Fe lawyer continued to urge its passage. He was especially active when the measure reached the Democratic-controlled Senate Committee on Territories on June 29. Writing to his friend Senator Platt, ranking Republican on the committee, he begged him to keep the pledge he had made the summer before when he vowed that although he would not vote for the bill he would do nothing to oppose or delay its passage. Playing upon the senator's known partisanship, as he had done before, Catron guaranteed an "absolutely republican state, with two republican senators, who will go there [Washington] not for free trade, but absolutely for protection." He attributed this overwhelmingly Republican sentiment in the territory to the threat of the Democrats in their Chicago plaform to place the industries of New Mexico on the free list. Catron assured Platt that the senators from New Mexico, Arizona, and Utah would enable the Republican party to regain control of the Senate and enact a worthy tariff bill.[52]

Knowing Senator Platt to be a man of strong convictions, Catron also wrote to his friend Elkins, whose good fortune since leaving New Mexico had been capped by his selection as a senator from West Virginia. After saying that it was his understanding that the New Mexico bill needed unanimous consent in the Senate, and that no Republican but Platt would oppose it, he asked the former New Mexico delegate to try to dissuade Platt from blocking the bill.[53] He also wrote another friend, Senator Stewart of Nevada, and asked him to assure Platt that New Mexico would be a Republican and pro-tariff state. However, he cautioned Stewart not to mention silver because Platt might think that Stewart wanted New Mexico in because it was a silver state.[54]

On July 19, a *New York Tribune* report stated that the subcommittees having charge of the statehood bills had been instructed to report them at the next meeting of the full committee. This action was voted by all members of the Committee on Territories except Senator Platt and Cushman K. Davis, Republicans, and Senator Wilkinson Call, Democrat. The New Mexico group met at once to prepare its report, and amended the bill so that the election of delegates and the constitutional convention would be held on the same dates as those provided in the Utah bill—November, 1894, for the election and March, 1895, for the convention. Another press report indicated that the Arizona bill would be considered at the same time as Utah's and New Mexico's.[55]

Nevertheless, when Democratic Senator Joseph C. S. Blackburn of Kentucky reported the bill favorably to the Senate on August 3, 1894, it was clearly revealed that the full committee had stemmed the original enthusiasm shown by the subcommittees. New Mexico's election of delegates to the constitutional convention was delayed until June, 1895, and the convention was not scheduled until the following month. However, the date for popular ratification remained November, 1895.[56] The bill was accompanied by a report that differed little from the Joseph report prepared the previous year.[57]

Favorable action on New Mexico and Arizona, such as that taken in Utah's case a month earlier, now seemed within the realm of possibility. But inaction became the rule of the day and several months passed as the two measures remained ignored. This provoked a "blame the other fellow" campaign in New Mexico. The *New Mexican* accused the Republicans of not following the "manly and straight forward course" regarding statehood that the Democrats had pursued. The *Silver City Enterprise* called all this "ridiculous nonsense"; the Democrats had absolute control of all departments, and it would be futile for the Republicans to offer any obstacle to admission, were they so inclined.[58] The same paper also reprinted a letter from D. V. Carr to the *Optic* that offered a new guess as to why the Democratic-controlled Senate was balking on statehood. Carr's opinion was that because the Arizona constitution, recently adopted, provided that silver as well as gold would be made legal tender in the new state, the "gold-bugs" in the party and the federal officials of both New Mexico and Arizona were greatly disturbed. These men had been speculating in various enterprises in both territories since their appointment by Cleveland and depended heavily upon the bonds sold to raise necessary money. Such bonds were more readily negotiated on a gold basis, so the attempt by Arizona to give silver equal recognition was a threat to the success of their ventures.[59]

Delegate Joseph received his share of the criticism for the delay of the statehood bill. Although the *Optic* defended him against severe attack by the influential *San Francisco Chronicle* for his opposition to the amendments requiring that teaching in the public schools be in English,[60] it later, on November 5, blamed him for the probable defeat of his bill by refusing to incorporate such amendments. This position would be inconsistent if it were not for the fact that election day was near and Catron was attempting a second time to become the territory's delegate to Congress.

Catron was successful this time, winning by nearly 3,000 votes. His substantial victory was probably due to the failure of Congress to take action on H. R. 353. Certainly it would be difficult to imagine a delegate achieving such a prized goal and being rejected at the polls the same year. Joseph laid almost exclusive emphasis upon this issue, using again and again the argument that he was the territory's only hope for statehood, and that Catron's position on the issue was doubtful.[61] Catron, on the other hand, counted on his large following in the northern counties and the Republican campaign to restore protective tariffs on wool and mining products as chief advantages.[62] As the campaign was fought on issues, Joseph could only blame the loss on the failure of his statehood campaign.

Joseph's defeat at the polls ended his long career as territorial delegate. Four months later, the demise of his statehood bill occurred as H. R. 353 remained on the docket, untouched, when the Senate adjourned. It was a remarkable tenure in that Joseph brought New Mexico to the brink of statehood on two occasions, only to be defeated in the upper chamber, which was becoming the traditional graveyard for the territory's statehood aspirations. He cannot be called a failure, especially in light of the fact that his active interest in this matter only began during his third term in Congress.

Joseph had his own very definite ideas as to why he failed to achieve statehood. In commenting on the defeat of his last bill, he blamed the Republicans, claiming they deliberately filibustered an appropriations bill in order to prevent consideration of New Mexico's enabling act. By these tactics they delayed action on the money measure until March 4, 1895, when it was too late to call up New Mexico's admission bill. Furthermore, he claimed that Republican senators received letters from prominent party men in the territory urging such action. Whether these charges are true or not, partisan politics was undoubtedly a very disruptive factor. Joseph also blamed the attitude of Eastern people for the defeat of his measure. He claimed both Wall Street and the American Protective Association opposed the territory's admission.[63] The A.P.A., a notorious nativist organization, bitterly opposed statehood because the Spanish-speaking population of New Mexico was "almost exclusively Catholic."[64]

Notwithstanding the potent impact of political partisanship, perhaps the key to Joseph's failure resides in his political philosophy. New Mexico's delegate did not equivocate on his stand regarding silver; he would not have dared. He introduced two memorials in Congress asking for the free and unlimited coinage of silver: one from New Mexico's legislative assembly, the other from the people of Las Vegas. He spoke on behalf of the issue in Congress and when he hesitated he was effectively needled by the territorial press. Upon retiring from politics to return to Ojo Caliente and lead a quiet life, he proudly stated that he was a "silver Democrat, true and strong."[65] His native background may have produced suspicion, his association with the controversial Knights of Labor in the territory may have angered big business,[66] but it was his association with silver that probably hurt him and his cause the most.

The silver question became an even more vital and emotional issue during Catron's term as delegate. The Democrats began to feud bitterly after Cleveland split the party right down the middle by his insistence that the Sherman Silver Purchase Act should be repealed. The Silver Democrats, as the new anti-administration forces were called, fought relentlessly to achieve some favorable silver legislation. The ranks of the Silverites were swelled by the presence of many Westerners who, regardless of political ideology, were sympathetic toward the cause of silver. Consequently, there were Silver Republicans as well as Silver Democrats.

Silver Republicans were often men of conservative leanings whose interests in silver mining outweighed the cautious approach that ordinarily characterized their political and economic beliefs. Prince, a Silver Republican, stretched his sympathies for the cause as far as party loyalty would allow him, realizing fully that the Republicans would eventually have to take a stand on the issue, probably contrary to his. For Tom Catron the silver question posed a real problem. He was a conservative, high-tariff Republican who saw eye to eye with the best party stalwarts. Yet, he, too, was interested in mineral development and was aware of the economic importance of this industry to the territory. At the same time, he knew that as a Republican, continued support of the silver cause could jeopardize his political influence nationally. Statehood, too, was endangered, for the close identification of New Mexico with the silver movement could only insure the hostility of the gold forces, which included the President and most of the powerful Eastern senators. On the other hand, silver sentiment was so strong that many in the territory preferred silver legislation to statehood if the choice had to be made. This dilemma would have confounded the most astute politician.

Tom Catron, however, counted astute, shrewd judgment among his talents and he was generally found on the winning side. He hoped to avoid the pitfalls of the silver issue, keeping the emphasis always on statehood, the tariff, or some other less controversial issue. But the very scope of Catron's political dominance in the territory made him the favorite whipping boy among Democrats. The *Albuquerque Citizen* claimed that "Democratic papers in a dull season always fall back on Catron and rend and tear him to tatters."[67] Tales of his greedy land bargains were generously distributed by Democratic journals,[68] but seemed to have little effect on the widespread popularity he enjoyed in the territory, especially among *Hispanos* in the northern counties.

But even Catron could not altogether avoid some public stand on silver. By now the silver issue was sweeping the country like a prairie fire. Governor Thornton upon returning from a trip to the East made the comment that "the first subject touched upon in conversation, whether political, social or of a business nature, invariably brought up the financial problem." He warned of the impending struggle, claiming that gold was the sole sentiment of businessmen to the east and north of Memphis, and that the remarkable growth of the double standard principle in the South and West had put the "Wall Street cohorts and their followers 'on the metal,' as it were."[69]

Regardless of the unknown consequences, Catron with characteristic energy pushed statehood in the 54th Congress by introducing four bills, two of which were tossed aside before the first session was more than eight days old.[70] He secured appointments to the Committee on the Territories and the Committee on Private Land Claims. These were his first and third committee choices, no doubt obtained chiefly because of his audacity. He had previously written "Czar" Thomas B. Reed of Maine, who was again slated for Speaker in case of a Republican triumph, requesting these assignments and putting in a good word for statehood.[71] Of the bills presented, the one that held most promise was introduced in the upper house by Senator John G. Gear, Republican from Iowa. This is not surprising in view of the acquaintances Catron had made in the upper chamber, several among the members of the Committee on Territories.

Catron greatly exerted himself to secure passage for the bill Gear introduced. He was particularly determined that the silver issue should not damage the bill's chances. He used all his influence to persuade territorial leaders to play down the silver cause. In a letter to Miguel A. Otero, a young political lieutenant of his from Las Vegas, he urged precaution.

Fearing that the territorial party convention, which was scheduled to meet in Albuquerque in less than three weeks, would take a drastic stand on silver, Catron urged his supporters to prevent any resolution being passed which would advocate the free and unlimited coinage of silver. He warned that such action would jeopardize the progress of the statehood bill, which he predicted would soon come to a vote in the Senate Committee on Territories. He felt that Republican territorial leaders should concentrate instead on strong resolutions which would urge statehood and favor the enactment of tariff laws. "Statehood and Tariff should be the watchwords."

Catron showed particular distress at the recent actions of Western senators who joined with the Democrats to substitute the so-called silver proposition for important measures such as the most recent tariff effort. The defeat of the tariff bill that resulted had caused much indignation among Eastern people, and many who had heretofore been committed to New Mexico's statehood were now under such pressure that they were "hesitating and holding back." It would help if the Albuquerque meeting passed a resolution condemning those Westerners who attempted "to tack on the free silver amendment to every proposition that comes along." But Catron realized that this would be too much to ask of any Western assembly.[72]

To Catron's relief, Otero was successful in achieving moderation, and later guided the party to an endorsement of the gold platform drafted at the Republican national convention on June 16, 1896.[73] Catron's final stand against silver had come about only because he was, above all else, an advocate of statehood for New Mexico. He was not completely unsympathetic toward the silver agitators, for after all he was a Westerner and silver was an important industry in the territory. The repeal of the Sherman Silver Purchase Act had closed every silver and lead mine in New Mexico, greatly affecting the territory's economy. But the free and unlimited coinage of silver was too extreme a measure for Catron's taste; he advocated a much more moderate course. His solution was to:

. . . Coin the product of the United States at some given standard, which might be fixed, and impose a duty upon all foreign silver so as to make it, with the duty, worth as much as the standard which we might fix the American dollar at. . . . [This] would be protection such as is desired. The United States could then take care of its own silver, because the balance of trade with Europe being generally in our favor at an average of nearly fifty millions a year, if we had to send our silver to Europe to make purchase with, they would send it back to us with an additional amount of fifty millions more, in order to purchase our staples, and thus we could take care of our silver, especially if we could abolish all currency under ten dollars except silver.

Catron also believed that the silver product was annually adding an "absolute wealth" of from fifty to sixty-five millions of dollars to the

United States. The addition of fifty millions that would come back to America in the shape of the balance of trade would make an aggregate of one hundred million dollars—"a very great item towards creating prosperity in the country, at a very early date."[74]

Catron's efforts to keep silver in the background and stress statehood instead were ultimately fruitless. In the Senate, not only was the New Mexico bill passed over and forgotten, but the delegate's reputation was severely damaged during the hearings that preceded consideration of the bill. Catron's controversial past had caught up with him, and at a most inopportune time. A fratricidal attack waged by the Blaine senators against Elkins, their political enemy, crippled Catron, too, because Elkins was one of the major supporters of the New Mexico bill. More disastrous was a deluge of letters from Republicans in New Mexico to Republican senators on and off the committee charging that both Catron and Elkins were land robbers. Catron especially was slandered, being called a "political freebooter" seeking to achieve his own selfish ends. He countercharged that the attack emanated from federal officials in the territory willing to sacrifice statehood in order to stay on the public payroll, but the damage was done.[75]

Catron was also disappointed in his attempt to pass an enabling act in the lower chamber, where he was accused of desiring statehood for the benefit of himself and his "political puppets."[76] The apportionment clause of one of his bills was labeled as unfair, a charge countered by Catron's claim that his bill was almost identical to one introduced by Joseph.[77]

The bitter attacks on Catron no doubt prejudiced New Mexico's case, and reinforced deep attitudes of opposition, according to the New York Tribune. Many people believed that the territory was not sufficiently settled to justify its assuming statehood, that the Spanish language was often used to the exclusion of English, and that the admission of the territory would increase the voting strength of the free silver men in the Senate by two votes.[78]

As election time in New Mexico approached, Catron became alarmed about his political future. His enemies kept hammering away at him and he was forced to answer one charge after another. The New Mexican told how his methods had disgusted Delegate Nathan O. Murphy of Arizona and Arizona now intended to stand alone in demanding admission.[79] Catron was forced to defend his friend Elkins in regards to private land claims in New Mexico,[80] matters in which he was often involved himself. And then there was the Borrego case which probably did more to tarnish the delegate's reputation than any other episode. The case involved Francisco Gonzales y Borrego, his brother, and two other men accused of murdering the former sheriff of Santa Fe, Francisco Chavez. Because the victim was a political enemy of Catron, and Catron vigorously defended the accused, the opposition press tried to implicate the portly delegate. When an attempt was made to disbar Catron for unprofessional conduct in this case, the story was given particular impetus.[81] It was so effectively employed and constantly repeated that Catron admitted later that the rumors might have reached even the President himself.[82]

But Catron did not submit without a fight. To Elkins, Catron wrote that while he had not made any final decision about running for re-election, he did have ideas for strategy in the coming campaign. He would have New Mexico Republicans declare themselves in favor of the coinage of the American product (the Catron substitute), but at the same time concentrate on the tariff question as the chief issue.[83] Also, Catron showed he was not beneath less honorable devices for assuring his election. His letter to tough Mark Hanna illustrates this. Knowing the tremendous influence this man had among the barons of big business, he suggested that perhaps Hanna could persuade the railroad companies owning the coal mines in the territory to transfer their employees from one district to another. His motive for doing this was simple. Most of the coal miners in New Mexico were, together with Populists and "all gold and silver miners," advocates of the free and unlimited coinage of silver and, therefore, opponents of his re-election. The laws of the territory required that all voters to be qualified had to reside in the territory six months, in the county three months, and in the precinct thirty days. By transferring these miners from one coal region to another their votes would be destroyed.[84]

Catron also diligently probed about in an effort to pick the winner in the upcoming Republican nominating convention. When advising Otero to throttle silver sentiment at the Republican territorial meeting, held almost four months before the national convention, he opined that it would not be advisable to endorse any particular individual for President, unless it be the reliable Elkins. Furthermore, this should be done only if his name came before the convention. Rather, the impression should be given that New Mexico planned to support those who supported New Mexico. However, long before giving this advice Catron had shown a definite partiality toward "Czar" Reed. In a letter to a friend the previous year, Catron called Reed "the coming man." As for McKinley, he had been too "boisterous" in his opposition to silver during the last election to make him strong in the West, and his tariff record was regarded as being extreme.[85]

In the months approaching November, 1896, the question of free and unlimited coinage of silver and gold at the ratio of sixteen to one became dominant. Democrats throughout the Western mining states flocked to the cause. Western Republicans joined the free silver "heresy" when Senator Henry M. Teller of Colorado led his fateful walkout of Republican dissenters at the stormy St. Louis convention. Both parties had platforms calling for admission of territories, but this issue was almost dead as the chant of "16 to 1" echoed throughout the West. New Mexico was captured by the excitement as Democrats nominated for territorial delegate the very able Harvey B. Fergusson. Fergusson was unequivocal in his support of the cause. Thus, the worst of Catron's fears had come true and silver would be the key issue. No course of moderation would now be possible.

The Democratic nominee was a fascinating person in many ways. A product of the Southern plantation aristocracy, he had become a dedicated champion of worthwhile, usually liberal causes. He ardently believed in public education and devoted much of his time to its attainment. A sincere believer in states' rights, he supported statehood for New Mexico. Although he was the son of an Alabama slave owner, he was sympathetic towards the plight of the Negro and on several occasions accepted invitations to address gatherings on Emancipation Day. He was a fiery, eloquent orator, never gruff or sharp-tongued as Catron was, although he could certainly match his Republican counterpart on the stump.[86] His popularity was immense, too. He had been offered the nomination two years before, but rejected it for personal reasons.[87] His nomination in 1896 was unanimous, assuring him strong support.

Democratic strength was enhanced by the addition of Populist strength. Populism, the reform movement that germinated in the late 1880's and the early 1890's, had sent nine congressmen and two senators to Washington in the 1890 election. In 1892, Populist elements united to form the People's Party of America which fielded an independent presidential candidate who polled more than a million votes. As economic conditions grew worse because of the depression of 1893, the new party was weakened because Democrats and Republicans began to take over the Populist program in states where the Populists had the most support. Populists were strongly attracted to free silver as a solution to many of the small farmer's economic ills. As a debtor group, the beleagured farmers found the prospect of cheaper and more available money an enticing answer to their then-mounting financial obligations, and consequently many of them were determined to attach themselves to this cause in the coming election. When the Democratic party nominated William Jennings Bryan and declared for free coinage, the People's party had no choice but to endorse the Democratic standard bearer. As a result, the dual causes of Free Silver and Populism were united under the Democratic banner and in New Mexico Fergusson inherited the support.

Populist backing did not come directly to New Mexico Democrats, however, for territorial Populists had first supported former Governor Prince, an outspoken Silver Republican. His forceful speeches had indicated that he would advocate unlimited silver coinage at a ratio with gold of 16 to 1. Acting on this assumption the local Populists nominated him as their candidate for governor. But Prince disappointed these friends by participating in the Republican convention which adopted the gold standard, and by refusing to follow the drastic example of Senator Teller who broke with the party. Thus, on October 7, the People's party angrily rescinded its support of Prince and agreed to follow the action adopted in other states and territories by fusing with the Democratic party "on equitable lines, in legislative and county affairs."[88]

Under the circumstances, adverse results for Catron were not unexpected. Delegate Catron, who had buried Joseph two years before by 2,762 votes, was defeated by a margin of 1,930. Silver was unquestionably the issue as both men advocated statehood.

The all-consuming interest in silver can best be appreciated by following the editorial line of the *Optic* during the eight months preceding this election. In March, this usually staunch Republican paper said that the protection of wool and statehood would be the party's battle cry and "he who would desert the republican ranks, this year, for any other party whatsoever, must only be considered as an enemy to his party and the Territory."[89] Certainly, as partisan a man as Catron could endorse this declaration. In July, the *Optic* confidently predicted that Catron could outdraw Fergusson by 5,000 votes.[90] But by October, the Las Vegas daily announced that in Fergusson the silver cause possessed an unusually well equipped candidate who, if elected delegate, would not "bring the blush of shame to the cheek of any citizen of this Territory."[91] Later in the month, the newspaper declared support for Fergusson, Catron and the gold Republicans of New Mexico having fallen into the "filth and mire of Hannaism." Furthermore, the *Optic* and all other "consistent, self-respecting republicans, who stand for principle rather than follow a name, who cannot change like a weather cock with every varying wind that blows —all of these, a host in number, will vote for Fergusson, and repudiate Catron at the polls in November."[92] After the election, the *Optic* praised the triumph of Fergusson as the new delegate to Congress and said of the defeated candidate: "The day is past when men like T. B. Catron may expect to hold the respect of the people of the great Territory of New Mexico. It was possible in the days of the 'Santa Fe ring' but not now."[93]

Thus Catron, only two years after his first big political victory, met defeat and was ringed with criticism from every quarter. Nevertheless, this conservative, orthodox Republican could hardly have expected to receive the criticism leveled at him by Congressman William P. Hepburn of Iowa, a fellow Republican, during the "lame duck" session. On December 10, 1896, Catron introduced a bill to amend an alien ownership act enacted in 1887. The law had long deprived New Mexico, Arizona, and Oklahoma of foreign investments because it allowed no foreigner to hold possession of, or own, real property. Catron opposed the law because he had large tracts of land to sell and he could make more money selling them undivided to wealthy foreigners.[94] The Populists had heretofore supported this law because they preferred to see the land divided among small, needy farmers. But foreign investments were needed and even active Populists were willing to support the change. Hence, the Catron amendment had the support of all the parties in the territory.

It was this fact that Hepburn had in mind when he sarcastically pointed out that this amendment was contrary to the fundamental principles of Populism which oppose acquisition of land in America by aliens. Hepburn demanded to know why Catron had gone against the desires of "his party" and people in presenting this bill. So Catron, the complete antithesis of everything Populism stood for, was suddenly identified with it and had to deny he was its representative. Answering Hepburn, he said his amendment would benefit all the parties in New Mexico, even the tiny Populist group numbering "500 or 600, or 1,000 or 1,200."

Hepburn was not satisfied and launched a vigorous attack that brought loud applause from the Republican side of the aisle. He shouted in ringing tones:

Oh, while they were upholding Populism as understood in the rest of the United States and the people where I live understand it, these gentlemen were sneaking away from the effects of Populism by attempting to modify it in their platform in their own locality, yet they voted for the party. The gentlemen can not deny that we are having an object lesson of the effect of these declarations of the platform—that the declarations of the platform that they support are destructive to their welfare. I want them to learn that they can not grow under Populism, and I want them further to be taught that they can not modify the general doctrines of Populism as they are understood in the whole country by the adoption of a little resolution that they sneak into their local platform and then vote for the Populist party upon the general platform.[95]

Although Catron eventually managed to get his amendment through the House, it was painfully evident that statehood prospects were intimately interwoven with New Mexico's association with Free Silver and Populism. New Mexico in the election of 1896 had emphatically endorsed the former and, by implication, approved the latter. But in this crucial election, the majority of Americans, especially in the populous East, had rejected both causes and would be suspicious of the "radical" influence of the territories for a long time to come.

TWELVE

A New Era

W ITH FERGUSSON'S VICTORY
in 1896 came a new political era in New Mexico. Much influence and
power slipped from the hands of the Old Guard, still called by its enemies
the Santa Fe Ring. An even more severe blow to the Ring and the status
quo came when on June 2, 1897, President McKinley unexpectedly appointed Miguel Otero the new territorial governor.[1] Otero, thirty-eight
years old and a native-born New Mexican, caused new tensions to divide
Ring members and their opponents. The Republican party had been
for years almost the private domain of Tom Catron, but now the stubborn Otero fought Catron bitterly with important consequences for the
statehood movement.

As territorial delegate, Harvey Fergusson's one handicap was that he
went to Washington as a Democrat during a Republican year. For all his
eloquence and integrity, his chances for achieving something as substantial
as statehood were next to nothing. However, the new delegate was loyal
to the cause and did what he could to accomplish this end. In his maiden
speech before the House, he asked for wool protection and at the same
time justified New Mexico's plea for statehood. Noting that hides were
placed on the free list while leather was given protection, Fergusson urged
justice for the "nearly 200,000 people" of New Mexico, who could not enforce their demand by a vote, because they were denied what they were
entitled to as "a matter of justice as well as a matter of law, under the treaty
of Guadalupe Hidalgo, admission to the sisterhood of states . . . ."[2] Fergusson attempted to act upon these words by introducing two enabling

acts[3] during his two-year term in Congress. Although the bills for statehood bore no fruit, he did secure passage of two significant laws. The first of these was a measure which would permanently locate the capital of the territory at Santa Fe. This was enacted to eliminate the "demoralizing effort" in every legislature to move the capital elsewhere.[4] The second was the famous land law which paved the way for New Mexico's admission into the Union.

The land measure was called the Fergusson Act and was introduced by him on February 16, 1898. According to the original terms of the bill, the Territory of New Mexico would receive immediately, before admission, sections 2, 16, 32, and 36 of every township for educational purposes. In addition, 100,000 acres of land would be granted for educational and other public institutions. Ordinarily such grants were conferred only upon the achievement of statehood, but it was argued that the operations of the recently created Court of Private Land Claims had opened for public entry thousands of acres of land on Spanish and Mexican grants which would be quickly taken if the school system were not provided for immediately.

The bill was submitted to the Committee on Public Lands which reported it favorably to the House with two major amendments, one of which cut the land allotment in half, granting only 2 sections from each township, and the other lowered the grant of 100,000 acres to 50,000. Iowa Congressman John F. Lacey, a member of the Public Lands Committee, said that because New Mexico had not been admitted, an injustice had been done to the people who for many years had been deprived of the usual grants given a territory upon achieving statehood. He also referred to the recent cases decided by the land court, claiming that the vast acreage released from litigation would be swallowed up and nothing would be left for the territory but desert land unless the bill were enacted. Fergusson was given credit for originating the proposal that took as its guide the enabling act of Utah, which had been proclaimed a state in 1896. Because of its aridity, Utah had enacted a four-section land grant system to provide financial support for its educational system. According to Lacey, it was the committee that suggested Fergusson should scale down his proposal for New Mexico to about one-half the land granted Utah and reserve the remainder until admission.

Although Lacey favored the bill, his speech belittled New Mexico's educational progress. The territory's slowness in raising educational standards was given as a reason for the feeling on both sides of the House that it was quite improbable that statehood would be granted soon. New Mexico's representative disliked any aspersions of this kind and spoke proudly of the public school system built by "voluntary taxation" of her citizens.

"If we are too ignorant for statehood, help us to become educated sufficiently, because you surely can not contemplate keeping us forever in a Territorial condition by refusing us the means of overcoming the objection of ignorance."

Fergusson referred to the impressive number of New Mexico volunteers for the Spanish-American War, then in progress. Despite the fact that Congress had "badly treated" the people of New Mexico, they were not embittered, and when the President in his call for 125,000 volunteers allotted to New Mexico four troops of cowboy cavalry to represent the territory's quota, "in a shorter time than the majority of the States responded New Mexico responded with a full quota . . . ." His report that the territorial Rough Riders were now on their way to Cuba and would be as brave in battle and as loyal to the government as any of the troops brought loud applause.[5]

But cheers for Fergusson's statehood boost did not bring action by the legislators. However, the Fergusson Act passed both houses of Congress and was signed into law on June 21, 1898. The act probably did more than any other one thing to promote education and prepare the people of New Mexico for statehood.

The Republican Old Guard was none too pleased by Fergusson's achievement, but its leaders—among them Catron—were not only displeased but angrily shocked by the appointment of Governor Otero. Territorial politicians had known a change would come in 1897 when McKinley would replace Cleveland's appointees with his own, but none thought the governorship would be given to a young party worker not even seeking the office.

McKinley had about twenty men from whom to choose, and among them Pedro Perea of Bernalillo probably had the strongest support as a friend of Catron, Elkins, Judge Waldo, and wealthy Solmon Luna. George H. Wallace, also a likely candidate, received the backing of Las Vegas banker Jefferson Raynolds. Former Governor Prince was sponsored by Max Frost and Edward L. Bartlett, founder of the New Mexico Bar Association. Other candidates included E. F. Hobart, cousin of Vice-President Garret A. Hobart; T. W. Collier; and William H. H. Llewellyn of Las Cruces.[6] The only office sought by Otero was the position of United States marshal in the territory. He had secured letters of recommendation from powerful national senators[7] and sought the support of Catron. Catron had promised to help, but, according to reports, actually worked in behalf of Luna.

When McKinley selected Otero to be chief executive rather than federal marshal, the would-be governors and their numerous backers were stunned. Catron was at a loss to explain the rejection of his candidate's bid. He had written a long letter to the President praising the virtues of Perea, whose selection as a governor would have won wide support from the native population.[8] The President selected a native politician, but it was not Perea. Reasons for the action were twofold. McKinley had made Otero's acquaintance at the 1892 nominating convention and liked him.[9] Elkins, probably Perea's most influential backer, had failed to keep an appointment with the President and the Secretary of Interior on Perea's behalf.[10]

Newspaper support was generally favorable to Otero's selection. One Chicago paper in praising the governor as the first of his race to fill the gubernatorial chair of territorial New Mexico called him "thoroughly American in every way."[11] The *Optic* termed the selection a splendid one[12] and, through Max Frost, even the powerful *Santa Fe New Mexican* supported Otero. Upon the governor's return to the territory after his Senate confirmation, he was received and feted at all the principal cities en route to the capital. At the inauguration in the summer of 1897, the ceremonies were the most "elaborate and impressive until that time ever seen in the ancient capital."[13] Delight and approval seemed to reign but an ominous note was struck for the future peace of the territory when several journals estimated that Otero's appointment marked the end of Catron's political career.

Rejection of his choice for governor following his own defeat in November was a galling experience for Catron. He would have preferred the appointment of someone like George H. Wallace. Wallace was an older man and a comparative newcomer to the territory and Catron could probably have bossed him.[14] But he could not dictate in any way to the "little Governor," as Otero came to be called. For a time, however, Catron made no move to challenge the new chief executive.

The tenuous nature of the Catron-Otero relationship was indicated in a letter Catron sent to Elkins regarding his desire to secure the post of United States attorney for New Mexico. Otero had promised the Santa Fe lawyer that he would use his influence with the President to help him get the position. But when Otero refused to make a clear statement regarding this upon his return from Washington, Catron wrote:

. . . The fact is that Otero is an ingrate and when he left here I raised the money for him to pay his expenses, on the positive promise that he would support me. I learn now that he has told others that if he supports me or recommends me he is afraid he will lose influence with McKinley. That is all bosh . . . .[15]

Despite this, Catron was able to write Elkins four months later that he and Otero were on the "best of terms." Furthermore, he praised him as being a good governor who merited the confidence that the President had bestowed upon him.[16]

But Otero's affront remained in the back of Catron's mind. Nor could he forget that he had once been boss and that the young man he had instructed to control silver sentiment at the Republican meeting a couple of years ago now held a position superior to his. Soon an open, bitter feud broke out—one of the most famous in New Mexico politics. For ambitious Republicans in the territory it was a matter of choosing one side or the other; there was no middle ground. Otero seemed to gain a fast advantage in numbers. Most of the promising young leaders—Colts as they were called—threw in their lot with him. Such names as Iowa-born Holm O. Bursum; Luna; Raynolds; Springer; Llewellyn; Charles A. Spiess, a former law partner of Catron; Doña Ana attorney Albert B. Fall; Rodey; Nathan Jaffa, one of the most successful merchants in the territory; and Clancy eventually sided with Otero. Catron had his allies too. According to Otero they included Eugene A. Fiske, a Santa Fean who had competed with Catron for the position of federal district attorney; Frederick "Fritz" Muller, a Rough Rider friend of Colonel Theodore Roosevelt; and William M. Berger, a New Yorker who operated the *Santa Fe Capital*, a paper which kept up a constant barrage against the governor.[17] Two old Ring members also were listed among the Otero detractors: Prince and Perea.

It is difficult to determine which factor played the more important role in the feud, political rivalry or personal animosity. Both were important and little attempt was made to conceal either. The domineering, dictatorial manner of each man accentuated conflicting political aspirations. The clash was quite evident in another letter from Catron to Elkins in which Catron noted that the governor's goal was to become United States senator when New Mexico was a state. "Otero is puffed up with [the] idea that he has grown to be a very great man . . . ."[18]

The impact of the Otero-Catron feud upon statehood was most unfortunate. Its effects were not felt, however, until Perea was elected as delegate over Fergusson in 1898 by a 2,163 vote majority. Perea's close association with Catron placed him right in the middle of the cross fire. Otero, recognizing the delegate as a Catron man, opposed him and later dismissed his term in Congress as a do-nothing one.[19] Perea in turn accused the governor of working against him.[20] The result was that little was accomplished at this time in the struggle for statehood.

Nevertheless, any honest evaluation of Perea's short tenure as delegate is difficult because of the political forces involved. It is apparent that the delegate was not a dynamic, forceful personality. The casual, dark-complexioned Republican introduced only one statehood bill in Congress and it was never reported by the House Committee on the Territories.[21]

On the other hand, the delegates from Arizona and Oklahoma, the neighboring territories, were exceptionally busy. Delegate John F. Wilson from Arizona introduced two statehood bills during the first session and was assisted in the upper house by Senator Clarence D. Clark of Wyoming who offered a companion measure. He received the support of the Arizona legislature which passed several memorials praying for statehood, one of which was couched in the most forceful terms.[22] Perea received no such support and, if inaction on his part is significant, he must have sensed little sentiment for statehood in New Mexico Territory. Oklahoma was also actively represented as three statehood bills for this territory were introduced during the 56th Congress.

Catron was impatient at the lack of concrete results during Perea's term. In one letter he advised the delegate to get hold of an enabling bill prepared by Republican Congressman Case Broderick of Kansas. The tone of his message was almost paternalistic:

I have been anxiously thinking that you would send me a copy of the Broderick Bill for admission. . . . I think you had better introduce it on the very first day the House meets. You can get one of the Bills and alter its date and change its numbers. All you have to do it [sic] to simply deposit it in the basket which sits on the corner of the Speaker's desk. It will be printed immediately and referred to the Committee on Territories. I wish you would send me also a copy of the Broderick Bill, as it may become necessary to make some changes and I will suggest them to you if I see any so that you may introduce the second bill. I think it is better that the bill, which you introduce and expect to pass[,] should not have any amendments put on it by the Committee. You can always avoid this by finding out what will be agreeable to the Committee and then introduce a bill in accordance with their understanding, . . .[23]

Athough the letter suggests that Perea was almost an incompetent, it must be remembered that Catron was a very domineering personality who took great joy in dictating to those who looked to him for leadership. Perea actually made a pleasant impression. There was much ignorance at the national capital concerning the native people of New Mexico, and Perea's mild manner, although not attracting as much attention as Catron's or Fergusson's more forceful conduct, helped to break down Eastern prejudices against his people.[24]

Otero's opposition to Perea only intensified the feud with Catron. When speculation about the governor's reappointment started, following McKinley's re-election, the true feelings of both men were revealed. Catron launched a campaign against Otero which, if Otero can be believed, must be described as vicious. He accused him of enriching himself in office, and being a gambler and frequenter of saloons before his appointment. Catron probably damaged the cause of statehood when he said that Otero opposed public education, and that in some outlying districts of the territory the Roman Catholic prayer book was the only textbook in use. Otero vigorously denied this. The man whom he appointed as Superintendent of Public Instruction, Colonel Amado Chaves, had a fine record as an advocate of state-supported education.[25]

The governor became especially angry at charges that his administration lacked fiscal responsibility and was alienating capital in the territory.[26] Otero was proud of the way he had improved the finances of the territory, and boasted that more capital and enterprises were attracted to New Mexico during his administration than had been the case since the coming of the Atchison, Topeka and Santa Fe Railroad Company.[27] He had sought and received the co-operation and support of the major enterprises in the territory, including the Santa Fe and all the banks and principal businesses.[28]

Otero also had the support of all members of the National Republican Committee, plus the chairman and 45 of 47 members of the Territorial Republican Central Committee. The only hostile members on the territorial committee were Prince and Catron.[29]

Thus, the preponderance of backing within and without the territory was for Otero. Vice-President Theodore Roosevelt intervened for the governor by laying letters of recommendation from the "best and most representative" men in the territory before the President together with his own "very strong note" stating his personal knowledge of the man.[30] Hence, Otero's reappointment was no surprise, and his selection by Roosevelt after McKinley's assassination was also expected.

Even after Otero's reappointment by Roosevelt on December 12, 1901, Catron and his allies continued a constant barrage of slander and innuendo. Otero's methods of administration were labeled "Oteroism,"[31] and the governor was said to head his own ring. Many years later Otero said of this accusation that "people who live in glass houses should not throw stones."[32] Otero's sympathy for statehood was even challenged when his enemies said that "Oteroism" stood for "double dealing in and treachery to the cause of statehood."[33]

The above charge was most unfair for after the turn of the century the campaign for statehood received a tremendous lift, largely due to Governor Otero, although much of the honor must be shared with the man elected as successor to Perea, Bernard S. Rodey. Rodey, an Albuquerque lawyer, had long been active in New Mexico politics. As a Republican he had served his constituents in the upper chamber of the territorial assembly, and was an active member of the body that framed the constitution of 1889. Born on the Emerald Island and termed a "wild Irishman" by one contemporary,[34] Rodey had a persistent, driving personality which lent strength to any cause to which he dedicated himself. Despite these dynamic characteristics his selection as party nominee to succeed Perea as delegate was the result of a political accident. Solomon Luna, the overwhelming choice of the convention delegates, unexpectedly withdrew his name, making Rodey's selection possible.[35] Curiously, he was nominated by Catron, although his choice obviously had the blessing of the "little Governor." Catron managed to justify this action to his political ally, Perea, on the basis that it would best facilitate statehood.[36] Later he attempted to win Rodey's allegiance by warning him against the Otero clique. Don't "give yourself up to them or support them for anything."[37] But regardless of this plea, the governor and the new delegate worked together harmoniously for four years.

The greatest accomplishment of this new team was that it silenced the opposition to statehood which had existed in the territory since the failure of the constitution of 1889. This was no easy task for although territorial papers made extravagant claims for statehood sentiment there was still an unmistakable undercurrent of opposition. The governor himself, as late as 1888, admitted he was not in favor of admission because of heavy taxation, among other reasons.[38] The religious, political, and economic reasons which brought about the rejection of the 1889 document were also used to oppose statehood. There was a noticeable slack in enthusiasm among Republicans after the defeat of their constitution, although it was not long before they were again in the midst of battle.

It is amusing to note that all through the political fight for statehood, the territorial parties changed policy without hestitation whenever they saw advantage on the other side. Thus, when the Democrats "stole" the legislative assembly in 1895, they became the leaders of the statehood crusade, while the Republicans played the role of critic. In this affair, Lorion Miller, secretary of the territory and a Cleveland appointee, had refused to swear in certain candidates who claimed to be victorious.[39] These gentlemen were all Republicans, and in anger they led the party faithful from the legislature. The howl of the Republican press was unremitting. "Statehood is dead" chimed many of them, while others spoke of it only in the remote future.[40] To vote for any constitution preparatory to statehood would be to perpetuate the power of the "disreputable gang" now illegally in the majority in both branches of the legislature, claimed one influential paper.[41] Democrats, however, were unabashed in their renewed enthusiasm for admission.

The "rump" Democratic assembly, to prove its statehood sentiments, decided to send a memorial to Congress, but in doing so ran into lively opposition. Much of it, of course, could be traced to partisan consideration, but some of the "anti" sentiments expressed were no doubt sincere. One legislator opposed the memorial on the grounds that statehood would raise taxes above the present figures and, when he was accused of near treason, he defiantly asserted that the only people who favor statehood are politicians and a "few damnable land grabbers." Notwithstanding this opposition, the resolution was passed in the lower chamber by a vote of 19 to 4.[42]

Although opposition had seemed to reach a high point in the middle of the nineties, it still persisted into the twentieth century. The old refrain that New Mexico was "ring ridden" and therefore not ready for statehood was repeated.[43] The alleged increase in taxation resulting from admission continued to be emphasized.[44] Fear of being dominated by native influences continued to arouse prejudices and antistatehood opinions.[45] The generally small numbers of immigrants to the newer states demolished a favorite argument of statehood sympathizers.[46] One of the most penetrating and effective of the antistatehood arguments was the question of why New Mexico should assume the burdens of statehood just to give two honorable men like Otero and Rodey seats in the Senate.[47]

Otero and Rodey, however, continued to strongly advocate early admission. In 1901, they began a tremendous effort which literally whipped the opposition into submission. They were materially aided in this campaign by New Mexicans who feared that New Mexico would be cheated of her rightful water resources by hungry neighbors to the north and south, unless statehood were achieved. There was a bill at this time before Congress which threatened to deprive New Mexico of water rights on the Rio Grande for the benefit of land speculators of the El Paso area.[48]

Rodey lent to the campaign a fighting aspect when he said, "every man who doesn't want statehood is our enemy."[49] He was backed by the New Mexican which again took leadership in the statehood movement. It editorialized that there should be "no man in New Mexico who has any ambition that he should place higher than New Mexico's right to statehood."[50] Colonel Ralph E. Twitchell of Santa Fe in writing to the Citizen on April 25, 1901, called for a campaign "to smoke out of their holes" those who were opposed to statehood. His method for doing this would be to ask each prominent businessman and the bigger taxpayers of the territory to endorse statehood in "black and white" so that it could be shown to the territorial committee and others in Congress. He implied that those who refused would probably no longer continue to enjoy business prosperity. Hence, the support of statehood became the criterion of patriotism, with the implied threat that those who opposed admission would no longer find it profitable to remain in New Mexico.

Rodey was extremely active after his election as delegate in 1900 by the comfortable margin of 3,700 votes. He plunged in with an infinite number of energetic ideas. Using his propensity for making friends, he quickly became acquainted with congressmen by employing a page to identify for him various members he wanted to meet.[51] Out of two thousand bills introduced in the House on the first day of the session, Rodey's statehood measure was number two.[52] He discussed statehood wherever he went and made a favorable impression on many national legislators. New Mexicans were impressed, too. Governor Otero called him Bernard "Statehood" Rodey.[53]

The imaginative Rodey undoubtedly deserved this praise. To one territorial journal, he suggested that five thousand letters advocating admission ought to be sent from citizens of New Mexico to members of Congress. From a patriotic view, he felt that this was the least any good citizen could do "for his country."[54] Mr. Rodey showed his vindictive side as he struck back at Judge A. A. Freeman, a critic who had spread the tale that Rodey wanted statehood merely for the sake of being one of the state's first senators. To charges that the judge, a native of Tennessee, was a carpetbagger, Rodey added that he would have been a copperhead in George Washington's day.[55] The judge, a former federal official whom Harrison had appointed to the territorial high court, was very unwise to have said anything about statehood, for federally appointed officeholders were constantly criticized by statehood promoters. Because they were on the federal payroll, they were suspected of fearing statehood as a move that might turn them out of office. Even Governor Otero was not above suspicion on this score.

Rodey later turned his energetic attack on S. M. Wharton, editor of the *White Oaks Weekly Eagle*, a Lincoln County paper. Wharton had contended through his newspaper that New Mexico was already prosperous as a territory and could gain nothing from statehood. He cited the increased costs of government and the higher taxes that would result. Rodey suggested he go somewhere else to live and characterized Wharton as "devoid of patriotism" and fearing native domination. He washed his hands of "Brother Wharton" with the remark: "Don't leave a record of your opposition to the territory's progress as a heritage to your son; he might yet be the governor of the great state of New Mexico . . . ."[56]

The *New Mexican* was as hard as Rodey on the opposition. Although more gentle in dealing with the statehood opposition of good Republicans such as Jefferson Raynolds, it was far less sympathetic when a Democratic politician stepped out of line. For instance, when Jacob Crist stated his opposition to New Mexico's admission in an interview with a Colorado journal, the *Antonito Ledger*, the *New Mexican* acidly remarked that the gentleman was "still a little sore over his defeat for the council last fall . . . ."[57] Even respected leaders such as Luna and J. Francisco Chaves were not immune from criticism. One New Mexico paper, the *San Marcial*

Bee, accused them of "knifing" the statehood cause. They were said to fear new settlers and Anglo influence. Luna was pictured as opposing statehood because it would bring new laws and force him to list his vast herds of sheep on the tax rolls.[58]

The first of the above accusations was a common one. There was considerable doubt about the statehood sentiments of the *Hispanos.*[59] New settlers could change their way of life and threaten their position of influence. The argument that statehood would bring immigration was not a popular one with the native people.

Although both Luna and Chaves could deny such charges and point to a host of defenders to substantiate their character and good motives, the attack was indicative of the new strength of the statehood movement. Territorial papers could without fear of challenge make such dubious claims as that nine out of ten were in favor of statehood,[60] or that less than five per cent were opposed.[61] The desire of Rodey and Otero that New Mexico present a unanimous front in favor of statehood was soon fulfilled. Anti-statehood opinions were expressed mainly in quiet places where men could talk heart-to-heart.[62]

Governor Otero had played an essential part in this forward swing of the statehood movement. His support of Rodey was consistent and he praised the delegate's "gallant struggle" publicly so that none could doubt his sincerity.[63] The governor, of course, had already established good relations with Washington. He was a McKinley find, so to speak, and had enjoyed harmonious relations with the man who first appointed him. The Roosevelt administration also held him in high regard. Otero had not, however, won McKinley to statehood. The late President's attitude on this issue had always been ambiguous. While passing through New Mexico, he caused some consternation at Deming by making only indefinite statements regarding statehood. Although this disappointed New Mexicans, the *Denver Republican* defended the popular executive by stating editorially that McKinley did not wish to appear as influencing the legislative branch of government.[64]

With Theodore Roosevelt it was a different matter. Otero had earned his gratitude by extending complete co-operation in raising the colonel's Rough Rider regiments in New Mexico.[65] The affection Roosevelt felt towards these men was as surprising as it was enduring. During the first Rough Rider reunion at Las Vegas in June, 1899, Roosevelt, who was then governor of New York, promised his full support if New Mexico wanted to become a state.[66] With McKinley's assassination and Roosevelt's accession to the presidency, the territory's hopes for statehood increased. But the President failed to mention anything about statehood in his first message to Congress on December 3, 1901, and the territory's citizens were surprised and disappointed. Delegate Rodey, however, could not be included among these for he publicly described the President as still friendly toward statehood, and claimed his omission of New Mexico occurred because one territory could not be mentioned without reference to all of them.[67]

At the start of the twentieth century, prosperity was returning to New Mexico. The depressed conditions which had produced such movements as Free Silver and Populism had also caused great suffering in New Mexico. The important industries—railroads, mining, and cattle—were at a low ebb as the result of the series of depressions during the eighties and the early nineties. By 1900, a gradual revival of these industries had begun and the population, which had been declining, started to rise again. Optimism soon replaced gloom, the change being generally regarded as a good omen for statehood.[68]

With such a combination of favorable circumstances Otero and Rodey might be expected to have been well pleased. But neither was satisfied, and at Rodey's request Otero called a statehood convention to meet in Albuquerque on October 15, 1901,[69] simultaneously with a territorial fair. At that convention the governor made a forceful address urging statehood. He spoke directly and sharply to those "timorous people" who were afraid of the expense and responsibility which full admission would bring. He suggested writing a strong resolution calling for statehood, and mixed a little bitter with the sweet by pointing to the ridiculously low tax assessment of the territory at present. The assessed value of the territory was less than forty million dollars, "while it is a notorious fact recognized by all who know anything about the subject" that it ought to be at least three times that amount. "You must see to it that proper men are elected to assess the property and equalize its value, so that we may appear to the world what we are in fact, as to our wealth and ability to pay our obligations."[70]

In response to the governor's plea, the convention passed a series of resolutions which were reported by a committee headed by L. C. Grove of San Juan County. These resolutions were essentially in the general style of the Declaration of Independence and contained an arraignment of Congress similar to that directed to George the Third of England.[71] Governor Nathan O. Murphy of Arizona, the territory's former delegate, attended the convention and spoke in behalf of statehood. Four days later Otero reciprocated by speaking at a convention for statehood held in Phoenix. His visit was an example of the tendency of the two territories to work together in their efforts to achieve statehood.

The result of all these encouraging developments initiated by Otero and Rodey was that the movement for immediate statehood was given new impetus. The New Mexican confidently predicted the territory would be admitted by the next Congress. It admonished all federal officeholders to "cut their cloth" by that fact, for if they retained their positions beyond next fall, it would be by the grace of the sovereign people of the State of New Mexico. "Put this in your pipes and smoke it gentlemen, for such is New Mexico's destiny."[72] Even the dethroned Catron would not fight Otero now, for increased land values under statehood meant more to him than political advantage. Prince, equally hostile to the changes wrought by Otero, had not lost his boundless affection for statehood, and for the tenth time he managed to get a resolution through the Trans-Mississippi Congress favoring statehood.[73] At that meeting, held in Cripple Creek, Colorado, Prince not only introduced the resolution but made an effective speech extolling the virtues of the territory.[74] Thus, despite the warfare precipitated by the political upheaval of 1896-1897, statehood in 1901 occupied a vaunted status, above petty partisanship, and New Mexico's prospects for admission appeared never better.

THIRTEEN

The Knox Bill

W ITH PROSPECTS FOR
statehood appearing so bright, the delegates from New Mexico, Arizona,
and Oklahoma decided to pool their resources and make the fight together. The result was an omnibus bill which bore the name of William
S. Knox of Massachusetts, chairman of the House Committee on the Territories. Rodey took credit for this combined action, telling, in a letter to
three New Mexico leaders, how he initiated the measure: "I managed to
get a conference of the delegates, and I suggested to them that nothing
could save us but an omnibus bill and I pointed out the reasons, such as
unity of action, unity of time for consideration, etc. . . ." Rodey did
give credit to Delegate Mark Smith of Arizona for having secured the
co-operation of the entire Democratic membership in the House to resolve in caucus to support the omnibus measure as a party.[1]

The result of this united effort was to wrap the fortunes of the three
territories in one package bill, H. R. 12543, which would enable the
citizens to form constitutions and state governments and be admitted into
the Union.[2] The bill was reported favorably on April 1, 1902. The committee gave affirmative answers to three questions which it had pro-
pounded: Do the people desire statehood? Is the population sufficient?
Do the territories possess adequate taxable wealth to maintain state
governments according to the American standard?

The bill was similar to recent enabling measures enacted by Congress
except for its provision that the constitutional convention in Oklahoma
should by "irrevocable ordinance" express its consent that Congress might

attach all or any part of the Indian Territory to the proposed new state. Another exception to the usual statehood bills was the issue of New Mexico's name. A provision empowered the constitutional convention of the territory to designate the name by which the new state would be known when admitted.[3]

On May 7, 1902, the House began consideration of the Knox bill. "Praise the Lord from whom all blessings flow," telegraphed an enthusiastic Rodey.[4] The bill seemed headed for success with Representative Knox, a respected Republican leader, lending the prestige of his name and committee chairmanship in support of the measure. Influential Republicans as well as Democrats backed the bid, and Knox delivered an extended speech in the House in its behalf. Taking cognizance of the affirmative stand on statehood in both party platforms, he emphasized the bipartisan aspect of the movement.[5]

Although rapid passage seemed likely, the bill did not lack opposition. Republican Representative Charles Grosvenor of Ohio conceded Oklahoma's worthiness, but opposed the admission of Arizona and New Mexico on the grounds that their membership would disturb the political and industrial equilibrium of the county. He compared the omnibus attempt to the old frontier custom of logrolling in which neighbors for miles around came in to help a man clean his land and roll in his logs. He likened the two Southwestern territories to a poor man, "poor in spirit, poor in industry, poor in everything except the genius to attach himself to somebody else . . . ." The "somebody else" was Oklahoma, a territory characterized as a big, enterprising man able to roll his own logs.[6] A number of Eastern newspapers repeated this charge and even the *Arizona Republican* praised Delegate Dennis T. Flynn of Oklahoma for staying with the omnibus measure when he could have had statehood for his territory any time he desired to desert New Mexico and Arizona.[7]

A most interesting development during the House debate was the proposal by Jesse Overstreet, Republican from Indiana, to admit Arizona and New Mexico as one state, rather than two separate ones, under the name Montezuma. It was argued that the measure would bring the two territories into the Union on such a basis as would make their representation in Congress bear some fair relation to their population. Debate on the amendment lasted most of the day, with Representative Lacey of Iowa acting as chief spokesman. Lacey argued that the area of the two was certainly not too big for one state and that the combined population would be sufficient for a state.[8] His assertion did not impress the territorial delegates, however. Rodey claimed that the range of mountains separating the two territories was sufficient reason geographically to keep them from becoming one state. Smith pointed to the new capitol building completed in

Arizona at great expense. Both delegates were relieved to see the Overstreet amendment rejected by a vote of 106 to 28.

On May 9, 1902, the omnibus measure passed the House. The quick success of the bill—only two days of debate were consumed—produced mixed reactions. The territorial press was delighted; one news organ hailed it as a "glorious victory for New Mexico."[9] However, there was still much opposition in the East. Two months before, the influential New York Tribune had said that the population of the two territories was largely of Mexican and Indian stock. It also warned Eastern manufacturers that the wool and livestock interests of Arizona and New Mexico would send representatives to Congress pledged to higher duties than they would desire.[10] There were also rumblings of discontent from the upper chamber. The Brooklyn Daily Eagle reported that leading Republican senators were very bitter about the passage of the bill. Only Oklahoma was looked upon with favor by this group. Furthermore, it was asserted that Senator Albert J. Beveridge, chairman of the Committee on Territories, would be helped in his fight against the measure by the restive attitude of senators anxious to have the session closed so they could return home.[11]

When the bill did reach the Senate, the figure of Senator Beveridge cast an ominous shadow. The measure was sent to his committee shortly after being reported to the Senate on May 12, and now came under the scrutiny of a man with definite ideas on statemaking. Beveridge was sincere in his belief that creation of a new state was of paramount concern to the entire nation because, once admitted, the act could not, by constitutional arrangement, be rescinded.[12]

The senator from Indiana was a colorful and powerful figure in Washington. Elected as a Republican to Congress' upper chamber in 1889 at the age of thirty-six, the young lawmaker soon established a national reputation for his oratorical ability. Always impeccably groomed, the hardworking and dignified Beveridge drew attention in any group. He was a fine conversationalist, and always courteous, but his fast wit and fluency of speech made him a devastating opponent in open debate.[13] Because he was an advocate of American imperialism, Beveridge was in close communion with President Roosevelt and other expansionists. This enhanced his power in the Senate as shown in his appointment as Chairman of the Senate Committee on Territories in December, 1901.

Beveridge was soon deluged with letters from citizens of the territories urging that his committee take favorable action on the omnibus measure. The former owner and editor of the Arizona Republican, using a political ploy, explained to Beveridge that the Territory of Arizona had been "slightly" Democratic in past elections because of the great personal popularity of the Democratic delegate, Marcus Smith, and because of apathy on the part of officials of the two great railroads running through the territory, the Santa Fe and the Southern Pacific, and the managers of the great mining corporations. The writer reasoned that as long as Arizona remained a territory, the class of men elected to the legislature would be very ordinary and easy to control. Consequently, there was little anxiety about statehood among these corporations, and the fact that the territorial delegate had no vote and little power only accentuated the disinterest.[14] Governor Nathan O. Murphy of Arizona echoed these sentiments. The Atchison, Topeka and Santa Fe and the Southern Pacific were both controlled by Republicans as were the other railroad corporations of the territory.[15]

New Mexico's Republican representation should have helped Arizona's cause, but Senator Beveridge found many drawbacks in New Mexico despite the territory's Republicanism. His suspicions were aroused by the unusual concern that certain corporate interests were displaying in New Mexico and Arizona statehood. An early progressive, Beveridge especially wondered why one of his committee members, Matthew S. Quay, was so deeply interested.

Senator Quay, known to be a shrewd and unscrupulous politician, dominated politics in Pennsylvania as if the state were his personal bailiwick. During Cleveland's second administration, he had admittedly speculated in sugar stocks while manipulating the sugar schedule of the Wilson-Gorman tariff.[16] He was a free lancer in the Senate, not belonging to the recognized oligarchy of the Old Guard, but preferring to look after his own interests in his own way. Despite Quay's unsavory reputation, even Beveridge was willing to admit he was brilliant. Notwithstanding his casual dress and unimpressive appearance, the Pennsylvania Republican was a man of great intellectual ability.[17] Beveridge felt that there must be more than mere interest in the territorial people behind Quay's concern with statehood and he determined for this reason, and also because of the many letters received asking favorable action on the bill, to fully acquaint himself with conditions in the territories before taking any action.

The bill remained before Beveridge's committee for five or six weeks without consideration. A disturbed Rodey wrote: "You have filled my cup of disappointment to overflowing . . . ." Favorable action would have meant thousands of votes for the Republican organizations in the territories.[18] Quay decided to take direct action. He wanted a majority of the members to take the bill out of the hands of the committee. Beveridge got wind of this, called a hasty conference with Quay and the three territorial delegates, Rodey, Smith, and Flynn, and warned them that continuation of such activities would cost them much support in the coming fall. Quay feigned agreement, but four days later, on June 23, made a motion in the Senate to discharge the Committee on Territories from further consideration of the omnibus measure. He cited several precedents to support such action and claimed that five of the eleven committee members wished to be excused from any additional consideration of the bill. He said that postponement would only defeat the bill and that the territories were ready for statehood. He then reminded his colleagues that the Republican platform of 1900 had favored early admission for the territories.[19]

Beveridge strongly protested, claiming it was impossible to give adequate consideration to the bill with adjournment so near. He agreed to take up the bill early in the next session but refused to set a specific date for his report. Quay continued his attack and finally forced Beveridge to promise a committee report on the third day of the second session which was scheduled to begin December 1. The Pennsylvanian finally withdrew his demand for immediate action when it was agreed by unanimous consent of the upper chamber that the bill should be taken up on December 10 and made the regular order of unfinished business until disposed of by that body.

About this time, Senator Beveridge decided to precede any report on the omnibus bill with a thorough investigation of the territories. His reasons for such a plan were probably several. First, his passion for investigation and research was well known. An interest in United States expansion once prompted him to travel to the Philippines in order to make a direct observation of conditions there. Also, Senator Orville H. Platt, a man whom Beveridge greatly admired, had proposed such an investigation himself several years ago. Platt's influence with Beveridge is discernible in a letter in which the Indiana senator praises him as one "who is as dear and close to me as if he were my father."[20] The senator's close friend, Dr. Albert Shaw, editor of the Review of Reviews, had also advised him to make the investigation. Shaw had counseled Beveridge as early as January not to make any hasty commitment on statehood for one or more of the territories.[21] Lastly, his suspicion of Quay's motives prompted him to take such action.

On June 27, Beveridge introduced a resolution in the Senate authorizing the Committee on Territories "to sit during the recess of the senate, at such times and places as it may desire, for the purpose of considering bills for the admission of the territories of New Mexico, Oklahoma, and Arizona to statehood . . . ." The resolution, which the Senate adopted, authorized the committee to send for persons and papers, take testimony, and employ a stenographer. Expenses incurred would be paid for from the contingent fund of the Senate.

When Congress adjourned on July 1, Beveridge made careful plans for his coming showdown with Quay. He was fortunate in having powerful friends in the journalistic fraternity. In addition to Shaw he was close to George H. Lorimer, editor of the *Saturday Evening Post*. He was also well acquainted with Frank Munsey, the noted publisher and editor of the *Washington Times*. His association with these men provided him with an excellent medium for influencing public opinion.

Before Beveridge left on his tour of investigation, he took advantage of these personal connections by arranging for additional testimony to be ready for the committee upon its return from the Southwest. He wrote Shaw urging him to approach such influential people as Frederick Remington and Owen Wister, both closely associated with the West. He also asked him to get in touch with professors from such institutions as Columbia, Yale, Harvard, and Princeton, who by their experience could testify as to "the soil, its aridity, the impossibility of further population till irrigation shall have done its work and the character of the present population."[22] Although proclaiming complete impartiality, he indicated to Shaw later that he hesitated to write these men himself, or call them before his committee, unless he knew to what they would testify.[23]

The Indianan tried to insure journalistic support for his coming venture by writing Lorimer and emphasizing to him the importance of having public opinion on their side.[24] He also wrote Dr. Lyman Abbott of the *Outlook*, stating that if the report of the committee were unfavorable to the admission of New Mexico and Arizona, there would probably be a desperate fight. He stressed the importance of having the committee reinforced by the "best and solidest public opinion of the country."[25] All of the letters seemed to indicate that Beveridge's approach in this investigation would be far from unbiased.

Although the senator received desired support from his friends in the press, he was not so successful in obtaining "well informed" witnesses for the committee. Shaw reported only "meager success" in securing the sort of people who would give Beveridge's committee report the prestige it needed.[26] However, Owen Wister did send a reply. Although he declared his testimony would have no weight because his personal knowledge ceased in 1895, he did advise:

But were I opposing the admission of Arizona, I should apply to the Wells-Fargo Express Company of San Francisco for a record of the hold-ups in which their safes have been dynamited or their messengers injured on the Southern Pacific Railroad, and also on the Santa Fe . . . crimes [are] so plentiful as to make holding-up rather than raising plums, the chief industry of the would-be state . . . .[27]

Beveridge began his investigation, then, having laid careful, although not entirely foolproof, plans for its success. Shaw, as early as July, 1902, began the fight against statehood. In an article appearing in his *Review of Reviews,* he opposed the omnibus bill because "grotesque" inequality of representation would exist in the upper chamber if six more members were added from states with sparse populations.[28] Six committee members were appointed by the Senate to accompany Beveridge on his tour through the territories, though only three made the trip. Two of them, Republicans Henry E. Burnham of New Hampshire and William P. Dillingham of Vermont, met Beveridge in Chicago on November 10, 1902. A third one, Populist Senator Henry Heitfield of Idaho, joined the committee en route. Accompanying the group was a staff of stenographers and interpreters. The schedule called for visits to New Mexico, Arizona, and Oklahoma, in that order.[29] On the eve of the committee's departure from Chicago, Beveridge set the tone of the investigation by insisting that this was not to be a mere junket but a trip of "serious hard work from early in the morning till late at night."[30]

The committee began its hearings at the Castañeda Hotel in East Las Vegas, New Mexico, on Wednesday, November 12. Although the members were greeted by a brass band, Beveridge refused to speak or take part in any festivities, saying he was under pressure of serious business.[31] The first witness called before the committee was William J. Mills, chief justice of the supreme court of the territory. When questioned as to the character of the population, he stated that in some counties it was predominantly "American" while in others, "Mexican." He admitted that interpreters were used in the courts to interpret the testimony of witnesses and arguments of counsel.[32] The committee made special note of the fact that the grocery store and meat market signs were in Spanish, and they were informed that the majority of people in that area were Spanish-speaking.[33]

Albuquerque was the committee's next stop. Here an elaborate reception was planned with two brass bands to greet the group, followed by supper at the Alvarado Hotel and a ball at the Commercial Club.[34] Despite a plea from Beveridge to Rodey to cancel these time-consuming activities, the reception invitation was accepted at the behest of Senator Heitfield, who knew that to decline the invitation would hurt those who had arranged the affair.[35] On November 14, the committee heard the mayor of Albuquerque, C. F. Myers, testify that the city was strictly "American," with a population of from seven to eight thousand. He claimed statehood would bring in necessary capital to finance the promising mineral development, as well as induce more people to settle in the territory.

Several days later at Las Cruces, the committee discovered that not all the internal opposition to statehood had been silenced. Martinez Amador, a volunteer witness, testified against admission on the ground that his people were not prepared for the changes statehood would bring. "My people all belong to the Mexican race. They come from Old Mexico and I think our people is not able now to support statehood, because most of the people here is ignorant, and I do not think we are ready to support statehood yet for about ten years, until our children grow up."[36] That this statement was extremely unpopular was revealed in a letter written by Amador's widow after his death three months later. "I doubt not," she stated, "but what the disease that carried him off was brought on by constant worry and mental strain caused by those who declared themselves his bitter enemies, for the truthful testimony rendered unsolicited by him . . . ."[37]

The committee concluded its New Mexican phase of the investigation at Carlsbad on November 21 after conducting hearings at Las Vegas, Albuquerque, Las Cruces, and Santa Fe. Although it had secured testimony from a number of important officials including Delegate Rodey, it had also brought before the committee census enumerators, justices of the peace, school teachers and superintendents, official interpreters, newspaper editors, postmasters, and ranchers. Its "flying trip"[38] through the territory provoked dissatisfaction from more than one newspaper. The editor of the *Roswell Weekly Record* had been particularly offended because that community's plan of welcome had been rebuffed. The committee arrived in Roswell in the darkness of night, stopped just long enough to have another engine attached to their private car "and rolled out . . . as quickly as they rolled in."[39]

In Arizona similar testimony was taken. More than a third of the witnesses questioned were census enumerators, indicating Eastern distrust of census procedures and figures.[40] In addition to questions regarding the accuracy of such tabulations, six of the ten census takers were questioned as to the nationality of their districts, while three were asked if interpreters were needed. Information concerning the aridity of the soil and provisions for its irrigation was also a source of interest to the committee.[41]

At Prescott, Judge Richard E. Sloan, associate justice of the territorial supreme court, said that although the land for irrigation was not limited, the amout of water was, unless storage dams were built to hold the water until it was needed. At Phoenix, Governor A. O. Brodie spoke proudly of the irrigation potentialities in the territory and praised the 7,000 or so Mormons in the territory as good citizens, not potential troublemakers.[42]

Of special value to Beveridge in his coming showdown with Quay was testimony that the brother of Senator Boise Penrose of Pennsylvania was part owner of the Commonwealth Mines of the territory. Penrose was Quay's close protege in state and national politics. In other testimony, it was discovered that statehood advocate Senator William A. Clark, a Montana Democrat, owned the profitable United Verde mine.

The committee moved quickly through Arizona, too, refusing offers of entertainment at both Phoenix and Tucson, and hastened on to Oklahoma, arriving at Woodward on November 22. This stop was followed by a brief hearing in Oklahoma City and the visit was completed at Guthrie on November 24. The line of questioning pertained to the willingness of the Oklahoma and Indian territories to unite and seek admission as a single state. The response was generally favorable. One witness testified that the legislature had repeatedly declared itself for such a union, the last declaration being a memorial to Congress in 1902 passed without a dissenting vote.[43]

The hearing at Guthrie terminated the investigation of the three territories which had begun in Las Vegas, New Mexico, only thirteen days before. Several days later Beveridge wrote to his friend, Frank Munsey, and gave him a detailed account of the investigation. The census enumerators, justices of the peace, and federal judges had been questioned because of their familiarity with the educational progress being made in the territories.[44] Careful perusal of this list would indicate that the senator intended to base much of his case on population figures, use of Spanish in legal transactions, law enforcement, and progress in education.

In another letter, this time to Shaw, Beveridge again revealed his suspicions concerning Quay's motives in advocating statehood for the territories. The Pennsylvanian's interest in New Mexico was attributed to his desire to help an old friend, William H. Andrews, secure a seat in the United States Senate and sell bonds for a new railroad being built in the territory.[45] Earlier, Beveridge had insinuated to Shaw that a good deal of Pennsylvania capital had been invested in this railroad.[46] The *Chicago Tribune* pictured the railroad's construction as the scheme of a large syndicate engaged in building railroads in Arizona and New Mexico. This syndicate wanted to see statehood for both territories because, in the event of success, the syndicate would be assisted by the two new states "to the amount of $15,000,000."[47] Beveridge felt statehood was desired by big business interests only because of their belief that if the territories were admitted the bonds of the road could be sold "for several points higher."[48]

Andrews was considered by Quay the greatest lobbyist in the world.[49] He had served as Quay's lieutenant in Pennsylvania politics and, as a state senator from Crawford County, had managed to run the state legislature exactly as his boss wanted. Andrews, an astute politician, had friends in both parties and often acted as representative for such powerful corporations as Standard Oil, the Pennsylvania Railroad, and the Pullman

Company. Andrews always had plenty of money on hand to help influence Pennsylvania's legislature, described as the most venal in the country. The tall Andrews with his flourishing mustache was a careful dresser, and often enjoyed an expensive cigar as he concluded deals in an unassuming manner.[50] While in Pennsylvania he acquired the sobriquet "Bull," a nickname which remained with him the rest of his life.

Andrews also served as chairman of the Pennsylvania Republican state committee and at that post proved that he knew how to manipulate "all the ins and outs of the great political organization."[51] As a fund raiser for the state committee, his aggressiveness in seeking contributions from federal as well as state employees prompted a polite but firm protest note to Quay from Theodore Roosevelt.[52] Despite this indiscretion, Quay's friendship with and faith in Andrews never changed. After the voters retired "Bull" from the upper chamber of the state body, Quay continued to regard him as a valuable friend.

Andrews came to New Mexico largely because of his interest in gold mining. This had started in the late 1890's as a result of talks with Llewellyn, who during the Spanish American War became a major in the Rough Riders and a close pal of Theodore Roosevelt. Andrews soon acquired a gold mine in Sierra County, eight miles from Hillsboro, called El Oro Mining Company or the Philadelphia Milling and Mining Company.[53] As this effort was not entirely successful, Andrews became interested in railroad building. He became acquainted with Willard S. Hopewell, a cattleman in Sierra County, who helped him secure a seat in the upper house of the territorial legislature. He in turn placed Hopewell in contact with W. H. Torrance, the head of a group of Pennsylvania capitalists.[54] The result of this alliance was the Santa Fe Central Railway, incorporated on December 7, 1901, under the original name of Santa Fe, Albuquerque, and Pacific Railroad Company.[55] The road, which was under construction from November, 1901, to December, 1903, stretched from Torrance, a town on the Southern Pacific Railroad, north to Santa Fe for a distance of approximately 116 miles.[56]

In addition to Quay's connection with Andrews, Beveridge also suspected that the senior senator from Pennsylvania was being influenced by his colleague from the Keystone State, Senator Penrose. Penrose was heir apparent to the leadership of the Quay Machine, having been trained in all the arts of the machine politician by the master himself.[57] The closeness of the two men, and the fact that Senator Penrose's brother was "a miner in Arizona," provoked Beveridge's suspicion on that score, too.

Beveridge concluded that the strong backing Quay and the other statehood supporters were receiving from the Democratic minority was due to purely political consideration. He felt certain that "these territories will after the first Senators constantly send Democratic Senators to Congress and that is their only reason [for such support]."[58]

When Congress convened in December, Beveridge was ready. On December 10, he gave the majority report of the committee which recommended that Oklahoma and the Indian Territory be admitted as one state, but that statehood for New Mexico and Arizona be withheld indefinitely. His major objection to the admission of the latter territories was that they lacked sufficient population to become states. Other criticisms in the report were that the majority of people in New Mexico were Spanish, and a large percentage of the people could speak only in their native tongue, necessitating such practices as the use of interpreters in court proceedings. Illiteracy was high, and the arid conditions of the Southwest imposed serious limitations on agriculture.[59]

Beveridge reaffirmed his belief in the importance of statemaking, claiming that the welfare of the nation must be considered as well as the interests of the proposed new states. Consequently, population was given great emphasis. In the Northwest Ordinance, 60,000 was fixed as the minimum population requirement for statehood. Although Beveridge regarded this as adequate for the United States in 1787 when the total population was only four million, he felt it was entirely too small for the twentieth century. Based upon the census of 1900 he reasoned that 1,530,000 would be a more realistic number.[60] Governor Otero's June 30, 1902, census estimate of 246,700, a figure almost 20 per cent above the 1900 figure, fell far short of that number.

The contrast between the majority report and the report to the Secretary of the Interior made by the Governor of New Mexico five months previous could not have been more pronounced. Otero, contradicting the 33.2 per cent illiteracy estimate in Beveridge's report, had said that less than 18 per cent of the population was illiterate. He praised the systems of irrigation which were being rapidly developed in the territory, claiming that more than 3,000 miles of irrigation ditches were in operation. Moreover, he described the stock industry as flourishing.[61]

Arizona did not fare much better in the Beveridge report. Although conceding that a majority of the people were Americans he estimated that there were 30,000 "Mexicans." Illiteracy was placed at 29 per cent of the total population, and 23.52 per cent of the people were reported as not speaking English.[62] Irrigation canals served but a fraction of the total acreage of the territory.

Only Oklahoma and the Indian Territory received the endorsement of Beveridge. He pointed out that these territories, unlike Arizona and New Mexico, did not need statehood for their development. The Indian Territory without any government at all had attracted hundreds of thousands of American citizens from the states. Beveridge advocated a single state government for the two neighboring territories.

Quay's report, released the same day, strongly disagreed with Beveridge's, claiming that it was unfair to say that New Mexico's population was insufficient. This question had played no part in the admission of other territories to statehood. Besides, the census, in his opinion, was poorly taken and incomplete. As for attacks on the Spanish-speaking population, the foreign element in the territory was smaller than anywhere in the country. Quay's report further stated that since New Mexico was acquired as a territory in 1848, all of its inhabitants, except for the very oldest, were born on American soil and therefore entitled to the rights and privileges of American citizens. The territory was complimented for the strides it had made in education. Arizona's right to statehood was defended, too, because the mines, forests, and grazing land of both territories would compensate for land made useless because of lack of water.

A minority report on the Beveridge findings was delivered five days later by Democratic Senator William B. Bate of Tennessee. It differed little from the Quay report and, like the latter, it urged passage of the Knox bill without amendment so that the long probationary period might come to an end. Congress, it felt, had no right to inquire into the character of a population if its numbers were sufficient to meet the requirements of the past.[63]

If these dissenting reports were comparatively mild, the editorial comments of the territorial papers were not restrained in the least. A highly indignant press soon made Senator Beveridge the most unpopular man in the Southwest. The Albuquerque *Evening Citizen* referred to the evidence gathered by the Beveridge committee as "insufficient, and incomplete testimony."[64] The *Optic* criticized the closed-door procedure used by Beveridge, and likened his refusal to receive voluntary statements to the course of a paid lawyer trying to secure evidence to justify an argument.[65] The *Denver Times*, owned by Colorado's Senator Thomas Patterson, a friend of the territories, was sure that the committee's sole purpose was to get adverse testimony.[66] Even Beveridge's home-state newspaper, the *Indianapolis Sentinal*, editorially attacked the logic of his report.[67]

A flock of telegrams from business and professional men of New Mexico and Arizona were sent to Quay. The consensus of these messages was that the Beveridge report grossly misrepresented conditions in the two territories.[68] Rodey also sent a letter to the Senate on February 15, 1903, in which he denied that New Mexico had reached the limit of her irrigation possibilities. His letter further stated that citizens of the territory resented being called "Mexicans" and "Foreigners." The committee investigation was dubbed a "cursory race" through New Mexico.[69]

Beveridge, however, received the support of many prominent newspapers in the East and Midwest. The *Indianapolis Journal* praised the committee's findings as an "unanswerable argument" against admission of the two Southwestern territories.[70] More important was the backing he received from President Roosevelt, who not only failed to mention statehood in his message to Congress, but in a letter to Quay stated that the facts presented to him regarding statehood for Arizona and New Mexico made "a strong case against the admission of these 2 territories."[71] Powerful Senate support for the Indianan was also assured. According to the Philadelphia *Press*, such Republican leaders as Platt, Nelson Aldrich, William B. Allison, Eugene Hale, Henry Cabot Lodge, and Mark Hanna were opposed to the admission of Arizona and New Mexico.[72]

Beveridge realized that the presence in Washington of a strong, vocal lobby for the territories meant there would be a head-on conflict in Congress. Proponents of the omnibus bill claimed they were in a majority and determined to override the adverse Beveridge report.[73] "We are in a fight for our lives," Beveridge wrote a friend.[74] Earlier he had predicted that interested politicians led by Senator Quay and the Democratic minority might attempt, for purely political reasons, "to 'bull' the bill through regardless of merit or argument."[75] The senator's prognostication was accurate enough, for on December 11, the day after the Beveridge report had been given, Senator Quay called for a vote on the Knox bill.

Beveridge, of course, protested this maneuver, maintaining that no intelligent consideration of the measure could be made until members of the upper chamber possessed a printed copy of the report plus other necessary evidence. Powerful men in the Senate, among them Aldrich of Rhode Island and Lodge of Massachusetts, supported Beveridge in his stand. Senator Hale of Maine accused Quay of trying to force a vote without alloting even the necessary time for debate. Their arguments were apparently sufficient for, following two days of debate, a postponement until after the Christmas vacation was secured by Beveridge on December 16, 1902.

Although the first clash between Quay and Beveridge lasted only two days, it was almost immediately apparent that Beveridge and his supporters intended to use the filibuster to prevent the admission of New Mexico and Arizona. One statehood supporter, Senator James K. Jones, an Arkansas Democrat, remarked cynically that, were he opposed to a bill and in the minority, he would resort to exactly the kind of tactics to defeat it that were being employed by the anti-statehood forces.[76]

Editorial comment throughout the nation paved the way for a bitter debate. The *Boston Daily Globe* on December 16 charged Beveridge and his Republican backers with political expediency. The recent elections in the territories were not satisfactory to the Republican managers in Congress, for, although Republicans won in New Mexico, they lost in Arizona and found their control in Oklahoma reduced to a "scanty" majority. The *Arizona Republic* remarked that newspapers which "are always ready to take up the cause of worthless half-breeds in South America, or the cause of savages in Samoa or Sula [sic], or the cause of the boxers in China against the forces of civilization, are always blind to some of the crying wrongs at home." It was referring to the influential *Chicago Tribune* and the New York *World* which were firmly convinced that the people of Arizona, New Mexico, and Oklahoma were "not deserving of sympathy" and were "unfit for statehood."[77] The *Optic*, however, maintained its sense of humor with a little poetic barb directed at Beveridge:

> We are knocking for admission.
> On the union's fast-barred gate;
> We are asking for permission
> To come in and be a state,
> But the congress cannot hear us,
> And they will not let us through—
> How can they hear when Beveridge
> is knocking—knocking, too?[78]

But Beveridge was not dissuaded from his course by the furor created by his opposition. "It is sickening—disheartening—to work on a problem . . . like this which affects the whole United States and which will affect the United States a hundred years from now to find a stumbling block in some man because of his personal ambitions," he wrote some years later. This obvious reference to Quay was followed by revelation of another motive. The idea that ten thousand votes in Nevada should be represented by two senators, while Indiana with three million people had the same voting power "is something awful."[79]

The Indianan showed his determination not to admit "unrepresented" territories in an optimistic letter to Shaw. "Thus far all is well. We have anticipated every move the enemy have made and checkmated them." He described his silencing of a move by Senator Hanna to allow the bill to come to a vote and rely upon a presidential veto, if necessary, and then reiterated his decision to oppose the passage of the omnibus measure. ". . . I myself would prevent it if I had to read the Century Dictionary, the Hebrew Scriptures and everything else in the course of the three weeks' speeches."[80]

On January 5, 1903, after the Christmas recess, Senate debate on the Knox bill resumed. Knute Nelson of Minnesota, a member of the Committee on Territories and a firm Beveridge supporter, opened the discussion. Selecting from a tall pile of manuscripts on his desk, he spoke movingly in behalf of Oklahoma, but firmly opposed the admission of Arizona and New Mexico. Then, in a Norwegian accent which had a disastrous effect on the Spanish words, he read passages from the early Spanish history of the area in order to prohibit constructive discussion.[81]

The Minnesota Senator wasted more than a week with his long-winded orations, and was succeeded by another colleague anxious that action be delayed. Beveridge's strategy was becoming clear. He would enlist the services of senators friendly to the cause and, instead of dissipating his own energies in prolonging debate, simply devote himself to keeping his supporters active. Beveridge's backers were primarily from New England and Eastern states, where fear of Western power seemed greatest, and included, in addition to Nelson, William P. Dillingham of Vermont, Eugene Hale of Maine, Chauncy M. Depew of New York, Henry E. Burnham of New Hampshire and John Kean from New Jersey.[82]

Arrayed against this powerful minority block was the Quay faction, including Democrats and a few influential Republicans. Foremost among the latter group were Senator Joseph B. Foraker of Ohio and New Mexico's old friend, Senator Elkins of West Virginia. Foraker, a fiery orator and intensely partisan individual, had won prominence during the Reconstruction period by waving the "bloody shirt." A child of the rough, tough generation of laissez-faire, he found it impossible to accept a more regulated, responsible form of business activity. He increasingly came into conflict with the more enlightened Roosevelt. His close association with big business made him one of the first politicians to be retired from office because of such connections.[83]

Foraker's motives in advocating statehood for Arizona and New Mexico were not as evident as were Quay's. He claimed that as a member of the Committee on Resolutions, which framed the Republican platform in 1900 pledging the admission of the remaining territories, he could take no other course. He expressed astonishment at the bitter opposition on the part of many leading Republicans to fulfilling their party pledge. Also, personal investigation had revealed to him the worthiness of these territories.[84] Perhaps the senator had a personal reason, too. His brother, C. M. Foraker, was United States marshal for New Mexico, and prior to this had been a prominent stockman in the southern part of the territory.[85]

Democrats active in support of the Knox bill included John T. Morgan of Alabama, Joseph L. Rawlins of Utah, and Henry M. Teller of Colorado. Morgan, one of the oldest members of the upper chamber in point of service, saw only "politics" behind Beveridge's opposition. Rawlins and Teller, representing neighboring states, felt a regional affinity for the aspirations of the Southwestern territories, although Teller had an additional motive. He and a friend had bought a farm in Arizona Territory near Yuma, and in 1904 they seriously considered raising Algerian dates for the market.[86] The Coloradan energetically defended the statehood aspirations of Oklahoma, New Mexico, and Arizona, equating the attack on these territories with an attack on the West. "They will be States some day in spite of the fear that there may be a preponderance of votes in this body against some other section of the country." He pointed accusingly to the New England delegation in which only one of twelve senators favored statehood. They were afraid of the "power of the West," he said, so they voted as a "solid Phalanx" against it in the Senate.[87]

Earlier, Teller had answered charges regarding the alleged Mormon threat in Arizona and New Mexico. Senator John C. Spooner of Wisconsin was particularly concerned about this "menace." Using recently admitted Utah as an example, he pointed to Mormon domination in politics. To be a candidate for the United States Senate, a person had to be an apostle of the church, hold a high office, or receive the consent of the hierarchy. He also questioned the allegiance of the 7,000 Mormons in Arizona and New Mexico. Teller corrected Spooner's population figures. The Mormon population of New Mexico did not exceed 500. Furthermore, he was confident that the citizens of both territories could handle the problem. As for the concern about the spread of polygamy, he charged that the opposition had previously admitted that only one of five Mormons in Arizona practiced polygamy. Colorado's senator also answered the "slanderous and libelous" criticism directed against native New Mexicans when he talked of the thousands of new European immigrants last year who were not ten per cent as good as the people of New Mexico.[88]

Teller was effective, but could speak only for the minority party. Foraker, on the other hand, was a power in the Republican party, which controlled the Senate, and he gave unceasing support to the Knox bill. When Senator Nelson challenged the Indian census in Arizona, implying that because 5,000 Indians were omitted from the count, the percentage of whites appeared greater than it actually was, Foraker lambasted the entire census. If the census enumeration could miss 5,000 Indians, he declared, how could the Beveridge committee have maintained that not a single white person was omitted in the 1900 count.

Having undermined the accuracy of the census, he turned to Beveridge's proposal to make the population requirements more in keeping with the tremendous influx of people since 1787. There was no sliding scale in the Ordinance of 1787. The only requirement for admission was that a territory should have 60,000 people. Foraker did accept the unit of representation rule also suggested in Beveridge's majority report. According to this, a new state should have at least a population equal to the ratio of representation as used in the previous census for apportionment of representatives. However, he claimed a third rule would make this implausible and unfair. If the Treaty of Guadalupe Hidalgo were to be applied to New Mexico and Arizona as it had been to California, these territorial people would now be granted citizenship regardless of population.

Taking note of Arizona's 1900 population count of 122,931—some 70,000 fewer than New Mexico's—Foraker directed attention to the fact that only two states, Maine and Utah, had a larger population at the census taken prior to their admission than did the Southwestern territory.[89] Foraker also felt that the opponents of the Knox bill were inconsistent in their statements regarding illiteracy in the territories. They held that Arizona must first build up a school system and educate herself for statehood, and at the same time urged that the Indian Territory be made a state in order to properly develop education and eliminate illiteracy. Referring to the committee's report that saloons and gambling houses stayed open night and day and even on Sundays,[90] Foraker noted that these same laws existed in several states of the Union.

It was said that slow land development and the desperate need for irrigation made New Mexico and Arizona poor prospects for either settlers or statehood. The Ohio senator emphasized that it was only natural for land development to be slow, considering the confused and unsettled legality of the Spanish grants. People coming west could not be certain that the land they settled upon in New Mexico would remain in their possession. Recently, however, the land grant situation had been greatly improved, and Foraker stressed the fact that a steady stream of land seekers were now entering the territory. If irrigation programs could be expanded, the area had great agricultural potential.

Along with Quay, Foraker thought it only honorable that Republicans fulfill their pledge to support that plank of the party platform calling for statehood for the territories. Beveridge replied that the senators were not bound by any plank of the platform which had not been an issue in the preceding campaign. Elaborating on his unique interpretation, he declared that not a single speech concerning statehood was made by either side and no newspaper outside the area directly concerned mentioned the subject.

The eloquent Foraker clashed openly with another power in the upper chamber, Senator Lodge of Massachusetts, who frankly opposed the admission of New Mexico and Arizona. Once, during the long filibuster, Lodge praised the balance which existed between the lower house where representation was according to population and the upper house where it was by states. The result of this balance was that the Senate of the United States was the only successful and powerful upper chamber "in all the history of parliaments." But he warned his colleagues of the unbalanced situation that would result if a minority in the country acquired a disproportionate amount of power in the upper house.[91]

The issue that brought Foraker and Lodge into direct controversy was the question of the Pima County railroad bonds. Pima County in Arizona had issued bonds to build a railroad within its borders. Although the securities had disappeared mysteriously from the safe of the county authorities and no railroad was ever constructed, the bonds had somehow fallen into the hands of holders anxious for payment.[92] A complicated legal tangle ensued with contradictory court decisions and legislative maneuvering. Lodge claimed that the citizens of the territory, although at one time agreeing to make the necessary payments in order to maintain a good credit standing, were now anxious to renege and believed that in achieving statehood they could avoid this obligation. Foraker told a different story and produced evidence that the territory did want to make payment on the bonds. A telegram from William Herring, former attorney general of the territory, was presented which declared that payments would be made as soon as it was known whether a recent court ruling had decided upon compound or single interest on the coupons. Foraker's evidence was accepted and the opposition dropped the subject.

Despite valiant efforts by Foraker and Teller to force consideration of the omnibus bill, the filibuster conducted by Beveridge and his colleagues continued to be effective. Some legislators stressed the tax relief the territories enjoyed under their present status, an obvious reference to the fact that the federal government paid the salaries of the governor, executive officers, and judges of the territory. Others cited the great need for irrigation in the Southwest. Elegant Senator Depew of New York described irrigation attempts in New Mexico and Arizona as futile. He ridiculed the shallowness of the Rio Grande, stating that "the peculiarity which those New Mexico rivers have, which belongs to no other streams in the world . . . [is] their bottoms are on top."[93] Several senators also contended that the people of the territories did not want statehood. The testimony of Amador, the simple Las Cruces farmer, was used repeatedly.

As the stormy congressional session drew to a close, the cause of statehood in the 57th Congress seemed doomed. For almost three months, the Knox bill had been debated and the Quay forces had not been able to bring it to a vote. The shrewd Pennsylvanian had made a total of twenty-seven motions to secure action on the matter. Some had called for an immediate vote while others merely attempted to establish a definite date for such a vote.[94]

Throughout the debate, Quay was confident he had the necessary support to enact the bill into law. They had the votes to pass the bill, he declared in January. The majority of senators were in favor of it, and "it is being willfully . . . obstructed by discussion, as no one knows better than the senator from Indiana." Quay refused to ease up on his attack and prevented action on any other measure until February 19. From that time until the close of the session in March, he contented himself by merely asking for a vote each day while allowing action on a tariff measure and appropriation bills.

The senator was a shrewd parliamentarian; on January 28, he introduced the omnibus bill as an amendment to both the agricultural appropriation bill and the sundry civil appropriation bill. On March 3, it was offered as an amendment to the Philippine tariff bill. Although none of these devices succeeded—Quay withdrew the latter proposal in discouragement—it was not because of any lack of effort on the senator's part.

Quay's conduct was generally supported throughout the territories even though he admitted to the press that his motives were personal and his efforts would benefit friends with property interests in the Southwest.[95] The New Mexican claimed that the name of Matthew Quay would live longer in the hearts and memories of New Mexicans than other public figures who might regard themselves as more esteemed.[96] The Arizona Daily Gazette on February 26 lauded the "magnificent" fight waged by Quay and the backing he had received from Foraker, Penrose, and others. Rodey's conduct also was recognized and New Mexico leaders solidly supported his effort. "He talks statehood everywhere and anywhere to anybody and everybody . . . he is never exhausted," commented one journal.[97]

Although Beveridge had dedicated himself to stopping Quay and his schemes, he had not underestimated the worth of his adversary. He regarded Quay as a genius and dealt with him accordingly. Beveridge managed his filibuster with great diligence, meeting Quay's thrusts with courtesy and firmness. Both men were afraid to leave the upper chamber during the lengthy filibuster without a trusted lieutenant on guard. Even when all precautions were taken, there was still danger of a surprise move. One day while Beveridge was out to lunch, Quay began to press energetically for an immediate vote. Beveridge was notified of the threat and came running into the Senate Chamber to launch into a long extemporaneous speech, clutching his napkin in hand the entire time. On another occasion, the Indianan had arranged for three men to give speeches and, when two failed to show up, he passed a note to the first speaker, Senator Depew, pleading: "Go on, for God's sake, or we are lost." When Beveridge ran out of parliamentary tactics, he hid in secret, as a last resort, in Gifford Pinchot's home for a week knowing that no vote could be taken unless he, as chairman of the Committee on Territories, were present. After that, he spent about three additional days "holed up" in a hotel at Atlantic City.[98]

The personal duel and the legislative stalemate it had produced at-tracted much attention. One journal referred to the debate and the ac-companying filibuster as the "longest continuous hold-up in the history of the country." It was compared with the famous deadlocks resulting over the repeal of the Sherman Silver Purchase Act and the controversy sur-rounding the Wilson-Gorman tariff measure.[99] Although a majority of the territorial newspapers tended to praise Quay and damn Beveridge, opinion outside the area was about equally divided. The *Washington Times*, the publication of Beveridge's friend Munsey, harshly denounced Quay's pol-icy of keeping the Knox bill before the Senate as one of "rule-or-ruin."[100] The *Kansas City Journal*, on the other hand, declared that the jealousy of the East and the insistence of that section on retaining a preponderance of power in Congress would always remain an obstacle to the admission of new states.[101] Regardless of which side had the most support, no doubt more people were now aware of the long struggle for statehood being waged by New Mexico and Arizona than at any other time.

A possible solution to the statehood issue was to join New Mexico and Arizona and admit them as one state along with Oklahoma. Rumors of such a compromise began to circulate in the cloakrooms and chambers of the capitol building during the month of January, 1903. According to the proposed solution, Oklahoma would enter the Union with the proviso that the Indian Territory should be annexed in 1907. The new state comprising the two Southwestern territories would be called Montezuma. When the Arizona section of the new commonwealth reached a population of 300,-000, it would be separated into another state and admitted under a new enabling act. A conference, which included such Republican leaders as Aldrich, Quay, Beveridge, Foraker, Hanna, Louis E. McComas, and Kean, decided to submit the compromise to the Democrats. But Democratic leaders rejected the proposal, ending the hope of any statehood action dur-ing the 57th Congress.

The attitude of Washington leaders toward this jointure proposal was a bit confusing. Although the scheme did not remove all the objections to admission, it did reduce them to minimum. By restricting the number of states erected within the area, the political power of the West would be curbed—by two senators, at least.[102] This satisfied a number of Easterners. There is evidence that Beveridge worked hard to bring about such a com-promise, although his own views regarding the prospects for its success were not optimistic.[103] Quay, too, seemed willing to accept such a solu-tion. Perhaps this is why Senator Thomas Patterson of Colorado felt that the senator from Pennsylvania did not keep up the fight to the last. The Democrats, of course, had no particular reason for supporting the com-promise, as they stood a good chance of capturing the seats of two of the three territories under the original omnibus bill. But the President, according to the *Denver Republican*, was in favor of such a proposition.[104]

In the territories there was, initially, much strong feeling against the jointure compromise. More material was printed in the newspapers of Arizona against joint statehood than about any other phase of the controversy.[105] On the other hand, there was a growing realization throughout the territories that acceptance of jointure was probably the only way to achieve statehood during the next session of Congress. Subsequent failure of the Knox measure only strengthened this belief.

With the adjournment of the Congress on March 4, 1903, the fate of the omnibus bill was sealed. Statehood was again denied to New Mexico and Arizona, but Oklahoma was a casualty, too, despite the lack of strong opposition and forceful arguments opposing her admission. The omnibus plan, which was a boon to the much-maligned territories of New Mexico and Arizona, proved a definite liability to Oklahoma. With the Democrats refusing to compromise on the jointure proposition, the Republican leadership in the Senate had to take all the territories or none at all. It chose the latter course.

Although Beveridge deserves most of the credit—or the blame—for defeat of the measure, there is evidence that a number of powerful Republicans exerted significant influence in this regard. It is difficult to estimate, for instance, how successful the filibuster would have been without the influence of Nelson Aldrich, the Republican leader in the Senate. One authority has claimed he was the real power behind the filibuster.[106] Whether this be true or not, it is evident that Senator Quay resented the support Aldrich gave to the opposition, and he and Teller and other disappointed advocates of statehood helped to defeat Aldrich's banking bill during the last days of the session in retaliation.[107]

Regardless of the crosscurrents of support and opposition, Beveridge and Quay were the leaders, and the Indianan had outgeneraled his opponent by use of parliamentary maneuvers. Quay's pride was hurt, but New Mexico, Arizona, and Oklahoma were, of course, the real losers. They could only take consolation in the fact that their case was given more publicity than at any time in the past.

FOURTEEN

The Jointure Movement

ALTHOUGH THE COMPROMISE
proposal to join Arizona and New Mexico as one state was rejected during
the 57th Congress, consideration of jointure subsequently took new forms
and dominated the statehood movement for the next four years. The Republican majority in Congress, led by the clever and energetic Beveridge,
confident after his victory over Quay, gave strength to the jointure movement. The proposed union was not without historical precedent since
Arizona had been part of the Territory of New Mexico until 1863. A need
for better government in the area, and a desire on the part of Arizonans
for independence, had brought separation. President James Buchanan, in
his message to Congress on December 8, 1857, had recommended the division,[1] which finally was accomplished six years later. The current proposal
for union, however, occupied a singular position among enabling acts.

There had been discussion of jointure for the territories as early as 1893,
when the *Washington Post* had commented unfavorably on the idea. The
fact that the total area of the combined territories would still be approximately 30,000 square miles less than that of Texas was considered by this
journal a poor argument for admitting another state of "abnormal and
uncomfortable size."[2] Senator John Sherman of Ohio wrote the following
year that there was "a strong feeling . . . to annex Arizona to New Mexico and admit the 2 as one state."[3] The Philadelphia *Press*, unfavorable to
separate statehood in 1902, had suggested jointure for the Oklahoma and
Indian territories as well as the two Southwestern ones, so that the four

territories would become two large states.[4] Finally there had been the effort in 1903 during the debate over the Knox bill.

There were numerous motives behind the movement. The East had long been jealous of the growing political power of the West. Representatives from that section resented Western states with their scant populations acquiring so much power in the Senate; jointure would limit that representation. In addition, Western tendencies to accept radical ideas such as Free Silver and Populism made this section suspect. Furthermore, the ceaseless agitation of the few remaining territories made the East fear that some Congress in the future might yield to their claims and grant the West eight additional senators.

One thing was certain. Joint statehood as a solution was not the result of any desire by residents of Arizona and New Mexico. The citizens of these territories had been asking for statehood for years but always for single statehood. There was no animosity between the two territories, but rather a lack of mutual interests. As Prince put it, the two territories were more disconnected with reference to personal, business, and social relations than many states separated by a greater distance. New Mexico in her business and trade relations faces east, while Arizona looks toward the west.[5] The people of the Oklahoma and Indian territories, on the other hand, were favorable to the jointure idea. One government would be less expensive and their consolidation would create an area of comparable size to such neighboring states as Kansas and Nebraska. Admitted singly, both territories would be dwarfed by their giant neighbor to the south, Texas.[6]

Despite the distinct lack of enthusiasm for jointure in Arizona and New Mexico, there was considerable pressure to admit them under some arrangement. The Republican party felt a special obligation, having been in power three years since its 1900 platform promise of statehood for territories. Republican President Roosevelt had been personally committed to the proposal since the first Rough Rider convention in 1899, and his attitude toward joint statehood was vital. Soon after Beveridge had issued his majority report in December, 1902, a group formed opposing both Quay and Beveridge and secured the President's support for a jointure attempt. But this support was immediately withdrawn, possibly on Beveridge's advice. Later, however, Beveridge reversed his stand and announced that he favored joint statehood because New Mexico and Arizona obviously desired jointure.[7]

Governor Otero indicates in his memoirs that Roosevelt was edging toward jointure as early as 1903. At the end of that year, Otero, Solomon Luna, and J. F. Wilson, the territorial delegate from Arizona, went to the White House to discuss the statehood proposition informally with the President. All three expressed the opinion that jointure would be unfair to both territories. According to Otero, their remarks did not make the slightest impression and they could plainly see Roosevelt was against them.[8]

One of the first important territorial figures to be converted to jointure was New Mexico's most enthusiastic statehood advocate, Delegate Rodey. A human dynamo in working for the cause of admission, Rodey had finally reached the conclusion that separate statehood was impossible. "Unless a majority of our people instruct to the contrary . . . ," he asserted in an interview with the *Evening Citizen*, "I am going to agree to jointure, if terms are favorable and we can get it."[9]

Rodey's support was timely, for on April 1, 1904, Edward L. Hamilton, a Michigan Republican who was chairman of the House Committee on the Territories, introduced a bill providing for the admission of the Oklahoma and Indian territories as one state, and Arizona and New Mexico as another. The latter two were to come into the Union under the name Arizona with the capital at Santa Fe. Although the location of the capital seemed a concession to New Mexico for the loss of its name, many objected to changing this historic designation, especially in view of the fact that Arizona had been a part of the territory until separation in 1863. "But it would be strange if when the daughter returns to its old home, the mother's name should be changed to that of the child, instead of the latter resuming its old position," declared Prince.[10]

The bill, labeled a Republican measure, passed the House on April 19, 1904, the vote being along strict party lines. It was sent to the Senate the following day, but when Congress adjourned a week later, no action had been taken. Delegate Rodey's agreeable attitude did not prevent a number of prominent territorial citizens from expressing their unhappiness with the situation. Governor Alexander O. Brodie of Arizona wrote Beveridge that the people in his territory were unalterably opposed to any union and would prefer indefinite territorial status to jointure.[11] His words echoed the sentiments offered in a resolution drawn up by the citizens of Phoenix during a mass meeting and sent to Beveridge on February 4, 1904.[12] Action followed words and, as the third session of Congress opened on December 5, 1904, former Arizona governor, Nathan O. Murphy, and several territorial officials joined their delegate in Washington to work against the bill.[13]

All was not serene in New Mexico, either, despite the pro-jointure stand taken by Rodey. The New Mexico territorial assembly memorialized the Senate not to pass the jointure bill.[14] Catron, who still had an influential voice in territorial affairs, opposed it with unyielding firmness. In a letter written to Elkins, he stated that nine-tenths of the people of New Mexico were opposed to jointure. Admitting that he would be the big gainer (Catron estimated that the value of his immense land holdings would double six months after statehood had been achieved), he still believed New Mexico was entitled to single statehood. He also thought it extremely unfair that under jointure New Mexico would assume a debt about four times the size of her own. The debt of Arizona was $4,000,000, according to his estimate, while New Mexico's was only $1,000,000.[15] This was one issue upon which Catron and Otero were agreed. The "little Governor" broke with his friend Rodey, saying jointure was neither acceptable or desired.[16]

While the bill was being considered in the Senate, the audacious Foraker intervened, offering an amendment which required a separate referendum on the matter in each territory. The joint statehood bill would not become law unless a majority of electors in both New Mexico and Arizona approved it. Thus, Arizona with her smaller population would not be forced into union with New Mexico if the impatient citizens of that territory were to choose jointure rather than no statehood at all.

The Foraker amendment, altering a Republican-sponsored measure, created a furor in the upper chamber. Democrats were delighted for, with thirty-three of them in the Senate, plus a formidable little group of Republicans, they could make their influence felt.[17] Separate statehood for the territories continued to be a more attractive alternative to them than jointure, for indications of Democratic sympathy by Southwesterners had not gone unnoticed. The first real test of strength occurred when Senator Thomas R. Bard, a California Republican, introduced an amendment that eliminated all reference to Arizona but conferred statehood upon New Mexico. This proposal proved to be the point around which most of the subsequent proceedings revolved. Although adopted by a close vote as the Senate sat as a committee of the whole, the amendment was finally rejected in a tie vote by the Senate proper.

Senator Augustus O. Bacon, a Democrat from Georgia, offered the next amendment, in which all reference to statehood for New Mexico and Arizona was eliminated and Oklahoma and the Indian Territory were admitted as one state. The motion was accepted by a vote of 39 to 36. No sooner had this action been taken than Senator Bard introduced another proposal. His second motion, which again called for the admission of New Mexico, had been only slightly revised to comply with necessary parliamentary procedure. This amendment was accepted in a close vote.[18]

The final decision would now be made in the House, where the jointure bill had originated. Considerable doubt was expressed that the House would recede from its original position in light of the large majority it had given the jointure measure the preceding year. Nevertheless, the New Mexico legislative council, delighted with the prospect of admission as a single state, urged the House to concur in the Bard amendment.[19] But the House refused to accept the Senate version and a conference was requested.

Hopes were high for an accord between the two bodies of Congress which would bring some form of statehood to New Mexico. Rodey was still convinced that only through the jointure arrangement would New Mexico be admitted, and he helped the Speaker of the House, "Uncle Joe" Cannon, to break a revolt of 33 recalcitrant Republicans by persuading 22 of them to drop their opposition to Cannon's desire that the bill be sent directly to conference.[20] Senator Teller, however, an opponent of jointure, cut hopes for a quick agreement by notifying Beveridge and the members of his committee that he was against sending the Senate version to conference. This refusal to compromise caused the dejected Rodey to feel that his four years of struggle to achieve statehood for New Mexico had come to naught. "The bill is dead. I feel it. It is like the shock of death."[21] The delegate's worst fears were borne out when the conferees failed to report and Congress adjourned without taking action on statehood.

The Territory of Arizona accepted the verdict with rejoicing and cautious optimism. The influential *Arizona Republican* warned editorially that the danger of jointure was as imminent as ever.[22] But the editorial opinion next door was of a different nature. The *Albuquerque Morning Journal* dejectedly predicted that statehood prospects would not be promising for the next four years because of the attitude of Arizona politicians.[23]

Meanwhile, politics in New Mexico were not peaceful. Rodey's determined advocacy of joint statehood had brought him into sharp conflict with Governor Otero. The split was widened over disagreement as to who should be appointed chairman of the Republican territorial committee. Rodey wanted to retain Frank Hubbell, the Republican boss of Bernalillo County, who had been instrumental, he felt, in his success at the polls. Otero was bitterly opposed to the retention of Hubbell at this or any job. The "little Governor" disliked the Albuquerque Republican and was aware of the rumors of graft that surrounded him.[24] Perhaps it was due more to Rodey's stubbornness on this issue than to his firm stand on jointure that Otero withdrew support.

Just prior to the nominating convention on September 12, 1904, Otero threw his support to a comparative newcomer, "Bull" Andrews, the Pennsylvania promoter and friend of Quay. The shrewd Andrews was quick to take advantage of the favorable development. His backers were alleged to have convinced Rodey supporters that it was not necessary for them to bear the expense of a long trip to the convention. They need only give a proxy to an Andrews worker who would vote for them. Needless to say, these proxies were cast for Andrews.[25] Another piece of deception was practiced by Major Llewellyn who had asked Rodey for the privilege of placing his name before the convention. When this was granted, Llewellyn arose and placed the name of Andrews before the convention. Delegations pledged to Rodey then cast their votes for Andrews, who was nominated.[26]

The campaign which followed showed that much of the area's wealth was supporting Andrews. The candidate, who was chief promoter and president of the Santa Fe Central Railroad and other enterprises, traveled the territory in a private car called the "Rocket." The car was part of a campaign train that included a parlor car for the band, a baggage car, plus an engine and full crew of trainmen to prevent any delays. On board was a larder filled with choice meats, poultry, fruits, and vegetables, as well as the finest liquors, cigars, and cigarettes.

Rodey was nominated by a group of independent Republicans. Democrats endorsed him, too, contributing $4,000 as an inducement to him to make the race. But Rodey had little if any chance against an officially endorsed, well-financed candidate. When final results were in, Andrews had a clear majority of 22,305 votes as opposed to the 17,125 votes cast for the Democratic nominee, G. P. Money. Rodey only polled 3,419.[27]

Throughout the rest of his term, Rodey continued his support of joint statehood. On April 8, 1905, a meeting was held in Albuquerque to organize a statehood league from which a great movement for jointure could be launched. Rodey was made secretary and a member of the league's executive committee. Other members of the group, auspiciously named the New Mexico Non-Partisan Joint Statehood League, included Judge A. A. Freeman, the chairman; William B. Childers; and former delegate Joseph.[28]

While sentiment was crystalizing in favor of jointure in New Mexico, it was being deliberately undermined in Arizona. Governor Joseph H. Kibbey's outspoken opposition to it had so angered Beveridge that he wrote an angry letter to the President questioning the right of territorial governors to interfere in such matters. "Does it not . . . appear to you that it would be well for the governors of these territories to keep their hands off on this question which is a policy affecting the nation?" he queried.[29] Roosevelt promptly answered, "Governor Kibbey is acting entirely within his rights, and . . . the people of Arizona are acting within theirs, in transmitting any kind of respectful protest they wish to make."[30] This fair presidential attitude must have been recognized by the citizens of Arizona, for agitation to defeat joint statehood continued unabated, and an anti-jointure convention was held in Phoenix on June 9, 1905.[31]

Beveridge, whose commitment to jointure was becoming firmer, was alarmed and angered at this resistance. To prevent any such ideas from taking root in New Mexico, he informed Rodey that if the Hamilton bill were defeated at the coming session, New Mexico and Arizona would not be admitted to the Union as separate states for fifty years. He also boasted to Rodey of his loyalty to the cause of joint statehood even though this position injured the statehood prospects of Oklahoma and the Indian Territory. "I could have passed Oklahoma and Indian Territory in fifteen minutes at any time by chopping New Mexico and Arizona, but I promised to stand by you and I did . . . ."[32]

Despite the petulant tone of Beveridge's letter, he and Rodey had become good friends. Their dedication to jointure had brought them together in a common cause. Because of this, Rodey felt no misgivings about asking favors of the Indiana senator. On May 2, 1905, still smarting over his defeat as delegate, Rodey suggested to Beveridge that if Otero were only in favor of jointure there would be practically no opposition to it in New Mexico. By June, Rodey came right to the point, stating he was in desperate need of a job and thought that the governorship was to his liking.[33] "If the President wants to aid the cause, he ought to appoint me governor of New Mexico. I will venture to say, that merely doing this will make New Mexico practically unanimous for jointure inside a month . . . ."[34] Rodey also revealed a revenge motive when he informed Beveridge on October 30, 1905, that Otero along with Frost and Bursum had called a meeting of the Republican central committee to pass an anti-jointure resolution, and that he was doing all he could to thwart it. "Oh: that Otero was [sic] fired."

Beveridge did recommend to the President that Rodey be made governor. "He is honest; he is loyal; he is industrious; he is brave."[35] Although Roosevelt did not accept the suggestion, he nominated Rodey as district judge of Puerto Rico, which prompted the delighted Beveridge to advise his friend "to drop all thought of the long struggle that has already eaten up so many of your best years."[36]

Two other pertinent situations developed about this time. One concerned the replacement of Otero as governor and the other the scandal which emerged regarding the past life of New Mexico's new delegate, Andrews. Both events were to have an important bearing on the statehood movement.

Although the President had not officially committed himself to joint statehood, he was obviously leaning in that direction. Otero's stubborn opposition could not have improved relations between the two men, which had never been particularly warm. Besides, Otero's dictatorial manner had made him numerous enemies, not to mention the undisguised ill-feeling Catron continued to bear him despite a common opposition to jointure.

Rodey's removal as delegate brought these differences to light. Otero had made a persistent attempt to dominate New Mexico politics; thus, Rodey was eliminated because he stood up for Frank Hubbell. Shortly after Beveridge's visit to New Mexico, the governor had removed Hubbell and his brother Tom from their offices as assessor and sheriff of Bernalillo County. Hubbell blamed the governor for a subsequent defeat suffered at the hands of a fusion ticket formed to oppose his control of county politics. In retaliation, he joined Catron and other enemies the governor had made during his nine years in office. This opposition badly disrupted the Republican party, already in a state of confusion. To restore party harmony, the President requested Otero's resignation in terms that could not be refused and the governor acceded.[37]

Although Otero's step down was not totally unexpected, Roosevelt's choice of Herbert J. Hagerman as his successor surprised all. Hagerman, who was the son of one of the territory's empire builders, J. J. Hagerman, was only thirty-four years of age at the time, and had spent three years prior to this appointment as assistant secretary of the American legation at St. Petersburg, Russia. His father had had both successes and failures as a railroad builder and reclamation promoter in the Pecos Valley.[38] Young Hagerman's selection over better-known men was probably as much due to his isolation from New Mexico politics as any other reason.

Roosevelt's choice did not please Beveridge. The senator had hoped to see Rodey appointed, but more than that, he suspected that Hagerman's views toward jointure were hostile ones. "I don't know him," he wrote his friend Pinchot, "and he may be all right; but it don't look or smell good to me."[39] The Denver Republican, however, a staunch friend of jointure, believed the views of the new governor would reflect those of the President and that he would support the cause.[40]

The other situation having an important bearing on the jointure campaign was the scandal caused by the suicide of a clerk at the Enterprise National Bank of Allegheny, Pennsylvania. This affair cast serious reflection upon the character of New Mexico's new delegate to Congress and adversely affected the movement toward statehood. In a note left by the unfortunate clerk, Andrews was blamed for a $300,000 shortage found in the bank's accounts. It seemed that the clerk, T. Lee Clark, used his position as bank cashier to advance Andrews funds to finance the activities of the Santa Fe Central Railroad. When the deception was discovered, the clerk took his life. The bank examiner investigated and brought a $52,000 suit against Andrews for money the delegate allegedly received.[41] Although Andrews later asserted he had paid back the money, he could not prove it.[42] His case was not helped when he made preparations to go to Europe just at the time the suit was announced. The Pittsburgh *Post* had no doubt about his guilt and felt that the incident would materially affect the actions of Congress on the question of making new states.[43]

Rodey quickly seized upon this incident to justify his position to Beveridge, saying, the national administration can now see "what sort of an outfit defeated me, and what sort of outfit Governor Otero and his minions hitched up with, and they may believe some of the report, that did not tell half the facts, as to corruption and bribery that my defeat and Andrews['] election was brought about by."[44]

Less than two months before the opening of the 59th Congress, Representative James A. Tawney of Minnesota, a number of fellow congressmen, and several personal friends began a tour through Arizona. This was a particularly interesting development because Tawney and his associates had been invited by Frank Murphy of the Santa Fe, Prescott and Phoenix Railroad, and their expenses were to be paid by the railroad company.[45] It was rumored that Arizonans hoped the visit would convert Tawney and his colleagues, supporters of jointure, to support of single statehood. In fact, this would have been a remarkable feat, as Congressman Tawney was the Republican whip in the House and a close personal friend of Speaker Cannon.

The Tawney party was given the red-carpet treatment, conducted through the territory on a special train consisting of two pullmans and eight private cars.[46] They were dined in the best hotels, and practically every town they visited expressed opposition to joint statehood. Rodey nonetheless did his best to present some jointure sentiment to the touring congressmen. Buttons plugging joint statehood were sent to citizens in Holbrook, Winslow, Gallup, Flagstaff, and other locations.[47] The Tawney junket's return through New Mexico was of particular concern to the pro-jointure citizens. One letter warned Beveridge of possible attempts by "anti's" to wire ahead to Kansas City in order to get interviews favorable to single statehood from members of the Tawney party as they arrived there.[48]

A series of interviews given to the *Kansas City Journal* by the returning lawmakers indicated that members of the group had indeed changed their minds about jointure. Tawney declared that his next vote would meet with Arizona's approval. Republican Representative Henry C. Adams of Wisconsin claimed he had voted for jointure earlier because of ignorance, but now was against the idea. Congressman Thomas F. Marshall, a North Dakota Republican, expressed the opinion that joint statehood would be a wrong to both territories.[49] Beveridge was unimpressed, noting that the entire expense of the trip was paid by the railroads and mining interests, and that three of the tour members had stock in Arizona mines.[50]

When Congress opened on December 4, 1905, there was great interest throughout the capital as to the opinion President Roosevelt would express on the jointure issue. Beveridge was quite concerned about Roosevelt's position. ". . . I am nervous and apprehensive lest our leader should fail us as the battle opens," he wrote Shaw.[51] This was surprising in view of the President's statement to Beveridge that a jointure recommendation would be part of his message to Congress despite "active intrigue" against it.[52]

True to his word, Roosevelt on December 5, 1905, recommended jointure in his presidential message to Congress. Calling for the admission of New Mexico and Arizona as one state and Oklahoma and Indian Territory as another, he expressed profound regret that so much time already had been spent on the question. Moreover, he felt that the present territorial subdivision should not be considered as binding on Congress.[53]

The President's call for statehood has been attributed to his love of the West and gratitude to the Rough Riders, but evidence does not justify such a conclusion. In one letter, the President, referring to jointure for the Southwestern territories, declared: "The only reason I want them in as one state now is that I fear the alternative is having them as two states three or four years hence."[54] Roosevelt evidently did not regard jointure as too important. Writing to Sir George Trevelyan on January 12, 1906, he placed joint statehood fifth in a five-item list of measures he hoped to see enacted while he was President.

Regardless of the motive, Roosevelt's call for joint statehood brought acclaim from jointure supporters. The Washington Evening Star commented that the President's recommendation would count for much because of his knowledge of the West and sympathy for its people.[55] Rodey described the "wild" delight of people in Arizona and New Mexico at hearing the proposal. "It has silenced the anti's in New Mexico," he assured Beveridge.[56]

But, of course, it was not true that opposition in New Mexico had ceased. The Optic viewed with suspicion the strong pro-jointure feeling in Albuquerque. Perhaps its citizens wanted joint statehood because they felt that Albuquerque with its central location would eventually become the capital of the new state.[57] Arizona papers were not dissuaded from their previous anticonsolidation stand either. With the exception of the Bisbee Evening Miner and a few other papers, most news organs in the territory continued their opposition.[58]

The President's official blessing resulted in several new statehood bills.

Representative Hamilton, as chairman of the territorial committee of the lower house, presented a joint statehood bill (H. R. 12707)[59] while Beveridge introduced a similar bill (S. 1158) in the upper chamber. Curiously, New Mexico's new delegate, "Bull" Andrews, introduced a measure calling for separate statehood. Although his was out of step with the Washington scene, it clearly showed a reluctance on the part of some Republican leaders in New Mexico to accept the jointure proposition.

Sensing a fierce struggle in the House, the Republican members met on December 14. After lengthy discussion, they decided unanimously in favor of admitting Oklahoma and the Indian Territory as one state. But there was no such unanimity regarding Arizona and New Mexico. Hamilton presented his over-all jointure plan, and was ardently supported by Speaker Cannon. But there was intraparty opposition as Tawney and Adams, back from their Arizona tour, spoke against jointure. A vote on joint statehood for New Mexico and Arizona was finally taken and the measure was approved as a binding commitment on House Republicans, 110 to 65.[60]

A hearing was held by the House Committee on the Territories, presided over by Hamilton, from January 16 to 20. A large anti-jointure delegation from Arizona gave their views on the proposed measure. Rodey and Andrews were on hand to put in a good word for joint statehood. The ex-delegate's position came as no surprise, but the apparent about-face of Andrews' was not entirely expected.

Prior to the hearing, jointure supporters received a setback as their bill became tied up with a Philippine sugar tariff measure. The Republican leadership in the House had hoped to displace the tariff bill with the joint statehood measure on January 8, but a stubborn minority of Western Republicans who opposed the joint admission of Arizona and New Mexico prevented this. The beet sugar group in Congress, sensing an opportunity to defeat the Philippine tariff measure, traded on this anti-jointure sentiment to form a bloc. By uniting, they had hoped to defeat jointure in return for such amendments to the sugar tariff as would render that bill unacceptable to the Senate.

The revolt, which not only represented definite sentiment against jointure but also a defiance of the wishes of the President and Speaker Cannon, was eagerly joined by Democrats. The House leadership managed to take up the Philippine bill first, this measure being strongly backed by the administration. This meant that the jointure opposition would have to kill the tariff measure merely on the promise that the sugar element would help them to achieve separate rather than joint statehood.[61] The new development caused much confusion and apprehension until John Sharp Williams of Mississippi, the minority leader, undermined the conspiracy with a speech in behalf of the Philippine measure which induced many

Democrats to withdraw from the bloc.[62] As a result, the tariff bill escaped relatively unscathed in the House as the anti-jointure bloc hoped to do better on the statehood issue.

Meanwhile, it appeared that the Hamilton bill, as the measure came to be called,[63] would not be reported until it was certain that there was enough support to insure the adoption of a favorable rule. The rule to be submitted by a majority of the Committee on Rules provided that the bill be debated briefly and voted upon without amendment. As long as the House leadership felt that a majority of Republicans might insist upon the right to offer amendments to the bill, the leaders seemed determined not to report the measure.[64]

Finally on January 23, 1906, the bill was reported, with the recommendations suggested by Roosevelt in his message to Congress. It also incorporated generous provisions for land and cash grants to the new, consolidated states. The state of Arizona, created from New Mexico and Arizona, was to receive four sections of non-mineral land in each township for the support of common schools. Oklahoma, being less arid, was to receive two sections. Both states were given $5,000,000 to be invested in a trust for common schools. Each was to receive 5 per cent of the cash realized from the sale of public lands for a permanent fund, the interest of which would be used to maintain public schools. As expected, the capital of Arizona was placed at Santa Fe, at least until 1915 when a popular referendum would be held to determine the permanent location. Guthrie was selected as the temporary capital of Oklahoma. Suffrage in both the states was well guarded and there was a strong antipolygamy clause in the measure.[65]

A stinging minority report was released under the name of Representative John A. Moon of Tennessee. The minority regarded the jointure bill as "oppressive, tyrannous, and vindictive," and called the proposed union of New Mexico and Arizona obnoxious to both. It contended that Arizona, because of her smaller population, could be forced into the consolidation regardless of a negative vote on the measure.[66] A series of reasons why each was entitled to separate statehood was inserted in the appendix.

The next day, debate on the bill began with consideration of the rule under which the measure would be managed. Almost immediately a resolution was presented making the statehood bill the special order of the day. Debate was to continue until the next day at 3:00 P.M., unless sooner exhausted. At that time, the House would consider the statehood measure as a committee of the whole, without "debate, intervening motion, or appeal." Discussion on the resolution was spirited and sometimes bitter. The opposition argued against the provision by which Oklahoma and the Indian Territory could not be admitted unless Arizona and New Mexico were admitted as well. Under the terms of the resolution, the former territories were not allowed a separate vote on whether they desired statehood under the present arrangement.

Insurgent Republicans as well as Democrats fought against the resolution. Representative Adams reiterated his opposition to the joint statehood plan, claiming he knew from personal observation that residents of Arizona were against it. He was joined in this resistance by a number of other congressmen. The big surprise of the day, interpreted by Arizona's delegate as "the cruelest cut of all," was the surrender of Congressman Tawney. Although maintaining that neither territory was ready for admission into the Union either separately or jointly, Tawney announced that as a member of the controlling party he would submit to the will of a majority of its members. His act was described by the *Indianapolis News* as the unfortunate failure of a man to act according to his convictions.[67] Tawney's desertion, however, brought the approval of the resolution by a vote of 188 to 158.

On the following day, January 25, 1906, the Hamilton bill passed the lower house by a comfortable margin, 195 to 150. The Republican leadership under its powerful Speaker, "Uncle Joe" Cannon, had won an important victory. The measure was sent the same day to the upper chamber where it was referred to the Senate Committee on Territories, to be favorably reported four days later by Senator Beveridge.

As expected Foraker again introduced an amendment very similar to the one he proposed the previous year. According to this proposition, introduced on February 9, 1906, it would be the duty of the governors of New Mexico and Arizona, within thirty days following the passage of the jointure bill, to proclaim a special election. Statehood would be the sole question to be decided. If a majority in either territory voted against the proposal to consolidate, the entire act would be invalidated.[68] Speculations as to why the Ohio senator again stepped into the fray to lead the fight against jointure varied. It may have simply been a part of Foraker's consistent pattern of opposition to the policies of President Roosevelt. Although Arizonans were high in their praise of Foraker and attributed only the loftiest motives to his support, the *Albuquerque Morning Journal* speculated that the senator had been deceived about the true condition in the territories, and in proposing the amendment he was allowing the mining corporations to use him to inflict the very condition on the people he was seeking to prevent.[69] But the Louisville *Courier-Journal* praised the "inherent merit" of the amendment and asserted that based upon its "abstract justice alone" it should not fail.[70]

Beveridge opposed Foraker's second attempt to amend the jointure proposition with characteristic determination. During a prolonged Senate debate extending from February 15 to March 8, he declared that if the

Foraker amendment were accepted, it would give 10,000 people in Arizona an opportunity to control the destinies of 300,000 to 400,000 people. He reasoned that there were only 21,000 voters in Arizona, and since it is never possible to get all registered voters to the polls, 10,000 of these would have control of the future of the entire population in both territories. There were 10,000 men employed by the Copper Queen Mining Company alone. The senator had long been leery of the special interests in Arizona whose opposition he believed was inspired by "nothing in the world except a desire to escape taxation."[71] The cattle interests would naturally oppose consolidation because the grazing lands from which they derived their wealth would be incorporated into school grants. Railroads would fight because under territorial jurisdiction they were totally exempt from taxation. Mining interests would fight because of the increased taxes they feared, while office seekers opposed jointure because there would be twice as many offices to fill under separate statehood.

Beveridge's arguments for the jointure bill were similar to those he gave in the last Congress, emphasizing that the two territories would be an economic as well as a physical unit if they were consolidated. The tax burden would be doubled, but only half the load would be placed upon the people. Jointure would cut in half the number of state officials, and the people would pay only half as many salaries.[72] Beveridge used his great eloquence to convert the members of the Congress to consolidation. His finest, most movingly rhetorical speech on the subject was his "Arizona the Great" oration, given on February 6, 1905:

And what a glorious State this new Arizona would be, . . . fit sister for that imperial Commonwealth upon her east on whose brow the the [sic] Lone Star shines, and of that mighty Pacific State upon her west which faces the greatest ocean of the world, with a coast line longer than that of most of the countries of the earth; Arizona, second in size and eminent in wealth among the States of the greatest of nations; Arizona, standing midway between California and Texas, three giant Commonwealths guarding the Republic's southwestern border; Arizona, scattering with one hand the fruits of the Tropics and with the other hand the products of the Temperate Zone; Arizona, youngest of the Union and the fairest; how proud of her her citizens would be; how proud of her the American people would be; how just a place she would hold in the nation's councils. Not querulous, irritable, and contentious because of her scant population, but large minded, generous, and conciliatory, because of the knowledge of her greatness; not apologetic for her numbers, but serene in her popular equality with her associated States; not Arizona the little, but Arizona the great; not Arizona the provincial, but Arizona the national; not Arizona the creature of a politician's device, but Arizona the child of the nation's wisdom! How its people and the people of the Republic will glory in such an Arizona!

At the end of this speech Beveridge categorically announced that the territorial people desired such a union. "No wonder selfish interests dare not let the people vote for or against such an Arizona, for all their wealth and all their organization could not defeat the people's will at the people's ballot box on such a question."[73] Thus, the senator chose to regard the powerful opposition to his program as representative of special organizations "and their money."

Despite Beveridge's support of the Hamilton bill, the Foraker amendment was adopted on February 9, 1906, by a vote of 42 to 29. But Senator Julius C. Burrows, who already had cast quite a shadow on the statehood movement, renewed the lengthy struggle by proposing an amendment which would remove from the joint statehood bill all reference to Arizona and New Mexico, leaving only the question of consolidating Oklahoma and Indian Territory. His proposition, carried by a close vote of 37 to 35, followed an earlier rejection by just one vote. Although the Burrows amendment came as a shock to proponents of consolidation, it caused great celebrating in Arizona. Half the population of the city of Tucson was said to be out on the streets rejoicing to the tune of band music after the news was heard.[74]

But the celebration was premature. The House had not yet taken action, and under its tough chief the probability of surrender was remote. Cannon disapproved the Senate's latest move and felt that the House should postpone action on the measure indefinitely rather than give in on the Burrows amendment. In his opinion, the prestige of the lower house was at stake.[75] During a Republican caucus on March 15, the party voted to stand by the statehood bill as enacted in the House and to call for a joint conference, a decision Speaker Cannon insisted was binding on all members.

Despite the strong stand taken by the party caucus, Representative Frank Mondell of Wyoming, acting on behalf of the insurgents, introduced a resolution calling for House agreement with the Burrows amendment to eliminate New Mexico and Arizona from the bill. The motion was overwhelmingly defeated by a vote of 123 to 43. Decisive on the surface, this ballot nevertheless did not include the votes of some 83 Republicans, who stayed away to avoid being bound by caucus action, and 137 Democrats, who were united in favoring the Senate version.[76] Regardless of the potential opposition, House leadership decided to act quickly. On March 22, the Rules Committee presented a special rule which provided that the statehood measure be taken from the Speaker's table with the Senate amendments rejected and a conference with the upper house be requested. This rule was adopted by a vote of 175 to 156, and the statehood measure was sent to conference.

As the Senate also proved obstinate, the Hamilton bill remained in conference for more than two months. The situation began to look black for the supporters of jointure, and it was even rumored that the administration would accept the Foraker amendment to allow a referendum if no better alternative were offered.[77] Finally, on June 12, a conference report, which became known as the Carter compromise, rescinded the Burrows amendment and recommended the passage of a measure somewhat similar to the one proposed by Foraker. Whereas the Foraker proposal allowed the people of Arizona and New Mexico to vote as separate territories at a special election solely on the question of consolidation, the conference amendment suggested that each territory should not only vote on the jointure question but should at the same time choose candidates for a constitutional convention and elect officers for the proposed state.[78]

On June 13, the Senate adopted the conference report, and similar action was taken by the House on the following day. With the acceptance of the Carter compromise, the long congressional fight over joint statehood came to an end. Roosevelt was delighted. "I'm particularly interested in seeing New Mexico and Arizona admitted to statehood while I'm president."[79] The bill was signed on June 16, 1906, and during the ceremony, the President reached across the table to shake the hand of Beveridge. "I congratulate you upon the great work finished and a great battle splendidly fought."[80]

Although the joint statehood bill as finally enacted was not precisely what Roosevelt and Beveridge wanted, they had accomplished much toward achieving their goal. The Carter compromise was considerably more palatable to them than the amendments offered by the Senate. The *Pittsburgh Dispatch* predicted that the candidates for state offices, whose fate was to be decided the same day as jointure, would influence all the voters they could to support consolidation.[81]

As the territories of New Mexico and Arizona were preparing to decide upon their future in the union of states, the arguments both pro and con regarding jointure began to circulate more rapidly than ever before. Arguments for jointure ranged all the way from the low tax rate that would result from consolidation to the blow that would be delivered against the selfish special interests opposing joint statehood. Adverse arguments included Arizona's apparent opposition to the movement, the differences between the people of the territories, and the huge size of the proposed state.

Regarding the belief that joint statehood was necessary because of the scarcity of population in the territories, *Harper's Weekly*, a pro-jointure organ, ridiculed the contention of opponents that representation should be based upon area rather than population. If such a premise were permitted, the Adirondacks with only a few persons per square mile would be able to balance out in the New York state legislature a one-mile fraction of Manhattan Island compromising a million inhabitants.[82] The magazine also insisted that separate statehood for New Mexico and Arizona was unjust to the nation as a whole because the two territories would never have a population exceeding a million and a half, while the states of New York, Pennsylvania, Illinois, Missouri, and Texas would someday have more than ten million apiece.[83]

Beveridge's favorite argument that selfish corporations would be severely crippled and hindered by jointure also became a major issue. The large railroad and mining interests were quite satisfied with territorial status because it meant a saving of millions of tax dollars each year. Therefore, statehood could hardly provoke enthusiasm among them. But if statehood had to come, a separate status for each state was preferred because, with the small voting population and large segment of people illiterate and irresponsible, these corporations could control two or possibly three of the new states and thereby secure the services of from four to six United States senators.[84]

Statistics provided by the Department of Commerce and Labor for this period reveal the light tax burden carried by the railroad companies of the two Southwestern territories. In New Mexico, the commercial value of railroads totaled $86,400,400, but their assessed value was only $8,511,538, so the value for taxation was a mere 9.9 per cent. In Arizona, the taxable value was even less, 9.7 per cent. In the state of California, on the other hand, where the commercial value of railroads was placed at $350,694,000, the assessed value amounted to $92,376,660 or a respectable 26.2 per cent. In Texas, the taxable value was even higher, 40 per cent.

This sizable discrepancy between the commercial value and assessed value of the territorial railroads existed because Congress had placed a blanket tax valuation amounting to $175 a mile on the Atchison, Topeka and Santa Fe Railroad within the two territories, to remain in effect until statehood was granted. Although the Santa Fe road north and east of Albuquerque was assessed on a valuation of $7,000 per mile, the rest of the road was practically exempt. However, when the Santa Fe crossed into Texas its valuation was raised from $175 per mile to $17,000 per mile.[85] It is not surprising, then, that the Santa Fe Railroad refused to contribute funds to promote the jointure effort in New Mexico Territory.[86]

The railroad had other motives too for objecting to jointure. At one time, the railroad owned several million acres of land in New Mexico and Arizona. Although much of the land was worthless, the company had shrewdly managed to have a large amount of it made into forest reserves, taking scrip in exchange. This scrip could be transferred to other lands, and a good deal of it had been used to block out huge tracts of territory for cattle ranches along the Pecos. It would be to the railroad's advantage to exchange the remainder of such tracts in this fashion before statehood was achieved and the new state had a chance to select the twenty-four million acres to which it would be entitled under the enabling act.[87]

What was true about the railroads was also true about the mining interests in the territory. Stevens' *Copper Handbook* shows that the large corporations were only taxed on a fraction of their real value. The giant Copper Queen Mining Company, if capitalized at 5 per cent of output would be valued at $120,000,000, yet, the value assessed for taxation amounted to only $56,513.50. A similar situation existed for the United Verde Mines and the Calumet Arizona Copper Company.[88]

Cattle barons were also lukewarm toward statehood as was evidenced by an anti-jointure memorial sent to Congress by the Arizona Cattle Growers' Association. Their motive was simply that the public domain would disappear with the coming of statehood. Men who had grazed thousands of head of cattle free of charge would be forced to make rental payments to the state school fund. Lumber barons opposed statehood because large holdings, such as those of the American Lumber Company in Valencia and McKinley counties, were assessed at less than one-tenth their value.[89] Statehood would undoubtedly change this situation.

So it was argued that jointure would benefit the people and bring to their knees the many greedy financial empires. Unbelievably low taxes would come with consolidation. A rate of one-half of one per cent would raise twice the money necessary to maintain state government. Revenue from the sale and rental of land grants, plus interest accrued from the school fund donation, would support the state educational system.[90]

The two territories were interdependent, and jointure would be of tremendous benefit to both. New Mexico possessed a smaller amount of gold, silver, and copper but had an adequate supply of fuel. Arizona was rich in precious metal but lacked suitable resources in coal and coke. Agriculturally, the two territories complemented each other. New Mexico raised the crops of the temperate zone while Arizona produced tropical fruits. ". . . Nature had made these two territories one," asserted Beveridge.[91] The issue soon was either one state or no state. The *Chicago Tribune* on June 14, 1906, noted that if Arizona did not vote for statehood now, it might be fifty years before she got another chance.[92]

Convincing as the arguments in favor of union were, the opposition kept pounding home their own. The population of the territories was shown as definitely sufficient to warrant separate statehood. New Mexico's population in 1900 was 195,310, an increase of 42,000 in ten years. With the unit of representation being only 194,000 in 1905, the people of the territory were entitled to admission. Arizona, having the smaller population, was also defended. Of the thirty-two states admitted since the founding of the nation in 1776, only five of them gained entrance into the Union with more people than Arizona possessed in 1905.[93]

Beveridge's oft-repeated story about the advantages and glory of a large consolidated state was controverted with convincing statistics. "Arizona the Great" was not looked upon as a blessing by a good many citizens in both territories. One congressman pointed out that the inconvenience to which Arizonans had been subjected had been the chief inducement for the separation of the territories by Congress in 1863. The principal center of population in Arizona was seven hundred miles from Santa Fe, and the journey was made more difficult by the continental divide, which ranged from 5,000 to 7,500 feet. Moreover, if the two territories were joined, they would comprise an area more than half the size of Europe.[94]

The proposition that largeness was an asset had little historical basis. Vermont had been taken from New York because it was thought that this state was becoming too large and powerful. More recently the Dakota Territory had been divided into two states because of its size. Dakota was only 149,000 square miles as compared with 235,000 square miles for the combined area of New Mexico and Arizona.

Differences in the people of the two territories and their contrasting backgrounds were brought out during the controversy. New Mexico's predominantly Spanish-speaking population and Arizona's Anglo majority seemed to many an incompatible combination. One newspaper crudely referred to the citizens of New Mexico as a mongrel population too ignorant and lazy to assume the privileges of full citizenship.[95] Different systems of law also divided the people. While Arizona statutes had their source in common law, the legal code of New Mexico was to a great extent derived from civil law, a necessity because the Spanish-speaking people of the territory were accustomed to laws and usages which prevailed in Mexico and Spain. Arizona also had a more progressive democracy providing for a primary election law and the Australian ballot, practices not found in New Mexico.

Financial disputes between the territories existed because Arizonans felt that certain counties in New Mexico having large debts and an insufficient amount of taxable property were practically bankrupt. However, Holm O. Bursum, chairman of the Republican central committee of New Mexico, declared in a letter to Senator Henry C. Hansbrough of North Dakota on January 9, 1905, that the public debt of Arizona was nearly four times as great as that of New Mexico.[96]

A constitutional reason for opposing jointure was found in Article IV, Section 3, of the Constitution of the United States, which stated that:

New States may be admitted by the Congress into this Union; but no new State shall be formed or erected within the Jurisdiction of any other State; nor any State be formed by the Junction of two or more States, or Parts of States, without the Consent of the Legislatures of the States concerned as well as of the Congress.

Although this provision applied to states, it was contended that most of the acts of Congress creating territories, such as the Ordinance of 1787, referred to the territories as states. This being the case, the principle enunciated in Article IV would be violated by uniting the two territories without their consent. The provision was used as part of a broader legal argument that each territory had the unquestionable right of ultimate statehood. Although the discretion of Congress on the matter was admitted, the denial of this right through the arbitrary act of forcing a distasteful union was considered extreme and revolutionary.[97]

As feelings of controversy and bitterness increased, anti-jointure arguments were feverishly advanced to combat the pressure being brought to bear by Washington. As significant as these were, they probably were not as important as the united and hostile opposition of the people of Arizona, who made no attempt to disguise their distaste for consolidation. Protests from business and social groups in the territory were commonplace, and it was claimed that ninety-five per cent of the people opposed union with New Mexico.[98]

Although Arizona's position seemed clear, New Mexico's was as yet uncertain. Old political hands Catron and Otero continued to work for separate statehood and to fight jointure. In December, 1905, Otero again declared that he was unalterably opposed to joint statehood.[99] Rodey, of course, had long been in the jointure camp, one of the first to add strength to the movement, and was aided by another influential convert, Prince. On February 1, 1905, Prince wrote Beveridge that although a majority of New Mexicans prefer separate status they "agreeably prefer any kind of statehood to none at all . . . ."

Of course, the support of Rodey and Prince would not insure success. New, younger political figures, such as Bursum, Luna, and the idealistic Governor Hagerman, were needed to swing the tide toward victory. The prestige of the popular Roosevelt naturally advanced the cause of joint statehood, but the final decision would be in the territories and local support was vital.

Evidence that Republican leaders of the territory were cool toward the idea is found in a letter written by former Judge A. A. Freeman of the territorial supreme court, an old foe of statehood. Addressed to Bursum, and printed in the *Albuquerque Morning Journal* on January 1, 1906, the letter said that a delegation of party leaders from New Mexico, including

Bursum, Luna, Judge Mills, Raynolds, and Major Llewellyn, had visited the President and reached an agreement whereby they promised to support consolidation if Roosevelt would not disturb the party machinery in the territory. Bursum heatedly denied that the President had to make a bargain to secure this support.[100] Although Bursum was part of a delegation which met with Roosevelt to discuss territorial matters, subsequent happenings seemed to confirm his denial. The President did not refrain from interfering in party organization, and gave his appointee, Hagerman, complete freedom to clean house in the politics of the territory.[101] Even Bursum was removed from his position as Superintendent of Prisons and prosecuted for alleged mishandling of funds. Moreover, if such a bargain were made, party leaders were certainly slow in fulfilling their promise. The Republican central committee did not officially endorse jointure until October 1, 1906,[102] nine months after publication of the controversial letter.

Even then, Republican support of jointure was probably prompted by expediency rather than conviction. Territorial Republicans did not want to lose favor with the President regardless of personal feelings toward joint statehood. As Arizona's attitude toward consolidation was intransigent, they had nothing to lose by supporting joint statehood. They would merely promote a favorable vote in their territory and receive the gratitude of the President, while being saved from jointure by Arizona.

The *Santa Fe New Mexican* and the *Las Vegas Daily Optic* demonstrated how quickly loyalties could change in the name of practicality. For a long time they were outspoken opponents of jointure, their outlook undoubtedly reflecting the attitude of important party figures in the territory. Max Frost was still editor of the *New Mexican*, and when Otero terminated the long reign of Tom Catron in territorial politics, Frost shifted to the new powers-to-be with little hesitation. That he remained in the good graces of the Republican leadership is evidenced by his frequent correspondence with Bursum and the award to his New Mexican Printing Company of a contract as public printer.[103] An even closer tie came into being on March 9, 1906, when Frost and his wife Maude turned over 18,750 shares of capital stock in the New Mexican Printing Company to Bursum and Luna at a price of $10,000.[104] Earlier, on January 30, 1905, Bursum and "Bull" Andrews purchased jointly 128 shares of stock in the Optic Publishing Company for $8,000. The publishing firm printed the *Las Vegas Daily Optic*. Four days after the enactment of the Carter compromise, the united front of these friends against jointure had changed to acceptance, and Frost wrote William J. Loeb, the President's secretary, stating that the *New Mexican* was now behind the jointure movement.

He declared that this decision was arrived at after due consultation with Republican leaders such as Bursum, Luna, and Andrews.[105]

Perhaps the strategy of the Republican leaders can be best summed up by Major Llewellyn's advice to the territorial heads during debate over the Hamilton bill. If the Foraker amendment were adopted, he declared, Arizona would vote it down and then New Mexico could make her demand for separate status.[106] Eleven days later, Llewellyn's views were confirmed when the Republican and Democratic parties in Arizona denounced consolidation in a joint session. Thus, the full burden of opposing the administratively sponsored jointure measure would be borne by Arizona, while New Mexico would support the measure and be admitted later on the basis of her loyalty to the national administration.

Once the party had committed itself to jointure, the difficult task was delivering the necessary votes. Party workers and a majority of voting citizens had to be convinced by Bursum and Frost that the Republican position was intelligent and that a vote for jointure would benefit the territory. Frost concentrated on average citizens, while Bursum used his influence as chairman of the central committee to convince loyal Republicans. Frost received help from a minority voice in Arizona, Louis C. Hughes of the *Arizona Daily Star*, who hoped to join Frost in an effort to blanket both territories with pro-union literature.[107]

Tom Catron, still the boss of Santa Fe County, refused to stop fighting jointure. On August 6, 1906, he expressed his fear that if jointure took place the Anglos of Arizona would dominate the new state and disenfranchise the Spanish-speaking citizens of New Mexico.[108] Although this opposition meant trouble, Bursum hopefully wrote to Rodey: "I shall do all within my power . . . towards securing the passage and acceptance of the bill." He then assured the former delegate that New Mexico would deliver a 20,000-vote majority for consolidation.[109] His strategy was to play upon the prejudices of those he attempted to convince. Sensing the lukewarm attitude toward jointure prevalent in the territory, he wrote to a Carlsbad citizen claiming that jointure would eventually lead to single statehood. With the aid of the national representatives and senators gained by statehood, he declared, Congress could be induced to permit the division of Arizona into two states.[110] In another letter, Bursum expressed doubts about Arizona's acceptance of joint statehood, but argued that New Mexico's support would increase her chances for favorable legislation in the next Congress.[111] He also wrote to Charles Spiess in Las Vegas declaring that support of jointure might mean a federal appropriation for a public building in the city.[112] Nor was appeal to party loyalty overlooked. As Bursum told one of his correspondents, this is "a republican measure" backed by Roosevelt, probably the "best friend the west ever had."[113]

Two problems faced by Bursum were general resistance to Andrews' re-election and his own feud with Governor Hagerman. Both questions were related, as far as Bursum was concerned, to the opposition against joint statehood. It was alleged, for instance, that anti-jointure Republicans were organizing to defeat Andrews. Charles Springer of Colfax County was to be their choice as delegate, according to Otero.[114] Hagerman was believed to be in the forefront of all efforts to stop Andrews and Bursum,[115] and therefore considered an enemy of consolidation. On September 5, 1906, during a meeting of the Republican central committee to decide whether to endorse Andrews as territorial delegate and Bursum as committee chairman, the committee retained both men in their posts. According to Bursum, Hagerman had attended the meeting solely to see him ousted. But the reverse occurred and Bursum was forced to prevent his friends from passing a motion of censure against the governor.[116]

Hagerman was an opponent of Bursum, but to say he was an enemy of jointure was unfair. The governor had been asked by Roosevelt to do all he could for joint statehood[117] and the record indicates he did. In a telegram to Beveridge dated June 18, 1906, Hagerman congratulated the senator on his jointure fight and predicted success for his efforts. The *Albuquerque Morning Journal* recognized the governor's good faith and claimed he used every spare moment to campaign for statehood.[118] Yet Hagerman was accused of using his influence to defeat jointure, probably because his feud with Bursum split the pro-statehood forces. Prior to the state party convention on September 29, 1906, there were rumors that although Lincoln, Luna, Torrance, and Sandoval counties had nominated candidates pledged to joint statehood,[119] forces opposed to Bursum and Andrews were gaining ground.[120] The failure of the New Mexico Bar Association to endorse jointure also posed a threat. But when the convention assembled, Andrews was renominated on the first day and consolidation was endorsed on the second.[121] Party discipline had evidently caused the Republican organization, which at this time completely dominated New Mexico politics, to support a cause that was hardly popular.

In Arizona, however, party discipline worked against the jointure movement. The two major political bodies worked closely together to defeat jointure. The holding of both party conventions at Bisbee, Arizona, on September 6, 1906, was more than a mere coincidence. E. E. Ellinwood, who strongly opposed jointure and was chairman of the Democratic territorial committee and attorney for the Copper Queen Mining Corporation, had great influence at both conventions. Jointure men were at a great disadvantage. Their delegations from Yuma and Mohave counties were refused recognition, while contesting bodies pledged against consolidation were seated.[122]

The press in Arizona, supposedly controlled by the copper trust, was almost solidly opposed to joint statehood and made it nearly impossible for pro-jointure forces to present their viewpoint to the public. The anti-union newspapers seemed to have formed a syndicate and employed a writer to prepare all articles since the same material appeared in most of the journals.[123] A typical *Arizona Republican* article spoke of growing sentiment to make permanent arrangements for the remaining territories. Thus, if Arizona's vote against consolidation should be apathetic and the majority small, Congress would interpret this as indifference and might decide to "clean up" Arizona during the following winter regardless of her wishes. If, however, a resounding majority were recorded against jointure, Congress would allow separate statehood for the territory.[124]

The fate of the few pro-jointure papers revealed the strength of separatist sentiment. The publishers of the *Arizona National* were forced to pay first class postage because the local postmaster insisted that the paper was published in the interest of one particular cause. Delivery of the paper was held up for as much as twenty-four hours in various post offices.[125]

Supporters of consolidation were infuriated by this prejudice. Beveridge received numerous letters of protest, most of them involving the activities of Arizona's partisan governor, Kibbey. Hughes declared: "A vigorous struggle is going on, but we need another governor at once. This man Kibbey has used his efforts both secretly and pubicly [sic] to defeat the purpose in view"[126] Andrews was also angry. "Kibbey is acting badly, but if we can get him out, I think it will help."[127] Beveridge was in a rage even before he received these letters, and earlier had written to the President strongly urging Kibbey's dismissal on the basis that he was a drunk, had misused proxies given to him to vote for jointure, and because his control of the election boards might prevent a fair count from being taken in Arizona, which would be a national disaster.[128]

In response to this complaint and others,[129] Roosevelt wrote Kibbey of the grave charges made against him. "I have no doubt that there is no truth in them," but "to avoid all criticism I direct that if you can in any-way arrange it, you have representatives of the statehood people present at the canvassing of the votes on [joint] statehood." He also directed Governor Hagerman to make the same arrangement in New Mexico.[130] The President told Beveridge that the removal of the governor would not only hurt the consolidation movement but would do serious damage to the Republican party throughout the nation.[131]

Andrews' dislike of Governor Kibbey was rather surprising in view of his own initially lukewarm attitude toward jointure.[132] Andrews soon came to regard Kibbey as his bitter foe as he carried the fight for union into both territories. His vigorous efforts to change the Arizona trend induced him to try to contact John Mitchell, president of the United Miners Association of America. Andrews hoped that his close connections with Senator Penrose, "a very good friend" of Mitchell, would influence the union chief to persuade 5,000 Arizona miners belonging to the Western Federation to vote for jointure.[133]

Andrews claimed in various letters to have borne all the expenses of his campaign for jointure in both Arizona and New Mexico. He requested that Beveridge help raise the money needed in the Arizona effort, around $6,000, assuring the senator that he had received not "one nickle" from any source for the jointure campaign.[134] Whether Beveridge was suspicious of the delegate's questionable financial reputation or not, he refused to help, claiming to be one of those financially poor senators. He did promise to send ten to fifteen thousand copies of his "Arizona the Great" speech if that was not too costly.[135]

In a further effort to change Arizona's attitude, Beveridge wrote to a Phoenix architect threatening dire consequences. If Arizona was foolish enough to reject this opportunity for statehood, he declared, there might not be another chance for fifty years, and certainly not for twenty-five.[136] President Roosevelt, too, told jointure supporter Dr. Mark Rogers that if the people allowed this chance to slip by they would have to wait many years, and eventual admission still might be on terms of jointure with New Mexico.[137]

But constant pressure to change their vote had little effect, if any, on the people of Arizona Territory. Local agitation for separate statehood was so persistent and loud that it seems to have deafened the ears of the people to any outside influence. On November 6, 1906, voting day, Arizonans killed the jointure proposal with a vote of 16,265 to 3,141. The final vote in favor of joint statehood was less than 20 per cent.[138] In New Mexico, however, where party and press were behind the movement, the reverse occurred. New Mexicans, casting their ballots on the same day, favored the measure by a vote of 26,195 to 14,735. Only five counties, Santa Fe, Taos, Rio Arriba, Sierra, and Union, recorded majorities against it.[139] This probably reflected the opposition of Catron and Otero. It is interesting to note that Arizonans did not need the protection provided by the Carter compromise or Foraker amendment, for the total majority cast against the proposition was 1,664—close, but decisive nonetheless.

Joint statehood efforts, however, were not a complete failure. Members of a constitutional convention elected by the people of Oklahoma and the Indian Territory on November 6, 1906, submitted a constitution for a consolidated state which was approved by a vote of 180,333 to 73,059. On November 16, 1907, President Roosevelt issued a proclamation declaring Oklahoma a state.[140] Thus, the Sooner territory by-passed her older sister territories and became a member of the Union.

Disappointment in New Mexico was not great, as a negative vote in Arizona had been expected. This was admitted on election day by the New Mexican, which proposed that a constitutional convention be held the following month at Santa Fe to formulate a constitution to be ratified by the legislative assembly and presented to Congress. The Albuquerque Morning Journal expressed a feeling shared by many when it said no Congress would be willing to punish New Mexico because of the attitude of Arizona.[141]

The outcome of the election in New Mexico was a political victory, however, for Bursum and the Republican organization. They had carried four-fifths of the counties and only the large anti-jointure vote in Arizona had negated the results. Only in the delegate race did they have cause for concern. Andrews squeaked by his Democratic opponent, Octaviano A. Larrazolo, by the narrow vote of 22,915 to 22,649.[142] But the closeness of the race should not necessarily be attributed to a weakness in the party machine, for Larrazola had come out in favor of separate statehood at an early date. This stand doubtless offered many voters a choice between party loyalty and a natural desire for separate status. Albert B. Fall probably faced such a dilemma when he wrote Larrazola expressing his personal preference for the man but questioning the effectiveness of a Democratic delegate before a Republican-dominated Congress.[143] Larrazola's background also was an important factor, especially with citizens of Spanish extraction, because he was born in Mexico.

Charges of irregular procedure and dishonesty characterized the jointure referendum in both territories. A rather amusing accusation was submitted in a complaint to Governor Hagerman. It seemed that certain ballots, pre-marked for consolidation, were changed by an election official in Socorro County during the count. Strange today, pre-marked ballots for a referendum were not uncommon in the territory.[144] In Arizona, Hughes charged that the ballots, which had been designed by the governor and the secretary of the territory, were confusing and misleading, especially as they pertained to jointure.[145] He was backed by the Albuquerque Morning Journal, which complained that 26 per cent of the voters had failed to cast their ballots because of this confusion. Moreover, less than 50 per cent of the registered voters had been against consolidation. This prompted the paper to speculate about the re-submission of the measure, as many jointure leaders felt that the issue could carry in a fair vote.[146]

Despite the disappointment of the joint statehood advocates, efforts for a new referendum were soon dropped. Even Senator Beveridge seemed willing to concede defeat for a measure which he regarded as a product of the best statesmanship. The jointure proposal was "the composite result of the thought of many minds,—the oldest, wisest, most experienced men in the legislative life."[147] The senator could not accept defeat without some bitterness. He wrote Shaw that twenty per cent of the vote in Arizona was cast for union despite the opposition of mining companies worth more than a thousand million dollars. As for Governor Kibbey, he along with men like Edward Kent, chief justice of the territorial court, had convinced the people that, although the President officially advocated jointure, he was in his heart opposed to it, as the activities of his appointees had revealed.[148]

Newspaper comment on the defeat of jointure varied. Territorial papers fairly well reflected their original stands on the issue. Nationally, newspaper opinion differed also. The *Los Angeles Times*, on November 10, rejected the Beveridge thesis that Arizona voters were controlled by interests such as the copper mining corporations. It declared that the largest percentage of the anti-union vote was cast in agricultural counties, despite the fact that miners, cattlemen, railroad workers, and lumber people contributed to the overwhelming rejection of consolidation. The *Denver Republican*, on the other hand, thought it a mistake and felt that the people of Arizona would some day realize that they had rejected a proposal which would have made their state "greater and stronger."[149] The *Washington Post* saw the $5,000,000 cash provision incorporated into the Hamilton bill as a bribe which was not accepted.[150] The Philadelphia *Press* was gratified, but for different reasons. It felt that both territories were unfit for statehood, separate or otherwise.[151]

The defeat was significant enough to quell all further talk of jointure. The movement had been stopped once and for all. Arizona had rejected it emphatically, and New Mexico had only supported it for questionable reasons—its certain defeat being the major one. Doubtless it would have been difficult at best to unite an agrarian, Spanish-speaking people with a territory dedicated to mining and industrial pursuits. But with the opposition of the big corporation executives and influential men of the territory, this initial difficulty was only increased.

The question remaining was when the two ill-fated territories would have another opportunity for admission.

FIFTEEN

The Enabling Act

Nᴇᴡ Mᴇxɪᴄᴀɴs ᴍɪɢʜᴛ plausibly have been totally discouraged by Arizona's rejection of jointure. But the prevailing spirit after 1906 was one of refusal to surrender hope. Bradford Prince was quick to point out in a letter to Beveridge that the territory gave a majority of more than 11,000 votes to the consolidation proposal. Nothing could show the intense desire of the people for self-government more forcibly than this vote for statehood, in spite of the "unnatural" union proposed and the loss of the historic name of New Mexico. The only course left for the territory was to hold a convention, form a constitution, and submit it to Congress. "We shall hope for your approval, and that of all true Americans everywhere, in this effort to obtain, after long unjust deprivation, that most fundamental right of American Citizenship,—Self-government."[1]

Statehood leaders throughout the territory now thought that if the election day suggestion of the *New Mexican* for a constitutional convention were followed, congressional action on an enabling act might still come in the near future. Nevertheless, pessimism was the mood of a number of territorial papers for some time after the defeat of jointure. The *Albuquerque Morning Journal* quoted an unnamed senator who declared that no other conditions for statehood would be considered except jointure.[2] Ex-delegate Rodey, now a federal judge in Puerto Rico, opined that it would be impossible for New Mexico to become a state for at least twenty years.[3] There was even talk that because of the failure of consolidation, Arizona might be joined with Nevada, adding to that state's area.[4]

Had Beveridge's view been widely known, this pessimism would have been more pronounced. The Indiana lawmaker's views were unchanged and, writing to Dr. Hamilton W. Mabie of *The Outlook*, he urged that the idea of separate admission be attacked exactly as it had been during the struggle over the Knox bill.[5] The influential *Harper's Weekly* was also approached. Because of scanty rainfall and an inadequate water supply, Beveridge was sure that the Western mountain states would never have more than 5,000,000 people. If the total population of the United States reached 200,000,000 in fifty years, this sparsely populated area, having only a fraction of the total, would constitute one-sixth of the voting power of the Senate, a "denial of representative government."[6]

In reply to a letter from George Curry, the new territorial governor, Beveridge reiterated his stand against the immediate admission of New Mexico.[7] Beveridge's opposition was a continuing detriment as he was still chairman of the Committee on Territories, and his judgments were considered seriously by Roosevelt.

Throughout most of 1907, a sensational land fraud scandal, centered in New Mexico, greatly jeopardized the territory's case for admission. Hagerman, Governor Curry's predecessor, was removed from office in the midst of serious charges and countercharges. The trouble probably began when Hagerman removed the politically powerful Bursum as superintendent of the state penitentiary for what the governor called "inefficient and irregular" administration.[8] Bursum said that the discrepancies which were discovered in the prison accounts were due to mistakes of his subordinates. Nevertheless, voluntarily or upon demand, the embattled superintendent paid back into the territorial treasury sums amounting to nearly $5,000. This rekindled smoldering hostilities that had kept the party split since the tumultuous administration of Governor Otero.

Roosevelt had appointed Hagerman because as an outsider he would not be aligned with any of the factions that had been formed as a result of Otero's feuds with Hubbell, Rodey, and Catron. Hagerman came in as a reform governor and had the initial backing of the President against certain territorial leaders whom the new executive labeled members of the "machine." In early disputes with men like Bursum; Wallace Raynolds, secretary of the territory; and Colonel George W. Pritchard, territorial attorney general; Hagerman received Roosevelt's warm support.

I entirely approve of your course. I shall give you an entirely free hand in the Territory because I hold you to an absolute responsibility for conduct of affairs. Remove whenever you deem wise the three men whom you report as unsatisfactory and improper Government officials, and any others whom you may thus find to be unsatisfactory and improper.[9]

Armed with such an endorsement Hagerman must have felt little apprehension in removing Bursum as superintendent of the territorial prison.

But opposition to the new governor within the territory was hardening.
He was accused of making a territorial reapportionment which would
favor certain large corporations and be adverse to the jointure cause. He
was severely criticized by the *New Mexican*, as Frost, a friend and political
ally of Bursum, tried to undermine the governor's reform movement.
Other political enemies included Delegate Andrews; Major Llewellyn,
then United States attorney for New Mexico; and Raynolds and Pritchard.
These men, most of whom were once powerful lieutenants of Otero, combined to bring about a deeper split in the Republican party.

Hagerman's support included a substantial number of Republican politicians and businessmen, plus the influential *Albuquerque Morning Journal*, which approved the governor's action. Democrats, of course, did all
they could to widen the breach.[10] Even old Tom Catron entered the dispute, and wrote the President that Hagerman would make a competent
governor, "healing up" all the differences existing in the Republican
party.[11] Elated by the replacement of Otero, the Santa Fe boss told
Hagerman's father, "I shall be very much pleased, especially if he will take
immediate steps to have the 'augean stables' cleaned as they ought to be
cleaned in one day, as Hercules was required to clean the ancient ones.
. . ." He suggested that the governor should appoint a new attorney
general and district attorney for the territory and replace such territorial
officials as the auditor and prison superintendent. "Criminal persecution
[sic] should be vigorously carried out against these plunderers of the Public Fund . . . ."[12] Catron and Hagerman appeared as political allies until
they disagreed over a reapportionment measure favored by the chief
executive.[13]

The enemies of the new governor were given an opportunity for revenge
as a result of his delivery of land deeds to the Pennsylvania Development
Company. To understand the episode, one must go back to the enactment
of the Fergusson Act, secured by Harvey Fergusson while he was delegate
to Congress in order to acquire for the territory several hundred thousand
acres of public land. It contained a section which restricted the sale of such
lands to only one quarter section per individual, corporation, or association. The purpose was to prevent the acquisition of large tracts of land. On
October 10, 1901, "Bull" Andrews on behalf of himself and his associates
offered to buy some ten thousand acres of timberland in Valencia County
at three dollars per acre. His offer was refused by the Board of Public
Lands in accordance with the restriction in the Fergusson Act. It was suggested, however, that the offer be modified by having various individuals
file applications for the land, and each person not ask for more than one

quarter section. This was done by Andrews' friend, W. S. Hopewell, who represented the delegate and the Pennsylvania Development Company, a corporation made up of Pennsylvania politicians and capitalists. Thousands of dollars worth of valuable timberland were acquired in this fashion by employees of the Pennsylvania Development Company, the Santa Fe Central Railway, or the New Mexico Fuel and Iron Company, corporations apparently under the control of the same men.[14] Hopewell, acting as attorney, deposited a bond for $10,000 to secure the options on this land. Deeds for the property were recorded in the Territorial Land Office but not delivered to the applicants. In August of 1906, Hopewell asked Hagerman to give him the deeds, which he did, accepting for them a check for the $10,000 bond and its accumulated interest—a sum totaling about $11,000.[15]

Although Andrews was a principal figure in the affair, he was among those who seized upon this episode to discredit the governor. Had not Hagerman consummated a transaction which was clearly fraudulent? Bursum was active, too, as he and his friends climaxed an intensive legislative campaign by securing tight control of the lower house of the territorial assembly.[16] On March 4, 1907, while the legislature was in session, one legislator offered a resolution which charged Hagerman with misconduct in the Pennsylvania Development Company matter, and provided for a committee of five members to be appointed by the speaker to investigate the charges and make a report to the House. The entire proceedings, according to Hagerman, were unfair and irregular. The speaker, R. L. Baca, a bitter opponent, appointed a committee hostile to the governor. Chairman for the group was E. C. Abbott, whom Hagerman had heretofore removed as district attorney of Santa Fe County. When the governor sent a message to the House to explain his side of the case it was ruled out of order by the speaker—a ruling sustained by a vote of the "gang." The committee report, which placed Hagerman in a very bad light, was subsequently put into the hands of an attorney in the Department of Justice and eventually reached the President.[17]

Andrews was in Washington, allegedly doing everything he could to make it appear that, unless the governor were removed, he would ruin the Republican party in New Mexico. Having persuaded Hagerman to approve their land steals, Andrews and his associates now intended to use this very transaction to bring about the governor's removal. Hagerman was called to Washington to explain his position, and on April 13, 1907, the day after his arrival, he was confronted with an unfavorable report of his activities prepared by Alvord W. Cooley, the President's assistant attorney general. He was given only a few hours to examine this report before seeing Roosevelt. The President appeared visibly shocked about the entire matter. After a brief interview, he asked Hagerman for his resignation.[18] As the President put it in a letter written some two weeks later: "It seems entirely clear that [your] . . . action was both illegal and improper." To appear magnanimous Roosevelt added: "If it were not for my knowledge of your previous career and of your standing in private life, and my consequent reluctance to believe that your motives were as improper as certain of your acts would indicate, I should have removed you instead of requesting your resignation . . . ."[19]

Hagerman had no alternative but a accede to the President's request. Nevertheless, he was to conduct a stout defense of his position in a series of long letters that passed between him and the President. He maintained that his reason for turning the deeds over to Hopewell was to secure compensation for valuable timber already cut. The $11,000 collected, then, was merely recompense. "A judgment in a suit by the Territory against that company [Pennsylvania Development] to recover the value of the timber would have been, to say the least of doubtful efficacy."[20] Therefore, half a loaf was better than none.

The legal position taken by the governor was scoffed at by Cooley. According to him delivery of the deeds gave the Pennsylvania Development Company a defensible title to the timber lands. Prior to this, the firm had only an equitable right to compel delivery of the deeds. Moreover, if the contract was illegal, as Cooley emphatically maintained, it could not be enforced. He also questioned Hagerman's contention that a suit by the territory would be of "doubtful efficacy." The territory had "ample power under the statutes to proceed either civilly or criminally" to recover the value of the timber cut.[21]

Although Hagerman ostensibly was removed because of his questionable activities in this affair, there were political reasons, too. There was little question that the President was not happy with Hagerman's performance as governor. "Hagerman is a good fellow, but has made an impossible Governor," Roosevelt once remarked to a friend.[22]

Hagerman regarded his dismissal as politically inspired from beginning to end. His father had written to Elihu Root on April 27, 1907, saying that Major Llewellyn, while in Roswell the previous week, had told several reputable men that he had received confidential information from Washington six weeks before that the President would remove Hagerman and appoint Curry. If this is true, it would appear that Roosevelt had made up his mind to remove Hagerman before he received the Cooley report telling of the governor's part in the Pennsylvania Development Company affair. The President, when thus charged, questioned the senior Hagerman's integrity. "Charges of a very grave character were made to me against your father himself in connection with his land transactions in the past," Roosevelt wrote the younger Hagerman. "Whether they were true or not I cannot say, because a preliminary investigation showed that action on them would be barred by the statute of limitations."[23]

The governor was infuriated by what he regarded as an "irrelevant assault" on his father, whose career as a railroad man and empire builder in the Southwest he defended. "He has never, to my knowledge, been accused of improper or fraudulent conduct." If the President would make these allegations specific, he promised that his father would not plead the statute of limitations.[24] Moreover, he proved that Major Llewellyn did make the statements in Roswell that were attributed to him. The evidence included a notarized written affidavit by one J. F. Hinkle, dated May 30, 1907, stating that Hinkle was told by Llewellyn on April 20, 1907, that he had known six weeks ago Curry would be appointed governor. Also, Curry at a banquet given in his honor at Roswell on August 6, 1907, stated in a speech that the position of Governor of New Mexico was tendered to him in February, 1907, while he was in the Philippines.[25] Curry's autobiography later corroborated this appointment date. While at Catbalogan, Samar, in the Philippines, Captain Curry received a cablegram in late February, 1907, from his old Rough Rider companion, Roosevelt, which asked: "In event of a vacancy in the governorship of New Mexico, will you accept the appointment?"[26]

Unquestionably, Hagerman was a political liability, and Roosevelt as President was his party's leader as well as chief executive. Hagerman's removal seemed to be a solution to the political turmoil in the territory. Whether the President considered Hagerman's mishandling of the Pennsylvania Development Company deeds as an inexcusable act or merely an excuse for removing him is another question. Senator Bronson Cutting, who claimed to be closer to the President than anyone else in New Mexico for many years, stated more than two decades later that it would be impossible to find an unprejudiced person in New Mexico who would support the position which Roosevelt took.[27]

Roosevelt appeared highly sensitive to any hints that he had been unfair or discriminating and was anxious to explain his actions even after the affair was over and forgotten by most people. To Hagerman's accusation that in December, 1903, Secretary Wallace Raynolds and Surveyor General Morgan Llewellyn, son of Major Llewellyn, had approved the sale of a large tract of timberland under conditions similar to those involving the Pennsylvania Development Company,[28] the President retorted he had no knowledge of any such transaction. Furthermore, by failing to report this earlier, the governor had only provided another reason for his dismissal.[29] Roosevelt did not, however, ignore Hagerman's charges. Raynolds was removed as interim governor of the territory on July 27, 1907.[30]

The President was not content merely to remove officials. Two attorneys from the Department of Justice, Ormsby McHarg and Peyton Gordon, were dispatched to New Mexico to investigate the situation. "McHarg is an excellent man, and if he is prejudiced, the prejudice is due to just such actions as this by Raynolds."[31] Roosevelt was especially anxious that the investigators co-operate and establish cordial relations with Curry. ". . . Curry is as straight as a string . . . I have asked him to see you immediately and I told him what you were striving to do . . . ," he wrote McHarg. "Remember, however, that the factional feeling in the Territory is very bitter, and that Hagerman as well as his predecessor, Otero, and their friends will do all they can to prejudice you against every man who they think is not of their crowd." The President included among the friends of Hagerman the Santa Fe Railroad "people" whom he declared were "red-hot" for the ex-governor and eager to oppose Curry in every way.[32]

McHarg and Gordon proved to be energetic investigators. During the months of August and September, 1907, they brought suits against the American Lumber Company, Clark M. Carr, Gross Kelly & Company, the Pennsylvania Development Company, J. A. Schomberg, and other firms and individuals involved in the illegal purchase of lands and timber from the territory. These were purchases made before Hagerman's administration, as the former governor was quick to point out. Although no indictments were made in connection with the territorial land sales, nineteen persons were indicted on account of alleged fraudulent coal land entries in the northwestern part of the territory. Among the indicted were Charles A. Spiess, former president of the Territorial Council, and Cleveland A. Dodge, a personal friend of the President. Dodge's firm, Phelps, Dodge & Company of New York, had invested several million dollars in New Mexico to develop mines and build railroads. Apparently, in so doing, they came into conflict with certain government land laws.[33]

The persistence and determination of the two agents quickly produced opposition. According to Hagerman, the "machine" men were initially gratified at the appearance of McHarg and Gordon, assuming they had come to find incriminating evidence against Hagerman and his friends. It was soon discovered, however, that the two agents had more in mind, and they were attacked by "Bursum's papers" as friends of the "late fake reform ex-Governor."[34] The President very soon became leery about Mc-Harg's capabilities. Although believing him to be honest, he felt McHarg was hardly big enough to grasp in its entirety such a "delicate and difficult matter" as the New Mexican situation. He was especially disturbed at his attitude toward Curry. McHarg had decided in advance and without the slightest knowledge of Governor Curry, that the governor "cannot successfully resist the territorial gang as he terms it."[35]

Curry and McHarg clashed openly when McHarg ordered distribution of the money received by Hagerman from the Pennsylvania Development Company for delivery of the now famous deeds.[36] Although Hagerman regarded this as vindication of his original position, Curry was furious. According to the November 24 issue of the New York Sun, the new governor accused McHarg of usurping his function and threatened to resign if the special investigator was not recalled. He told Roosevelt that McHarg was trying to make a record as a prosecutor that would give him a real reputation.

The President lent a sympathetic ear to Curry's charges. He was not pleased by the indictment of his Harvard classmate, Cleveland Dodge, and publicly revealed his disbelief that Dodge could be a land grafter by inviting him to lunch. At another important luncheon, attended by Major Llewellyn and his assistant, Captain David J. Leahy, Governor Curry, and others, the White House announced that Major Llewellyn, United States district attorney, and his son, Morgan, surveyor general, had submitted their resignations to be effective January 1, 1908.[37] Although this would appear a victory for McHarg and Gordon—Llewellyn having been accused of not co-operating with them—such was not the case. The two agents were to complete their investigation the following month and turn all unfinished business over to Leahy, who succeeded Llewellyn. All nineteen indictments in the coal land cases eventually were dropped, and there was a report in the December 16 issue of the Los Angeles Times that suits pending against firms involved in the timberland frauds would be settled out of court.

The investigating team was most unhappy at the outcome of the legal action taken in the coal and land fraud cases. McHarg was outspoken on this matter and laid much of the blame on the shoulders of Roosevelt. In 1909, when McHarg resigned from government service, he placed the new President, William Howard Taft, in a very awkward position. As Taft phrased it:

. . . I should like very much to express to McHarg my high appreciation of his efficiency in the Department, because I believe we have had nobody who has done harder work, or more conscientious work, than he. But I am embarrassed in so doing by reason of the fact that he has also worked with his mouth, and has been reported as saying things, if he did say, would certainly call for discipline on our part because they reflected seriously on my predecessor, Mr. Roosevelt, for whom I have the highest respect, and whose administration we are trying to follow, and whom it would be very deplorable for us in any way to criticize or hold up to public ridicule.

If it were necessary to prove the loyalty of Roosevelt's hand picked successor—at least in 1909—the above is prime evidence. The discreet Taft was, however, quite relieved that McHarg denied "having said anything derogatory to President Roosevelt."[38]

With the appointment of Curry as governor on April 1, 1907,[39] about two weeks before Hagerman was asked to resign, a modicum of peace was restored. Territorial Republicans could now think in terms of statehood rather than party warfare. The new governor's friendship with Roosevelt seemed to brighten prospects for early admission. The Albuquerque *Evening Citizen* interpreted Curry's appointment as an indication that Roosevelt had at last consented to support a single statehood campaign for New Mexico.[40] Catron wrote Elkins that "Curry is the best man who has ever been appointed for Governor of New Mexico; he seems to be entirely satisfactory to the entire people . . . ."[41]

A wave of optimism spread throughout the territory. A statehood league was formed in Santa Fe, and the *Evening Citizen* recommended such an organization for Bernalillo County.[42] Curry, however, was not blind to the many obstacles still blocking admission. Roosevelt had told him bluntly, "Captain, I know your ambition is to have New Mexico made a state, but before you can get statehood you must clean house in New Mexico and show to Congress that the people of New Mexico are capable of governing themselves."[43]

The attitude displayed publicly by Roosevelt was of tremendous importance. He had advocated jointure, and his admiration and respect for Beveridge had not lessened. Nevertheless, he now apparently had misgivings about his earlier stand. This was confirmed in August, 1907, when an Associated Press dispatch from Oyster Bay, New York, carried an announcement by James R. Garfield, Secretary of the Interior, that no further effort would be made by the administration to bring up the jointure matter.[44]

Press comment on Roosevelt's decision was in large part commendatory. The *Los Angeles Times* praised the President's move as one which would eliminate the sole cause for friction between New Mexico and Arizona—that being their opposing stands on joint statehood.[45] The territory's friends in Congress were greatly encouraged. Senator Teller of Colorado introduced a bill for separate statehood in December, 1907, during the early days of the 60th Congress. Andrews also presented a statehood measure, and was instrumental in having his friend from Pennsylvania, Senator Penrose, introduce a companion bill in the upper chamber. Consequently, the path was cleared for action in 1908.

A crucial event that year was the Republican National Convention's decision to include for the first time an unequivocal statehood plank in the party platform. "We favor the immediate admission of the Territories of New Mexico and Arizona as separate States in the Union." Responsibility for this simple, forthright statement has been attributed to Holm Bursum, who was not only a delegate to the convention but was made a member of the important committee on resolutions. By obtaining control of the seven votes which represented the combined voting strength of all the territories, he was able to make a trade with certain key Eastern delegates, including Frank H. Hitchcock, the Republican national chairman. According to this exchange Bursum would use his influence to see that an injunction compromise was incorporated into the platform in return for a favorable statement on admission. Bursum was in an excellent bargaining position as the administration wanted an anti-injunction plank in the platform in order to attract the labor vote, although many delegates and committee members construed this as an undesirable curb on the judiciary and refused support. Bursum's seven votes could insure victory for the party leadership. He cast them in favor of a modified anti-injunction pledge, but at a price—the immediate admission of New Mexico and Arizona.[46]

Perhaps as significant as the party pledge was the shifting attitude of the administration. Roosevelt was edging toward support of separate statehood. In his message to the Sixteenth National Irrigation Congress meeting in Albuquerque in September, he expressed hope that he would have an opportunity to sign statehood bills for New Mexico and Arizona during the coming winter.[47] More surprising was his letter to Beveridge. He told the Senator that it would be "mere folly" to hold out against the territories any longer. "You will have to take them both in. You can not take them both in together, and by keeping them out you merely irritate the people there against the Republican party."[48] Roosevelt took the final leap in his message to the 60th Congress on December 8, 1908. "I advocate the immediate admission of New Mexico and Arizona as States. This should be done at the present session of the Congress. The people of the two Territories have made it evident by their votes that they will not come in as one State. The only alternative is to admit them as two, and I trust that this will be done without delay."

Unfortunately, Roosevelt's heartening words came from a "lame duck" President. If statehood were opposed during this last session of the 60th Congress, Roosevelt's official influence being greatly reduced, the viewpoint of President-elect Taft would then be decisive. Governor Curry called upon Taft at Hot Springs, Virginia, shortly before Roosevelt's statehood message. Taft advised him that he was warmly in favor of admission, but having no official capacity could not promise any help during the coming session.[49]

Losing no time in the new atmosphere of hope, "Bull" Andrews on December 7, the day before the President recommended statehood, introduced H. R. 22273, a bill calling for New Mexico's admission. Seven days later an old friend of statehood, Senator Foraker, offered a similar measure to the Senate. Perhaps the platform pledge coupled with clear stands taken by the President and President-elect would be of sufficient weight to bring passage.[50]

Almost two months passed, however, before any action was taken. Finally on February 3, 1909, Representative Hamilton introduced H. R. 27607, an omnibus measure which called for separate statehood for both New Mexico and Arizona. The bill passed the House unanimously on February 15 and was sent to the Senate where its approval was predicted. A poll taken by the Hearst publications reported that three-fourths of the senators were in favor of it, and only Beveridge was reported in opposition. He was pictured as standing practically alone.[51]

But even alone the senator was a man to be reckoned with. As chairman of the Committee on Territories he could do much to obstruct action. The scandal initiated by Hagerman's dismissal provided him with the necessary ammunition. When his committee met on February 27, he and Senator Nelson read statements charging corruption among certain New Mexico officials. A statement from Ormsby McHarg was also read, in which he claimed that Governor Curry and his attorney general, Albert B. Fall, had hampered work in uncovering this corruption. Also, former Governor Hagerman sent a telegram containing derogatory remarks about the character of officials in the territory.[52]

Perhaps most damaging was the statement submitted by a stenographer who had assisted McHarg in gathering evidence in these land fraud cases. Among other things, the woman, Miss Kathleen Lawler, indicated that the federal agents not only faced opposition and hostility but McHarg was threatened with physical violence if he persisted in the investigation. His private office was broken into repeatedly and at will, his desk opened, his personal affairs ransacked, and his private letters read. Moreover, he was "grossly insulted and repulsed" in his efforts to look into the penitentiary situation. The statement named as obstructionists Governor Curry, Major Llewellyn, Catron, Fall, Pritchard, and Max Frost of the New Mexican, a paper described as the "organ and mouthpiece of the 'gang'."[53] Beveridge was impressed and even tried to arrange an interview between the stenographer and Taft.[54]

Beveridge followed up these revelations by introducing a resolution which would authorize the committee to conduct an investigation in New Mexico before taking action on admission. The committee then adjourned without motion for additional meetings on the statehood bill.

Statehood proponents were shocked. The New Mexico scandal was "sprung with deliberate intent," a Tucson banker was quoted as saying.[55] The *New Mexican* protested that no basis existed for these charges of fraud and corruption. It contended that what irregularities had occurred were approved by the Department of the Interior. Moreover, the alleged irregularities had not been the result of fraudulent intent but rather imperfect legislation[56]—an obvious reference to the restrictive sections in the Fergusson Act which limited to one-quarter section the amount of land that could be sold to any one person, corporation, or association. This interpretation was supported by the Assistant Attorney General who failed to find anything to justify the conclusion that these officers derived or intended to derive personal gain from the transactions in question, or that they were not acting in their official capacity as they conceived it to be "in the best interests of the Territory."[57]

Despite the *coup de grace* delivered to the statehood measure by Beveridge, a final effort was made to save it on the last day of the session. Senator Robert L. Owen, a Democrat from Oklahoma, proposed that the bill be added as an amendment to a House resolution directing the Secretary of State to renew negotiations with the Russian government in an effort to achieve a treaty that would prohibit discrimination against American Jews in Russia. Although the resolution was adopted, the proposed statehood amendment was laid on the table.[58] This terminated the struggle for statehood during the 60th Congress. Theodore Roosevelt's great reputation as a friend of the West had not spelled admission for New Mexico and Arizona.

The territories fared no better during the first session of the 61st Congress, despite the known friendship of the newly inaugurated Taft. This led some to believe that the President's professions of interest and understanding were less than sincere. Such fears were unfounded because Taft's support never wavered. The admission of New Mexico and Arizona had been a Roosevelt policy in 1908 and would be continued during his administration. However, strong pressures were brought to bear. Beveridge persevered, and having failed with Roosevelt tried to convince Taft that the territories were not ready for admission. His approach was frankly political. Arizona could have one congressman and New Mexico two. Should they be Democratic, they might be sufficient to make the next Congress Democratic. He also warned the President that Arizona would send two Democratic senators to Congress, while New Mexico would send Andrews and Curry. Beveridge made particular capital of Andrews' unsavory reputation. "If it is said by anyone in New Mexico that Andrews could not succeed in being elected senator, you have only to consider his former success, the methods which he employs and the powerful forces back of him."[59] But Taft remained unmoved by the senator's plea that statehood be put off until after the 1910 census.

Even insults hurled at the President did not alter his support of the territories. In October, 1909, Taft was a guest at the Alvarado Hotel in Albuquerque, where Albert Fall, who was supposed to deliver an address extolling the virtues of the President, instead devoted his time to questioning Taft's sincerity on the statehood issue. New Mexico leaders in attendance were shocked, fearing that Fall's remarks would alienate the President's cherished support. But the President handled the embarrassing situation with dignity. When Fall had concluded his remarks, Taft rose to his feet and told a story about a young lawyer who had engaged in an extended argument with a judge. After their exchange, the judge told the man that he agreed with him on the law and was with him "in spite of the reasons" given. "Judge Fall," Taft concluded, "I have heard your argument and am for your cause in spite of it."[60]

Friends of statehood were concerned when Curry resigned as governor of New Mexico. But this was not due to a policy difference between the President and Curry. Rather, it was the result of a personality difference between the governor and Taft's controversial Secretary of the Interior, Richard A. Ballinger. Curry and Ballinger first clashed when the latter was Commissioner of Public Lands in Roosevelt's administration. Curry had gone over his head to the President in order to rescind a directive requiring homesteaders in the vicinity of Clovis to surrender their claims and take options on the public domain elsewhere. Ballinger never forgave him, and according to the governor extended his vengeful attitude toward "practically everything having to do with New Mexico's welfare, including our efforts for statehood."[61] Because of this, the governor resigned, giving financial difficulties as the reason. Although Taft eloquently praised Curry's "honesty and loyalty" in accepting the resignation,[62] he apparently was not alarmed over Ballinger's alleged persecution of the governor. "I have sent the enclosed letter accepting Governor Curry's resignation," wrote Taft to his Secretary of the Interior. "I don't think it necessary to pay any attention to the charges."[63]

Notwithstanding all the pressures, insults, and intrigue, when the second session of the 61st Congress began, Andrews, when speaking of the new statehood bill being prepared by Hamilton, was able to say:

The President is a strong advocate of the measure and his cabinet is enthusiastic. The House is absolutely for the bill . . . and an overwhelming majority of senators favor statehood for the territory . . . .[64]

Curry's successor, Judge William J. Mills, who was sworn in on March 1, 1910, was also a statehood man. According to Curry his conservatism and judicial background were attractive to the President, as well as many members of Congress who believed he might be the first governor or one of the senators if statehood were achieved.

On January 14, 1910, Representative Hamilton, still chairman of the House territorial committee, introduced H. R. 18166, an act to enable the people of New Mexico and Arizona to form separate constitutions and state governments and be admitted into the Union "on an equal footing with the original States."[65] New Mexico would be allowed two representatives to the lower house of Congress, while Arizona would be allowed one. Capitals would be established at Santa Fe and Phoenix, and remain there until 1915 when elections would determine permanent sites. Land provisions were generous. New Mexico was to receive two sections of nonmineral land in each township in addition to the two sections previously granted or reserved for the common schools under the Fergusson Act. Each new state was to be given approximately 3,000,000 acres of nonmineral land for the payment of valid, subsisting debts incurred by the territorial administrations and county governments. Both new states were to establish nonsectarian schools and insure the "teaching of English therein." The estimated date for final admission of the territories was January 1, 1911.[66]

After several days of consideration the Hamilton bill, as it was often called, passed the House by a two-thirds majority[67] and was sent to the Senate where it was referred to the Committee on Territories. New Mexicans were both delighted and frustrated at the results. The Deming Graphic praised the "indefatigable efforts" of Representative Hamilton, ably assisted by Andrews. It warned, however, of Senate amendments which might delay final admission until 1912.[68] Sensing the growing split between the Taft and Roosevelt forces, the Graphic cautioned patience with the President. Bear with Taft and do not expect him to "drive his way through with the big stick," for Taft was Taft, splendidly trained, widely experienced, and, above all, tactful. The President's "inexorable firmness" in the Pinchot affair also was cited to indicate his potential toughness.[69]

But even now there were enemies such as the Outlook, a magazine close to Beveridge, which brought up the old, timeworn population argument. Estimating the population of New Mexico to be about 230,000, it declared that New Mexico had less than half the population of Baltimore, "but a single city in one of the smallest eastern States."[70] In answer to this, the Deming Headlight seethingly denounced the "little junta" of New England financiers who feared that the West, South, and Southwest might gain control and give the government back to the people.[71]

Senator Beveridge was now tiring of his long campaign against state-hood. The party platform, the stand of the Taft administration, and the vote on jointure all made further opposition quite futile. Beveridge, there-fore, accepted the inevitable, but determined to push a statehood measure free of "jokers" hurting the people's interests.[72] To this end, Senator Dill-ingham, in the absence of Beveridge, introduced on January 31 a separate statehood bill, S. 5916, which was referred to the Committee on Ter-ritories. After a series of hearings in consideration of both the Hamilton and Beveridge bills, the Hamilton bill was reported favorably on March 14 with an amendment which left nothing of its original form except the enacting clause.

The alterations, which were the handiwork of Beveridge, slashed many of the generous land provisions and put the process of constitution-mak-ing under the close supervision of the federal government. The ratified constitutions of the new states would be returned to the President and the Congress for final approval. Beveridge's strongly held philosophy that national interests must be placed above those of territories seeking ad-mission was thus incorporated. This surveillance was justified on the basis that it would prevent "unsound or harmful provisions in the constitutions of the proposed new states."[73] Logical as was the reasoning behind the amendment, it was a departure from past practice. Previous enabling acts usually required that a constitution be returned to Congress for approval, or, if the enabling act specified, to the President for his proclamation of admission. The Beveridge version would require action by both the Presi-dent and Congress. One territorial journal asked why, if the enabling act provided for New Mexico's admission on an equal footing with the other states, it placed restrictions on the people of the territory which had never been placed on any other state admitted into the Union.[74]

Land provisions in the amended Hamilton bill undoubtedly reflected Beveridge's suspicions of fraud and corruption in the territory. Exhibit A in the Senate Report, entitled "Memorandum Relative to the 'Fall Tim-ber' Cases in New Mexico," cited the sensational violations of the Fer-gusson Act and made reference to the 1907 investigation conducted by McHarg and Gordon. Harsh restrictions on the handling of public lands in the Senate version thus may be traced back to the land fraud scandals.

The amount of public land granted in the Senate version was drastically reduced. To lessen temptation, New Mexico and Arizona only received 1,000,000 acres of land apiece. One reason for such a reduction was to insure that the citizens of the two territories would pay all just debts in-curred while living under territorial status. Revenue derived from the reduced land allotment, then, would be enough to cover exactly those debts validated by Congress. Included in this category would be the controversial Pima County bonds, plus bonds voted by the people of Santa Fe and Grant counties as early as 1879.

Reductions in the land allotment were accompanied by rigid safeguards. Whereas the original Hamilton bill contained no restrictions, the Senate version placed "careful and rigid, though entirely reasonable and practical restrictions." Lands granted were placed in a trust to be disposed of by a specified procedure. Mortgages were forbidden, while sales and leases were made only to the highest bidder at public auction. Appraisals were required, and no property could be sold for less than the appraised value.[75] The minimum price for such lands was relatively low and varied according to aridity.[76] Lands susceptible to irrigation, however, or under federal or other irrigation projects could not be sold for less than $25 an acre. Reflecting Beveridge's determination to guarantee an effective school support provision was a careful leasing procedure for sections 13 and 26 of each township, which protected the value of these lands by prohibiting the cutting of timber.[77]

One especially interesting provision called for the withdrawal of saline lands previously granted to the University of New Mexico. Because the definition of saline lands in reference to the area had been vague, the House abolished the grant to the university. The Senate version concurred in this action, but because of efforts to acquire a monopoly of saline lands lying near the Santa Fe Central Railroad line, it went a step further and withdrew all such land from public entry until Congress could take further action.[78] In the Senate report, the Beveridge committee revealed an attempt by the Santa Fe Central to open negotiations with the board of regents of the university in 1903 for leasing of the Laguna del Perro, largest of the salt lakes, so as to develop it and establish a market for salt. Although nothing came of these negotiations, they illustrated how valuable resources granted for the public good could be exploited by selfish interests. As Andrews was president of the railroad, this move was a well-directed slap at New Mexico's official voice in Congress.

The Senate version of the bill reflected the Eastern viewpoint to a far greater degree than had the original. Whereas the House bill permitted the teaching of languages other than English, the Senate version provided that schools should be conducted in English and struck out the provision "that nothing in this act shall preclude the teaching of other languages in said public schools." The Senate version required state legislators as well as state officers to read, write, and understand the English language sufficiently well to conduct the duties of office without aid of an interpreter.[79] Fear of Mormonism, especially in Arizona Territory, prompted the Senate to add a strong polygamy restriction. Polygamy, if practiced under the form of polygamous habitation, was permitted in the House bill. Finally, the Senate judiciously refused to recognize an Arizona election law because it contained an "educational" test which could disfranchise a large number of Spanish-speaking residents of the territory.[80]

While the Senate committee was rewriting the Hamilton bill, New Mexicans became greatly alarmed over reports of the drastic reductions in the land allotment. The Senate bill was wrong and unjust, Catron wrote. "We should have all the lands which were provided for the State in the House Bill . . . ."[81] The territorial Democratic and Republican central committees both met, passed resolutions protesting certain provisions in the Senate substitute, and appointed committees to go to Washington to attempt to eliminate "objectional features" of the bill.[82] But once the amended Hamilton bill was reported, New Mexicans had no alternative but to support it. Knowing that statehood would only be achieved on Beveridge's terms, Bursum on March 16 wrote the senator: "I have told our friends down here that New Mexico will obtain statehood by the grace and good offices of Senator Beveridge."

With the two houses of Congress taking such opposing positions on statehood for the territories, a further wait was no surprise. But the waiting had been so long and so drawn out that at last there were even sympathizers among Eastern newspapers. "Let the New Sisters Come In," urged the Baltimore Sun, implying that because the new states might side with Thomas Jefferson, Republican leaders were willing to violate their platform pledge.[83] The Arizona Republican blamed the delay on "long and tiresome speeches and long and tiresome debates . . . ."[84]

After the substitute bill had been reported by the Senate territorial committee on March 14, a favorable vote by the entire body was the next goal. Fortunately for New Mexico, opposition to statehood had been waning in recent months, largely because of a bargain between Senator Aldrich and the Democrats. Aldrich, who was in charge of the controversial Mann-Elkins bill for more effective railroad regulation, had agreed to support the statehood measure, in return for which the Democrats would back his railroad bill against the objections of insurgent Republicans, who insisted that the bill did not go far enough. Apparently it was conceded by both parties in the Senate that the two territories would be Democratic once admitted, despite the notable Republican successes in New Mexico during the past several years. The removal of opposition by the powerful Republican, Aldrich, an old foe of statehood, brightened New Mexico's hopes as never before.[85]

To get any vote in the Senate, however, the Hamilton bill had to compete with one of the administration's pet measures, a conservation bill providing for the withdrawal of certain public lands. Early in June, the conservation measure was made the unfinished business of the Senate, which meant that it would be brought up each day until enacted upon. An attempt was made to place the statehood bill next in line, but this was ruled out of order despite Beveridge's expressed intention to take up the statehood measure immediately after disposal of the conservation bill. Another motion was made to have the statehood bill take precedence as unfinished business but it, too, was ruled out of order.[86] Not until June 15, after the Senate had taken action on the conservation measure, was Senator Beveridge able to make the statehood bill the unfinished business of the upper house. On the following day at two o'clock, the bill was placed before the Senate. After a brief discussion, a vote was taken on the Senate amendments to the Hamilton bill. These were approved 42 to 19 in a ballot which closely followed party lines, Democrats preferring the original measure.[87] On the final vote, the bill was passed unanimously. After so many years, the Senate, chief stumbling block for statehood, now approved admission of the territories.

Supporters of statehood hoped that the considerable prestige of President Taft would help to accomplish a reconciliation of the differing views of the House and Senate. Despite fears on the part of a number of senators that corporate interests would dominate the new states, contributing four more "pocket borough" members to the upper chamber, the President regarded admission of the terriitories as "must" legislation.[88] In his famous letter to Roosevelt on May 26, 1910, in which he tried to halt the growing split between them, he listed as one of the chief accomplishments of his administration Roosevelt's statehood measure. "The Statehood bills have passed the House and will in some form pass the Senate . . . ."[89] Taft could be counted on to pressure the two houses to come to some agreement.

The President had been reported to favor the House measure with certain modifications, and had made it known through his advisers that he wanted a conference called to work out an agreement. Representative Hamilton, after arranging for such a meeting, called upon the President on June 17 to discuss the matter. To his amazement and chagrin, he was told that the Senate measure was preferred and that the House should accede.[90] Beveridge's close consultation with the President on this bill, and particularly with Taft's sympathetic postmaster general, Frank Hitchcock, had produced results. In light of Taft's wishes, the House concurred, and on June 18, 1910, unanimously accepted the Senate version.

New Mexicans were delighted, and Hamilton was praised for unselfishly surrendering his position in order that the territory might have its long-sought enabling act. There was evidence that to achieve statehood, supporters had been willing to pressure the more flexible House of Representatives despite a decided distaste for certain Senate amendments. Stephen Elkins, as one of his last official acts, went with Catron to the House of Representatives to insist that the House concur in the Senate amendments. Elkins had assured Catron that unless this were done statehood would be "deferred indefinitely."[91] Catron, who was in Washington on private business, spent "seven weary weeks" lobbying for statehood without compensation.[92] Doubtless, the appearance of these two old champions of the statehood movement had its effect.

Taft, anxious to leave Washington for New Haven, where he was to attend the Yale commencement, expressed a desire to sign the bill promptly. The long document was prepared and signed by the proper officers of the House and Senate and then taken to the President on June 20, 1910. At 1:40 P.M., in the presence of Senator Beveridge, Representative Hamilton, Postmaster General Hitchcock, Delegate Andrews, Delegate Ralph H. Cameron from Arizona, and other prominent figures, including Catron and Ira M. Bond from New Mexico, Taft affixed his signature to the enabling act.[93] "As the last stroke of the eagle quill pen crossed the 't' one era in the history of the American republic ended and another began . . . the age of the territories, with all it ment [sic] of adventure, of romance and of National glory, has closed . . . ."[94]

Friends of the territory had only effusive praise for the President. ". . . It has certainly made President Taft immensely popular, we believe that it was due to his deep interest in the matter and persistent effort that statehood was finally accomplished," one prominent Arizonan was quoted as saying. There was even speculation that Taft's action might help to reconcile the growing differences between him and Roosevelt. The timing of Taft's signature was significant. Roosevelt had returned from his world travels two days before and was greeted at the dock by a large contingent of Arizonans and New Mexicans, including his old wartime comrades, Llewellyn and Curry.[95]

But the political storm clouds which accompanied Roosevelt's arrival had little impact on the elated spirits of Southwesterners. "Rejoice together in the new day that is borned unto us."[96] And New Mexicans and Arizonans rejoiced. Accolades and best wishes were received from outsiders, among them a Denver paper which was sure that the new states would rise to the occasion and never dishonor the privilege that had been given them.[97] Still, some newspapers, such as the New York World, repeated the tiresome argument that the "sagebrush commonwealths" did not have the population to merit statehood.[98] Some in New Mexico resented the provision that their constitution had to receive the approval of both the President and Congress. But an enabling act had finally been achieved, and that was most important.

SIXTEEN

The Constitutional Convention of 1910

Almost immediately after New Mexico's enabling act had been signed into law, citizens of the territory began preparations for the election of delegates to a constitutional convention, which according to the act was to be held not less than sixty nor more than ninety days after passage of the bill. On June 29, 1910, Governor Mills issued a proclamation calling for an election on September 6, 1910. One hundred delegates would be chosen from the twenty-six counties in accordance with an apportionment made by the governor, chief justice, and secretary on June 28, based upon the vote cast for delegate to Congress in 1908.[1]

Neither the Democratic nor Republican party held a state convention to advise delegates on how they should vote or what features should be incorporated into the new instrument. There was a significant move to have a nonpartisan convention. "There is but one primary issue envolved [sic] in this election—that is the CONSTITUTION. All other issues are secondary . . . ."[2] The Non-Partisan Voters' League of Bernalillo County was launched, pictured by one unfriendly newspaper as having a platform of sixteen articles "advocating initiative, referendum and other Socialist doctrines."[3] Despite good intentions, nonpartisanship went the way of all such movements in a two-party democracy. The dominant Republican party refused to agree to a proposal by the Democratic central committee to have a nonpartisan convention. Moreover, they were alleged to have "audaciously" proclaimed their purpose to have a Republican constitutional convention to frame a Republican constitution.[4] The *Las Cruces*

Citizen ridiculed such charges of arbitrary conduct on the part of territorial Republicans. "We don't seem to hear any sharp shrill shrieks for nonpartizanship [sic] from the Democratic counties. What piffle!"[5] Rival party tickets soon appeared in a majority of the counties.[6]

The overshadowing issue in most of these contests was whether direct legislation in the form of initiative, referendum, and recall should be written into the constitution. The continual debates on this subject were often similar to one between Elias S. Stover, a former lieutenant governor of Kansas, and Francis E. Wood, an attorney, held at the Young Men's Republican Club in Albuquerque. Stover defended the new techniques of direct democracy while counselor Wood called the initiative the "destroyer of all law."[7] Not merely a local issue, direct legislation was one of the key reforms of the Progressive movement. Pioneered in states such as Oregon, Wisconsin, and South Dakota, direct legislation found particular acceptance in the West as many state constitutions in this area underwent amendment. New Mexico and Arizona, as the last contiguous continental territories to be admitted, had new constitutions to formulate, and consequently these territories were real battlegrounds for the great political issues of the day.

Harvey Fergusson, a man swept by the mood of the times, was leader of the fight for direct legislation in the territories. Praising a speech on this subject by Senator Jonathan Bourne, Jr., progressive Republican from Oregon, he wrote a correspondent: "It is a most useful document for the widest possible circulation in New Mexico at this important juncture, for the reason that Oregon is a republican state,—our constitution[al] convention, I fear, under the probable apportionment soon to be announced, being republican . . . ." Fergusson was pessimistic that "certain elements" of the Republican party would gain control. "They may dish us out such a constitution that we shall, as honest and good citizens, have no alternative but to fight it."[8] If only the native people would appreciate the overshadowing importance of the referendum to them as a race, Fergusson wrote a Spanish-speaking citizen. It would be "a shield and protection" to them. He warned that future legislatures might attempt to disfranchise New Mexico's Spanish population.[9]

The territorial Republican party apparently was noncommittal on many of the important political and social issues of the day. A platform adopted by the party in Doña Ana County declared itself for direct primaries, restriction of corporations, purity of the ballot, wise educational provisions, the safeguarding of school lands and school funds, "and the submission to a vote of the people of the question of whether or not initiative and referendum, statewide prohibition or local option[,] shall be engrafted upon and made a part of the Constitution." In other words, direct legislation and prohibition, the two burning issues of the day, would be passed along like the proverbial "buck." The Republican central committee, in endorsing this platform, urged the election of Republican nominees in Doña Ana County to the constitutional convention scheduled to begin on October 3, 1910.[10]

As election day approached, the outcome was never much in doubt. Republicans had dominated New Mexico since the turn of the century, except in a few areas like Grant and Luna counties, and the eastern part of the state where a number of Texans had migrated. So it was perfectly normal when more than two-thirds of the votes cast at the September election were for Republicans, and of 100 delegates elected to the convention 71 were Republicans and 29 were Democrats.[11] With Republicans now in command, it remained to be seen if they were those "certain elements" of which Fergusson spoke so apprehensively.

The *Albuquerque Morning Journal* was concerned. All the candidates the paper had attacked as "bosses, railroad attorneys and corporation lawyers" were elected.[12] One newspaper interpreted the election results as meaning a sane constitution. "New Mexico declared herself proud and dealt a heavy blow to the initiative, referendum and recall advocates."[13] A somewhat different attitude was taken by a contributor to the New York *Sun* who declared that 32 of the 100 delegates elected were Spanish-speaking, insuring that the constitutional convention would resemble "some bull fight in a Mexican village." Furthermore, provisions in the enabling act requiring use and knowledge of the English language were being totally ignored.[14] Charges of "frauds on the ballot box" also were heard,[15] despite the fact that the election was a comparatively fair one.

Convention delegates knew that regardless of the nature of the constitution they wrote, it would be extremely difficult to insure the necessary approval of both Congress and the chief executive. The rising tide of Progressivism pointed to Democratic gains in the coming congressional election, with the lower house most vulnerable. Could a conservative constitution meet with the approval of such a body?[16] Taft had warned New Mexico to adopt "a safe and sane constitution."[17] Would such a constitution be in harmony with the views expressed by the influential Roosevelt, who capped his tour through the West by proclaiming his New Nationalism at Osawatomie, Kansas, on August 31, 1910. Roosevelt had intervened openly by warning the people of New Mexico and Arizona against the dangers of having an "iron-clad" constitution, not easily amended. Speaking at Pueblo, Colorado, he cautioned friends who had written for his advice to be on guard against "doctrinaires" and designing corporation lawyers who would incorporate "jokers or impractical propositions" into the new constitutions.[18]

There were other pressures, too—pressures not faced to any great degree by constitution-makers of the last century. Women were on the march, either as suffragettes or prohibitionists. Although only nineteen of the delegates were reported in favor of statewide prohibition, women had started an organized effort to secure a prohibition clause for the constitution and vowed to work on every delegate to achieve this end. The strength of this group was growing. At the last annual meeting, it was shown that eight new branches of the Woman's Christian Temperance Union had been established in the territory.[19]

As the appointed date for the convention drew near, delegates began to assemble at Santa Fe. A number of familiar faces were in evidence. The aging Catron, running fifth in a field of five delegates elected by Santa Fe County,[20] was present to lend his prestige and vast experience. Bursum, then only forty-three, was in attendance to impress his conservative viewpoint on assembled members. Fall, who had matched his noted legal career with investments in cattle and mining, was there as a spokesman for the livestock industry.[21] Solomon Luna, the wealthiest sheep owner in the territory, attended as leader of the native element. It was later reported that to stop any proposal which he deemed against the best wishes of his people he had "only to lift a finger or his eyebrows."[22] Fergusson represented Bernalillo County, and was listed among the so-called "irreconcilables," a faction of the Democratic minority that would be satisfied with nothing less than "a thoroughly progressive constitution."[23] Other prominent leaders were Charles A. Spiess, now practicing law in San Miguel County; Charles Springer; Jose D. Sena; Harry M. Daugherty, a Socorro Democrat; Colonel George W. Pritchard; attorney Reed Holloman; and Jacob H. Crist.[24]

In terms of occupations and special interests represented, this group was particularly interesting. The thirty-two attorneys present reflected the leading role played by tough frontier lawyers in the history of the territory. Perhaps this explains why one "irreconcilable" declared that the land grant group was the most powerful special interest at the convention.[25] Twenty stockmen comprised the second largest occupational group in attendance. This figure indicates the significant strength of the sheep and cattle interests which, together with the mining and railroad lobbies, were to exert an important influence on convention proceedings. Other groups represented included fourteen merchants, seven farmers, six general businessmen, four saloonkeepers, three bankers, three physicians, three editors, three territorial officers, two county officers, one college president, one mining man, and one lumber and sawmill man.[26]

One important interest group which was not anchored on an economic base was the sizable delegation of Spanish-speaking people. They had an understandable concern for the welfare of their traditional customs and culture. Since the American occupation, they had feared that the "Gringos" might dispossess them of their inheritance, deprive them of their voting rights, and threaten their common welfare. This group would doubtless be a formidable force at the convention.

Proceedings of the constitutional convention commenced at noon, on Monday, October 3, 1910. The meeting place was the House Chamber of the old capitol. The brass rail was removed and desks were placed almost to the back wall.[27] Catron, acting as temporary chairman, called the meeting to order and delivered the opening remarks.[28] One of the first projects was a feeble effort to establish a nonpartisan convention. On the second day it was decided that delegates should be seated according to their county. This was tried but without success. The twenty-nine Democrats were so widely distributed that a spontaneous effort to achieve anything on the floor was impossible.[29] The pretense of nonpartisanship probably was doomed from the beginning. Early in the summer Catron had written:

We are sure to have a two-thirds republican majority in the convention, and we think we are better able to make a good constitution than the democrats. We know they would not hold a non-partisand [sic] convention if they were in the majority. To make it non-partisan means that we would have to give away some of our strength, and I do not believe any political party can succeed by surrendering a part of its strength.[30]

One of the earliest decisions the convention had to make was the choice for convention chairman. Catron had been considered fairly certain for the position prior to the election for delegates, but his narrow victory at the polls forced him to release his claims for the job.[31] The choice then fell to Charles Spiess, a former Catron law partner, who because of his dark, handsome features was known as the "Black Eagle of San Miguel County."[32] Nominated by Fall and receiving the backing of the Republicans, he easily won over Fergusson in a 68 to 29 party-line vote.[33] His victory was interpreted as a triumph for the railroads. "If Charles A. Spiess is given the leading role in the convention, the corporation taint will be there."[34]

Other officers elected included George W. Armijo as chief clerk and the elderly Major Harry R. Whiting as sergeant-at-arms. These elections, too, followed party lines. Cesario Pedregon's selection as interpreter was without contest. But the election of convention officials was not nearly as important as the committee system established by the leadership of the convention. On the third day, a resolution was introduced calling for the formation of a Committee of Committees, consisting of twenty-six members, which would be responsible for the selection of other convention committees. Approval of the master committee assured caucus control of convention proceedings. Luna was appointed chairman and Charles Springer, secretary, while men such as Fall, Daugherty, Bursum, Holloman, and Catron served as members on the new power trust.[35]

The Committee on Committees set to work and established twenty-seven committees, each assigned the job of drafting a section of the constitution. In attempting to cover every phase of state government, Luna's committee set up divisions ranging all the way from the Committee on the Legislative Department to the Committee on Liquor Traffic and Prohibition.[36] Although Democrats were represented, the chairman and a majority on each committee were Republicans. The constitution of 1889 and copies of the constitutions of other states were used as guides.[37] Each group after completing a tentative draft of its section submitted the work to the Republican caucus where it was carefully considered before being submitted to the convention. On the floor, it was debated and voted upon. Because the Republicans committed all their members in caucus, substantial changes rarely were made in the original draft, despite the heated and partisan debate which often ensued.[38]

Other forms of control exercised by the Republican majority included the so-called gag rules. One prevented a roll call vote so that it was impossible for the public to know how each delegate voted.[39] Another prevented a delegate from speaking more than twice on a certain subject. A third allowed any member the right to demand the previous question,[40] thus making it possible to stop debate at any time. Of special significance was the refusal of the majority to allow a verbatim record of the convention proceedings to be made. Only the most formal actions, such as committee reports, key votes and the like, were printed. A Democratic effort to have stenographers take down the full proceedings each day was defeated by the majority.[41] Democrats even complained that the reading of the journal was suspended for a time so that only the convention officers knew whether an accurate account of the deliberations was being printed.[42]

Despite tight control exercised by the Republican leadership, fairly cordial relations existed between members—at least at first. A round of parties, receptions, dinners, and buggy rides in Santa Fe reduced tension between Republicans and Democrats and between advocates of a "safe and sound" constitution and a progressive constitution. Some Democrats realized the hopelessness of their position and were willing to compromise from the beginning. Although Fergusson later labeled them as representatives for "special interests, such as the railroads, the land grants, coal companies,"[43] these members doubtless created a more harmonious working relationship.

Bipartistanship was easy to achieve on a number of the earlier actions.

A motion to invite President Taft to the convention was unanimously approved. Another to send compliments to the Arizona constitutional convention which assembled October 10 received quick approval. No objection was voiced to receiving a gavel from Mary Prince, wife of the former governor, who was state regent of the territorial chapter of the Daughters of the American Revolution. And in true bipartisan fashion, portraits of Antonio Joseph and J. Francisco Chaves were placed side by side on the wall of the convention hall.[44] But such harmony could not last indefinitely. Soon partisanship reached a high pitch whipped by the emotional oratory of Fergusson, who denounced the greedy rich and corporate interests who sought to control the convention. Fall's antics did not make for a smooth-functioning convention, either. The delegate from Otero County was a hot-tempered, emotional man who carried a gun. His wife and daughter, aware of his ugly disposition, sat in the House Chamber every other day in such a way that they could keep their eyes on him. One day, Fall took offense to a remark by Jacob Crist, the eloquent Democratic delegate, whose quote from Shakespeare had the remarkable effect of causing Fall to jump to his feet and approach the pale Crist with shaking fists and loud invectives. Although Fall was finally persuaded to take his seat, Crist left the convention and never returned.[45] Even if the personalities at the convention had been more compatible, it would have been impossible to avoid controversy over such issues as direct legislation, the method to be used in amending the constitution, prohibition, woman's suffrage, what powers to give a corporation commission, handling of the public land allotment, and the establishment of judicial and legislative districts.

According to one delegate, there was never any doubt that provisions for initiative or recall would be adopted.[46] But since all Democratic delegates were pledged to both a liberal initiative and liberal referendum, and many favored recall, a stirring fight was inevitable. A recall proposal was introduced October 17 and three days later two initiative and referendum proposals were presented.[47] The Republican majority, determined to draft a "safe, sound and fundamentally simple constitution,"[48] looked with suspicion at these comparatively new and untried instruments of democracy. But even Republicans could not give too negative a response to the most popular issues of the day. Finally a watered-down referendum measure was approved. Rather than give the people power over all legislation except "laws necessary for the immediate preservation of the public peace, health or safety," as many states had done, New Mexico's referendum listed a series of exemptions in addition to the ones regarding "public peace, health or safety."[49] The effectiveness of the referendum provision was thus seriously hampered. Exempted were general appropriation laws, enactments regarding payment of the public debt "or interest thereon" and creation and funding of the debt, laws for the maintenance of public schools or state institutions, and local or special laws.[50]

The demand for an easily amended constitution, such as Roosevelt felt New Mexico should adopt, was also met with a compromise which provided that a two-thirds vote of the entire membership in each house of the state legislature would be necessary to propose an amendment. But in the third year after the constitution's adoption, and every eighth year thereafter, a majority vote in each house would suffice. The proposed amendment would have to be ratified by a popular majority, and the number of votes cast must be equal to forty per cent of all votes cast in the general election and must be approved by at least one-half of the counties.[51] Although it was obvious that the aim of the convention was to make it exceedingly difficult to amend the constitution, the amendment provisions were adopted by a vote of 83 to 10. Obviously, only the "irreconcilables" held out for a workable amending procedure.

Constitutional safeguards of the rights of *Hispanos* were made nearly impossible to amend. Voting and educational rights in particular were specifically mentioned in the constitution. Section 3 of Article VII protected, among other things, the right of a citizen to vote regardless of his "religion, race, language or color," and regardless of his inability to handle effectively either the English or Spanish languages "except as may be otherwise provided in this constitution." Section 10 of Article XII declared that "children of Spanish descent" would never be denied the right of admission to the public schools, nor ever "classed in separate schools, but shall forever enjoy perfect equality with other children in all public schools . . . ." To amend these provisions, three-fourths of the members of each house were required to propose any change, while at least three-fourths of the electorate voting in the "whole state" and not less than two-thirds of those voting in each county were required for ratification.[52]

The stringent provisions regarding equality for the Spanish-speaking citizen were intended to overcome the fears and apprehensions of the native population that they might be discriminated against by the Anglo majority. One delegate described the inclusion of such clauses as being part of a compromise. In return for the Spanish-speaking delegates' agreement to permit women to vote in school elections—a provision contrary to the traditional role of women in their culture—these safeguards were enacted.[53] Native delegates were especially adamant against any provision for separate schools, even for Negroes.[54] This caused one Southern newspaper, the *El Paso Times*, to warn New Mexicans after the national elections in November that the recently elected Democratic House would reject their constitution because separation of the races was not mentioned.[55]

One powerful pressure group that failed to achieve its objectives at the convention was the Woman's Christian Temperance Union. They, along with the Anti-Saloon League, waged a vigorous campaign to put a prohibition provision into the new constitution. They had the support of all the Democrats from the eastern part of the territory. Fergusson counted the prohibitionists, together with insurgent Republicans, among the party's best allies in the fight for a more progressive constitution.[56] Upon a motion by Catron, five members of the W.C.T.U. were issued tickets to the convention where they could engage in lobbying activities. Petitions calling for statewide prohibition were presented,[57] and appropriate motions were introduced. The Republican leaders found it very awkward to maneuver in this difficult situation. And they faced a real dilemma when on November 18 the majority and minority reports of the Committee on Liquor Traffic and Prohibition were presented. E. A. Miera, of Sandoval County, chairman of the group, introduced the majority statement which declared that the regulation of liquor traffic was the proper subject of legislative regulation under the police power of the state, and not "a proper matter" to be incorporated into the constitution. The minority report, although agreeing that the question was not a proper one for incorporation, did recommend that this and other important measures should be submitted to a vote of the people through an initiative and adequate referendum.[58] The majority report was adopted by a vote of 57 to 25.

The women of the state also failed to achieve adequate suffrage. Although widely discussed at the convention, only a limited franchise to vote in school elections was given. This limited measure, introduced by Democrat Reuben Heflin from Farmington, did, however, receive approval and support from such powerful Republicans as Bursum and Luna.[59]

Proponents of both reforms were disappointed by their lack of success, the prohibitionists being particularly bitter. A group of New Mexico citizens insisted that the "liquor interests" were the strongest in a convention controlled by special interests. They claimed an examination of internal revenue records would show that fifteen of the delegates were liquor dealers, while "special inside information" indicated there were as many as twenty.[60] A New Jersey official of the Anti-Saloon League echoed these charges and accused Miera, the chairman of the liquor traffic committee, of being one of the liquor dealers. Miera and his committee, by "juggling," prevented a representative of the Anti-Saloon League, who represented the Christian and temperance sentiment of the territory, from being heard by the committee.[61] One distraught W.C.T.U. member, a mother from Belen, wrote Hamilton, "I ask you in the name of the Lord to help . . . put whiskey out of New Mexico . . . I have a boy and a girl to be protected and a husband[,] and the Saloon men have every thing their own way and if we don't do something I do not know what will become of us."[62]

Two other issues which were heatedly contested at the convention were control of corporate institutions and legislative apportionment. Monopoly control and restrictions on big business had become major objectives of the Progressive crusade. Beveridge's continued fight to keep New Mexico out of the Union had much to do with his distaste for the tremendous influence of large corporations in territorial affairs. For varying reasons, everyone waited to judge New Mexico's corporation provisions. The selection of Bursum as chairman of the Corporation Committee made very lax rulings a certainty.

The Republican leader believed that New Mexico needed to attract capital investment in order to fulfill its economic potential. Consequently, he was eager to prevent the inclusion of any provision which would discourage corporations from coming into the new state or hamper the activities of those already there. The result was the establishment of a weak corporation commission which could fix and regulate the "rates of railway, express, telegraph, etc. . . . ,"[63] but could not regulate the rates of utilities. Moreover, what regulatory powers were given the commission did not alarm the railroad corporations, which "heartily" endorsed the constitution and recommended its support to the voters in the upcoming election on ratification.[64]

The controversy over legislative apportionment took its traditional American form. A gerrymandering operation was so effectively employed by the Republican majority that although the Democrats elected their governor and their candidate to Congress, plus about half of the state officers, at the first state election, the Republicans achieved a two-thirds majority in both the senate and the house of the state legislature. Using their numerical superiority and playing on the desire of delegates from sparsely populated counties for at least one representative in the legislature,[65] the Republicans carved up the state to their liking and won a favorable vote for their apportionment on the last day of the convention.

The convention then enacted a bill of rights in which Spanish-speaking natives were further protected. "The rights, privileges and immunities, civil, political and religious, guaranteed to the people of New Mexico by the treaty of Guadalupe Hidalgo shall be preserved inviolate."[66] Attention was also paid to state offices. The move to have judges elected rather than appointed received overwhelming support, but a motion to establish civil service for state employees died for want of a second.[67] Article XXI was of special importance because it was in the form of a compact with the federal government. All the stipulations made by Congress in New Mexico's enabling act were fulfilled in this article and made "irrevocable" without the consent of Congress.

All provisions proposed for the constitution were sent to the Committee on Revisions and Arrangements where they were scrutinized for clarity, grammar, spelling, and punctuation. The result was at last a constitution—conservative, longer than most, but nevertheless a fundamental document to guide the destinies of the new state.

On the final day of the convention, November 21, 1910, a roll call vote was taken on the constitution and, as expected, the document was adopted by a vote of 79 to 18 with 3 not voting.[68] Only eight Democrats voted for the constitution although a majority later signed it. Of the small group of Democrats who refused to the end to sign the constitution, Fergusson was probably the most vociferous. "This constitution is wholly reactionary, has not a progressive principle in it; the so-called REFERENDUM therein being wholly impracticable because of its prohibited [sic] labor and expense to make it effective." Fergusson urged his colleagues and supporters to stand by their progressive principles.[69]

Despite the bitter controversy which had characterized deliberations at the convention, differences were forgotten on the last day. Whether this was due to the three barrels of bottled beer and the large supply of sandwiches contributed by an unknown benefactor on closing night, or whether the delegates were simply exhausted from their extended labors, is not known. But forgiving and forgetting occurred on all sides. Chairman Spiess was presented with a beautiful silver service set, a gift of the entire convention. His remarks upon receiving the gift were unusually complimentary to the minority Democrats.[70] At 11:15 P.M., according to the official *Proceedings*, the convention adjourned *sine die*.[71]

On November 22, the day after adjournment, Governor Mills proclaimed January 21, 1911, as the day the voters could either ratify or reject the new constitution. "Those voting in favor of the ratification of said Constitution shall vote, in either English or Spanish, 'For the Constitution,' and those opposed to the ratification of said Constitution shall vote in either English or Spanish, 'Against the Constitution.' "[72] Mills, who was thought to be completely sympathetic with the conservative constitution, predicted its ratification by 25,000 votes.[73]

The ease with which approval would come depended to a large extent upon the attitude of the Democratic party in the territory. Memories of twenty years ago when the Republican leaders formulated the constitution of 1889, only to have it rejected by the people, were too real to merit a feeling of complete confidence. A clue to the Democratic position would be provided at Santa Fe on December 19, 1910. William B. "Billy" Walton, party chairman, had called a delegate convention for that day at which time the party would determine whether to support or work against the proposed constitution. Prospects looked good as the *Silver City Independent*, a paper owned and edited by Walton, came out in favor of adoption of the new instrument. The New Mexico constitution like the United States constitution was a compromise which represented "the best composite labors of 100 men, and it does compare favorably with other states."[74]

The Democratic convention which assembled at Santa Fe found itself hopelessly divided and, although it drew up a list of thirteen objections, it decreed that party loyalty would not be tested by any member's vote upon the constitution. First among the objections was the charge that the document was too difficult to amend. Also cited were the "inequitable" apportionment and the omission of an initiative and practical referendum. High salaries to be paid state employees and the alleged increase in taxation were questioned. Lack of provisions for a direct primary or an advisory selection of United States senators were felt to be weaknesses of the new constitution. Curiously, the Democrats remained silent on woman's suffrage and prohibition in their list of objections.[75]

With Democrats free to vote according to the dictates of their own consciences, it remained for individuals to carry much of the burden in implementing the thirteen objections. Fergusson was in the forefront of this campaign. Writing to Judge C. R. Worral of Clovis, he declared:

. . . It is the patriotic duty of every citizen, in my humble opinion, to defeat this first draft of a constitution, made by the gang which has corruptly governed New Mexico for the past twenty years. . . . Read the Organic Act and find plainly stated that if the first draft of the constitution is defeated by the people, it is the duty of the Governor within twenty days after such defeat, to reconvene this convention to make another draft. This will only delay statehood beyond this present congress and leave it to some extent in the hands of the 62nd Congress which is heavily democratic.[76]

Fergusson labeled the article relating to the amendment of the constitution as "most difficult and improbable" as the powers in control had evidently intended it to be. Once every eight years it would be possible for twelve men in the senate, out of a total membership of seventy-three in the legislature, to prevent an amendment from being submitted. "All the balance of the time, it will require only nine or seven men in the senate to prevent any effort by the people to amend their constitution . . . ." As for the absence of any effective direct legislation, it ought to be defeated for this omission alone. The referendum provided in the constitution was described as "mere make believe." The provision that three-fourths of the counties and ten per cent of the total vote cast in the last election were required to petition for a referendum was certainly prohibitory. This three-fourths figure meant nineteen counties. "Think of the long railroad trips, of the long distances between towns and settlements and the expense, time and labor required in getting . . . voters scattered over nineteen counties."[77]

Fergusson also claimed that corporations were the "controlling influences" in the convention and were stalwart supporters of the constitution as written. He called the provision for corporation control an ineffective one. Although the commission established by it could regulate railroad rates, railroad attorneys and agents were active in the preparation of the corporation article, and corporations were understood to be in favor of it. The commission was powerless to force obedience to its own orders, while its procedures for action were considered expensive.[78] Fergusson capped his attack on the work of the convention with a discussion of the Hagerman affair and the land fraud cases, tying in these scandals with the "bosses" of the convention.

Fergusson's charges were answered point by point by Frank W. Clancy, attorney general for the territory. Clancy defended the amending procedure by declaring that in only three states, or at the most four if Oklahoma be included, could constitutions be "as easily amended as here."[79] He asserted that the omission of an initiative and recall was not enough to justify rejection of statehood. Although nearly half of the members of the convention favored some sort of an initiative, they were never at any time able to agree upon the details of what they wanted, while a large portion, "probably a majority of the convention," regarded the initiative as "highly objectionable." As for the recall advocated by Fergusson, this was considered dangerous, especially as it pertained to elected judges. The independence of the judiciary must not be subject to the "sudden impulses of mere majorities."[80] The corporation commission was defended as being only a scale model of the Interstate Commerce Commission. Whereas the I.C.C. can only enforce its orders through the federal courts, so the corporation commission must rely upon the supreme court of the state to make its decrees effective. As for the charge that railroad attorneys and agents were active in the preparation of the corporation article, Clancy asked just who these railroad attorneys and agents were. He also denied that corporations were in favor of the commission. After all, this was a body established for their regulation.[81]

Although the fight against advocates of the initiative and a stronger referendum was conducted on a territorial basis, local appeals were also effectively made. For instance, the people of San Juan County were approached with an appeal to their selfish interests. Having an abundance of water and irrigable land, many of them apparently believed the ancient irrigation laws and customs found throughout much of the territory were not applicable in San Juan. Consequently, direct legislation would be a threat. "It would be possible under the initiative for a majority in some parts of the territory to impose these ancient laws and customs upon us, and we would be helpless to prevent it."[82] Calls to come to the aid of the party were frequently sounded by Republicans who knew that their party's reputation depended upon ratification of the constitution. Andrews borrowed $500 to contribute to Republican efforts for decisive ratification. "This is more than my share, but I am willing to help."[83]

Newspapers were especially active in the campaign for ratification. The large majority supported the constitution, admitting that, while it did not please everyone, it was on the whole a good document. The threat that statehood would be delayed if the constitution were not approved was also effectively employed. The *Deming Graphic* commended the hundred delegates at the convention for turning out the best constitution they could produce.[84] The Socorro *Chieftain* called the convention an honorable body, and denounced the "ill-tempered attack" of the Democratic newspapers on the majority members of the convention for not seeing fit to do the will of the minority in the matter of initiative and referendum.[85]

Some newspapers, however, bitterly opposed ratification, concentrating their attack on the difficult amending clause and the absence of an initiative and practical referendum. They asked for a new constitution and urged rejection of the present instrument. Most outspoken was the *Deming Headlight*, still a crusading little paper in the Edmund Ross tradition. Statehood could be a boon and it could be a heavy burden, and the most enthusiastic statehood booster "should not blind himself" to the fact that a progressive and just constitution was necessary to make statehood desirable. Referring to the alleged special treatment given business interests at the convention, the paper warned that the farmer of today was no hayseed, but was "up on all progressive subjects."[86] It compared the initiative procedure with the king's petition of the past. No king in recent times in any country claiming to be free had had the hardihood to deny the right of petition; therefore, New Mexicans should insist on this safeguard in their constitution. As for the charge that direct legislation and other "socialistic measures" kept capital out of the territory, the *Headlight* pointed to the amount of money corporations had turned loose in Oregon since direct legislation was introduced there. "In face of actual facts, this argument, like every other against direct legislation vanishes into thin smoke."[87]

Despite the unpopularity of the conservative features of the constitution, desire for statehood was too great to permit the constitution's defeat at the polls. The document was approved by a vote of 31,742 to 13,399. The constitution carried in all counties except Roosevelt, Lincoln, San Juan, and Sierra.[88] It now remained for Congress and the President to render the final decision.

SEVENTEEN

The Final Steps

NEW MEXICANS CONSIDERED
their conservative constitution a likely candidate for approval despite a
national Democratic victory in the 1910 congressional election. At the
time the constitution was completed, a "lame duck" Republican Congress
was still in session, and a President known to be cautious and scrupulously
legal was in the White House.

But in 1910 it was not Santa Fe or Washington that halted the march
toward statehood, it was Phoenix. There on December 9, Arizona Territory completed its constitution. Long, liberal, and very unlike New
Mexico's, it contained measures for initiative, referendum, and recall, and
a child labor provision. In every phase of legislation, Arizona's constitution reflected a liberal mood, astounding those who had been sure Arizona was a corporation-controlled baliwick. President Taft may have
understood the situation a little better. He had visited the territory in
1909 and observed that strong labor forces under the guidance of a prominent businessman, George W. P. Hunt, had gained control of the
Twenty-fifth Territorial Legislature. Taft had subtly warned the territory
at that time to refrain from radical provisions in its constitution.[1] The
Progressivism spreading throughout America at this time could not, however, have been checked by President Taft or any one else. In Arizona,
where workers, farmers, and small businessmen had long been under the
yoke of big business, Progressivism grew as dissatisfaction with the status
quo mounted.[2] The election for constitutional convention delegates
showed the strength of the workers by giving 41 out of 52 seats to Demo-

crats, and Democrats triumphed again when Hunt, who had travelled to Oregon and California to study Progressive laws and constitutions, was elected president of the convention.[3] After nearly two months of debate and maneuver, Progressivism prevailed and a constitution considered almost radical for its time was adopted.

The recall provision in the new document was thought to be most dangerous. Prior to Arizona's adoption of the measure, only Oregon had incorporated such a provision into her constitution. Although California was to follow shortly thereafter, the newness of this instrument of direct legislation caused lifted eyebrows. The inclusion of judges in the provision only made it more unacceptable. According to the Arizona recall, any elective officer, having been in office six months or more, was subject to a recall election upon the petition of 25 per cent of the voters who participated in the last election.[4] Other provisions for direct legislation included an initiative in which 10 per cent of the voters could propose a law and, if a majority approved it at the next election, the law would be final. A referendum was also provided whereby 5 per cent of the vote could, by petition, order the submission to the people of any enactment of the legislature, except for those acts immediately necessary to preserve "public peace, health or safety."[5]

Before Arizonans voted approval or disapproval of their constitution, the press across the nation had much to say on the subject. The *El Paso Herald*, three days before the February 9 election to ratify the new instrument, recommended that if Arizona really wanted a constitution, the smartest thing that she could do would be to reject the instrument adopted by the Phoenix convention. The President would never approve the document and this would cause unnecessary delay. If the people rejected the constitution, they would have a chance to vote on it again in a few weeks without the objectionable recall provision.[6] The New York *Evening Post*, although sharing the dislike for recall—especially recall of judges—felt the threat was exaggerated. " . . . The Union will survive even if Arizona does her worst; nor need the judges of the Supreme Court at Washington tremble for what may be done at Phoenix . . . ."[7] Perhaps this was sagacious advice, because Arizonans ratified the constitution by a vote of 12,187 to 3,302.

Prominent individuals had their opinions about the new constitution too. Catron adamantly opposed the provisions for direct legislation. "I do not believe in either the initiative, referendum, or recall; they are heresies and constitute the first movement in the direction of anarchy in this government of ours; that is, we will all be nihilists in a few years or in a nihilist government if those radicals who are starting such a movement are allowed to get control."[8] However, a much more potent figure, former

President Roosevelt, gave the new document his wholehearted support[9] and alienated his more conservative following a year later by coming out for the recall of judicial decision by popular vote.

New Mexicans little realized that the controversy over Arizona's constitution would affect them. They were having their own problems, for the territorial vote which had ratified the constitution was being challenged. Local prohibitionists, including three ministers from Albuquerque, had aroused the national W.C.T.U. and Anti-Saloon League with accusations of "fraud, bribery, violence, and intimidation." Letters and telegrams poured into the House of Representatives and Senate asking for a congressional investigation of the January 21 election.[10] A former senator from New Hampshire, Henry W. Blair, was leader of the attack in Washington. Acting as attorney for protesting New Mexicans he produced a letter from a Republican leader in New Mexico to the members of the Republican central committee with the admonition: "Be sure if you can . . . [to] see that no ballots against the constitution are printed."[11] The House Committee on the Territories felt compelled to draft four resolutions, three of which endorsed the constitution and relieved the committee of responsibility for investigating the matter. The fourth resolution, which required action, stated that the committee desired further information "upon the question of the validity of the elections for the ratification or rejection of the Constitution."[12]

Andrews, sensing the seriousness of the situation, wired officers and citizens of the territory for affidavits testifying as to the fairness of the election.[13] These were presented to the House committee along with a copy of the governor's proclamation of January 20, 1911, requesting peace officers and district attorneys to inquire into all complaints of fraud or intimidation and "vigorously prosecute" them.[14] The affidavits showed that ballots were printed and distributed in every county and precinct of the Territory of New Mexico, that saloons were closed all day on January 21 and in many places did not open until the following morning, and that order and peace prevailed throughout the territory on an election day free from "intimidation, bribery or corruption."[15]

The affidavit from Santa Fe County was an especially forceful one, signed by such prominent residents as Catron, Nathan Jaffa, secretary of the territory, and Benjamin M. Read, a prominent prohibitionist. It contended that the charges made regarding the election were "wicked and malicious slanders on our good people." It denied that the registration lists were fraudulent, and that saloonkeepers gave voters liquor and forced them to vote for the constitution. Every saloon in Santa Fe was closed from midnight of January 20 to midnight of January 22, the day after election being Sunday. It also swore that an equal number of ballots for and against the constitution had been delivered to opposition workers as well as Republicans in every precinct of the county.[16]

The territory's problems with prohibitionists were largely resolved by President Taft, who on February 24, 1911, formally approved the constitution and sent it to Congress with a recommendation that approval be given.[17] The House quickly acceded to the President's wishes. Four days after receiving Taft's recommendation, the Committee on Territories accepted the constitution, and on March 1, 1911, the House gave its approval. The measure, called House Joint Resolution No. 295, was then sent to the upper house, where Andrews seemed encouraged about favorable action. "We have a lot of good friends in the senate," he wrote Catron, but admitted that Senator Beveridge was the key to success or failure. Although the Indianan had been defeated for re-election, he was still chairman of the Senate territorial committee until the 61st Congress adjourned. "The President said he would make him report it off the bat and if so, why it will require no debate in the senate."[18] Apparently Andrews was right, for three days later the Beveridge committee reported the resolution.

Senator Robert Owen from Oklahoma shattered the prevailing confidence when he objected during the last hours of the 61st Congress to passing the resolution until it included approval of the controversial Arizona constitution. He threatened to prevent passage of the sundry civil conference report, a post office bill, and a post roads bill,[19] and launched into a filibuster which tied up legislation for hours. Adjournment being imminent, the senator's action was regarded as a serious threat to the legislative program. Finally, the President and members of the upper house took action to end the filibuster. The Senate agreed to vote on House Joint Resolution No. 295, as amended by Owen to include the Arizona constitution. The result was an adverse vote of 45 to 39[20] and a defeat for the statehood aspirations of both territories. But to get action, Taft had to assure Owen that an extraordinary session would be called immediately after the close of the 61st Congress to deal with the Canadian reciprocity treaty, at which time the statehood question could again be considered. This message, sent through Vice President James S. Sherman, apparently was satisfactory as the Oklahoman agreed to end his filibuster, enabling the 61st Congress to complete its legislation and adjourn.[21]

Owen's filibuster caused bitterness in New Mexico despite the fact that the territory would have another chance during the extra session convening on April 4. Catron vented his anger by writing: "Its too bad that we failed; but when things get to the point where one louzy [sic] whelp can make trouble and do harm you will always find the individual who is equal to the occasion." The fact that Owen came from Oklahoma, a state which had labored with New Mexico for many years to achieve statehood, particularly irked Catron. "One would have thought that Owen was the last man who would have obstructed us. . . . This is ingratitude of the basest kind and one that our people will never forget."[22] Fall saw partisan politics in Owen's action. "Naturally, the Democrats want Arizona admitted along with New Mexico, as the latter will probably send two Republican senators and the former two Democrats."[23]

The *El Paso Times* saw another motive in the filibuster. It declared that the *New York Tribune* had information proving that Owen was not devoted to Arizona's liberal constitution, but rather hoped that by filibustering he could prevent another bill from coming up which would have questioned the deals which had brought him possession of many acres of rich land belonging to the Indians, "to which race the senator himself belongs." According to the story, for two years the sundry civil bill had carried an appropriation of $50,000 "to give the law department the means to get after this defendant, and others in the attempt to restore the lands in question to the defrauded Indians."[24]

Senator Owen had his own explanation for the much publicized filibuster. "My fight against the New Mexico bill was made primarily to bring the issue of the initiative and referendum squarely before the American people." The senator vowed to oppose the admission of New Mexico not because he wished to keep the territory out of the Union, but because he felt Arizona was equally entitled to admission.[25] He also had aroused the ire of many New Mexico papers by supporting the prohibitionists and threatening to investigate the election that had resulted in the adoption of the constitution.[26]

About three weeks before the opening of the special session, Andrews confidently wrote Catron that if no action were taken during the extra session, he had been assured by the Attorney General, George W. Wickersham, that he would rule that New Mexico had complied with the terms of the enabling act and should be brought into the Union at the end of the first regular session of the 62d Congress, providing she was not disapproved by Congress or the President in the meantime.[27] In another exchange between the two men, the delegate spoke bitterly of Beveridge's last-ditch obstructionism in reporting House Joint Resolution No. 295. ". . . Beveridge refused to do anything with it and at 12:00 midnight Friday, March 3d, it took the combined efforts of four Senators and Postmaster General Hitchcock to make Beveridge give up and allow Dillingham to report it . . . ."[28]

The correspondence between the pair revealed the amazing power that Catron wielded after long years in New Mexico's rough and tumble political scene. On March 11, Andrews felt compelled to deny reports reaching the Santa Fean that he and Fall had made a deal regarding the two senatorships the territory would receive. Through Catron's pressure, Andrews took great pains to make sure that a certain appointment would not be made on the commission authorized by congressional action to relocate the old Clark boundary line north of El Paso between Texas and New Mexico.[29]

The first day of the extra congressional session brought to the floor Representative Henry D. Flood, a Democrat from Virginia, who had taken Hamilton's position as chairman of the Committee on the Territories in the new Democratic House. He introduced a joint resolution calling for the admission of Arizona and New Mexico on the basis of their submitted constitutions. Andrews also introduced a joint resolution which provided for the admission of New Mexico singly,[30] while Delegate Smith of Arizona did the same for his territory. These early maneuvers were followed by a series of committee hearings conducted by Flood on his proposal, House Joint Resolution No. 14, which extended from the middle to the latter part of April. If the hearings accomplished nothing else, they forced New Mexicans to air their dirty linen before a national audience. Hostile Democrats like Fergusson, J. D. Hand, and Andrieus A. Jones were there to castigate the new constitution, and insurgent Republicans such as Hagerman and Richard H. Hanna of Santa Fe were there to help them.[31] Jones, who had chaired the Democratic meeting that issued the thirteen objections to the Santa Fe constitution, attacked the awkward amending procedure of the document, declaring that a majority of members at the convention had been pledged to an initiative and referendum but had failed to fulfill their commitment. He decried the apportionment and corporation articles and denounced the language qualification.[32] Fergusson and Hand requested that the Flood committee adjourn for a week to enable them to prepare a better-documented case against the constitution.[33] Critics of New Mexico were aided by former Senator Blair who testified that the election to ratify the constitution was crooked.

Defenders of the new document also fought to be heard. Fall gave what Andrews described as "a bully good talk"[34] defending the provisions of the constitution; the convention had only done what he had heard Taft recommend several times—adopt a "safe and sane" constitution. Curry, who with Andrews and Clancy gave testimony, provided the only important break in the defense. He indicated that he was not personally opposed to any move that would make the constitution easier to amend. The majority of people had heretofore opposed tampering with the amendment clause because they felt it would delay admission.[35]

The press was in an uproar after hearing the testimony of the Democratic leaders. Republican papers in the territory were downright bitter. If the people of New Mexico wanted to experiment with recall, they might wait a hundred years before finding a more opportune time than the present for using it on J. D. Hand, A. A. Jones, and H. B. Fergusson, "self styled leaders who are now engaged in fighting statehood."[36] New Mexico's position was pictured as greatly injured by the testimony of these three.[37] So constant were the attacks of the Republican papers that the *El Paso Times* remarked: "It was no crime for the machine bosses to hogtie the free men of that territory in the proposed constitution in such a manner as would serve to perpetuate Republican rule for at least a quarter of [a] century. The crime lies in the effort that is being made to break up the unholy combination."[38] Watching sympathetically from the sidelines, the *Boston Herald* provided the only comedy relief during the stormy controversy by suggesting that the territory change its name to Jefferson "to win friends and hold them strongly."[39]

Although they resented the attacks on their constitution, many Republican leaders began to see the handwriting on the wall. The *New Mexican*, always a good barometer of Republican sentiment, expressed the belief that a greater part of the people of New Mexico would not mind having a clause put into the constitution to make it more easily amendable, if that would bring statehood. The paper did hope, however, that the protection given the Spanish-speaking people would not be tampered with, for native New Mexicans had a right "to protest against being put in the same status as the negro in Mississippi."[40] Jones predicted accurately what action the committee would eventually take. Writing to a friend in Albuquerque, he stated that a substitute for the amendment article would be voted upon by New Mexicans at the first state election. "This substitute provides for the submission of amendments by a majority thereon." Arizona, too, would have to vote upon a substitute for her recall article.[41] This, in substance, was the final form of House Joint Resolution No. 14, better known as the Flood resolution, which was reported by the Committee on the Territories on May 12, 1911, about two weeks after the hearings ended, and which the House passed by a *viva voce* vote on May 23.[42]

Once the resolution reached the Senate, the usual delay was encountered. Republican Senator William Alden Smith of Michigan, the new chairman of the Senate Committee on Territories, was absent from Washington and was not expected back until about the middle of June. Senator Owen had been called to Oklahoma to mend his "political fences."[43] Consequently, the bill was bottled up in committee for a month and a half. Fergusson, one of the New Mexicans most responsible for the Flood amendment,[44] became impatient. Writing to Owen, he insisted that there were enough Democratic and progressive Republican votes in the Senate to pass the resolution.

The scheme of the corruptionists in New Mexico and of the old standpat element in Washington and in the Senate,—more and more made plain with each passing day, is to prevent the admission of Arizona altogether, and to delay the admission of New Mexico, by preventing a vote on the Flood resolution in the Senate, until after the end of the next regular session of Congress to convene next December, when by operation of the law of the enabling act of June 20th, 1911 [1910], New Mexico will be in the Union under its drastic special interest constitution as made by the gang: Arizona remaining a Territory.[45]

Senate action was not the only concern; Taft's position was a constant source of worry. One report had the President promising Curry and Flood that although he would not use his influence to push statehood under the Flood resolution, he would sign the resolution if the Senate approved.[46] Taft denied this. Notwithstanding his approval of the New Mexico constitution, he declined to commit himself on the resolution.[47]

The Senate territorial committee took action on the measure after conducting hearings on June 16, 17, and 23. The resolution was favorably reported to the Senate, but three days later, on July 13, Senator Nelson of the committee offered an alternative. The clause in the Arizona constitution providing for recall of judges would have to be eliminated as a "fundamental condition" of admission. The Flood resolution had provided for a referendum on the recall clause, the territory to be admitted regardless of the vote, but under the substitute the people must veto the recall provision. Regarding New Mexico's constitution, Nelson would not require the people to vote on an easier amending procedure as specified in the original resolution.[48]

With two such proposals in abeyance, the conservative and liberal camps in the Senate each had a measure to champion. Although recall was an important feature of the progressive program, its application to judges caused real alarm. Even Senator William E. Borah of Idaho, who usually voted as a progressive Republican, expressed his concern. "Without a free and independent judiciary popular government would be tantamount to a tormenting delusion." The senator was opposed to the recall because he believed judges would be dissuaded from their convictions and legal guidance by the will of the majority, and this would undermine the stability of legal protection now afforded to American citizens.[49] Senator Elihu Root of New York, usually a calm, analytical speaker, was emotionally roused by the subject too,[50] and stated that while judges were supposed to decide cases by evidence, the judges themselves would now be judged by newspaper accounts of the case, "necessarily brief and partial." Newspapers were looking for the sensational features of a trial, and people form their opinion largely from these accounts.

Despite these strong opinions held by powerful men, the Nelson amendment was voted down on August 8 by a vote of 43 to 26, while the Flood resolution was approved, 53 to 18. Evidently a majority felt, as Republican Senator Miles Poindexter of Washington did, that it would be "a travesty on self government" to try to compel the people of Arizona to adopt a resolution, which they themselves did not want, but which the people of other states thought they should have.[51]

What would President Taft do now that both houses of Congress had approved the Flood resolution? It was well known that the President disliked recall as heartily as Root and Borah. But Congressman Flood felt confident that Taft would not veto his resolution in view of the record vote given it in the Senate, where a more than two-thirds majority was achieved.[52] Some felt that the President would allow the bill to become law without his signature, while others predicted a veto.[53] The latter speculation seemed most valid, as the New York World reported that the President on August 8 had informed opponents of recall in the Senate that he would never stand for the provision.[54] Also, on the day after the vote, he announced to a visiting delegation of New Mexico Democrats led by Fergusson, Jones, and Hand his intention to veto the Flood resolution, even though he "heartily" endorsed New Mexico's constitution. Privately, Taft was greatly irked. "What a lot of cowards they are in the Senate! There is not a handful of men there, either Democrats or Republicans, who believe in the Recall of the Judiciary, and yet they send me the Constitution of Arizona with this provision in it."[55]

True to his word, President Taft vetoed the Flood resolution in a message kept a carefully guarded secret until the day it was read in Congress, August 15, 1911.[56] Referring to the controversial recall, the President declared: "This provision of the Arizona constitution, in its application to county and State judges, seems to me so pernicious in its effect, so destructive of independence in the judiciary, so likely to subject the rights of the individual to the possible tyranny of a popular majority, and, therefore, to be so injurious to the cause of free government, that I must disapprove a constitution containing it."[57] The rejection was explosive. Conservatives were delighted and, when the message was read to the House, a burst of applause rose from the Republican side while Democrats remained silent.[58] Leading newspapers like the Chicago Tribune and the New York World supported the action.[59] The World hailed Taft's veto as a measure that would halt the drift of unenlightened opinion being exploited by demagogic leaders.[60] Because New Mexico was included in the Flood resolution, her statehood hopes were smashed, too. This provoked stinging criticism of Taft by much of the territorial press. The *Roosevelt County Herald* labeled the veto an "act of wanton, without reason, without justification and without precedent." This was the first time in America's history that a President had refused to approve a properly presented constitution.[61] The *Pecos Valley News* was especially bitter. "It seems to us that Mr. Taft has assumed, first, that the people of the southwest are not possessed of sufficient judgment and ability to form a state constitution and again, that communities are not capable of self government."[62]

The President was quite sensitive to public reaction. Responding to a telegram sent by a group of Las Vegas citizens, he stated: "The spirit with which you bear the disappointment of delayed Statehood reassures me and strengthens my conviction with respect to the performance of an unpleasant duty."[63] A look at the Taft correspondence following his veto reveals that the President was grateful for all the support he could get.

There was talk in Congress of overriding the presidential veto. One Democratic representative from the House territorial committee was especially critical and insisted upon overriding the veto by pushing the Flood resolution through Congress. Other Democrats insisted that if an acceptable compromise could not be worked out the veto should be made a national issue.[64] But cooler heads won out. Senator Smith, on the day the veto message was read, introduced Senate Joint Resolution No. 55, which would amend the Flood measure by requiring that the recall clause be eliminated from the Arizona constitution—such action to be voted upon by the people of the territory. New Mexico would still vote on an easier amendment clause, although the vote would have no bearing on her admission.[65] A joint committee from both houses met to consider the plan. Because two Democratic moderates were willing to vote with the Republicans from the House side, the Smith proposal was accepted. Smith, in behalf of the Senate territorial committee, reported the resolution, known as Senate Joint Resolution No. 57,[66] to the floor of the Senate on August 17. A vote taken the following day approved the compromise resolution by 53 to 9, and on August 19 the House passed it without a roll call. Democratic fears that Republican New Mexico might enter the Union alone under the terms of her enabling act doubtless facilitated action on the resolution.

Anticipating presidential approval, a gleeful Andrews telegraphed Catron: "I will have accomplished what the people of New Mexico sent me to Congress for."[67] At 3:08 P.M., August 21, 1911, President Taft signed the new compromise resolution promising statehood to New Mexico and Arizona if the terms of the resolution were met. "Well, gentlemen, it's done," remarked Taft to the delegation on hand to witness the ceremony.[68]

The President used three pens for the occasion. One he gave to Delegate Ralph Cameron of Arizona, another to Senator Smith, and a third to Andrews.[69] Overjoyed New Mexicans held statehood meetings throughout the territory—"the people being anxious to express their satisfaction at the successful termination of the half century fight for statehood."[70] Andrews quickly registered at the Navy Department to have the next new dreadnaught battleship being constructed named after the new state. ". . . You will soon see our name on the high seas."[71]

On August 22, 1911, the extraordinary session of the 62d Congress adjourned and President Taft went to his home at Beverly, Massachusetts, for a rest.[72] The territories now acted according to the specifications in the compromise. Governor Mills issued a proclamation calling for the first state election on November 7, 1911. Among the officials to be chosen were the governor, two representatives to Congress, members of the first state legislature, and a host of county and state officers. Aside from this, New Mexicans were to vote on a proposal to make the constitution easier to amend. A change could be proposed by a simple majority of all members in each legislative house, and this action could be ratified by a majority at the "next election after adjournment," or in a special election held in not less than six months after adjournment. The amendment ballots would be separate, and "printed on paper of the blue tint, so that they might be readily distinguishable from the white ballots provided the election of county and state officers . . . ."[73] Because of the color specification, this amendment became known as the "Blue Ballot" amendment.

The governor's proclamation, coming as it did so soon after Taft's approval, found Fergusson in real distress. Writing to William Jennings Bryan, he complained: "The enabling act provided for the election not less than sixty nor more than ninety days after the governor's call. As a willing tool of corruptionists long in control here, the governor called the election for November 7, the shortest time possible. They know their machine is all ready with abundance of money,—that we are without money or effective organization." This cry of distress was followed by a warning. ". . . You know how the local bosses and corrupt corporations make political contributions as investments certain to bring big returns. As a state, the inducements to put up money are many times multiplied. Outside, the prospect of two corrupt or stand-pat senators and one member of the House; within, the rich picking for the local gang, with the alternative of the penitentiary for many of them if they lose." The letter concluded with an urgent plea for money. ". . . Democrats have no special interests to draw upon for money . . . [but with] one dollar we can get [more] than our opponents can do with ten."[74]

Fergusson's belief that money could do the trick was not without substantial basis. Republicans were sharply divided, and events of the next few months were to show how severe the split was. Marked dissension was revealed at their convention in Las Vegas on September 28. Bursum's selection as gubernatorial candidate met with bitter opposition, while the choice of Curry as candidate for one of the two seats allowed the new state in the House made many delegates unhappy. Colorful Elfego Baca of Socorro County, the other choice, endorsed the stand taken by the convention against the Blue Ballot, but Curry told convention members that the condemnation of the Blue Ballot was a mistake. ". . . I could not ask the people of New Mexico for their support and at the same time tell them they were incapable of amending their own constitution."[75]

Disharmony at the Las Vegas gathering was augmented by developments at the Democratic meeting in Santa Fe on October 2. Here it was announced that a group of "Independent Republicans" headed by former Governor Hagerman and Hanna would join the Democrats in forming a fusion ticket. They were given two spots on the ticket while top jobs went to leading Democrats. William C. McDonald of Lincoln County, chairman of the Democratic central committee, was nominated for governor, and Fergusson and Paz Valverde were selected as candidates for the national House of Representatives. Moreover, it was announced that Hagerman and Hanna under the banner of "Progressive Republicans" would conduct a separate campaign chiefly against the candidacy of Holm Bursum.[76]

This combination was so strong that Bursum was defeated by McDonald, and a resurgent Democratic organization elected Fergusson and gained control of about half the state offices. Curry was elected because he refused to campaign against the Blue Ballot. In the legislative elections, the apportionment provision of the new constitution saved the day for Republicans, who elected 15 of the 24 state senators and 32 of the 49 representatives. The Blue Ballot amendment carried by a vote of 34,897 to 22,831.[77]

Curry interpreted the election results as a victory for the Democrats and declared that Republican opposition to an easier amendment process was the chief cause. He was willing to admit that there were other reasons, such as overconfidence of Republican leaders, opposition of Independent Republicans, and revival of charges against Bursum's conduct as prison superintendent. He might also have added the opposition of prohibitionists. But the crusade against the Blue Ballot was the costliest blunder; only 7 of the 26 counties of the territory polled majorities against the proposal for a workable amending clause. "The fact is that rigid provisions in the constitution, making amendment almost impossible, had been written into it by powerful corporate interests for entirely selfish ends. The people knew this and resented it. The Democrats took full advantage of this popular feeling in the ensuing campaign.[78]

The first state election did not complete the slate of officials who would govern the new commonwealth. New Mexico's first two senators were to be chosen by the newly elected legislature which was scheduled to convene in the spring. These two posts were regarded as rightful prizes by some of the territory's more vigorous fighters for statehood. Catron, Andrews, Fall, and Governor Mills were all top contenders whose various supporters were busy as early as September, securing all the backing they could.

Andrews seemed by all odds certain to be one of the first senators. As delegate to Congress when the enabling act was passed, he had increased his popularity with the people of New Mexico. His determination, skill as a lobbyist, and national political connections with men like the late Matthew Quay, still remembered in New Mexico for his support of the Knox bill, were other advantages. Senator Boise Penrose, heir to Quay as a political boss of Pennsylvania, had assured Taft in the presence of Andrews that he would support the delegate's political aspirations.[79] Penrose was quite popular among many New Mexicans because of his support of statehood. Early in May, 1911, the *Ft. Sumner Review* remarked: "If New Mexico receives statehood from the special session of Congress . . . it will not be because of the lack of his friendship and his active support . . . ."[80]

Andrews' early start gave him further advantage. As early as August 16, 1910, he felt compelled to deny in a speech that he and Catron had formed a coalition to assure their election to the United States Senate. "Statehood for New Mexico is bigger than any personal ambition of mine or Mr. Catron['s] . . . ."[81] In September, 1911, he came out for a direct primary in the election of senators. Apparently sensing a lack of support for his candidacy among Republican leaders of the territory, he declared: "No Republican could object to going before the people of his party and letting them make the choice at the polls."[82] In November, 1911, following the first state election, a more direct bid for support was attempted. "I am a candidate for United States Senator, I would be obliged if you will see your members of the Legislature in my behalf, some of the corporation managers are against me and I need your help . . . ."[83]

But Andrews, despite political support and backing from Eastern financial interests, was doomed to failure. His competition was too shrewd, too well entrenched. Although Mills was not an active candidate, Fall and Catron were, and two more formidable opponents could not be found. Bronson Cutting, a transplanted New Yorker and new leader of the Pro-

gressive Republicans in New Mexico, called Catron the "most unscrupulous man in the Southwest" and easily the "ablest of the bunch." Fall was
also regarded with trepidation—the "most dangerous man of the bunch."[84]

The actual account of how Catron and Fall won the new state's two
Senate seats is a confused one. One report states that Andrews nobly withdrew his candidacy during a secret meeting attended by Luna, Bursum,
Catron, and other party leaders. According to this version, Andrews, Fall,
Catron, and Mills were high men when the new state legislature met in
the spring of 1912, but the balloting went on for days and days without
the legislature being able to narrow the choice to two men. Fall clearly
had the advantage as Luna, the national committeeman, was championing
the cause of Fall and Catron, while Bursum, the former state chairman,
was supporting Fall and Andrews. At the secret meeting, called one night
in Andrews' home in Santa Fe, the former delegate withdrew his name
for the "sake of party harmony."[85]

This version fails to account for Andrews' bitterness following the
selection of Catron and Fall on March 28. He, along with Governor Mc-
Donald and the Albuquerque Journal-Democrat, questioned the legality
of Fall's election. Apparently, seventeen members of the House joined
the Senate in a little pre-election maneuver and decided upon Fall, the
legislature in joint assembly merely ratifying the action the following day.
This procedure caused such an uproar that Fall wrote: "Their continual
yawping and talk about the illegality of my election and that I could not
be re-elected by this legislature etc., simply aggravates me to the point of
stubbornness."[86] In stubbornness Fall continued a public career which
was in all respects sensational.

Even more damaging was an account of four Spanish-speaking legislators, all supporters of Andrews, being lured into the old Palace Hotel in
Santa Fe by Elfego Baca, where they were arrested for allegedly trying to
sell their votes. The four were forced to resign their offices and were jailed
for two nights and a greater part of two days. A request by the sergeant-
at-arms that they be released was ignored for eighteen hours. Upon their
release, they were exonerated of the charges preferred against them and
declared entitled to their seats. The conclusion of the report was that the
whole incident was a frame-up initiated by Baca, Apolonio Sena of the
state mounted police, Spiess, Springer, Major Llewellyn, and Bursum to
advance the candidacy of Fall, who would be assured of victory if the four
were removed.[87] It was obvious that steamroller tactics had won for Fall,
despite Andrews' skill and experience in political manipulation.

Statehood had, however, been safely achieved before the election of
Catron and Fall. Arizona had complied with the wishes of the President
and a majority in Congress by eliminating the recall provision, at least

until a state government was formed.[88] Although the two new congressmen, Curry and Fergusson, were told by the President on January 3, 1912,
that he would sign the proclamation the following day, on January 5 the
last of a long series of delays occurred. Crowds gathered in Santa Fe to
hear the eagerly awaited news, but suddenly, in Washington, Andrews received a message from the White House to the effect that the Department
of Justice wanted the signing of the statehood proclamation delayed until
it could take final action in the old timber cases. The Alamogordo Lumber
Company was one of the concerns involved, and the Department of Justice
wanted to issue a writ of error to transfer the case from the dying Territorial Supreme Court to federal jurisdiction so that the interest of the
federal government in certain public lands could be protected. Taft was
displeased and anxious that there be no additional delay, and his irritation
brought results. The Department wired its representatives in New Mexico
to take immediate action so that statehood could be proclaimed.[89] Although quickly solved, this last difficulty was symbolic of New Mexico's
entire, frustrating statehood fight.

Very frequently over the years, the territory's political inclinations were
in direct opposition to the prevalent mood in the nation's capital, resulting in indifference, and often hostility, to New Mexico's statehood aspirations. As early as 1850, the territory's fate was affected by national issues.
The bitter slavery debate was finally, momentarily, calmed by the Compromise of 1850 which gave to New Mexico the territorial status in which
she would remain for more than sixty years. Although the Civil War and
difficult Reconstruction years disrupted any systematic admission policy
for the territories, Nevada, despite a tiny population, was admitted because her three electoral votes would aid Lincoln's re-election and help
gain approval of the Thirteenth Amendment. Unfortunately, when Colorado was admitted in 1876, her three electoral votes went to Hayes in the
"Stolen Election," causing Democrats to balk at the admission of any
more Western states. In 1889, however, the Springer omnibus bill did
bring statehood to the Dakotas, Washington, and Montana, despite
failure of Democratic efforts to include New Mexico in the bill. In the
turbulent decade of the nineties, New Mexico allied herself with Free
Silver and Populism, thus losing the support of conservatives and "gold-
bugs" in Washington who viewed these causes as Western radicalism. In
the first years of the twentieth century, New Mexico shifted to conservatism but by this time most of the country was caught up in the reform
spirit of the Progressive Era. But for once New Mexico's long and continual association with Arizona was fortunate, because the conservative
constitution written by the territory's leaders in 1910 was balanced by the
liberal constitution Arizonans had written. Taft, a man torn by the poli-

tical currents of the day, was pleased with the New Mexico document and in 1912 would personally help end the long quest for statehood.

New Mexico's conservative leanings and connections with big business interests, especially those in Pennsylvania, made Albert Beveridge the territory's most implacable and powerful enemy over the years. To one of the leading progressives of his day, the special economic interests supporting both the New Mexico and Arizona statehood movements simply could not be allowed to bring about statehood for their own financial benefit. Beveridge also embodied some of the common and widespread prejudices of Easterners toward the *Hispano*, Catholic population of New Mexico. The general feeling of Anglo-Saxon superiority was certainly present in Beveridge, a leading spokesman for the new American imperialism. The Indianan remained suspicious of the territory to the very end, and when the final enabling act was being prepared, it was he who attached provisions and safeguards which he ardently hoped would prevent any corrupt "ring" of politicians from controlling the new state.

Outside forces cannot be totally blamed for New Mexico's long wait to join the Union. Internal dissension and periodic loss of interest were major problems. The early bid in 1850 was crippled by the feud between Weightman's statehood group and Houghton's territorial group. In 1866, a statehood convention dissolved, having accomplished nothing because the group was so lacking in interest and enthusiasm that it failed to obtain a quorum. The territory certainly did not appear eager to receive statehood when it failed to approve the fairly progressive constitution of 1872. Again, in 1889, a constitution was defeated at the polls by partisanship, opposition to secular schools, and a belief by many citizens that primarily "land grabbers" wanted statehood. Although a dedicated campaign by Governor Otero and Delegate Rodey significantly weakened opposition to statehood, subsequent opposition to jointure alienated not only Otero but also Tom Catron from the statehood movement, at least temporarily. Even after the prized enabling act had been passed, New Mexicans quarreled over the conservative constitution and its lack of provisions for direct legislation.

From the time the Treaty of Guadalupe Hidalgo was signed, there were New Mexicans who for varying reasons honestly preferred territorial status to statehood. Some feared increased taxation under a state government, and it was frequently charged that federal officials in the territory objected to a change that would jeopardize their jobs. Some Anglos and *Hispanos* feared that statehood would result in a domination of one group by the other, with ensuing complications in Church-state relations. Nevertheless, there were throughout the years numerous important champions of statehood.

The early self-promoting efforts for admission by Weightman were followed by the rather half-hearted actions of a few governors, such as Connelly and Giddings, who tried to instill in New Mexicans a desire for statehood. An effective and unswerving advocate was Bradford Prince, whose zeal for the cause was matched by such fighters as Bernard "Statehood" Rodey and the forceful Stephen Elkins. Tom Catron and Edmund Ross both fought for admission, although increased value for his vast land holdings appears to have been a prime motivation for Catron, not to mention Prince and Elkins, while Ross's concern was that statehood be granted only when a good public school system was established and corrupt "land grabbers" were under control. Delegate Andrews desired statehood as much as he desired to be one of the new state's first senators, although this ambition proved to be futile.

Why was New Mexico so long denied statehood despite increasing numbers of inhabitants determined to rise above the second-class citizenship of territorial status? Examination reveals that the principal arguments openly used by Easterners and others opposing New Mexico statehood applied with equal veracity to the other Western territories. Small populations and the fear that Westerners would hold a disproportionate amount of power in the Senate did not prevent Idaho and Wyoming from receiving statehood at a time when each had a smaller population than New Mexico. Certainly they were overrepresented in the upper house. These territories were also slow to develop economically, a favorite argument against New Mexico, and much of their land was arid, a fact which was used to refute the hope of natural development when applied to New Mexico, but which did not prevent these two territories from becoming states more than two decades before the Southwestern territory.

Factional strife and political discord do not fully account for the fact that New Mexico was never considered in the same light as the other territories. The unique population of New Mexico profoundly separated the territory from most of the remainder of the West where Anglo pioneers had slowly filled the frontiers with a fairly homogeneous population of Western European stock. In the long years between 1846 and 1912, frequent newspaper articles and speeches by congressmen indicated a strong prejudice toward the Spanish-speaking, Roman Catholic people of New Mexico. Nativism in America, sometimes concealed and at other times brought out into the open, was thus the major obstruction to the territory's statehood aspirations. Some remarks concerning the widespread use of Spanish in the schools, courts, and businesses of the territory had merit, but many reflected a most unfair bias against a people labeled by one congressman "a race speaking an alien language" and not representing the "best blood on the American continent." The actions of the territory's

Catholic hierarchy, especially its determined opposition to the constitution of 1889 because of a secular school provision, only aggravated the prejudice and dislike of a predominantly Protestant nation. Thus, an unfortunate but instinctive distrust of New Mexico's essentially foreign culture was the last and most durable brick added to the strong wall of opposition that prevented the territory from joining the Union until 1912.

But now the last barrier was removed, and on January 6, 1912, a delegation including Andrews and the two congressmen-elect from New Mexico gathered at the White House and proudly witnessed the making of their new state at exactly 1:35 P.M. After affixing his signature to the proclamation, Taft turned and smilingly said: "Well, it is all over. I am glad to give you life. I hope you will be healthy."[90] Arizona, so long associated with New Mexico in the long fight, was proclaimed a state on February 14, 1912.[91] Consequently, almost sixty-four years after the signing of the Treaty of Guadalupe Hidalgo, the sister territories of the Southwest were brought into the Union.

Chapter Notes

CHAPTER I

1. Milo Milton Quaife (ed.), *The Diary of James K. Polk: During His Presidency, 1845 to 1849* (Chicago: A. C. McClurg & Co., 1910), I, 384-85. According to Polk's entry of May 9, his cabinet a few hours before receiving news of the clash had all agreed except for one that he should deliver a war message to Congress.

2. Dwight L. Clarke, *Stephen Watts Kearny: Soldier of the West* (Norman: University of Oklahoma Press, 1961), pp. 114-15, 134. Kearny was not notified of his promotion until August 15 when his army was approaching Las Vegas, New Mexico.

3. The term means Spanish-speaking and will be used from time to time to refer to the native population of New Mexico.

4. Polk first made this charge in his war message delivered on May 11, 1846. James D. Richardson (ed.), *A Compilation of the Messages and Papers of the Presidents, 1789-1897*, Vol. IX (Washington, D.C.: Published by authority of Congress, 1900), p. 442.

5. Confidential Circular, James Buchanan to Manuel Alvarez, May 14, 1846, Benjamin Read Collection, State Records Center and Archives, Santa Fe.

6. June 2, 1846, U.S. War Department, Letters Sent, Records Group 107, National Archives, Washington, D.C. Hereafter cited as NA, RG 107.

7. Marcy to Kearny, May 27, 1846, NA, RG 107. It was hoped that this person, who would bear a letter of introduction from Bishop Kenrick or one of two other clergymen and would speak Spanish, would be "useful in removing the false impressions of the Mexicans in relation to the United States and their objects in taking possession of New Mexico,—and inducing them to confide in the assurance you will make that their institutions will be respected,—the property of the Church protected,—their worship undisturbed—in fine, that all their religious rights will be in the amplest manner preserved to them."

8. Sister Mary Loyola, "The American Occupation of New Mexico, 1821-1852," *New Mexico Historical Review*, XIV (April, 1939), 160, 166.

9. Capt. W. M. D. McKissack to Maj. Gen. Thomas S. Jesup, November 7, 1848, "California and New Mexico Documents, 1846-1850 (Documents accompanying the Annual Message of President Polk [Dec. 5, 1848] and other papers relating to the Civil Government of California and New Mexico)," U.S. Executive Collection, Division of Manuscripts, Library of Congress, Washington, D.C.

10. Stella M. Drumm (ed.), *Down the Santa Fe Trail and into Mexico: The Diary*

of *Susan Shelby Magoffin, 1846-1847* (New Haven: Yale University Press, 1926), introduction, pp. 84, 263-65; LeRoy R. Hafen and Carl Coke Rister, *Western America: The Exploration, Settlement, and Development of the Region Beyond the Mississippi* (Englewood Cliffs, New Jersey: Prentice-Hall, Inc., 1962), pp. 298-99; Thomas Hart Benton, *Thirty Year's View* (New York: D. Appleton and Company, 1856), p. 683. Senator Benton takes credit for the Magoffin mission claiming that he persuaded Magoffin to go with Kearny's army and introduced him to the President prior to the mission.

11. Kearny Proclamation (original), August 22, 1846, Read Collection. The proclamation is in both Spanish and English, side by side in a double column. According to a handwritten notation by Benjamin Read, this was the first official paper printed in Santa Fe under American rule. It was printed on the so-called Father Antonio Jose Martinez printing press. Photostat of Spanish version found in the collection called New Mexico Miscellaneous, Division of Manuscripts, Library of Congress, Washington, D.C.

12. Frank D. Reeve, *History of New Mexico*, II (New York: Lewis Historical Publishing Company, Inc., 1961), 61.

13. Both Doniphan and Hall were lawyers. To assist them in drafting the Code, Doniphan chose Francis P. Blair, Jr., an army scout, also a lawyer, and John F. Hughes, whose book, *Doniphan's Expedition*, became the early standard account of the conquest of New Mexico. See Clarke, pp. 148-49.

14. As quoted in Loomis Morton Ganaway, "New Mexico and the Sectional Controversy, 1846-1861," *New Mexico Historical Review*, XVIII (July, 1943), 207.

15. New Mexico, *Organic Law of the Territory of New Mexico* (1846). Original belonging to Col. A. W. Doniphan, Library, Division of History, Museum of New Mexico, Santa Fe.

16. Appointments made by Brig. Gen. S. W. Kearny are listed on a document under the heading "Notice." Governors' Papers, State Records Center and Archives, Santa Fe. Printed in both Spanish and English.

17. U.S. *Congressional Globe*, 29th Cong., 2d Sess., 1846, Appendix, p. 68.

18. January 11, 1847, NA, RG 107.

19. Extract of a dispatch from John Y. Mason, Secretary of the Navy, dated January 11, 1847, and enclosed in the Marcy to Kearny letter of the same date.

20. Col. George A. McCall, military representative of the federal government in New Mexico to Lt. Col. N. W. Bliss in Washington, July 16, 1850, New Mexico Miscellaneous.

21. Paul A. F. Walter, "The First Civil Governor of New Mexico Under the Stars and Stripes," *New Mexico Historical Review*, VIII (April, 1933), 120-22; Hubert Hugh Bancroft, *The Works of Hubert Hugh Bancroft*, XVII: *History of Arizona and New Mexico, 1530-1888* (San Francisco: The History Company, Publishers, 1889), pp. 428-33. Governor Bent's daughter, Mrs. Teresina Scheurich, many years later gave a vivid description of the murder of her father to L. Bradford Prince, a territorial governor.

22. June 11, 1847, NA, RG 107.

23. September 24, 1847. Photostatic copies of *The Republican*, Library, Division of History, Museum of New Mexico, Santa Fe.

24. Proceedings of the General Assembly including Vigil's address are discussed in Ralph Emerson Twitchell, *The Leading Facts of New Mexican History* (5 Vols., Cedar Rapids, Iowa: The Torch Press, 1911-17), II, 264-66. Vigil's address is also included in William G. Ritch, *The Legislative Blue-Book, of the Territory of New Mexico* (Santa Fe: Charles W. Greene, Public Printer, 1882), pp. 98-99.

25. *The Republican*, December 11, 1947; Ritch's *Blue-Book*, p. 98. Although the upper house is designated the Legislative Council in the Kearny Code, the *Republican* calls it the Senate in all its references to that body.

26. December 25, 1847.

27. January 1, 1848.

28. The population estimate for the United States was probably quite low, but understandably so considering the rapid growth in the country at this time. The 1850 census showed 23,191,876 persons not counting Indians, a 35.9 per cent increase over the 1840 count. The population of Mexico in 1850 has been placed at 7.7 million, an increase of approximately 700,000 persons over the 1840 estimate. See U.S. Bureau of Census, *Statistical Abstract of the United States: 1958* (79th ed., Washington: U.S. Government Printing Office, 1958), p. 5, and Howard F. Cline, *Mexico: Revolution to Evolution, 1940-1960.* Issued under the auspices of the Royal Institute of International Affairs (London: Oxford University Press, 1962), p. 83.

29. *The Republican*, January 15, 1848.

30. An election was held in January to choose delegates to the convention. Consequently, the inaction of the convention delegates must have been somewhat reflective of the attitude of many New Mexicans.

31. U.S. Congress, Senate, *Treaties, Conventions, International Acts, Protocols and Agreements Between the United States of America and Other Powers, 1776-1909* (Compiled by William M. Malloy under resolution of the Senate of January 18, 1909), 61st Cong., 2d Sess., 1910, Senate Doc. 357, I, art. v, 1109-10; art. xii, 1113; art. xv, 1114.

32. *The Republican*, July 19, 1848.

CHAPTER II

1. U.S. Congress, *Treaties, Conventions, International Acts* . . . , Senate Doc. 357, p. 1112.

2. James Quinn to James Buchanan, August 20, 1848, as quoted in Ganaway, July, 1943, p. 209.

3. U.S. *Congressional Globe*, 30th Cong., 1st Sess., 1848, p. 1002.

4. As quoted in Bancroft, p. 443. Polk states in his diary that the letter was addressed to the people of California only. See Quaife (ed.), *The Diary of James K. Polk*, pp. 136, 140.

5. *The Diary of James K. Polk*, pp. 136-37, 140-43. According to Polk's entries of September 30 and October 3, 1848, the Benton letter was discussed in two cabinet meetings before the President and his cabinet finally agreed to have Secretary of State Buchanan prepare the warning.

6. Price, receiving orders to leave for Mexico, departed from Santa Fe on February 7, 1848, and captured the city of Chihuahua during the following month. "California and New Mexico Documents, 1846-1850 (Documents accompanying the Annual Message of President Polk [Dec. 5, 1848] and other papers relating to the Civil Government of California and New Mexico)," U.S. Executive Collection. *The Republican* reported on February 12 that Price and his staff left on the morning of February 8 rather than on the 7th. Washington, the new commander, was a war hero. On February 23, 1847, he was brevetted a lieutenant colonel for gallantry in action during the battle of Buena Vista.

7. Benjamin M. Read, *Illustrated History of New Mexico* (Santa Fe: The New Mexican Printing Company, 1912), pp. 453-54; Ritch's *Blue-Book*, p. 99. According to W. H. H. Davis, *El Gringo* (New York: Harper & Brothers, Publishers, 1857), p. 109, Colonel Washington, sensing excitement concerning the issue, commanded the inhabitants to abstain from "participating in or being movers of seditious meetings." Davis also cited the role of Angeny in the affair.

8. Twitchell, *The Leading Facts of New Mexican History*, II, 267.

9. See footnote 30, chapter one.

10. Ganaway, July, 1943, p. 210.

11. Ritch's *Blue-Book*, pp. 99-100. Other convention officials were Henry Henrie, interpreter, and Thomas White, doorkeeper.

12. Original memorial with signatures and unsigned Spanish version, New Mexico Territorial Papers Collection, Records Group 46, National Archives, Washington, D.C. This collection of bills, memorials, and other materials of the U.S. Senate pertinent to New Mexico will be hereafter cited as NA, RG 46. Memorial quoted in U.S. *Congressional Globe*, 30th Cong., 2d Sess., 1848, p. 33; Ritch's *Blue-Book*, pp. 99-100; Read, p. 454; and Ralph Emerson Twitchell, *The Military Occupation of New Mexico, 1846-1851* (Denver: Smith-Brooks Company, 1909), pp. 154-55. Quoted passages are from original memorial in English.

13. Although only an accompanying letter addressed to Clayton was found (see note 14), Twitchell claims that the memorial was sent to both Clayton and Benton and that Clayton, like his colleague from Missouri, had earlier advised the people of New Mexico to establish their own government until Congress could take action. Twitchell, *The Leading Facts of New Mexican History*, II, 268. Ritch claims that Benton, too, was sent a copy. Ritch's *Blue-Book*, p. 100.

14. Houghton to Clayton, October 16, 1848, U.S. Department of State, Miscellaneous Letters, Records Group 59, National Archives, Washington, D.C. Hereafter cited as NA, RG 59.

15. U.S. *Congressional Globe*, 30th Cong., 2d Sess., 1848, p. 33.

16. Ganaway, April, 1943, p. 136.

17. December 21, 1848. The antislavery provision of the New Mexico memorial is quoted in this issue.

18. U.S. *Congressional Globe*, 29th Cong., 2d Sess., 1847, Appendix, p. 356.

19. January 29, 1848.

20. Ganaway, April, 1943, p. 122.

21. Joseph H. Parks, "John Bell and the Compromise of 1850," *Journal of Southern History*, IX (August, 1943), 342.

22. Charles W. Ramsdell, "The Natural Limits of Slavery Expansion," *The Mississippi Valley Historical Review*, XVI (September, 1929), 160. Ramsdell sets natural limits to slavery expansion in the Southwest and in Kansas and Nebraska, and concludes that the extension of slavery was an unrealistic cause of the Civil War.

23. William C. Binkley (ed.), "Reports from A Texas Agent in New Mexico, 1849," *New Spain and the Anglo-American West: Historical Contributions*, Presented to Herbert Eugene Bolton, Vol. II (Los Angeles: Privately printed, 1932), 167.

24. J. J. Bowden, "The Texas-New Mexico Boundary Dispute Along the Rio Grande," *The Southwestern Historical Quarterly*, LXIII (October, 1959), 224.

25. Polk to Andrew Jackson Donelson, special commissioner for the United States to Texas, June 15, 1845, as quoted in William C. Binkley, *The Expansionist Movement in Texas, 1836-50*, Vol. XIII of Series *University of California Publications in History* (Berkeley: University of California Press, 1925), 126.

26. Kearny Proclamation (original). The natives of New Mexico referred to the upper Rio Grande as the Rio del Norte or just Del Norte. The upper course of the Rio Grande is still called Rio del Norte in Mexico.

27. October 12, 1848, NA, RG 107.

28. Historical Society of New Mexico, *Journal of New Mexico Convention of Delegates to Recommend A Plan of Civil Government*[,] September, 1849, No. 10 (Santa Fe: The New Mexican Printing Company, 1907), p. 5, State Records Center and Archives, Santa Fe. This is a reprint of U.S. Congress, House, *New Mexico-Convention of Delegates: Journal and Proceedings* . . . , 31st Cong., 1st Sess., 1850, House Miscl. Doc. 39, pp. 1-13. A printed copy of the journal also is included with a letter from Hugh N. Smith, the representative from New Mexico who presented the journal to Congress, to Stephen A. Douglas, chairman of the Senate Committee on Territories. February 18, 1850, NA, RG 46; Davis, p. 110. James S. Calhoun, first territorial governor, mentions the Beall proclamation in a letter to T. Ewing, Secretary of Interior, dated October 16, 1849. Annie H. Abel (ed.), *The Official Correspondence of James S. Calhoun*. Collected mainly from the files of the Indian Office (Washington: Government Printing Office, 1915), pp. 58-59. Oddly enough, Ritch makes no mention of the 1849 convention in his legislative Blue-Book.

29. *Journal of New Mexico Convention of Delegates* . . . , p. 6. Quinn was chosen by a vote of 15 to 4 over a man listed in the *Journal* as William J. Pillon. This was probably an error as in all likelihood the man referred to was Palmer J. Pillans, an influential Anglo attorney.

30. The minority report was in the form of a series of instructions to the delegate who would represent the convention in Congress. The minority proposal, instructing the delegate to ask for state government if this seemed most practicable, was rejected by the convention on the last day of the meeting.

31. Earlier, on April 21, 1849, Colonel Washington by proclamation called attention to art. viii of the Treaty of Guadalupe Hidalgo, which stated that within one year from the date of the "exchange of ratifications" of the treaty, *Hispanos* must declare their intention of becoming citizens of Mexico, otherwise they "shall be considered to have elected to become citizens of the United States." Consequently, the provision adopted by the convention constituted a new and more positive requirement for acquiring United States citizenship. Proclamation in Ralph Emerson Twitchell Collection, State Records Center and Archives, Santa Fe.

32. *Journal of New Mexico Convention of Delegates* . . . , p. 18. Proposed boundary unanimously adopted on the last day of the meeting, p. 10 and p. 21.

33. Davis, p. 109.

34. *Journal of New Mexico Convention of Delegates* . . . , pp. 7-10.

35. A list of persons holding office under the Kearny Code is included in Twitchell, *The Leading Facts of New Mexican History*, II, 268-69.

36. *Journal of New Mexico Convention of Delegates* . . . , pp. 20-22. The instructions pertaining to religious guarantees, peonage, and Indian protection were first included in the minority report presented by Naugle. See Document 10, pp. 17-19.

37. Lt. Col. W. Gilpin to Gen. R. Jones, August 1, 1848, "California and New Mexico Documents . . . ," U.S. Executive Collection.

38. Calhoun to Orlando Brown, Commissioner of Indian Affairs, November 2, 1849, *The Official Correspondence of James S. Calhoun*, pp. 68-69. An earlier but less complete account of the affair is reported in Calhoun's letter to Col. W. Medill, October 29, 1849, pp. 63-66. The attempted rescue of Mrs. White was reported in *The New Mexican*, November 24, 1849. Originals of this issue are in the Special Collections

Division, University of New Mexico Library, Albuquerque, and the Library, Division
of History, Museum of New Mexico, Santa Fe. Carson's comment found in Twitchell,
in whose version the tragic emigrant leader is called Dr. White. See Twitchell, *The
Leading Facts of New Mexican History*, II, 125. White Wolf was the leader of the
Apache raiding party according to M. Morgan Estergreen in an account which varies
somewhat from Calhoun's report. See his *Kit Carson: A Portrait in Courage* (Norman:
University of Oklahoma Press, 1962), pp. 199-201.

39. Calhoun to Ewing, October 16, 1849, *The Official Correspondence of James
S. Calhoun*, p. 59. According to Calhoun, Smith was quite concerned and commented
on the colonel's stubborn position before he left for the national capital.

40. Calhoun to Medill, October 15, 1849, p. 53.

41. November 24, 1849.

42. Circular (1850), translated from Spanish, Miscellaneous Territorial Papers,
State Records Center and Archives, Santa Fe.

43. A commission signed by James Buchanan announcing Alvarez's appointment as
commercial agent is in the Read Collection.

44. *The New Mexican*, November 24, 1849.

45. Report 220, New Mexico Territorial Papers Collection, Records Group 233,
National Archives, Washington, D.C. This collection of bills, memorials, and other
materials of the U.S. House of Representatives pertinent to New Mexico will be hereafter cited as NA, RG 233.

46. U.S. *Congressional Globe*, 31st Cong., 1st Sess., 1850, Part 2, p. 1407. For
additional discussion of this pamphlet, which was in the form of a public letter, see
Howard R. Lamar, *The Far Southwest, 1846-1912: A Territorial History* (New Haven:
Yale University Press, 1966), p. 76.

47. U.S. *Congressional Globe*, 31st Cong., 1st Sess., 1850, Part 2, pp. 1386-88.

Chapter III

1. Theodore Grivas, *Military Governments in California, 1846-1850: With a
Chapter on Their Prior Use in Louisiana, Florida and New Mexico* (Glendale, California: The Arthur H. Clark Company, 1963), pp. 203-22.

2. Richardson, *Messages and Papers of the Presidents*, V, 18-19.

3. U.S. Congress, House, *California and New Mexico: Message from the President . . . Transmitting Information . . . on the Subject of California and New
Mexico*, 31st Cong., 1st Sess., 1850, Ex. Doc. 17, pp. 1-2. This message, along with
the reports prepared by Taylor's department heads, was sent to both houses of Congress. The House message was dated January 21; the Senate message, January 23.

4. Crawford to Taylor, January 18, 1850, Zachary Taylor Papers, Division of Manuscripts, Library of Congress, Washington, D.C.

5. April 3, 1849, U.S. Congress, *California and New Mexico . . .*, House Ex.
Doc. 17, pp. 9-11. Italics are the author's.

6. A third person may have been sent to New Mexico to carry out certain presidential
desires. William Carey Jones, a lawyer adept in Spanish and knowledgeable about
Spanish colonial titles, was to be sent to Mexico City and California to gather pertinent
information. See Clayton to Thomas Ewing, Secretary of Interior, July 11, 1849,
House Ex. Doc. 17, p. 112. Upon Jones' return he was authorized to "proceed to
Santa Fe, the capital of New Mexico, and there obtain access to the archives of that
country, and to furnish similar information as to all titles which have emanated from

the authorities when New Mexico was a province of Spain, and subsequently under the government of the Mexican republic." See J. Butterfield, Commissioner of the General Land Office, to Jones, July 5, 1849, House Ex. Doc. 17, p. 115.

7. Davis, p. 111.

8. *The Official Correspondence of James S. Calhoun*, introduction.

9. November 12, 1849, U.S. Congress, *California and New Mexico . . .*, House Ex. Doc. 17, p. 280. On June 10, 1850, while on his New Mexico mission, McCall was elevated to the rank of colonel and will be designated by that rank throughout the remainder of the chapter.

10. Ganaway, July, 1943, p. 215.

11. Twitchell, *The Leading Facts of New Mexican History*, II, 271.

12. McCall to Lt. Col. N. V. Bliss in Washington, April 15, 1850, New Mexico Miscellaneous.

13. Bancroft, p. 451.

14. McCall to Bliss, April 15, 1850, New Mexico Miscellaneous.

15. U.S. Congress, Senate, *Message from the President of the United States, Communicating . . . Information in Relation to Military Orders Issued to United States Officers in Santa Fe . . .* , 31st Cong., 1st Sess., 1850, Ex. Doc. 56, p. 14. The proclamation, in both English and Spanish, is reproduced in this document. The signers, in addition to Houghton, were T. S. J. Johnson, E. W. Prewitt, J. W. Folger, Jose M. Abreo, Domingo Fernandez, Ceran St. Vrain, Merrill Ashurst, Murry F. Tuley, Donaciano Vigil, and Francisco Ortiz y Delgado.

16. Munroe was assigned on May 26, 1849, by Asst. Adj. Gen. W. G. Freeman, responding to a command by Maj. Gen. Winfield Scott, to "immediately repair to Santa Fe, via Fort Leavenworth, and relieve Brevet Colonel Washington . . . ."

17. April 23, 1850, proclamation in English and Spanish, U.S. Congress, Senate, *Message from the President of the United States, in Answer to a Resolution of the Senate Calling for Information in Relation to the Formation of a State Government in New Mexico*, 31st Cong., 1st Sess., 1850, Ex. Doc. 60, Part II, pp. 2-3.

18. Calhoun to Orlando Brown, August 13, 1850, *The Official Correspondence of James S. Calhoun*, p. 253.

19. Webster to P. H. Bell, governor of Texas, August 5, 1850, as quoted in U.S., Congress, House, *Message from the President of the United States, in Reference to the Texas Boundary*, 31st Cong., 1st Sess., 1850, Ex. Doc. 82, p. 8.

20. Munroe to Maj. Gen. R. Jones, May 13, 1850, as quoted in U.S. Congress, *Message from the President of the United States . . . [Regarding] State Government . . .* , Senate Ex. Doc. 60, Part II, p. 2.

21. *Constitution of the State of New Mexico (1850)*. One of three extant Spanish copies in Constitutional Convention Papers, State Records Center and Archives, Santa Fe. Also consulted, *Constitution of the State of New Mexico, 1850* (Santa Fe: Stagecoach Press, 1965), pp. 13-46, an exact reproduction of one of three extant English copies, this one being in the National Archives, Washington, D.C. Quotations will be from the English version.

22. McCall to Bliss, May 21, 1850, New Mexico Miscllaneous. This letter contained the following notation: "Copy, or rather substance of a letter to Col. Bliss—The language of Constitution (State of N. Mexico) in Convention." Only seventeen delegates signed the constitution unless Robert Carey and Donaciano Vigil, whose names appear at the bottom of the list as convention secretaries, are included. Apparently, several delegates refused to endorse the document, as in one of the convention votes McCall claimed there were as many as twenty-two delegates entitled to vote.

23. McCall in his letter to Bliss put this statement in quotes.

24. Twitchell, *The Leading Facts of New Mexican History*, II, p. 272. There is evidence that the constitution was written several months before the convention and sent to certain senators in Washington for approval before being returned to the convention for use. Lamar, *The Far Southwest, 1846-1912*, p. 77.

25. McCall to Bliss, June 11, 1850, New Mexico Miscellaneous. McCall went to great lengths to keep his superiors informed about all of the proceedings. For instance, he sent a copy of the new constitution to Colonel Bliss. "I now enclose you a copy . . . in the Spanish language, the English version not yet having issued from the press."

26. *Constitution of the State of New Mexico (1850)*, art. i, sec. 1, "Declaration of Rights." Although Negro slavery was outlawed, Negroes were not allowed the vote. See art. viii, sec. 1, "Suffrage."

27. All the convention delegates who endorsed the constitution also signed this address.

28. McCall to Bliss, May 24, 1850, New Mexico Miscellaneous.

29. *Constitution of the State of New Mexico (1850)*, "Preamble."

30. Art. vii, secs. 1, 2, "Education."

31. Art. viii, sec. 1, "Suffrage."

32. Art. ix, sec. 8, "General Provisions."

33. Spanish copy of proclamation, Governors' Papers; U.S. Congress, Senate, *Correspondence on the Subject of Civil Affairs in New Mexico*, 31st Cong., 2d Sess., 1850, Ex. Doc. 1, Part 2, pp. 93-94.

34. McCall to Bliss, July 16, 1850, New Mexico Miscellaneous.

35. Ballots used in the 1850 election are in the Read Collection. One ballot indicates that the Weightman faction was pushing its state and national candidates even before the May 6 election of delegates to the constitutional convention.

36. McCall to Bliss, July 16, 1850, New Mexico Miscellaneous. McCall, in this list of leaders of the Weightman faction, is referring to Palmer J. Pillans and has misspelled the name.

37. Father Leyva to Alvarez, Read Collection.

38. McCall to Bliss, June 11, 1850, New Mexico Miscellaneous. McCall did not mention Calhoun by name, but merely referred to him as the "U.S. Indian Agent."

39. 1850 election ballots, Read Collection; McCall to Secretary of War Crawford, July 15, 1850, as quoted in U.S. Congress, Senate, *Report to the Secretary of War, Communicating, in Compliance with a Resolution of the Senate*, Colonel McCall's Reports in Relation to New Mexico, 31st Cong., 2d Sess., Ex. Doc. 26, p. 16; McCall to Bliss, July 16, 1850, New Mexico Miscellaneous. A county-by-county breakdown of the votes found in U.S. Congress, Senate, *Message from the President . . . Transmitting a Copy of the Constitution . . . of New Mexico, Together with a Digest of Votes for and Against it . . .*, 31st Cong., 1st Sess., 1850, Ex. Doc. 74, p. 2, showed the following results: Taos, 1,339 for and 25 against; Rio Arriba, no vote recorded; San Miguel, 203 to 0; Doña Ana, 1,146 to 0; Bernalillo, 1,504 to 1; Valencia, 2,008 to 1; and Santa Fe, 571 to 2. The omission of the Rio Arriba vote may account for the fact that this tally was 1,660 votes short of the final count.

40. Calhoun to Orlando Brown, July 15, 1850, *The Official Correspondence of James S. Calhoun*, p. 217. An interesting but opinionated discussion of the election results is included in this letter.

41. McCall to Crawford, *Report to the Secretary of War . . .*, Senate Ex. Doc. 26, p. 16. Weightman interpreted Alvarez's victory as an "overwhelming" one. See

Weightman to President Millard Fillmore, December 30, 1850, Manuel Alvarez Papers, State Records Center and Archives, Santa Fe.

42. House Report No. 20 refusing to seat Messervy, February 6, 1851, NA, RG 233. In trying to deprive Hugh Smith of a presidential appointment at a later date, Weightman claimed that "Mr. Messervy . . . [was] elected over Mr. Smith by a majority on the face of the returns of more than fourteen hundred . . . ." See Weightman to Millard Fillmore, December 26, 1850, Alvarez Papers.

43. McCall to Bliss, July 16, 1850, New Mexico Miscellaneous. A certificate signed by Alvarez on July 15, 1850, indicated that Weightman was selected as senator on July 11. NA, RG 46. Weightman, in his December 26, 1850, letter to President Fillmore, claims that he was the choice of "nineteen twentieths of the vote of the legislature." Alvarez Papers.

44. Calhoun to Brown, July 15, 1850. The Official Correspondence of James S. Calhoun, p. 217.

45. Letter sent to editor of the St. Louis Union, October 7, 1850, as quoted in Speech [of the] Hon. Richard H. Weightman of New Mexico, Delivered in the House of Representatives, March 15, 1852 (Washington: Congressional Globe Office, 1852), p. 7.

46. Quotation taken from the body of Weightman's speech on page 27.

47. Alvarez Papers. The vote suppressed, Weightman charged, amounted to 500 apiece in the counties of Valencia, Bernalillo, and possibly San Miguel. The vote not only included Anglos and "Mexicans" but also Pueblos, as some 500 votes from the Zuñi Pueblo were stolen. Weightman also charged that a campaign of character assassination was waged against Alvarez. Because of his Iberian origin, he was called, among other things, a gachupine, a name contemptuously reserved for Spanish loyalists during Mexico's War for Independence. See Weightman to Alvarez, December 30, 1850, Alvarez Papers.

CHAPTER IV

1. Bancroft, pp. 450-51.
2. Art. v, sec. 9, "Judicial Department."
3. McCall to Bliss, July 16, 1850, New Mexico Miscellaneous.
4. McCall and Weightman both mention Connelly's absence, but neither of them offer any explanation as to why the newly elected governor failed to be present at this crucial moment. McCall merely states that Connelly was "in the U.S.," while Weightman, without elaboration, asserts that "in the absence of the Governor elect . . . [Alvarez] performed his duties under trying circumstances, to the great approbation of a large majority." Davis, Bancroft, and Twitchell all make reference to Connelly's absence but give no reason for it.
5. Weightman to Fillmore, September 14, 1850, Alvarez Papers. Alvarez's "Inaugural address and first message to the Legislature" along with other materials pertinent to the statehood effort were later submitted to the President by Weightman.
6. Enclosure in letter from McCall to Bliss, July 16, 1850, New Mexico Miscellaneous. Despite McCall's accusation of undue speed on the part of Alvarez, the acting Governor did inform Colonel Munroe on July 12, 1850, that he was proceeding "to nominate those officers which the [state] constitution provides shall be filled in that manner." See U.S. Congress, Correspondence on . . . Civil Affairs in New Mexico, Senate Ex. Doc. 1, Part 2, p. 95.

7. This description, and those of other Alvarez appointees, was found in a separate communication enclosed in McCall's July 16 letter. The Colonel, in this particular statement, again misspelled Pillans' name as Pillons. According to Davis, p. 111, Pillans was one of the prominent leaders of the Weightman faction.

8. McCall in his report to Bliss crossed out the reference to *Hispanos* being "led by the nose" and the statement pertaining to his belief that New Mexico natives had delusions of grandeur. Even so, his strong bias against the Spanish-speaking people of the territory is unmistakable.

9. U.S. Congress, *Correspondence on . . . Civil Affairs in New Mexico*, Senate Ex. Doc. 1, Part 2, pp. 94-95.

10. McCall to Bliss, July 16, 1850, New Mexico Miscellaneous.

11. As quoted in a letter from Alvarez to Munroe, July 13, 1850, in U.S. Congress, *Correspondence on . . . Civil Affairs in New Mexico*, Senate Ex. Doc. 1, Part 2, pp. 95-98.

12. The resolution was signed by Angeny, speaker of the House; Joseph Naugel, president of the Senate; and Lewis D. Sheetz, secretary of state.

13. July 12, 1850, as quoted in U.S. Congress, *Correspondence on . . . Civil Affairs in New Mexico*, Senate Ex. Doc. 1, Part 2, p. 99.

14. Munroe to Houghton, March 26, 1852, as quoted in Joab Houghton, *Reply of Joab Houghton, Late Chief Justice of the Supreme Court of the Temporary Civil Government of the Territory of New Mexico, to the Personal and Slanderous Attack of R. H. Weightman, in His Printed Pamphlet, Purporting to a "Speech" Delivered in the House of Representatives on the 15th of March, 1852*, p. 5, Miscellaneous Territorial Papers. Also found in James S. Calhoun folder, U.S. Department of State, Appointments and Recommendations, Records Group 59, National Archives, Washington, D.C. Hereafter cited as NA, RG 59. Some of the words in the title of this printed pamphlet have been capitalized by the author.

15. Calhoun to Orlando Brown, July 15, 1850, *The Official Correspondence of James S. Calhoun*, p. 218.

16. July 19, 1850, Alvarez Papers.

17. Calhoun to Orlando Brown, August 13, 1850, *The Official Correspondence of James S. Calhoun*, p. 253.

18. Munroe's message to the prefects, trans. from Spanish, Alvarez Papers. Message drafted and signed by Donaciano Vigil, who was still serving as Munroe's territorial secretary.

19. Description supplied by Samuel Ellison, a prominent early settler from Kentucky, as quoted in J. Manuel Espinosa, "Memoir of a Kentuckian in New Mexico, 1848-1884," *New Mexico Historical Review*, XIII (January, 1938), 7.

20. U.S. Congress, *Correspondence on . . . Civil Affairs in New Mexico*, Senate Ex. Doc. 1, Part 2, p. 107. Also enclosed in August 13 letter from Calhoun to Orlando Brown, *The Official Correspondence of James S. Calhoun*, p. 254. Although the exchange appears to be a compromise, Calhoun was bewildered. "The precise object of the two documents is beyond my comprehension. . . ."

21. He is ambiguous as to whether elections were held anywhere else in the territory. "The elections under the proposed state organization have come off on yesterday, but no elections were held in this city, nor was any attempt made to induce the people to assemble at the polls . . . ."

22. *New Orleans Delta* as quoted in *The Republican*, August 31, 1848.

23. August 31, 1848.

24. Binkley, *The Expansionist Movement in Texas, 1836-1850*, p. 179. A helpful

map of these four Texas counties is found on this page. For a contemporary description of the new Texas counties, see Maj. J. Van Horne, Headquarters Batallion, 3d Inf. Paso del Norte (El Paso) to Lt. L. McLaws, February 23, 1850, in *The Official Correspondence of James S. Calhoun*, p. 163. "The country from Presidio del Norte to 70 miles below is called Presidio county; thence to San Diego above Dona Ana, El Paso county, thence north is divided into Worth and Santa Fe counties."

25. The colonel also gave the judicial authorities created by Texas the same protection. Munroe to Beall and others, March 12, 1850, *The Official Correspondence of James S. Calhoun*, p. 164. The same proclamation, with some slight variation in the words, was published in *The Telegraph* (Houston) on May 23, 1850. Consequently, the position of the federal government on the Neighbors' mission eventually became public knowledge. See N. A. Gant, "A History of the Texas Boundary Disputes" (unpublished Master's thesis, Department of History and Political Science, Colorado State Teachers College, 1930), p. 77.

26. *The Texas Republican* (Marshall), May 11, 1850, as quoted in Gant, p. 77.

27. Davis, p. 111.

28. McCall to Bliss, May 21, 1850, New Mexico Miscellaneous.

29. Enclosure in letter from McCall to Bliss, July 16, 1850, New Mexico Miscellaneous. McCall accused Weightman of having "great presumption" and of being guilty of "unscrupulous chicanery." He claimed that Weightman had been "droped" [sic] from the army and was a poor "apology for an attorney."

30. Ganaway, July, 1943, p. 213.

31. J. L. Collins, *Answer to Certain Infamatory Representations of R. H. Weightman* (Santa Fe: 1852), pp. 10-12, trans. from Spanish, Miscellaneous Territorial Papers.

32. Calhoun, as early as October 15, 1849, speculated as to the possibility of a "State or territory" being formed "immediately west of the Rio Grande," but made no mention of Weightman in this connection. See Calhoun to Medill, *The Official Correspondence of James S. Calhoun*, p. 53.

33. In mentioning Baird's appointment in a letter to Alvarez on February 9, 1852, Weightman expresses particular warmth. Alvarez Papers. He also speaks of Baird as an ally in the fierce political struggles in the territory during the 1850's. See *Speech [of the] Hon. Richard H. Weightman . . .*, pp. 24-26.

34. According to McCall, Facundo Pino, whom Alvarez nominated as state treasurer, was "a stray boy from a Mexican college [who] arrived . . . in the last six months with no character and little brains[,] strongly Mexican and no love for the U.S. or its institutions—the tool of a corrupt priesthood being related to the Mexican Vicar of the Territory."

35. *The Official Correspondence of James S. Calhoun*, p. 233.

36. Davis, p. 111. Calhoun also claimed that the Texas election never came off, there being not one "solitary effort" to enforce Baird's proclamation.

37. Calhoun to Orlando Brown, July 31, 1850, *The Official Correspondence of James S. Calhoun*, p. 232.

38. Binkley, *The Expansionist Movement in Texas, 1836-50*, p. 193.

39. U.S. Congress, *Message from the President . . . in Reference to the Texas Boundary*, House Ex. Doc. 82, pp. 4-5.

40. August 6, 1850, U.S. War Department, Letters Sent, NA, RG 107.

41. Weightman to Alvarez, August 26, 1850, Alvarez Papers.

42. Dexter Perkins and Glyndon G. Van Deusen, *The United States of America: A History*, Vol. I to 1876 (New York: The Macmillan Company, 1962), p. 572.

43. There was some apprehension before Taylor took office as to whether Clay would

support his administration. According to one Clay confident, Taylor once used "offensive" language in speaking about Clay. See Thomas B. Stevenson to Clay, April 30, 1849, Henry Clay Papers, Division of Manuscripts, Library of Congress, Washington, D.C. Taylor was aware of this problem and tried to assure Clay of his respect. "I . . . thought from the course I had uniformly pursued towards you for many years, of which you must be aware, you ought to have entertained no doubts in relation to that matter." May 28, 1849, Henry Clay Papers.

44. Parks, p. 349.

45. U.S. Congress, Senate, Report: To Accompany Bills S. No. 225 and S. No. 226, 31st Cong., 1st Sess., 1850, Rept. 123, p. 6.

46. U.S. Congressional Globe, 31st Cong., 1st Sess., 1850, Part 1, p. 945. The committee in making its report to the Senate admitted that there was "great diversity of opinion" among members regarding the western boundary of Texas. Some claimed it was the Nueces River; others, the Rio Grande from "its mouth to its source." Consequently, a majority of the committee members insisted on their determination to "abstain from expressing any opinions as to the true and legitimate western and northern boundary of that State."

47. U.S. Congress, Report . . . , Senate Rept. 123, p. 7.

48. Parks, pp. 349-51.

49. Quoted in U.S. Congressional Globe, 31st Cong., 1st Sess., 1850, Part 2, Appendix, p. 1556. For more details on Seward's two speeches see George E. Baker (ed.), The Works of William H. Seward, Vol. I (New York: Redfield, 1853), pp. 51-93, 119-31.

50. U.S. Congressional Globe, Part 2, p. 1555.

51. S 307, NA, RG 46; "Organic Act Establishing the Territory of New Mexico: Approved September 30, 1850," New Mexico Statutes Annotated, Compiled and Annotated by Stephen B. Davis, Jr., and Merritt C. Mechem (Published by authority; Denver: The W. H. Courtright Publishing Company, 1915), p. 36. The northwestern boundary of Texas also was defined in the final settlement. "The State of Texas will agree that her boundary on the north shall commence at the point at which the meridian of one hundred degrees west from Greenwich is intersected by the parallel of thirty-six degrees thirty minutes north latitude, and shall run from said point due west to the meridian of one hundred and three degrees west from Greenwich . . . ."

52. The financial commitment was contained in President Fillmore's December 13, 1850, proclamation declaring the new boundary in force.

53. U.S. Congress, House, Acts of Congress Local or Temporary in Nature: Texas, 46th Cong., 3d Sess., 1881, Ex. Doc. 47, Part 2, p. 1100. The President would authorize the issuance of stock in favor of Texas upon receiving the act.

54. J. J. Bowden, "The Texas-New Mexico Boundary Dispute Along the Rio Grande," The Southwestern Historical Quarterly, LXIII (October, 1959), 221-37, and William C. Binkley, "The Question of Texas Jurisdiction in New Mexico Under the United States, 1848-1850," The Southwestern Historical Quarterly, XXIV (July, 1920), 1-38, are especially valuable accounts of the boundary dispute.

55. Needless to say, there was great controversy over the Foote proposal, and included with S 170 was an amendment offered by antislavery Senator John P. Hale of New Hampshire that would have prohibited slavery altogether. The amendment was rejected.

56. S 170, NA, RG 46; U.S. Congressional Globe, p. 1583. The remainder of the boundary, not so clearly defined by Douglas, was drawn along the 37th parallel to the western border of California and south along that boundary "to the place of beginning."

57. There was one minor difference between the two versions. In the Senate bill, there was a provision for "a library and for public buildings" which was not included in the Boyd proposal. Interestingly enough, this same provision for public facilities was included in the Senate bill proposing territorial government for Utah, also being considered at this time.

58. U.S. *Congressional Globe*, p. 1764.

59. Weightman is not too definite about the time of his arrival. "I arrived in Washington on the morning of Thursday . . . (I believe) . . . . The boundary bill as it is called . . . had passed both houses of Congress the day of my arrival or the next day following. I do not recollect which—It had passed the Senate before my arrival and the day after my arrival the House of Reps." As the amended bill, S 307, passed the House on September 6, it seems likely from Weightman's remarks that he arrived in Washington on Thursday, September 5. See Weightman to Alvarez, September 14, 1850, Alvarez Papers.

60. Addresses by Alvarez; statehood memorials, including one from the 1850 constitutional convention; and other pertinent materials also were forwarded to the President of the Senate, William R. King, whom Weightman erroneously addressed as the Vice President of the United States. These materials located in NA, RG 46 include a letter from Weightman to King, dated September 11, 1850, in which he defends the new state government.

61. Weightman to Alvarez, September 14, 1850, Alvarez Papers. Fillmore, in submitting the New Mexico constitution without recommendation on September 9, informed the Congress that this was done in compliance with a request from Alvarez, and he included with the constitution a digest of votes cast for and against the constitution at the June 20 election.

62. Secretary of State Clayton, on behalf of the cabinet, urged the President in several letters to be more careful about his health: August 13, 1849; August 15, 1849; and August 29, 1849. In the latter message, Clayton expressed deep concern about an attack of cholera which Taylor suffered in Buffalo while on a presidential tour. "The deep anxiety that is felt by everyone of us, arises from no mere personal feeling; but from a reflection upon the alarming consequences to the people of the United States in the event that the constant excitement and exposure to which you will be subjected, should be attended with fatal results." Taylor Papers.

63. Weightman to Alvarez, September 14, 1850, Alvarez Papers. On his way to Washington, Weightman met Smith in St. Louis and got a firsthand report on the impact of Taylor's death. Smith was pessimistic. As Weightman put it: "General Taylor's death Hugh Smith (also is here) tells me is unfortunate for us—His whole influence would have been in favor of our admission." See Weightman to Alvarez, August 26, 1850, Alvarez Papers.

64. Weightman to Alvarez, September 14, 1850, Alvarez Papers. Weightman often used dashes instead of periods at the end of his sentences. To avoid confusion, the author has substituted a period whenever necessary.

65. Weightman to Alvarez, August 26, 1850, Alvarez Papers.

66. September 14, 1850, Alvarez Papers.

67. Hardy was appointed as a "bearer of dispatches" from the War Department to Munroe in Santa Fe. He was ordered to leave on the morning of September 11 and to go by way of St. Louis and Ft. Leavenworth, receiving an escort at Leavenworth. Conrad to Hardy, September 10, 1850, U.S. War Department, Letters Sent, NA, RG 107.

68. Conrad to Munroe, September 10, 1850, U.S. War Department, Letters Sent,

NA, RG 107. Conrad also informed Munroe of congressional passage of the bill establishing the Territory of New Mexico and of the boundary settlement, which would not go into effect "until the assent of Texas shall have been given to the boundary established by the Act."

69. *Speech [of the] Hon. Richard H. Weightman*, p. 15. Weightman later charged Munroe with suppressing the contents of his instructions until the legal territorial government was installed in March of 1851, thereby enabling him to continue interfering in the civil affairs of New Mexico.

70. Webster to P. H. Bell, Governor of Texas, U.S. Congress, *Message from the President . . . In Reference to the Texas Boundary*, House Ex. Doc. 82, p. 11.

71. October 18, 1850, Alvarez Papers.

72. September 14, 1850, Alvarez Papers.

73. September 18, 1850, Alvarez Papers.

74. Bancroft, p. 630; Twitchell, *The Leading Facts of New Mexican History*, II, 283. According to Twitchell, Weightman, while serving as delegate to Congress some months later, was able to defeat the Smith bid, but was unable to secure the position for Alvarez, apparently because Alvarez was not a United States citizen.

75. U.S. *Congressional Globe*, 31st Cong., 1st Sess., 1850, Part 2, p. 1934.

76. U.S. *Congressional Globe*, pp. 1948-49.

CHAPTER V

1. *Speech [of the] Hon. Richard H. Weightman . . .* , p. 4.

2. Calvin Horn, *New Mexico's Troubled Years: The Story of the Early Territorial Governors*, foreword by John F. Kennedy (Albuquerque: Horn & Wallace, Publishers, 1963), pp. 31-32.

3. This was the press in the possession of the military, which Weightman erroneously claimed that Kearny had brought with him when he came to New Mexico. Controversy over Captain Reynold's allegedly illegal sale of the printing press to the leaders of the Houghton faction was bitter. Charges continued to be directed against the Houghton group after it gained possession of the press, one of the more damning ones being that the leaders of the faction, as owners of the newspaper, refused to print the communications or ballots of the state party during the June, 1850, election.

4. *Speech [of the] Hon. Richard H. Weightman . . .* , p. 21. There is some confusion about the ownership of the Gazette as the territorial party was somewhat reluctant to have its control of the newspaper publicized. In one of the issues, St. Vrain was listed as the proprietor. The Weightman faction later secured a printing press and published a partisan little newspaper called *El Amigo del Pais* (The Friend of the Country). See Weightman to Alvarez, September 10, 1852, Alvarez Papers, and *Al Publico* by J. L. Collins, Miscellaneous Territorial Papers, for comment about this newspaper.

5. Arie W. Poldervaart, *Black-Robed Justice* (Santa Fe: Historical Society of New Mexico, 1948), pp. 25-27. Recall also Houghton's apparent authorship of the antislavery 1848 memorial to Congress.

6. "Address to the inhabitants of New Mexico and California, on the omission by Congress to provide them with a territorial government, and on the social and political evils of slavery," as quoted in Weightman's letter to the editors of the St. *Louis Republican*, November 13, 1851, *Speech [of the] Hon. Richard H. Weightman . . .* , p. 18. Also in *Letter of R. H. Weightman, Delegate from New Mexico*, November 13, 1851, printed in Spanish, Twitchell Collection.

7. Weightman to Senator H. S. Foote of Mississippi, December 16, 1851, *Speech [of the] Hon. Richard H. Weightman . . . ,* p. 4.

8. Weightman, serving under Gen. Sterling Price, was killed at the battle of Wilson's Creek. According to Price, Weightman was one of the first to take up arms in the Confederate cause.

9. Horn, p. 85.

10. Ganaway, July, 1943, pp. 239-41. By the terms of this code, which affected only a small number of Negro slaves, a sentence of from four to ten years would be given to anyone helping a slave escape; the distribution of arms to slaves was prohibited; sentences could be imposed upon individuals caught inciting slaves to revolt; and any individual guilty of molesting or killing a slave would be tried as if the offense had been committed against a Caucasian.

11. As quoted by Alexander M. Jackson, a friend of Jefferson Davis who was appointed territorial secretary in September, 1857.

12. *Extract of a Letter Addressed to the Editor of the Santa Fe Gazette, for Publication in New Mexico,* a published pamphlet dated March 12, 1852, and signed with the pseudonym, "Russell," James S. Calhoun folder, U.S. Department of State, Appointments and Recommendations, Records Group 59, National Archives, Washington, D.C.

13. *Speech [of the] Hon. Richard H. Weightman . . . ,* p. 7. Horn states that the trouble dated back to 1849 when control of the Indians was removed from the military and placed under the jurisdiction of the Department of Interior. Munroe's response to this transfer was to cut off immediately all military supplies from Calhoun's order. See Horn, p. 29.

14. March 3, 1851, U.S. Department of State, Territorial Papers: New Mexico, I, Records Group 59, National Archives, Washington, D.C.

15. The exact number of members of the new legislative assembly was designated in Section 5 of the Organic Act.

16. April 24, 1851, census report, U.S. Department of State, Territorial Papers: New Mexico, I, NA, RG 59. A county breakdown is included in the census report. Calhoun, nine days after his inaugural address, ordered the census which was to include all people in New Mexico except Indians, the results to be in his possession by April 15. See March 12, 1850, proclamation in the Territorial Papers: New Mexico, I. Census report was published in the *Bulletin from the Gazette Office* (*Gazette* of Santa Fe), April 26, 1851, Library, Division of History, Museum of New Mexico, Santa Fe. Calhoun was required to take a census before the first election.

17. Horn, p. 28. The rate of illiteracy was even higher across the border, in northern Mexico, where it was estimated that 19 out of 20 could not read or write. David R. Diffendeiffer, U.S. consul in Paso del Norte, to Secretary of State Lewis Cass, April 10, 1858, U.S. Department of State, Diplomatic Despatches, 1789-1906, NA, RG 59, Washington, D.C.

18. Petition from Santa Fe dated February 5, 1851, to the Postmaster General in Washington, Alvarez Papers.

19. "Memorial of A. W. Reynolds contesting the legality of the election of R. H. Weightman, as delegate from New Mexico," NA, RG 233.

20. *Speech [of the] Hon. Richard H. Weightman . . . ,* p. 16.

21. Judge Spruce Baird to Weightman, January 31, 1852, *Speech [of the] Hon. Richard H. Weightman . . . ,* pp. 21-22.

22. J. L. Collins to President Millard Fillmore, April 20, 1852, Appointments and Recommendations, NA, RG 59.

23. Evidence and testimony from the United States vs. Juan Cristobal Armijo as quoted in *Speech* [*of the*] *Hon. Richard H. Weightman* . . . , pp. 24-26.

24. Loyola, July, 1939, p. 276.

25. *Speech* [*of the*] *Hon. Richard H. Weightman* . . . , p. 24.

26. Collins to President Fillmore, April 20, 1852, Appointments and Recommendations, NA, RG 59.

27. As quoted in *Speech* [*of the*] *Hon. Richard H. Weightman* . . . , p. 24.

28. April 20, 1852, Appointments and Recommendations, NA, RG 59.

29. Collins to Fillmore, April 24, 1852, Appointments and Recommendations, NA, RG 59. Collins was supported in two letters: J. N. Ward to Collins, April 7, 1852, and Edwin M. Kern to Collins, April 21, 1852 (enclosed in letter from Collins to Fillmore, April 27, 1852). Calhoun's position was supported in a letter from Bvt. Lt. Col. J. M. Washington, undated, and in a letter from Weightman to Fillmore, April 1, 1852. Weightman claims that Collins, the accuser, was the "official Spanish interpreter" at the treaty proceedings and was one of the treaty signers.

30. Messervy to Daniel Webster, Secretary of State, November 19, 1851, Appointments and Recommendations, NA, RG 59. Messervy, who apparently changed sides in the factional fight, was enthusiastic in recommending Calhoun calling him "a steadfast Whig" and a man of "high character and ability." Messervy and Weightman to Fillmore, December 11, 1850, Appointments and Recommendations, NA, RG 59.

31. December 29, 1851, letter from the members of the Council and the House of Representatives of the New Mexico Legislative Assembly. Also a testimonial letter to Calhoun from the members of the Legislative Assembly dated July 12, 1851, in which the governor's conduct, "both public and private," was commended. All the members who signed had Spanish names except Spruce Baird and George Gold. Appointments and Recommendations, NA, RG 59.

32. *Extract of a Letter Addressed to the Editor of the Santa Fe Gazette, for Publication in New Mexico*, Appointments and Recommendations, NA, RG 59.

33. Letter received on April 5, 1852, Appointments and Recommendations, NA, RG 59.

34. April 8, 1852, Appointments and Recommendations, NA, RG 59.

35. *Speech* [*of the*] *Hon. Richard H. Weightman* . . . , pp. 1-29. Missouri merchants supplying the army were behind Reynold's selection. Lamar, *The Far Southwest, 1846-1912*, p. 96.

36. Alvarez Papers. The Tullis Weightman refers to is John R. Tullis, who served in the upper house of the 1847 legislative assembly.

37. This attack on Houghton's integrity, which was supported by specific charges, was contained in a letter from Weightman to Munroe dated December 1, 1849. Also Weightman and seven other prominent attorneys petitioned Houghton on July 24, 1849, asking him to resign his judgeship because in their view he was "incompetent to fill the office."

38. *Reply of Joab Houghton* . . . , pp. 1-15.

39. Houghton in a letter to Weightman on September 9, 1849, demanded an "unequivocal retraction" of his slanders, or "the satisfaction due from one gentleman to another." *Speech* [*of the*] *Hon. Richard H. Weightman* . . . , p. 9.

40. Twitchell, *The History of the Military Occupation of the Territory of New Mexico*, p. 392.

41. Some of the early Mountain Men may provide a possible exception, many of them taking native wives and adopting certain native customs. Unfortunately, few of them left a record of their opinions.

42. Many of these accounts have been published and make for illuminating, if not fascinating, reading. Some have appeared in books first published in the nineteenth century, such as Garrard's *Wah-To-Yah and the Taos Trail* and Cooke's *Conquest of New Mexico and California*. Shorter accounts, including diaries and other commentaries, are found in the *New Mexico Historical Review* and other pertinent journals.

43. Collins, *Answer to Certain Infamatory Representations by R. H. Weightman*, pp. 13-16.

44. McCall to Crawford, July 15, 1850, as quoted in U.S. Congress, . . . *Colonel McCall's Report in Relation to New Mexico*, Senate Ex. Doc. 26, p. 2.

45. Representation of election ticket, which according to Weightman was Messervy's handiwork, found in *Speech [of the] Hon. Richard H. Weightman . . .* , p. 23.

46. Gallegos to Alvarez, March 21, 1851, trans. from Spanish, Alvarez Papers.

47. Gallegos to Alvarez, July 18, 1850, trans. from Spanish, Alvarez Papers.

48. *Speech [of the] Hon. Richard H. Weightman . . .* , p. 22.

49. Weightman to Alvarez, September 10, 1852, Alvarez Papers. According to Weightman, the newspaper was published under the supervision of the archbishop in that city.

50. *Reply of Joab Houghton . . .* , p. 1.

51. Munroe to Maj. Gen. R. Jones, Adj. Gen., U.S. Army, July 16, 1850, as quoted in U.S. Congress, *Correspondence on . . . Civil Affairs in New Mexico*, Senate Ex. Doc. 1, Part 2, p. 92.

52. Original memorial of April 5, 1851, and summary of it in synopsis prepared by Secretary of State Webster, Appointments and Recommendations, NA, RG 59; *Speech [of the] Hon. Richard H. Weightman*, p. 28. Quoted from Weightman's speech because the punctuation is more effective and logical.

53. Collins, *Answer to Certain Infamatory Representations by R. H. Weightman*, p. 16.

54. "The military would be recalled[,] . . . again to be superior to the civil power, and again to harass a law-abiding people."

55. Weightman to the editors of the *St. Louis Republican*, as quoted in *Speech [of the] Hon. Richard H. Weightman*, pp. 17-19.

CHAPTER VI

1. *The Official Correspondence of James S. Calhoun*, introduction. Calhoun had intended to return to the states earlier, and had appointed Alvarez to serve as acting governor in his absence, effective April 1, 1852. (See March 30, 1852, proclamation of appointment, Read Collection.) However, due to "physical inability" Calhoun canceled his trip and revoked Alavarez's appointment. April 2, 1852, Read Collection.

2. "Biographical Sketch of Governor William Carr Lane, Together with His Diary of His Journey from Saint Louis, Mo., to Santa Fe, N.M.[,] July 31st, 1852[,] to September 9th[,] 1852, with Annotations by R. E. Twitchell, esq.[,] Vice-President of the New Mexico Historical Society," (pages unnumbered), Twitchell Collection.

3. Horn, p. 38.

4. *The Republican Review* (Albuquerque), June 10, 1871, Library, Division of History, Museum of New Mexico, Santa Fe. The newspaper article alluded to here was a report of Greiner's death in Toledo, Ohio. As part of the eulogy, Greiner was lauded as "an enthusiastic Whig in the old Van Buren and Harrison days, and . . . author of those famous campaign song[s], 'Old Zip Coon,' 'Tippecanoe and Tyler too,' and 'The Wagoner Boy.' "

5. Lansing Bloom, "The Governors of New Mexico," *New Mexico Historical Review*, X (April, 1935), 156. Bloom, in a complete list of New Mexico governors prior to statehood, lists Greiner as ad interim governor in 1852 between Calhoun and Lane.

6. In a July 16, 1852, letter, Weightman urged Alvarez to introduce Lane to the "Mexican gentlemen of Santa Fe and of New Mexico generally . . . ."

7. Espinosa, p. 8.

8. Undated letter quoted in "Biographical Sketch of Governor William Carr Lane . . . ," Twitchell Collection.

9. *Message of William Carr Lane, Governor of the Territory of New Mexico, to the Legislative Assembly of the Territory at Santa Fe, Dec. 7, 1852* (Santa Fe: Gazette Office, 1852), pp. 3-10, Read Collection.

10. Lane even criticized the operation and rationale of territorial governments. On March 16, 1854, he scored the inadequacy of such governments, and the error of changing personnel each time a new President takes office. Perhaps his most serious charge against New Mexico was contained in a letter of March 5, 1854, in which he claimed that the territorial treasury was plundered almost as a matter of course. See Ralph P. Bieber (ed.), "Letters of William Carr Lane, 1852-1854," *The New Mexico Historical Review*, III (April, 1928), 179-203.

11. Charles M. Conrad, Secretary of War, to Sumner, September 9, 1852. Sumner also was admonished by Conrad for assigning inadequate rooms in the Palace of Governors to Judge Grafton Baker for holding court. October 11, 1852. In an even more blunt letter Conrad ordered Sumner to stop interfering in civil affairs. December 23, 1852. Correspondence in U.S. War Department, Letters Sent, NA, RG 107.

12. As quoted in Bancroft, pp. 632-33.

13. *Message of William Carr Lane . . . ,* p. 3

14. Report quoted in *Santa Fe Weekly Gazette*, February 19, 1853, Library, Division of History, Museum of New Mexico, Santa Fe.

15. Arnold L. Rodriguez, "New Mexico in Transition," *New Mexico Historical Review*, XXIV (July, 1949), 186.

16. *Santa Fe Weekly Gazette*, February 19, 1853.

17. One historian, P. M. Baldwin, describes *La Mesilla* or the Mesilla Valley as that area lying between Elephant Butte dam to the north and Juarez to the south, and including portions of Sierra and Doña Ana counties in New Mexico and El Paso County in Texas. The apparent inclusion of the east bank of the Rio Grande as part of *La Mesilla* would not be accepted by some historians. See Baldwin, "A Short History of the Mesilla Valley," *New Mexico Historical Review*, XIII (July, 1938), 314.

18. U.S. Congress, *Treaties . . .* (Compiled by Malloy), Senate Doc. 357, I, art. v, 1109-10.

19. Secretary of State Marcy to David Meriwether, Governor of New Mexico, May 28, 1853, as quoted in J. Fred Rippy, *The United States and Mexico* (New York: Alfred A. Knopf, Inc., 1926), p. 119.

20. "Biographical Sketch of Governor William Carr Lane . . . ." The size of the Texas land grants, generally 640 acres, explains, perhaps more than anything else, why the Anglos came and why the pressure on these regional owners was so great.

21. Rippy, pp. 115-16. As an indication of the minority status of Anglo-Americans in the settlement of Mesilla, there were only a hundred or so of them in 1859 as compared to almost 4,000 inhabitants of Mexican extraction. See W. Clement Eaton, "Frontier Life in Southern Arizona, 1858-1861," *The Southwestern Historical Quarterly*, XXXVI (January, 1933), 174.

22. August 25, 1851, petition, *The Official Correspondence of James S. Calhoun,* p. 405.

23. Proclamation, bearing the name of Miguel A. Otero, Lane's private secretary, Read Collection.

24. May 12, 1853, in Rippy, pp. 118-19.

25. Photostatic copy of March 19, 1853, letter from Lane to Colonel D. S. Miles, Joseph King Fenno Mansfield Papers, U.S. Army Collection, Division of Manuscripts, Library of Congress, Washington, D.C. The letter was apparently written at Ft. Fillmore, across the Rio Grande from Mesilla, several days after Lane had issued his controversial proclamation. In it the governor not only attacked the neutral position assumed by Colonel Miles and his superior, Colonel Sumner, but vigorously asserted the superiority of civil authority over the military.

26. Paul Neff Garber, *The Gadsden Treaty* (Philadelphia: Press of the University of Pennsylvania, 1923), pp. 130-32. Congress balked at the Gadsden Treaty for a variety of reasons and trimmed the original sum we agreed to pay Mexico from 15 to 10 million dollars. (The amount involved in the Mexican Cession was only 15 million!) The exact number of square miles acquired by the United States was 45,535.

27. Garber was one of those who felt that Governor Lane had brought the issue to a head and thereby forced federal intervention.

28. The Committee on Elections of the House of Representatives, to whom Lane had appealed in the hopes of being seated, ruled in favor of Gallegos in Report 121, which was issued on February 24, 1854. Also found in the New Mexico Territorial Papers Collection, NA, RG 233, were affidavits from two Santa Ana County citizens claiming an election judge had received 140 illegal Indian votes, plus a list of the Indians involved, and some 44 poll books or precinct tally sheets used in the disputed election. Final legal tally showed 2,806 for Gallegos to 2,267 for Lane. Lane blamed his defeat on the fact that he was an Anglo. "They say they have no personal objection to me, but they are determined to elect one of their own race . . . ." See August 30, 1853, letter from Lane to his wife as quoted in Bieber, p. 198.

29. Twitchell, *The Leading Facts of New Mexican History,* II, 309; Bancroft, pp. 650-51.

30. U.S. *Congressional Globe,* 33d Cong., 1st Sess., Part 1, p. 492.

31. LeRoy R. Hafen (ed.), *Colorado and Its People: A Narrative and Topical History of the Centennial State* (New York: Lewis Historical Publishing Co., Inc., 1948), p. 221. The area severed from New Mexico, which extended north along the 103rd meridian to the 38th parallel and west along that line to the crest of the Rockies, was known as the New Mexico notch.

32. Frank Hall, *History of the State of Colorado* (Chicago: The Blakely Printing Company, 1888-95), I, 258-60.

33. Henry Connelly, who became governor of the Territory of New Mexico in 1861, estimated in an address to the territorial legislature on December 6, 1865, that there were 4,000 inhabitants living in the New Mexico notch at that time.

34. Fillmore to L. Barlow and others, December 16, 1859, Millard Fillmore Papers, Division of Manuscripts, Library of Congress, Washington, D.C. This letter was in response to a request that the former President attend a public meeting in New York City sponsored by a group deeply concerned about the growing division within the country.

35. Warren A. Beck, *New Mexico: A History of Four Centuries* (Norman: University of Oklahoma Press, 1962), p. 147. Bancroft contends that there was very little

enthusiasm for national politics in New Mexico, "apathy being the leading characteristic, with a slight leaning on general principles to southern views." Bancroft, p. 680.

36. F. S. Donnell, "The Confederate Territory of Arizona, as Compiled from Official Sources," *New Mexico Historical Review*, XVII (April, 1942), 150-59; B. Sacks, *Be It Enacted: The Creation of the Territory of Arizona* (Phoenix: Arizona Historical Foundation, 1964), 58-63.

37. William Clark Whitford, *Colorado Volunteers in the Civil War: The New Mexico Campaign in 1862* (Denver: The State Historical and Natural History Society, 1906), pp. 11-14. This book includes some interesting quotations from Major Trevanion T. Teel's account of Confederate aspirations in the West. Teel was an officer in the Confederate army that invaded New Mexico.

38. Whitford, p. 14.

39. Rencher to Secretary of State William H. Seward, April 14, 1861, U.S. Department of State, Territorial Papers: New Mexico, II, NA, RG 59.

40. Connelly to Seward, November 17, 1861.

41. Printed copy of "Address of the Legislative Assembly of New Mexico," NA, RG 46. The address was adopted unanimously.

42. Donnell, p. 154.

43. This was the conclusion reached by Col. William Steele, the officer in charge of troops at El Paso, in a July 12, 1862, letter to Gen. S. Cooper, adjutant general at Richmond. Steele did, however, believe that the difficulties encountered with the native population were due more to the obvious fact that the Confederates were losing the war and were about to abandon the territory than to any great fervor for the Union cause.

44. Bancroft was quite emphatic on this point. ". . . The old hatred of the Texans . . . [was] the strongest popular feeling of the natives, far outweighing their devotion to either the south or north." p. 684.

45. October 26, 1861, as quoted in U.S. War Department, *The War of the Rebellion: A Compilation of the Official Records of the Union and Confederate Armies*, Series 3, I (Washington: U.S. Government Printing Office, 1880-1900), 600-01.

46. Scott to Maj. Gen. John C. Frémont, Western Department, Cairo, August 6, 1861, O.R., Ser. 1, III, 428.

47. Canby to Assistant Adjutant General, Headquarters of Western Department, St. Louis, August, 16, 1861, O.R., Ser. 1, IV, 65.

48. Canby to Adjutant General of the Army, Washington, January 13, 1862, O.R., Ser. 1, IV, 84-85.

49. *The Fourth Annual Message of S. E. D. Henry Connelly, to the Legislative Assembly of New Mexico, Given December, 1865* (Santa Fe: Manderfield and Tucker, Printers, Office of *The New Mexican*), p. 30. English version enclosed in U.S. Department of State, Territorial Papers: New Mexico, III, NA, RG 59. Spanish version enclosed in Council Journal, p. 9, and House Journal, p. 123, Legislative Papers, State Records Center and Archives, Santa Fe. Quotations will be from English version, pp. 24-30.

50. Paraje was considerably south of Socorro and south of San Marcial, at approximately 33° 35', according to an 1870 map found in the L. Bradford Prince Papers, State Records Center and Archives, Santa Fe.

51. Thomas E. Farish, *History of Arizona* (8 vols., San Francisco: The Filmer Brothers Electrotype Company, 1915-1918), I, 322 cited in Sacks, pp. 10, 47. Sacks' book, *Be It Enacted*, is the most up-to-date account of the secessionist movements in

southern and western New Mexico prior to 1863, the photographs and reproductions of original petitions, addresses, convention proceedings, and constitutions making the appendix invaluable.

52. New Mexico Territorial Papers Collection, NA, RG 46.

53. The Tucson memorial bore the names of more than 260 people. NA, RG 46.

54. The memorial so called because the signature of M. E. Bradley heads the list of petitioners.

55. Sacks, pp. 10, 47.

56. Joint resolution of the Council and House of Representatives of the New Mexico legislature, NA, RG 46.

57. Joint memorial of the New Mexico legislature, NA, RG 46. Delegate Otero, reflecting the same sentiment, also reported in 1860 H. R. 192, a bill to organize Arizona as a separate territory.

58. New Mexico Governor Abraham Rencher, in a dispatch to Seward, mentions the creation of a provisional government in this area as early as 1858. "In 1858 they withdrew all connexion [sic] with this Territory, and established what they call a provisional Government, wishing thereby to obtain from Congress a separate territorial organization, which has been a complete failure." Rencher cited the Jornada del Muerto as a particularly imposing geographical barrier. See Rencher to Seward, May 18, 1861, U.S. Department of State, Territorial Papers: New Mexico, II, NA, RG 59.

59. Sacks, pp. 69-80.

60. Later surveys located the boundary precisely at 109° 2' 59.25".

61. Congressman John Addison Gurley of Ohio, a supporter of the Arizona bill, reported to the House that more than a million dollars had been expended to open the gold and silver mines of Arizona, and that the federal government was honor bound to protect those who had embarked upon such operations. Sacks, p. 73.

62. Memorial referred to the House Committee on the Territories on July 9, 1865, New Mexico Territorial Papers Collection, NA, RG 233. Also found, a petition signed by 98 citizens of El Paso County plus the officers and soldiers of a local military unit, and petition signed by 47 citizens of Doña Ana County asking for the organization of the Territory of Montezuma.

63. December 9, 1865, Library, Division of History, Museum of New Mexico, Santa Fe.

64. Memorial, referred to the House Committee on the Territories on February 18, 1867, with names of 33 citizens from Doña Ana and El Paso counties, NA, RG 233. A majority of the names are Spanish.

65. Undated article found in the Thomas B. Catron Papers, Special Collections Division, University of New Mexico Library, Albuquerque. Hereafter cited as Catron Papers.

66. December 9, 1865.

67. December 16, 1865.

68. "An Act authorizing the Governor to call a Convention to frame a Constitution for a Government of State," U.S. Department of State, Territorial Papers: New Mexico, III, NA, RG 59; Daily Rocky Mountain News (Denver), February 13, 1866, Library of Congress, Washington, D.C. According to the Daily Rocky Mountain News, only two legislators opposed the act.

69. Governor Connelly approved it on January 31, 1866, according to an entry in the U.S. Department of State, Territorial Papers: New Mexico, III, NA, RG. 59.

70. The repeal of the Free Negro law was approved by the governor on January 19,

1866, while the action taken on the peonage matter was approved January 26, 1866. U.S. Department of State, Territorial Papers: New Mexico, III, NA, RG 59. Peonage in all forms was finally abolished by the Congress in 1867.

71. February 3, 1866, NA, RG 46.

72. U.S. Department of State, Territorial Papers: New Mexico, NA, RG 59.

73. Joint memorial of the Council and House of Representatives of the New Mexico legislature, NA, RG 46. Arny in a letter to Schuyler Colfax, Speaker of the House, dated February 10, 1866, claimed that the memorial had been unanimously adopted. See U.S. Congress, House, *Memorial of the Assembly of New Mexico, in Regard to a State Government for that Territory,* 39th Cong., 1st Sess., 1866, III, Misc. Doc. 57, 1.

74. *Daily Rocky Mountain News,* February 13, 1866.

75. Miguel E. Pino, president of the Council, and Samuel Ellison, speaker of the House, to Secretary of State Seward, December 6, 1865, U.S. Department of State, Territorial Papers: New Mexico, III, NA, RG 59.

76. *Daily Rocky Mountain News,* June 12, 1866.

77. The controversial Cummings even went to Washington to urge President Johnson to veto a Colorado statehood measure passed by Congress, a good example of the damage a powerful federal appointee could do to a statehood effort. Frank Hall, one of the statehood proponents, a former secretary of the territory and an appointee of Cummings, provides a highly critical account of Cummings' opposition in pp. 369-70 of his book.

78. *Daily Rocky Mountain News,* April 12, 1866, May 4, 1866. The first of these two newspaper accounts reported that two powerful senators, Wade and Charles Sumner, had been won over to Colorado statehood; the second revealed that a Colorado statehood bill had passed both houses of Congress. Sumner originally opposed the state movement because of the exclusion of one hundred Negroes from voting privileges. He also felt that the population of Colorado was insufficient, and that the would-be state did not deserve two senators.

79. *Daily Rocky Mountain News,* June 1, 1866.

80. Hall, p. 383.

81. U.S. Department of State, Territorial Papers: New Mexico, III, NA, RG 59.

82. *Daily Rocky Mountain News,* June 12, 1866.

83. *The Valedictory Address of Governor Henry Connelly, and the Inaugural of Robert B. Mitchell, Delivered in Front of the Palace, Santa Fe, N.M., Monday, July 16th, 1866* (Santa Fe: Office of the Weekly Gazette, 1866), pp. 3-7, U.S. Department of State, Territorial Papers: New Mexico, III, NA, RG 59.

84. September 27, 1866, NA, RG 46.

85. September 26, 1866, U.S. Department of State, Territorial Papers: New Mexico, III, NA, RG 59.

86. Memorial, translated from Spanish, Papers Pertaining to Nominations, Records Groups 46, National Archives, Washington, D.C. The memorial, which was certified by the Secretary of the Territory on March 8, 1869, urged that Houghton be replaced by John D. Bail of Grant County. Houghton had many difficulties as judge of the third district, stemming for the most part from his inadequate legal training, and President Grant did replace him in 1869 with Abraham Bergen. See Reeve, pp. 306-07.

87. September 15, 1866, Twitchell Collection.

88. Twitchell, *The Leading Facts of New Mexican History,* II, 400.

89. February 10, 1871, as quoted in Horn, p. 143.

90. September 15, 1866, Twitchell Collection.

91. Horn, pp. 142-43.

92. H. R. 2276, handwritten copy submitted to the House Committee on the Territories on June 20, 1870, NA, RG 233. Interestingly enough, Lincoln would have incorporated a section of Old Mexico, as the southern boundary was to be drawn from the Rio Grande westward along the latitude of 31° 20'. Southwestern Colorado also was to be a part of the proposed state, as the northwestern boundary would extend along the 38th parallel from the 109th meridian to the Sangre de Cristo range. The bill called for a constitutional convention, the handiwork of which would be submitted to the people for their approval on the first Monday of June, 1871. See Bancroft, p. 721, for a list of government documents pertaining to the Lincoln statehood movement.

CHAPTER VII

1. Giddings claims that the two senators from Michigan, Zachariah Chandler and Thomas W. Ferry, recommended his appointment in his absence, and without his "knowledge or desire." They did so because of concern over Giddings' failing health, and in the hope that a change of climate would help the governor.

2. Giddings to Secretary of Interior Columbus Delano, April 3, 1873, U.S. Department of Interior, Appointments File, 1849-79, Records Group 48, National Archives, Washington, D.C. Hereafter cited NA, RG 48.

3. Daily Rocky Mountain News as quoted in The Daily New Mexican (Santa Fe), January 18, 1872. The article in the Denver paper was entitled, somewhat appropriately, "The New Mexican Muddle." Newspapers cited in this chapter will be from the Division of History, Museum of New Mexico, Santa Fe, unless otherwise indicated.

4. As quoted in The Daily New Mexican, January 18, 1872.

5. Giddings to Delano, April 3, 1873, NA, RG 48.

6. Charges made in statement prepared by Governor Giddings, in response to an investigation of his conduct ordered by President Grant. See Selected Letters Received by Appointment Division and Miscellaneous Division, Concerning Gov. Marsh Giddings, National Archives, Washington, D.C., as quoted, in part, in Horn, pp. 165-66. The statement, not dated by Horn, is very similar—identical in parts—to the April 3, 1873, letter Giddings sent to Delano, which leads this writer to believe that the statement and letter were prepared from the same draft, copied from one another, or could even be one and the same. A May 19, 1873, memo, signed by U. S. Grant, ordering the investigation of Giddings, was found in the governor's Appointments File, 1849-73, NA, RG 48. "Have charges investigated and if true removal will be ordered," stated Grant. The President, however, cautioned investigators not to act on statements made in local newspapers, particularly the one edited by "a man who has been removed from office for cause . . . ," probably a reference to Sullivan. Judge Benedict also was critical, publishing a local Democratic newspaper in which both Giddings and Chief Justice Palen were attacked.

7. Giddings to Delano, April 3, 1873, NA, RG 48. The term was Giddings'.

8. The Daily New Mexican, January 11, 1872.

9. The indomitable Diego Archuleta was elected as the new council president by a vote of 8 to 4.

10. Political partisanship was at its highest. The Borderer (Las Cruces), described by the Daily New Mexican as "a scurrilous democratic weekly," seemed just as determined to see the Democrats retain control of the House. It editorially slammed the Republicans for not recognizing the removal of three Taos Republicans, a position vigorously assailed by the Daily New Mexican on January 12, 1872. Governor Giddings

also found *The Borderer* offensive, calling it the "vilest newspaper in the territory." Giddings to Delano, April 3, 1873, NA, RG 48.

11. Horn fittingly entitled the chapter dealing with this incident "The Revolution in Santa Fe." See p. 156.

12. *The Daily New Mexican*, January 11, 1872.

13. Giddings to Delano, April 3, 1873, NA, RG 48.

14. *The Daily New Mexican*, January 22, 1872.

15. Horn, p. 163.

16. According to Giddings, the compromise was brought about largely because of the constructive efforts of federal officials and certain "excellent" citizens of the territory.

17. Giddings to Delano, April 3, 1873, NA, RG 48.

18. *Santa Fe New Mexican*, October 29, 1890, Marion Dargan Papers, Special Collections Division, University of New Mexico Library, Albuquerque. This collection, which contains a great amount of material pertinent to the statehood movement, including many newspaper articles, will hereafter be cited as the Dargan Papers.

19. *Weekly New Mexican* (Santa Fe), January 23, 1872. In 1872, Catron, Elkins, Giddings, and two other prominent New Mexicans formed the first incorporated cattle company in the territory, the Consolidated Land, Cattle Raising and Wool Growing Company. See Reeve, p. 211.

20. Giddings to Delano, April 3, 1873, NA, RG 48.

21. March 22, 1872.

22. *The Daily New Mexican*, March 25, 1872.

23. House Journal (unpublished and in Spanish), p. 114, Legislative Papers. Diego Archuleta, president of the council, presided over the joint session.

24. Council Journal (unpublished and in Spanish), pp. 194-199, Legislative Papers. The bill, No. 39, was not even referred to committee, but was promptly passed after the third reading.

25. House Journal, p. 114, Legislative Papers.

26. *The Daily New Mexican*, May 29, 1872.

27. New Mexico, *Constitution* (1872), art. v, Railroads, sec. 7, Constitutional Convention Papers. According to the accompanying legislative act one thousand copies of the *Constitution of the State of New Mexico* were to be printed. Three hundred of them were to be in English, seven hundred in Spanish. Quotations are from the English version.

28. Art. v, Railroads, secs. 1, 3, 4, 5.

29. *The Daily New Mexican*, May 29, 1872.

30. April 13, 1872. In the same issue, the editor of the *Republican* ridiculed a pamphlet in Spanish, circulated by proponents of statehood, entitled *Manifesto Dirigido a los Mejicanos de Nuevo Mejico*. Statements in the leaflet predicting the speedy arrival of the railroads were answered by a prediction that it would take an "indefinite number of centuries" before railroad corporations would overcome the "insurmountable physical obstacles, to say nothing of a grave political obstacle to railroad building provided by the State Constitution . . . ."

31. New Mexico, *Constitution* (1870), art. iv, Legislative Department, sec. 6.

32. Art, v, Education, sec. 3.

33. Art. ii, Bill of Rights, sec. 3.

34. June 10, 1871. Remarks of *The Borderer* in this issue.

35. New Mexico, *Constitution* (1872), art. v, Suffrage.

36. April 6, 13, 1872.

37. "An Act Providing for a General Election for the Purpose of Submitting to a

Vote of the People a State Constitution and State Officers," sec. 1, Constitutional Convention Papers. The act was included in the same booklet with the constitution, and according to section 6 of the enactment, 1,000 copies were to be printed, 300 in English and 700 in Spanish.

38. March 25, April 5, 1872.

39. April 13, 1872.

40. Quoted in *The Republican Review*, April, 13, 1872. Also, see June 1, 1872, issue.

41. April 20, 1872.

42. Charge contained in May 8, 1871, letter from Mesilla to the editor of *The Borderer* found in an undated newspaper clipping, Catron Papers.

43. *The Republican Review*, April 6, 1872.

44. *Ibid.*, March 16, 1872.

45. April 20, 1872. The paper estimated that the people of the proposed State of New Mexico would have to be taxed every year to the amount of "from two hundred thousand to five hundred thousand dollars to pay interest on this debt."

46. Letter from Cimarron, signed TRUTH, in April 2, 1872, issue.

47. *The Daily New Mexican*, May 29, 1872. *The Republican Review*, in its May 18, 1872, issue, ridiculed the whole idea of "Colorado biting off a piece of New Mexico."

48. An especially unique feature of the Chaffee plan was its inclusion of states, i.e., Nebraska, Nevada, and the lower half of California. In discussing the plan in its February 15, 1872, issue, the *New Mexican* questioned the combined population for Colorado and Wyoming, claiming that census reports do not even show half that number.

49. March 9, 1872.

50. *The Republican Review*, June 1, 1872. The group, which had gathered in a public meeting at the county courthouse on May 19, 1872, had requested both the *Republican* and *The Borderer* to publish its proceedings.

51. As quoted in Horn, p. 165. Although Gallegos felt strongly about Giddings, he did not bother to come to New Mexico during the congressional recess and campaign against the constitution. According to a Washington correspondent, the delegate planned to spend the summer and fall, during the congressional recess, in New York and Philadelphia, and other Eastern cities. *The Daily New Mexican*, June 13, 1872.

52. The charge, made by Gallegos in his letter to Grant, and apparently elsewhere, was vigorously refuted in Giddings to Delano, April 3, 1873, NA, RG 48.

53. Accusation of *The Borderer*, carried first in *The People* (Pueblo, Territory of Colorado), and reprinted from that paper in *The Daily New Mexican*, March 28, 1872. February 28, 1872, apportionment proclamation of Governor Giddings attached to p. 87, Executive Record, Territory of New Mexico, July 25, 1867, to November 8, 1882, State Records Center and Archives, Santa Fe. The apportionment, made during the last two hectic days of the legislative session, was necessitated by the confusion and partisanship, and yet, in the governor's words, it would have "to stand for the next ten years."

54. Although admitting the appointment was made during the busy two remaining days of the legislature, Giddings defended it on the basis of his son's business experience.

55. Giddings to Delano, April 3, 1873, NA, RG 48.

56. Proclamation in Executive Record, Territory of New Mexico, July 25, 1867, to November 8, 1882, State Records Center and Archives, Santa Fe. The governor was required to make his proclamation by "An Act Providing for a General Election . . . ," sec. 1. See footnote 37 for full citation.

57. "An Act Providing for a General Election . . . ," secs. 4, 5.

58. Although its Albuquerque rival was not mentioned by name, the Santa Fe daily almost read the *Republican* out of the party.

59. April 5, 1872.

60. March 13, 1872.

61. May 29, 1872.

62. June 1, 1872.

63. As quoted in *The Republican Review*, April 27, 1872.

64. April 6, 1872. In this article, the changing ratios of apportionment are listed, starting with the first census in 1790. In a list of fifteen states: Vermont, Kentucky, Tennessee, Ohio, Louisiana, Indiana, Mississippi, Illinois, Missouri, Arkansas, Florida, Iowa, Oregon, Nevada, and Nebraska, the newspaper in its March 30 issue pointed out that all but the last three "were admitted on the basis of the ratio of apportionment existing at the time of their admittance . . . ." The *New Mexican*, obviously not regarding this consideration as an important one, boasted on March 25, 1872, about the territory's substantial population, which ranged from "92,000 to 100,000 people."

65. April 27, 1872.

66. March 16, 1872.

67. May 18, 1872.

68. May 4, 1872.

69. March 30, April 6, April 13, 1872.

70. "An Act Providing for a General Election . . . ."

71. April 27, 1872.

72. May 4, 1872.

73. As quoted in *The Republican Review*, June 1, 1872.

74. June 15, 1872.

75. Sec. 5 of the *Laws of the Territory of New Mexico Enacted by the Legislative Assembly of 1871-1872* (Santa Fe: A. P. Sullivan, Public Printer, 1872), pp. 55-56. The printed laws were located in the National Archives by John Porter Bloom, Editor of The Territorial Papers of the United States, who graciously sent a Xerox copy to the writer.

76. The following words appear at the end of the act: "Approved February 1, 1872. [Translation.]"

77. The original law probably is no longer in existence. It is not in the State Archives and Record Center, Santa Fe. The writer is grateful to Dr. Myra Ellen Jenkins, Senior Archivist, for making a careful search for it in the Archives and elsewhere.

78. Sec. 6 of the *Laws of the Territory of New Mexico* . . . 1871-1872, p. 56, and of "An Act Providing for a General Election . . . ."

79. *The Republican Review*, June 15, 1872.

80. Proclamation of April 2, 1872, Executive Record, Territory of New Mexico. A published version of the proclamation in *The Republican Review* did add the following sentence: "And the returns of such election and the vote: to be cast, to be made and returned to the Governor of the Territory ot [sic] his office in Santa Fe within the time prescribed by law." Interestingly enough, despite its determined opposition to the constitution, the *Republican* publicized the election proclamation, with its vague reference to sending returns to Santa Fe, on almost a weekly basis. See April 6, April 13, April 20, April 27, May 4, May 18, May 25, and June 1 issues. *The Daily New Mexican* also printed the proclamation, in Spanish and English, on April 3, 1872.

81. According to sec. 6 of the law, election judges also were to receive printed copies of the constitution.

82. As quoted in *The Republican Review*, June 15, 1872.

83. June 11, 1872.

84. *The Borderer* as quoted in *The Republican Review*, June 29, 1872.

85. *The Daily New Mexican*, March 22, 1872.

86. June 8, 1872.

87. *The Borderer* as quoted in *The Republican Review*, June 15, 1872.

88. *The Daily New Mexican*, June 10, 1872.

89. As quoted in *The Republican Review*, June 1, 1872.

90. They were San Ildefonso and Tesuque. The precinct of Agua Fria also was rejecting it. Voting for the constitution and state government were the precincts of Galisteo, Cienega, Pojoaque, Upper and Lower Santa Fe, and Old and New Placer.

91. June 6, 1872.

92. June 10, 1872.

93. *The Daily New Mexican* as quoted in *The Republican Review*, June 15, 1872.

94. June 8, 1872. Three choices were offered the voting citizens of Bernalillo. They could vote for state government, against it, or elect to remain a territory. The editors of the *Republican* arrived at their whopping majority by adding the 79 votes cast for territorial status to the 619 cast against statehood, making a total of 698. By subtracting the meager 24 votes cast for state status from 698, they reached the 674 figure.

95. *The Republican Review*, June 15, 1872. The paper was using the Las Vegas *Mail* and the *New Mexican* as its sources.

96. *Message of Governor Marsh Giddings, to the Legislative Assembly of New Mexico, December, 1873* (Santa Fe: Manderfield & Tucker, Public Printers, 1873), pp. 17-18, Governors' Papers, State Records Center and Archives, Santa Fe.

97. It is interesting to note that the secretary of the territory, Henry Wetter, a Giddings opponent, was not placed on the commission.

98. June 15, 1872. The *Republican* also challenged its Santa Fe rival to name the precinct that gave four hundred votes to statehood.

99. *The Republican Review*, June 29, 1872.

Chapter VIII

1. *The Daily New Mexican*, March 16, 1874. Memorial quoted in *Admission of New Mexico as a State—Her Resources and Future: Speech of Hon. Stephen B. Elkins, Delegate from New Mexico in the House of Representatives, May 21, 1874* (Washington: Government Printing Office, 1874), p. 4, Edmund G. Ross Papers, State Records Center and Archives, Santa Fe. Hereafter cited as Ross Papers.

2. *Message of Governor Marsh Giddings . . . December, 1873*, p. 18.

3. H.R. 2418, NA, RG 233.

4. *Admission of New Mexico . . . Speech of Hon. Stephen B. Elkins*, pp. 1-33. An analysis of Elkins' motives is included in the next chapter.

5. Elkins placed the population of the Pueblo Indians at a "little short of 10,000," which was somewhat in excess of the estimate offered by Governor Giddings.

6. March 18, 1848, dispatch from Buchanan as quoted on p. 17.

7. The two medical authorities quoted were Dr. Kenon, a Santa Fe physician, who commented on the low incidence of disease, and a Dr. McKee, author and former professor at Jefferson College, Louisville, who remarked favorably on the climate.

8. Statement from the 1868 report of the commissioner.

9. Comment of George Colin McKee, a Republican from Mississippi and supporter

of the bill, as quoted in U.S. *Congressional Record*, 43d Cong., 1st Sess., 1874, Part 5, p. 4130.

10. May 31, 1874, Stephen B. Elkins Papers, West Virginia Collection, University of West Virginia Library, Morgantown. Hereafter cited as Elkins Papers.

11. Hubbell to Elkins, June 9, 1874, Elkins Papers. Another letter of congratulation was sent to Elkins by one M. C. Meigs on May 22, 1874. Expressing a belief that state governments should be organized as soon as possible "in the interior of the continent," the writer, who was apparently an Easterner—the letter was sent from Washington—had nothing but praise for New Mexico's qualifications for statehood.

12. Fifth Annual Message as quoted in Richardson, *A Compilation of the Messages and Papers of the Presidents*, VI, 4209. Grant, in his December 1 message, also proposed that a canal be built from private resources, for purposes of irrigation, from the eastern slope of the Rocky Mountains to the Missouri River. This would claim for man's use "an arid belt of public land from 300 to 500 miles in width . . . ."

13. Charles S. Thomas, "The Pioneer Bar of Colorado," *The Colorado Magazine*, I (July, 1924), 201; Elmer Ellis, *Henry Moore Teller: Defender of the West* (Caldwell, Idaho: The Caxton Printers, Ltd., 1941), p. 89. The quarrel occurred possibly as early as 1872 and news of it allegedly became common knowledge. The account of Thomas is particularly interesting as Thomas, a pioneer lawyer, claimed to have heard the rumor while practicing law in Denver.

14. Hall, II, 158.

15. The fight also had economic overtones as McCook was accused of making profits off Indian beef contracts, and Elbert was labeled by McCook as a front man for a land-stealing ring. Lamar, *The Far Southwest, 1846-1912*, pp. 286-89.

16. Although Grant did not mention Colorado statehood in his Sixth Annual Message, sent to Congress on December 7, 1874, this is not to say he worked against the mountain territory. In a letter to Chaffee dated March 13, 1875, he expressed his continuing approval of Colorado. "From the date of my first visit to Colorado to the present I have believed that the Territory had the Mineral and Agricultural resources to make it a populous and prosperous state, and an intelligent and energetic population calculated to develop these resources and to maintain republican government." See Ulysses S. Grant Papers, Division of Manuscripts, Library of Congress, Washington, D. C.

17. The Colorado bill was reported by the Senate Committee on Territories on June 11.

18. U.S. *Congressional Record*, 43d Cong., 2d Sess., 1875, Part 3, pp. 1673, 1678.

19. *Ibid.*, p. 1691.

20. *The Daily New Mexican* erroneously reported the vote as 31 to 11 in the March 5, 1875, edition.

21. March 5, 1875.

22. February 26, 1875. A majority of Eastern and Midwestern newspapers used in this chapter and throughout the rest of the book are from the Newspaper Reference Room, Library of Congress, Washington, D.C.

23. March 5, 1875.

24. Population estimates for the two territories in 1875 gave New Mexico 100,000 and Colorado, 65,000, a considerable increase for both territories, if accurate.

25. February 26, 1875.

26. The comment of this journal may have been more bitter because of an erroneous assumption that Colorado and New Mexico had already been admitted as states. The *St. Louis Daily Globe* of March 5, 1875, playfully needled the *Commercial* for its

error, claiming that the Cincinnati paper was entitled to "ignore facts."

27. March 3, 1875.

28. This was Democrat Thomas M. Patterson's evaluation, who at the time was Colorado's delegate-elect to Congress. "Whether the Republicans did make their admission a caucus measure I never learned with positiveness, but it was understood at the time the bills were introduced that the Republicans of both houses would, with practical unanimity, support the measure." See *The Rocky Mountain News* (Denver), April 23, 1909, "Golden Jubilee Number" for Patterson's recollection of final congressional action on the Colorado and New Mexico statehood bills. This special edition was to commemorate the fiftieth anniversary of the newspaper's founding.

29. E. Merton Coulter, *The South During Reconstruction, 1865-1877*, Vol. VIII of *A History of the South*, ed. Wendell Holmes Stephenson (10 vols.; Baton Rouge: Louisiana State University and The Littlefield Fund for Southern History of the University of Texas, 1947), pp. 366-67.

30. *The Rocky Mountain News*, April 23, 1909, "Golden Jubilee Number." This was the view of Patterson.

31. Elected as delegate in the summer of 1874, Patterson decided to go to Washington in 1875, after the New Year, and add "whatever influence" he could to the fight for statehood.

32. March 4, 1875.

33. The vote, 145 to 95 in the affirmative with 48 abstentions, fell considerably short of the required two-thirds. The *Times* erroneously recorded 93 votes against the Butler resolution.

34. *The Rocky Mountain News*, April 23, 1909, "Golden Jubilee Number."

35. *U.S. Congressional Record*, p. 2237.

36. *The Rocky Mountain News*, April 23, 1909, "Golden Jubilee Number"; *The Daily New Mexican*, March 15, 1875. Patterson and the *New Mexican* disagree on when the Colorado bill was finally taken up. In Patterson's recollection, printed in *The Rocky Mountain News*, it was two o'clock, but the *New Mexican*, in a garbled report, claimed the measure was reached as early as 1:00 A.M.

37. *U.S. Congressional Record*, pp. 2238-39.

38. According to Patterson, defeat for the New Mexico measure was recognized "even before those not voting and who asked to have their votes recorded" at the end of the roll call, were accommodated. *The Rocky Mountain News*, April 23, 1909, "Golden Jubilee Number."

39. *U.S. Congressional Record*, p. 2239. John Cessna, a Pennsylvania Republican, tried to save the New Mexico measure, insisting that a simple majority was all that was needed for concurrence with the Senate amendments. His objection, however, was overruled by Blaine, who upheld the ruling that a two-thirds vote was necessary to remove the New Mexico bill from the table.

40. March 15, 1875.

41. Denver *Mirror* as quoted in *The Daily New Mexican*, March 26, 1875.

42. March 26, 1875.

43. March 4, 1875. When the *New Mexican* published this over-all evaluation of Elkins, the final fate of the New Mexico bill was unknown. However, one senses little optimism in the chances for statehood.

44. March 20, 1875, as quoted in *The Daily New Mexican*, March 25, 1875.

45. March 5, 1875.

46. The *New Mexican* confuses the three ballots taken on proposals to suspend the rules. Although obviously referring to the vote on Hoskins' resolution, the paper

erroneously claims that vote was taken on March 4. Moreover, in an apparent misprint, the *New Mexican* records this vote as 164 to 85 instead of 164 to 84, the actual count, which was two shy of the necessary two-thirds.

47. March 5 and 15, 1875.

48. March 20, 1875, as quoted in *The Daily New Mexican*, March 25, 1875. Although partisan politics were momentarily suspended in this grateful evaluation of Patterson's contribution, the staunchy Republican *Tribune* was not totally uncritical. "We don't know whether he actually persuaded all those [Democrats] to voluntarily forego the privilege of voting against the bill, or whether he beguiled some of them into listening to a fascinating tale of how he scooped the Republicans of Colorado— how things were fixed for him in the north, and how he corraled the Mexican vote in the south—and thus distracted their attention from what was going on until the critical moment had passed."

49. *The Daily New Mexican*, March 5 and 25, 1875.

50. *Boston Post*, March 1, 1875. The charge also was published in the *St. Louis Daily Globe*, March 1, 1875.

51. James G. Blaine, *Twenty Years of Congress: From Lincoln to Garfield* (Norwich, Connecticut: The Henry Bill Publishing Company, 1884-93), II, 543-66.

52. As quoted in the *St. Louis Daily Globe*, March 8, 1875.

53. *The Rocky Mountain News*, August 2, 1901.

54. U.S. *Congressional Record*, 59th Cong., 1st Sess., 1906, Part 4, p. 3512. Also, see Mary Fonda Adams, "Thomas M. Patterson, Some Aspects of His Political Career" (unpublished Master's thesis, Dept. of Political Science, University of Colorado, 1933), pp. 19-20, for a helpful account of Patterson's role in the incident.

55. *The Rocky Mountain News* (Denver), April 23, 1909, "Golden Jubilee Number."

56. Patterson's apt and colorful description.

57. U.S. *Congressional Record*, 43d Cong., 2d Sess., 1875, Part 3, p. 1925.

58. *The Rocky Mountain News* (Denver), April 23, 1909, "Golden Jubilee Number." Although Patterson is apparently the only primary source for this incident, it has been repeated in many secondary accounts, such as Twitchell, *The Leading Facts of New Mexican History*, II, 403-06; Reeve, II, 324; Beck, pp. 229-30; Lamar, *The Far Southwest, 1846-1912*, pp. 166-67. There seems little question as to the veracity of Patterson's account, as both Elkins and Burrows were serving in the Senate when Patterson related the incident in the upper house, in 1906, and neither man contradicted or questioned his version. As a matter of fact, Patterson in his speech referred to both men as his colleagues, and expressed his warm regard, although insisting, in a teasing reference, that Elkins was no longer as impulsive. See U.S. *Congressional Record*, 59th Cong., 1st Sess., 1909, Part 4, p. 3512.

59. Hafen, *Colorado and Its People*, I, 345-59.

Chapter IX

1. Marion Dargan, "New Mexico's Fight for Statehood, 1895-1912, III: The Opposition Within the Party (1888-1890)," *New Mexico Historical Review*, XV (April, 1940), 137. This conclusion is generally accepted.

2. L. Bradford Prince, *New Mexico's Struggle for Statehood: Sixty Years of Efforts to Obtain Self-Government* (Santa Fe: The New Mexican Printing Co., 1910), p. 37.

3. Twitchell, *The Leading Facts of New Mexican History*, II, 406. According to Twitchell, although Elkins received a majority of the votes as shown by the official

returns, he did not receive a majority of those actually cast, for, unbeknown to the delegate, he had been "counted in by the leaders of the republican party."

4. H. R. 2418 renumbered H. R. 1022, with Elkins' corrections inserted by hand, NA, RG 233.

5. U.S. *Congressional Record*, 44th Cong., 1st Sess., 1876, Part 2, p. 1617.

6. Beck, p. 170.

7. *News and Press* (Cimarron) as quoted in Horn, pp. 176-77. At a meeting held in Santa Fe that same month, which was reported in the New York Sun on December 22, 1875, it was claimed that Tolby's murderers implicated "the principal members of the Colfax County branch of the 'Ring' as instigators of the crime . . . ." One of those implicated in Tolby's death was Cruz Vega, who was strung from a telegraph pole near Cimarron by a drunken mob in an equally shocking death. Poldervaart, pp. 97-98.

8. A damning letter Axtell sent in 1876 to Benjamin Stevens, territorial district attorney, was the prime evidence for the charge that Axtell had planned to murder Springer. It so convinced Frank Warner Angel, special investigator for the Department of Interior and the Department of Justice, that he was certain of Axtell's guilt. "Was there ever a cooler devised plot with a Governor as sponsor?" A copy of Angel's report on the charges made against Axtell is in the Papers Pertaining to Nominations, RG 46, National Archives, Washington, D.C.

9. Beck, pp. 163-165; William A. Keleher, *Violence in Lincoln County, 1869-1881* (Albuquerque: University of New Mexico Press, 1957), pp. 38-40.

10. The legal matter, which caused the outbreak of violence in Lincoln County, was the $10,000 insurance policy of Emil Fritz, Murphy's deceased partner in the mercantile firm. Fritz's heirs had been encouraged by Dolan and Riley to sue McSween for his refusal to release the insurance money because of unforeseen expenses he incurred in New York while collecting on the policy. Reeve speculates that the real motive for the suit was a fear on the part of Fritz's heirs that McSween might look at the firm's books and discover that Fritz and Murphy had been involved in some questionable deals in connection with government contracts to supply the Mescalero Apaches. Reeve, II, 312-14.

11. The business connections between Axtell, Catron, and Rynerson and the Murphy faction, sometimes called the Murphy-Riley-Dolan group, were quite close. In May, 1876, Riley loaned Governor Axtell $1,800. Horn, p. 182. Murphy had retained Catron and Rynerson as attorneys in an effort to recover the money collected by McSween in the Fritz affair. Note preceding footnote.

12. Amnesty proclamation quoted in Keleher, pp. 194-195.

13. Susan E. Wallace to her cousin, E. F. Test, March 4, 1879, Lewis Wallace Papers, State Records Center and Archives, Santa Fe. Governor Wallace did not necessarily agree with his wife, having at least an aesthetic appreciation for New Mexico, which he described in a letter to his critical mate on October 20, 1878, Keleher, pp. 172-73. The governor also acquired extensive mining interests, which gave him a material interest in the territory. A deed from "Lew" Wallace to L. Bradford Prince, dated November 20, 1882, provides evidence as to the eventual extent of these interests. According to the document, the following mining claims in the Cuchillo Negra and Apache mining districts of Socorro County were transferred from Wallace to Prince: the Independence, the Emmet, the Black, the Summers, the North Star, the Copper Glade, the Filagree, the Coral Reef, the Santa Fe, the Albion, the Gray Friar, and the Treasury Vault Tunnel Site. Deed located in the Prince Papers.

14. Twitchell, *The Leading Facts of New Mexican History*, II, pp. 438-40.

15. Geronimo, like Victorio, spent much of his time in mountainous northern Mexico during his escape from the San Carlos reservation. After his surrender, he and all the Chiricahuas were sent to Florida, where they remained for over a quarter century, before 187 of them were allowed to return to New Mexico and live on the Mescalero reservation. The rest of the Chiricahuas settled in Oklahoma. Reeve, p. 206.

16. The exact figure was 68,408, a seventy-four per cent increase. U.S. Bureau of the Census, *Historical Statistics of the United States, Colonial Times to 1957* (Washington: U.S. Government Printing Office, 1960), pp. 12-13.

17. Horn, p. 218.

18. Beck, p. 260.

19. Ross to John O'Grady (copy), March 26, 1887, Ross Papers. Also quoted by Lamar in his chapter on the Santa Fe Ring. *The Far Southwest, 1846-1912*, pp. 148-51.

20. What Ross probably had in mind, when he wrote of Cattle Rings and Public Land Stealing Rings, was the activities of Stephen W. Dorsey, former senator from Arkansas, and his cattle associates in the broad range country around Springer. The governor claimed that Dorsey, whose earlier involvement in the Star Route frauds brought him disgrace, had incorporated within his "great stock range" portions of the public domain. "Dorsey's range is made up, in part, of fraudulently entered public land. Much of it, also, is fraudulently fenced, as are several others . . . ." As this practice was in violation of a proclamation by President Cleveland calling for the removal of fences from the public domain, Ross wrote Cleveland for advice, enclosing in the letter an extract from the *Springer Stockman* challenging the Cleveland position. See Ross to Cleveland, August 16, 1885, Grover Cleveland Papers, Division of Manuscripts, Library of Congress, Washington, D.C.

21. Ross to John O'Grady, March 26, 1887, Ross Papers.

22. Petition for receivership to complete partition of Mora Grant, brought by Stephen B. Elkins against Carmen Arce and others, "In the District Court of the Fourth Judicial District of the Territory of New Mexico for the County of Mora the day of September [no date given] 1888." Also Chain of Titles for Mora Grant, Land Grant Papers. Preceding items in Prince Papers.

23. Elkins got Congress to confirm the claims of 76 grantees. This brought about a petition, signed by 920 citizens of Mora, protesting the confirmation, claiming it would jeopardize the livelihood of 8,000 inhabitants, many of whom had lived on the grant for "nearly 50 years as pioneers." The methods whereby the "Mexican Mora Land Grant" fell into the hands of these grantees were similar to those later described by Governor Ross. ". . . A few adventurers . . . came among us ten or fifteen years ago and . . . went about slowly and quietly buying of poor illiterate persons, heir to the grant—all their interest in same, at the rate of from five to fifteen dollars per head —After these purchases had been made of all the heirs that could be found our late Delegate to Congress—S.B. Elkins—without warning to at least eight thousand souls, and without giving Congress a fair discription [sic] of the present condition of the grant—succeeded in having the same confirmed, and now threatens us with a partition of the grant, and a demand to pay or leave." The petitioners also commented on how careless the Mexican government was in making such grants, pointing out that within the Mora Grant it issued another one called the La Junta Grant. This, they contended, was proof that "the Government of Mexico did not know or care what it did." See "Petition of 920 citizens of Mora [o. New Mexico] praying Congress to reconsider the Act confirming the Mora Land grant," January 21, 1878, Accompanying Papers File, RG 233, National Archives, Washington, D.C.

24. Elkins to Catron, August 15, 1879; S. M. Janney to Elkins, March 9, 1888. Elkins Papers. Both letters confirm Elkins' stake in the grant.

25. *Las Vegas Daily Optic*, May 13, 1892, Dargan Papers.

26. Notes on an interview with Colonel Jose D. Sena, Dargan Papers.

27. *Santa Fe New Mexican*, January 13, 1883, Dargan Papers.

28. Otero Folder, Dargan Papers. For additional evidence of Catron's and Elkins' interest in the Mora Grant see Elkins to Catron, August 15, 1879, Elkins Papers. Catron once asked Elkins to make him attorney for the Mora Grant. Catron to Elkins, December 9, 1890, Catron Papers.

29. Abstract of Title, Rio Arriba County Clerk's Office, Book 15a, p. 235, in Vioalle Clark Hefferan, "Thomas Benton Catron" (unpublished Master's thesis, Department of History, University of New Mexico, 1940), p. 24.

30. *Dictionary of American Biography*, ed. Dumas Malone (New York: Charles Scribner's Sons, 1928-44), XV, 229-30; Mary Elizabeth Sluga, "The Political Life of Thomas Benton Catron, 1896-1921" (unpublished Master's thesis, Department of History, University of New Mexico, 1941), p. 8. Elkins endorsed Prince for the judicial post. "I think he will make a good officer, probably as good if not better than we can get for the place. I can hear nothing affecting his integrity—all agree he is an honest man . . . ." Papers Pertaining to Nominations, RG 46, National Archives, Washington, D.C.

31. Miguel A. Otero, *My Life on the Frontier, 1882-1897: Death Knell of a Territory and Birth of a State* (Albuquerque: University of New Mexico Press, 1939), II, 4.

32. Mining deed from Sophie L. Utter and husband to L. Bradford Prince, August 28, 1890, transferring mining property in the Apache mining district, Black Range area, Socorro County. Prince Papers. There are five document cases of Prince's mining affairs in the Prince Papers. See footnote 13.

33. *New York Tribune*, November 4, 1889, Dargan Papers.

34. Hefferan, p. 36.

35. Undated, unsigned memo entitled "Gildersleeve Clique," Santa Fe Ring Folder, Ross Papers.

36. Gildersleeve is accused of using his influence and Catron's money to purchase the Ritaca Land Grant. Catron supplied the money which Gildersleeve used to buy the claims of the natives, taking the deeds in his own name, and later dividing the property with Catron and paying back the loan. Catron's business relationship with Elkins was even closer. They held extensive tracts of land in each other's name such as the Ortiz Grant, some "grants near Santa Fe," and land tracts along the Puerco River, not to mention their common interest in the vast Mora Grant. Their joint mining interests included the Aztec mine and coal lands near Galisteo. See Elkins to Catron, August 15, 1879, Elkins Papers.

37. Memo entitled "Gildersleeve Clique," Santa Fe Ring Folder, Ross Papers.

38. Otero, p. 241.

39. Frost Folder, Dargan Papers; Victor Westphall, *The Public Domain in New Mexico, 1854-1891* (Albuquerque: The University of New Mexico Press, 1965), pp. 106-10. Although Frost, who had been Register of the Land Office in Santa Fe, was convicted by one jury, he was acquitted in a new trial, despite evidence of official misconduct.

40. May 16, 1894, Catron Papers.

41. Catron to Don Matias Contreras, July 30, 1896, Catron Papers.

42. Dargan, April, 1940, p. 157.

43. *Santa Fe New Mexican*, January 21, 1870, as quoted in Archie M. McDowell, "The Opposition to Statehood Within the Territory of New Mexico, 1889-1903" (unpublished Master's thesis, Department of History, University of New Mexico, 1939), p. 33.

44. Howard R. Lamar, "Edmund G. Ross as Governor of New Mexico Territory: A Reappraisal," *New Mexico Historical Review*, XXXVI (July, 1961), 178-83, 187. Not all Kansans condemned Ross for his refusal to vote against Johnson's removal. One admiring Kansas Democrat called Ross's appointment "an instance of historic justice . . . to this man who by his vote in the U.S. Senate 16 years ago saved this nation from a calamity worse than civil war—the bravest, most courageous, most momentous vote ever cast in the Senate of the United States." Thomas R. Fenlon to Cleveland, May 26, 1885, Cleveland Papers. Enclosed with the letter was an article from the *Leavenworth Standard* endorsing these views.

45. Ross to John O'Grady, March 26, 1887, Ross Papers.

46. "Constitution and By-Laws of the Association of the Brotherhood for the Protection of the Rights and Privileges of the People of New Mexico," art. i (handwritten copy), Prince Papers.

47. Letter from Ross to I. S. Struble, chairman of the Committee on Territories, March 31, 1890, printed in pamphlet entitled "Public Schools and Statehood for New Mexico," Statehood Folder, Ross Papers; Lamar, "Edmund G. Ross as Governor of New Mexico Territory: A Reappraisal," pp. 183-84, 205-06. Lamar believes that Ross was a sincere and determined advocate of statehood, but only after the federal government established a public school system.

CHAPTER X

1. U.S. *Congressional Record*, 50th Cong., 1st Sess., 1888, Part 3, p. 2021. Springer had introduced an omnibus bill incorporating these states as early as December 13, 1886.

2. Joseph and Springer apparently enjoyed a good relationship. Springer once intervened in behalf of the New Mexico delegate, urging Cleveland to listen to Joseph's views regarding another appointment for Judge William A. Vincent, whom the President had removed from the territorial supreme court because he was allegedly too intimate with the notorious Stephen W. Dorsey. Springer to Cleveland, July 3, 1888, Cleveland Papers.

3. Dargan, April, 1940, p. 137.

4. Nathaniel Wright Stephenson, *A History of the American People*, II (New York: Charles Scribner's Sons, 1934), 346.

5. Marion Dargan, "New Mexico's Fight for Statehood, 1895-1912, VI: Advertising the Backyard of 'the United States'," *New Mexico Historical Review*, XVIII (January, 1943), 69.

6. *Chicago Tribune*, January 10, 1889.

7. Quoted in the *Las Vegas Daily Optic*, January 28, 1889.

8. February 2, 1889.

9. February 9, 1889.

10. H. R. 8466, NA, RG 233.

11. Prince, pp. 60-61.

12. Report No. 1025, NA, RG 233. Copies of H. R. 8466 and Report No. 1025 in Statehood Folder, Ross Papers.

13. U.S. Congress, House, Committee on the Territories, *Admission of Dakota*,

Montana, Washington, and New Mexico into the Union, 50th Cong., 1st Sess., 1888, H. Rept. 1025 to accompany H. R. 8466, pp. 16-17.

14. *Santa Fe New Mexican*, March 8, 1888, as quoted in Dargan, April, 1940, p. 143.

15. Ross had also persuaded Joseph to introduce an earlier memorial in the spring of 1887, and, after Cleveland's defeat in 1888, the governor, knowing he would probably be replaced, continued to push for statehood, advocating admission in his message to the 28th Assembly.

16. Petition, sent by the citizens of Las Vegas in support of the Springer bill, NA, RG 233.

17. Two petitions dated April 12, 1888, presented, one from the residents of San Antonio and vicinity, Socorro County, and the other from the citizens of Anthony, Doña Ana County, NA, RG 233.

18. January 27, 1889, Catron Papers.

19. January 27, 1889, Catron Papers.

20. January 18, 1889, Dargan Papers. Prince also made reference to the earlier constitutional conventions, and the almost forty years of legislative experience enjoyed by New Mexicans, as evidence of their preparation.

21. April 13, 1888, Dargan Papers.

22. For an account of the significant role German Jewish merchants have played in the development of New Mexico see William J. Parish, "The German Jews and the Commercial Revolution in Territorial New Mexico, 1850-1900," *New Mexico Historical Review*, XXXV (January, 1960), 1-20; (April, 1960), 129-50.

23. *U.S. Congressional Record*, 50th Cong., 2d Sess., 1889, Part 2, p. 1233.

24. Petition of February 11, 1889, signed by E. S. Stover, L. S. Trimble, and others, and forwarded to Congress by resolution of the Territorial Council, NA, RG 233. Another counterpetition from Albuquerque, dated February 16, 1889, found in NA, RG 233.

25. *Las Vegas Daily Optic*, January 2, 1889.

26. Joseph to Prince, December 7, 1888, Prince Papers.

27. *Silver City Enterprise*, January 25, 1889, Dargan Papers.

28. *El Paso Herald-Post*, January 9 and 19, 1889, Dargan Papers.

29. *Silver City Enterprise*, February 8, 1889, Dargan Papers.

30. *U.S. Congressional Record*, p. 1905.

31. *Silver City Enterprise*, January 18, 1889, Dargan Papers.

32. *U.S. Congressional Record*, pp. 1906-10.

33. Stephenson, p. 346.

34. *Silver City Enterprise*, January 18, 1889, Dargan Papers.

35. *Santa Fe New Mexican*, January 19, 1888, Dargan Papers.

36. Quoted in the March 24, 1888, issue of the Santa Fe *Herald*, Dargan, April, 1940, p. 147.

37. Catron to O. H. Platt, January 27, 1889, Catron Papers.

38. New Mexico, Legislature, *Acts of the Legislative Assembly of New Mexico*, 28th Sess. (Santa Fe: New Mexico Printing Co., 1889), pp. 235-40.

39. Dargan, April, 1940, p. 156.

40. Prince, pp. 49-50.

41. June 25, 1889, as quoted in Dargan, April, 1940, p. 156.

42. "Resolution of the Democratic Central Committee, June 22, 1889, in re Constitutional Convention" bearing name of Edmund G. Ross, Governor, Executive Office, Territory of New Mexico, in Statehood Folder, Ross Papers.

43. Even though Ross expected to be replaced because his party was out of power,

he had a glimmer of hope that President Harrison, a former United States senator like himself, might reconsider. See Lamar, "Edmund G. Ross as Governor of New Mexico Territory: A Reappraisal," p. 207.

44. New Mexico, Executive Record, III, 486.

45. August 3, 1889, Dargan Papers.

46. New Mexico, Executive Record, III, 489-90.

47. August 7, 1889.

48. August 11, 1889, Dargan Papers.

49. Joseph to daughter, Sofia Joseph, November 21, 1888, Joseph Folder, Dargan Papers.

50. New Mexico, "Journal of the Constitutional Convention, Territory of New Mexico: September 3 to 21, 1889, and August 18 to 19, 1890" (unpublished), p. 7, State Records Center and Archives, Santa Fe. Microfilm of journal in Special Collections Division, University of New Mexico Library, Albuquerque.

51. On the first day Chaves was authorized to appoint members to these committees. "Journal of the Constitutional Convention . . . ," p. 15.

52. Twitchell, The Leading Facts of New Mexican History, II, 501.

53. Quoted in Rio Grande Republican, July 13, 1889, Dargan Papers.

54. Rio Grande Republican, September 7, 1889, Dargan Papers.

55. New Mexico, Constitution (1889), art. ix, sec. 1, Special Collections Division, University of New Mexico Library, Albuquerque. Microfilm copy used.

56. September 24, 1889.

57. D. V. Carr to Prince, September 9, 1889, Prince Papers.

58. M. W. Mills to Prince, September 3, 1889, Prince Papers.

59. Benjamin Harrison Papers, Division of Manuscripts, Library of Congress, Washington, D.C.

60. November 4, 1889, Dargan Papers.

61. New Mexico, "Journal of the Constitutional Convention . . . ," p. 104. When Perea during the convention moved to make the vote on the education provision unanimous, his affirmative vote was greeted with loud applause.

62. Albuquerque Morning Democrat, September 24, 1889.

63. New Mexico, Constitution (1889), art. xiii, sec. 8.

64. Art. xviii, sec. 6 states: "The ordinances and provisions in this article contained are hereby declared to be irrevocable without the consent of the United States and the people of this state."

65. Silver City Enterprise, September 20, 1889, Dargan Papers.

66. September 24, 1889.

67. September 24, 1889.

68. September 20, 1889, Dargan Papers.

69. Dargan, April, 1940, p. 160. Although the group claimed to be representative, only one Hispano made the trip.

70. January 16, 1890, Dargan Papers.

71. Santa Fe New Mexican, May 12, 1890, quoted in McDowell, pp. 35-36. Although Judge Waldo remained neutral, the Santa Fe did not oppose statehood despite the belief of many that admission would mean higher taxation for the railroads. W. C. Hazeldine, delegate and attorney for the Atlantic and Pacific, even favored the movement.

72. Albuquerque Morning Democrat, November 20, 1889.

73. March 28, 1890, Dargan Papers.

74. Santa Fe New Mexican, April 2, 1890, Dargan Papers.

75. U.S. *Congressional Record,* 51st Cong., 1st Sess., 1890, Part 3, p. 2995.

76. July 3, 1889, Prince Papers.

77. Joseph's father, Antonio Joseph Treviz, was Portuguese and a native of the Azores. He had been shipwrecked on the gulf coast and later in 1840 arrived in New Mexico to open up a general store in Taos.

78. J. D. Huff, Secretary, Montezuma Lodge No. 1, AF&AM, Santa Fe, to Sister Ida Catherine, October 20, 1943. Joseph Folder, Dargan Papers.

79. Joseph to Senora Dona Emiliana Luna, March 14, 1881, Joseph Folder, Dargan Papers.

80. *Santa Fe New Mexican,* June 23, 1890, Dargan Papers.

81. New Mexico, "Journal of the Constitutional Convention . . . ," p. 141.

82. New Mexico, *Constitution* (1889), amended version, art. ix, sec. 5.

83. *Las Vegas Daily Optic,* August 21, 1890.

84. Joseph once advised his daughter to dissuade her in-laws from selling their part of a grant because he was working to get land grant titles confirmed. Joseph to daughter, Sofia Joseph, February 8, 1888, Joseph Folder, Dargan Papers.

85. *Las Vegas Daily Optic,* August 21, 1890.

86. *Santa Fe New Mexican,* August 19, 1890, Dargan Papers.

87. October 3, 1890, Dargan Papers.

88. Quoted in *Santa Fe New Mexican,* September 1, 1890, Dargan Papers.

89. *Las Vegas Daily Optic,* October 31, 1890.

90. September 20, 1890, Dargan Papers.

91. *Socorro Industrial Advertiser,* September 13, 1890, Dargan Papers.

92. January 9, 1891, Dargan Papers.

93. Quoted in the *Santa Fe New Mexican,* September 29, 1890, Dargan Papers.

94. *Colfax County Stockman* (Springer) as quoted in the *Santa Fe New Mexican,* September 29, 1890, Dargan Papers.

95. September 22, 1890, Dargan Papers. Ross was offered the job on the *Headlight* by an old friend, S. M. Ashenfelter, when he left the governorship. He accepted the position a year later after surprising many by accepting, temporarily, a job on the *New Mexican.* Lamar speculates that Frost extended the offer out of admiration for his old rival, while Ross accepted it to advance the cause of statehood. "Edmund G. Ross as Governor of New Mexico Territory: A Reappraisal," p. 207.

96. Unidentified newspaper clipping, May 1, 1890, Dargan Papers.

97. Perea was not the only Catholic politician to oppose a nonsectarian school system. During the legislative session preceding the vote on the constitution, Juan Jose Baca, a staunch Catholic and Council member from Socorro County, announced his unequivocal opposition to any measure favoring nonsectarian schools. See *Silver City Enterprise,* March 3, 1889, as quoted in Dargan, April, 1940, p. 184.

98. October 6, 1890, Dargan Papers.

99. September 24, 1890, Catron Papers.

100. October 6, 1890, Catron Papers.

101. April 23, 1890, Dargan Papers.

102. A copy of a proposed "Constitution of the State of New Mexico" is in the Statehood Folder, Ross Papers, with the following notation from George W. Lane, Territorial Secretary, to Governor Ross: "Thought perhaps you had not seen Clancy's proposed Constitution. Notice that he provides for the election of the gov. & legislature only. All others to be apptd. by gov."

103. One rather persistent writer, D. V. Carr, in a second letter to Prince, insisted

that no one be allowed to vote "unless he could read and write in the English language."
September 23, 1889, Prince Papers.

104. Prince, p. 55.

105. October 10, 1890, Dargan Papers.

106. Speech by Miguel A. Otero delivered at a constitutional convention in Albuquerque on October 16, 1901, Miguel A. Otero Papers, Special Collections Division, University of New Mexico Library, Albuquerque, New Mexico. Hereafter cited as Otero Papers.

CHAPTER XI

1. Statistics presented by Delegate Joseph in a speech before the House on April 3, 1890, U.S. *Congressional Record*, 51st Cong., 1st Sess., 1890, Part 3, p. 2993.

2. Manzanares was New Mexico's delegate to the 48th Congress, and remained one of the prominent leaders of the Democratic party until his death in 1904. Upset because his beloved territory had been "unjustly slandered and unmercifully vituperated," Manzanares once urged President Harrison, through a friendly Republican senator, to make federal appointments from the "*right material*," thus preventing unscrupulous politicians from taking over. Manzanares to Senator Preston B. Plumb of Kansas, March 15, 1889, Harrison Papers.

3. The vote for Joseph was 12,271 to 9,930 for Prince and 5,192 for Rynerson.

4. The national Democratic sweep in 1890 which reduced Republican strength in the House to 88 also was a factor in Joseph's fourth victory. One Republican described it as a landslide and "fearful defeat." George W. Honey to Prince, November 20, 1890, Prince Papers.

5. Statement by W. A. Chapman, a Raton insurance man and an acquaintance of Joseph, Dargan Papers.

6. October 14, 1892, Dargan Papers.

7. *An Illustrated History of New Mexico* (Chicago: The Lewis Publishing Co., 1895), p. 665; Marion Dargan, "New Mexico's Fight for Statehood, 1895-1912, I: The Political Leaders of the Latter Half of the 1890's and Statehood," *New Mexico Historical Review*, XIV (January, 1939), 6.

8. The first measure, H. R. 12592, was presented by Joseph on February 15, 1889; the second, H. R. 12646, was presented on February 26.

9. Twitchell, *The Leading Facts of New Mexican History*, II, 520.

10. *Chieftain* (Socorro), November 15, 1889, Dargan Papers.

11. According to Catron's own admission in a letter to Robert Black dated April 9, 1895, Catron Papers.

12. Vioalle C. Hefferan, "Thomas Benton Catron," (unpublished Master's thesis, Department of History, University of New Mexico, 1939), pp. 28, 35.

13. *Santa Fe New Mexican*, January 6 and 10, 1890, Dargan Papers.

14. February 28, 1890, Dargan Papers. Joseph responded to criticism of his position with an open letter to the press on March 5, 1890, in which he claimed that a majority of members on the House Committee on the Territories favored his measure and opposed Springer's. *Santa Fe New Mexican*, March 11, 1890, Dargan Papers.

15. U.S. *Congressional Record*, 51st Cong., 1st Sess., 1890, Part 3, pp. 2991-2995.

16. Joseph's population estimate is far above 153,076, the number given New Mexico in the 1890 census.

17. *Santa Fe New Mexican*, November 11, 1891, Dargan Papers.

18. U.S. Congress, House Committee on the Territories, *Admission of New Mexico*, 52d Cong., 1st Sess., 1892, H. Rept. 736 to accompany H. R. 7136, pp. 3-45.

19. For more details on Joseph's reapportionment scheme and other proposals and arguments advanced by the delegate during his long tenure in Congress, see Robert W. Larson, "Statehood for New Mexico, 1888-1912" (unpublished Ph.D. dissertation, Department of History, University of New Mexico, 1961), pp. 60-90.

20. The congressman undoubtedly was referring to the section of the report entitled "Does New Mexico Desire Admission!" in which the chief documents included a memorial to Congress adopted by the legislative assembly in 1872 and two speeches by Governor Prince and former Governor Axtell. The evidence on the whole was repetitious and outdated, and although it left little doubt where the politicians stood, it did not indicate complete unanimity among the people. See Marion Dargan, "New Mexico's Fight for Statehood, 1895-1912, IV: The Opposition Within the Territory During the Nineties," *New Mexico Historical Review*, XVI (January, 1941), pp. 70, 73.

21. *U.S. Congressional Record*, 52d Cong., 1st Sess., 1892, Part 6, p. 5088.

22. U.S. Congress, Senate, Committee on Territories, *Senate Reports*, Vol. V, 52d Cong., 1st Sess., 1892, S. Rept. 1023 to accompany H. R. 7136, p. 9.

23. *Denver Times* quoted in the *Santa Fe New Mexican*, April 22, 1890. Dargan Papers.

24. Prince to Platt, June 25, 1892, as quoted in L. Bradford Prince, *Admission of New Mexico* (Santa Fe: New Mexican Printing Co., no date), pp. 11-12, Library, Division of History, Museum of New Mexico, Santa Fe. Prince placed the population of the territory at from 180,000 to 185,000.

25. *Santa Fe New Mexican*, October 6, 1890, Dargan Papers.

26. Prince to Joseph, November 27, 1890 (unsent), Prince Papers.

27. July 12, 1892, Dargan Papers.

28. October 5, 1892, Dargan Papers.

29. *Denver Republican* quoted in *Las Vegas Daily Optic*, June 16, 1892; *Denver News* quoted in *Las Vegas Daily Optic*, June 20, 1892.

30. June 28, 1892.

31. Kirk H. Porter, *National Party Platforms* (New York: The Macmillan Co., 1924), pp. 165, 176. The Democratic platform adopted in late June even commended the House of Representatives, which was controlled by Democrats, for passing the statehood bills of New Mexico and Arizona on June 6.

32. *U.S. Congressional Record*, 52d Cong., 2d Sess., 1893, Part 1, p. 902.

33. February 7, 1893, Catron Papers.

34. February 24, 1893, Dargan Papers.

35. September 1, 1893, Dargan Papers.

36. June 4, 1893, Catron Papers.

37. Measure introduced by Joseph on September 6, in NA, RG 233.

38. House Report 155, NA, RG 233; U.S. Congress, House, Committee on the Territories, *Admission of New Mexico*, 53d Cong., 1st Sess., 1893, H. Rept. 155 to accompany H. R. 353, p. 16. A territorial fair and a Southwestern silver convention held at the same time may have been more instrumental in drawing people to Albuquerque than the statehood convention.

39. Letter quoted in *Silver City Enterprise*, October 13, 1893, Dargan Papers.

40. Interestingly enough, word of the Republican stand was brought to the attention of the House by Colorado's Populist representative, Lafe Pence, who urged Wheeler to make a pledge in behalf of Oklahoma's cause.

41. *U.S. Congressional Record*, 53d Cong., 2d Sess., 1893, Part 1, p. 274.

42. Prince, *New Mexico's Struggle for Statehood*, p. 47.

43. Joseph to Ambrosio Valdes, March 12, 1894, trans. from Spanish, Joseph Folder, Dargan Papers.

44. *Silver City Enterprise*, March 9, 1894, Dargan Papers. The actual Democratic majority in the House was 81.

45. November 17, 1893, Dargan Papers.

46. Catron to Carey, January 22, 1894, Catron Papers.

47. U.S. *Congressional Record*, 53d Cong., 2d Sess., 1894, Part 7, p. 6917.

48. Quoted in the *Silver City Enterprise*, July 13, 1894, Dargan Papers.

49. Quoted in the *Las Vegas Daily Optic*, January 4, 1894, Dargan Papers.

50. *Ibid.*, February 1, 1894, Dargan Papers.

51. *Silver City Enterprise*, July 13, 1894, Dargan Papers.

52. July 18, 1894, Catron Papers.

53. July 18, 1894, Catron Papers.

54. July 18, 1894, Catron Papers.

55. *Silver City Enterprise*, July 27, 1894, Dargan Papers.

56. *Ibid.*, August 10, 1894, Dargan Papers.

57. U.S. Congress, Senate, Committee on Territories, *Admission of New Mexico*, 54th Cong., 1st Sess., 1895, S. Rept. 628 to accompany H. R. 353, pp. 1-38.

58. August 17, 1894, Dargan Papers. *New Mexican* quoted in this issue.

59. September 14, 1894, Dargan Papers.

60. July 13, 1894, Dargan Papers.

61. *Las Vegas Daily Optic*, November 27, 1894, Dargan Papers.

62. *George Curry, 1861-1947: An Autobiography*, ed. H. B. Hening (Albuquerque: University of New Mexico Press, 1958), pp. 81-82. Curry, who was territorial governor of New Mexico from 1907 to 1909 and a longtime resident of the territory, regarded these two factors as most decisive.

63. *Santa Fe New Mexican*, March 18, 1895, Dargan Papers.

64. *El Paso Herald*, January 19, 1895, Dargan Papers.

65. *Santa Fe New Mexican*, March 18, 1895, Dargan Papers.

66. Joseph to Ambrosio Valdes, January 30, 1893, trans. from Spanish, Joseph Folder, Dargan Papers. Joseph gratefully acknowledges support from this labor group in a letter to his son-in-law.

67. Quoted in the *Santa Fe New Mexican*, June 3, 1891, Dargan Papers.

68. He also was accused of opposing the division of land grants among small farmers for fear of reducing land prices. See Report of Democratic Auxiliary Committee, Washington, D.C., October 13, 1892, Catron Folder, Prince Papers.

69. *Santa Fe New Mexican*, June 26, 1895, Dargan Papers.

70. U.S. *Congressional Record*, 54th Cong., 1st Sess., 1895, Part 1, pp. 49, 97, 720; Part 4, p. 3569. Report No. 2259, submitted by Catron with H. R. 7909, last of the four statehood bills, in NA, RG 233.

71. August 2, 1895, Catron Papers.

72. Catron to Otero, March 5, 1896, Dargan Papers.

73. Mary Elizabeth Sluga, "The Political Life of Thomas Benton Catron, 1896-1921" (unpublished Master's thesis, Department of History, University of New Mexico, 1941), p. 26.

74. Catron to Platt, July 18, 1894, Catron Papers.

75. *Santa Fe Sun* quoted in an undated, unnamed Las Vegas paper, 1896, Dargan Papers.

76. *Santa Fe New Mexican*, December 20, 1895, Dargan Papers.

77. *Silver City Enterprise*, January 24, 1896, Dargan Papers. The luckless Catron even incurred the wrath of his usually loyal Santa Fe constituency when he supported an amendment to one of his bills which would have validated some unpopular railroad bonds issued by Santa Fe County. See *Las Vegas Daily Optic*, March 10 and 26, 1896, Dargan Papers.

78. *New York Tribune*, March 11, 1896, Dargan Papers.

79. April 16, 1896, Dargan Papers.

80. Letter to the *Wheeling Intelligencer*, Wheeling, West Virginia, from Catron and six other New Mexicans, January 3, 1895, Dargan Papers.

81. Hefferan, pp. 31-33; Twitchell, *The Leading Facts of New Mexican History*, II, 510-13.

82. Catron to Colonel Richard C. Kerens, October 26, 1897, Catron Papers. The President referred to was William McKinley, a fellow Republican whom Catron did not wish to alienate.

83. July 30, 1896, Catron Papers.

84. September 7, 1896, Catron Papers.

85. Catron to Colonel Richard C. Kerens, January 23, 1895, Catron Papers. Later, Catron came around to supporting Senator William B. Allison of Iowa until it appeared that McKinley would be nominated. See Sluga, p. 20.

86. Fergusson Folder, Dargan Papers.

87. Albert B. Fall to A. H. Garland, October 4, 1894, Cleveland Papers. Fall, who was a Democrat at this time, claimed the nomination was also offered to Frank Manzanares and E. V. Chavez before it was again extended to Joseph. Curry, on the other hand, asserted that Fergusson was defeated for the nomination by "a handful of votes." See *George Curry, 1861-1947: An Autobiography*, p. 80.

88. *Las Vegas Daily Optic*, October 8, 1896.

89. March 20, 1896, Dargan Papers.

90. July 9, 1896, Dargan Papers.

91. October 5, 1896, Dargan Papers.

92. Quoted in the *Albuquerque Morning Democrat*, October 16, 1896, Dargan Papers.

93. November 5, 1896.

94. Report of Democratic Auxiliary Committee, Washington, D.C., October 13, 1892, Prince Papers.

95. U.S. *Congressional Record*, 54th Cong., 2d Sess., 1896, Part 1, pp. 77-78.

CHAPTER XII

1. Miguel A. Otero, *My Nine Years as Governor of the Territory of New Mexico*, ed. Marion Dargan (Albuquerque, University of New Mexico Press, 1940), p. 1.

2. *Las Vegas Daily Optic*, April 8, 1897, Dargan Papers.

3. U.S. *Congressional Record*, 55th Cong., 2d Sess., 1897, Part 1, p. 13; 3d Sess., 1898, Part 1, p. 245. H. R. 4067, statehood bill introduced during second session, in NA, RG 233. Senator Elkins of West Virginia also introduced a New Mexico statehood bill during the 55th Congress.

4. H. R. 4066, bill to keep the capital at Santa Fe, NA, RG 233.

5. U.S. *Congressional Record*, 55th Cong., 2d Sess., 1898, Part 6, p. 5191.

6. Otero, *My Life on the Frontier*, 1882-1897, II, 288.

7. Knute Nelson of Minnesota to McKinley, April 22, 1897; Allison and Gear of Iowa to McKinley, April 10, 1897, Otero Papers.

8. Catron to McKinley, April 30, 1897, Catron Papers.

9. Otero, *My Nine Years as Governor* . . . , p. 1.

10. Twitchell, *The Leading Facts of New Mexican History*, II, 523; Elkins-Perea Folder, Dargan Papers.

11. *Chicago Times-Herald*, June 11, 1897.

12. June 2, 1897.

13. Twitchell, *The Leading Facts of New Mexican History*, II, 524-25.

14. Sluga, p. 36.

15. April 19, 1898, Catron Papers.

16. August 23, 1898, Catron Papers.

17. Otero, *My Nine Years as Governor* . . . , pp. 146-49, 194.

18. February 10, 1900, Catron Papers.

19. Otero, *My Nine Years as Governor* . . . , p. 135.

20. Perea to Catron, September 29, 1900, Dargan Papers.

21. *U.S. Congressional Record*, 56th Cong., 1st Sess., 1899, Part 1, p. 10.

22. Memorial, introduced during first session of 56th Congress, in Part 3, p. 2044, of *Record*.

23. November 24, 1899, Catron Papers.

24. Unidentified manuscript, Elkins-Perea Folder, Dargan Papers; *Albuquerque Journal-Democrat*, January 13, 1901, Elkins-Perea Folder, Dargan Papers.

25. Otero to Daniel H. McMillan, May 14, 1901, Otero Papers.

26. Catron to Colonel Richard C. Kerens, April 4, 1901, Catron Papers; Otero to E. A. Cahoon, May 7, 1901, Otero Papers.

27. Otero to McMillan, May 14, 1901, Otero Papers.

28. Otero claimed he had the endorsement of the El Paso and Northwestern as well as the Santa Fe, and of such major business interests as Gross Blackwell and Company and Brown and Manzanares. See Otero to George W. Bowen, May 13, 1901, Otero Papers. According to Catron's son, although Tom Catron was attorney for the Santa Fe, Otero's claim of support by the powerful railroad was due to his friendship with Judge Henry Waldo, solicitor for the Santa Fe. Interview with Fletcher Catron, July 12, 1960.

29. Otero to George W. Bowen, May 13, 1901, Otero Papers.

30. Roosevelt to Otero, June 17, 1901, Otero Papers.

31. Pamphlet entitled "Cogent Reasons for Statehood," dated June, 1902, and enclosed in a letter from Albert J. Beveridge to Otero, December 19, 1902, Otero Papers.

32. Otero, *My Nine Years as Governor* . . . , p. 197.

33. Pamphlet entitled "Oteroism and Andrews," Albert J. Beveridge Papers, Division of Manuscripts, Library of Congress, Washington, D.C. Hereafter cited as Beveridge Papers.

34. Notes from an interview with Colonel Jose D. Sena, Dargan Papers.

35. Undated newspaper clipping from the *Capital* (Santa Fe), A. M. Bergere Scrapbook, photostat copy, Special Collections Division, University of New Mexico Library, Albuquerque.

36. Catron to Perea, October 17, 1900, Catron Papers.

37. Catron to Rodey, November 8, 1900, Catron Papers.

38. Otero, *My Life on the Frontier, 1882-1897*, II, 235-36.

39. *Denver Republican*, quoted in the *Evening Citizen* (Albuquerque), January 16, 1895, Dargan Papers. The Albuquerque journal was sometimes called the *Daily Citizen*.

40. Dargan, January, 1941, pp. 87-92.

41. *Evening Citizen*, January 17, 1895, Dargan Papers.

42. *Albuquerque Morning Democrat*, January 25, 1895, Dargan Papers. In the Council, where the resolution also passed, Perea was one of the opposition leaders, but the two most outspoken foes of statehood were a native politician named J. A. Ancheta and a former Indianan, Walter C. Hadley. See Dargan, January, 1941, pp. 99-101. Hadley was once accused of writing influential Senator Platt letters which placed New Mexico's statehood qualifications in a very unfavorable light. Frank W. Clancy to Catron, February 22, 1895, Catron Papers.

43. *Albuquerque Journal-Democrat*, October 13, 1901, Dargan Papers.

44. *Evening Citizen*, January 27, 1902, Dargan Papers.

45. Marion Dargan, "New Mexico's Fight for Statehood, 1895-1912, V: The Silencing of the Opposition at Home," *New Mexico Historical Review*, XVI (October, 1941), 397-400.

46. S. M. Wharton, editor of *White Oaks Weekly Eagle*, as quoted in *Santa Fe New Mexican*, September 17, 1901, Dargan Papers.

47. Judge A. A. Freeman as quoted in the *Santa Fe New Mexican*, October 14, 1901, Dargan Papers.

48. *Evening Citizen*, April 23, 1901, as quoted in McDowell, p. 82.

49. *Hustler* (Farmington), March 28, 1901, Dargan Papers.

50. June 22, 1901, Dargan Papers.

51. *Evening Citizen*, March 3, 1903, Dargan Papers.

52. *Hustler*, December 15, 1901, Dargan Papers.

53. Otero, *My Nine Years as Governor* . . . , p. 218. One New Mexico newspaper lauded Rodey for being "full of the project." *San Marcial Bee*, February 1, 1902, Dargan Papers.

54. *Hustler*, November 14, 1901, Dargan Papers.

55. *San Marcial Bee* (undated), Dargan Papers.

56. Quoted in the *Santa Fe New Mexican*, September 17, 1901, Dargan Papers.

57. November 11, 1901, Dargan Papers.

58. Story in *Albuquerque Journal-Democrat*, September 24, 1901, as quoted in McDowell, pp. 86-87.

59. Four years after the defeat of the 1889 constitution, the *Optic* had to admit that the native people were still skeptical about the advantages of statehood. See November 20, 1894, issue.

60. *Albuquerque Journal-Democrat*, October 23, 1901, Dargan Papers.

61. *Evening Citizen*, April 21, 1901, Dargan Papers.

62. Interview with J. H. Purdy in *Evening Citizen*, February 17, 1902, Dargan Papers.

63. Speech by Otero at an Albuquerque reception for Rodey (undated), Otero Papers.

64. Quoted in the *Evening Citizen*, May 9, 1901, Dargan Papers. Otero had invited McKinley to New Mexico after hearing that the President was contemplating a trip to the Pacific Coast. "I know of no portion of the U.S. where you are held in greater esteem." Otero to McKinley, April 28, 1899, William McKinley Papers, Division of Manuscripts, Library of Congress, Washington, D.C.

65. L. A. Hughes to Roosevelt, November 20, 1905, Dargan Papers; Twitchell, *The Leading Facts of New Mexican History*, II, 530-32.

66. *Las Vegas Daily Optic*, June 26, 1899.

67. *Hustler*, December 15, 1901, Dargan Papers.

68. *Albuquerque Journal-Democrat*, September 8, 1901, Dargan Papers.

69. New Mexico, *Executive Record*, V, 383.

70. Otero's speech to the statehood convention at Albuquerque, October 16, 1901, Otero Papers.

71. Resolutions in NA, RG 233.

72. June 22, 1901, Dargan Papers.

73. *Evening Citizen*, July 26, 1901, Dargan Papers.

74. *Santa Fe New Mexican*, July 23, 1901, Dargan Papers.

CHAPTER XIII

1. Rodey to Otero, Luna, and F. A. Hubble, May 10, 1902, Dargan Papers.

2. H. R. 12543, NA, RG 233.

3. House Report 1309, NA, RG 233; Congress, House, Committee on the Territories, *Admission of Certain Territories into the Union*, 57th Cong., 1st Sess., 1902, H. Rept. 1309 to accompany H. R. 12543, p. 1.

4. Rodey to Otero, May 6, 1902, Otero Papers.

5. Interestingly enough, there was considerable opposition to the bill in Knox's own state. Resolutions and memorials against the measure were received from the Massachusetts State Board of Trade and the New England Shoe and Leather Association. The first was dated May 7, 1902; the second, June 2, 1902. NA, RG 233.

6. *U.S. Congressional Record*, 57th Cong., 1st Sess., 1902, Part 5, p. 5179.

7. May 10, 1902, Dargan Papers.

8. Lacey also claimed that political considerations would be eliminated because New Mexico was Republican and Arizona Democratic.

9. *Santa Fe New Mexican*, May 10, 1902, Dargan Papers.

10. March 3, 1902.

11. June 26, 1902, Dargan Papers.

12. Charles Edgar Maddox, "The Statehood Policy of Albert J. Beveridge: 1901-1911" (unpublished Master's thesis, Department of History, University of New Mexico, 1938), p. 117.

13. Claude G. Bowers, *Beveridge and the Progressive Era* (Cambridge, Massachusetts: The Riverside Press, 1932), p. 158. James E. Watson, a congressional colleague from Indiana, ranked Beveridge with Theodore Roosevelt and Senator Reed Smoot of Utah as the most diligent workers he ever knew in public life. See James E. Watson, *As I Knew Them* (Indianapolis and New York: The Bobbs-Merrill Co., 1936), p. 62.

14. S. M. McGowan to Beveridge, May 29, 1902, Beveridge Papers.

15. Murphy to Beveridge, May 13, 1902, Beveridge Papers.

16. Louis H. Hacker and Benjamin B. Kendrick, *The United States Since 1895* (rev. ed.; New York: F. S. Crofts & Co., 1936), p. 96.

17. Bowers, p. 196.

18. Rodey to Beveridge, June 14, 1902, Beveridge Papers.

19. *U.S. Congressional Record*, 57th Cong., 1st Sess., 1902, Part 7, pp. 7198-99.

20. Beveridge to Albert Shaw, November 10, 1904, Beveridge Papers.

21. Shaw to Beveridge, January 8, 1902, Beveridge Papers.

22. October 19, 1902, Beveridge Papers.

23. November 3, 1902, Beveridge Papers. In a second letter to Shaw, on November

9, Beveridge stated he would rather write these men himself but that it was too risky. Beveridge Papers.

24. November 10, 1902, Beveridge Papers.

25. November 10, 1902, Beveridge Papers.

26. November 28, 1902, Beveridge Papers.

27. Wister to Shaw, December 4, 1902, Beveridge Papers.

28. *The American Monthly Review of Reviews*, July, 1902, pp. 15-16.

29. Dorothy E. Thomas, "The Final Years of New Mexico's Struggle for Statehood, 1907-1912," (unpublished Master's thesis, Department of History, University of New Mexico, 1939), pp. 11-12.

30. Beveridge to Shaw, November 10, 1902, Beveridge Papers.

31. *Los Angeles Times*, November 13, 1902, Dargan Papers.

32. U.S. Congress, Senate, Committee on Territories, *New Statehood Bill: Hearing Before the Subcommittee of the Committee on Territories on House Bill 12543* . . . , 57th Cong., 2d Sess., 1902, Senate Doc. 36, p. 1.

33. The committee did observe, though, that in neighboring West Las Vegas, across the Gallinas River, the population was primarily Anglo.

34. *Albuquerque Journal-Democrat*, November 12, 1902, Dargan Papers.

35. Senator Heitfield to Dr. Marion Dargan, February 20, 1936, as quoted in Maddox, p. 53.

36. U.S. Congress, *New Statehood Bill* . . . , Senate Doc. 36, p. 104.

37. Mrs. Martinez Amador to Beveridge, March 20, 1903, Beveridge Papers.

38. *Evening Citizen*, December 8, 1902, Dargan Papers.

39. November 28, 1902, Dargan Papers.

40. La Moine Langston, "Arizona's Fight for Statehood in the Fifty-seventh Congress" (unpublished Master's thesis, Department of History, University of New Mexico, 1939), p. 45.

41. U.S. Congress, *New Statehood Bill* . . . , Senate Doc. 36, pp. 121-72.

42. At Tucson the committee discovered internal dissension as L. C. Hughes, editor of the *Arizona Daily Star*, loudly claimed that the Knox bill was gerrymandered and that Pima County was cheated of its rightful representation.

43. U.S. Congress, *New Statehood Bill* . . . , Senate Doc. 36, p. 219.

44. December 4, 1902, Beveridge Papers.

45. November 29, 1902, Beveridge Papers.

46. November 3, 1902, Beveridge Papers.

47. Quoted in *Literary Digest*, December 20, 1902, p. 829.

48. Beveridge to Shaw, November 3, 1902, Beveridge Papers.

49. Bronson Cutting to James Roger Addison, December 11, 1911, Bronson Cutting Papers, Division of Manuscripts, Library of Congress, Washington, D.C. Hereafter cited as Cutting Papers.

50. Notes on an interview with Billy Bayer, private secretary to Andrews, Dargan Papers. Also, see interview with Colonel Jose D. Sena in Dargan Papers.

51. *Santa Fe New Mexican*, September 13, 1911, William H. Andrews Scrapbook, Special Collections Division, University of New Mexico Library, Albuquerque, New Mexico. Hereafter cited Andrews Scrapbook.

52. September 27, 1902, Matthew S. Quay Papers, Division of Manuscripts, Library of Congress, Washington, D.C. Hereafter cited Quay Papers.

53. Notes on an interview with Billy Bayer, private secretary to Andrews, Dargan Papers.

54. *George Curry, 1861-1947: An Autobiography,* p. 190.

55. U.S. Interstate Commerce Commission, *Decisions of the Interstate Commerce Commission of the United States: Valuation Reports, October, 1925-February, 1926,* CVI, 445.

56. U.S. Interstate Commerce Commission, *Decisions of the Interstate Commerce Commission of the United States: Finance Reports, June-November, 1928,* CXLV, 242.

57. Wayland Fuller Dunaway, *A History of Pennsylvania* (New York: Prentice-Hall, Inc., 1935), pp. 573-74.

58. Beveridge to Shaw, November 3, 1902, Beveridge Papers.

59. U.S. Congress, Senate, Committee on the Territories, *New Statehood Bill,* 57th Cong., 2d Sess., 1902, S. Rept. 2206 to accompany H. R. 12543, Part 1, 1-31.

60. The Beveridge report was quite specific in its prejudices against the people and geography of New Mexico, citing the "Spanish, mixed Spanish, and Indian descent" of the majority, and the insufficient water supply for agriculture and stock raising.

61. U.S. Department of Interior, *Report of the Secretary of the Interior for the Fiscal Year Ended June 30, 1902* (Washington: U.S. Government Printing Office, 1902), pp. 103, 106-07. Personal copy of Hon. Miguel A. Otero, Otero Papers.

62. U.S. Congress, *New Statehood Bill,* S. Rept. 2206, pp. 14-16.

63. Quay report and Bate report in U.S. Congress, *New Statehood Bill,* S. Rept. 2206, Part 2, pp. 1-21 and Part 3, pp. 1-10.

64. December 8, 1902, Dargan Papers.

65. January 8, 1903.

66. Quoted in the *Evening Citizen,* December 5, 1902, Dargan Papers.

67. December 24, 1902.

68. U.S. *Congressional Record,* 57th Cong., 2d Sess., 1902, Part 1, pp. 660-62.

69. Arizona's delegate, Marcus Smith, was indignant, too, calling the investigation "a secret star-chamber proceeding from first to last."

70. Editorial, December 16, 1902, Dargan Papers.

71. December 4, 1902, Quay Papers.

72. December 2, 1902, Dargan Papers.

73. *Indianapolis Journal,* December 3, 1902, Dargan Papers. Because the senator was so closely identified with this report, many newspapers gave his name to it.

74. Beveridge to Charles E. Smith, December 4, 1902, Beveridge Papers.

75. Beveridge to Abbott, November 29, 1902, Beveridge Papers.

76. To this remark, Senator Hale replied prophetically, "The tactics have not yet begun."

77. Quoted in the *Evening Citizen,* December 23, 1902, Dargan Papers.

78. January 3, 1903.

79. Beveridge to Shaw, December 15, 1904, Beveridge Papers.

80. December 19, 1902, Beveridge Papers.

81. *Washington Post,* January 8, 1903, Dargan Papers.

82. For an analysis of the motives of these senators and the arguments they advanced, see Beatrice Arline Cottrell, "Senate Action on the Omnibus Statehood Bill of 1902," (unpublished Master's thesis, Department of History, University of New Mexico, 1938), pp. 22-47.

83. Everett Walters, *Joseph Benson Foraker: An Uncompromising Republican* ("Ohio Governors Series"; Columbus: The Ohio State Archaeological and Historical Society, 1948), pp. 2-4; Benjamin B. Kendrick, "McKinley and Foraker," *Political Science Quarterly,* XXXI (December, 1916), 592.

84. Joseph Benson Foraker, *Notes of A Busy Life* (3d ed.; Cincinnati: Stewart & Kidd Company, 1917), II, 184-85.

85. Unidentified newspaper article dated December 1, 1897, J. W. Crumpacker Scrapbook, Library, Division of History, Museum of New Mexico, Santa Fe.

86. Teller to Hal Sayre, January 14, 1904, as quoted in Ellis, p. 375.

87. U.S. *Congressional Record*, 57th Cong., 2d Sess., 1902, Part 3, pp. 2972-75.

88. Teller was eloquent in his praise of the Spanish language calling it the "equal to any other language in the world."

89. Foraker claimed that only nine states had as large a population at the time of their admission as Arizona did in 1900.

90. U.S. Congress, *New Statehood Bill . . .* , Senate Doc. 36, p. 131.

91. Senator Burnham of New Hamsphire lent support to Lodge's contention, pointing out that New Mexico was so sparsely populated that it had only 1.6 inhabitants per square mile, while Arizona was not even entitled to a single representative in the lower house.

92. U.S. Congress, Senate, Committee on Territories, *An Act Enabling the People of New Mexico and Arizona to Form a Constitution and State Government, Etc.*, 61st Cong., 2d Sess., 1910, S. Rept. 454 to accompany H. R. 18166, p. 17. Contains an excellent summary of this controversy from its inception to its final disposition.

93. U.S. *Congressional Record*, 57th Cong., 2d Sess., 1902, Part 3, Appendix, pp. 111-12.

94. Langston, p. 114.

95. *Evening Citizen*, January 31, 1903, as quoted in Cottrell, p. 30.

96. February 3, 1903, Dargan Papers.

97. *Washington Post*, December 19, 1902, Dargan Papers.

98. Bowers, pp. 199-201. The home of Pinchot was an excellent sanctuary as the head of the Forestry Service honestly believed that practically everyone in New Mexico coveted the federal forest reserves in the territory. See Howard R. Lamar, "The Relunctant Admission: The Struggle to Admit Arizona and New Mexico into the Union," in *The American West: An Appraisal*, ed. Robert G. Ferris (Santa Fe: Museum of New Mexico Press, 1963), pp. 169-70.

99. *New York Evening Post*, February 20, 1903, Dargan Papers.

100. Quoted in "Holding Up the United States Senate," *Literary Digest*, March 7, 1903, p. 327. Beveridge's home-state newspaper, the *Indianapolis Journal*, praised its junior senator for his generalship and persistence in defeating the Pennsylvanian. February 26, 1903, Dargan Papers.

101. February 26, 1903, Dargan Papers.

102. *Press* (Philadelphia), February 4, 24, and 25, 1903, Dargan Papers.

103. Beveridge to Shaw, February 24, 1903, Beveridge Papers.

104. February 5, 1903, as quoted in Mary J. Masters, "New Mexico's Struggle for Statehood, 1903-1907" (unpublished Master's thesis, Department of History, University of New Mexico, 1942), p. 17.

105. Langston, p. 101.

106. Ellis, p. 377.

107. Nathaniel Wright Stephenson, *Nelson W. Aldrich: A Leader in American Politics* (New York: Charles Scribner's Sons, 1930), pp. 210-11. Aldrich, always the good party man, blamed Teller for the defeat of his measure, which did not disturb the Coloradan, who was quite frank in announcing his purpose to defeat the banking bill if Knox's bill were rejected. See U.S. *Congressional Record*, 57th Cong., 2d Sess., 1902, Part 3, p. 2975.

CHAPTER XIV

1. Richardson, *Messages and Papers of the Presidents*, V, 456. See chapter VI for an account of the movement to separate Arizona from New Mexico as an independent territory.

2. Quoted in the *Santa Fe New Mexican*, December 23, 1893, Dargan Papers.

3. Sherman to A. L. Morrison, January 27, 1894, as quoted in the *Silver City Enterprise*, February 9, 1894, Dargan Papers.

4. Quoted in the *Santa Fe New Mexican*, April 28, 1902, Dargan Papers.

5. Prince, *New Mexico's Struggle for Statehood*, p. 107.

6. Roy Gittinger, *The Formation of the State of Oklahoma*, 1803-1906 (Berkeley: University of California Press, 1917), p. 205.

7. Bowers, pp. 198-99, 216-18.

8. Otero, *My Nine Years as Governor* . . . , p. 218.

9. Quoted in the *El Paso Herald*, February 1, 1904, Dargan Papers. Rodey followed up this admission with a letter to Beveridge on March 1, 1904, in which he asserted that jointure was the only solution to the problem. Beveridge Papers.

10. Prince to Beveridge, March 12, 1904, Beveridge Papers.

11. March 17, 1904, Beveridge Papers.

12. Maddox, p. 92.

13. *Arizona Republican*, January 23, 1905, Dargan Papers.

14. Memorial, filed in Office of the Secretary of New Mexico on January 18, 1905, was signed by John S. Clark, president of the Council; Carl A. Dalies, Speaker of the House; Miguel A. Otero, governor; and James W. Raynolds, secretary. Copies in NA, RG 233.

15. April 13, 1904, Catron Papers.

16. Notebook No. 2, pp. 121-22, Otero Papers.

17. *Evening Star* (Washington), February 6, 1905, Dargan Papers.

18. U.S. *Congressional Record*, 58th Cong., 3d Sess., 1905, Part 2, pp. 1982-84, 2001, 2004.

19. Telegram from the Council of the 36th Legislative Assembly of the Territory of New Mexico to Joseph G. Cannon, Speaker of the House, dated February 9, 1905. According to the petitioning legislators, the Bard amendment "embodies the hopes[,] aspirations and rights of the people of New Mexico." Two telegrams were sent to Rodey on February 9 and 10 urging him to persuade House members to concur in the Senate version. The citizens of Socorro, New Mexico, sent telegrams urging House concurrence to Rodey and Cannon, the one to Rodey being received by the House Committee on Territories on February 17, 1905. NA, RG 233.

20. *Evening Star*, February 14, 1905, Dargan Papers. For additional information on the revolt against Speaker Cannon see the *New York Tribune*, February 11, 1905, Dargan Papers.

21. *Evening Star*, February 21, 1905, Dargan Papers.

22. March 24, 1905, Dargan Papers.

23. March 7, 1905, Dargan Papers. Foraker underscored this general tone of pessimism by advising New Mexicans to wait until after the next census before making another try for statehood. Foraker to Holm Bursum, March 13, 1906, Holm O. Bursum Papers, Special Collections Division, University of New Mexico Library, Albuquerque. Hereafter cited as Bursum Papers.

24. Otero, *My Nine Years as Governor* . . . , p. 229.

25. *Morning Gleaner* (Gallup), December 6, 1904, Dargan Papers.

26. Twitchell, *The Leading Facts of New Mexican History*, II, 544.

27. Otero, *My Nine Years as Governor* . . . , pp. 233, 236-38.

28. Letterhead on letter from Rodey to Hamilton, November 20, 1905, Beveridge Papers.

29. March 20, 1905, Beveridge Papers.

30. March 20, 1905, Beveridge Papers. Roosevelt added that Congress in receiving such protests must "act as it deems best, paying only such heed to the petition as in its judgment the needs of the nation warrant."

31. *Albuquerque Morning Journal*, June 9, 1905, Dargan Papers.

32. October 7, 1905, Beveridge Papers.

33. June 7, 1905, Beveridge Papers.

34. August 15, 1905, Beveridge Papers.

35. October 4, 1905, Beveridge Papers.

36. May 25, 1906, Beveridge Papers.

37. *George Curry, 1861-1947: An Autobiography*, p. 192.

38. William S. Greever, "Railway Development in the Southwest," *New Mexico Historical Review*, XXXII (April, 1957), 178.

39. October 22, 1905, Beveridge Papers.

40. December 3, 1905, as quoted in Masters, p. 50.

41. Clipping from the *Indianapolis News*, November 2, 1905, Beveridge Papers.

42. Notes on interview with Billy Bayer, 1907 Folder, Dargan Papers.

43. November 11, 1905, Dargan Papers.

44. October 22, 1905, Beveridge Papers.

45. Beveridge to Gifford Pinchot, October 23, 1905, Beveridge Papers.

46. *Albuquerque Morning Journal*, October 8 and 20, 1905, Dargan Papers.

47. Rodey to Beveridge, October 15, 1905, Beveridge Papers.

48. Rodey to Beveridge, October 22, 1905, Beveridge Papers.

49. Clipping from October 16, 1905, issue attached to letter from Keith K. Gordon to Beveridge, October 17, 1905, Beveridge Papers.

50. Beveridge to Gifford Pinchot, October 23, 1905, Beveridge Papers.

51. November 20, 1905, Beveridge Papers.

52. Roosevelt to Beveridge, November 8, 1906, as quoted in Elting Morison (ed.), *The Letters of Theodore Roosevelt* (Cambridge: Harvard University Press, 1952), V, 135.

53. Roosevelt placed only one qualification on the admission of the territories: the abolition of licensed gambling.

54. Roosevelt to B. I. Wheeler, January 18, 1906, as quoted in Morrison, V, 135.

55. December 5, 1905, Dargan Papers.

56. Rodey to Beveridge, December 7, 1905, Beveridge Papers. Rodey had earlier written to Hamilton to endorse the linking of the four territories in an omnibus bill. Rodey to Hamilton, November 20, 1905, Beveridge Papers.

57. Quoted in the *Albuquerque Morning Journal*, December 5, 1905.

58. Although Beveridge boasted with delight about the Bisbee paper's conversion, his optimism regarding Arizona newspaper support was unfounded. Beveridge to Shaw, October 28, 1905, Beveridge Papers. The *Albuquerque Morning Journal* on December 20, 1905, attributed Arizona's resistance to the selfish attitude of special interest groups in the territory.

59. Hamilton also introduced another joint statehood bill the day Roosevelt made his recommendation, but no action was taken on it. H. R. 3186, NA, RG 233.

60. *Evening Star*, December 15, 1905, as quoted in Masters, p. 59.

61. *Pittsburgh Dispatch*, January 8, 1906, Dargan Papers.

62. *New York Times*, January 10, 1906.

63. Beveridge wanted the joint statehood bill to bear Hamilton's name, and instructed Shaw on October 28, 1905, to speak of it as the "Hamilton Bill" when referring to it in the *Review of Reviews*. Beveridge Papers.

64. *Houston Post*, January 21, 1906, Dargan Papers.

65. U.S. Congress, House, Committee on the Territories, *Statehood for the Territories*, 59th Cong., 1st Sess., 1906, H. Rept. 496 to accompany H. R. 12707, pp. 2-3.

66. Moon report on pp. 14-19.

67. January 28, 1906, Dargan Papers.

68. U.S. *Congressional Record*, 59th Cong., 1st Sess., 1906, Part 3, p. 2332.

69. February 24, 1906, Dargan Papers. Actually, on this occasion, Foraker had been persuaded by Delegate Mark Smith of Arizona to introduce the amendment. Smith, a good politician who shrewdly cultivated all major economic interests in Arizona including mining, was responsible for drafting the Foraker amendment, according to Lamar, "The Reluctant Admission . . . ," p. 171.

70. February 12, 1906.

71. Beveridge to Shaw, December 7, 1905, Beveridge Papers.

72. U.S. *Congressional Record*, 58th Cong., 3d Sess., 1905, Part 4, p. 3520.

73. U.S. Congress, Senate, *Speech of Hon. Albert J. Beveridge, of Indiana, Closing the Debate on the Statehood Bill in the Senate of the United States*, 58th Cong., 2d Sess., 1905, pp. 25-26.

74. *Evening Star*, March 10, 1906, Dargan Papers.

75. *Sun* (New York), March 13, 1906, as quoted in Masters, p. 80.

76. *Houston Post*, March 16 and 17, 1906, Dargan Papers.

77. Denial of jointure would also hurt Oklahoma and Indian Territory, and the White House feared the political consequences of such a move. *Houston Post*, March 23, 1906, Dargan Papers.

78. U.S. *Congressional Record*, 59th Cong., 1st Sess., 1906, Part 9, pp. 8834-35.

79. *Albuquerque Morning Journal*, June 19, 1906, Dargan Papers.

80. Bowers, p. 235.

81. June 6, 1906, Dargan Papers.

82. "The Statehood Bill Should Pass," *Harper's Weekly*, January 14, 1905, pp. 45-46.

83. "The Joint Statehood Bill Should Pass," *Harper's Weekly*, October 28, 1905, p. 1547.

84. "Do We Want Four New Partners?" *Outlook*, December 16, 1905, p. 911.

85. U.S. *Congressional Record*, 59th Cong., 1st Sess., 1906, Part 2, pp. 1508, 1554-55 and Part 4, p. 3535.

86. H. L. Miedo to Bursum, October 17, 1906, Bursum Papers. According to this letter, written on company stationery, the matter of contributing to the jointure fund drive was presented to President Ripley of the Santa Fe, who claimed that because of the severe criticism corporations were receiving for their participation in public affairs, he was unwilling to take an active part in any program to influence public sentiment, especially as it concerned elections.

87. *Albuquerque Morning Journal*, November 18, 1905, Dargan Papers.

88. U.S. *Congressional Record*, 59th Cong., 1st Sess., 1906, Part 4, p. 3535. When Governor Kibbey forced an upward evaluation of the tax assessment in Arizona by removing one of the members of the territorial board of equalization, the territorial

supreme court, acting upon an appeal by the mine owners, reversed the board and reduced the tax assessment by nine million dollars.

89. *Santa Fe New Mexican*, April 9, 1906, Dargan Papers.

90. *Albuquerque Morning Journal*, February 25, 1906, Dargan Papers.

91. U.S. *Congressional Record*, 58th Cong., 3d Sess., 1905, Part 2, p. 1928.

92. Masters, p. 87.

93. U.S. *Congressional Record*, 58th Cong., 3d Sess., 1905, Part 2, p. 1130.

94. High transportation costs were often cited. The fare from Phoenix to Santa Fe,
a distance of 651 miles, was $30.05 one way. Averaging the fare at five cents per mile,
the transportation costs to Santa Fe, using the shortest mail routes, would be $23.65
from Tucson, $35.50 from Prescott, and $40.25 from Yuma. *Boston Transcript*,
December 26, 1905, Dargan Papers.

95. *Pittsburgh Times* as quoted in the *El Paso Times*, March 13, 1906, Dargan
Papers. The failure of most native New Mexicans to acquire the use of English as their
major tongue, an old criticism, was also mentioned during the jointure controversy.
See the *Boston Transcript*, March 12, 1906, Dargan Papers.

96. Cited in U.S. *Congressional Record*, 58th Cong., 3d Sess., 1905, Part 2, p. 1921.

97. U.S. Congress, *Statehood for the Territories*, H. Rept. 496, p. 19.

98. U.S. *Congressional Record*, 59th Cong., 1st Sess., 1906, Part 3, p. 2407. For a
more detailed account of the arguments for and against joint statehood, see Masters,
pp. 89-105.

99. *New York Tribune*, December 23, 1905, Dargan Papers.

100. *Evening Citizen*, January 4, 1906, as quoted in Donald D. Leopard, "Joint
Statehood: 1906" (unpublished Master's thesis, Department of History, University
of New Mexico, 1958), p. 13. A summary of this thesis was published in the October,
1959, issue of the *New Mexico Historical Review*, pp. 241-47.

101. Roosevelt to Hagerman, March 3, 1906, as quoted in Morison, V, 177.

102. *Santa Fe New Mexican*, October 1, 1906.

103. Contract signed by J. G. McNary on March 1, 1906, Bursum Papers.

104. Contract addressed to Bank of Commerce, Albuquerque, Bursum Papers. Bursum and Luna were each entitled to 9,375 shares to be paid for over a five-year period.

105. June 16, 1905, Bursum Papers.

106. Telegram from Ira M. Bond to the *Santa Fe New Mexican*, May 17, 1906,
Frost Folder, Bursum Papers.

107. Hughes to Frost, July 11, 1906, Bursum Papers. Hughes, a former territorial
governor and a Democrat, was an old political foe of Delegate Smith and his Democratic cohorts in Arizona, most of whom stubbornly opposed consolidation. See Lamar,
The Far Southwest, 1846-1912, pp. 480-81.

108. Catron to Thomas D. Burns, Catron Papers.

109. July 27, 1906, Bursum Papers.

110. Bursum to L.C. Pullen, July 21, 1906, Bursum Papers. He also presented the
possibility that the constitution of the new state might contain a provision to allow
districting, whereby the new commonwealth could be divided into two almost autono-
mous units corresponding to the present boundaries of the two territories. Bursum to
Otero, March 28, 1906, Otero Papers; Bursum to Daniel H. McMillan, July 21, 1906,
Bursum Papers; Bursum to Hughes, August 15, 1906, Bursum Papers; Leopard, pp.
26-27. A discussion of the constitutionality of this "two-in-one" proposal is contained
in these letters and the Leopard thesis.

111. Bursum to McMillan, July 21, 1906, Bursum Papers.

112. September 8, 1906, Bursum Papers.

113. Bursum to Joe Brown, August 23, 1906, Bursum Papers.

114. Frost to Bursum, August 14, 1906, Bursum Papers.

115. Frost to Bursum, August 25, 1906, Bursum Papers.

116. Bursum to McMillan, September 8, 1906, Bursum Papers. Lamar speculates that this bitter Bursum-Hagerman feud finally compelled Roosevelt to agree to remove Hagerman in return for support of jointure by the Bursum-led Republican organization. See *The Far Southwest, 1846-1912*, p. 496.

117. Herbert J. Hagerman, *A Statement in Regard to Certain Matters Concerning the Governorship and Political Affairs in New Mexico in 1906-1907*. (Printed for Private Circulation, 1908), p. 29, Special Collections Division, University of New Mexico Library, Albuquerque.

118. October 8, 1906, Dargan Papers.

119. Leopard, p. 43.

120. Bursum to Luna, September 8, 1906, Bursum Papers.

121. *Santa Fe New Mexican*, October 1, 1906.

122. Garret J. Ryan to Beveridge, October 9, 1906, Beveridge Papers. According to the *Albuquerque Morning Journal*, small groups of politicians gathered at Bisbee prior to the meeting and consulted and agreed that neither convention would favor jointure. September 6, 1906, Dargan Papers.

123. *Albuquerque Morning Journal*, June 25 and August 3, 1906, Dargan Papers.

124. Quoted in *Albuquerque Morning Journal*, July 9, 1906, Dargan Papers.

125. Ryan to Beveridge, October 18, 1906, Beveridge Papers.

126. October 5, 1906, Beveridge Papers.

127. September 23, 1906, Beveridge Papers.

128. September 20, 1906, Beveridge Papers.

129. Roosevelt to Dr. Mark A. Rogers, Secretary of the Arizona Statehood Association, June 27, 1906, Beveridge Papers. Roosevelt in answering Rogers' protest regarding Kibbey told him that federal officials have as much right as any other citizen to express their sentiments and vote as they please.

130. Roosevelt to Kibbey, September 20, 1906, and William Loeb, Jr., secretary to the President, to Hagerman, September 20, 1906, as quoted in Morison, V, 417.

131. September 22, 1906, Beveridge Papers.

132. Notes on interview with Billy Bayer, 1907 Folder, Dargan Papers. Bayer, Andrews' secretary, claimed the delegate never heartily supported jointure.

133. Andrews to Beveridge, September 10, 1906, Beveridge Papers.

134. September 23, 1906, Beveridge Papers. In his September 10 letter to Beveridge, Andrews urged the lawmaker to raise the needed cash among his Indiana cronies. Beveridge Papers.

135. September 18, 1906, Beveridge Papers.

136. Beveridge to James M. Creighton, June 19, 1906, Beveridge Papers.

137. June 27, 1906, Beveridge Papers.

138. Rufus Kay Wyllys, *Arizona: The History of a Frontier State* (Phoenix: Hobson and Herr, 1950), p. 302. Even the predictions of defeat by the *Albuquerque Morning Journal* proved to be optimistic. It had indicated, after checking with its most reliable sources in Arizona, that the territory would poll for jointure a vote something in excess of 25 per cent—15 per cent less than the crusading advocates of consolidation predicted. November 6, 1906, Dargan Papers.

139. Twitchell, *The Leading Facts of New Mexican History*, II, 545.

140. Gittinger, pp. 213-14; Edward Everett Dale and Morris L. Wardell, *History of Oklahoma* (New York: Prentice-Hall, Inc., 1948), p. 312.

141. June 15, 1906, Dargan Papers.

142. Larrazolo contested the results charging the Republican managers of Socorro, Colfax, Valencia, and Torrance counties with fraud and irregularities in the conduct of the election.

143. October 22, 1906, Bursum Papers.

144. C. B. Allaire to Hagerman, November 7, 1906, Bursum Papers. Hagerman, perhaps because Socorro was Bursum's county, urged quick action in prosecuting these election frauds. Hagerman to W. A. Wolford, November 10, 1906, Bursum Papers.

145. Hughes to Beveridge, November 2, 1906, Beveridge Papers.

146. November 14 and 27, 1906, Dargan Papers.

147. U.S. *Congressional Record*, 59th Cong., 1st Sess., 1906, Part 4, p. 3537.

148. November 16, 1906, Beveridge Papers. Beveridge also blamed the railroads, cattlemen, and newspapers of Arizona for the defeat.

149. November 11, 1906, Dargan Papers.

150. November 12, 1906, as quoted in Masters, p. 134.

151. November 14, 1906, Dargan Papers.

Chapter XV

1. Undated, Beveridge Papers.

2. January 7, 1907, Dargan Papers.

3. *Roosevelt County Herald* (Portales), September 25, 1907, Dargan Papers.

4. *Washington Post*, September 7, 1907, Dargan Papers. The *Post* editorially attacked this idea, commending the independent spirit of Arizona.

5. October 26, 1907, Beveridge Papers.

6. Beveridge to George Harvey, October 26, 1907, Beveridge Papers.

7. October 19, 1907, Beveridge Papers.

8. Hagerman, *A Statement in Regard to . . . Political Affairs in New Mexico in 1906-1907*, p. 9. Copies of booklet, in which Hagerman conducts a vigorous defense of his position, in Special Collections Division, University of New Mexico Library, Albuquerque; Herbert J. Hagerman Papers, State Records Center and Archives, Santa Fe; and U.S. Social and Economic Branch, Private Papers Given to the National Archives, Records Group 316, National Archives, Washington, D.C. Hereafter cited as NA, RG 316. Also entitled *Matters Relating to the Administration and Removal of Herbert J. Hagerman[,] Governor of New Mexico[,] 1906-1907*. Booklet will be cited under author's name in subsequent references.

9. Roosevelt to Hagerman, March 13, 1906, as quoted in Hagerman, pp. 63-64.

10. *George Curry, 1861-1947: An Autobiography*, p. 195.

11. November 24, 1905, Catron Papers.

12. Catron to J. J. Hagerman, November 22, 1905, Catron Papers.

13. Hagerman, p. 13.

14. "Exhibit A: Preliminary Report of Assistant Attorney General Cooley, Department of Justice," H. W. Cooley to Roosevelt, April 12, 1907, as quoted in Hagerman, pp. 84-87. The federal government apparently felt that two of these corporations were under the control of the same group of men, as a suit was later filed in the Sixth Judicial District of the Territory of New Mexico naming as defendants the Pennsylvania

Development Company, the New Mexico Fuel and Iron Company, and W. S. Hopewell. See File No. 955, Part 1, NA, RG 316.

15. Hagerman to Roosevelt, May 15, 1907, Theodore Roosevelt Papers, Division of Manuscripts, Library of Congress, Washington, D.C. Hereafter cited as Roosevelt Papers.

16. When the legislature met the governor was constrained to veto eight or nine bills.

17. Hagerman, pp. 21-22.

18. According to Hagerman's version of the interview, Roosevelt declared that what Hagerman had done was so bad that his usefulness was ended, and if the President had not known him to be honest he would have "summarily" removed him solely on the basis of the report of his assistant attorney general. However, Roosevelt agreed to write two letters, a public and private one. The public letter, which could be used for publication, would say that the governor was "strictly honest, upright and fearless." See pp. 25-31.

19. Roosevelt to Hagerman, May 1, 1907, Roosevelt Papers.

20. Hagerman to Roosevelt, May 15, 1907, Roosevelt Papers.

21. Cooley to Roosevelt, May 23, 1907, Roosevelt Papers.

22. Roosevelt to Philip Bathell Stewart, April 16, 1907, Roosevelt Papers. He also quoted a correspondent from New Mexico who claimed that the governor was "not only absolutely ignorant of things and conditions in New Mexico, but has no knowledge of the people . . . ."

23. May 1, 1907, Roosevelt Papers. The judgments of Curry and Rodey added substance to this suspicion. Curry believed the elder Hagerman was a "crook," while Rodey suspected that he had been engaged in some "very questionable" land transactions in connection with the exchange of scrip. See Roosevelt to Ormsby McHarg, July 31, 1907, Roosevelt Papers.

24. Hagerman to Roosevelt, May 15, 1907, Roosevelt Papers.

25. Hagerman, pp. 68-69.

26. George Curry, 1861-1947: An Autobiography, p. 186.

27. U.S. Congress, Senate, Subcommittee of the Committee on Indian Affairs, Hearings, Survey of Conditions of the Indians in the United States, 71st Cong., 3d Sess., 1931, p. 4352. Cutting made the statement while defending Hagerman during an investigation of the former governor's connection in a scandal involving oil leases on Indian lands.

28. Hagerman to Roosevelt, May 15, 1907, Roosevelt Papers.

29. William Loeb, Jr., Secretary to the President, to Hagerman, May 23, 1907, as quoted in Hagerman, pp. 52-53.

30. What had infuriated the President was Raynolds' appointment of Colonel Pritchard, the very man who had advised Hagerman to deliver the deeds. Even Hopewell received an appointment. "This action on Raynolds' part," Roosevelt remarked righteously, "has been to me wholly inexplicable, save on the ground that he thought I was really removing Hagerman for other reasons than those I gave . . . ." Roosevelt to Major Llewellyn, July 29, 1907, as quoted in Morison, V, 733.

31. Roosevelt to Major Llewellyn, July 29, 1907. Although Roosevelt was referring specifically to the appointment of Pritchard and Hopewell (see preceding note), he no doubt had in mind the illegal sale of timberland sanctioned by Raynolds.

32. Roosevelt to McHarg, July 31, 1907, Roosevelt Papers.

33. Sun (New York), November 24, 1907, as quoted in Hagerman, p. 77.

34. Hagerman, p. 70.

35. Roosevelt to Charles Bonaparte, August 15, 1907, Roosevelt Papers. One historian regards the territorial "gang" or "machine" as another Santa Fe Ring and Bursum as its head. Lamar, *The Far Southwest, 1846-1912*, p. 496.

36. McHarg to R. P. Ervien, Commissioner of Public Lands, Santa Fe, New Mexico, October 7, 1907, as quoted in Hagerman, p. 75.

37. *Sun*, November 24, 1907, as quoted in Hagerman, pp. 76-79.

38. Taft to Charles Nagel, Secretary of Commerce and Labor, September 1, 1909, William Howard Taft Papers, Division of Manuscripts, Library of Congress, Washington, D.C. Hereafter cited as Taft Papers.

39. *George Curry, 1861-1947: An Autobiography*, pp. 186-87. Curry includes Roosevelt's cablegram announcing his appointment of Curry.

40. October 4, 1907, Dargan Papers. Curry claimed he received such a pledge as a condition to his acceptance of the governorship.

41. January 8, 1908, Catron Papers. Other New Mexico leaders praised the appointment. Max Frost in an undated letter to Secretary of the Interior James R. Garfield claimed that the territory's leading citizens strongly approved Curry's selection. A. L. Morrison in another letter to Garfield, dated April 18, 1907, claimed the appointment would give "universal satisfaction" to New Mexicans. See U.S. Department of the Interior, General Correspondence Files, 1907-53, Records Group 48, National Archives, Washington, D.C.

42. October 16, 1907, Dargan Papers.

43. *George Curry, 1861-1947: An Autobiography*, p. 208.

44. *Deming Headlight*, September 12, 1907, Dargan Papers.

45. September 11, 1907, Dargan Papers.

46. Maddox, pp. 103-04; Thomas, pp. 46-48. Personal interviews with Holm O. Bursum included in both works. One on March 4, 1938, the second on March 18, 1939.

47. *Carlsbad Argus*, October 2, 1908, Dargan Papers.

48. November 19, 1908, Roosevelt Papers. One scholar places Roosevelt's warm regard for Curry even above this political consideration in his ultimate shift to single statehood. Bowers, pp. 267-68.

49. *Washington Herald*, December 5, 1908, Dargan Papers. Andrews had doubts about Taft's sympathies, feeling that despite Roosevelt's new commitment the President-elect was opposed to granting statehood during the remainder of his predecessor's term. Lamar, "The Reluctant Admission . . . ," pp. 172-73. Shortly after Curry's meeting with Taft, the governor requested that the New Mexico legislative assembly appropriate money to send a special delegation of New Mexicans to Washington to work for statehood. This was done, the members even refusing to accept the $3,000 appropriated for their expenses. See *George Curry, 1861-1947: An Autobiography*, pp. 239-41.

50. The *Denver Republican* was optimistic, advising New Mexico politicians to mend political fences in preparation for elections to state and national offices. January 23, 1909, Dargan Papers.

51. *El Paso Herald*, February 5, 1909, as cited by Thomas, pp. 63-64.

52. *Arizona Republican* (Phoenix), February 28, 1909, Dargan Papers.

53. "Statement of Miss Lawler in connection with the prosecution of so-called land fraud cases in New Mexico, growing out of the law of 1898," Beveridge Papers.

54. In an unmailed letter dated April 20, 1909, Beveridge wrote the new President "I suggest again that by all means you have a personal interview with Miss Lawler, who was the stenographer of the late Senator Platt of Connecticut, and who is one of the best and most competent women I have ever known . . . ." Beveridge Papers.

55. *Arizona Republican*, February 28, 1909, Dargan Papers.

56. February 27, 1909, Dargan Papers.

57. James R. Garfield, Secretary of the Interior, to Roosevelt, May 27, 1907, Roosevelt Papers.

58. U.S. *Congressional Record*, 60th Cong., 2d Sess., 1909, Part 4, p. 3742.

59. Beveridge to Taft, September 2, 1909, as quoted in Maddox, pp. 107-08.

60. *George Curry, 1861-1947: An Autobiography*, p. 245.

61. Every contact with the Interior Department was an unpleasant one, according to Curry. *George Curry, 1861-1947: An Autobiography*, p. 226.

62. Taft to Curry, November 15, 1909, Taft Papers.

63. November 15, 1909, Taft Papers. Also in General Correspondence Files, 1907-53, NA, RG 48. Taft took this position despite his knowledge of Curry's wide acceptance in the territory. During the President's first month in office, he received a number of letters from leading citizens urging him not to accept a resignation submitted by Curry, probably in response to another Ballinger action which denied the governor permission to come to Washington to lobby for statehood. See Elmo R. Richardson, "George Curry and the Politics of Forest Conservation in New Mexico," *New Mexico Historical Review*, XXXIII (October, 1958), 283. The tone of the letters was very complimentary to Curry. J. M. Cunningham, president of the San Miguel Bank of East Las Vegas, asked Taft in behalf of the business interests and "good people" of the territory not to accept the resignation. March 22, 1909. I. Sparks of Santa Fe made a similar request on the same day insisting that Curry had rendered "a great service." Other letters in behalf of Curry include Secundino Romero of East Las Vegas to Taft, March 22, 1909; H. W. Kelly, president of Gross-Kelly Company of East Las Vegas, to Taft, March 22, 1909; and George Klock of Albuquerque to Taft, March 23, 1909. General Correspondence File, 1907-53, NA, RG 48.

64. *Deming Graphic*, January 7, 1910. Dargan Papers.

65. U.S. *Congressional Record*, 61st Cong., 2d Sess., 1910, Part 1, p. 654. Four versions of H. R. 18166 in NA, RG 233, including the one introduced by Hamilton, the one passed by the House, the one amended by the Senate, and the one passed by Congress and submitted to the President. A Senate amended version of H. R. 18166 in Special Collections Division, University of New Mexico Library, Albuquerque.

66. House Report No. 152, NA, RG 233; U.S. Congress, House, Committee on the Territories, *Statehood for the Territories*, 61st Cong., 2d Sess., 1910, H. Rept. 152 to accompany H. R. 18166, pp. 1-4.

67. As the House was sitting as the Committee of the Whole House on the State of the Union, a two-thirds vote was needed to suspend the rules and discharge the committee so the bill could be passed. In the opinion of the chair, such a vote was achieved following a rather lengthy debate.

68. January 21, 1910, Dargan Papers.

69. January 28, 1910, Dargan Papers.

70. As quoted in the *Deming Headlight*, February 24, 1910, Dargan Papers. As for Arizona, its population of approximately 157,000 was many thousands fewer than Providence, "a city in the very smallest Eastern State."

71. February 24, 1910, Dargan Papers.

72. Bowers, p. 379.

73. U.S. Congress, Senate, Committee on Territories, *An Act Enabling the People of New Mexico and Arizona to Form a Constitution and State Government, Etc.*, 61st Cong., 2d Sess., 1910, S. Rept. 454 to accompany H. R. 18166, pp. 1-2. The pro-

vision for presidential and congressional approval is in Sec. 22 of H. R. 18166 (amended version).

74. *Deming Headlight*, July 28, 1910, Dargan Papers.

75. U.S. Congress, *An Act Enabling the People . . . to Form a Constitution and State Government . . .* , S. Rept. 454, pp. 15-18.

76. H. R. 18166, Sec. 10 (amended version). "Lands east of the line between ranges eighteen and nineteen east of the New Mexico principal meridian [105th] shall not be sold for less than five dollars per acre, and lands west of said line shall not be sold for less than three dollars per acre . . . ."

77. U.S. Congress, *An Act Enabling the People . . . to form a Constitution and State Government . . .* , S. Rept. 454, p. 36. A good school-lands clause was Beveridge's major motive for holding up the bill for two months, according to Lamar, *The Far Southwest, 1846-1912*, p. 497.

78. U.S. *Congressional Record*, 61st Cong., 2d Sess., 1910, Part 8, p. 8227.

79. U.S. Congress, *An Act Enabling the People . . . to Form a Constitution and State Government . . .* , S. Rept. 454, pp. 25-26. If Beveridge had had his way on this issue, no one who could not read or speak English would be allowed to vote or hold office. Curry to Andrews, February 16, 1910, as cited by Lamar, *The Far Southwest, 1846-1912*, p. 497.

80. The House Committee on the Territories had approved the election law, perhaps being persuaded to some degree by a letter from an Arizonan who claimed the territory was "over run with ignorant and often vicious Mexican voters," most of whom were "purchasable." N. A. Vyne of Prescott to Hamilton, December 17, 1909, Papers Accompanying Specific Public Bill H. R. 18166 and H. J. Res. 289, NA, RG 233.

81. Catron to Elkins, February 1, 1910, Catron Papers.

82. *Deming Headlight*, March 10, 1910, Dargan Papers. Another concern of statehood advocates was a campaign to change the name of the state to "Acoma," supported by Rodey and others. Andrews disowned the idea after a survey conducted by Curry showed great opposition. *George Curry, 1861-1947: An Autobiography*, pp. 252-53.

83. May 21, 1910, Dargan Papers.

84. May 25, 1910, Dargan Papers.

85. George E. Mowry, *The Era of Theodore Roosevelt, 1900-1912* (New York: Harper and Brothers, 1958), p. 260. Curry rather naively believed that Aldrich's backing was due to a promise he made to Curry in the presence of Judge Henry L. Waldo in December, 1908. Because the Republican platform of 1908 had called for the admission of New Mexico and Arizona as separates states, Aldrich, although still opposed to statehood for New Mexico, told Curry that he would vote for the territory's admission. *George Curry, 1861-1947: An Autobiography*, pp. 228-29. In the end Aldrich cast no vote at all.

86. *Arizona Republican*, June 7, 1910, as cited by Thomas, pp. 76-77.

87. U.S. *Congressional Record*, 61st Cong., 2d Sess., 1910, Part 8, p. 8237. The remaining 31 senators were recorded as not voting.

88. *Kansas City Star* as quoted in the *Tribune-Citizen* (Albuquerque), March 16, 1910, Dargan Papers.

89. Taft Papers. For a more detailed discussion of the relationship between the two men as it pertained to New Mexico statehood, see Robert W. Larson, "Taft, Roosevelt, and New Mexico Statehood," *Mid-America: An Historical Review*, VL (April, 1963), 99-114.

90. New York *World*, June 18, 1910, as cited by Thomas, p. 81.

91. Elkins died on January 4, 1911, and Catron related this incident to his widow in a letter acknowledging her congratulations upon his selection to the United States Senate. Catron to Mrs. Hallie D. Elkins, March 28, 1912, Catron Papers. Andrews was selected by the Speaker as a member of a House committee to attend Elkins' funeral in Elkins, West Virginia. Andrews to Catron, January 5, 1911, Dargan Papers.

92. Copy of speech by Andrews, August 16, 1910, Dargan Papers. Andrews claimed that Taft had delivered a speech in Paterson, New Jersey, two months before in which he stated he might not be able to secure statehood for the territories, because of the possibility that they might go Democratic or send Republicans who would oppose his policies. Shortly thereafter, Andrews called upon Catron to help out at this crucial point.

93. Prince, *New Mexico's Struggle for Statehood*, p. 127. According to Taft's military aid, Archie Butt, Taft used six pens in signing the statehood measure. "I can see some day conflicting claims of museums as to which was the pen he actually used in signing the statehood bills." Butt to his sister-in-law, Clara Butt, June 26, 1910, as quoted in Archibald W. Butt, *Taft and Roosevelt: The Intimate Letters of Archie Butt, Military Aid*, Vol. I (Garden City, New Jersey: Doubleday, Doran & Company, Inc., 1930), p. 413.

94. *Inter-Ocean* (Chicago) as quoted in the *Evening Citizen*, June 24, 1910, Dargan Papers.

95. *Washington Herald*, June 19, 1910, Dargan Papers. According to the New Mexican, Llewellyn, Curry, and David J. Leahy, also a former Rough Rider, left New Mexico on June 5 for New York City where they were to greet their former colonel.

96. *Melrose Enterprise* as quoted in *Literary Digest*, June 16, 1910, p. 87.

97. *Rocky Mountain News*, June 20, 1910, Dargan Papers.

98. June 19, 1910.

CHAPTER XVI

1. New Mexico, *Proceedings of the Constitutional Convention of the Proposed State of New Mexico Held at Santa Fe, New Mexico: October 3rd, 1910, to November 21st, 1910* (Albuquerque: Press of the Morning Journal, 1910), pp. 271-72, microfilm, Special Collections Division, University of New Mexico Library, Albuquerque; New Mexico, *Executive Record*, VII, 357-59.

2. Undated clipping from Mora County newspaper, Andrews Scrapbook.

3. Undated newspaper clipping, Andrews Scrapbook.

4. *Deming Headlight*, July 21, 1910, Dargan Papers.

5. Undated, Andrews Scrapbook.

6. Undated newspaper clipping, Andrews Scrapbook. County primaries or nominating conventions in McKinley, Valencia, and Otero cited.

7. Undated newspaper clipping, Andrews Scrapbook.

8. Fergusson to James D. Whelan, June 27, 1910, Harvey Butler Fergusson Letter Collection (1910-1911), Special Collections Division, University of New Mexico Library, Albuquerque. Hereafter cited as Fergusson Letters.

9. Fergusson to Antonio Lucero, July 30, 1910, Fergusson Letters.

10. Republican central committee to citizens of Las Cruces, Doña Ana County, August 20, 1910, undated newspaper clipping, Andrews Scrapbook.

11. *Santa Fe New Mexican*, undated, Andrews Scrapbook; Thomas J. Mabry, "New

Mexico's Constitution in the Making—Reminiscences of 1910," *New Mexico Historical Review*, XIX (April, 1944), 170. Mabry lists one delegate, Green B. Patterson, as a socialist.

12. Thomas C. Donnelly, *The Government of New Mexico* (2d ed.; Albuquerque: University of New Mexico Press, 1953), p. 37.

13. Undated newspaper clipping, Andrews Scrapbook.

14. *Sun,* September 24, 1910, enclosed in letter from Ira M. Bond to Catron, September 24, 1910, Dargan Papers. Bond, a Washington correspondent for New Mexico newspapers, believed Edward D. Tittman, a Democratic delegate from Sierra County, wrote the letter to the *Sun,* and, as a good Republican, Bond urged Catron to publicize this criticism but to imply that Fergusson or William B. Walton, the Democratic leaders, wrote the article.

15. Fergusson to Senator R. L. Owen, July 5, 1911, Fergusson Letters.

16. Undated newspaper clipping, Andrews Scrapbook.

17. *Santa Fe New Mexican,* undated, Andrews Scrapbook.

18. Undated newspaper clipping (probably *Santa Fe New Mexican*), Andrews Scrapbook.

19. Undated newspaper clipping, Andrews Scrapbook.

20. *Santa Fe New Mexican,* undated, Andrews Scrapbook.

21. Donnelly, p. 41.

22. Mabry, p. 172. Octaviano A. Larrozolo, a naturalized Mexican with a legal background, also championed the interests of the *Hispanos* at the convention, although he was not a delegate. Reeve, p. 333.

23. Mabry, p. 173.

24. *New Mexico Constitutional Convention Book* (Denver: C. S. Peterson, n.d.), pp. 1-98. Pictures and brief biographical sketches of many of the members are included in this special commemorative book.

25. Reuben W. Heflin, "New Mexico Constitutional Convention," *New Mexico Historical Review*, XXI (January, 1946), 62.

26. Undated newspaper clipping, Andrews Scrapbook.

27. Mabry, p. 170.

28. New Mexico, *Proceedings of the Constitutional Convention* . . . , pp. 3-4.

29. Edward D. Tittman, "New Mexico Constitutional Convention: Recollections," *New Mexico Historical Review*, XXVII (July, 1952), 177.

30. Catron to William H. H. Allison, June 28, 1910, Catron Papers.

31. Undated newspaper clipping, Andrews Scrapbook.

32. Interview with Eleanor Spiess, his granddaughter, July 27, 1959.

33. New Mexico, *Proceedings of the Constitutional Convention* . . . , p. 7.

34. Undated newspaper clipping (probably *Santa Fe New Mexican*), Andrews Scrapbook. According to a memorial from citizens of Albuquerque and other communities protesting the election of delegates to the constitutional convention, Spiess was a "salaried attorney for a railroad of the territory, and one or more other large corporations, with an enormous fee contingent upon the adoption of the constitution" and subsequent validation of Santa Fe County railroad bonds. "A Memorial and Petition," Papers Accompanying Specific Public Bill H. R. 18166 and H. J. Res. 289, NA, RG 233.

35. The inclusion of Daugherty, a Democrat, on this powerful committee was the result of a nonpartisan selection of convention delegates from Socorro County, as well as Daugherty's friendship with Republican leaders. *George Curry, 1861-1947: An Autobiography*, p. 254.

36. New Mexico, *Proceedings of the Constitutional Convention* . . . , pp. 13-18. A list of all the committees is included in these pages.

37. Catron introduced the 1889 constitution for consideration and study, but on a motion by Fall it was not printed.

38. Donnelly, p. 44.

39. If any objection to a motion for roll call were recorded, the roll call motion would have to be sustained by a vote of at least thirty delegates. There were only twenty-nine Democrats.

40. New Mexico, *Proceedings of the Constitutional Convention* . . . , pp. 276-77.

41. Heflin, p. 65.

42. Tittman, p. 178.

43. Fergusson to E. C. de Baca, December 3, 1910, Fergusson Letters.

44. New Mexico, *Proceedings of the Constitutional Convention* . . . , pp. 9, 24, 34, 284-85.

45. Tittman, pp. 182-83; Heflin, pp. 62-63; Mabry, p. 176. All three writers were Democratic delegates to the convention, each saw the altercation and each came up with a slightly different version of it. According to Mabry, Crist demanded a public apology from Fall, and not receiving one refused to return.

46. Mabry, p. 177.

47. New Mexico, *Proceedings of the Constitutional Convention* . . . , pp. 36, 40.

48. Two undated newspaper clippings, Andrews Scrapbook. Quotations extracted from Republican party pledge to the citizens of New Mexico.

49. Opinion of Justice Daniel K. Sadler of the state supreme court regarding direct legislation in the New Mexico Tobacco Tax case, as quoted in Mabry, pp. 179-80. According to Judge Sadler, of some twenty states employing the referendum, none defined the exemptions as carefully as New Mexico.

50. New Mexico, *Constitution*, art. iv, sec.1, microfilm, Special Collections Division, University of New Mexico Library, Albuquerque. Constitution as originally drafted at Santa Fe used.

51. Art. xix, sec. 1.

52. Art. vii, sec. 3; art. xii, sec. 10; art. xix, sec. 1. Amending procedure repeated in each of the preceding articles.

53. Tittman, p. 182.

54. *Santa Fe New Mexican*, undated, Andrews Scrapbook. A provision for separate schools for Negroes was reported by the Committee on Education to the floor of the convention where it was defeated because of native influence.

55. As quoted in the *Outlook* (Carrizozo), undated, Dargan Papers.

56. Fergusson to James A. Hall, December 3, 1910, Fergusson Letters. Fergusson had particular reference to their help in his post-convention fight against ratification of the constitution.

57. One petition from the W.C.T.U. of Quay County was presented on November 3.

58. New Mexico, *Proceedings of the Constitutional Convention* . . . , p. 210.

59. *Santa Fe New Mexican*, undated, Andrews Scrapbook.

60. "A Memorial and Petition," Papers Accompanying Specific Public Bill H. R. 18166 and H. J. Res. 289, NA, RG 233.

61. Thomas B. Shannon, state superintendent of the Anti-Saloon League, Newark, New Jersey, to House Committee on Territories, February 16, 1911, NA, RG 233.

62. Mrs. Minnie B. Owens to Hamilton, January 30, 1911, NA, RG 233.

63. New Mexico, *Constitution*, art. xi, sec. 7.

64. William E. McGrath, chairman of Joint Legislative Board of Railway Organizations, to Charles A. Spiess and members of the constitutional convention, November 21, 1910, as quoted in New Mexico, *Proceedings of the Constitutional Convention* . . . , p. 244.

65. Tittman, pp. 179-80.

66. New Mexico, *Constitution*, art. xi, sec. 5.

67. Mabry, pp. 173, 176.

68. New Mexico, *Proceedings of the Constitutional Convention* . . . , p. 252.

69. Fergusson to C. A. Scheurich, December 7, 1910, Fergusson Letters.

70. Mabry, pp. 175-76.

71. Although the official account gives 11:15 P.M. as the adjournment time (p. 253), Mabry asserts it was 4:00 A.M. the following morning, while Tittman gives 3:10 A.M. as the time. Both Mabry and Tittman claim that the time for the convention to expire was November 21, 1910, but because the proceedings were not complete by that time the clock was turned back.

72. New Mexico, *Proceedings of the Constitutional Convention* . . . , (Appendix), pp. 291-92; New Mexico, *Executive Record*, VII, 417. The second citation refers to a proclamation made January 11, 1911, in which the governor declared Saturday, January 21, 1911, as a legal holiday and ordered all territorial and county offices closed that day.

73. Undated newspaper clipping, Andrews Scrapbook.

74. Newspaper clipping (dateline: Silver City, New Mexico, December 2), Andrews Scrapbook.

75. Donnelly, pp. 48-49. The thirteen objections signed by Andrieus A. Jones, convention chairman, in Lansing B. Bloom and Thomas C. Donnelly, *New Mexico History and Civics* (Albuquerque: The University Press, 1933), pp. 236-39.

76. November 29, 1910, Fergusson Letters.

77. Actually, it would take 20 counties to achieve the necessary three-fourths as there were 26 counties in New Mexico in 1910.

78. Harvey B. Fergusson, *The Constitution: Its Dangers and Defects*, pp. 1-13, campaign pamphlet, Bursum Papers.

79. H. B. Fergusson, Frank Springer, and Frank W. Clancy, *New Mexico in 1910: Letters and Addresses Relating to the Constitution* (Printed for Frank W. Clancy, n.d.), pp. 78-79.

80. Although the opposition to recall was insurmountable, it is perhaps quite possible that had proponents of direct legislation not advocated the so-called Oregon plan, which required only five per cent of those voting in the previous election to refer a measure and ten per cent to initiate one, both reforms might have been adopted. According to Reed Holloman, a delegate from Quay County, most of the delegates felt this was too small a percentage, but would have been willing to accept a 25 per cent requirement to refer and initiate legislation. December 11, 1938, interview with Reed Holloman, as quoted in Thomas, p. 99.

81. Fergusson, Springer, and Clancy, pp. 68-69.

82. Arthur M. Edwards and Willard Belknap, *To The People of San Juan County*, campaign leaflet, Bursum Papers.

83. Andrews to Catron, December 28, 1910, Dargan Papers. Andrews borrowed the money from Catron for four months at 8 per cent interest.

84. January 20, 1911, Dargan Papers.

85. As quoted in the *News* (Columbus), November 18, 1910, Andrews Scrapbook.

86. December 21, 1910, Dargan Papers.

87. January 12, 1911, Dargan Papers.

88. "Certificate of the Governor, Secretary and Chief Justice of the Territory of New Mexico, as to Vote on Constitution of Proposed State of New Mexico, at Election Held Saturday, January 21, 1911," included in booklet which contains breakdown by counties of vote cast, with signatures of Governor Mills, Secretary Nathan Jaffa, and Chief Justice William H. Pope, Papers Accompanying Specific Public Bill H. R. 18166 and H. J. Res. 289, NA, RG 233.

CHAPTER XVII

1. Edward H. Peplow, Jr., History of Arizona (New York: Lewis Historical Publishing Company, Inc., 1958), II, 17.

2. N. D. Houghton, "Arizona's Experience with the Initiative and Referendum," New Mexico Historical Review, XXIX (July, 1954), 183.

3. Lamar, The Far Southwest, 1846-1912, p. 502; Peplow, pp. 18-21.

4. Saturday Evening Post as quoted in Deming Headlight, February 9, 1911, Dargan Papers; Arizona, Constitution, art. viii, secs. 1 and 5, as quoted in Arizona Code, compiled under supervision of the members of the Supreme Court of Arizona (Indianapolis: The Bobbs-Merrill Co., 1939), I, 153.

5. Arizona, Constitution, art. iv, secs. 2 and 3.

6. February 6, 1911, Dargan Papers.

7. February 8, 1911, Dargan Papers.

8. Catron to Andrews, March 16, 1911, Catron Papers.

9. El Paso Times, April 21, 1911, Dargan Papers. Roosevelt believed the Arizona constitution to be an "unusually good" one, although in 1910 he preferred the removal of judges by legislative action to a recall election. The former President did insist, however, that it would be a "negation of popular government" to deny the people of Arizona the right to establish for themselves what their judicial system should be. See Theodore Roosevelt, "Arizona and the Recall of the Judiciary," Outlook, June 24, 1911, pp. 378-79. Roosevelt's support of New Mexico was unequivocal, urging his friend Senator Lodge to take "a special interest in the New Mexico Bill." May 23, 1911, as quoted in Morison, VII, 269.

10. Andrews to Catron, February 24, 1911, Dargan Papers. Among the critical letters, telegrams, and night letters which reached Congress were those from Rev. S. Alonzo Bright, state superintendent of the Methodist Mission and other pastors, Rev. James Seder, superintendent of the state Anti-Saloon League, and Pitt Ross, president of the Albuquerque Good Citizens League, February 15, 1911; S. E. Nicholson, legislative superintendent of the Anti-Saloon League of America, February 11, 1911; Mrs. J. W. Collins, president of the New Mexico W.C.T.U., undated; Mary E. Burger of Belen, January 31, 1911; and Mrs. Lucy Lies, secretary of W.C.T.U. of Valencia County and public school teacher, undated. NA, RG 233. Other messages of protest include a night letter sent on February 23, 1911, by a group of Santa Fe citizens complaining about the "illegalities" of the election and a February 26, 1911, night letter from D. L. Pond of Denver, who not only protested the election but complained that six Catholic hospitals were receiving state aid. Such aid to Roman Catholic hospitals and schools was also protested in a petition form entitled "A Memorial and Petition," of which there were eight signed by prominent Protestant clergymen and citizens. Papers Accompanying Specific Public Bill H. R. 18166 and H. J. Res. 289, NA, RG 233.

11. Letter from Jose D. Sena enclosed in Blair to Beveridge, February 11, 1911. Senator Blair also wrote another letter to Beveridge on February 8 and one to President Taft on February 7. On March 3, 1911, he filed a critical statement with the Senate Committee on Territories. See pamphlet entitled *Constitution of New Mexico* enclosed in packet with H. J. Res. 14, NA, RG 233.

12. Statement by Andrews regarding the four resolutions adopted February 21, 1911, by the Committee on the Territories and contained in a file box entitled "Statement and papers relating to the New Mexico Constitution, 1911," Special Collections Division, University of New Mexico Library, Albuquerque. Hereafter cited as Andrews File.

13. Affidavits in Andrews File. Other letters and affidavits in support of the fairness of the election include correspondence from H. A. Wolford, Republican chairman of Sierra County, February 20, 1911; officials and citizens from Valencia County, February 20, 1911; citizens from Quay County, February 20, 1911; citizens from Farmington, San Juan County, February 20, 1911; John V. Conway, superintendent of the Santa Fe County public schools, February 20, 1911; Damacio Tafoya, chairman of the county commissioners of Mora County, February 20, 1911; Father Florentine Meyers of Gallup, undated and notarized; citizens of San Juan County, February 22, 1911; Roosevelt County Democrats, undated; and T. J. Walrath, president of Belen Commonwealth Club, February 23, 1911. The gist of these letters was that the election was a clean one and the saloons were closed the entire day. Papers Accompanying Specific Public Bill H. R. 18166 and H. J. Res. 289, NA, RG 233.

14. Andrews File. Included with this is a certificate signed on February 22, 1911, by Nathan Jaffa, secretary of the territory, declaring this copy of the proclamation to be the same as the original. Also in the file is a letter from Frank W. Clancy, attorney general, advising Jaffa to write each probate clerk instructing him to have printed an equal number of ballots for or against the constitution, and Jaffa's response which indicated he had done this.

15. Statement by Andrews used as a cover letter for the affidavits, Andrews File.

16. Andrews File. There was a heated controversy in Rio Arriba County over election ballots, an Edwin L. Broadwell of Ranchitos charging on April 20, 1911, that the only ballots provided were those used to vote for the constitution. When Broadwell asked the election judge if he could cross out "for" and write in "against," he was told that his vote would only count if he used an official ballot. About sixty brown-colored ballots from Rio Arriba County labeled in both English and Spanish "Against the Constitution" were, however, submitted to Congress to refute Broadwell's charge. Letters and ballots enclosed in packet with H. J. Res. 14, NA, RG 233. Broadwell was supported by Benedicto Naranjo who claimed that 200 people who opposed the constitution could not vote because the appropriate ballots had not been printed. Naranjo to Hamilton, February 19, 1911, Papers Accompanying Specific Public Bill H. R. 18166 and H. J. Res. 289, NA, RG 233.

17. Copy of President Taft's message, Andrews File.

18. February 24, 1911, Dargan Papers.

19. Account by Andrews in *Albuquerque Morning Journal*, undated, Andrews Scrapbook.

20. U.S. *Congressional Record*, 61st Cong., 3rd Sess., 1911, Part 5, pp. 4319-20.

21. Twitchell, *The Leading Facts of New Mexican History*, II, 591.

22. Catron to Andrews, March 2, 1911, Catron Papers.

23. As quoted in the *Outlook* (Carrizozo), April 21, 1911, Andrews Scrapbook.

24. *El Paso Times*, April 1, 1911, Dargan Papers.

25. As quoted in the *Rock Island Tribune*, March 16, 1911, Andrews Scrapbook.

26. *El Paso Times* as quoted in the *Santa Fe New Mexican*, March 13, 1911, Andrews Scrapbook.

27. March 11, 1911, Dargan Papers.

28. March 11, 1911, Dargan Papers. (Separate letter.)

29. Proper delineation of boundaries was, of course, a necessary part of any action taken on statehood. There had been rumors that the governor of Texas would appoint a General Anson Mills to the commission authorized to relocate the Clark line. The boundary line, which started at the point where the Rio Grande intersected the 32nd parallel, was named after John H. Clark, a United State commissioner, who completed the boundary survey in 1860. Mills had participated in an earlier survey that validated Texas claims in the area. As a result of Catron's complaints, Andrews investigated and discovered that the Texas governor had never considered Mills for that post. For additional information see W. H. Austin to Catron, January 31, 1911; George W. Wickersham to Andrews, March 22, 1911; W. H. Austin to Catron, March 29, 1911; George W. Wickersham to Andrews, April 6, 1911, Dargan Papers.

30. *U.S. Congressional Record*, 62d Cong., 1st Sess., 1911, Part 1, p. 28. Both joint resolutions on this page.

31. *Las Vegas Daily Optic*, April 19, 1911, Andrews Scrapbook.

32. U.S. Congress, House, Committee on the Territories, *Hearings Before the Committee on the Territories of the House of Representatives on House Resolution No. 14: Approving the Constitutions Formed by the Constitutional Conventions of the Territories of New Mexico and Arizona*, 62d Cong., 1st Sess., 1911, p. 117.

33. *Las Vegas Daily Optic*, April 19, 1911, Andrews Scrapbook.

34. Andrews to Catron, April 23, 1911, Dargan Papers.

35. U.S. Congress, *Hearings . . . on House Resolution No. 14 . . .* , pp. 6, 45-47.

36. *Evening Herald* (Albuquerque) as quoted in the *Santa Fe New Mexican*, April 22, 1911, Andrews Scrapbook.

37. *Outlook* (Carrizozo), May 12, 1911, Andrews Scrapbook. The *Optic* was among the newspapers which equated the opposition of Fergusson, Hand, and Jones to the constitution with opposition against statehood. April 26, 1911, Andrews Scrapbook.

38. May 15, 1911, Dargan Papers.

39. As quoted in the *Deming Headlight*, April 20, 1911, Dargan Papers. This suggestion did not even get as far as the proposal to name the territory Lincoln if statehood were granted in the early 1870's. See note 92, chapter 6.

40. May 9, 1911, Andrews Scrapbook.

41. Jones to Sumner Burkhart as quoted in *Las Vegas Daily Optic*, May 12, 1911, Andrews Scrapbook.

42. An effort to recommit the bill failed by a vote of 215 to 58. *U.S. Congressional Record*, 62d Cong., 1st Sess., 1911, Part 2, pp. 1528-29. Enrolled copy of House Joint Resolution No. 14 bearing the signatures of Speaker Champ Clark and Vice President James S. Sherman in NA, RG 233.

43. *Evening Herald*, June 7, 1911, Andrews Scrapbook.

44. There is some dispute as to whether Fergusson or Jones was the parent of the Flood resolution. According to one account, Fergusson began corresponding with Flood after the constitutional convention rejected his ideas, and the result of the exchange was House Joint Resolution No. 14. Ferguson Folder, Dargan Papers. Twitchell, on the other hand, regarded Jones as the moving force, one of the prominent Democrats who quietly met at Albuquerque to draft the Flood resolution and dis-

patch a committee to Washington to lobby for its passage. Twitchell, *The Leading Facts of New Mexican History*, II, 590.

45. July 5, 1911, Fergusson Letters. The enabling act, of course, was signed on June 20, 1910.

46. *Santa Fe New Mexican*, June 5, 1911, Andrews Scrapbook.

47. *Evening Herald*, June 7, 1911, Andrews Scrapbook.

48. *Raton Daily Range*, August 7, 1911, Andrews Scrapbook. See U.S. *Congressional Record*, 62d Cong., 1st Sess., 1911, Part 4, p. 3633 for the Nelson amendment.

49. *Raton Daily Range*, August 7, 1911, Andrews Scrapbook.

50. Philip C. Jessup, *Elihu Root* (New York: Dodd, Mead & Company, 1938), II, 243.

51. Remarks of both Root and Poindexter quoted in *Raton Daily Range*, August 7, 1911, Andrews Scrapbook.

52. *Chieftain* (Socorro), August 12, 1911, Andrews Scrapbook.

53. *Ft. Sumner Review*, August 12, 1911; *Chieftain*, August 12, 1911. Andrews Scrapbook.

54. August 9, 1911, Dargan Papers.

55. Archie Butt to Clara Butt, August 9, 1911, as quoted in Butt, II, 742. For details about Taft's meeting with the New Mexico delegation see Mabry, p. 181.

56. On one of the original, unpublished copies of the veto message were these words of warning: "*CONFIDENTIAL*[.] To be held in confidence, and no portion, synopsis, or intimation to be published or given out until its READING has been begun in the Senate. While this message is dated Tuesday, August 15, 1911, some contingency may arise to prevent its delivery to the Senate on that date, and extreme care must therefore be exercised to avoid premature publication." NA, RG 233.

57. U.S. Congress, House, *Special Message of the President of the United States Returning Without Approval House Joint Resolution No. 14*, H. Doc. 106, 62d Cong., 1st Sess., 1911, p. 2 (referred to the Committee on the Territories and ordered to be printed, August 15, 1911).

58. *Rock Island Tribune*, August 17, 1911, Andrews Scrapbook.

59. Taft to Franklin MacVeagh, Secretary of the Treasury, August 16, 1911, Taft Papers. Taft expressed relief that the *Tribune* was supporting him. "The Chicago *Tribune* attitude is very valuable."

60. August 16, 1911, Dargan Papers.

61. August, 17, 1911, as quoted in *Portales Daily News*, January 3, 1939, Dargan Papers.

62. August 17, 1911, Andrews Scrapbook.

63. Taft to Secundino Romero and others, August 16, 1911, Taft Papers.

64. *Santa Fe New Mexican*, August 16, 1911, Andrews Scrapbook.

65. U.S. *Congressional Record*, 62d Cong., 1st Sess., 1911, Part 4, p. 3939.

66. Original and amended and engrossed S. J. Res. 57, NA, RG 46.

67. August 19, 1911, Dargan Papers.

68. *News* (Clovis), August 24, 1911, Andrews Scrapbook.

69. *Las Vegas Daily Optic*, August 26, 1911, Andrews Scrapbook. Andrews gave his pen to Prince, who was then president of the New Mexico Historical Society, where it was placed in the historical museum in the Old Palace alongside the pen used by the President to sign the enabling act.

70. *Pecos Valley News*, August 24, 1911, Andrews Scrapbook.

71. Andrews to Catron, August 23, 1911, Dargan Papers.

72. *Pecos Valley News*, August 24, 1911, Andrews Scrapbook.

73. New Mexico, *Executive Record*, VII, 490-94. The requirement for a separate blue-tinted ballot was in both the Flood and Smith resolutions.

74. September 15, 1911, Fergusson Letters. Fergusson should have known that New Mexico was entitled to two representatives to Congress.

75. *George Curry, 1861-1947: An Autobiography*, p. 259.

76. The two dissident Republicans and their followers officially organized as the Republican Progressive League on October 4. Reeve, p. 333.

77. Bloom and Donnelly, p. 243; *George Curry, 1861-1947: An Autobiography*, p. 261.

78. *Ibid.*, p. 258.

79. Andrews to Catron, September 5, 1911, Dargan Papers.

80. May 6, 1911, Andrews Scrapbook. The *Raton Daily Range* also regarded Penrose as a champion of statehood (see July 17, 1911, issue, Andrews Scrapbook), although it is interesting to note that Penrose's support was qualified by his conservative Republicanism. He voted against the Flood resolution and for the Nelson amendment.

81. Copy of speech, 1910 Folder, Dargan Papers. According to Catron's son, Fletcher, his father and Andrews never made any deal regarding New Mexico's two Senate seats. Personal interview with Fletcher Catron, July 12, 1960.

82. *Cincinnati Times-Star*, September 4, 1911, as quoted in *Rio Grande Republican* (Las Cruces), September 15, 1911, Andrews Scrapbook.

83. Andrews to Catron, November 15, 1911, Dargan Papers.

84. Cutting to James Roger Addison, December 11, 1911, Cutting Papers.

85. *Santa Fe New Mexican*, March 27, 1912, as quoted in seminar paper by Charles M. Martin, Dargan Papers. According to Curry, Bursum persuaded Andrews to withdraw in favor of Catron. There were Democratic aspirants too, such as Jones and Felix Martinez, but a bipartisan compromise effort to make Fall and Martinez the first two senators failed because of Fall's opposition. *George Curry, 1861-1947: An Autobiography*, pp. 265-66.

86. Fall to Catron, November 16, 1912, Albert Bacon Fall Papers, Special Collections Division, University of New Mexico Library, Albuquerque

87. C. J. Smith to Cutting, November 15, 1913, plus enclosed report by Burn's Detective Agency and copy of letter from Smith to Mark Sullivan, in care of *Collier's Weekly*, November 16, 1913, regarding investigation of Fall's election by the agency, Cutting Papers. Supporters of Andrews advanced $40,000 in behalf of his candidacy, the money to be distributed by Bursum and Major Llewellyn. Andrews was so incensed at the way the fund was disbursed that he visited Llewellyn's home in Socorro and threatened him.

88. Peplow, pp. 26-27. During the general election on November 5, 1912, an amendment to restore the recall provision in the state constitution was "quietly but firmly" approved by the voters of Arizona.

89. *Albuquerque Morning Journal*, January 6, 1912, as quoted in Thomas, p. 117; Poldervaart, p. 210. According to Poldervaart, Jose D. Sena, the clerk of the Territorial Supreme Court, was at a dance on the night of January 4 when he received a telegram from the Department of Justice, and immediately hustled over to the capital to prepare the writ.

90. *George Curry, 1861-1947: An Autobiography*, p. 262. Proclamation in United States Government Documents Having General Legal Effect, NA, RG 11.

91. Arizona proclamation, NA, RG 11.

Bibliography

Manuscript Collections

* Manuel Alvarez Papers. State Records Center and Archives, Santa Fe.
William H. Andrews File. Special Collections Division, University of New Mexico Library, Albuquerque.
William H. Andrews Scrapbook. Special Collections Division, University of New Mexico Library, Albuquerque.
A. M. Bergere Scrapbook (photostat copy). Special Collections Division, University of New Mexico Library, Albuquerque.
Albert J. Beveridge Papers. Division of Manuscripts, Library of Congress, Washington, D.C.
Holm O. Bursum Papers. Special Collections Division, University of New Mexico Library, Albuquerque.
Thomas B. Catron Papers. Special Collections Division, University of New Mexico Library, Albuquerque.
Henry Clay Papers. Division of Manuscripts, Library of Congress, Washington, D.C.
Grover Cleveland Papers. Division of Manuscripts, Library of Congress, Washington, D.C.
Constitutional Convention Papers. State Records Center and Archives, Santa Fe.
J. W. Crumpacker Scrapbook. Library, Division of History, Museum of New Mexico, Santa Fe.
▼ Bronson Cutting Papers. Division of Manuscripts, Library of Congress, Washington, D.C.
Marion Dargan Papers. Special Collections Division, University of New Mexico Library, Albuquerque.
Stephen B. Elkins Papers. West Virginia Collection, University of West Virginia Library, Morgantown.
Albert Bacon Fall Papers. Special Collections Division, University of New Mexico Library, Albuquerque.
Harvey Butler Fergusson Letter Collection (1910-1911). Special Collections Division, University of New Mexico Library, Albuquerque.
Millard Fillmore Papers. Division of Manuscripts, Library of Congress, Washington, D.C.
Governors' Papers. State Records Center and Archives, Santa Fe.

Ulysses S. Grant Papers. Division of Manuscripts, Library of Congress, Washington, D.C.

Herbert J. Hagerman Papers. State Records Center and Archives, Santa Fe.

Benjamin Harrison Papers. Division of Manuscripts, Library of Congress, Washington, D.C.

Legislative Papers. State Records Center and Archives, Santa Fe.

William McKinley Papers. Division of Manuscripts, Library of Congress, Washington, D.C.

Miscellaneous Territorial Papers. State Records Center and Archives, Santa Fe.

New Mexico Miscellaneous. Division of Manuscripts, Library of Congress, Washington, D.C.

Newspaper Collection. Newspaper Reference Room, Library of Congress, Washington, D.C.

Newspaper and Rare Book Collection. Library, Division of History, Museum of New Mexico, Santa Fe.

Newspaper and Rare Book Collection. Special Collections Division, University of New Mexico Library, Albuquerque.

Miguel A. Otero Papers. Special Collections Division, University of New Mexico Library, Albuquerque.

L. Bradford Prince Papers. State Records Center and Archives, Santa Fe.

Matthew Quay Papers. Division of Manuscripts, Library of Congress, Washington, D.C.

Benjamin Read Collection. State Records Center and Archives, Santa Fe.

Theodore Roosevelt Papers. Division of Manuscripts, Library of Congress, Washington, D.C.

Edmund G. Ross Papers. State Records Center and Archives, Santa Fe.

William Howard Taft Papers. Division of Manuscripts, Library of Congress, Washington, D.C.

Zachary Taylor Papers. Division of Manuscripts, Library of Congress, Washington, D.C.

Ralph Emerson Twitchell Collection. State Records Center and Archives, Santa Fe.

U.S. Army Collection. Joseph King Fenno Mansfield Papers. Division of Manuscripts, Library of Congress, Washington, D.C.

U.S. Department of Interior. Appointments File, 1849-79. Records Group 48, National Archives, Washington, D.C.

————. General Correspondence Files, 1907-53. Records Group 48, National Archives, Washington, D.C.

U.S. Department of State. Appointments and Recommendations. Records Group 59, National Archives, Washington, D.C.

————. Diplomatic Despatches, 1789-1906. Records Group 59, National Archives, Washington, D.C.

————. Miscellaneous Letters. Records Group 59, National Archives, Washington, D.C.

————. Territorial Papers: New Mexico. Records Group 59, National Archives, Washington, D.C.

U.S. Executive Collection. Division of Manuscripts, Library of Congress, Washington, D.C.

U.S. House of Representatives. Accompanying Papers File. Records Group 233, National Archives, Washington, D.C.

————. New Mexico Territorial Papers Collection. Records Group 233, National Archives, Washington, D.C.

U.S. Proclamations in United States Government Documents Having General Legal Effect. Records Group 11, National Archives, Washington, D.C.

U.S. Senate. New Mexico Territorial Papers Collection. Records Group 46, National Archives, Washington, D.C.

U.S. Senate. Papers Pertaining to Nominations. Records Group 46, National Archives, Washington, D.C.

U.S. Social and Economic Branch. Private Papers Given to the National Archives. Records Group 316, National Archives, Washington, D.C.

U.S. War Department. Letters Sent. Records Group 107, National Archives, Washington, D.C.

✦ Lewis Wallace Papers. State Records Center and Archives, Santa Fe.

PUBLIC DOCUMENTS

Arizona. *Constitution* as quoted in *Arizona Code*. Compiled under the supervision of the members of the Supreme Court of Arizona. Indianapolis: The Bobbs-Merrill Co., 1939.

New Mexico. *Constitution* (1850).

————. *Constitution* (1872).

————. *Constitution* (1889).

————. *Constitution*.

————. Council Journal, 1865, 1872 (unpublished and in Spanish).

————. Executive Record, Territory of New Mexico, July 25, 1867, to November 8, 1882 (unpublished).

————. *Executive Record*. Vols. III, V, VII.

————. House Journal, 1865, 1872 (unpublished and in Spanish).

————. "Journal of the Constitutional Convention, Territory of New Mexico: September 3 to 21, 1889, and August 18 to 19, 1890" (unpublished).

————. *Laws of the Territory of New Mexico Enacted by the Legislative Assembly of 1871-1872*. Santa Fe: A. P. Sullivan, Public Printer, 1872.

————. Legislature. *Acts of the Legislative Assembly of the Territory of New Mexico.* 28th Sess. Santa Fe: New Mexico Printing Co., 1889.

————. *Message of Governor Marsh Giddings, to the Legislative Assembly of New Mexico, December, 1873.* Santa Fe: Manderfield & Tucker, Public Printers, 1873.

————. *Message of William Carr Lane, Governor of the Territory of New Mexico to the Legislative Assembly of the Territory at Santa Fe, Dec. 7, 1852.* Santa Fe: Gazette Office, 1852.

————. "Organic Act Establishing the Territory of New Mexico: Approved September 30, 1850," *New Mexico Statutes Annotated.* Compiled and annotated by Stephen B. Davis, Jr., and Merritt C. Mecham (published by authority). Denver: The W. H. Courtright Publishing Company, 1915.

————. *Organic Law of the Territory of New Mexico.* 1846 (Kearny Code).

————. *Proceedings of the Constitutional Convention of the Proposed State of New Mexico Held at Santa Fe, New Mexico: October 3rd, 1910, to November 21st, 1910.* Albuquerque: Press of the *Morning Journal*, 1910.

————. *The Fourth Annual Message of S. E. D. Henry Connelly, to the Legislative*

Assembly of New Mexico Given December, 1865. Santa Fe: Manderfield and Tucker, Printers, Office of The New Mexican, 1865.

—————. The Valedictory Address of Governor Henry Connelly, and the Inaugural of Robert B. Mitchell, Delivered in Front of the Palace, Santa Fe, N.M., Monday, July 16th, 1866. Santa Fe: Office of the Weekly Gazette, 1866.

U.S. Bureau of Census. Historical Statistics of the United States, Colonial Times to 1957. Washington: U.S. Government Printing Office, 1960.

—————. Statistical Abstract of the United States: 1958. 79th ed., Washington: U.S. Government Printing Office, 1958.

U.S. Congressional Globe, 1846-73.

U.S. Congressional Record, 1873-1911.

U.S. Department of Interior. Report of the Secretary of Interior for the Fiscal Year Ended June 30, 1902. Washington: U.S. Government Printing Office, 1902.

U.S. House of Representatives. Acts of Congress Local or Temporary in Their Nature: Texas. Ex. Document No. 47, Part 2, 46th Cong., 3d Sess., 1881.

—————. Admission of New Mexico as a State—Her Resources and Future: Speech of Hon. Stephen B. Elkins, Delegate from New Mexico in the House of Representatives, May 21, 1874. Washington: U.S. Government Printing Office, 1874.

—————. Annual Report of the Department of the Interior: Governor of New Mexico. Document No. 5. 59th Cong., 2d Sess., December 3, 1906-March 4, 1907.

—————. Biographical Directory of the American Congress, 1774-1927. Document No. 783. 69th Cong., 2d Sess., 1928.

—————. California and New Mexico: Message from the President of the United States, Transmitting Information in Answer to a Resolution of the House of the 31st of December, 1849, on the Subject of California and New Mexico. Ex. Document No. 17. 31st Cong., 1st Sess., 1850.

—————. Memorial of the Assembly of New Mexico, In Regard to a State Government for that Territory. Misc. Document 57. 39th Cong., 1st Sess., 1866.

—————. Message from the President of the United States, in Reference to the Texas Boundary. Ex. Document No. 82. 31st Cong., 1st Sess., 1850.

—————. New Mexico-Convention of Delegates: Journal and Proceedings . . . . Misc. Document No. 39. 31st Cong., 1st Sess., 1850.

—————. Special Message of the President of the United States Returning Without Approval House Joint Resolution No. 14. Document No. 106. 62d Cong., 1st Sess., 1911.

—————. Speech [of the] Hon. Richard H. Weightman of the House of Representatives, March 15, 1852. Washington: Congressional Globe Office, 1852.

—————, Committee on the Territories. Admission of Dakota, Montana, Washington, and New Mexico into the Union. Report No. 1025. 50th Cong., 1st Sess., 1888.

—————, Committee on the Territories. Admission of New Mexico. Report No. 736. 52d Cong., 1st Sess., 1892.

—————, Committee on the Territories. Admission of New Mexico. Report No. 155. 53d Cong., 1st Sess., 1893.

—————, Committee on the Territories. Admission of Certain Territories into the Union. Report No. 1309. 57th Cong., 1st Sess., 1902.

—————, Committee on the Territories. Statehood for the Territories. Report No. 496. 59th Cong., 1st Sess., 1906.

————, Committee on the Territories. *Statehood for the Territories.* Report No. 152. 61st Cong., 2d Sess., 1910.

————, Committee on the Territories. *Hearings Before the Committee on the Territories of the House of Representatives on House Resolution No. 14: Approving the Constitutions Formed by the Constitutional Conventions of the Territories of New Mexico and Arizona.* 62d Cong., 1st Sess., 1911.

U.S. Interstate Commerce Commission. *Decisions of the Interstate Commerce Commission of the United States: Valuation Reports, October, 1925-February, 1926.* Vol. CVI.

————. *Decisions of the Interstate Commerce Commission of the United States: Finance Reports, June-November, 1928.* Vol. CXLV.

U.S. Senate. *Correspondence on the Subject of Civil Affairs in New Mexico.* Ex. Document No. 1, Part 2, 31st Cong., 2d Sess., 1850.

————. *Message from the President of the United States, Communicating . . . Information in Relation to Military Orders Issued to United States Officers in Santa Fe . . . .* Ex. Document No. 56. 31st Cong., 1st Sess., 1850.

————. *Message from the President of the United States, in Answer to a Resolution of the Senate Calling for Information in Relation to the Formation of a State Government in New Mexico.* Ex. Document No. 60, Parts 1 and 2, 31st Cong., 1st Sess., 1850.

————. *Message from the President of the United States, Transmitting a Copy of the Constitution . . . of New Mexico, Together with a Digest of Votes for and Against It . . . .* Ex. Document No. 74. 31st Cong., 1st Sess., 1850.

————. *Miscellaneous: Election and Recall of Federal Judges.* Document No. 87. 62d Cong., 1st Sess., April 4-August 22, 1911.

————. *Report: To Accompany Bills S. No. 225 and S. No. 226.* Report No. 123. 31st Cong., 1st Sess., 1850.

————. *Report to the Secretary of War, Communicating, in Compliance with a Resolution of the Senate.* Colonel George A. McCall's reports in relation to New Mexico. Ex. Document No. 26. 31st Cong., 2d Sess., 1850.

————. *Speech of Hon. Albert J. Beveridge, of Indiana, Closing the Debate on the Statehood Bill, in the Senate of the United States.* 58th Cong., 2d Sess., 1905.

————. *Treaties, Conventions, International Acts, Protocols and Agreements Between the United States of America and Other Powers.* (Compiled by William M. Malloy under resolution of the Senate of January 18, 1909.) Document No. 357, Vol. I, 61st Cong., 2d Sess., 1910.

————, Committee on Territories. *Senate Reports,* Vol. 5, Report No. 1023. 52d Cong., 1st Sess., 1892.

————, Committee on Territories. *Admission of New Mexico.* Report No. 628. 54th Cong., 1st Sess., 1895.

————, Committee on Territories. *New Statehood Bill: Hearing Before the Subcommittee of the Committee on Territories on House Bill 12543 . . . .* Document No. 36. 57th Cong., 2d Sess., 1902.

————, Committee on Territories. *New Statehood Bill.* Report No. 2206. 57th Cong., 2d Sess., 1902.

————, Committee on Territories. *An Act Enabling the People of New Mexico and Arizona to Form a Constitution and State Government, Etc.* Report No. 454. 61st Cong., 2d Sess., 1910.

————, Committee on Territories, *H. R. 18166* (amended version). Calendar No. 388. 61st Cong., 2d Sess., March 14, 1910.

————, Subcommittee of the Committee on Indian Affairs. *Hearings, Survey of Conditions of the Indians in the United States.* 71st Cong., 3d Sess., 1931.

U.S. War Department. *The War of the Rebellion: A Compilation of the Official Records of the Union and Confederate Armies.* Series 1, Vols. III, IV; Series 3, Vol. I. Washington: U.S. Government Printing Office, 1880-1900.

Original and Edited Accounts by Contemporaries

Abel, Annie Heloise (ed.). *The Official Correspondence of James S. Calhoun: While Indian Agent at Santa Fe and Superintendent of Indian Affairs in New Mexico.* Collected mainly from the files of the Indian Office. Washington: U.S. Government Printing Office, 1915.

Baker, George E. (ed.). *The Works of William H. Seward.* Vol. I. New York: Redfield, 1853.

Benton, Thomas Hart. *Thirty Years' View.* New York: D. Appleton and Company, 1856.

Blaine, James G. *Twenty Years of Congress: From Lincoln to Garfield.* Vol. II. Norwich, Connecticut: The Henry Bill Publishing Company, 1884-1893.

Binkley, William C. (ed.). "Reports from a Texas Agent in New Mexico, 1849" (Text of seven letters written by Spruce M. Baird), pp. 157-183, *New Spain and the Anglo-American West: Historical Contributions.* Presented to Herbert Eugene Bolton. Vol. II. Los Angeles: Privately Printed, 1932.

Butt, Archibald W. *Taft and Roosevelt: The Intimate Letters of Archie Butt, Military Aid.* 2 vols. Garden City, New Jersey: Doubleday, Doran & Company, Inc., 1930.

Collins, J. L. *Answer to Certain Infamatory Representations of R. H. Weightman.* Santa Fe, 1852.

Davis, Britton. *The Truth About Geronimo.* New Haven: Yale University Press, 1927.

Davis, W. W. H. *El Gringo, or New Mexico and Her People.* New York: Harper & Brothers, Publishers, 1857.

Drum, Stella M. (ed.). *Down the Santa Fe Trail and into Mexico: The Diary of Susan Shelby Magoffin, 1846-1847.* New Haven: Yale University Press, 1926.

Edwards, Arthur M. and Willard Belknap. *To the People of San Juan County.* 1910 campaign leaflet.

Fergusson, H. B., Frank Springer, and Frank W. Clancy. *New Mexico in 1910: Letters and Addresses Relating to the Constitution.* Printed for Frank W. Clancy, n.d.

Fergusson, Harvey B. *The Constitution: Its Dangers and Defects.* 1910 campaign pamphlet.

Foraker, Joseph Benson. *Notes of a Busy Life.* Vol. II. 3d ed. Cincinnati: Stewart & Kidd Company, 1917.

George Curry, 1861-1947: An Autobiography. Edited by H. B. Hening. Albuquerque: University of New Mexico Press, 1958.

Hagerman, Herbert J. *A Statement in Regard to Certain Matters Concerning the Governorship and Political Affairs in New Mexico in 1906-1907.* Printed for Private Circulation, 1908.

Historical Society of New Mexico. *Journal of New Mexico Convention of Delegates to Recommend a Plan of Civil Government[,] September, 1849.* No. 10. Santa Fe: The New Mexican Printing Company, 1907.

Houghton, Joab. *Reply of Joab Houghton, Late Chief Justice of the Supreme Court of the Temporary Civil Government of the Territory of New Mexico, to the Personal and Slanderous Attack of R. H. Weightman, in His Printed Pamphlet, Purporting to a "Speech" Delivered in the House of Representatives on the 15th of March, 1852,* n.d.

Lewis, Alfred Henry (ed.). *A Compilation of the Messages and Speeches of Theodore Roosevelt.* 2 vols. New York: Bureau of National Literature & Art, 1906.

Morison, Elting E. (ed.). *The Letters of Theodore Roosevelt.* Vols. V, VII. Cambridge: Harvard University Press, 1952-1954.

New Mexico Constitutional Convention Book. Denver: C. S. Peterson, n.d.

Otero, Miguel A. *My Life on the Frontier, 1882-1897: Death Knell of a Territory and Birth of a State.* Vol. II. Albuquerque: University of New Mexico Press, 1939.

————. *My Nine Years as Governor of the Territory of New Mexico.* Edited by Marion Dargan. Albuquerque: University of New Mexico Press, 1940.

Prince, L. Bradford. *Admission of New Mexico.* Santa Fe: New Mexican Printing Co., n.d.

————. *New Mexico's Struggle for Statehood: Sixty Years of Effort to Obtain Self Government.* Santa Fe: The New Mexican Printing Co., 1910.

Quaif, Milo Milton (ed.). *The Diary of James K. Polk: During His Presidency, 1845 to 1849.* Vol. I. Chicago: A. C. McClurg Co., 1910.

Richardson, James D. (ed.). *A Compilation of the Messages and Papers of the Presidents, 1789-1897.* Vols. V, VI, IX. Washington: U.S. Government Printing Office, 1897.

Ritch, William G. *The Legislative Blue Book, of the Territory of New Mexico.* Santa Fe: Charles W. Green, Public Printer, 1882.

Russell (pseudonym). *Extract of a Letter Addressed to the Editor of the Santa Fe Gazette, for Publication in New Mexico.* March 12, 1852.

Watson, James E. *As I Knew Them.* Indianapolis and New York: The Bobbs-Merrill Co., 1936.

NEWSPAPERS

Albuquerque Morning Democrat, 1889-1896.
Albuquerque Morning Journal, 1889-1911.
Albuquerque Journal-Democrat, 1901-1902.
Arizona Daily Gazette (Phoenix), 1903.
Arizona Republican (Phoenix), 1905-1910.
Borderer (Las Cruces), 1871.
Boston Globe, 1902.
Boston Post, 1875.
Boston Transcript, 1905-1906.
Brooklyn Daily Eagle, 1902.
Capital (Santa Fe), undated.
Carlsbad Argus, 1908.
Chicago Times-Herald, 1897.
Chicago Tribune, 1875-1889.
Chieftain (Socorro), 1889-1911.
Cincinnati Commercial, 1875.
Colfax County Stockman (Springer), 1890.

Courier-Journal (Louisville), 1906.
Deming Graphic, 1910-1911.
Deming Headlight, 1907-1911.
Denver Republican, 1906-1909.
El Paso Herald, 1895-1911.
El Paso Herald Post, 1889.
El Paso Times, 1905-1911.
Evening Citizen (Albuquerque), 1895-1911.
Evening Herald (Albuquerque), 1911.
Evening Post (New York), 1903-1911.
Evening Star (Washington), 1905-1906.
Ft. Sumner Review, 1911.
Houston Post, 1906.
Hustler (Farmington), 1901.
Indianapolis Journal, 1902-1903.
Indianapolis News, 1905-1906.
Indianapolis Sentinal, 1902.
Kansas City Journal, 1903-1911.
Las Cruces Citizen, 1902-1910.
Las Vegas Daily Optic, 1889-1911.
Los Angeles Times, 1906-1907.
Morning Gleaner (Gallup), 1904.
National Era (Washington), 1848.
New York Times, 1875-1906.
New York Tribune, 1894-1905.
News (Clovis), 1911.
News (Columbus), 1910.
Outlook (Carrizozo), 1910-1911.
Pecos Valley News, 1911.
Pittsburgh Dispatch, 1906.
Portales Daily News, 1939.
Post (Pittsburgh), 1905-1906.
Press (Philadelphia), 1902-1906.
Raton Daily Range, 1911.
Republican (Santa Fe), 1847-1848 (photostat copies used).
Republican Review (Albuquerque), 1871-1872.
Rio Grande Republican (Las Cruces), 1889-1911 (title varies).
Rock Island Tribune, 1911.
Rocky Mountain News (Denver), 1866-1910.
Roosevelt County Herald (Portales), 1907.
Roswell Weekly Record, 1902.
San Marcial Bee, 1902.
St. Louis Daily Globe, 1875.
Santa Fe New Mexican, 1849-1911 (title varies and there are weekly as well as daily
    issues).
Santa Fe Weekly Gazette, 1853-1865.
Silver City Enterprise, 1888-1896.
Silver City Independent, 1910.
Socorro Industrial Advertiser, 1890.
Sun (Baltimore), 1910.

Sun (New York), 1910.
Texico Trumpet, 1911.
Tribune Citizen (Albuquerque), 1910.
Washington Herald, 1908-1910.
Washington Post, 1902-1906.
Wheeling Intelligencer, 1895.
World (New York), 1911.
Newspapers used in this study are from the Newspaper Reference Room, Library of Congress, Washington D.C.; the Library, Division of History, Museum of New Mexico, Santa Fe, including items in the J. W. Crumpacker Scrapbook; the Special Collections Division, University of New Mexico Library, Albuquerque, including items in the Marion Dargan Papers, the William H. Andrews Scrapbook, and the A. M. Bergere Scrapbook; and the Albert J. Beveridge Papers, Division of Manuscripts, Library of Congress, Washington, D.C. Because of variations in newspaper titles, Gregory's list was consulted whenever necessary.

BOOKS

An Illustrated History of New Mexico. Chicago: Lewis Publishing Co., 1895.
Bancroft, Hubert Hugh. *The Works of Hubert Hugh Bancroft, XVII: History of Arizona and New Mexico, 1850-1888.* San Francisco: The History Company, Publishers, 1889.
Beck, Warren. *New Mexico: A History of Four Centuries.* Norman: University of Oklahoma Press, 1962.
Binkley, William C. *The Expansionist Movement in Texas, 1836-50.* Vol. XIII of series *University of California Publications in History.* Berkeley: University of California Press, 1925.
Bloom, Lansing M., and Thomas C. Donnelly. *New Mexico History and Civics.* Albuquerque: The University Press, 1933.
Bowers, Claude G. *Beveridge and the Progressive Era.* Cambridge, Massachusetts: The Riverside Press, 1932.
Clarke, Dwight L. *Stephen Watts Kearny: Soldier of the West.* Norman: University of Oklahoma Press, 1961.
Cline, Howard F. *Mexico: Revolution to Evolution, 1940-1960.* Issued under the auspices of the Royal Institute of International Affairs. London: Oxford University Press, 1962.
Coan, Charles F. *A History of New Mexico.* 3 vols. Chicago and New York: American Historical Society, Inc., 1925.
Coulter, E. Merton. *The South During Reconstruction, 1865-1877.* Vol. VIII of *A History of the South.* Edited by Wendell Holmes Stephenson. 10 vols. Baton Rouge: Louisiana State University and The Littlefield Fund for Southern History of the University of Texas, 1947.
Dale, Edward Everett, and Morris L. Wardell. *History of Oklahoma.* New York: Prentice-Hall, Inc., 1948.
Davis, Ellis Arthur (ed.). *The Historical Encyclopedia of New Mexico.* 2 vols. Albuquerque: New Mexico Historical Association, 1945.
Dictionary of American History. Vols. XV, XVI. Edited by Dumas Malone. New York: Charles Scribner's Sons, 1935.
——————. Vol. IV. Edited by James Truslow Adams. New York: Charles Scribner's Sons, 1940.

Donnelly, Thomas C. *The Government of New Mexico.* 2d ed. Albuquerque: University of New Mexico Press, 1953.

Dunaway, Wayland Fuller. *A History of Pennsylvania.* New York: Prentice-Hall, Inc., 1935.

Ellis, Elmer. *Henry Moore Teller: Defender of the West.* Caldwell, Idaho: The Caxton Printers, Ltd., 1941.

Estergreen, M. Morgan. *Kit Carson: A Portrait in Courage.* Norman: University of Oklahoma Press, 1962.

Faulkner, Harold Underwood. *American Political and Social History.* 7th ed. New York: Appleton-Century-Crofts, Inc., 1957.

Gittinger, Roy. *The Formation of the State of Oklahoma, 1893-1906.* Berkeley: University of California Press, 1917.

Graber, Paul Neff. *The Gadsden Purchase.* Philadelphia: Press of the University of Pennsylvania, 1923.

Gregory, Winifred (ed.). *American Newspapers, 1821-1936: A Union List of Files Available in the United States and Canada.* Under the Auspices of the Bibliographical Society of America. New York: The H. W. Wilson Company, 1937.

Grivas, Theodore. *Military Governments in California, 1846-1850: With a Chapter on Their Prior Use in Louisiana, Florida and New Mexico.* Glendale, California: The Arthur H. Clark Company, 1963.

Hacker, Louis H., and Benjamin B. Kendrick. *The United States Since 1865.* Revised ed. New York: F. S. Crofts & Co., 1936.

Hafen, LeRoy (ed.). *Colorado and Its People: A Narrative and Topical History of the Centennial State.* New York: Lewis Historical Publishing Co., Inc., 1948.

—————, Carl Coke Rister. *Western America: The Exploration, Settlement, and Development of the Region Beyond the Mississippi.* Englewood Cliffs, New Jersey: Prentice-Hall, Inc., 1962.

Hall, Frank. *History of the State of Colorado.* Vol. I. Chicago: The Blakely Printing Company, 1888-1895.

Jessup, Philip C. *Elihu Root.* Vol. II. New York: Dodd, Mead & Co., 1938.

Keleher, William A. *Violence in Lincoln County, 1869-1881.* Albuquerque: University of New Mexico Press, 1957.

Lamar, Howard R. *The Far Southwest, 1846-1912: A Territorial History.* New Haven: Yale University Press, 1966.

—————. "The Reluctant Admission: The Struggle to Admit Arizona and New Mexico to the Union," in *The American West: An Appraisal.* Edited by Robert G. Ferris. Santa Fe: Museum of New Mexico Press, 1963.

Marshall, James. *Santa Fe: The Railroad That Built an Empire.* New York: Random House, Inc., 1945.

Mowry, George E. *The Era of Theodore Roosevelt, 1900-1912.* New York: Harper and Brothers, 1958.

Peplow, Edward H., Jr. *History of Arizona.* Vol. II. New York: Lewis Historical Publishing Co., Inc., 1958.

Perkins, Dexter, and Glyndon Van Deusen. *The United States of America: A History,* Vol. I to 1876. New York: The Macmillan Company, 1962.

Poldervaart, Arie W. *Black-Robed Justice.* Santa Fe: Historical Society of New Mexico, 1948.

Porter, Kirk H. *National Party Platforms.* New York: The Macmillan Co., 1924.

Pringle, Henry F. *The Life and Times of William Howard Taft.* 2 vols. New York: Farrar and Rinehart Co., 1939.

————. *Theodore Roosevelt: A Biography.* New York: Harcourt, Brace & Co., 1931.

Read, Benjamin M. *Illustrated History of New Mexico.* Santa Fe: The New Mexican Printing Co., 1912.

Reeve, Frank D. *History of New Mexico.* Vol. II. New York: Lewis Historical Publishing Company, Inc., 1961.

Rippy, J. Fred. *The United States and Mexico.* New York: Alfred A. Knopf, Inc., 1926.

Roberts, Frank H. H., and Ralph Emerson Twitchell. *History and Civics of New Mexico.* Albuquerque: Charles Ilfeld Co., 1914.

Sacks, B. *Be It Enacted: The Creation of the Territory of Arizona.* Phoenix: Arizona Historical Foundation, 1964.

Stephenson, Nathanial Wright. *A History of the American People.* 2 vols. New York: Charles Scribner's Sons, 1934.

————. *Nelson W. Aldrich: A Leader in American Politics.* New York: Charles Scribner's Sons, 1930.

Twitchell, Ralph Emerson. *The Leading Facts of New Mexican History.* Vol. II. Cedar Rapids, Iowa: The Torch Press, 1912.

————. *The Military Occupation of New Mexico, 1846-1851.* Denver: Smith-Brooks Company, 1909.

Walters, Everett. *Joseph Benson Foraker: An Uncompromising Republican.* "Ohio Governors Series," Vol. I. Columbus: The Ohio State Archaeological & Historical Society, 1948.

Waters, L. L. *Steel Trails to Santa Fe.* Lawrence: University of Kansas Press, 1950.

Westphall, Victor. *The Public Domain in New Mexico.* Albuquerque: The University of New Mexico Press, 1965.

Whitford, William Clark. *Colorado Volunteers in the Civil War: The New Mexico Campaign in 1862.* Denver: The State Historical and Natural History Society, 1906.

Wish, Harvey. *Contemporary America: The National Scene Since 1900.* Revised ed. New York: Harper & Bros., 1955.

Wyllys, Rufus Kay. *Arizona: The History of a Frontier State.* Phoenix: Hobson & Herr, 1950.

ARTICLES AND PERIODICALS

Baldwin, P. M. "A Short History of the Mesilla Valley," *New Mexico Historical Review,* XIII (July, 1938).

Bieber, Ralph P. (ed.). "Letters of William Carr Lane, 1852-1854," *New Mexico Historical Review,* III (April, 1928).

Binkley, William C. "The Question of Texan Jurisdiction in New Mexico Under the United States," *The Southwestern Historical Quarterly,* XXIV (July, 1920).

Bloom, Lansing. "The Governors of New Mexico," *New Mexico Historical Review,* X (April, 1935).

Bowden, J. J. "The Texas-New Mexico Boundary Dispute Along the Rio Grande," *The Southwestern Historical Quarterly,* LXIII (October, 1959).

Carson, William G. B. (ed.). "William Carr Lane, Diary," *New Mexico Historical Review,* XXXIX (October, 1964).

Dargan, Marion. "New Mexico's Fight for Statehood, 1895-1912, I: The Political Leaders of the Latter Half of the 1890's and Statehood," *New Mexico Historical Review,* XIV (January, 1939).

————. "New Mexico's Fight for Statehood, 1895-1912, II: The Attitude of the

Territorial Press (1895-1901)," *New Mexico Historical Review*, XIV (April, 1939).
————. "New Mexico's Fight for Statehood, 1895-1912, III: The Opposition Within the Party (1888-1890)," *New Mexico Historical Review*, XV (April, 1940).
————. "New Mexico's Fight for Statehood, 1895-1912, IV: The Opposition Within the Territory During the Nineties," *New Mexico Historical Review*, XVI (January, 1941).
Dargan, Marion. "New Mexico's Fight for Statehood, 1895-1912, V: The Silencing of the Opposition at Home," *New Mexico Historical Review*, XVI (October, 1941).
————. "New Mexico's Fight for Statehood, 1895-1912, VI: Advertising the Backyard of 'the United States'," *New Mexico Historical Review*, XVIII (January, 1943).
————. "New Mexico's Fight for Statehood, 1895-1912, VII: The Part Played by the Press of the Southwest," *New Mexico Historical Review*, XVIII (April, 1943).
"Do We Want Four New Partners?" *Outlook*, LXXXI (December 16, 1905).
Donnell, F. S. "The Confederate Territory of Arizona, as Compiled from Official Sources," *New Mexico Historical Review*, XVII (April, 1942).
Eaton, W. Clement. "Frontier Life in Southern Arizona, 1858-1861," *The Southwestern Historical Quarterly*, XXXVI (January, 1933).
Espinosa, J. Manuel. "Memoir of a Kentuckian in New Mexico, 1848-1884," *New Mexico Historical Review*, XIII (January, 1938).
Ganaway, Loomis Morton. "New Mexico and the Sectional Controversy, 1846-1861," *New Mexico Historical Review*, XVIII (April, July, 1943).
Greever, William S. "Railway Development in the Southwest," *New Mexico Historical Review*, XXXII (April, 1957).
Heflin, Reuben W. "New Mexico Constitutional Convention," *New Mexico Historical Review*, XXI (January, 1946).
"Holding Up the United States Senate," *Literary Digest*, XXVI (March 7, 1903).
Houghton, N. D. "Arizona's Experience with the Initiative and Referendum," *New Mexico Historical Review*, XXIX (July, 1954).
Keen, Effie R. "Arizona's Governors," *Arizona Historical Review*, III (October, 1930).
Kendrick, Benjamin B. "McKinley and Foraker," *Political Science Quarterly*, XXXI (December, 1916).
Lamar, Howard R. "Edmund G. Ross as Governor of New Mexico Territory: A Reappraisal," *New Mexico Historical Review*, XXXVI (July, 1961).
————. "Political Patterns in New Mexico and Utah Territories, 1850-1900," *Utah Historical Review*, XXVII (October, 1960).
Larson, Robert W. "Statehood for New Mexico, 1888-1912," *New Mexico Historical Review*, XXXVII (July, 1962).
————. "Taft, Roosevelt, and New Mexico Statehood," *Mid-America: An Historical Review*, VL (April, 1963).
Leopard, Donald D. "Joint Statehood: 1906," *New Mexico Historical Review*, XXXIV (October, 1959).
Loyola, Sister Mary. "The American Occupation of New Mexico, 1821-1852," *New Mexico Historical Review*, XIV (April, July, 1939).
Mabry, Thomas J. "New Mexico's Constitution in the Making—Reminiscences of 1910," *New Mexico Historical Review*, XIX (April, 1944).
Parish, William J. "The German Jew and the Commercial Revolution in Territorial New Mexico, 1850-1900," *New Mexico Historical Review*, XXXV (January, April, 1960).
Parks, Joseph H. "John Bell and the Compromise of 1850," *Journal of Southern History*, IX (August, 1943).

Ramsdell, Charles W. "The Natural Limits of Slavery Expansion," *The Mississippi Valley Historical Review*, XVI (September, 1929).

Richardson, Elmo R. "George Curry and the Politics of Forest Conservation in New Mexico," *New Mexico Historical Review*, XXXIII (October, 1958).

Rodriguez, Arnold L. "New Mexico in Transition," *New Mexico Historical Review*, XXIV (July, 1949).

Roosevelt, Theodore. "Arizona and the Recall of the Judiciary," *Outlook*, XCVIII (June 24, 1911).

The American Monthly Review of Reviews, XXVI (July, 1902).

"The Joint Statehood Bill Should Pass," *Harper's Weekly*, XLIX (October 28, 1905).

"The New States on Statehood," *The Literary Digest*, XLI (July 16, 1910).

"The Statehood Bill Should Pass," *Harper's Weekly*, XLIX (January 14, 1905).

Thomas, Charles S. "The Pioneer Bar of Colorado," *The Colorado Magazine*, I (July, 1924).

Tittman, Edward D. "New Mexico Constitutional Convention: Recollections," *New Mexico Historical Review*, XXVII (July, 1952).

Walter, Paul A. F. "The First Civil Governor of New Mexico Under the Stars and Stripes," *New Mexico Historical Review*, VIII (April, 1933).

Westphall, Victor. "The Public Domain in New Mexico, 1854-1891," *New Mexico Historical Review*, XXXIII (January, April, 1958).

"What Makes a Territory Fit for Statehood?" *The Literary Digest*, XXV (December 20, 1902).

DISSERTATIONS AND MASTERS' THESES

Adams, Mary Fonda. "Thomas M. Patterson, Some Aspects of His Political Career." Unpublished Master's thesis, Department of Political Science, University of Colorado, 1933.

Cottrell, Beatrice Arline. "Senate Action on the Omnibus Statehood Bill of 1902." Unpublished Master's thesis, Department of History, University of New Mexico, 1938.

Gant, N. A. "A History of the Texas Boundary Disputes." Unpublished Master's thesis, Department of History and Political Science, Colorado State Teachers College, 1930.

Hefferan, Vioalle Clark. "Thomas Benton Catron." Unpublished Master's thesis, Department of History, University of New Mexico, 1940.

Langston, La Moine. "Arizona's Fight for Statehood in the Fifty-seventh Congress." Unpublished Master's thesis, Department of History, University of New Mexico, 1939.

Larson, Robert W. "Statehood for New Mexico, 1888-1912." Unpublished Ph.D. dissertation, Department of History, University of New Mexico, 1961.

Leopard, Donald D. "Joint Statehood: 1906." Unpublished Master's thesis, Department of History, University of New Mexico, 1958.

Maddox, Charles Edgar. "The Statehood Policy of Albert J. Beveridge: 1901-1911." Unpublished Master's thesis, Department of History, University of New Mexico, 1938.

Masters, Mary J. "New Mexico's Struggle for Statehood, 1903-1907." Unpublished Master's thesis, Department of History, University of New Mexico, 1942.

McDowell, Archie M. "The Opposition to Statehood Within the Territory of New Mexico, 1888-1902." Unpublished Master's thesis, Department of History, University of New Mexico, 1939.

Sluga, Mary Elizabeth. "The Political Life of Thomas Benton Catron, 1896-1921." Unpublished Master's thesis, Department of History, University of New Mexico, 1941.

Thomas, Dorothy E. "The Final Years of New Mexico's Struggle for Statehood, 1907-1912." Unpublished Master's thesis, Department of History, University of New Mexico, 1939.

INTERVIEWS

Fletcher Catron, son of Thomas B. Catron, Santa Fe, July 12, 1960.

Eleanor Spiess, granddaughter of Charles A. Spiess, Albuquerque, July 27, 1959.

Index